W9-AVM-827

Beginning JSP Web Development

Jayson Falkner

Ben Galbraith

Romin Irani

Casey Kochmer

Meeraj Moidoo Kunnumpurath

Sathya Narayana Panduranga

Krishnaraj Perrumal

John Timney

Wrox Press Ltd. ®

Beginning JSP Web Development

Published by Wrox Press Ltd,
Arden House, 1102 Warwick Road, Acocks Green,
Birmingham, B27 6BH, UK
Printed in the United States
ISBN 1-861002-09-2

Trademark Acknowledgements

Wrox has endeavored to provide trademark information about all the companies and products mentioned in this book by the appropriate use of capitals. However, Wrox cannot guarantee the accuracy of this information.

Credits

Authors
Jayson Falkner
Ben Galbraith
Romin Irani
Casey Kochmer
Meeraj Moidoo Kunnumpurath
Sathya Narayana Panduranga
Krishnaraj Perrumal
John Timney

Additional Material
Grant Palmer

Technical Reviewers
Rich Bonneau
Simon Brown
Carl Burnham
Chris Crane
Jeremy Crosbie
Brian Hickey
Andrew Jones
Sachin S. Khanna
Vidar Langberget
Sing Li
Chris Lightfoot
Alex Linde
Jim MacIntosh
Jacob Mathew
Ramesh Nagappan
Massimo Nardone
Joel Peach
James Scheinblum
David Schultz
Rick Stones
Geoff Taylor
John Timney

Category Manager
Viv Emery

Technical Architect
Richard Huss

Technical Editors
Benjamin Hickman
Christian Peak
Daniel Richardson

Author Agent
Nicola Phillips

Project Manager
Simon Brand

Production Manager
Simon Hardware

Production Coordinator
Pip Wonson

Production Assistant
Paul Grove

Figures
Paul Grove

Index
Adrian Axinte
Andrew Criddle

Cover
Dawn Chellingworth

Proof Reader
Agnes Wiggers

About the Authors

Jayson Falkner

Jayson is a full time student at the University of Miami pursuing a degree in Information Technology. He has been programming in Java for the past two years and specializes in Servlets and JSP. Jayson is the CTO of Amberjack Software LLC and webmaster of JSP Insider. In his spare time Jayson likes to program in binary and write not-so-funny jokes using XML.

Jayson is an avid supporter of the open-source community and regularly contributes to various Java and JSP related projects. He may be reached at Jayson@jspinsider.com or by visiting his on-going efforts to provide good free information to the JSP community at http://www.jspinsider.com.

Jayson contributed chapters 10 and 17 to this book.

To family, friends and cherished memories. My dreams are built from their love.

Ben Galbraith

Ben Galbraith first started programming when he was eight years old. He spent a considerable amount of his youth as a hobby programmer. In his late teens, he was hired by a Silicon Valley computer manufacturer to develop Windows-based client-server applications. In 1995, Mr. Galbraith began developing for the web and fell in love with Unix, VI, and Perl. After some years as an Internet consultant, Mr. Galbraith now leads the Java development team at an insurance company in Salt Lake City. He regularly lectures, evangelizes, and gives classes on Java technology.

Ben contributed chapters 1 and 7 to this book.

To my best friend and all the good times that lie ahead of us. I love you.

Romin Irani

Romin Irani works as a Senior Software Engineer with InSync Information Systems, Inc in Fremont, California. He has a Bachelors degree in Computer Engineering from University of Bombay, India. At InSync Information Systems, he was in the design and development team for a distributed eProcurement application which used a variety of J2EE technologies. His primary skills and interests lie in J2EE Technologies especially JSP/Servlets, Java-XML and Web Services. He loves listening to all kinds of music and of course following the fortunes of the Indian Cricket Team, who have caused him more grief than he can ever remember.

Romin contributed chapters 5, 8, and 12 to this book.

First and foremost, to Wrox Press for giving me the opportunity to write. Thanks especially to Nicola and Richard. I would also like to thank my lovely wife, Devyani, who completely understands why I need to keep on working even after returning from work. I wish to devote the chapters I wrote to my loving parents, Khushru and Gulrukh, for all that they have taught me in life. And of course to my 4 Pomeranians (Ricky, Rambo, Fifi , Brandy) and a Dachshund (Elsa).

Casey Kochmer

Casey Kochmer's professional programming experience spans the past 11 years. Since 1996 his emphasis has been on web development using the server-side web languages. Now actively promoting JSP, Casey is a co-founder of JSPInsider.com, a web site devoted to technical support for programmers making the jump to this development environment. Casey is also President of Amberjack Software LLC. When not programming Casey loves to spend time with his family at a lake or hiking in the Olympic Mountains near his home.

Casey contributed chapter 9 to this book.

To Jailyn,
because she cared
and because I will always
have a smile for her.

Meeraj Moidoo Kunnumpurath

I work as a senior developer with Mutant Technology Ltd. My key areas of expertise include enterprise application development using J2EE and XML. I would like to thank mighty Allah for all the work I've done for this book. One of my dreams is for Chelsea to win the Premiership ;-)

Meeraj contributed chapters 2, 3, 18, 19, and 20 to this book.

Sathya Narayana Panduranga

I am a Software Design Engineer living in Bangalore, the silicon valley of India. My areas of interest and experience include Distributed and Component based Application Architectures, Object Oriented Analysis and Design, Voice Over IP and Convergence platforms. I frequently write articles for Codeguru, a web site for developers.

Sathya contributed chapters 11 and 13 to this book.

I would like to thank Nicola Philips and Emma Batch of Wrox Press for giving me an opportunity to work on this book and my family for being with me all the time.

Krishnaraj Perrumal

I am a Sun Certified Java Programmer, founder and director of Adarsh Softech, a consultancy firm providing Web solutions to businesses. I also regularly give presentations on Java and XML. I love to spend most of my time and earnings on books to keep up with the new technologies.

I have been developing software systems using C++, Delphi and Java for the past 15 years.

Perrumal contributed chapters 14, 15, and 16 to this book.

I would like to thank the team at Wrox for their encouragement, and to all who have made my work look better. I would also like to thank my parents, Krishnaraj and Pushpa for their love. Special thanks go to my wife Girija and my son Adarsh for their support and inspiration.

John Timney

John lives in the UK with his lovely wife Philippa in a small town called Chester-Le-Street in the North of England. He is a Postgraduate of Nottingham University having gained an MA in Information Technology following a BA Honours Degree from Humberside University. John specialises in Internet Solutions and his computing expertise has gained him a Microsoft MVP (Most Valuable Professional) award. His hobbies include Martial Arts, and he has black belts in two different styles of Karate.

John contributed chapters 4 and 6 to this book.

Thanks Pippa, for letting me spend hours glued to the web, feeding me biscuits, bringing me tea and just being you.

Congratulations to my dear Mother-in-Law Brenda for succesfully completing her BA Honours Degree at Newcastle University. You have done us all proud.

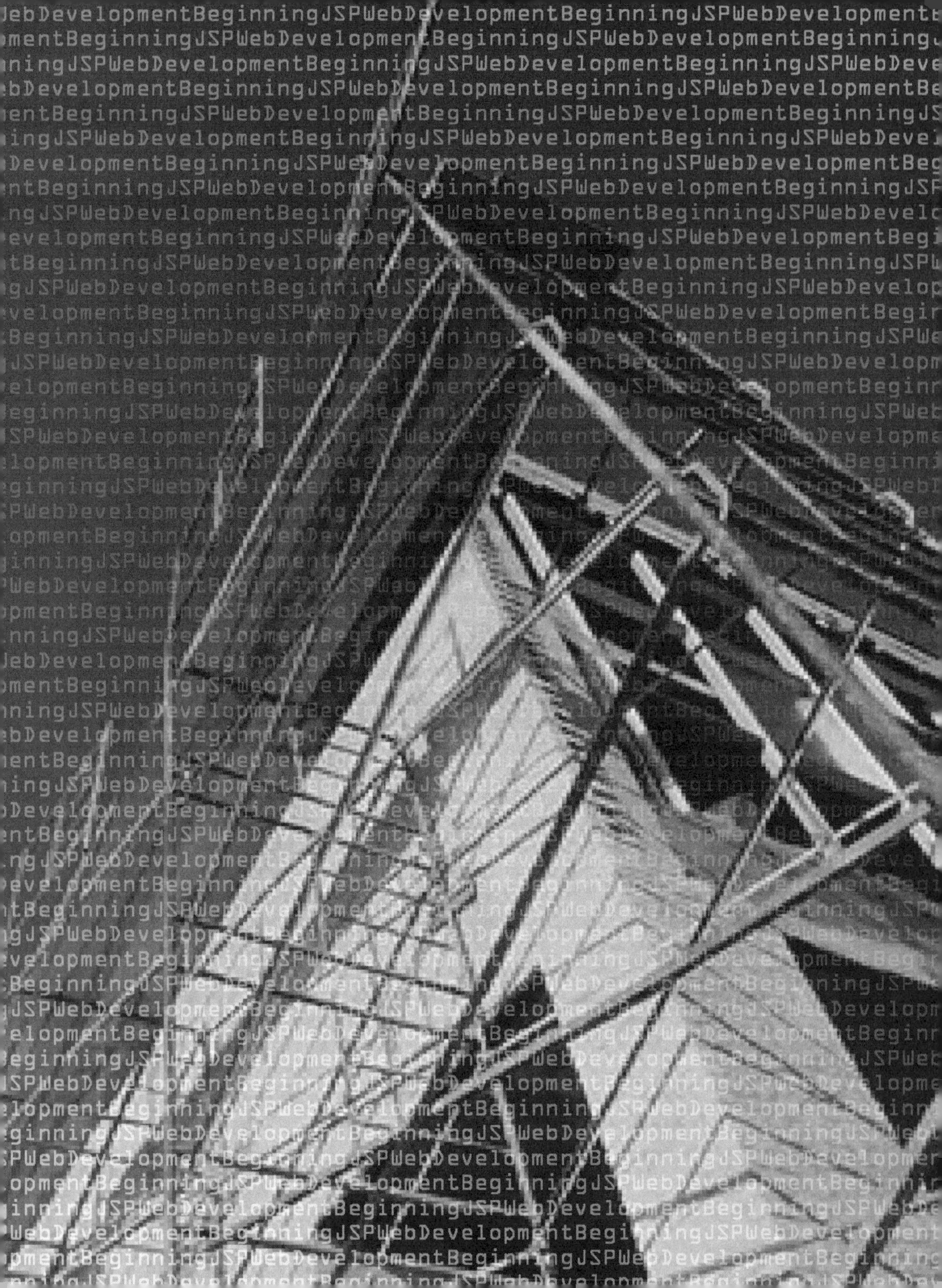
BeginningJSPWebDevelopment

Table of Contents

Table of Contents

Table of Contents

Table of Contents

Table of Contents

Table of Contents

Table of Contents

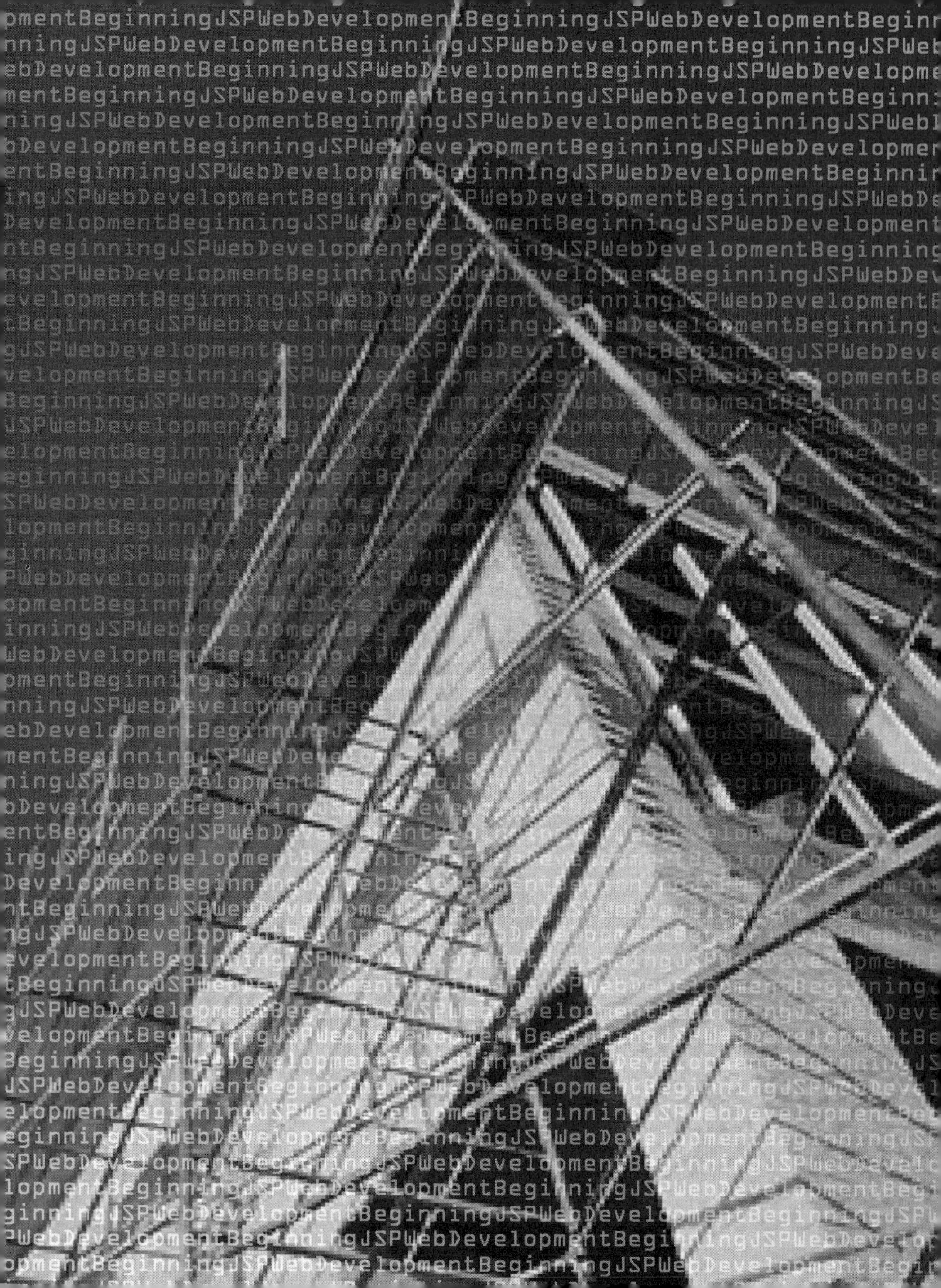
BeginningJSPWebDevelopment

Introduction

JavaServer Pages, or JSP for short, is a technology for creating interactive, dynamic web sites, based on the Java programming language. Indeed, much of the power of JSP comes from its ability to make use of the full facilities of the Java language. JSP builds on an earlier Java technology for creating dynamic web content, Java Servlets. In fact, JSP pages and Servlets are often used together, and we'll be looking later in the book at their different approaches as well as how they can complement each other.

Web applications, as opposed to static web sites, are pervasive nowadays. Everyone – including, presumably, yourself, wants their web presence to be **dynamic**: to present the latest information, to allow users to log on and customize the appearance of the site, or to offer the ability to purchase your services online. A site built with plain HTML can't do that, which is where server-side programming technologies like JSP come in.

This book teaches you about web programming using JSP, Java, and Servlets, from the ground up. We'll teach you:

❑   What JSP is.

❑   How to get your first JSP pages up and running.

❑   The JSP syntax, and that of the Java language on which it is based.

❑   The best ways of using Java technologies to build interactive web applications.

As we go along, we will explain things thoroughly, with plenty of complete, working examples to show you how things work.

Who is This Book For?

This is a *Beginning ...* book, and so we'll show you everything you need to know, from scratch.

In order to get the most out of this book, you'll need to have an understanding of HTML and how to create a static web page. If you don't know HTML you should spend some time familiarizing yourself with HTML before you start to learn about JavaServer Pages.

We won't assume that you have any programming experience; this book will teach you all you need to know in order to create dynamic web applications. However, this book will also suit you if you have some programming experience in a language other than Java, and would like to turn your hand towards web programming. If you know a fair amount about computing concepts but not as much about web technologies, then this book is for you.

Whoever you are, we hope that this book lives up to your expectations.

What's Covered in This Book?

This book aims to teach you the basics of the Java language, so that you can create JSP web applications.

Chapter 1 lays the foundation for the rest of the book by showing you how to install the software you'll need in order to use JavaServer Pages and Java. Then we'll create our very first working example of a JSP page. We finish by discussing web servers, how they work with JSP, and how they communicate with your web browser.

Chapters 2–5 are where we start doing some more serious programming. We'll start by looking at how our web applications can store data and perform simple calculations. Then, in Chapter 3, we'll see in more detail how JSP can read and process information supplied by a user – normally someone accessing your application with a web browser. As our applications get more complex, the JSP code will be getting harder to understand. To get around this, in Chapter 4 we start to look in more detail at the Java language and how to program **JavaBeans**, which help us to make our code easier to read by splitting it up into smaller, more independent pieces. Chapter 5 introduces us to **control structures** that allow our applications to do more complex tasks.

Chapter 6 introduces a cool new feature of JavaServer Pages – **tag libraries**. These allow you to create a set of HTML-like tags that can be used in a JSP page in place of Java code; like JavaBeans, they help to keep our code readable. There are a lot of tag libraries freely available to download from the web, and we'll show you the type of thing they can accomplish as well as how to use a ready-made tag library.

Chapters 7 and 8 concentrate on how to create and use **objects**. We've reached the point where we need to learn more about the Java language, and in Chapter 7 we will learn about one of Java's most useful features – object-orientation. In Chapter 8 we look at some of the useful objects that the Java language provides.

Chapters 9–13 take us firmly back to web programming. It's an unfortunate but inescapable fact that things don't always go according to plan where computers are concerned; however, Java provides us with a mechanism for keeping note of things that go wrong and responding to them intelligently. Chapter 9 also looks at how we can track down **errors** (bugs) in our code. By Chapter 10 we've learned enough to return to tag libraries and see how to **create our own tags**, rather than being limited to using tags that other people have written. Chapter 11 introduces the important **session** and **application** objects, which allow our web applications to deal intelligently with users by tracking information about who's using our site and where they've got to in the application. Whilst JavaBeans and tag libraries are important ways of making your code more manageable, there's still more to learn on this; Chapter 12 looks at further ways of **structuring our applications**. Rounding off this section, Chapter 13 takes a behind-the-scenes look at what's *really* going on when we write a JSP-based application. We'll discover that it's all built on the **Servlet API**, which we'll then investigate.

Chapters 14–17 look at different aspects of **managing data**. Any practical web application will need to be able to read data from a variety of sources and store it for long periods. These chapters look at three different aspects of this: reading and writing **files**, using **databases**, and managing **e-mail**.

Chapters 18-20 round the book off by looking at **Struts**, a popular framework that makes creating JSP- and Java-based web applications much easier by providing a lot of the basic infrastructure for you (hence the name – Struts is what holds the rest of your application up). In Chapter 18 we look at the facilities that Struts provides, then in the final two chapters we'll see how we can apply everything we've learned in the book to build a working database-powered application for a local tourism authority.

The **Appendices** cover a range of useful reference material on the syntax of JSP and its implicit objects, the various XML-based document formats you'll encounter in the course of the book, and where to get more information.

What You Need To Use This Book

The first thing you'll need to use this book is a computer for which the Java programming language is available. We'll be particularly addressing people using Microsoft Windows (including Windows 95, 98, Me, NT, and 2000), but Java is also available as a free download for a wide variety of other operating systems including Solaris and Linux.

You'll also need appropriate web server software for running your JSP and Servlet applications. We'll use Tomcat, which is available free-of-charge and is the official "reference implementation" of the JSP and Servlet technologies. In Chapter 1 we'll walk you through installing the Java environment and Tomcat version 4.0, and running your first JSP.

In later chapters you'll need some additional software, and we'll show you where to download them from and how to go about installing them as required:

❑   In Chapters 15-16 and 19-20 you'll need the MySQL database.

❑   For Chapter 17 you need the JavaMail and JavaBeans Activation Framework, in order to send and receive e-mail from your web applications.

❑   For Chapters 18-20 you need the Struts application framework; this provides an excellent basis on which we can build complex web applications without our code becoming too hard to follow and maintain.

Conventions

To help you understand what's going on, and in order to maintain consistency, we've used a number of conventions throughout the book:

When we introduce important new terms, we **highlight** them.

Advice, hints and background information comes in an indented, italicized font like this.

> Important bits of information that you shouldn't ignore come in boxes like this!

Try It Out

After learning something new, we'll have a *Try It Out* section, which will demonstrate the concepts learned, and get you working with the technology.

How It Works

After a *Try It Out* section, there will usually be a further explanation within a *How It Works* section, to help you relate what you've done to what you've just learned.

Words that appear on the screen in menus, like the File or Window menu, along with URLs are in a similar font to what you see on screen, for example: http://www.wrox.com.

The command line and output is shown as follows:

```
> java runMe
When the command line is shown, it's in the above style, whereas terminal output
is in this style.
```

Keys that you press on the keyboard, like *Ctrl* and *Enter*, are in italics.

Definitions of Java methods and structures are shown in a bold, fixed pitch font, for example:

```
void write(byte barray [], int offset, int numBytes)
```

We use two font styles for code. If it's a word that we're talking about in the text, for example, when discussing doGet() method or the HttpServletRequest object, it will be in a fixed pitch font. File names are also displayed in this font.

If it's a block of code that you can type in and run, then it's also in a gray box:

```
<%@ page info="If Example JSP"%>
<html>

  <head>
    <title>Chapter 5 Examples</title>
  </head>

  <body>
    <b>IF Statement Example ( Response ) <br /></b>
    <br />

    <%
      int quantity = Integer.parseInt(request.getParameter("quantity"));
      if (quantity > 0) {
        out.println("Thank-you for your order!!");
      } else {
        out.println("Sorry, please enter a positive quantity");
```

```
      }
    %>

  </body>
</html>
```

Sometimes you'll see code in a mixture of styles, like this:

```
<%@ page info="If Example JSP"%>
<html>

  <head>
    <title>Chapter 5 Examples</title>
  </head>

  <body>
    <b>IF Statement Example ( Response ) <br /></b>
    <br />

    <%
      int quantity = Integer.parseInt(request.getParameter("quantity"));
      if (quantity > 0) {
        out.println("Thank-you for your order!!");
      } else {
        out.println("Sorry, please enter a positive quantity");
      }
    %>

  </body>
</html>
```

In this case, we want you to consider the code with the gray background in particular, for example to modify it. The code with a white background is code we've already looked at, and that we don't wish to examine further.

Downloading the Source Code

As we move through the chapters, there will be copious amounts of code available for you, so that you can see exactly how the JSP principles being explained work. We'll also be stopping frequently to try it out, so that you not only see how things work, but can make them work yourself.

The source code for all of the examples is available for download from the Wrox site (see below). However, you might decide that you prefer to type all the code in by hand. Many readers prefer this, because it's a good way to get familiar with the coding techniques that are being used.

Whether you want to type the code in or not, we have made all the source code for this book available at our web site, at the following address:

http://www.wrox.com

If you're one of those readers who likes to type in the code, you can use our files to check the results you should be getting – this should be your first stop if you think you might have typed in an error. If you're one of those readers who don't like typing, then downloading the source code from our web site is a must!

Either way, it'll help you with updates and debugging.

Tell Us What You Think

We've worked hard to make this book as relevant and useful as possible, so we'd like to get a feel for what it is you want and need to know, and what you think about how we've presented things.

If you have anything to say, let us know at feedback@wrox.com.

Errata & Updates

We've made every effort to make sure there are no errors in the text or the code. However, to err is human, and as such we recognize the need to keep you informed of any mistakes as they're spotted and amended, so errata sheets are available at http://www.wrox.com.

More details on obtaining support, finding out about errata, and providing us with feedback, can be found in Appendix E.

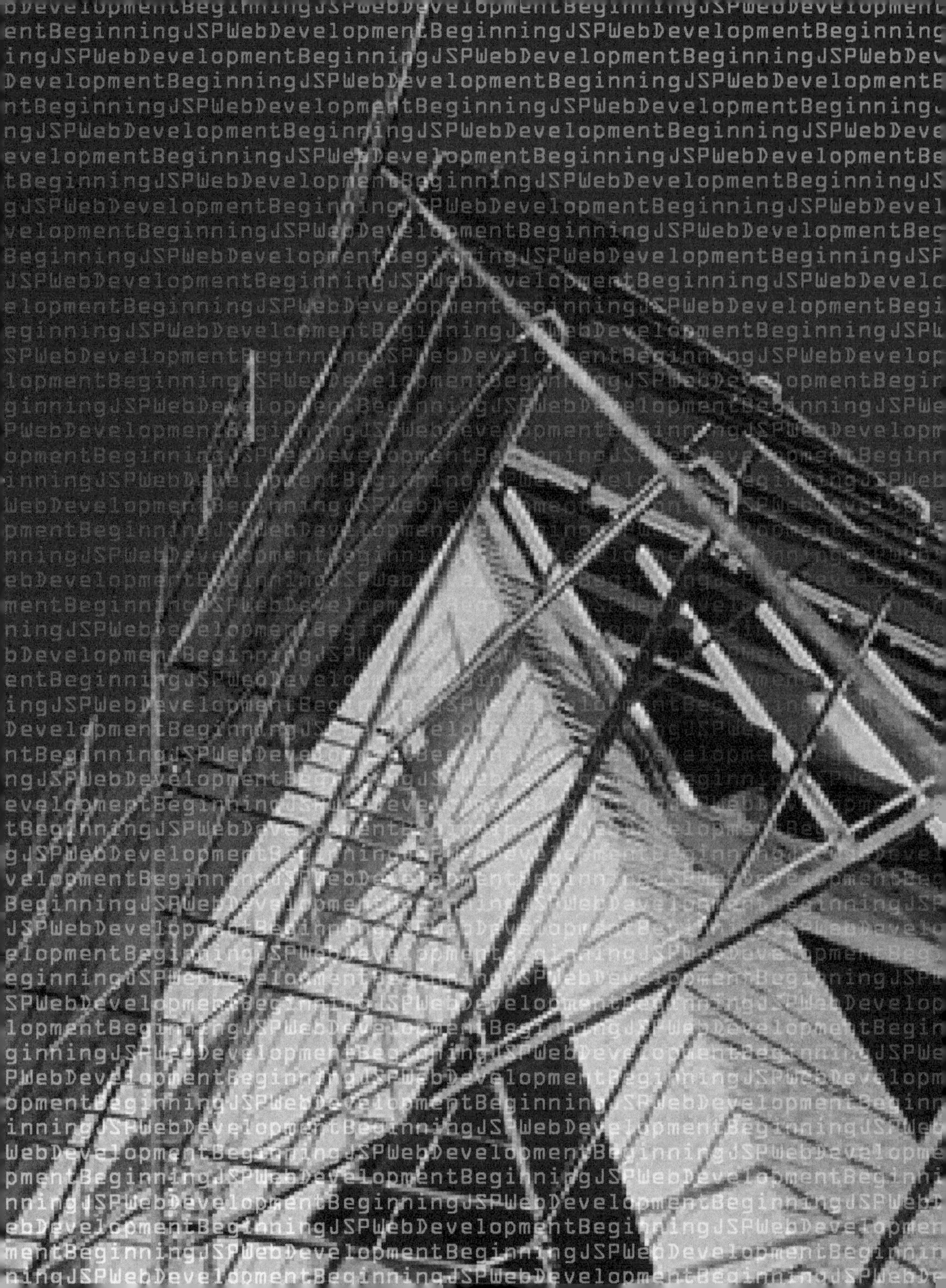
BeginningJSPWebDevelopment

Starting Web Programming

Java has enjoyed a tremendous growth in use among web developers over the past few years to become one of the Web's pre-eminent development platforms. In fact, Java has become such a major player so rapidly that many in the industry aren't really sure exactly what Java does or how it works; they just know they need to learn it fast. If you fall into this category, keep reading – you're about to get some answers.

The goal of this chapter is to get all the tools installed on your machine that you'll need to develop Java web applications. We'll also go through the process of writing a simple Java web application as well.

At the end of the chapter, I've also included some optional material that explains a little about how the web itself works, and Java's role in the web.

Installing the Software

The first step to writing Java web applications is installing the necessary software; let's get to it!

Installing Java

The first thing you need is the Java software development kit:

❑ **Download Java**. Point your web browser to http://java.sun.com/j2se/. You're looking for the latest version of the "Java 2 SDK, Standard Edition", disregarding any beta versions that may be available. As of this writing, the latest version is 1.3.

❑ **Install Java**. After your browser finishes sucking down Java, execute the file that you've downloaded. For version 1.3 on Windows the installer's default folder (or directory) for the Java is C:\jdk1.3, but feel free to install it wherever you want (however, substitute your custom path for C:\jdk1.3 wherever you see it in this book).

Note that in these instructions and throughout the rest of the chapter I use the Windows notation for paths. To make these into Unix paths, substitute forward slashes (/) instead of back slashes (\) and remove the drive prefix at the beginning of the path – for example, C:\jdk1.3 becomes /jdk1.3.

Installing Tomcat

You've now got Java, but for creating web applications, we'll need one more tool: **Tomcat**. Tomcat is what's known as a **servlet container**. In the Java world, a servlet container is responsible for receiving web requests and passing them to Java web applications. (For the curious, see the history lesson at the end of this chapter to learn exactly why it's called a servlet container.)

❑ **Download Tomcat**. Tomcat's home is http://jakarta.apache.org/tomcat/. Surf on over there and grab the latest version of Tomcat 4.x (as of this writing, it's Tomcat 4.0 beta 5).

❑ **Extract Tomcat**. You may extract the Tomcat archive into any location you desire; we suggest that you extract it into C:\, which will place the files in a folder called something like C:\jakarta-tomcat-4.0-b5. (The exact folder will depend on which version of Tomcat 4.x you downloaded; this is the correct folder for beta 5.)

Configuring Your Environment

That's the software installed; we're nearly done now. However, you do need to set up your computer's environment so that Tomcat knows where it can find the various bits of software we need such as the Java software development kit.

To do this you need to set or modify several environment variables. We'll look at how to do this in a moment; first, let's see which variables we need to set:

❑ JAVA_HOME tells Tomcat where it can find the Java software development kit; you must set it to the folder where you installed this, such as:

    C:\jdk1.3

❑ CATALINA_HOME needs to point to the folder where you installed Tomcat, such as:

    C:\jakarta-tomcat-4.0-b5

❑ CLASSPATH is used to help the Java software find extra bits of program code; it contains a list of places to look, separated by semicolons (;) on Windows or colons (:) on Unix. We need to include a file called servlet.jar, which can be found in Tomcat's common\lib folder – this contains various bits of useful code that we'll need in later chapters. So, if you're on Windows and have been following our recommendations so far you've set CLASSPATH to:

    C:\jakarta-tomcat-4.0-b5\common\lib\servlet.jar;.

❑ PATH is used by your operating system to find programs you want to run; like CLASSPATH, it consists of a list of places to look separated by semicolons (on Windows) or colons (on Unix). You'll find that PATH is already set but you need to *add* the C:\jdk1.3\bin folder to the list. For example, on Windows your PATH might currently be:

    C:\WINDOWS;C:\WINDOWS\COMMAND

which would need to be changed to:

```
C:\WINDOWS;C:\WINDOWS\COMMAND;C:\jdk1.3\bin
```

So, let's move on to seeing how you actually set these environment variables.

Setting Environment Variables On Windows 2000

Let's start by seeing how to do so on Windows 2000:

1. Go into the Control Panel and open up the System control panel application.

2. You should have a window entitled System Properties on your screen; select the Advanced tab, and click on the Environment Variables button:

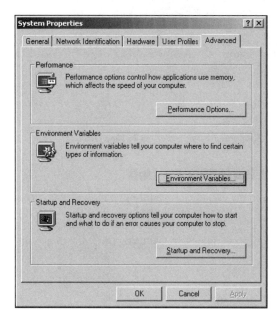

3. A new window named Environment Variables should have opened. Click on the New button in the System Variables section.

4. The New System Variable window should now be on your screen. Enter JAVA_HOME for as the name and the path to your JDK (such as c:\jdk1.3) for the value, as shown below:

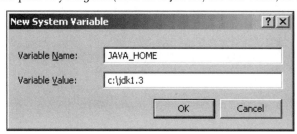

5. Repeat steps 3 and 4, substituting first the values CATALINA_HOME and c:\jakarta-tomcat-4.0-b5 (or whichever is the correct folder) for those given above, and again for CLASSPATH.

6. The procedure for setting PATH is similar, except that as the PATH variable already exists, you need to select it in the list of system variables and click Edit..., rather than using the New... button. Then amend the value as described above.

Setting Environment Variables On Windows 95/98

In Windows 95 and 98, environment variables are set by editing the C:\autoexec.bat file (with an editor like Notepad) and adding set commands; for example, :

```
set JAVA_HOME=C:\jdk1.3
set CATALINA_HOME=C:\jakarta-tomcat-4.0-b5
set CLASSPATH=C:\jakarta-tomcat-4.0-b5\common\lib\servlet.jar;.
set PATH=C:\WINDOWS;C:\jdk1.3\bin
```

You'll also need to increase your "environment space": edit C:\config.sys and add the following line at the end:

```
shell=c:\command.com /e:1024 /p
```

You'll need to restart Windows for these changes to take effect.

Setting Environment Variables On Unix

On Unix, you set environment variables by editing your shell start-up script, such as .bashrc if you use **bash** as your shell or .tcshrc if you use **tcsh**.

❑ In bash, environment variables are set using the following syntax in your .bashrc file:

```
JAVA_HOME=/jdk1.3
export JAVA_HOME
CATALINA_HOME=/jakarta-tomcat-4.0-b5
export CATALINA_HOME
CLASSPATH=/jakarta-tomcat-4.0-b5/common/lib/servlet.jar:.
export CLASSPATH
PATH=/usr/bin:/usr/local/bin:/jdk1.3/bin
export PATH
```

❑ In tcsh, the setenv command is used in your .tcshrc file to set environment variables, for example:

```
setenv JAVA_HOME /jdk1.3
setenv CATALINA_HOME /jakarta-tomcat-4.0-b5
setenv CLASSPATH /jakarta-tomcat-4.0-b5/common/lib/servlet.jar:.
setenv PATH /usr/bin:/usr/local/bin:/jdk1.3/bin
```

You'll need to start a new shell for these changes to take effect.

For the purposes of this book, we're done with installing Java. However, when you get a chance check out http://java.sun.com/j2se/1.3/install.html for some additional steps that make Java easier to use; it's also a good resource if you need more help with the installation process.

Try It Out – Testing Tomcat

We're all done with installing and setting environment variables – time to try out Tomcat!

❑ On Windows, the command to run Tomcat is:
```
c:\jakarta-tomcat-4.0-b4\bin\startup.bat
```

❑ On Unix, the command is:
```
/jakarta-tomcat-4.0-b4/bin/startup.sh
```

Elsewhere in the book we'll be using the notation `%CATALINA_HOME%` to refer to the folder that the `CATALINA_HOME` environment variable refers to; using this, we could have referred to the `%CATALINA_HOME%\bin\startup.bat` command on Windows.

Once Tomcat is up and running, open your favourite web browser and go to http://localhost:8080/. You should see something like the following page:

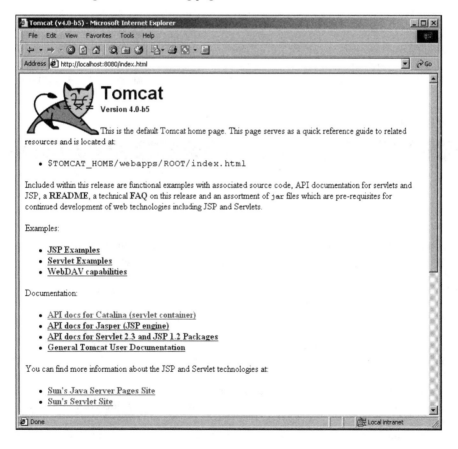

Click on the **JSP Examples** link and try out the example programs to verify that everything is working properly. If you can't get the examples to work, double-check to ensure that you have correctly followed these instructions.

When you're done working with Tomcat, you'll want to shut it down.

- ❑ On Windows, the command to shut it down is:
  `c:\jakarta-tomcat-4.0-b5\bin\shutdown.bat`
- ❑ On Unix, it's:
  `/jakarta-tomcat-4.0-b5/bin/shutdown/sh` ,

Your First Web Application

Okay, we've got Java, we've got Tomcat, now we're ready to write a simple web application. What could be better for your first application than a variation of the timeless "Hello World" program? Far be it from me to break from long-standing tradition. To add a dynamic flair, we'll make it dynamically display today's date, too. For this example, we'll be using **JavaServer Pages (JSP)** technology, which allows Java developers to mix Java code with normal HTML.

Before we start coding, let's talk a little bit about web applications. In the Java world, the term **web application** is an official label, referring to the many different files that make up a web-enabled application. Hereafter, "web application" will be used in this Java-centric sense. Java web applications are designed to automatically configure themselves to run on any servlet container. It's actually not as complex as it sounds, but it is really neat. We'll get into the nitty gritty of web applications in subsequent chapters.

Now, let's get started.

Try It Out - Creating a Simple Web Application

We'll start by creating a new web application, and calling it `begjsp-ch01` (because this is the first chapter of the book). To do this, we create a new folder with that name, in Tomcat's `webapps` folder. In other words, we need to create a new folder called something like `C:\jakarta-tomcat-4.0-b5\webapps\begjsp-ch01`.

Inside this folder we need to create some more folders. We won't actually *use* them in this chapter, but they're needed to get Tomcat to recognize our application. Inside the `begjsp-ch01` folder you just created, make a folder called `WEB-INF`, and inside that `WEB-INF` folder create two new folders called `classes` and `lib`. We'll see what these folders are for from Chapter 4 onwards.

Now that we've created the web application folder, `begjsp-ch01`, we can put all sorts of resources in it – for example, HTML pages. For example, if you created a web page file called `hello.html` and saved it in the `begjsp-ch01` folder, you could point your web browser at http://localhost:8080/begjsp-ch01/hello.html and see that page.

We, on the other hand, are going to create a JSP page; the difference here is that a JSP page can include special program code that is run *inside the web server* (in other words, inside Tomcat) that affects what is sent to the browser. It's important to be clear on this difference – in this book the web server and web browser programs are actually going to be running on the same computer, but that's not normally the case.

Now, using Notepad, or vi, or whatever your favorite editor is, let's create a JSP page. Create a file called `index.jsp`, in your `C:\jakarta-tomcat-4.0-b5\webapps\begjsp-ch01` folder, and enter these lines into it:

```
<html>
  <head>
    <title>My First JSP</title>
  </head>

  <body>
    Hello world!<br>
    The current date and time is <%= new java.util.Date() %>
  </body>
</html>
```

Save the file, and we're done! Now, let's view your JSP with a web browser.

Start Tomcat (if it's still running from earlier, shut it down and then start it again so it will recognize our new web application) and then enter the URL http://localhost:8080/begjsp-ch01/index.jsp into your browser.

You should see a screen looking something like this:

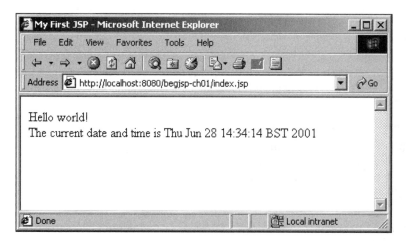

Congratulations! You've created your first JSP, and you're on the way to a larger world of Java fun. If all this still seems a bit hazy to you, don't panic, that's why this is the first chapter!

How It Works

If you've done any work with HTML, the JSP we wrote should have looked very familiar to you. In fact, the only JSP-centric code we wrote was:

```
The current date and time is <%= new java.util.Date() %>
```

JSP introduces a special tag, `<%= ... %>`, to distinguish itself from normal HTML. The servlet container will attempt to execute any Java code within those tags, which are called **expression scriptlet tags** (not to be confused with JavaScript).

The words `new java.util.Date()` tell Java to create a new `Date` object, and the `<%= %>` symbols tell Java to print the contents of that object (today's date) to the HTML.

If you select View | Source in your web browser, you'll see that what the browser received is not exactly the same as the JSP code you entered: the expression scriptlet tag was replaced with the current date and time – the Java code was run *within the server* and never made it as far as the browser:

```
<html>
  <head>
    <title>My First JSP</title>
  </head>

  <body>
    Hello world!<br>
    The current date and time is Thu Jun 28 14:34:14 BST 2001
  </body>
</html>
```

Finally, let's pick apart the URL we used to request the page, http://localhost:8080/begjsp-ch01/index.jsp. There are five parts to this:

❑ http – We're using the HTTP protocol, in other words the World Wide Web, to retrieve a resource from a web server.

❑ localhost – This is the name of the web server. localhost is a special, reserved name that refers to the local machine – the machine you're running the browser software on. Although you normally use a web browser to access a server somewhere else in the world, in this case our web server is running on the same machine as the browser.

You can also use 127.0.0.1 to specify the local machine, rather than localhost.

❑ 8080 – This is the port number that the web server is listening on. A computer can have various server programs listening for clients (such as web browsers) to connect to them; each must have a different port number. Normally web servers use port 80, but Tomcat installs itself to use port 8080 by default so that it can coexist with another web server on the same machine.

You can change the port number by editing Tomcat's `server.xml` configuration file, found in the `%CATALINA_HOME%\conf\` folder. However, it's not necessary to do so to use any of the code in this book.

❑ begjsp-ch01 – This is the name of the web application we created.

❑ index.jsp – This is the actual resource we requested. The `.jsp` filename extension told Tomcat that it should treat the file as a JavaServer Page and read through it checking for Java code to execute. If we had placed the same text in a file called index.html the Java code would have been left untouched and sent directly to the browser.

We can also, of course, place web resources in folders within our `begjsp-ch01` folder, maybe in one called `images`. That would not make `images` a web application – only folders that are within Tomcat's `webapps` folder form web applications.

Brief History of Java and the Web

For the curious, in these next few sections, I've written a summarized history of the Web and Java. If you'd rather just get down to business, go ahead and skip to the next chapter. If you're interested in understanding a bit more about how things work and why things are the way they are, read on!

The Web

Back in the sixties, as computers began their prolific distribution across the nation, the United States constructed a military computer network called the ARPANET, which linked key computers across the nation. The network was decentralized and so somewhat impervious to a large-scale attack on the United States.

The attack never happened, but the network's well-designed architecture ensured its survival for many years. The academic community's use of it soon overtook that of the military. The network become primarily an educational tool and was renamed the **Internet**.

The early days of the Internet were not for the layman. Few people outside of the scientific disciplines were even aware that the Internet existed, and fewer still had access to it. This first generation of Internet users had to learn many command-line driven utilities such as Telnet, FTP, and Gopher to get anything useful done. Ease of use was not a concern.

The seeds of an easier to use Internet, and hence widespread use, were sown in 1989 when Tim Berners-Lee, a computer scientist working for the European Organization for Nuclear Research (CERN), invented the **World Wide Web**. Berners-Lee aimed to create an interactive **hypertext** system on top of the existing Internet, that would facilitate greater communication amongst the world community of physicists. Hypertext refers to any system where words function as links to other documents or sections of a document – Macintosh users will remember the classic Hypercard, which for many was the first hypertext application they used.

The Web began to gain momentum, and by 1993 comprised around 50 web servers. At this time an event occurred that would light the fuse of the Internet explosion; the National Center for Supercomputing Applications (NCSA) at the University of Illinois released the first version of the Mosaic web browser for Unix, PC, and Macintosh systems. Prior to Mosaic, the only fully featured browser available was on the NeXT platform.

With the Mosaic foundation laid, 1994 saw the emergence of the Web into pop culture. The Web became the "killer application" that encouraged the general public to explore the Internet for themselves. In the same year, a small Silicon Valley company, that would eventually become Netscape, was founded by some of the same folks who had created Mosaic. The so-called "New Economy" consisting of e-land grabs and irrationally valuated companies was just around the corner. And the rest is, well, history.

For more information on the history of the Internet, see http://www.isoc.org/internet/history/.
For more information on the history of the web, see
http://public.web.cern.ch/Public/ACHIEVEMENTS/web.html.

How the Web Works

There can be confusion as to what exactly the Internet is and how it's different from the Web. The Internet is the physical computer network that links computers around the world. The Web on the other hand is a **service** that sits on the foundation of the Internet. The Web allows interconnected computers to do something worthwhile. The Web is one of many different services that utilize the Internet; others include e-mail, streaming video, and multiplayer games.

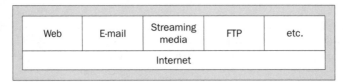

As a service, the Web defines how two parties, a **web client** (or web **browser**) and a **web server,** use the Internet to communicate. When you visit a web site, you are creating a relationship between these two parties. In this relationship, the two parties communicate by sending a series of brief messages. First, the web browser sends a message to the web server requesting a particular web page that it wishes to receive, and the web server responds with an appropriate message. For each additional page that is viewed, the web browser sends additional requests to the web server, which likewise responds with the appropriate messages.

This type of relationship is called a **request/response model**. The client, in this case the web browser, requests a specific resource (for instance, a web page) and the server then responds with the requested resource, if it's available. The Web is based on this request/response model, which is implemented via the **Hyper Text Transfer Protocol (HTTP)**. Just as "protocol" in diplomatic settings governs how two parties should conduct discussions, a "protocol" in the networking sense is a definition of how one device or program communicates with another. HTTP is a networking protocol that defines how a web client and a web server communicate.

The important point to remember is that the request the client sends to server is known as the **HTTP request**, and the response sent by the server back to the client is called the **HTTP response**. You will often deal with HTTP requests and responses as you develop web applications.

Common Gateway Interface (CGI)

When browsing the web, you've certainly come across both static pages, which return the same document to every user, and pages that are specially generated just for you. While you can get a fair amount of use from returning static files, the real excitement and usefulness comes from creating dynamic HTML documents.

The **Common Gateway Interface (CGI)** provided the original mechanism by which web users could actually execute programs on web servers, not just request HTML pages. Under the CGI model:

1. The web browser sends a request just as it would for an HTML page.

2. The web server is configured to know that the requested resource corresponds to an external program.

3. The web server then executes the external program, passing it the HTTP request that it received from the browser.

4. The external program does its work.

5. The web server passes the program's output back to the browser as an HTTP response.

CGI was enormously popular in the early days of the Web as the standard means of generating web pages on the fly (such pages are said to be **dynamic**). Almost every programming language imaginable has been used to implement some kind of CGI-based solution; Perl has been an especially popular language for CGI development.

However, as the Web grew in popularity and the traffic demands placed on web sites increased, CGI wasn't efficient enough to keep up. This is because, with CGI, each time a request is received the web server must start running a new copy of the external program. If only a handful of users request a CGI program simultaneously, this doesn't present too much of a problem.

But that's not the case if hundreds or thousands of users request the resource at the same time – imagine the web server attempting to launch a separate copy of a CGI program for each of those requests. With each new program requiring its share of CPU and memory use, the server's resources would be rapidly used up. The situation is even bleaker when one considers that CGI programs written in interpreted languages such as Perl will result in the launch of large run-time interpreters with each request.

Alternatives To CGI

Over the years, many alternative solutions to CGI have surfaced. The successful CGI replacements provide an environment that lives *within* an existing web server, or even functions as a web server on its own.

Many such CGI replacements have been built on top of the popular open-source **Apache web server** (http://www.apache.org/). This is because of Apache's popular module API, which allows developers to extend Apache's functionality with persistent programs. The modules are loaded in memory when Apache starts up, and Apache passes the appropriate HTTP requests to these in-memory modules and passes the HTTP responses back out to the browser. This means that the cost of loading an interpreter into memory is removed, and scripts can begin executing faster.

While few developers actually create modules themselves (because they are relatively difficult to develop), many third-party modules exist that provide a basis for developers to create applications that are much more efficient than normal CGI. A few examples:

❑ mod_perl – Maintains the Perl interpreter in memory, thus freeing Perl scripts from the overhead of loading a new copy of the Perl interpreter for each request. This module is very popular.

❑ mod_php4 – Does for the popular PHP language what mod_perl does for Perl.

❑ mod_fastcgi – Similar to plain vanilla CGI, but enables programs to stay resident in memory rather than terminate when each request is completed.

While the Apache name originally referred only to the Apache web server, a legion of open-source programs have been developed under the auspices of the Apache Project, including the Tomcat server which we're using in this book.

Java and the Web

At last we come to Java. Java was initially released in the mid-1990's as a way to liven up dull, static web pages. It was platform-independent (Java programs could run on computers running a variety of different operating systems, rather than being tied to just, say, Windows) and allowed developers to have their programs executed right in the web browser. Many an industry sage prognosticated that these **Java applets** (applet meaning a "mini-application" that executed within the browser) would catch on, make the Web more exciting and interactive, change the way we bought computers, and commoditize all of the various conventional operating systems – they'd just be platforms for web browsers.

One of my favorite applets; find more at http://java.sun.com/applets/.

Turns out Java applets never really caught on to the degree people predicted, and other technologies such as Macromedia Flash became much more popular for creating really stylish websites. However, Java wasn't just good for applets; it could also be used for creating stand-alone applications that were also platform-independent. While these too could threaten the strength of entrenched incompatible operating systems, Java applications haven't really caught on yet either.

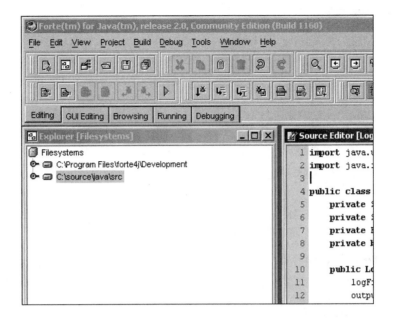

This is a screenshot of Forte (http://www.sun.com/forte/ffj/), a popular Java programming environment; it's an example of a stand-alone Java application.

But like a prize-fighter that won't stay knocked down, those innovative Java architects had another trick up their sleeve: **Java Servlets**. Servlets (a "mini-server") are another alternative technology to CGI. Servlets themselves are not stand-alone applications; they are loaded into memory by a **servlet container**. The servlet container then functions as a web server, receiving HTTP requests from web browsers and passing them to servlets. Alternatively, the servlet container can integrate with an existing web server – for example, a popular Apache module integrates Apache with the Tomcat servlet container.

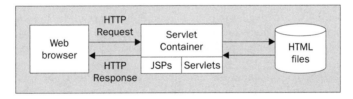

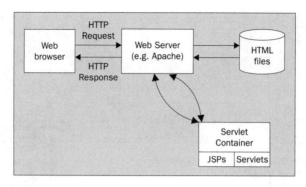

The simplicity of the Java programming language, its platform-independent nature, Sun's open-source and community-driven attitude towards Java, and the elegance of the servlet model itself have all made Java Servlets an immensely popular solution for creating dynamic web content.

JavaServer Pages (JSP)

To make creating dynamic web content even easier, Java has introduced **JavaServer Pages** (also called **JSPs**). While Servlets can require some pretty extensive knowledge of Java to write, a newbie to Java can learn how to do some pretty neat things with JSPs in a hurry. JSPs were also designed to make it easier for users of Microsoft's **Active Server Pages (ASP)** technology to migrate to Java.

> *The JSP technology is actually built on top of servlets; as we'll see later in the book, the two technologies actually work well together. It is common to use both in the same web application.*

JavaScript

In closing, let's talk about JavaScript. JavaScript is a technology that enables web pages to have some programmatic functionality *in the browser*. While Java applets are isolated applications that are simply displayed on a web page, JavaScript works with and can manipulate the HTML page.

Some folks, after coding some JavaScript code here and there, are under the impression that they know Java and have programmed in Java. Surprisingly, that's not at all true. **JavaScript is not Java**; it's an entirely distinct programming language that was developed about the same time that Java was released.

Originally called LiveScript, the name was changed by Netscape to JavaScript because it employed a syntax similar to Java's, and because those behind it wanted to capitalize on the exposure and popularity of the Java language. However, Microsoft introduced its own scripting language, JScript, and after a while a neutral standard was developed. Today, JavaScript and JScript are based on the open **ECMAScript** standard (also called ECMA-262) but Netscape and Microsoft persist in using their proprietary names for their implementations of it.

To understand the distinction between JavaScript and JavaServer Pages better, it may help you to remember that **JavaScript code is generally executed by the web client (browser)** after the web server sends the browser the HTTP response, and **JavaServer Pages are executed by the web server** before the web server sends the HTTP response. In fact, the JSP is what creates the HTTP response. Thus, JavaScript is said to be a "client-side" technology and its underlying code can be viewed (and copied) by web users, while JavaServer Pages are a "server-side" technology and its underlying code is not exposed to web users; it is processed by the web server before it reaches the client.

Summary

In this chapter, you've accomplished a lot:

- ❑ You installed the basic tools you need to create Java web applications.

- ❑ You also created your first simple web application.

- ❑ You also understand the difference between static and dynamic web content, the history of the web, different approaches to creating dynamic content, and the difference between client-side programming (like JavaScript) and server-side programming (like JSPs or Servlets).

In subsequent chapters, you'll build on this foundation to create increasingly complex and useful web applications, and you'll also be taught more details about how the Java language works.

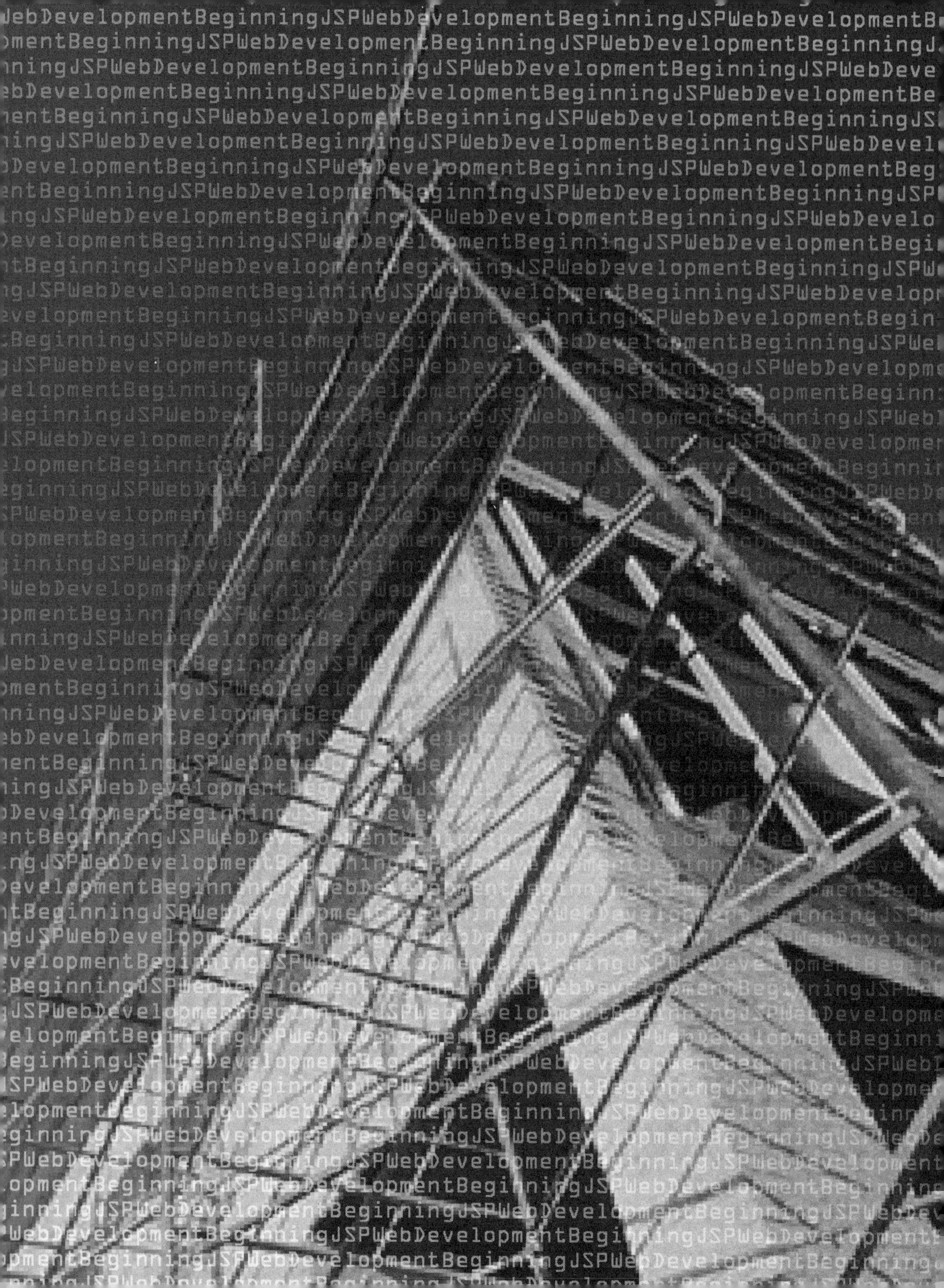
BeginningJSPWebDevelopment

Storing Data and Performing Calculations

If you want to create a dynamic and interesting web site you will need to be able to store data, and to perform calculations with that data. In this chapter we will look at how you can store data in Java and JSP, and the differences in storing different types of data, such as numbers and characters.

It is also important for the JSP engine, for example Tomcat, to be able to understand which parts of a JSP page should be sent to the client, for example the HTML markup, and which parts are Java code that contains data and calculations that it should execute. Scriptlet elements are used to make this separation, and we will look at the different types of scriptlet elements available as well as discussing how to best use them.

We will cover:

- ❏   How data is stored in variables
- ❏   The different types of data we can store
- ❏   How we can perform calculations using variables
- ❏   How to store and manipulate textual data (strings)
- ❏   The different types of scriptlet elements used in JSP pages
- ❏   How to output the result of calculations to the client

Let's start by looking at how we store data in Java.

Variables

A **variable** is a named piece of memory in which you can store some data. Each variable will be able to store a particular **type** of data. So, if you have a variable that stores integers you cannot use it to store a character.

Each variable has a name, which is the variable's **identifier**, and this identifier is used to reference the variable in your code. Before you can use a variable you must **declare** it, which specifies the name of the variable and the type of data that it will store.

If you wanted a variable to store a character in you would declare it as follows:

```
char myChar;
```

A variable declaration begins with the type of the variable. In this case we declare a variable named myChar, and we say that it is "of type char". If we wanted to declare an integer type variable named myInt we would write:

```
int myInt;
```

If you want you can declare more than one variable at once – so long as they are of the same type. For example, the following code declares three variables of type int:

```
int myFirstInt, mySecondInt, myThirdInt;
```

A variable also has a **value**, the actual data that it's currently storing, which you can change in your code. Setting the value of the variable is easy; if you wanted to set the value of myChar to 'a' you would write:

```
myChar = 'a';
```

Note the single quotes around the value of the char; this tells Java that a is a character, not (say) the name of a variable. (Make sure that you use single quotes and not double quotes.) These quotes are only needed for char variables; if you were setting the value of myInt to 7 you would simply write:

```
myInt = 7;
```

If you want, you can combine the declaration of a variable and setting its value, this is known as **initializing** the variable. To declare and initialize a char variable, myChar, you could write:

```
char myChar = 'a';
```

You saw before that you can declare more than one variable at once; similarly you can declare and initialize more than one variable at once. For example:

```
char myFirstChar = 'a', mySecondChar = 'b', myThirdChar = 'c';
```

Of course, we can create variables that hold data of types other than characters and integers, but before we look at the different types available we should mention a few rules about naming variables.

Variable Names

There are some rules about what names you can use for your variables. They must begin with a letter, an underscore, or a dollar sign. (In practice you should avoid using names that begin with the dollar sign and stick to letters and an underscore; this is because the dollar sign is used to signify particular types of variables.)

After the first character your variable names can include any characters you want, except for certain special characters that have special meanings like =, +, and -. In addition your variable names cannot have any spaces, so `myInt` is a valid name but `my Int` is not. You should also keep in mind that Java is a **case-sensitive** language, which means that `myint` is not the same as `myInt`.

There is one final naming rule; there are certain **keywords** that you cannot use for variable names, such as `char` and `int`, as these are words that have special meanings in Java code. If you stick to simple, descriptive names for your variables you shouldn't run into any trouble.

> *You can check the complete naming rules, as well as other coding coventions, in the Java Language Specification at http://java.sun.com/docs/books/jls/index.html and the Java Coding Conventions at http://java.sun.com/docs/codeconv/html/CodeConvTOC.doc.html.*

The Primitive Data Types

Java has eight **primitive data types**. These are used to store data that falls in one the following three categories:

❑ Numeric variables, both integer and floating point

❑ A single character

❑ Logical values that represent `true` or `false`

Let's take a closer look at these different types of data and the data types used to store them. We will begin with numeric variables, which can be further categorized into **integer** and **floating point** data types.

Integer Data Types

Integer data types are used for declaring variables that can store integer values (whole numbers) and Java defines four such data types: `byte`, `short`, `int`, and `long`. All four data types store both negative and positive whole numbers, but differ in the range of data they can store. Therefore, your choice of which type to use is determined by the size of the data you will need to store. The following table describes the range of values each data type can store:

Data Type	Description
byte	Can have values from -128 to +127 inclusive
short	Can have values from -32768 to +32767 inclusive
int	Can have values from -2147483648 to +2147486347 inclusive
long	Can have values from -9223372036854775808 to +9223372036854775807 inclusive

If you try to set the value of a variable outside of the range that its data type can store, your code will not work. For example, an error will occur if you try to use the following piece of code:

```
byte b = 1000;
```

You need to be careful when you use an integer data type other than int. This is because by default an integer "literal" value, such as 1000000, is assumed to be of type int.

> A value of any kind specified directly in your Java code is referred to as a literal; so 10000000, 'a', and "Hello World" are all examples of literals.

If you want to define a variable of type long and the value you want to assign to the variable is larger than that supported by int you need to append an L to the end of the integer literal. For example, if you wanted to assign the value 10000000000, which is too large for an int, to a variable of type long you would write:

```
long l = 10000000000L;
```

Floating-Point Types

Java defines two floating-point data types, float and double, for storing non-integral numeric values. These data types store values such as 123.67, or using the scientific notation 1.2367E2.

Like the integer data types, the two floating-point data types can store a different range of numbers – and to a different level of precision:

Data Type	Description
float	Can have values from -3.4E38 to +3.4E38. Values are represented with approximately 7 digits accuracy.
double	Can have values from -1.7E308 to +1.7E308. Values are represented with approximately 17 digits accuracy.

Just as integer literals were assumed to be of type int, floating point literals, for example 1.234, are assumed to be of type double – even if they are within the range of float. Therefore, just as you place an L after a literal to store it as a long, you place an F after a floating point literal to store it as a float. For example:

```
float f = 1.234F
```

So we've seen how to declare and initialize integer and floating point data types and we can change the value stored in the variable, but this isn't much use on its own. What we need now is to discover how we can use these variables in calculations; for this we need to learn about **arithmetic operators**.

Arithmetic Calculations

The result of a calculation is stored in a variable using an **assignment statement**. An assignment statement consists of a variable name, followed by an **assignment operator**, followed by an **arithmetic expression**. For example:

```
totalGoals = leagueGoals + cupGoals;
```

In this code snippet, the assignment operator is the = sign. The value of the expression to the right of the = sign is calculated and stored in the variable to the left of the = sign. In this case, the values of leagueGoals and cupGoals are added together and the result is stored in totalGoals.

Addition, subtraction, multiplication, and division expressions all follow the same syntax. We've already seen how to add two values, now let's look at the other three.

To subtract the value of a variable goalsConceded from the value of a variable goalsScored, and store the result in a variable goalDifference, you would write:

```
goalDifference = goalsScored - goalsConceded;
```

To multiply the value of a variable gamesWon and the value of a variable pointsForAWin, and store the result in a variable points, you would write:

```
points = gamesWon * pointsForAWin;
```

Finally, to divide the value of a variable goalsScored by the value of a variable gamesPlayed, and store the result in a variable goalsGamesRatio, you would write:

```
goalsGameRatio = goalsScored / gamesPlayed;
```

Operator Precedence

You can combine more than one of these operators into a single expression, for example:

```
totalPoints = gamesWon * pointsForAWin + gamesDrawn * pointsForADraw;
```

This is valid code, but you might have noticed a problem. Which operation in the expression should be performed first: the addition or the multiplication? The answer is easy to work out, because Java has a consistent operator **order of precedence**. Multiplication and division operations are evaluated first, from left to right, followed by addition and subtraction operations, again from left to right. So, in the above code the expressions:

```
gamesWon * pointsForAWin
```

and

```
gamesDrawn * pointsForADraw
```

are calculated, and the results are then added together.

Although we can rely on operator precedence to combine expressions it is easy to make mistakes and it makes the code harder to read – two things we should always try to avoid. Also, you might want the addition part of an expression to be executed *before* the multiplication. These problems can be overcome by the use of **parentheses**. Parentheses are used to explicitly group expressions as well as to make your code easier to read. For example, consider the following two calculations:

```
d = a + b * c;
d = (a + b) * c;
```

In the first of these the value of b is multiplied by c and the result added to the value of a. However, in the second the parentheses mean that the value of a will be added to b and the result multiplied by c. As you can see, parentheses are very useful for ensuring that calculations will proceed in the order you want them to.

Let's see how we can use what we have learnt about variables and operators in a JSP page.

Try It Out – Using Operators With Integers

Open your favorite editor and enter the following code:

```html
<html>
  <head>
    <title>Using Operators</title>
  </head>
  <body>

    <h2>Using Operators</h2>

    <%
       int numberWins = 18;
       int numberDraws = 10;
    %>

    We won
    <%
       out.print(numberWins);
    %>
    games and drew
    <%
       out.print(numberDraws);
    %>
    games.

    <br />
```

```
<%
  int totalPoints = (numberWins * 3) + (numberDraws * 1);
%>

We won a total of
<%
  out.print(totalPoints);
%>
points.

  </body>
</html>
```

Create the directory %CATALINA_HOME%\webapps\begjsp-ch02\WEB-INF\classes\, and save
the above code as operators.jsp in %CATALINA_HOME%\webapps\begjsp-ch02\.

Start up Tomcat and navigate to http://localhost:8080/begjsp-ch02/operators.jsp; you should see the
following page:

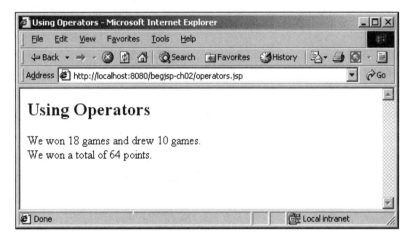

How It Works

The first piece of JSP code in operators.jsp is the declaration and initialization of two variables of
type int:

```
<%
  int numberWins = 18;
  int numberDraws = 10;
%>
```

In Chapter 1 you were introduced to scriptlet expression tags, they enclosed a JSP expression with <%=
and %>. The tags we use here are slightly different, they are simply called **scriptlet tags** and they enclose
code with <% and %>. We can include any Java code we want within these tags.

> **Java code is made up of statements. A statement is a piece of Java code, terminated by
> a semi colon.**

31

Next we print the number of games won and the number of games drawn:

```
We won
<%
   out.print(numberWins);
%>
games and drew
<%
   out.print(numberDraws);
%>
games.
```

In Chapter 1 we created output from Java code using an expression scriptlet tag and we could have used an expression tag to output the values of numberWins and numberDraws. Instead we take the opportunity to introduce the out.print() **method**.

A method is a bit of code, specially bundled up so that we can make use of it over and over again. A method takes one or more arguments, performs some operations with them, and may also return a value that we can use in an expression. In this case the out.print() method takes a variable as an argument and inserts a string representation of the variable into the HTML that is sent to the browser.

Next, we calculate the total points scored, according to the number of wins and the number of draws. We give 3 points for a win and 1 point for a draw:

```
<%
   int totalPoints = (numberWins * 3) + (numberDraws * 1);
%>
```

You can see from this that it is perfectly legal to initialize a variable, in this case totalPoints, using an expression. We have included parentheses to make the code easier to follow, although because of operator precedence they are not strictly necessary.

Finally, we include the value of totalPoints into the HTML sent to the client, using the out.print() method:

```
We won a total of
<%
   out.print(totalPoints);
%>
points.
```

Integer Division

When you divide an integer by another integer the result will not always be what you expect. For example the result of the division 5/2 is 2 and the result of 13/3 is 4. As you can see the remainder of the division is discarded. If you want to know what the remainder of an integer division is you must use the **modulus operator**, %. For example, if you wanted to know what the remainder of 27 divided by 5 was you would write:

```
remainder = 27%5;
```

The modulus operator has the same level of precedence as multiplication and division, and so is executed in any expression before addition and subtraction.

Increment and Decrement Operators

A commonly performed operation is to add or subtract one from the value of a variable. As this is such a common occurrence there are two special operators you can use to achieve this. These operators are different from those we have seen so far as these act on a single variable, therefore they are known as **unary operators**.

If you had a variable `counter` you could increment its value by one using:

```
++counter;
```

And you could decrement its value by one by using:

```
--counter;
```

This is rather more concise than:

```
counter = counter + 1;
```

However, the real benefit of using these operators is that they can be used within an expression. For example:

```
totalPoints = (numberWins++ * 3) + (numberDraws * 1);
```

After this expression has been executed the value of the variable `numberWins` is incremented by one.

We can also write the ++ operator *before* the variable name, for example:

```
totalPoints = (++numberWins * 3) + (numberDraws * 1);
```

This has an important impact on the expression. The value `numberWins` is now incremented *before* the expression is executed. You must be careful when using the increment and decrement operators to think about whether the value should be changed before or after the expression is executed.

More Assignment Operators

There are a number of other assignment operators available to use in your code, designed primarily to make the code easier to write. Commonly you will perform an operation on a variable, for example adding to another variable, and then store the result in the original variable. For example:

```
numberGoals = numberGoals + numberCupGoals;
```

Using one of these special operators we can write this as:

```
numberGoals += numberCupGoals;
```

There are equivalent assignment operators for the -, *, /, and % operations.

Arithmetic Promotion

So far, we have been careful to use the same type of variable in our expressions. However, it is possible to mix the basic types within the same expression. For example:

```
double d = 23.4;
int i = 4;
double result = d + i;
```

This works because the value of the variable i is converted to type double before the expression (d + i) is executed; this result can then be stored in the variable result, which is of type double.

These conversions follow a simple rule: if either of the operands is of type double, float, or long the other operand is converted to the correct type before the expression is executed.

Casting

If the default conversion of variable type is not what you require, you can explicitly state what type to convert a variable to; this is called **casting**. For example, if you had the following expression:

```
double result = 2.3 + 3/2;
```

The value of result will be 3.3 because the division expression is performed on variables of type int. If you wanted the result of 3 divided by 2 to give the result 1.5, you need to cast at least one of the int values to type double. To do this you write:

```
double result = 2.3 + (double)3/2;
```

Now, the value of result will be 3.8, because we're dividing the double value 3.0 by 2. You can cast any of the basic types to each other but you need to be careful that you don't lose any information when you do so. Obviously casting from an int to a double won't result in any loss but if you cast from a long to an int, or a double to an int, there will be some loss of precision.

What happens if the result of an expression on the right-hand side is not of the same type as the variable on the left-hand side in which the result is to be stored? The answer is that the result is automatically cast into the type of the left-hand side variable. For example:

```
long result = 4 + 2;
```

The result of the expression on the right-hand side is an int with a value of 6. It is automatically cast to a long so that it can be stored in the variable result, which is of type long. This automatic casting occurs so long as we are casting to a type that can hold more information. So you can automatically cast from an int to a double but you cannot automatically cast from a double to an int. If you want to cast the result of an expression to a type that holds less information you must use an *explicit* cast, for example:

```
int result = (int)(2.3 + 1.2);
```

Boolean Data Types

A somewhat different primitive data type is `boolean`. This is a data type that has only two possible values: `true` or `false`, which are `boolean` literals. An important difference between `boolean` data types and the other primitive data types is that you cannot cast a `boolean` to another type, or any other primitive type to a `boolean`.

Boolean data types are useful when we need to make decisions in our code based on whether or not a particular condition currently exists. We will cover this in Chapter 5, but we mention `boolean` data types here for completeness.

Character Data Types

The data type `char` is used to store a single character. You declare and initialize `char` variables in a slightly different way from those of integer and floating point data types:

```
char myChar = 'a';
```

This declares and initializes a `char` variable. Note the use of the single quotes around the character to be stored in the variable, like we saw earlier. As we saw then, the quotes are necessary so that the literal character value `'a'` can be distinguished from a variable named a.

Character Escape Sequences

You may wish to store characters that are not available from within your editor. Fortunately, variables of data type `char` may also be initialized using their hexadecimal codes. The example below shows a `char` variable can be initialized to the character `'A'` using its hexadecimal code:

```
char myChar = '\u0041';
```

This is a character **escape sequence**. The backwards slash `'\'` means that what follows is a code that corresponds to a particular character. The `'u'` after the escape means that the code is in hexadecimal.

For more information on character codes visit http://www.unicode.org.

Some of the more commonly used unavailable characters have special escape codes; here are some useful ones:

Escape Code	Meaning
\b	Backspace
\f	Form feed
\n	New line
\r	Carriage return
\t	Tab

Operating on Characters

You saw how you could perform operations on integer and floating point data types, so what type of operations can be performed on character data types?

Well, we can use the increment operator on a `char`:

```
char myChar = 'A';
myChar++;
```

The variable `myChar` will now hold the character `'B'`. You can even perform more complicated operations on characters like:

```
char myChar = 'A';
myChar = (char)(2 * myChar);
```

In this case `myChar` now holds the character `'?'`. Although there are situations where character arithmetic is useful, we won't need it in this book.

Most of the time you will want to use more than one character. Words and sentences are collections of characters, and if we had to create each character in turn it would be tedious to code and difficult to make changes to our application. Fortunately Java provides a type of variable that can hold and manipulate a collection of characters – `String`.

Strings

Strings are collections of characters that we can manipulate. We introduced you earlier to literal values. Java also contains **string literals**; `"I am a string"` is an example of a string literal and we can create a `String` variable as follows:

```
String str = "I am a String of characters";
```

Note that a string literal is contained within *double* quotes, unlike a `char` which is contained in single quotes.

It's important to understand that a variable of type `String` is not a primitive type like `int` or `double`. Instead it is an object; you don't need to worry about the definition of an object for now – you'll be introduced to them properly in Chapter 4. But because a variable of type `String` is an object, you can perform lots of very useful operations on it, such as searching within it, and extracting other strings from it.

Variables of the `String` type may be initialized two ways. The first way is assigning the character sequence directly to the variable as we saw above; the second is as follows:

```
String str = new String("I am a String of characters");
```

What this says is that a new `String` object named `str` should be created, and it should contain the collection of characters specified by the string literal `"I am a String of characters"`.

Operating on Strings

We said before that, because a `String` variable is an object, we can do lots of interesting things with it.

One of the most common operations performed is to join two or more string variables, this is known as **concatenation**. We can do this in two ways; first we can use the + operator in much the same way as we used it with integer and floating point data types:

```
String stringOne = "Hello ";
String stringTwo = "World";
String joinedString = stringOne + stringTwo;
```

The variable `joinedString` now has a value of `"Hello World"`. The second way is by calling **methods** on the variable; we can join strings using the `concat()` method:

```
String stringOne = "Hello ";
String stringTwo = "World";
String joinedString = stringOne.concat(stringTwo);
```

This achieves the same result, with `joinedString` having a value of `"Hello World"`. Effectively, we are telling `stringOne` to add `stringTwo` to itself, and to give us the resulting new `String`.

So, let's create a simple JSP that concatenates strings.

Try It Out - Using Strings

Open your editor and enter the following code:

```
<html>
  <head>
    <title>Using Strings</title>
  </head>
  <body>
    <h2>Using Strings</h2>

    <%
      String stringOne = "Hello";
      String stringTwo = "World";
      String joinedString = stringOne + " " + stringTwo + "!";
      out.print(joinedString);
    %>

  </body>
</html>
```

Save this as `joinedString.jsp` in `%CATALINA_HOME%\webapps\begjsp-ch02\`, start up Tomcat and navigate to http://localhost:8080/begjsp-ch02/joinedString.jsp. You should see this page:

37

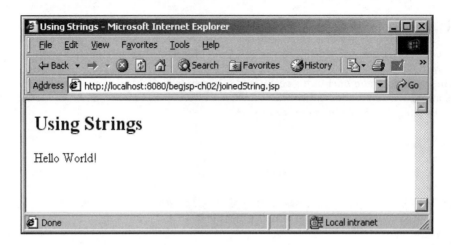

How It Works

This example simply puts into practice what you have learnt about `String` variables up to this point. We begin by declaring and initializing two `String` objects, `stringOne` and `stringTwo`:

```
String stringOne = "Hello";
String stringTwo = "World";
```

We then construct a third `String`, named `joinedString`. This `String` contains the collection of characters from both `stringOne` and `stringTwo`, as well as two other string literals, `" "` and `"!"`:

```
String joinedString = stringOne + " " + stringTwo + "!"
out.print(joinedString);
```

Now, let's take a look at some of the other methods we can use with strings: `length()`, `trim()`, and `substring()`.

length()

Use the `length()` method to get the number of characters in a `String`:

```
String str = "Use length() to find my length";
int len = str.length();
```

In the above code the value of the variable `len` is 30 – the number of characters in the variable `str`.

trim()

Often a string will have excess whitespace at either the start or the end (or both) of the collection of characters it contains. The following characters are treated as whitespace:

Character	Meaning
'\b'	Backspace
'\f'	Form feed
'\n'	New line
'\r'	Carriage return
'\t'	Tab

We can use `trim()` to get a `String` that does not have these characters at the start or end. For example:

```
String str = "      Hello World \t\n ";
String newStr = str.trim();
```

The `String` variable `newStr` now contains the text `"Hello World"`.

substring()

You can use `substring()` to extract a string from within another string. The `substring()` method is used to return a specified number of characters starting from a specified position in the `String`. For example:

```
String str = "Hello World";
String newStr = str.substring(6, 11);
```

In the above code we extract characters from `str` starting at character 6 and ending at character 10. (Note that we're counting from *zero* – the characters are numbered from 0 to 10.) Therefore, `newStr` will contain the string `"World"`. The substring begins at the index specified by the first parameter and extends to the character *before* that specified by the second parameter.

Now, let's see how we can put `trim()` and `substring()` to some use.

Try It Out – More With Strings

Open your editor and enter the following code:

```
<html>
  <head>
    <title>More With Strings</title>
  </head>

  <body>

  <h2>More With Strings</h2>

  <%
    String str = "Using trim() and substring() can be very useful";
    out.println(str);
```

```
    %>

    <br />

    <%
       str = str.substring(5, str.length());
       str = str.trim();
       out.println(str);
    %>

    </body>
</html>
```

Save this as `moreStrings.jsp` in `%CATALINA_HOME%\webapps\begjsp-ch02\`, start up Tomcat and navigate to http://localhost:8080/begjsp-ch02/moreStrings.jsp. You should see the page shown below:

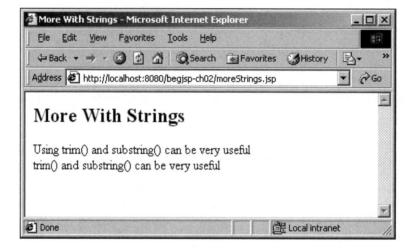

How It Works

We begin by creating a `String` that we will manipulate in the example, and printing it out:

```
    <%
       String str = "Using trim() and substring() can be very useful";
       out.println(str);
    %>
```

Then we extract a new `String` from `str`, using the `substring()` method. We start at the fifth character in `str` and use the `length()` method to ensure that string is extracted up until the last character:

```
    <%
       str = str.substring(5, str.length());
```

Then we trim any excess whitespace from the start of `str`, and print it once more to show the result:

```
     str = str.trim();
     out.println(str);
  %>
```

Note that when we call methods on `str` we cannot simply call the method on the object; we also have to save the result back into the `str` variable. This is because `String` objects are **immutable.**

Immutability of Strings

Strings are **immutable**; this means that the collection of characters they contain does not change. If we change the collection of characters that a `String` contains, we must instead create a whole new `String` object. As you can imagine, if we were constructing a large `String` bit by bit, this constant creation of new `String` objects would be very inefficient. For circumstances such as this we have another type of object called `StringBuffer` that *is* mutable. `StringBuffer` is very similar to `String`, except that the collection of characters that it contains can change. So using `StringBuffer` can, under certain circumstances, be more far more efficient than `String`.

We won't go into the details of `StringBuffer` in this chapter; we mention it only so that you are aware of the limitations of `String`, due to its immutability, and the existence of an alternative.

Objects Versus Primitive Data Types

So what *is* the difference between an object and a primitive data type such as `int`? We'll see the answer to this in much more detail in later chapters, but for now here are the most important differences:

❏ An object can contain more than one piece of data. An `int` variable can only hold one integer value at a time; an object could store (say) an `int` and a `char`, together, under the one name.

❏ An object can not only contain several pieces of data but can also provide **methods** for working with that data. For example, we saw that a `String` object has a method called `trim()` that works on the data stored in that object by trimming off any whitespace at the start or end of it. The data and the code that manipulates that data are bundled together into the object.

❏ An object is free-standing. This is a subtle one: when you declare a variable of type `String`, that variable *doesn't* actually store the `String` object. Instead, it stores a **reference** to the `String` object, and the object itself exists separately from the variable. You can even have several variables each of which references the same object. For example, if we wrote this code:

```
String first = "Hello";
String second = first;
String third = second;
```

there is only one `String` object! The three variables, `first`, `second`, and `third`, all refer to the *same* object. If we were working with a different type of object that wasn't immutable like `String`, then any changes we made to `first` would automatically be made on `second` and `third` as well, since there's only *one* object.

Scriptlet Elements

So far, you have encountered two types of script elements – **expressions** and **scriptlets**. There are two other types of elements you will use, **declarations** and **comments**. In this section we will look at all four of these types and discuss where they should be used.

Comments

Comments are designed to help you make your JSP easier to understand. The content of a comment element is not passed to the client; comments are stripped out of the page prior to transmission. If you want your comments to be visible in the markup sent to the client you need to place them in HTML comments.

JSP comments have the following syntax:

```
<%-- This is a comment and will be stripped out. --%>
```

You can also write comments within Java code – in other words, within a script element. There are two types of Java comments:

```
<%
    // This type of Java comment starts with two forward slash characters
    // and continues to the end of that line.

    /* This type of Java comment starts with a forward slash and an asterisk
       and continues for as many lines as you like until an asterisk and a
       forward slash. */
%>
```

Declarations

Declarations are used to define variables and methods for use in subsequent scriptlets and expressions, or other declarations. The syntax of a declaration is:

```
<%! JavaDeclaration %>
```

where `JavaDeclaration` is one or more Java declarative statements or method definitions, for example:

```
<%! int counter = 0; %>
```

We can also define methods for our use, for example:

```
<%!
    double calculateInterest(double loan,
                             double interestRate,
                             int numYears) {
      double interest = numYears * (interestRate * loan/100);
      return interest;
    }
%>
```

Let's break down this method declaration into its separate parts. First we define the **return type** of the method, in this case `double`. This defines the type of the value that the caller of the method will receive when the method has finished.

Next is the name of the method, `calculateInterest`, this is how we can refer to the method within code. After the method name come the **arguments** or **parameters** that the method will take. This method takes three arguments: `loan`, `interestRate`, and `numYears`. In addition to the names of the arguments we also specify the type of variable that must be passed to the method. In our method two of the arguments are of type `double` and the third is of type `int`.

We then have the **body** of the method, within the curly brackets. In the body of the method we provide instructions to perform any calculations we need, using the arguments passed to the method as required. Finally, we **return** a value to the caller of the method.

Expressions

You met expression elements in Chapter 1. Expression elements are an evaluation of a Java expression; the general syntax is:

```
<%= JavaExpression %>
```

where `JavaExpression` is a Java expression like those we've already seen. The result of the expression will then be included in the output of the page. For example, if we had a `String` named `helloString` that held the string literal `"Hello World"` and we include the expression:

```
<%= helloString %>
```

in a JSP page, then Hello World would be included in the output of the page. You should note that the semi colon is not included in an expression element.

Scriptlets

You can include any Java code within scriptlet elements. We have been using scriptlets in the examples in this chapter and they follow the general syntax:

```
<% JavaCode %>
```

Let's see how we can use these different scripting elements in a JSP page that calculates a loan repayment.

Try It Out - Loan Calculator

Open your editor and enter the following code:

```
<%-- VARIABLE DECLARATIONS --%>
<%! double loanAmount; %>
<%! double interestRate; %>
```

```
<%! int numYears; %>

<%-- METHOD DECLARATIONS --%>
<%!
  double calculateInterest(double loan,
                           double interestRate,
                           int numYears) {
    return numYears*interestRate*loan/100;
  }
%>

<html>
  <head>
    <title>Loan Calculator</title>
  </head>


  <body>
    <h1>Loan Calculated</h1>

    <%
      loanAmount = 1000;
      interestRate = 9;
      numYears = 1;
    %>

    Loan Amount: <%= loanAmount %>
    <br />
    Interest Rate: <%= interestRate %>
    <br />

    ************************
    <br />
    Number of Years: <%= numYears %>
    <br />
    Total Interest: <%= calculateInterest(loanAmount,
                                           interestRate,
                                           numYears) %>

    <br />

    <%-- CHANGE THE VALUE OF numYears --%>
    <% numYears++; %>

    ************************
    <br />
    Number of Years: <%= numYears %>
    <br />
    Total Interest: <%= calculateInterest(loanAmount,
                                           interestRate,
                                           numYears) %>

    <br />
    ************************

  </body>
</html>
```

Save this as `loanCalculator.jsp` in `%CATALINA_HOME%\webapps\begjsp-ch02\`. Start Tomcat, navigate to http://localhost:8080/begjsp-ch02/loanCalculator.jsp and you should see this page:

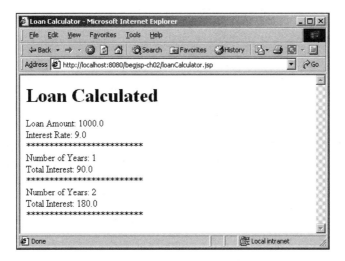

How It Works

We begin by declaring the variables we will use in this page:

```
<%-- VARIABLE DECLARATIONS --%>
<%! double loanAmount; %>
<%! double interestRate; %>
<%! int numYears; %>
```

Note the comment just before the declarations; comments can be used in this way to make the structure of the code clearer. We then define a method that we will use:

```
<%-- METHOD DECLARATIONS --%>
<%!
  double calculateInterest(double loan,
                           double interestRate,
                           int numYears) {
    return numYears*interestRate*loan/100;
  }
%>
```

This method is actually the one that we described when we introduced method declarations earlier. It takes three arguments, a loan amount, an interest rate and the number of years and returns the amount of interest to be paid on that loan. We then have some simple HTML until we reach a scriptlet in which we set the values of the variables we declared at the start of the page:

```
<%
  loanAmount = 1000;
  interestRate = 9;
  numYears = 1;
%>
```

We then print out the values of `loanAmount` and `interestRate` using expression elements:

```
Loan Amount: <%= loanAmount %>
<br />
Interest Rate: <%= interestRate %>
```

Then we print out the number of years over which to calculate the interest payments, again using an expression element:

```
Number of Years: <%= numYears %>
```

Now we use the method we defined earlier. We pass `calculateInterest()` our variables that we declared and set values for and print out the value the method returns using an expression element.

```
Total Interest: <%= calculateInterest(loanAmount,
                                       interestRate,
                                       numYears) %>
```

Then the value of `numYears` is incremented and the previous process of printing out the number of years and the interest paid is repeated.

```
<%-- CHANGE THE VALUE OF numYears --%>
<% numYears++; %>

*************************
<br />
Number of Years: <%= numYears %>
<br />
Total Interest: <%= calculateInterest(loanAmount,
                                       interestRate,
                                       numYears) %>
```

Note once more the use of a comment, so that when you come to change the code it is easy to understand what your original intention was. Using comments is one part of employing good coding practices, which we will look at in a little more detail next.

Good Coding Practices

The example JSP pages we have seen so far have been relatively simple affairs and it is relatively easy to follow what the code is doing. As they are simple it is not difficult to make changes to the code to alter the functionality of the page. However, you will inevitably create larger and more complex pages as you create your own web applications, and it is equally inevitable that if you do not follow good coding practices it will be difficult to reliably maintain your code.

Part of the difficulty of maintaining JSP code is that the scriptlets are mixed up with the HTML markup. Using the different scripting elements in a sensible and consistent way can help alleviate this. As we did with our previous example, you can use declaration elements to declare all your variables at the start of your page; this makes it easy to check what variables are available and to make any necessary changes. Equally, it is sensible to define any methods together at the start of the page. Comment elements can be used to make clear what the code is intended to do.

One of the themes of this book is to show you how to build easily maintained web applications and you will be introduced to a number of solutions to the problems of scriptlets. However, scriptlets are an almost inevitable part of JSP pages, and in your early applications you will undoubtedly use them a great deal. If you are aware of the dangers of excessive scriptlet use, and use the ways we have outlined to reduce these dangers, your applications will be the better for it.

Summary

You have been introduced to the basic building blocks of Java in this chapter. There is a great deal more to Java, as you will see in later chapters, but you will find yourself using the primitive data types, String objects, and scripting elements throughout this book and in your applications.

You saw how to declare and initialize variables. These variables included the primitive data types – byte, short, int, long, float, double, char, and boolean. You learned how to perform operations and calculations on these variables, such as addition and multiplication. You were also introduced to String objects, which are used to manipulate collections of characters. You learned how to create a String and how to invoke methods on it.

We then went on to look at scripting elements in JSP pages. You saw how to use the four different elements – comments, declarations, expressions and scriptlets. Finally, we talked about the dangers of scriptlet use and how sensible use of the different scripting elements can help reduce these dangers.

You have learned the basics of Java and are now in a position to create simple JSP web applications, but to create interesting web applications you need to be able to get input from the user – which we cover in the next chapter.

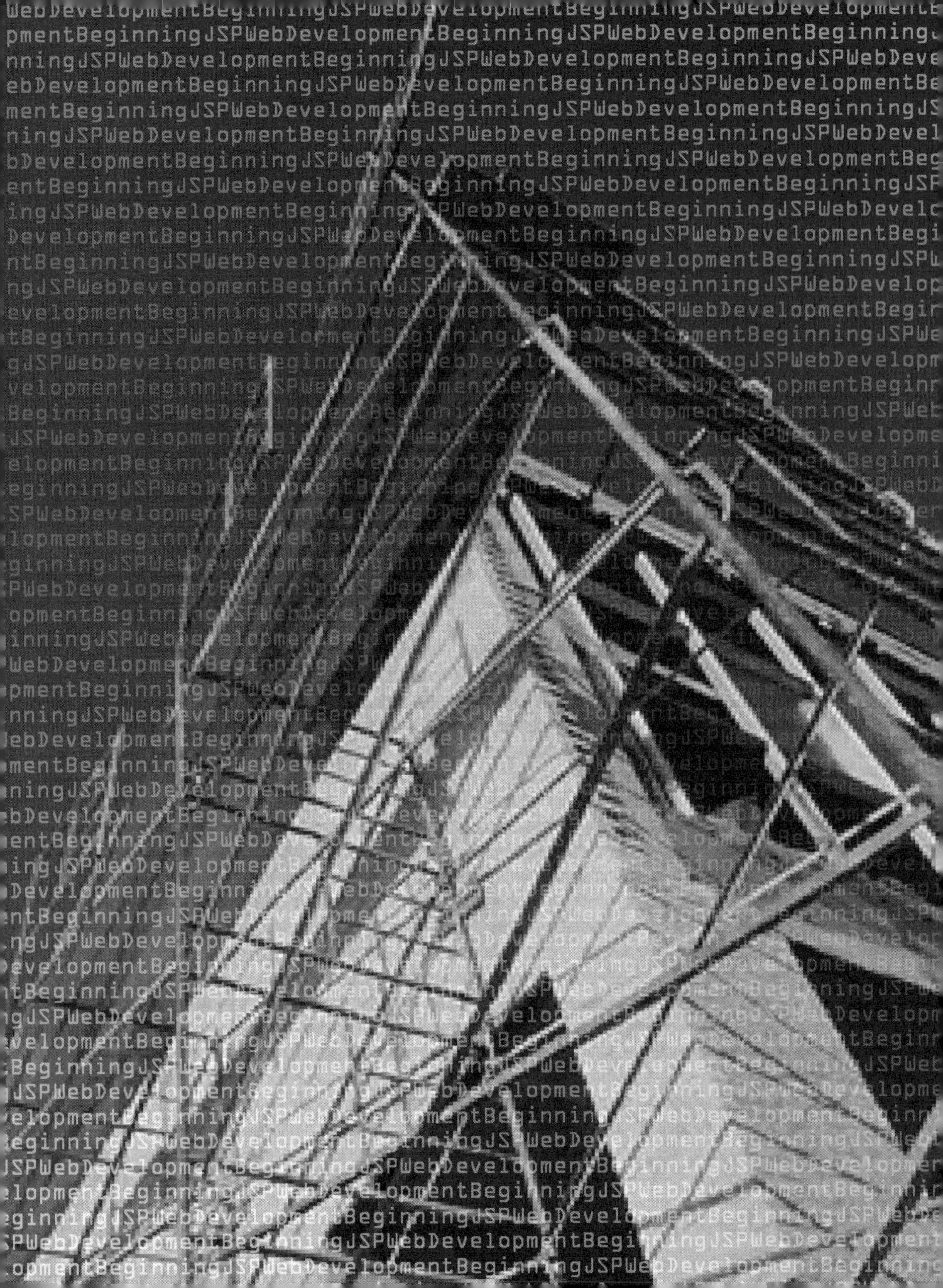

Getting Data from the Browser

In Chapter 2 we covered the fundamentals of the Java language, and we introduced you to the idea of using scriptlets to embed Java code fragments within JSPs. We also showed you how to declare methods and variables, and how to return data back to the browser. However, sending data back to the browser from the server is only one half of developing a successful web application. To make a web application more interactive, the users of the application should be able to enter data into their browser and send it back to the server, for further processing.

In this chapter, we will be covering how to make web applications more interactive by providing forms into which the client enters data. We will follow this by discussing the techniques we can use to pass this data to the server, so that it can be read and processed.

We will be introducing and using various HTML **form controls**, including:

❑   Text boxes and text areas (text boxes that allow us to type multiple lines)

❑   Radio buttons

❑   Checkboxes

❑   Select control (used for rendering dropdown listboxes and multi-select listboxes)

❑   Submit and Reset buttons

Finally, data from the client sent to the server is placed in the **request object**; we will finish this chapter by explaining how to retrieve the data from this object, so that we can process the data on the server.

Retrieving Client Data Using HTML Forms

If we wish to capture data from the client and send it to the server, the method usually employed to achieve this is to ask the user to fill in an **HTML form**. The information that the user provides may be textual (for instance the user's name), or it may be a selection from a number of choices ("choose your holiday destination"). On completion of the form, a **Submit** button will need to be clicked, to initiate the **request** (the transfer of the data from the client to the server).

HTML provides you with a number of different form controls that you can present to the user. We will meet these shortly; first let's look at the basic building block we need to construct any HTML form – a `<form>` element.

Using the <form> Element

All forms within an HTML page are enclosed within starting `<form>` and ending `</form>` element tags. However, you should note that the form element itself doesn't render any visual control on the browser screen. We place specific form controls within this element, and these controls then become part of the form. It is the controls that are rendered onto the browser for the client to interact with.

The `<form>` tag contains **attributes**, which are configuration settings for the form. For example, there is more than one method we can use to send the client data to the server, and we must choose which method is most suitable. Also, the form needs to know which page to jump to once the form has been submitted. Let's now look more closely at the attributes of the `<form>` tag.

The action Attribute

As we have already mentioned, the `<action>` attribute is used to specify the page to move to when the form is submitted. We need to specify the server-side resource – for example, a JSP – responsible for processing the form data submitted by the user. This server-side resource may then produce an HTML page that is sent back to the client as the **response** to the client's request.

The name of the form attribute used to specify this resource is `action`, and its value may be specified in various ways. First, as an *absolute* URL, as shown below:

```
<form action="http://myServer.com/process.jsp"></form>
```

You should note the use of the starting tag `<form>` in which we've specified the value of `action`, and the presence of a closing `</form>` tag. Here, on form submission, the page to jump to will be at the URL http://myServer.com/process.jsp.

Alternatively, the URL may be specified *relative* to the URL of the page that contains the form:

```
<form action="process.jsp"></form>
```

In this case, if the current HTML is produced by http://myServer.com/input.jsp, the request is sent to the resource http://myServer.com/process.jsp. In other words, the page we move to is in the same web directory as the page containing the form.

Finally, if a form is submitted without an `action` attribute, the request is sent back to the page that contains the form.

The name Attribute

If we are going pass data, we need to label the data too, otherwise we won't know which form or form control the data came from. Therefore, the `name` attribute is used to identify a particular form or form control within the HTML page. We will see this attribute being used in examples to come.

The method Attribute

As well as a choice of where to send the form data to, we also get a choice of how to send it. The "how" is specified by the value of the `method` attribute. Although we could potentially send the data to any page, there are only two commonly used methods you can choose to send the data:

❑   GET

❑   POST

We would specify which of these to use like this:

```
<form action="process.jsp" method="post"></form>
```

Here we are sending form data to the `process.jsp` page using the `post` method. You should note that the default value of `method` is `get`.

Let's take a closer look at how these methods work.

Using Get and Post

When the user submits the form data, the browser collates the data entered or selected by the user into name-value pairs. The name in this pair is the value of the `name` attribute of the control, while the value denotes the data value. For example, say we had a textbox called `username` for the user to enter his name. The name value pair for user "Meeraj Kunnumpurath" is:

```
?username= Meeraj+Kunnumpurath
```

Note how a name-value pair is prefixed by the ? symbol, and the whitespace in the middle of the name value has been replaced with a + character. This begs the question: what happens when we write a + character into the textbox? The answer is that some characters are replaced with a special code. This is known as **URL encoding**.

Now, if we choose to use the GET method of transferring data to the server, this name-value pair is passed to the server by appending it onto the end of the URL of the target page that we are sending the form to. For example:

```
process.jsp?userName=Meeraj+Kunnumpurath
```

Here the target page for the form data is `process.jsp`. Note that we can include several name-value pairs in this **query string** by linking them together in the URL with an & character:

```
process.jsp?userName=Meeraj+Kunnumpurath&userGender=Male
```

Here we have two input fields in the form named `userName` and `userGender` to which the user has entered the data `Meeraj Kunnumpurath` and `Male`.

You may have spotted that a possible disadvantage of this technique is that placing name-value pairs in the URL string is a rather public way of passing information. What if we have data that is personal or private, and we don't want it visible for all to see? This is where the POST method comes in. When we specify that data should be transferred using POST, the name-value pairs are sent within the body of the HTTP request instead.

So when should we use GET, and when should we use POST? Opinions differ here; some advocate that POST should always be used due to the public nature of GET requests. However, there are advantages to GET too: for instance, pages that are loaded using POST cannot be bookmarked properly, while those loaded by GET (for example, the result of a form submission on Alta Vista) can be bookmarked easily. Also, while POST is a more secure way of sending data than GET, the data is not encrypted during a POST, so it would not be very difficult to retrieve any data if we really wanted to.

The target Attribute

We noted earlier that the server-side resource identified in the action attribute might produce an HTML page when the form is submitted. The target attribute may be used to identify a frame or window within the browser to which the resulting HTML page should be sent, if it is different from the frame or window containing the form. This attribute may take the following values.

❑   _blank: The resulting HTML page is sent to a new window.

❑   _parent: The resulting HTML is sent to the parent of the current frame.

❑   _self: The resulting HTML page overwrites the current page. This is the default value used when one is not specified.

❑   _top: The resulting HTML page will occupy the entire browser window, ignoring all the nested framesets.

Now that we know how to create a form, let's find out how to fill it with controls.

Using HTML Controls

HTML controls are used for rendering the different boxes, lists and switches that may be used by the users for entering the data that they wish to submit to the server. The various HTML controls that may be used within a form can be defined using the following elements.

❑   <input> – used for rendering controls like text fields, radio buttons, and checkboxes

❑   <select> – used for rendering multi-select listboxes and dropdown listboxes

❑   <textarea> – used for rendering multi-line edit controls

Let's take each of these elements in turn and review them.

The <input> Element

The HTML <input> element may be used for rendering the controls that can be used for creating textboxes, radio buttons, and checkboxes within HTML forms. The element is defined as below:

```
<input [attribute list] >
```

The <input> element has a set of attributes that may be used for setting various properties, such as the name of the control, and the type of the control to be rendered. We will now review the most common of these.

The type Attribute

One of the most important attributes we need to define is the type of control we want, using the type attribute. This attribute may take a variety of values:

Attribute Value	Description
TEXT	Used for rendering text fields. This value is the default if the attribute is not specified
PASSWORD	Used for rendering password controls
HIDDEN	Used for defining **hidden controls**. Hidden form elements are used for storing information on the page that doesn't have to be displayed to the users. They are typically store values used by the processing logic on the server across multiple requests
CHECKBOX	Used for rendering checkboxes
RADIO	Used for rendering radio buttons
RESET	Used for rendering a button control that is used for resetting the contents of the form to its original default values
SUBMIT	Used for rendering a button control that is used for submitting the form
IMAGE	Used for rendering an image map
BUTTON	Used for rendering a button control that may be linked with a client-side script
FILE	Used for rendering a file control that may be used for browsing and selecting files from the local file system to be uploaded by the server

Here's an example, where we create a textbox:

```
<input type="TEXT">
```

The name Attribute

After we have chosen the type of control we need, we should give it a name if we want data from the control to be passed to the server on form submission. In fact, we have already encountered the name attribute used to do this, when we were talking about naming forms. Here is an example of how we can name our controls:

```
<input type="text" name="address">
```

Here we create a textbox called address. Therefore, when we send this information to the server as a name-value pair, the name will be address, and the value will be the URL-encoded version of whatever the user enters into the textbox before submitting the form.

The maxlength Attribute

This `maxlength` attribute may only be used if the `type` attribute is defined as either `text` or `password`, and is used for defining the maximum number of characters that may be entered into the control. For instance, we could impose a limit of 30 characters on the textbox we created earlier:

```
<input type="text" name="address" maxlength="30">
```

The size Attribute

This attribute may be used if the `type` attribute is defined as either `text` or `password`. The `size` attribute is used for defining the visible width of the control in number of characters (note that `maxlength` doesn't change the actual width of a textbox, just the number of characters that will be accepted). So, say we wanted to define the width of our textbox:

```
<input type="text" name="address" maxlength="30" size="30">
```

Here the width of our text box is defined to be 30 characters.

Now that we know how to create a control, let's take a break from discussing the attributes of the `<input>` element and throw in an example showing how to create a page with a few controls in it.

Try It Out – Adding Textboxes To an HTML Form

In this example and the next, we are going to build up a form that a client could use to order a pizza over the Internet. First, we are going to need a couple of textboxes to hold the client's name and address. Save the following page as `pizza.html`:

```html
<html>
<head>
  <title>Wrox Pizza's...Order Now!!!</title>
</head>

<body>
  <form action="process.jsp" method="post">
    <b>Name:</b>
    <input type="text" name="name" size="30"><br>
    <b>Address:</b>
    <input type="text" name="address" size="70">
  </form>
</body>

</html>
```

Create a new directory under your `%CATALINA_HOME%\webapps` folder:

`...\begjsp-ch03\WEB-INF\classes`

Now place your `pizza.html` page inside the `begjsp-ch03` folder. Start up Tomcat and navigate to the URL http://localhost:8080/begjsp-ch03/pizza.html. You should see the following:

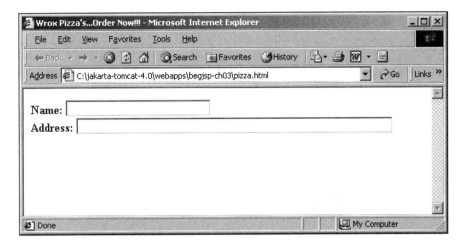

How It Works

As you can see, the example renders textboxes for a hungry client to write in his name and address when he orders a pizza online. Let's skip to the section of the HTML page we're really interested in, the body:

```
<body>
  <form action="process.jsp" method="post">
```

As you can see, we have created a form using the `<form>` element, that will send its form data via the `post` method to the `process.jsp` page when the form is submitted.

```
    <b>Name:</b>
    <input type="text" name="orderName" size="30"><br>
```

Next we create two textboxes using the `<input>` element, and specifying `type` to be `text`. In the first case, we name the textbox `orderName` and make the box 30 characters long, and for the second box we name it `orderAddress` and give it a length of 70 characters (addresses tend to be longer than names).

```
    <b>Address:</b>
    <input type="text" name="orderAddress" size="70">
  </form>
</body>
```

And that's all we need to do to create a few textboxes. But our pizza order page is still under construction; after all, we haven't given our client a choice of pizzas or even provided a submit button so that we can send the form data! But, let's first discuss some more of the attributes of `<input>` before we start changing our page.

The checked Attribute

This attribute of the `<input>` element may be used if the `type` attribute is defined as either a `radio` or `checkbox`. If this attribute is present, the radio button or the checkbox is checked by default. For example:

```
<input type="radio" name="gender" checked>
```

This code would create a radio button called `gender` that is checked by default.

The value Attribute

The `value` attribute works differently in the `<input>` element depending on the contents of the `type` attribute. For selectable controls like radio buttons and checkboxes, the contents of this attribute defines the value that is sent as part of the name-value pair, when the form is submitted. For text and password controls, this attribute can be used for pre-populating the control with specific data. For button controls the contents of this attribute is displayed on the button.

Here's an example of how we would use the `value` attribute with a textbox:

```
<form action="process.jsp">
  <input type="text" name="name" value="Meeraj">
</form>
```

The above form will render a text field named `name` pre-populated with the string `Meeraj`.

You should note that more than one control in a form may have the same value for the `name` attribute; this occurs when we have a group of controls that we intend using together. For example, we might have a group of radio buttons, each called `rdb`:

```
<form action="process.jsp">
  <input type="radio" name="rdb" value="123">
  <input type="radio" name="rdb" value="456">
</form>
```

For radio buttons, the user can select only one of the buttons. If the first radio button is selected when the above form is submitted, the name-value pair `rdb=123` is sent to the server. If the second radio button is selected, the name-value pair `rdb=456` is sent instead.

For other controls the users may select any combination of them. In scenarios where multiple controls have the same value for the `name` attribute, the key-value pairs sent to the server can contain duplicate values for the key. For instance:

```
<form action="process.jsp">
  <input type="checkbox" name="cbx" value="123">
  <input type="checkbox" name="cbx" value="456">
</form>
```

When the above form is submitted the name-value pairs `cbx=123` and `cbx=456` are both sent back to the server, if both checkboxes are checked.

Finally, we can also use the `value` attribute with buttons. In this case, the value of the `value` attribute is the text that is rendered on top of the button. For instance, the line below creates a reset button called `dataReset` that displays the name **Reset Form**:

```
<input name="dataReset" "type="reset" value="Reset Form"/>
```

Along the same lines, here's an example of creating a submit button called `dataSubmit` with **Submit Form** written on the top:

```
<input name="dataSubmit" type="submit" value="Submit Form"/>
```

Now we have all of the information we need to create a cool pizza order page. So let's build on the page we started earlier.

Try It Out – Adding Buttons and Checkboxes to an HTML Form

In this example we are going to add more HTML controls to the `pizza.html` page we created earlier. Specifically, we are going to introduce a set of checkboxes so that the pizza client can choose the toppings on his pizzas, a pair of radio buttons so that he can choose whether he wants home delivery or not, and a submit button so that he can submit his order to the `process.jsp` page.

Add the highlighted lines below to your `pizza.html` file, and resave the file:

```
<html>
<head>
  <title>Wrox Pizza's...Order Now!!!</title>
</head>

<body>
  <form action="process.jsp" method="post">
    <b>Name:</b>
    <input type="text" name="name" size="30"><br>
    <b>Address:</b>
    <input type="text" name="address" size="70">

    <br><br>
    <input type="radio" name="purchaseType" value="Home Delivery">
    <b>Home Delivery</b>
    <br>
    <input type="radio" name="purchaseType" value="Take Away">
    <b>Take Away</b>
    <br><br>

    <b>Select your pizza(s)...</b>
    <br>
    <input type="checkbox" name="margherita" value="Yes">
    <b>Margherita</b>
    <br>
    <input type="checkbox" name="hawaiian" value="Yes">
    <b>Hawaiian</b>
    <br>
    <input type="checkbox" name="pepperoni" value="Yes">
    <b>Pepperoni</b>
    <br><br>

    <input type="submit" value="Place Order">
  </form>
</body>

</html>
```

After you have resaved the file, refresh the browser from the previous example, and as if by magic the pizza order page becomes full of new and exciting options!

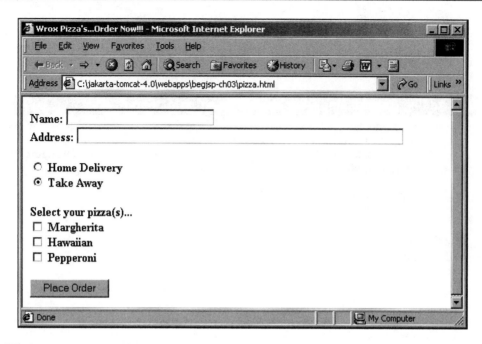

How It Works

As with the previous example, we will focus on how we added the new controls. First we add a set of two radio buttons called purchaseType. By giving the buttons the same value of name, we make sure that only one of the two buttons can be selected at any time. Each button is labeled using its value attribute:

```
<br><br>
<input type="radio" name="purchaseType" value="Home Delivery">
<b>Home Delivery</b>
<br>
<input type="radio" name="purchaseType" value="Take Away">
<b>Take Away</b>
<br><br>
```

Next we get the client to select his pizza from a choice of three checkboxes. Remember that the value attribute for a checkbox indicates the value that will be sent if the checkbox is checked.

```
<b>Select your pizza(s)...</b>
<br>
<input type="checkbox" name="margherita" value="Yes">
<b>Margherita</b>
<br>
<input type="checkbox" name="hawaiian" value="Yes">
<b>Hawaiian</b>
<br>
<input type="checkbox" name="pepperoni" value="Yes">
<b>Pepperoni</b>
<br><br>
```

Our final step is to add a submit button. Here the `value` attribute indicates the text of the button label:

```
<input type="submit" value="Place Order">
```

You should note that although we now have a submit button, filling in the form and clicking on the button results in an error message, because the page tries to send the form data to `process.jsp`, which doesn't exist yet! Indeed, we could create a blank page called `process.jsp` in the `begjsp-ch03` folder that the `pizza.html` page would jump to, but we don't know how to retrieve the form data yet anyway. However, don't worry, we will see how to extract this data later in the chapter.

The <select> Element

The `<select>` element is used within HTML forms for rendering drop-down listboxes and multi-select listboxes. The individual items within the select control are defined using `<option>` elements nested within the `<select>` element. Select elements can be defined within an HTML form as follows:

```
<select>
  <option>Item 1</option>
  <option>Item 2</option>
</select>
```

As with the `<input>` element, the `<select>` and `<option>` elements have attributes that allow us to configure the form controls.

Let's review some of the attributes, starting with attributes of the `<select>` element.

The name Attribute

As usual, the `name` attribute for a `<select>` element is used to define the name in the name-value pair that is sent back to the server, when the form is submitted.

The size Attribute

If the value of the `size` attribute is 1, the control is rendered as a dropdown listbox; if it is greater than 1 the control is rendered as a listbox, and the value of the attribute defines the number of items in the list that are visible at a time. The default value for this attribute is 1 if the attribute is not specified.

The multiple Attribute

If the `multiple` attribute is present, the select control will allow multiple selections in the listbox. Please note that if the form is submitted with multiple entries selected, all of the selected values are sent back to the server against the `name` defined for the `<select>` element.

The `<option>` element is used to render the individual entries within a `<select>` control. Let's review the two most important attributes for the `<option>` element.

The value Attribute

This attribute is used to define the value that is sent back to the server when a particular item is selected from the list. For example, say we had a list of employees at our Wrox Pizza company, and these employees had a special company ID code. If we wanted to choose one of them to deliver the pizza, we might want the form to return the ID of the employee, not the name:

```
<select name="delivery">
  <option value="07">Johnny Wrox</option>
  <option value="15">Leanne Dean</option>
</select>
```

In this case, the dropdown listbox would contain two entries, **Johnny Wrox** and **Leanne Dean**. If we selected Johnny to make the delivery, the form would pass the name-value pair `?delivery=07` to the server.

If the `value` attribute is not present, the data between the start and end `<option>` tags would be passed instead. For instance:

```
<select name="delivery">
  <option>Johnny Wrox</option>
  <option>Leanne Dean</option>
</select>
```

If we selected Johnny this time, we would get `?delivery=Johnny+Wrox` passed to the server instead.

The selected Attribute

If this attribute is present for an `<option>` element, the contents of this `<option>` are displayed in the control as default.

Now that we know how to create a listbox, let's incorporate it into our Wrox Pizza scenario.

Try It Out – Adding Listboxes To HTML Forms

We are going to improve the customer service of Wrox Pizza by giving the customer three pizza sizes to choose from. To do this we will introduce the options in a dropdown listbox.

Add the following highlighted lines of code to your `pizza.html` file:

```
    ...
        <input type="checkbox" name="pepperoni" value="Yes">
        <b>Pepperoni</b>
        <br><br>

        <b>Options...</b>
        <select name="size">
          <option>Small</option>
          <option selected>Medium</option>
          <option>Large</option>
        </select>
        <br><br>

        <input type="submit" value="Place Order">
      </form>
  </body>

  </html>
```

As in the previous example, resave your `pizza.html` file when you have added the new lines, and then refresh your browser. You will see:

60

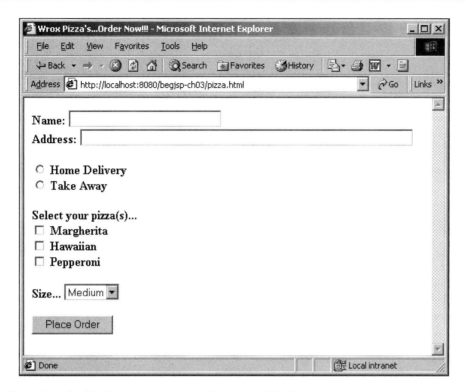

You will see that the Medium size option is selected as default.

How It Works

Let's look at the code we added to pizza.html. We added a <select> element called size so that we create a listbox.

```
<b>Size...</b>
<select name="options">
```

Then we create three size options for the list: small, medium, and large. The second, medium, is the option that is selected when the page loads:

```
    <option>Small</option>
    <option selected>Medium</option>
    <option>Large</option>
</select>
<br><br>
```

We're nearly finished with our pizza order page now. We have just one minor modification to make... but more on that in a moment.

The <textarea> Element

The <textarea> element is used in an HTML form to render multi-line textboxes. These elements are defined using the start tag <textarea> and the end tag </textarea>. All the text appearing between the start and end tags are displayed in the control:

```
<textarea>
    line of text
    another line of text
    ...
</textarea>
```

Let's have a look at the attributes of the <textarea> element.

The name Attribute

As with the other controls, the name attribute defines the name in the name-value pair that is sent to the server when the form is submitted.

The rows and cols Attributes

The rows attribute defines the number of rows of characters displayed in the control. The default value of this attribute varies with the browser and the operating system. Similarly, the cols attribute defines the number of columns of characters displayed in the control. The default value of this attribute varies with the browser and the operating system.

Let's now finish off our Wrox Pizza example by incorporating a multi-line textbox.

Try It Out – Adding Multi-line Textboxes To HTML Forms

Our Wrox Pizza order page looks pretty cool at the moment, but there is one improvement we could make. The Address textbox doesn't look quite right as a 70-character long textbox, does it? Since an address is often composed of several lines of text, we would be better off using a multi-line textbox instead. So let's replace the original textbox for the Address with a multi-line one.

Open up your pizza.html file, and replace the line:

```
<input type="text" name="address" size="70">
```

with the following line:

```
<textarea rows="4" cols="40" name="address"></textarea>
```

Now resave the file.

After you have resaved pizza.html, simply refresh the page again. Hey presto!

We have now replaced the original one-line text field with a multi-line textbox.

How It Works

Obviously we only replaced one line of the original file:

```
<textarea rows="4" cols="40" name="address"></textarea>
```

We created a multi-line textbox called `address`, using the `<textarea>` element. We specified that it should have a size of 4 rows by 40 columns.

Request Processing

So far in this chapter, we have seen how HTML forms and form elements may be used for rendering different input controls on the user's browser screen, enabling the user to enter data into a form. However, that is only one side of web application development. As we have already seen, when the users submit the forms, the data entered into the form is sent back to the server. Hence, the server needs to be able to read and interpret this data. How this task is performed on the server depends very much on the technology used at the server. In this section, we will see how the JSP/Servlet API may be used for processing the requests sent to the server from the client browser.

Using the Request Object

In the last chapter, we saw that before we can use a variable in Java programs we need to *declare* the variable, by specifying its data type. However, J2EE web containers provide a set of implicit variables that can be used within your JSP pages without such explicit declaration. One such variable is the `request` object, which contains data from client requests; this `request` object may be used within your JSP pages for accessing request data, such as form data.

Introducing Objects and Methods

Now the obvious question is: what is an "object" in this sense? In its loosest sense an object is simply a way of storing data. We will be discussing the concept of an object in far more depth in Chapter 4. Objects also have associated **methods**, which as we saw in the last chapter are self-contained bundles of functionality. In other words, a method is kind of like a black box: we can feed data values into the box, the box will process the data, and it will return the processed data to us. We don't really need to know how the method works; only that the method does what it is supposed to. For example, the `request` object has a method called `getParameter()` that allows us to retrieve the value of a name-value pair from the object, if we tell it the name:

```
<%
   String specialReq = request.getParameter("specialRequest");
%>
```

Note the syntax used here. The name of the name-value pair we want to retrieve from the `request` object is `specialRequest`, and this is written between the parentheses at the end of the method name. We want the method to retrieve a value from the `request` object, so we tell the method this by writing the name of the object (`request`), then a period, then the method name we want to use on the object. Finally, we want the value returned by the method to be stored in a `String` variable called `specialReq`, so we link the method to this variable using the equality sign (=).

Now, since an object stores data, it bears similarities to a variable. Therefore, the next question that you may ask is: what is the data type of an object? The answer is that there are lots of different object data types; in fact, the real power of using objects to store data is that we can create our own object data types, as we will see in chapters to come. For example, the data type for our `request` object is called `HttpServletRequest`. Each object data type has its own associated collection of methods that it can use too, so `getParameter()` is a method associated with the `HttpServletRequest` data type.

Now, say we use a multi-select listbox, and we get more than one item in the list selected. We have already noted earlier in the chapter that in such a scenario several name-value pairs, each with the same name, are passed to the server with the form data. So does this mean that if we used the `getParameter()` method, all of the values associated with this name will be returned? The answer is no, only the first name-value pair will get its value returned. If we wish to retrieve the values of all of the pairs with the same name, then we must use the `getParameterValues()` method, like this:

```
<%
   String[] myList = request.getParameterValues("myListboxName");
%>
```

You can see that this is very similar to the way that we used the getParameter() method before, except that in the variable declaration at the start, we have String[]. We saw in Chapter 2 that this refers to a collection of String variables called an **array** of Strings. Therefore, the getParameterValues() method returns a String array. We will be discussing arrays in much more depth in Chapter 5.

One last thing to note about the request object is that, unlike variables and objects of many other data types, it is **implicit**. This means we do not have to declare the object to create it; it is created for us.

Let's now use our knowledge of the request object to retrieve the data sent from the Wrox Pizza order page (in the examples we built earlier).

Try It Out – Retrieving Data from the Request Object

In this example we are going to create the page that our pizza.html page sends form data to. This page, as we noted from earlier examples, is called process.jsp:

```
<html>
  <head>
    <title>Wrox Pizza's: New Order</title>
  </head>

<body>

  <b>Name:</b>
  <% out.println(request.getParameter("name")); %>
  <br>
  <b>Address:</b>
  <% out.println(request.getParameter("address")); %>
  <br>
  <b>Delivery:</b>
  <% out.println(request.getParameter("purchaseType")); %>
  <br>
  <b>Margherita?</b>
  <% out.println(request.getParameter("margherita")); %>
  <br>
  <b>Hawaiian?</b>
  <% out.println(request.getParameter("hawaiian")); %>
  <br>
  <b>Pepperoni?</b>
  <% out.println(request.getParameter("pepperoni")); %>
  <br>
  <b>Size:</b>
  <% out.println(request.getParameter("size")); %>
  <br>

</body>

</html>
```

Save this process.jsp file in the begjsp-ch03 folder. Then start up Tomcat and direct your browser to the now familiar order page:

65

http://localhost:8080/begjsp-ch03/pizza.html

Fill in your order, and click on the Place Order button:

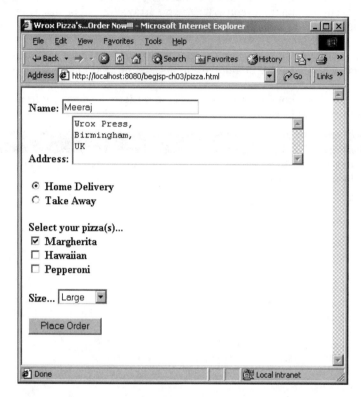

You should see the following summary of your order:

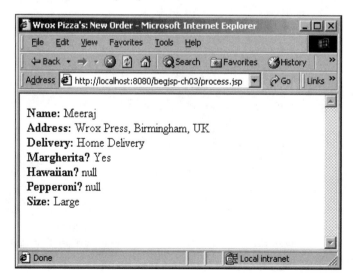

You should note that when a particular pizza topping is not ordered, we get "null", not "No". We'll come back to this issue in a moment.

How It Works

This script looks quite long, but it's actually incredibly simple. Let's look at how we retrieve the first value, of the customer's name:

```
<b>Name:</b>
<% out.println(request.getParameter("name")); %>
<br>
```

The line that we're interested in here is the second line, containing a scriptlet. As we described before, we use `request.getParameter("name")` to retrieve the value associated with `name` from the `request` object. Then we print out this value to the browser using the `out.println()` command. Then we do exactly the same thing for every name-value pair in the form data, so we won't go through each one.

The null Value

You may have noticed in the previous example that if we don't check a checkbox in the order page, the value we receive from the `request` object is not "No", as we might expect, but something called `null`. What is this?

A `null` entry represents a missing data value. You should note that while it doesn't belong to any particular data type, but a `null` can be used to represent missing data of any data type. A `null` returned from a variable simply means that there is no value available for this variable. This does not mean that the variable contains zero, because zero is a value. For `String` variables, it does not mean that the variable contains an empty `String` or a `String` consisting of one or more whitespaces, because these are still `String` values. Any arithmetic or other processing involving a `null` will return `null` too; after all we can't process data properly if some of the data is missing. Remember that a `null` is *nothing*: no data type, and no value.

Summary

In this chapter we have a looked at how to use forms to send data from the browser to the server in web applications. We have seen the HTML `<form>` element and the various basic controls that may be embedded within it, such as:

- ❑ Textboxes and text areas
- ❑ Radio buttons
- ❑ Checkboxes
- ❑ Dropdown listboxes and multi-select listboxes
- ❑ Submit and Reset buttons

We saw how to use the `<input>`, `<textarea>`, `<select>`, and `<option>` elements, and their attributes, to create these controls. We noted that form data can be passed from the client to the server in name-value pairs using two methods:

Chapter 3

❑   GET

❑   POST

We have also explained how the form data submitted by the users at the browser may be retrieved from the implicit `request` object, using the `getParameter()` and `getParameterValues()` methods. We finished by discussing the meaning of "`null`".

In this chapter, during our discussion of the `request` object, we briefly mentioned that objects provide a way of storing data, and that we can create our own object data types. In the next chapter, we will be looking more closely at objects, and we will also be showing how objects called JavaBeans can be used with JSP pages to simplify them.

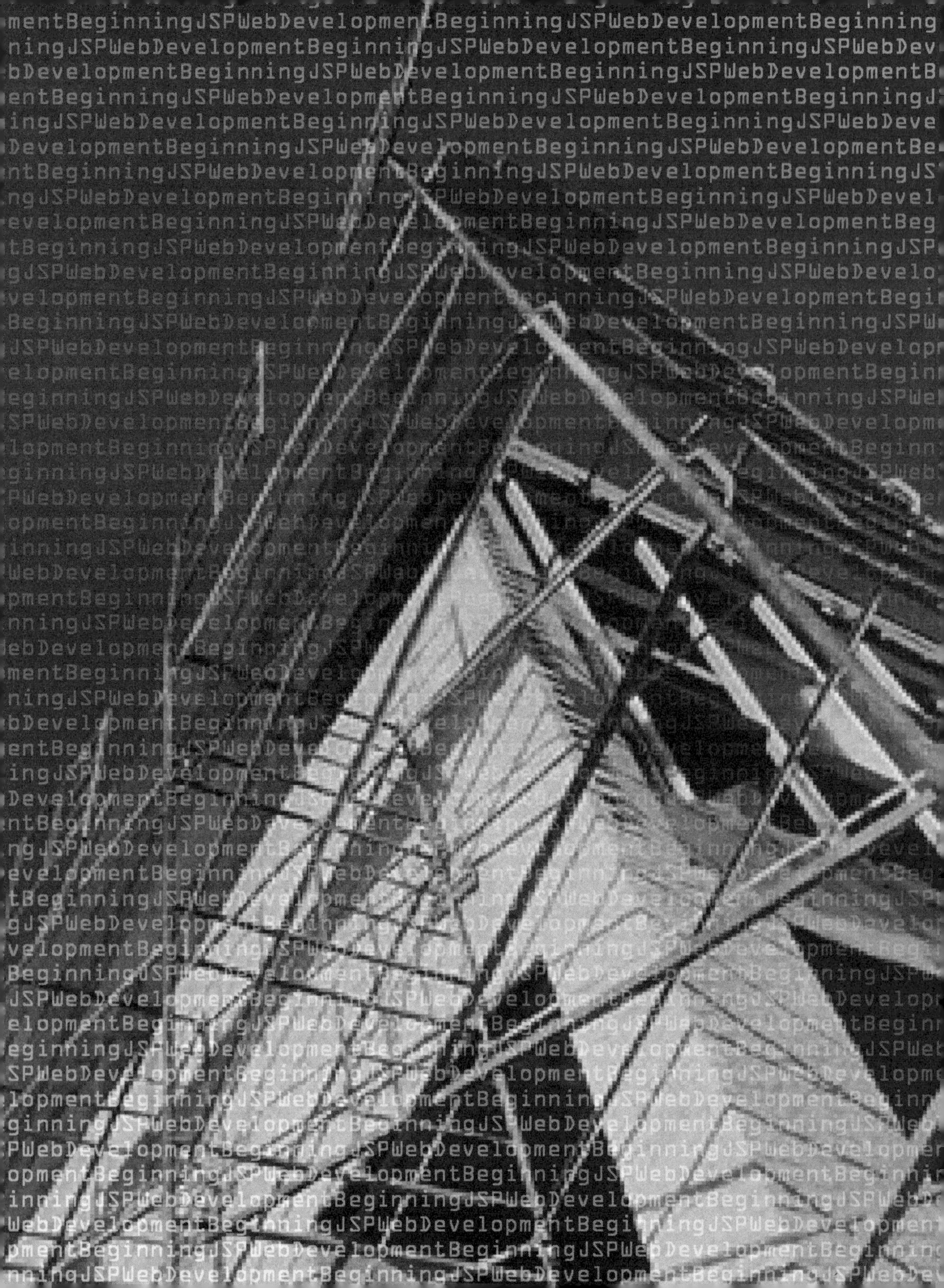
BeginningJSPWebDevelopment

Introducing JavaBeans

In Chapter 2 we introduced scriptlets, and touched on the problem associated with their excessive use in JSP pages: as your JSP pages and application become more complicated, embedded scriptlets often become longer and more complex. This will make your JSPs difficult to understand, and therefore difficult to maintain. Not only this, but the functionality implemented in a scriptlet is tied to its JSP, making it awkward to reuse this logic elsewhere.

In this chapter we are going to learn how to get around these problems by reorganizing our code into **components**. One way to do this is move the data and functionality present in the scriptlets into **JavaBeans ("beans")** instead. So, in this chapter we will be discussing:

❑ How and why you should organize your code

❑ How to use components to organize your code

❑ What **objects** and **classes** are, and how to use them as components

❑ How to create and use JavaBeans

Let's start then by considering how best to organize our code.

Organizing Your Code

When you are designing any application based upon JSPs there are three important considerations:

❑ What are the tasks that the application will perform (and are any tasks repeated)?

❑ What type of maintenance will the application require?

❑ Who is responsible for the different parts of the application?

Let's now tackle each of these questions in turn.

Code Reuse

In simple applications that consist of only a small number of JSP pages, like the examples we have seen in the first few chapters, any particular task may well be performed only once in the application. However, in larger applications, the same task may be performed many times by many different parts of the application. Rather than rewrite the same code time after time wouldn't it be better if we could reuse code?

Why Reuse Code?

Intuitively, we know that reusing code is a great idea. But let's think about why this is true. By reusing code we can:

❑   Speed up application development.

Obviously, if we reuse code, we have less code to write, so we can develop our application more quickly. Not only this, but if we reuse code, the final application will be smaller, and therefore will probably have fewer bugs. Indeed, debugging the application should be easier anyway, because there will be fewer lines of code to wade through.

❑   Ease maintenance of the application.

Consider a JSP web application that stores data in a database. Connecting to the database and retrieving data are tasks that the application performs.

Using the techniques we have learnt so far, the Java code to perform these tasks would be contained in scriptlets. The scriptlets would have to be repeated in every JSP page that required database access.

But what happens if we want to change the database system used by the application, for example from Oracle to SQL Server? In this case, the application developer would have to change the database access code in every scriptlet. In a small application this could mean changing the code in only a few pages. However, in a large application the code in hundreds or thousands of pages would have to be changed.

There are two reasons why such a change is a problem. Firstly, the changes are tedious and time consuming to make. And we all know that "time is money"; the developer's time could be better spent improving the application. Secondly, the more code the developer changes, the more danger there is of introducing new errors into the code.

Both of these problems can be avoided if instead of repeating the same code in many different parts of an application, the code is written once and accessed by the different parts of the application when they need it.

Separation of Roles

If we consider a typical e-commerce web site which uses JSPs, the maintenance of the site often falls to two distinct groups of people: the **designer** and the **developer**. The role of the designer is to maintain the **presentation**, or look and feel, of the site. The developer is responsible for the **functionality** or **logic** of the application. The logic of the application is the Java code that provides things like database access and the business rules.

There may be a clear separation of these roles or there may be some degree of overlap between them. The key point is that when you are thinking about the design of the page, you do not want to have to worry about the Java code that provides functionality. As a designer you want to treat tasks like database access as "black boxes". That is, you put something in and get something out but you are not interested in what actually happens inside. As a developer, you don't want to worry about how the data that you look after is displayed or passed to web site clients.

This separation of roles leads to the organization of the application into **layers** or **tiers**. It was explained in Chapter 1 that JSP is the presentation tier of the J2EE architecture. There are other parts of the architecture that are responsible for data access and business logic, some of which we will come across later in this chapter and in Chapter 12. In our JSP web applications we should adopt a similar approach.

Components

You can see from our discussion above that we have two important objectives when we design a JSP web application: code reuse, and the grouping of code into layers depending on the code's role within the application. But what is the best way to achieve these objectives?

A common approach is to break the code up into **components**. Componentization allows a complex piece of code consisting of lots of kinds of functionality to be broken down into its constituent bits of functionality, or **modules**. Each module of functionality can then be written and tested independently from the others, making it easier to write and debug. Of course, this speeds up application development. Another bonus is that if any kind of functionality is repeated in the application, when we split it up into modules we only need to write this functionality once, because then we can reuse the module. Also, since modules tend to contain simple functionality, there's a good chance that a developer elsewhere has already written the module you need: meaning more time (and money) saved!

So we've established that splitting your code into components is a cool thing to do. So how do we do this for a JSP-based web application?

Creating Components in Java

Since JSP is scripting language based on Java, then we are obviously talking about creating modules in Java if we wish to componentize our web applications.

Now, it turns out that Java lends itself naturally to the concepts of code reuse and components that we have been talking about. This is because Java is an **object-orientated** language. An object-orientated language makes use of **objects** to model "things" in our code, and the ideas behind objects are closely related to those of components.

Object orientation is an important subject and we will cover it in greater detail in Chapter 7. Our intention in this chapter is just to give you a basic understanding of object orientated concepts.

What are Java Objects?

Objects can seem strange at first, but they are actually a very logical way to think about problems and organize code.

We mentioned before that an object represents some "thing". For instance a *Newspaper* is an object. It has certain properties that make it distinct from any other object – a *Tree*, a *Car*, whatever.

These distinctive properties of an object are defined in something called a **class**. A class is therefore a template we would refer to if we wanted to make another of these objects: another newspaper maybe. If we did print another *Newspaper*, we would have two occurrences of the newspaper; each of these is an **instance** of the *Newspaper* object.

In Java, an object is a bundle consisting of variables containing data, and components containing functionality that may use this data. The variables are called **attributes** and the components are called **methods**. If we wish to create an object, we must refer back to the definition of the attributes and methods contained by the object. This definition is in a file called the class: it provides the template more making more of these objects.

Methods can be passed data to manipulate – this data is called an **argument** – and can pass values back (**return** them) too. Actually, you have already encountered and used object methods in Chapter 3. You saw how to use the `request` object and you invoked methods on it.

One of the great advantages of object orientation is that we can build new class templates on top of existing ones. This is known as **inheritance**. For example, we could make a new class of objects, *Sunday Newspaper*, that "inherits" of all of the attributes and methods of *Newspaper* objects but adds new ones of its own too. We say that the *Sunday Newspaper* class is a **subclass** of *Newspaper*, while *Newspaper* is the **superclass** of *Sunday Newspaper*. We will discuss inheritance in greater detail in Chapter 7 too.

Classes fulfill the requirements we discussed earlier for a component. By using classes we divide up functionality and associated data into methods and attributes. Class methods provide us with components of "black box" functionality that we can use without needing to know how they work. Class inheritance enables our code to be more reusable, because we reuse the code needed to create one class by using it in the class definition for a new class.

Introducing JavaBeans

We have discussed what components are and why you would want to use them in your web applications, and how Java objects can be used as components. So, how do you actually use components with JSP pages? The answer is that you use JavaBeans (often referred to as 'beans').

JavaBeans are components that expose pieces of data that are called **properties**. We can use beans to store this data and then retrieve it at a later date. For instance, we might have a bean that modeled a bank account. This bean might have account number and balance properties.

Formally, a JavaBean is really nothing more than a class that maintains some data (the properties) and follows certain coding conventions. These conventions provide a mechanism for automated support. This automated support means that the JSP engine, for example Tomcat, can inspect the bean and discover what properties it has.

Properties

Each piece of information that a bean exposes is called a **property**.

For an example of public properties we need look no further than HTML.

```
<font face="Arial, Helvetica, sans-serif" color="#330099">
  JSP Bean Properties Syntax
</font>
```

In HTML with reference to the `<font>` tag for example, `face` and `color` are both examples of properties that can be set against the standard HTML `<font>` tag. You may already be very familiar with this type of property.

Like HTML properties, properties in JavaBeans provide a simple approach to being able to pass information to set or retrieve a value to use in your JSP code.

The properties of a JavaBean are publicly exposed using getter and setter methods. These methods follow simple naming conventions, easiest understood by example. If we have a property called `color` the getter and setter methods would be called `getColor()` and `setColor()`. The method names are simply the capitalized name of the property preceded by either `get` or `set`.

To build a JavaBean of our own all we have to do is to write a Java class, and obey these rules.

Building a JavaBean

So what does a JavaBean look like? Let's define a JavaBean class called `CarBean` that we could use as a component in a car sales web site. It will be a component that would model a car and will have one property – the make of the car.

```
public class CarBean {

  public CarBean(){
  }

  private String make = "Ford";

  public String getMake() {
    return make;
  }

  public void setMake(String make) {
    this.make = make;
  }

}
```

There are several things to note here. The first line is where we define the name of the class:

```
public class CarBean {
```

Don't worry about the `public` keyword; we'll explain this later. The definition of the contents of the class goes inside the braces following the class name. First up, we see the definition of a special method called the **constructor**:

```
public CarBean() {
}
```

A constructor is called when an instance of a new bean is requested, and always has the same name as the class. You should note that this constructor is empty (there is nothing between the braces) but this is often not the case: we can set properties at instantiation time between these braces.

Next we define a `String` property called `make`, and we set its value to "Ford":

```
private String make = "Ford";
```

Again, ignore the `private` keyword for the time being.

Moving through the code we can see this property has "getter" and "setter" methods.

```
public String getMake() {
  return make;
}
```

The `getMake()` method returns the value of `make`. It does not get passed any arguments. The `setMake()` method is however passed an `String` argument also called `make`; the method then sets the value of the `make` property to the same value as the argument:

```
public void setMake(String make) {
  this.make = make;
}
```

The `void` keyword indicates that this method returns no value. `this` is a way of referring to the current `CarBean` object, so `this.make` is simply the `make` property of the current object.

Variable Scope and Accessibility

In the last section, we ignored the presence of two Java keywords associated with the attributes and methods within the class:

❑   `public`

❑   `private`

What do these keywords refer to? The answer is that they refer to the **accessability or scope** of an attribute variable or method. The scope defines the parts of the code in which the variable or method is recognized, and so we can use them. The scope of a variable or method depends upon where it is defined (**declared**).

Variables that are defined within a method have **local** scope. This means that they can only be used within the confines of the method in which they were declared. However, variables declared as attributes within the class can be used anywhere within the class definition.

But what about when we come to use an object of this class? Which variables declared within the class can we use? The answer to this is that it depends. We cannot directly access variables (with local scope) declared within class methods. If an attribute is declared as being `public`, we can access the attribute from outside the class. However, if an attribute is declared as being `private`, we can only use it within the class.

The same is true for the scope of methods in the class. If the method is declared as being `public` it can be called from outside the class; if it is `private`, it cannot.

You should note that all our attributes have been made `private`, while all of the getter/setter methods are `public`. There is a good reason for this: it forces us to use these methods to access and modify attribute values. This is much safer than allowing direct access to attributes. For example, using the setter method forces us to provide a value for the attribute that is of the correct data type, otherwise the resetting of the value won't work. In other words, we can make sure that any user who wants to access the data in the bean does so without modifying the data in unpredictable ways.

We now understand the code required for a JavaBean, but there is another step to take before it can be used – compilation.

Class Files and Compilation

Before a JavaBean, or any class, can be used in an application it must be **compiled**. The process of compilation is converting **source code** into **byte code**. It is this byte code that the **Java Virtual Machine (JVM)** that runs Java programs can understand and execute.

Classes are compiled using the **javac** compiler that comes as part of the Java SDK you installed in Chapter 1. We will see exactly how this is done in the example to follow.

However, if we want to use a compiled JavaBean in a JSP web application, the JSP engine, for example Tomcat, also needs to know where to look for it.

You saw in Chapter 1 that web applications are stored under the `%CATALINA_HOME%\webapps` directory. If you had a web application called "cars" you would create a directory `cars` in `%CATALINA_HOME%\webapps`.

By default Tomcat checks for classes in the `\WEB-INF\classes` directory under the web application directory, and any subdirectories of this. So, for our "cars" web application Tomcat would look for JavaBeans in directory `%TOMCAT_HOME%\webapps\cars\WEB-INF\classes` and all directories below this. While it is possible to store your JavaBeans elsewhere, in this chapter we will store our JavaBeans in this default location.

Using a JavaBean

We have now defined a JavaBean, and we know that we need to compile it and put in a directory where Tomcat can see it. Now we will create the `CarBean` class we described in the previous section and see how we can use it in a JSP page.

Try It Out – Using a JavaBean in a JSP

Open up your editor and enter the following text:

```
package com.wrox.cars;

import java.io.Serializable;

public class CarBean implements Serializable {

  public CarBean(){
  }

  private String make = "Ford";

  public String getMake() {
    return make;
  }

  public void setMake(String make) {
    this.make = make;
  }

}
```

Save it in a file named `CarBean.java` in `%CATALINA_HOME\WEB-INF\classes\begjsp-ch04\WEB-INF\classes\com\wrox\cars\`. Don't worry about the directory structure at this point. We will explain why we need this directory in a moment.

Now create the JSP page that will use our bean:

```
<html>
  <head>
    <title>Using a JavaBean</title>
  </head>
  <body>

    <h2>Using a JavaBean</h2>

    <% com.wrox.cars.CarBean myCar = new com.wrox.cars.CarBean(); %>

    I own a <%= myCar.getMake() %> <br />

    <% myCar.setMake("Ferrari"); %>

    Now I own a <%= myCar.getMake() %>

  </body>
</html>
```

Save this as `carPage.jsp` in `%CATALINA_HOME%\webapps\begjsp-ch04`.

We first need to compile `CarBean.java`. Open a command prompt and change directory to `%CATALINA_HOME%\begjsp-ch04\webapps\begjsp-ch04\WEB-INF\classes\` and then run the following command to compile the class.

> **> javac com\wrox\cars\CarBean.java**

If you get any errors go over the code and make sure you entered it exactly as it is written. When compilation is complete you will have a file, `CarBean.class`, in the directory.

Now start up Tomcat and point your browser to http://localhost:8080/begjsp-ch04/carPage.jsp. You should see something like this:

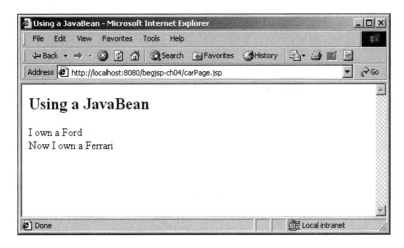

How It Works

Let's walk through our code and explain it. The first line in our JavaBean class is:

```
package com.wrox.cars;
```

What is this? Java classes are stored in collections called **packages**. These packages provide an easy way to organize related classes. The names of packages follow a very simple structure. You have already come across packages in Chapter 1 when you used the `Date` class. The `Date` class is stored in the `java.util` package.

The name of the package has a direct relation to the directory in which the class is stored under the `classes` folder. For example, since the `Date` class is in the package `java.util`, it would need to be stored under a `...\classes\java\util\` directory structure. Similarly our `CarBean` class is stored under the `...classes\com\wrox\cars\` directory.

Next we have to import a class to use with our class:

```
import java.io.Serializable;
```

This tells the compiler that we want to use the `Serializable` class which is in the `java.io` package. Now we declare our class:

```
public class CarBean implements Serializable {
```

You don't need to worry too much about what `implements Serializable` means. It simply allows the class and its data to be saved to disk.

We've seen and explained the rest of the class, so we don't need to go through it again, so now let's take a look at the JSP code in `carPage.jsp`.

We start off with some simple HTML, defining the title of the page and displaying a heading of "Using a JavaBean":

```
<html>
  <head>
    <title>Using a JavaBean</title>
  </head>
  <body>

    <h2>Using a JavaBean</h2>
```

Before we can use our JavaBean we need to create an instance of it. To create an instance of any class, we must declare the class type and call the constructor:

```
<% com.wrox.cars.CarBean myCar = new com.wrox.cars.CarBean(); %>
```

The class type is simply the class name, but we must remember to state the full package name. The constructor method for our class is therefore `com.wrox.cars.CarBean()`, and when we create a new instance of a bean using a call to the constructor, we must remember to also place the `new` keyword in front of the call.

Then we call the `getMake()` method on the instance of the bean, to return the value of the `make` property:

```
I own a <%= myCar.getMake() %> <br />
```

We then change the value of this `make` property of the bean by calling the `setMake()` method.

```
<% myCar.setMake("Ferrari"); %>
```

Finally we call the `getMake()` method once more to show off our new make of car to the world.

We have now seen how we can create our own bean class and use it in a JSP page. No doubt our `CarBean` class could be given additional properties and methods to make it more interesting and useful. However, part of our aim was to eliminate excessive scriptlet use, in order to make the code easier to follow, but all we have done up to now is introduce more scriptlets containing bean method calls into our JSP code. This is where we can introduce you to the real power of JavaBeans.

Remember how we insisted that the getter and setter methods followed a strict naming convention? In the previous example the need for this convention wasn't clear. Next, we will introduce **bean tags**, which will allow us to remove the need for scriptlets to call bean methods from the JSP.

Bean Tags

JSP provides an approach to utilizing JavaBeans that is based on the concept of tags. These tags are really no more complicated than the standard HTML tags: they have a name, and they take attributes.

Tags are designed to make the page developer's job easier as they allow the designer to use JavaBeans without knowing any Java. There are three tags provided by the specification to support the use of JavaBeans in your JSP pages:

- ❑ `<jsp:useBean>`
- ❑ `<jsp:setProperty>`
- ❑ `<jsp:getProperty>`.

In this section we will tell you about each of these tags and how to use them when working with your JavaBeans.

The <jsp:useBean> Tag

The `<jsp:useBean>` tag locates and instantiates a JavaBean. For example:

```
<jsp:useBean id="myCar" class="com.wrox.cars.CarBean" />
```

Here, an object of class `com.wrox.cars.CarBean` will be located and created. We can refer to this bean later in the page, using the value set for the `id` attribute (`myCar`).

Note that for the `<jsp:useBean>` tag we have two ways of closing the tag. We can use the short notation of `/>` shown above to close the tag. Or, if you wish to populate values at instantiation rather than after instantiation you can use the full `</jsp:useBean>` end tag instead:

```
<jsp:useBean id="myCar" class="com.wrox.cars.CarBean" ></jsp:useBean>
```

The <jsp:setProperty> Tag

The `<jsp:setProperty>` element sets the value of a property of a bean using the setter method.

If we have instantiated a JavaBean with an `id` of `myCar`, as we did in the previous section, we can use the following tag to set the value of a property of the bean.

```
<jsp:setProperty name="myCar" property="make" value="Ferrari" />
```

Here we are setting the property `make` to the value `Ferrari`. This is where the usefulness of the method naming conventions becomes apparent. This tag takes the bean instance with an `id` of `myCar` and calls the `setMake()` method on it. It passes `Ferrari` to the method as the argument.

The <jsp:getProperty> Tag

The `<jsp:getProperty>` element gets a property value using the getter method and returns the property value to the calling JSP page.

As with the `<jsp:setProperty>` tag, you must create or locate a bean with `<jsp:useBean>` before you can use `<jsp:getProperty>`. Here's an example of using the tag:

```
<jsp:getProperty name="myCar" property="car" />
```

We get the value of the property `car` from the bean instance `myCar`.

> Remember to specify the `<jsp:useBean>` tag before using either the `<jsp:setProperty>` or the `<jsp:getProperty>` tags, otherwise your JSP will throw a compile error.

Now, let's rewrite our previous example using these three tags rather than Java code in scriptlets.

Try It Out – Using a JavaBean Tags in a JSP page

We can use our `CarBean` in a JSP page using the bean tags. We have already written and compiled our bean, so let's go straight onto the JSP page and show you how to incorporate the tags.

Create and save the following as `carPage1.jsp` in `%CATALINA_HOME%\webapps\begjsp-ch04`:

```html
<html>
  <head>
    <title>Using a JavaBean</title>
  </head>
  <body>

    <h2>Using a JavaBean</h2>

    <jsp:useBean id="myCar" class="com.wrox.cars.CarBean" />

    I have a <jsp:getProperty name="myCar" property="make" /> <br />

    <jsp:setProperty name="myCar" property="make" value="Ferrari" />

    Now I have a <jsp:getProperty name="myCar" property="make" />

  </body>
</html>
```

Now start up Tomcat and enter the following URL into your browser:

http://localhost:8080/begjsp-ch04/carPage1.jsp

You should see something like this:

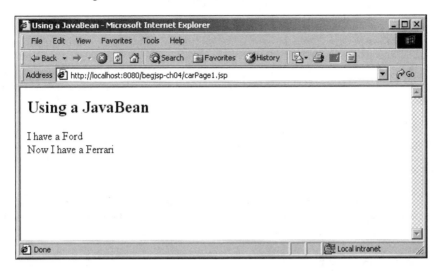

In other words the same message should be displayed as in the previous example.

How It Works

If we look through the code for myCar.jsp we can see that the JSP page is very easy to follow.

We issue a <jsp:useBean> request to the tag handler which in turn instantiates the JavaBean:

```
<jsp:useBean id="myCar" class="com.wrox.cars.CarBean" />
```

The <jsp:useBean> tag provides an ID for this instance called myCar. The ID can be used to identify the JavaBean in the page. Because each bean instance is given an ID you could instantiate many JavaBeans of the same type if you wanted to, all with different ID attributes.

The <jsp:useBean> tag also identifies a class that is the location of the compiled code for the JavaBean.

Next we use the <jsp:getProperty> and <jsp:setProperty> tags to retrieve the initial value of the make property for this instance, and display it, then reset this property to "Ferrari".

```
I have a <jsp:getProperty name="myCar" property="make" /> <br />

<jsp:setProperty name="myCar" property="make" value="Ferrari" />
```

We finish by displaying this new property value:

```
Now I have a <jsp:getProperty name="myCar" property="make" />
```

A Closer Look At JavaBean Methods

Although we have only used getter and setter methods in our bean so far, you should realize that we don't have to have just methods that get and set properties. Methods in our bean could contain any kind of functionality. For example, we might include a method that establishes a database connection, and this method is called from another method in the bean. However, the important thing to remember is that, unless you include getter and setter methods, you will not be able to retrieve or set values in the bean using tags.

Another important point that may not be clear to you at the moment is that the properties we get do not have to be bean attributes. Although the bean we created earlier uses getter and setter methods to retrieve/set attribute values, we can return the value of any variable from a getter method using a tag, not just object attributes.

For example, say we wanted to calculate the cost of a car after sales tax. We could add two new attributes to our class, which represent the cost before tax (cost) and the tax rate (taxRate):

```
private double cost = 10000.00;
private double taxRate = 17.5;
```

We can also easily add a method that calculates the sales tax:

```
public double getPrice() {
   double price = (cost + (cost * (taxRate/100)));
   return price;
}
```

Now note that this method follows the standard conventions for a getter method: it returns a value but takes no argument, and it follows the standard naming convention. Therefore there is no reason why we shouldn't be able to retrieve the value returned by this method using a tag... except that we also need a corresponding setter method too. We don't really want to use this setter method, so we can just construct a method that contains no functionality, as long as it follows the standard conventions for a setter method: that it takes an argument and returns no value:

```
private void setPrice(double newPrice) {
}
```

Since the name of the getter method implies that the value returned by the method corresponds to a property called price, we can retrieve this value from a bean instance using a
<jsp:getProperty> tag:

```
<jsp:getProperty name="myCar" property="price" />
```

Here the bean instance ID is myCar. Let's now create a new version of our CarBean bean that includes the ability to get the price of the car.

Try It Out – Playing with Bean Methods

Make the following changes to `CarBean.java`. The additions to the original are highlighted.

```java
package com.wrox.cars;
import java.io.Serializable;

public class CarBean implements Serializable {

  public CarBean(){
  }

  private String make = "Ford";

  public String getMake() {
    return make;
  }

  public void setMake(String make) {
    this.make = make;
  }

  private double cost = 10000.00;
  private double taxRate = 17.5;

  public double getPrice() {
    double price = (cost + (cost * (taxRate/100)));
    return price;
  }

  private void setPrice(double newPrice) {
  }
}
```

Now create a new JSP page, `carPage2.jsp`, under `%CATALINA_HOME%\webapps\begjsp-ch04` and enter the following code:

```jsp
<html>
  <head>
    <title>Using a JavaBean</title>
  </head>
  <body>

    <h2>Using a JavaBean</h2>

    <jsp:useBean id="myCar" class="com.wrox.cars.CarBean" />

    I have a <jsp:getProperty name="myCar" property="make" /> <br />

    My car costs $<jsp:getProperty name="myCar" property="price" />

  </body>
</html>
```

You will need to recompile the JavaBean. Open a command prompt and change directory to
`%CATALINA_HOME%\webapps\begjsp-ch04\WEB-INF\classes\`. Then run the
following command:

> **javac com\wrox\cars\CarBean.java**

Restart Tomcat and point your browser to http://localhost:8080/begjsp-ch04/carPage2.jsp. You should
see something like this:

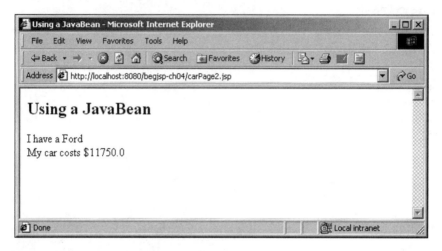

How It Works

Let's skip to the bits we've added to the bean. We have added our two attributes, `cost` and `taxRate`,
used to hold the pre-tax cost of the car and the sales tax rate:

```
private double cost = 10000.00;
private double taxRate = 17.5;
```

Then we have our method for getting the taxed price of the car:

```
public double getPrice() {
  double price = (cost + (cost * (taxRate/100)));
  return price;
}
```

And the empty method for setting the `price` property:

```
private void setPrice(double newPrice) {
}
```

Now let's see how we use the `getPrice()` method in the JSP. As usual we use the `<jsp:useBean>`
tag to create a bean instance, which is given an ID of `myCar`:

```
<jsp:useBean id="myCar" class="com.wrox.cars.CarBean" />
```

86

Then we retrieve the `make` of the car as in our previous example:

```
I have a <jsp:getProperty name="myCar" property="make" /> <br />
```

Finally we retrieve the post-tax cost of the car, represented by the property `price`, and display it on the web page:

```
My car costs $<jsp:getProperty name="myCar" property="price" />
```

Pretty simple stuff – and notice that by replacing all of the scriptlet code in the JSP with tags that use a bean, we have made the JSP far simpler and easier to understand.

JavaBeans or Enterprise JavaBeans?

We explained in Chapter 1 that Java Server Pages are one part, the "presentation tier", of the J2EE architecture. Another part of this architecture is **Enterprise JavaBeans (EJBs)**. EJBs are an advanced topic, and beyond the scope of this book. However, as you create bigger and better JSP web applications you will inevitably come across the term.

Our intention here is to warn you not to confuse the JavaBeans we have learnt about in this chapter with Enterprise JavaBeans. Although they share a similar name they have very different capabilities, design, and uses.

JavaBeans are designed to be simple general-purpose components that can be used either on the client side, or on the server-side (as we are doing), as part of a JSP page for instance.

EJBs, on the other hand, are components designed to implement enterprise business logic, and they are always used on the server-side. The main selling point of EJB components is that many useful features needed by enterprise businesses, such as support for transactions, database connection pooling, and security, is automatically handled when you use EJBs, so you don't need to write code to do this. Don't worry about what these features do; the point is that they are pretty useful for enterprise commerce. However, EJBs are considerably more complicated to understand, use, and maintain than JavaBeans, so we won't encounter them in this book.

Summary

We started off this chapter by discussing why you would want to organize your code in order to maximize code reuse. We also discussed how applications are easier to create and maintain if the different roles are defined and separated. Then we introduced components as a means to achieve these aims.

You were introduced to object-orientation and shown how Java classes fulfill the requirements of components. We covered the basics of using object methods, and showed you how to compile a class, and where to store it in a web application.

We then looked at a specific type of Java class, a JavaBean. You saw how to use these beans to organize your code. You also learnt how to use bean tags to instantiate a bean, and to set and retrieve data vales from the beans. We noted how the simplicity of these tags can make your JSP code easier to understand and maintain.

In the next chapter we are going to look at Java control statements, which allow us to make decisions within our code and then change the flow of execution through our code. You will see that using control statements wisely can allow us to reuse even more of our code. We will also introduce the idea of an array, as a way to collect together groups of variables. We will see how this can make our code simpler too.

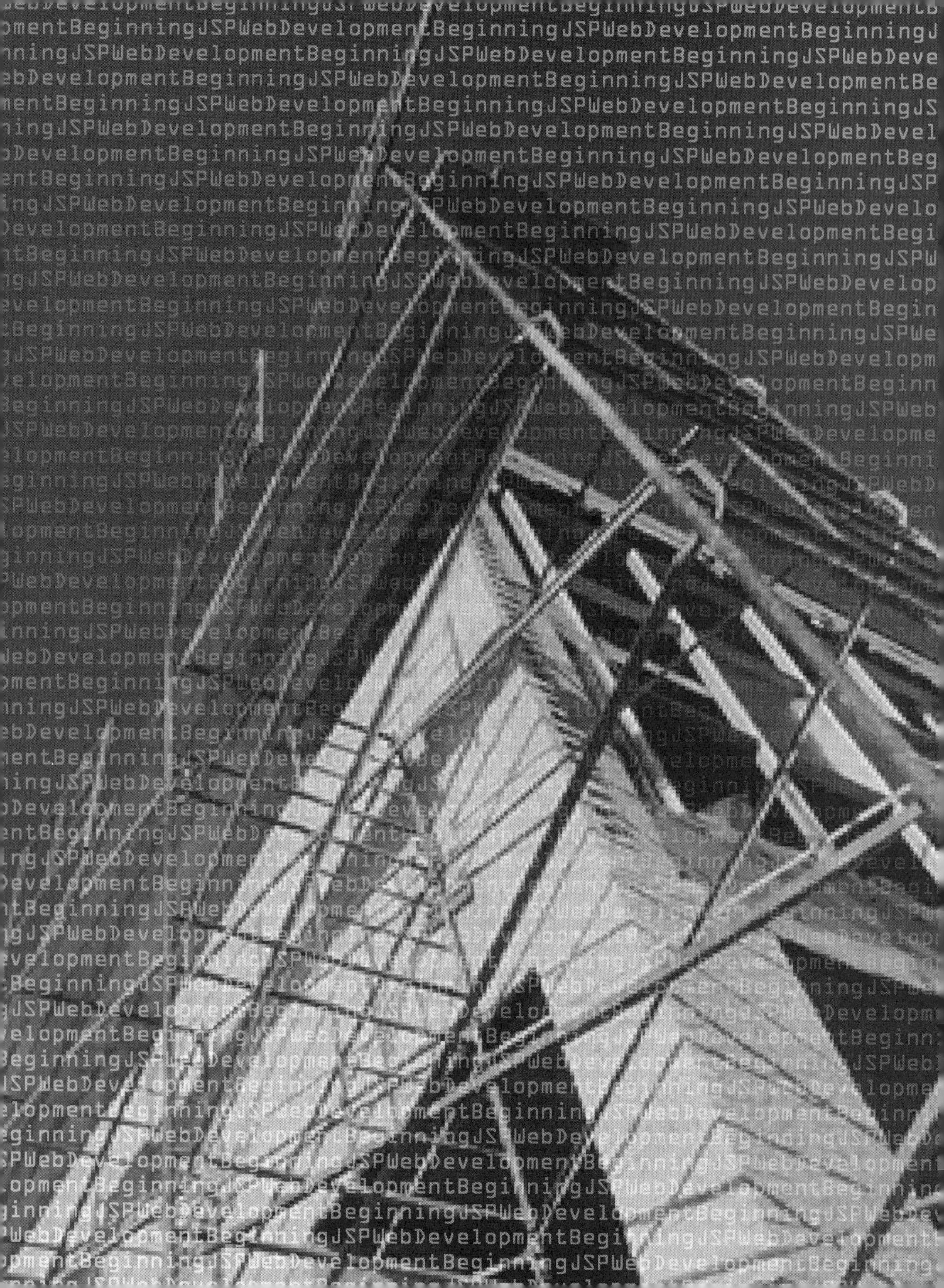
BeginningJSPWebDevelopment

Decisions, Decisions

As your Java code becomes more and more complex you will find that you will need to execute different blocks of code, depending on the circumstances. In other words, you will need a way to control the flow of execution through your code. In order to do this, we need to provide a *control statement*, where the result of evaluating this statement influences the flow of execution.

So what kinds of program flow control will we need? Examples include:

❑ Conditional statements: evaluating a condition in the program and executing code depending on whether the condition evaluates to "true" or "false"

❑ Iterative statements: repeating (*looping* through) sections of code

❑ Branching statements: transferring execution of the program to a particular section of the code

Fortunately, Java provides ways to do all of these things. Java also provides you with an easy way of manipulating multiple variables of the same type, using **arrays**.

In this chapter we will discuss:

❑ How to compare values

❑ How to easily incorporate logic in your code

❑ The `if`, `if-else` and `if-else-if` statements

❑ The `while`, `do-while` and `for` loops

❑ The `break`, `continue` and `return` statements

❑ How and where to use arrays

Before we can make decisions, we need to compare some values, so let's begin by looking at ways of comparing data values in Java.

Comparing Data Values

Before you can make any decisions in your code you need to know how to compare data values. The data values being compared are known as **operands** and these operands can be variables, constants or expressions.

The basic syntax for comparing two data values is shown below:

```
operand1  relational_operator  operand2
```

The six relational operators that Java provides are shown below:

Operator	Operator Name	Explanation
<	Less Than	Evaluates to true if operand1 is less than operand2, otherwise false.
<=	Less Than Or Equal To	Evaluates to true if operand1 is less than, or equal to, operand2, otherwise false
>	Greater Than	Evaluates to true if operand1 is greater than operand2, otherwise false.
>=	Greater Than Or Equal To	Evaluates to true if operand1 is greater than, or equal to, operand2, otherwise false.
==	Equal To	Evaluates to true if operand1 is equal to operand2, otherwise false
!=	Not Equal To	Evaluates to true if operand1 is not equal to operand2, otherwise false.

The example shown below demonstrates the comparison of two integer variables x and y.

```
boolean compareValue = false;
int x = 10;
int y = 20;
```

First, the variable x is initialized to 10, and the variable y is initialized to 20. The boolean variable compareValue will contain the result of the comparison: either true or false. Let's now compare x and y using some operators:

```
compareValue = (x < y);
compareValue = (x <= y);
compareValue = (x != y);
```

All of the above expressions evaluate to true. For instance (x < y) evaluates to true because 10 is less than 20. The expressions below evaluate to false:

```
compareValue = (x > y);
compareValue = (x >= y);
compareValue = (x == y);
```

This is all well and good, but what happens if we want to make decisions that depend on more than one condition? For example, say that I get an additional 10% discount if I have bought items worth more than $100 AND if I shop during the Christmas week? To allow us to evaluate more than one decision at once, we need to use Boolean logical operators.

Using Boolean Logic

In the above section, we saw how to use a relational operator to compare values. But what if we wanted to create more complex conditions by combining two or more conditions?

Java provides Boolean operators that allow you to construct more complex expressions based on two or more conditions. The Boolean operators are listed below. Remember that the operands can be values, variables or expressions.

Operator	Usage	Explanation
`||`	`operand1 || operand2`	Returns `true` if operand1 OR operand2 is `true`. It returns `false` if both the operands are `false`. It evaluates operand2 only if operand1 is `false`.
`&&`	`operand1 && operand2`	Returns `true` if operand1 AND operand2 are `true`. In other words, if any of the operands are `false`, it returns `false`. Note that operand2 is evaluated only if operand1 is `true`.
`!`	`!operand1`	Returns `true` if operand1 is `false`. Else if operand1 is `true`, it returns `false`.
`|`	`operand1	operand2`	Returns `true` if operand1 or operand2 is true. It returns `false` if both the operands are `false`. It differs from the `||` operator in that it always evaluates both operand1 and operand2.
`&`	`operand1 & operand2`	Returns `true` if operand1 AND operand2 is `true`. It returns `false` if either of the operands is `false`. It differs from the `&&` operator in that it always evaluates both operand1 and operand2.
`^`	`operand1 ^ operand2`	Returns `true` if either of operand1 or operand2 is `true` but not both.

Let's have some examples of their use. Imagine a situation where if a shopper purchases 4 items AND the total of the items is greater than $100, then shipping is free. What expression can we use to evaluate this? First we create two integer variables, `itemcount` and `totalcost`, and initialize their values. These variables will hold the number of items bought by the customer and the total cost of these items respectively:

```
int itemcount = 6;
int totalcost = 130;
```

Next we create and initialize a `boolean` variable, `freeShipping`, that will tell us whether shipping is free for this customer:

```
boolean freeShipping = false;
```

Now we can write an expression which can tell us whether shipping should be free or not:

```
freeShipping = ((itemcount >= 4) && (totalcost >= 100));
```

Of course, since the customer bought 6 items (greater than the 4 required) and paid $130, then `freeShipping` will contain `true`. Now say the store changes its policy so that customer needs only one of the criteria (4 items or more, or $100 or more spent) to qualify for free shipping. Here's the expression that represents this:

```
freeShipping = ((itemcount >= 10) || (totalcost >= 100));
```

Finally, here's a simple expression that we can use to evaluate whether an integer n is a negative number or not:

```
int n = -1;
boolean isNegativeNumber = false;
isNegativeNumber = !(n >= 0);
```

You can see that we initially set n to a value of `-1`, and then we create the `isNegativeNumber` `boolean` variable which will hold `true` or `false` depending on whether n is negative or not. Finally we test to see whether n is greater than or equal to 0: `(n>=0)`, and if it is not (expressed using the `!` operator) then `isNegativeNumber` will store `true`.

Making Decisions

In the previous sections, we saw how we can compare values and also how to use Boolean logic to create more complex expressions (or "decisions"). Therefore we now have the tools to help us to control the flow of execution of the program. But just how are we likely to want to change the normal, sequential, flow of a program? Here's a few ideas:

❑   We might want to execute different sections of code depending on the condition. For example, only if I spend over $100 do I get a 10% discount; this means that the line(s) of code which discounts 10% from my bill only gets executed if my bill is over $100.

❑   Perhaps we might want to repeat certain blocks of code. For instance, there might be several customers besides me that we wish to check for discount. It seems like a waste of time to write the same lines of code to check for and apply discount for each customer; it would be better to reuse the same code block for each customer.

❑ We may need to transfer execution of the program to a certain section of the code. Say that we have a block of code that searches for a product in the product catalog. If the product is found early in the catalog, we need to exit from the search block rather than needlessly carry on with the search until we reach the end of the block.

All the above scenarios are accomplished in Java using **control statements**; in other words, statements that control the flow of program execution. We are now going to take a look at three types of control statement:

❑ **Conditional statements**: here the statement is evaluated, and the code block executed depends upon the value returned by the statement

❑ **Iterative statements**: the same block of code is executed again and again ("iterated")

❑ **Branching statements**: the statement moves execution to a particular point within the code

So, let's start by taking a look at conditional statements.

Introducing Conditional Statements

While writing new programs you will continually come across situations where you need to evaluate a condition in your program and proceed accordingly. We have already seen an example of this: "If greater than four items are ordered then shipping is free". There are two main types of this conditional statement:

❑ if statement (and its variations)

❑ switch statement

The difference between the two is that an if statement demands a true or false answer, whereas switch allows for a whole variety of different answers to the statement.

The if Statement

Let's start with an example of an if statement:

```
if ( itemQuantity > 0 ) {
   System.out.println("The Quantity is greater than 0");
   System.out.println("No. of items : " + itemQuantity);
}
```

In English, what this basically says is "if the value of itemQuantity is greater than zero, then display

The Quantity is greater than 0

No. of items :

followed by the value of itemQuantity".

Note that this `if` statement follows the general form of `if` statements:

```
if (expression) {
   Statement Block
}
```

The expression is evaluated first; if it evaluates to `true`, the statement block (which consists of one or more Java statements) is executed.

You should also note that the `if` statement also has a shorthand form. If the statement block consists of only one line then you can omit the braces from your code, as shown below:

```
if (itemQuantity > 0)
   System.out.println("The Quantity is greater than 0");
```

This is fine, but what if we want to specify a code block to execute if the expression evaluates to `false`?

The if-else Statement

If the expression evaluates to `false`, we can direct the flow of execution to a particular code block by using an `if` statement that has an `else` clause tagged on the end. The syntax of such an `if-else` statement is shown below:

```
if (expression) {
   Statement Block 1
} else {
   Statement Block 2
}
```

As before, the expression is evaluated first, and if the expression gives `true`, the first statement block after the `if` is executed. However, on `false`, the block of code inside the braces after the `else` is executed instead.

Here's an example of the `if-else` statement in action. Here we build an `if-else` statement that evaluates whether we have 4 or more items to ship. If this is the case, no shipping costs are incurred by the customer. If not, the shipping cost is found by multiplying the number of items to ship by the cost of shipping an item:

```
if (itemQuantity >= 4) {
   shippingCost = 0.0;
} else {
   shippingCost = basicShippingCost * itemQuantity;
}
```

Assume that the `basicShippingCost` is $3.00 in the above code snippet. Given below is a table that shows the shipping costs for different numbers of items to ship:

itemQuantity	shippingCost
2	$3 x 2 items = $6 because `itemQuantity` is not $>=4$
4	$0 since `itemQuantity` $>=4$
6	$0 since `itemQuantity` $>=4$

Let's now try and put into practice what we have learned about the `if` and `if-else` statements, through a Try-It-Out example that you can run.

Try It Out – Using an if-else Statement

In this example we will see how we can use the `if-else` statement within the context of a JSP page. This is a simple JSP page that contains a form that allows the user to enter the quantity of a particular item. The scenario is that of a typical shopping cart at an e-commerce site where the user has to select the number of items that he wishes to purchase, and then submit the order.

First off, you will need to create a new folder under webapps to hold the JSPs we will be using in this chapter. Create a new directory:

`%CATALINA_HOME%\webapps\begjsp-ch05\WEB-INF\classes\`

Then open up your text editor, type in the following, and save it as `ifexample.jsp` under `%CATALINA_HOME%\webapps\begjsp-ch05`.

```html
<html>

  <head>
    <title>Chapter 5 Examples</title>
  </head>

<body>
  IF Statement Example
    <form method="POST" action="ifexamplehandler.jsp">
    <table border="0" cellpadding="0" cellspacing="0" width="439">
      <tr>
        <td width="157"><b>Shopping Cart</b></td>
        <td width="128"></td>
        <td width="148"></td>
      </tr>
      <tr>
        <td width="157" bgcolor="#C0C0C0">
          <font color="#FFFFFF">Product</font>
        </td>
        <td width="128" bgcolor="#C0C0C0">
          <font color="#FFFFFF">ListPrice</font>
        </td>
        <td width="148" bgcolor="#C0C0C0">
          <font color="#FFFFFF">Quantity</font>
        </td>
      </tr>
      <tr>
```

97

```
        <td width="157">Wrox Press Beginning JSP</td>
        <td width="128">$49.99</td>
        <td width="148">
          <input type="text" name="quantity" size="4" />
        </td>
      </tr>
    </table>

    <p>
      <input type="submit" value="Place Order" name="PlaceOrderBtn" />
    </p>

  </form>

  </body>
</html>
```

The number entered into the form (produced by the JSP above) is submitted to the
ifexamplehandler.jsp file. This file is listed below; again save this JSP into your
%CATALINA_HOME%\webapps\begjsp-ch05 folder:

```
<%@ page info="If Example JSP"%>
<html>

  <head>
    <title>Chapter 5 Examples</title>
  </head>

  <body>
    <b>IF Statement Example ( Response ) <br /></b>
    <br />

    <%
      int quantity = Integer.parseInt(request.getParameter("quantity"));
      if (quantity > 0) {
        out.println("Thank-you for your order!!");
      } else {
        out.println("Sorry, please enter a positive quantity");
      }
    %>

  </body>
</html>
```

Now start up Tomcat, and enter the following URL into your browser:

http://localhost:8080/begjsp-ch05/ifexample.jsp

Enter a positive number in the Quantity field as shown:

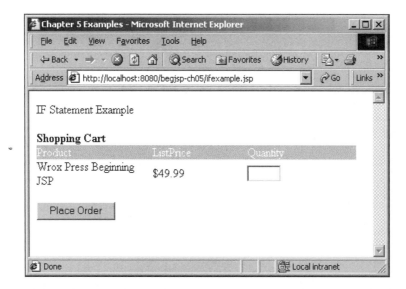

Next, click on the **Place Order** button. You should see the following output in the browser:

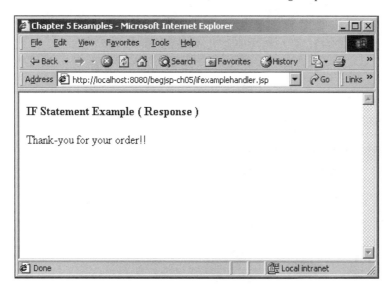

How It Works

Let's now walk through the JSPs, explaining how the code works.

First, we execute the `ifexample` JSP. This JSP is actually just plain HTML, and it generates a form for the customer to enter the number of items being purchased. This quantity is stored in the form field `quantity`:

```
<input type="text" name="quantity" size="4" />
```

When the form is submitted (in other words the user clicks on **Place Order**), the value of `quantity` is passed via the `POST` method to our other JSP, `ifexamplehandler.jsp`:

```
<form method="POST" action="ifexamplehandler.jsp">
```

The flow of execution now passes to the `ifexamplehandler` JSP. Our first step is to retrieve the value of the `quantity` variable and convert it into an integer value:

```
int quantity = Integer.parseInt(request.getParameter("quantity"));
```

Next, using the `if-else` construct, we check to see if the value of `quantity` is positive (greater than zero):

```
if (quantity > 0) {
```

If this evaluates to `true`, we print a message "Thank-you for your order!!":

```
out.println("Thank-you for your order!!");
```

Finally, if the expression evaluates to `false`, we print the message "Sorry, please enter a positive quantity":

```
} else {
  out.println("Sorry, please enter a positive quantity");
}
```

A Note About Input Validation

You may have noted that in this example there was nothing to stop a user entering letters or other non-numerical characters into the **Quantity** box. If you try this yourself, you will see that the result is often a set of vague error messages; something like "A Servlet Exception Has Occurred":

As a programmer, you should get into the habit of including input validation in your programs, to anticipate bad user input. This may involve checking the input value after submission, and displaying your own error messages if the input is not of the correct type. The handling of possible errors (known as **exceptions** in Java) thrown by your code is an important consideration for any programmer. We will explore this topic in more detail later in Chapter 9.

Time to get back on track. We have overlooked another potential scenario for using our if statement. What if there are more than two options; for instance, what if there were several levels of discount available to customers, depending upon how much money they each spent? There might be no discount for purchases below $100, but between $100 and $500 the customer gets 10% off, while above $500 they get 15% off. How do we cope with multiple options like this, using our if statement?

The if-else-if Statement

Coping with lots of possible options, using the if statement, is achieved by placing else-if clauses after the if block. The basic syntax of the resulting if-else-if statement is shown below:

```
if (expression1) {
  Statement Block 1;
} else if (expression2) {
  Statement Block 2
}
More else if Blocks !
...
```

Only any statement block where the associated expression has evaluated to true will be evaluated in this case.

Consider the code snippet shown below. Here we test the value of the integer variable n against several possible scenarios: is it less than zero (negative); is it equal to zero; or is it greater than zero (positive)?

```
int n = 10;

if (n < 0 ) {
  System.out.println("n is negative");
} else if (n == 0) {
  System.out.println("n is zero");
} else if (n > 0) {
  System.out.println("n is positive");
}
```

Since n is set equal to 10 at the start of the code snippet, the output will be "n is positive".

There are a couple of extra things to note about the if-else-if statement:

❑ If several else if expression blocks evaluate to true then each of these statement blocks will be executed. This is different from an else block, where once the if-block is executed, there is no chance of the else block getting executed as well.

❑ All of the expressions in the else-if should refer to the same variable. This ensures that the same variable is being compared against different conditions.

Next we'll put the if-else-if statement to use in another Try-It-Out.

Try It Out – Using if-else-if Statements

In this example, the user is presented with a drop-down list containing a list of books. The user can select a particular book and click on the **Get Details** button to retrieve the details of the book. We will use an `if-else-if` statement to select the correct details for the book chosen by the user.

First let's take a look at the file which builds the initial form displayed to the user. This JSP is similar in many ways to the corresponding file in the previous Try-It-Out. Save this file as `ifexample2.jsp` in your `begjsp-ch05` folder:

```html
<html>

  <head>
    <title>Chapter 5 Examples</title>
  </head>

  <body>
    IF ELSE IF Statement Example<br />

      <form method="POST" action="ifexamplehandler2.jsp">
        <table border="0" cellpadding="0" cellspacing="0" width="439">
          <tr>
            <td width="157"><b>View Book Details</b></td>
            <td width="128"></td>
            <td width="148"></td>
          </tr>
          <tr>
            <td width="433" colspan="3">
              <select size="1" name="book">
                <option selected value="1">Beginning JSP</option>
                <option value="2">Professional JSP</option>
                <option value="3">Beginning Java</option>
              </select>
              <input type="submit" value="Get Details" name="GetDetailsBtn" />
            </td>
          </tr>
        </table>
        <p> </p>
      </form>
  </body>
</html>
```

Control is passed to the following `ifexamplehandler2.jsp` file when we click on the **Get Details** button:

```jsp
<%@ page info="If Else If Example JSP"%>

<html>

  <head>
    <title>Chapter 5 Examples</title>
  </head>
```

```
<body>
  <b>IF ELSE IF Statement ( Response ) </b><br /><br />

  <%
    int bookid = Integer.parseInt(request.getParameter("book"));
    if (bookid == 1) {
      out.println("Beginning JSP");
      out.println("Price : $39.99, September 2001");
    } else if (bookid == 2) {
      out.println("Professional JSP");
      out.println("Price : $59.99, May 2001");
    } else if (bookid == 3) {
      out.println("Beginning Java");
      out.println("Price : $49.99, July 2000");
    }
  %>

</body>
</html>
```

Enter the following URL into your browser: http://localhost:8080/begjsp-ch05/ifexample2.jsp. You should see the following dropdown listbox:

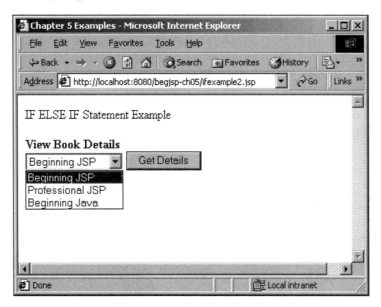

You can now select a book. If you choose **Beginning JSP** and click on the **Get Details** button, you should see the following response, showing the book's price and its date of publication:

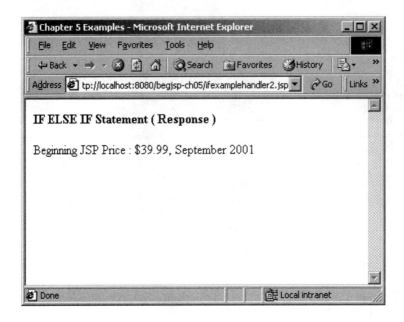

How It Works

Starting in `ifexample2.jsp`, the user selects a particular book from the dropdown listbox. The form field to capture the value of the book chosen is named (unsurprisingly) `book`:

```
<select size="1" name="book">
  <option selected value="1">Beginning JSP</option>
  <option value="2">Professional JSP</option>
  <option value="3">Beginning Java</option>
</select>
```

When the user clicks the **Get Details** button, the form field variable is submitted to `ifexamplehandler2.jsp`:

```
<form method="POST" action="ifexamplehandler2.jsp">
```

In `ifexamplehandler2.jsp`, we first retrieve the value of the `book` option and then store it in a variable `bookid`:

```
int bookid = Integer.parseInt(request.getParameter("book"));
```

Finally, using the `if-else-if` construct, we select the appropriate details for the chosen book, by cycling through all of the possible values of `bookid` until we find the one we need:

```
if (bookid == 1) {
  out.println("Beginning JSP");
  out.println("Price : $39.99, September 2001");
} else if (bookid == 2) {
  out.println("Professional JSP");
  out.println("Price : $59.99, May 2001");
```

```
  } else if (bookid == 3) {
    out.println("Beginning Java");
    out.println("Price : $49.99, July 2000");
  }
```

So now we know how to select one option from a set of options. But there are many situations in which choosing one option leads to another set of choices. How do we model this in Java?

Nested if Statements

We can model this "choice within a choice" in Java by embedding an `if` statement or an `if-else` statement inside another `if` or `if-else` statement. This is known as *nesting* of `if` statements, and is shown in a general way below. The nested statements are highlighted:

```
if (expression1) {
  if (expression2) {
    Statement Block 1
  }
} else {
  if (expression3) {
    Statement Block 2
  } else {
    Statement Block 3
  }
}
```

This ability to nest statements should not be entirely unexpected. Since a statement block is simply one or more lines of Java code, there is no reason why an `if` statement block should not contain further `if` and `if-else` statements.

Let's have a code snippet that helps to illustrate our point. We'll return to our earlier shipping cost scenario. Here, our customer is only allowed free shipping if more than 4 items are purchased. If he spends more than $100 on his 5 or more items then the customer gets 5% discount as well. However, if over $2000 is spent on the 5 or more items, the customer gets a free television too! What a generous offer!

```
if ( itemQuantity > 4 ) {
  System.out.println("Free Shipping for You!!");
  if (itemCost > 100) {
    System.out.println("5% Discount for You!!");
    if (itemCost > 2000) {
      System.out.println("Free Television for You!!");
    }
  }
}
```

You should have noted that we have more than one layer of nesting here: we can have as many layers as we need.

The Conditional Operator

Java provides a short version of the if-else statement via the conditional (?:) operator. The general syntax for using this operator is shown below:

> operand1 ? operand2 : operand3

The ?: operator returns operand2 if operand1 is true , or returns operand3 if operand1 is false. This may seem mildly confusing until we see this being using in a snippet of Java code:

```
int itemCost = 150;
boolean freeShipping = (itemCost > 100)?true:false;
```

In the above example, itemCost is $150. Since the expression itemCost > 100 evaluates to true, the freeShipping boolean variable gets initialized to the second operand, which has the value of true.

Take a look at another example:

```
int x = 20;
int y = (x > 50)?x+10:x-15;
```

Here the integer variable x is initialized to 20. Since (x > 50) evaluates to false, the variable y is assigned the value of the third operand, which has the value x-15 (which in turn evaluates to 5).

The switch Statement

We have already seen that there is a way to deal with a selection of options using if-else-if statements. However this method can be somewhat untidy. A cleaner alternative is to use the switch statement, the basic syntax of which is shown below:

```
switch (expression) {
  case <expressionValue 1>
    StatementBlock1;
    break;
  case <expressionValue 2> :
    StatementBlock2;
    break;
  default :
    DefaultStatementBlock;
    break;
}
```

Take a deep breath – this is not nearly as complicated as it looks at first sight! Let's walk through what this syntax really means.

The first thing to note is that we have an initial expression to evaluate. Second, we have case blocks nested inside the switch block; each case block has an associated expressionValue. Third, we have a default case too.

So what happens when the switch block is executed?

1. The expression is evaluated, and its value is compared to each expressionValue.

2. If a matching expressionValue is found, the associated case is executed (in other words, the StatementBlock belonging to the case is executed).

3. If a matching expressionValue is not found, the DefaultStatementBlock belonging to the default case is executed instead.

There are several things you should note about the switch block:

❑ The expression must return a value of type byte, char, short or int

❑ The default statement is optional

❑ The break statement, which will be discussed in detail later in the chapter, is used to knock the flow of execution out of the switch block. On reaching break the program control is transferred to the first statement following the enclosing switch block.

> **If you do not include the break statement, then the program control will fall through the remaining case options and execute all the statement blocks there.**

Let's now take a look at an example, given below. Here we display a list of options, the contents of which depend on the value of the menuOption variable:

```
int menuOption = 1;

switch (menuOption) {
  case 1 :
    System.out.println("1. Add User");
    System.out.println("2. Edit User");
    System.out.println("3. Delete User");
    System.out.println("4. List Users");
    System.out.println("5. Exit");
    break;
  case 2 :
    System.out.println("1. List Users");
    System.out.println("2. Exit");
    break;
  default :
    System.out.println("Incorrect Option!!!");
    break;
}
```

In the above code snippet, the value of menuOption is set to 1, so you should be able to work out that the output displayed will be:

1. Add User
2. Edit User
3. Delete User
4. List Users
5. Exit

If the value of menuOption was changed to 5, then the switch statement would fall through to the default case and the output will be:

Incorrect Option!!!

Note that there is no restriction on the order in which you check the values in the switch statement. We could have written the same code in the following manner by checking for case 2 first instead.

```
switch (menuOption) {
  case 2 :
    ...
    break;
  case 1 :
    ...
    break;
  default :
    System.out.println("Incorrect Option!!!");
    break;
}
```

Let's revisit the if-else-if block from the previous Try-It-Out example. It is shown below:

```
if (bookid == 1) {
  out.println("Beginning JSP");
  out.println("Price : $49.99, September 2000");
} else if (bookid == 2) {
  out.println("Professional JSP");
  out.println("Price : $59.99, May 2000");
} else if (bookid == 3) {
  out.println("Beginning Java");
  out.println("Price : $39.99, July 99");
}
```

We can replace the above code with the following switch statement:

```
switch (bookid) {
  case 1 :
    out.println("Beginning JSP");
    out.println("Price : $49.99, September 2000");
    break;
  case 2 :
    out.println("Professional JSP");
    out.println("Price : $59.99, May 2000");
    break;
  case 3 :
    out.println("Beginning Java");
    out.println("Price : $39.99, July 99");
    break;
  default:
    out.println("Invalid Option");
    break;
}
```

The end result is the same, except that the switch provides a much cleaner way of writing code because it not only makes it easier to add new options, but also improves the readability.

As an exercise to the reader, you might like to open the file ifexamplehandler2.jsp and replace the if-else-if block with the switch block shown above.

Iterative Statements

Consider a situation where we would want to execute the same block of code more than once. A classic example of this would be if we had written a block of code that could find the interest on our bank balance, and we wanted to work out how much our account would grow over, say, five years. Rather than writing five blocks of code which all have the same functionality, we would like to be able to feed the initial balance into the code block, work out the interest after the first year, add this to the initial balance, and then feed this new balance back into the start of the block of code again. We would then obtain the balance after two years, and by repeating the process three more times we would obtain the balance after five years.

Executing the same block of code over and over is known as **iteration**, or **looping**. Iterative statements in Java allow us to loop through a section of code in this way. There are three types of iterative statement that we will be looking at in this section:

- ❑   while statements
- ❑   do-while statements
- ❑   for statements

We will start by introducing you to the while statement.

The while Statement

In many situations, you will want to continue looping through a code block while an expression remains true. For example, say a bank had loaned you some money. Each month a percentage of your wages went to repaying the loan. You don't want to make more repayments than you need to, so we could say that *while* the money owed is greater than zero dollars, we will make a monthly repayment. In this case, of course, the expression is "money owed is greater than zero dollars".

The basic syntax of a while statement is therefore pretty simple, and is shown below:

```
while (expression) {
  Statement Block
}
```

Here's a brief example of using a while statement in Java code:

```
int count = 1;

while (count < 6) {
  System.out.println(count);
  count = count+1;
}
```

We have an integer variable, count, which we initialize to 1. The while statement itself says that the statement block should be executed over and over until the value of count jumps reaches 6. Each time we loop through the statement block, the value of count is displayed, and 1 is added to the value of count, so we expect that we get count displayed five times before the while expression returns false. Indeed, the above code will display the following:

```
1
2
3
4
5
```

Let's now move on and look at a variation of the while statement, the do-while statement.

The do-while Statement

The do-while statement is similar in function to the while statement: it executes the statement block while the expression remains true. However, the notable difference between these two types of iterative statement is that for do-while, the expression in the while clause is evaluated at the end, not the start, of the statement block. We can see this if we study the basic syntax of a do-while statement, as shown below:

```
do {
   Statement Block
} while (expression);
```

If the expression evaluates to true, then the statement block is executed repeatedly until the condition evaluates to false.

On first glance it looks like we can achieve the same results using the while and the do-while statements, and indeed in many situations they give similar results.

However, let's now go back to the counting example we used for the while statement. This time though we'll give the count variable a value of 6 instead. Consider what happens as we proceed through the loop:

```
int count = 6;

while (count < 6) {
   System.out.println(count);
   count = count+1;
}
```

Since the while loop will only iterate while the value of count is less than 6, setting the initial value of count to 6 means that the loop never gets executed.

Now consider what happens if we set up the same counting example using the do-while loop:

```
int count = 6;

do {
   System.out.println(count);
   count = count+1;
} while (count < 6);
```

In this case, because the exression is not checked until the end of the loop, one iteration is allowed to occur, and we can see the value of `count` displayed:

6

So, importantly, we can use the `do-while` loop in situations in which we need the contents of the statement block to execute **at least once**.

Try It Out – Using the while Statement

It's time for another Try-It-Out example that you can have a go at running yourself. For this example, we will discuss how you can go about building a simple mathematics quiz which makes use of the `while` statement. The quiz will consist of three questions, and you have to answer all of them correctly to pass.

Shown below is the JSP file, `quiz.jsp`, which displays the quiz. As usual, place this file in your `begjsp-ch05` folder below `webapps\`:

```
<html>

  <head>
    <title>Chapter 5 Examples</title>
  </head>

  <body>
    Mathematics Quiz ( Please answer the questions below.
    You must answer all the questions correctly to pass!!!)
    <br />
    <form method="POST" action="quizhandler.jsp">
      <table border="0" cellpadding="0" cellspacing="0" width="645">
        <tr>
          <td width="347">1. Is 2 an even or odd number ?</td>
          <td width="127">
            <input type="radio" value="even" name="answer1" />even
          </td>
          <td width="165">
            <input type="radio" name="answer1" value="odd" />odd
          </td>
        </tr>
        <tr>
          <td width="347">2. Is 7 a prime number ?</td>
          <td width="127">
            <input type="radio" name="answer2" value="yes" />yes
          </td>
          <td width="165">
            <input type="radio" value="no" name="answer2" />no
          </td>
        </tr>
        <tr>
          <td width="347">3. What is ((1 + 1) x 4) /(2 + 2 + 2 + 2)</td>
          <td width="127">
            <input type="radio" name="answer3" value="1" />1
          </td>
        </tr>
```

```
        <td width="165">
          <input type="radio" name="answer3" value="2" />2
        </td>
      </tr>
      <tr>
        <td width="347"></td>
        <td width="127"></td>
        <td width="165"></td>
      </tr>
      <tr>
        <td width="639" colspan="3">
          <input type="submit" value="Submit Answers" name="SubmitBtn" />
        </td>
      </tr>
    </table>
    <p> </p>
  </form>
</body>
</html>
```

When the **Submit Answers** button produced by this JSP is clicked, control is passed to the quizhandler.jsp file listed below:

```
<%@ page info="Quiz Handler JSP"%>

<html>

  <head>
    <title>Chapter 5 Examples</title>
  </head>

  <body>
    <b> Your Result : </b> <br /><br />
    <%
      String answer1 = request.getParameter("answer1");
      String answer2 = request.getParameter("answer2");
      String answer3 = request.getParameter("answer3");

      boolean bChecking = true;
      boolean bPassed   = true;

      while (bChecking) {
        if (answer1 != "even") {
          bPassed = false;
        }

        if (answer2 != "yes") {
          bPassed = false;
        }

        if (answer3 != "1") {
          bPassed = false;
        }
```

```
        bChecking = false;
      }

      if (bPassed) {
        out.println("Congratulations, You Passed !!!");
      } else {
        out.println("Sorry !!! Better Luck Next Time!");
      }
    %>
  </body>
</html>
```

First, open your browser and enter the following URL: http://localhost:8080/begjsp-ch05/quiz.jsp.
When viewed in the browser, the quiz appears as shown below:

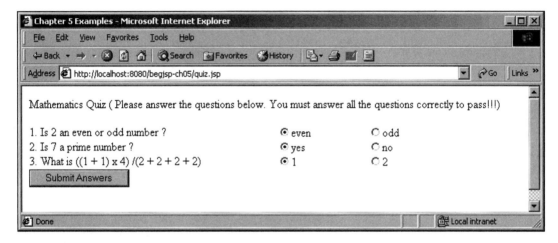

Enter your answers for the quiz, and then click on the **Submit Answers** button. If all of the answers are
correct, you will get the message:

Congratulations, You Passed !!!

If your math ain't too hot, you'll get:

Sorry !!! Better Luck Next Time!

How It Works

In `quiz.jsp`, we produce three pairs of radio buttons corresponding to form variables `answer1`,
`answer2`, and `answer3`. When the **Submit Answers** button is clicked, these variables are passed via
POST to our other JSP, `quizhandler.jsp`:

```
<form method="POST" action="quizhandler.jsp">
```

In `quizhandler.jsp`, we retrieve the answers to all the quiz questions as shown below:

```
String answer1 = request.getParameter("answer1");
String answer2 = request.getParameter("answer2");
String answer3 = request.getParameter("answer3");
```

After we have retrieved the answers, we use a `while` statement to check the answers to the quiz. We first create two boolean variables. The first, `bChecking` is used as the expression for the `while` statement. It holds a value of initial value of `true`. When all of the answers have been checked within the `while` loop, it is made `false` and the flow of execution drops out of the loop because the `while` expression returns `false`.

```
boolean bChecking = true;
boolean bPassed   = true;

while (bChecking) {
        if (answer1 != "even") {
          bPassed = false;
        }

        if (answer2 != "yes") {
          bPassed = false;
        }

        if (answer3 != "1") {
          bPassed = false;
        }

        bChecking = false;
}
```

The second boolean that we set, `bPassed`, also takes an initital value of `true`. If any of the answers are incorrect, we reset this variable to `false`. This means that the user has failed the test. If all the answers are correct, the `bPassed` variable remains set to `true`. Finally we select the appropriate congratulations or commiserations message on the basis of the value of `bPassed`:

```
if (bPassed) {
  out.println("Congratulations, You Passed !!!");
} else {
  out.println("Sorry !!! Better Luck Next Time!");
}
```

Variable Scope Within Statement Blocks

Before we move any further, it's time to throw in a cautionary note about variable scope and statement blocks. Consider the following code snippet:

```
int myVar1 = 100;
System.out.println(myVar1);

if (myVar1 > 0) {
```

```
      int myVar2 = myVar1 * 2;

      System.out.println(myVar1);
      System.out.println(myVar2);
   }
   System.out.println(myVar2);
```

In this code, we create two integer variables myVar1 and myVar2, assign values to them of 100 and 200 respectively, and attempt to print them out twice. Therefore we might expect the execution of this code to result in:

100
100
200
200

Actually, attempting to print myVar2 for the second time results in an error. Why? This is because myVar2 is declared *inside* the for statement block, so this variable only has scope *local to this statement block*. If we attempt to use the variable outside of the block, it will not be recognized, and an error will be thrown.

You should note, however, that variables declared *outside* of the statement block may be used within the statement block as well. This is why we are able to print out myVar1 inside and outside of the for statement.

The for Statement

The while and do-while statements are very useful for situations when we don't know when the expression will return false. However, in many scenarios we know how many times we want the loop to iterate. Remember the bank interest example we used earlier? In this case, we had a block of code that found the interest on an account balance, and we wanted to find the interest accumulated over five years. In other words, we knew that we needed to iterate through the loop 5 times.

A fixed number of iterations can be achieved using the for statement. To illustrate its use, let's jump straight into an example.

Consider the simple for statement shown below:

```
for (int num=1; num<=5; num++)
   System.out.println(num);
}
```

Before we consider what this statement does, let's take a closer look at the statement itself. You should have spotted that the for expression is actually made up of three expressions:

```
int num=1
num<=5
num++
```

The first is known as the *initialization expression*, the second is the *termination expression*, and the third is the *increment expression*. In other words, a general syntax for the for loop is:

```
for(initialization; termination; increment) {
  Statement Block
  }
```

The `for` loop also introduces the notion of a **loop counter**: a variable that allows us to keep track of how many iterations have been made by the statement. In this example, num is the counter. Let's now see how these expressions and the loop counter are used in the `for` statement:

1. For the first iteration, the value of the loop counter is given by the initialization expression (=1).

2. Before proceeding through the statement block, the value of the loop counter is fed into the termination expression, and this expression is evaluated. We find that the value of the loop counter num is indeed less than or equal to 5, so this expression returns `true`.

3. The value returned by the termination expression governs whether the flow of execution continues through the statement block or not. If it returns `true`, we continue, if `false`, we break out of the `for` statement. The termination expression has returned `true`, so we execute the statement block, printing out the value of the loop counter.

4. When the flow of execution reaches the end of the first iteration, we feed the value of the loop counter into the increment expression (num++) which increments the value of the counter by one.

5. The next step is to feed the new value of the counter into the termination expression and evaluate this expression, to check that we are allowed to execute the statement block again. In other words, we are revisiting step 2.

6. We proceed through all of the steps after 2 again with the new value of the counter, and then increment the counter again, and so on, until the flow of execution breaks out of the `for` statement because the termination expression returns `false`.

You should therefore be able to see that the code snippet will print out numbers one through five:

```
1
2
3
4
5
```

You should note that the `for` statement is very flexible. For instance, the loop counter doesn't need to be incremented by one; it can be any number. We may want to increment by 5, or even by -5. Indeed, we don't need to "increment" at all: the increment expression might be a more complex mathematical expression, such as num=num*num. And although we will often start the loop counter at 1, we could start and terminate with any number.

Furthermore, we can include other variables aside from the counter in our expressions. For instance, a more complicated `for` expression might be:

```
(int num=minNum; num<=maxNum; num=num*num)
```

Here we are initializing the num loop counter with the value of the minNum variable, incrementing by num*num, and terminating when num exceeds the value of maxNum.

Finally, it is also worth noting the variable scope for the variable num. As you can see, the variable num is declared inside the for statement, so it is accessible only within the for statement block.

Branching Statements

Earlier in the chapter when we discussed switch statements, we noted that we needed to include a break statement at the end of each case block, in order to move the flow of program execution to the end of the switch statement. Statements like this, which direct the flow of execution to a particular point in a program, are known as **branching** (or "flow control") statements.

There are three branching statements that we will cover in this section:

❑   break

❑   continue

❑   return

Since we've already mentioned the break statement, let's start with that.

The break Statement

The break statement can be used to terminate any enclosing for, do-while or while loops as well as the switch control statement. The program control gets transferred to the next statement after the enclosing loop.

An example of the break statement in a for loop is shown below (this is a modification of the example we used to explain the for loop):

```
for(int num=1; num<=5; num++) {
  System.out.println(num);
  if ( num == 3) {
    break;
  }
}
```

In the above code snippet, if the value of the num variable is equal to 3, the break statement is executed. This will result in the termination of the enclosing for statement, so the for loop for values of num equal to 4 or 5 will not be iterated. The output of the above code snippet will therefore be:

1
2
3

You should note that a **labeled** break statement is also available to you. This is useful because it means that we can jump to the end of any particular enclosing statement using break and a label. To illustrate this, consider what would happen if we nested the for statement from the example above inside another for statement:

```
OuterLoop:
for(int counter=1; counter<=2; counter++) {
  InnerLoop:
  for(int num=1; num<=5; num++) {
    System.out.println(num);
    if ( num == 3) {
      break OuterLoop;
    }
  }
} // break directs execution flow to this point
```

Note that we have labeled the `for` statements with `OuterLoop` and `InnerLoop` labels respectively, and that we have labeled `break` too:

```
break OuterLoop;
```

Now when program execution reaches this line, it will jump to the end of the outer `for` statement, *not* to the end of the inner `for` statement (as an unlabeled `break` would). We will see that other types of statement can be labeled in a similar way.

The continue Statement

The unlabeled `continue` statement is used to skip the current iteration of the enclosing `for`, `do-while` or `while` loop. A `continue` statement with a label is used to skip the current iteration of the loop that is referred to via that label.

An example of the `continue` statement is shown below:

```
for(int num=1; num<=5; num++) {
  if (num == 3) {
    continue;
  }
  System.out.println(num);
}
```

You can see that when the value of num is 3, the expression `(num == 3)` evaluates to `true`, and the `continue` statement is called. This will terminate the current iteration of the `for` loop and the incremental expression will be called. Therefore this `for` statement will not print out the number 3:

```
1
2
4
5
```

The return Statement

A `return` statement is used to transfer control out of the current executing method. Remember that a Java method is a block of code functionality that can be executed ("called") from within another block of code, simply by including the name of the method in this code. The result of a method call may be a returned value or `void`. In the case of a non-void `return` value, the `return` statement **must** include the variable of that particular data type. We will see many examples of this in later chapters.

We have now discussed all of the important control statements. We will move on now to discuss how to group together variables of the same data type into arrays, and how combining the use of control statements with arrays can make our code simpler and easier to manage.

Introducing Arrays

Consider the following code snippet shown below:

```
String str1 = "S1";
String str2 = "S2";
String str3 = "S3";
...
String str1000 = "S1000";
```

Imagine we had a thousand `String` variables as above. Remembering and managing them all would be troublesome. Also, say we wanted to perform the same action on every variable – process each `String` using the same method. We would have to call the method a thousand times, and we could end up with a thousand more variables!

```
newStr1 = myMethod(str1);
newStr2 = myMethod(str2);
newStr3 = myMethod(str3);
...
newStr1000 = myMethod(str1000);
```

This is a time-consuming and untidy way of using lots of variables. Wouldn't it be nice if you could refer to all of the above variables using a single variable that represents all of them, and then access a particular variable as and when you need it? This is where **arrays** come in.

An array provides us with an easy method of collecting together and referencing many variables of the same data type. By type, we mean an array of `Strings`, or an array of `int`'s, or array of `char`'s, and so on. We can have an array of any of the basic primitive data types, as well as other non-primitive data types such as user-defined objects. We can even have arrays of arrays (of arrays...)! Note that we cannot however have an array of mixed data types.

Array Elements and Index Values

Each variable in the array is known as an **element**. In order to be able to reference a particular element within the array, a number called the **index** is assigned to each element. The first element has an index of zero, the second has an index of 1, and so on. You should note that the index value has no effect on the value of the element itself. For example, we might have an array called `numbers`, in which the fourth element of the array contains a value of 93. Since it is the fourth element of the array, the index of this element would be 3.

Creating Arrays

In this section we will walk through the process of array creation. In order to create an array, we need to do three things:

1. *declare* the array

2. *define* the array

3. *initialize* the array

Let's look through each of these steps in turn.

Declaring an Array

So how do we name (or **declare**) an array? Here's an example:

```
int[] numbers;
```

In this case we have declared an array of integers called `numbers`. You should note the use of the brackets `[]` to denote an array. Here's another example, where we declare a `String` array called `names`:

```
String[] names;
```

So, we can see that the standard syntax for declaring an array is:

```
DataType[] array_variable_name;
```

However, you should note that we could also use:

```
DataType []array_variable_name;
DataType array_variable_name[];
```

These are also valid forms of array declaration.

Defining an Array

After we have declared an array, the next step is to **define** it. This means that we need to state the **length** of the array – the number of elements that it will contain – so that the correct amount of memory can be allocated to it. Here's a few examples of array definition using the arrays we have just declared:

```
numbers = new int[4];
names = new String[3];
```

In both of these examples, we have defined arrays containing three elements – in other words three elements in length. Obviously the basic syntax for defining an array is therefore:

```
array_variable_name = new DataType[array_length];
```

You should note that the default value of each of the elements when the arrays above are created is zero. Indeed the default value of any primitive data type in an array is zero; the default value of objects in arrays is `null`.

Initializing and Resetting Array Values

Our final step is to place initial values into our array elements. We can assign values to each of the elements individually, as below:

```
numbers[0] = 39;
names[0] = "Chris";
```

The number between the brackets is the index of the element that we wish to initialize.

You should note that we can **reset** the values contained by the elements in an array at any time during the array's lifetime in exactly the same way. So if Jim changed his name to Kurt, we could reset the value of the second element of the names array using:

```
names[1] = "Kurt";
```

Creating an Array the Easy Way

Although we have taken you through each step of array creation one at a time for illustrative purposes, we can actually perform all of these steps at the same time, in one line of code. Here's a few examples:

```
int[] numbers = {39, 21, 8, 93};
String[] names = {"Chris","Jim","Nancy"};
```

On the left-hand side, we declare the data types and names of the arrays, and on the right-hand side we initialize them. Note that we don't need to initialize each element one at a time if we use comma-delimited values between braces. But what happened to array definition? Cleverly, Java notes the number of initialization values and creates an array large enough to hold them – in other words Java performs array definition for you.

Finally, the easiest way to create a new array is to initialize it using an existing array. For instance, now that we have created the numbers array, we could use it to initialize a new array, moreNumbers:

```
int[] moreNumbers = numbers;
```

In this case, Java creates a new integer array, moreNumbers, that has the same number of elements (4) as the numbers array. Each element of moreNumbers will contain the same value as the corresponding element of numbers.

Determining the Array Length

As the size of an array is such an important property, Java provides us with an easy way to find the length of any given array, using *array_name*.length. For example, referring to the arrays we created earlier:

```
System.out.println(numbers.length);
System.out.println(names.length);
```

As we expect, these lines will print:

4
3

Note that `length` will return the declared length of the array, not the number of elements that have been initialized in the array. For instance, consider the following code snippet:

```
int[] moreNumbers;
moreNumbers = new int[4];
moreNumbers[0] = 37;
moreNumbers[0] = 71;

System.out.println(names.moreNumbers);
```

The last line will display "4" because the `moreNumbers` array has been declared as being four elements in length, even though only two of its elements have been initialized.

Let's now put our new-found knowledge of arrays to good use in a Try-It-Out example.

Try It Out – Using Arrays

We will now demonstrate the use of arrays within a JSP page. In this example we will simulate a form-based survey in which the user is asked to select items that he or she has purchased online in the last 6 months. The example consists of two JSPs: the first generates the selection form, and passes the form field variables (stored in an array) to the second JSP that processes the information. Here's the first JSP, `arrayexample1.jsp`. Place it (along with the rest of the JSPs in the chapter) in your `webapps\begjsp-ch05` folder.

```html
<html>
  <head>
    <title>Chapter 5 Examples</title>
  </head>

  <body>
    Array Example 1 <br>
    <form method="POST" action="arrayexamplehandler1.jsp">
      <table border="0" cellpadding="0" cellspacing="0" width="625">
        <tr>
          <td width="619"><b>Survey - I </b></td>
        </tr>
        <tr>
          <td width="619">
            1. In the last 6 months, which of the following items
            did you purchase online :
          </td>
        </tr>
        <tr>
          <td width="619">
            <input type="checkbox" name="surveyquestion"
                   value="Technical Books" /> Technical Books
            <input type="checkbox" name="surveyquestion"
                   value="Music CD" /> Music CD
            <input type="checkbox" name="surveyquestion"
                   value="DVD" /> DVD
          </td>
        </tr>
      </table>
      <p>
        <input type="submit" value="Process Survey" name="ProcessBtn" />
      </p>
    </form>
  </body>
</html>
```

This page displays three checkboxes. The contents of the form field variable array, corresponding to the state of these checkboxes, is passed via POST to the second JSP `arrayexamplehandler1.jsp` (below), when the **Process Survey** button is pressed:

```
<%@ page info="Array Example1 JSP"%>

<html>

  <head>
    <title>Chapter 5 Examples</title>
  </head>

  <body>
    <b>Array Example 1 ( Response ) </b><br /<br />

    <%
      String[] surveyquestion =
                request.getParameterValues("surveyquestion");
      if (surveyquestion != null) {
        for(int i=0;i<surveyquestion.length;i++) {
          out.println(surveyquestion[i] +  "<BR>");
        }
      } else {
        out.println("You did not answer any questions!!");
      }
    %>
  </body>
</html>
```

Open your browser and enter this URL: http://localhost:8080/begjsp-ch05/arrayexample1.jsp. You should see a page that looks something like this:

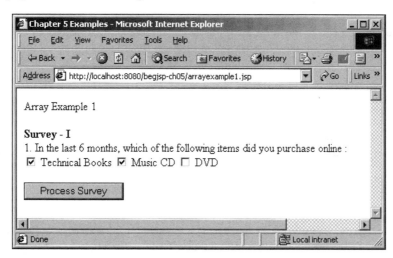

Fill in the survey, and then click on the **Process Survey** button. You should get a response that looks like this (depending on the items you chose):

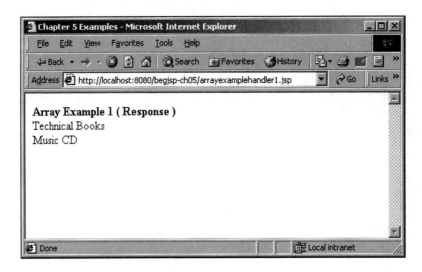

How It Works

First, let's look at the important lines within the `arrayexample1.jsp` code. Pay special attention to the HTML below, where we save the state of each checkbox into a variable called `surveyquestion`:

```
<input type="checkbox" name="surveyquestion"
       value="TechnicalBooks" /> Technical Books
<input type="checkbox" name="surveyquestion"
       value="Music CD" /> Music CD
<input type="checkbox" name="surveyquestion"
       value="DVD" /> DVD
```

Since all of our checkboxes in our form have this same variable name, this implies that `surveyquestion` must be an array, otherwise it wouldn't be able to hold more than one value. You should note that this array is created implicitly: we do not need to include an array declaration and definition, like:

```
String[] surveyquestion;
surveyquestion = new String[3];
```

This `String` array is then passed via POST to `arrayexample1handler.jsp`:

```
<form method="POST" action="arrayexample1handler.jsp">
```

In `arrayexample1handler.jsp` we first retrieve the array from the `request` object, and place its contents into a new `String` array called `surveyquestion`:

```
String[] surveyquestion = request.getParameterValues("surveyquestion");
```

Hopefully what we have is an array of `String` variables that contains all the options that selected. However, we first check that there are values within the array:

```
        if (surveyquestion != null) {
```

If there are values, we iterate through the `surveyquestion` array, printing out all the values within it:

```
        if (surveyquestion != null) {
          for(int i=0;i<surveyquestion.length;i++) {
            out.println(surveyquestion[i] +  "<BR>");
          }
```

Finally, if there are no values in the array, we print out an error message:

```
        } else {
          out.println("You did not answer any questions!!");
        }
```

Imagine for a moment that we did not use an array; we would have to think of different names for each of the choices made for every survey question. If we modified the survey so that it consisted of tens of questions, this would become a major maintenance issue. So, we can see that arrays can make our code much, much simpler.

Using JavaBeans with Our JSPs

You may have noted that the scriptlet code in our examples is becoming increasingly long and untidy. In Chapter 4 we discussed the need to move logic code out of the JSP and into JavaBean classes, in order to simplify the JSP script, and to make the JSP easier to maintain (through separation of business logic from presentation code).

In this chapter we will not use beans with our JSPs, because we want to keep our examples as simple as possible. However, you may have noticed that our scriptlet code is becoming increasingly long and more difficult to maintain. If we wanted to make our JSP examples easier for page designers to understand, and easier to maintain, we should seriously consider moving the code from scriptlets into beans. We will, however, leave it to the reader to attempt a version of the previous example that makes use of beans, as an exercise.

Iterating Through Arrays

Did you notice the way that we used the array in the previous example in tandem with the `for` statement? If we want to process lots of variables (of the same data type) in a similar way, we can do this using `for` statements and arrays. Note how we used ***array_name***`.length` above to determine how many elements we needed to process, and used this figure to set the termination expression:

```
        for(int i=0;i<surveyquestion.length;i++) {
```

We also processed one element per iteration, by referring to the element by its index:

```
        out.println(surveyquestion[i] +  "<BR>");
```

Using a `for` loop in conjunction with an array in this way is often called *iterating through the array*, and it is a technique that is widely used in programming.

Chapter 5

Arrays of Arrays

So far, we have played with arrays of primitive types and arrays of objects. Let's now turn our attention to using arrays of arrays (two-dimensional arrays). Essentially this means that each element of the first array dimension is itself an array.

For instance, say we had two houses in our street, and each house had three occupants. We could create a two dimensional array in which each element of the first array dimension represented a house, and elements of the second array dimension represented the names of the occupants of a particular house. We would need a 2 x 3 `String` array (the array would have 6 elements in total).

How would we create such an array? To create the 2-D `houses` array described above, we would need the following code:

```
String[][] houses = {
   {"Richard", "Dan", "Chris"},
   {"Jeelani", "Stephen", "Romin"},
};
```

You should be able to see that this is a minor variation on ordinary 1-D array creation, for instance:

```
String[][] house = {"Richard", "Dan", "Chris"};
```

All that we have done is replace each single initialization value between the braces with a array of values instead, grouped together in another set of braces. So the general syntax for creating 2-D arrays of size M x N (where M and N are positive integers) in Java is:

```
DataType[][] array_variable_name = {
   {value1, value2, ..., valueN},
   {value1, value2, ..., valueN},
   ...
   {value1, value2, ..., valueN}, // Mth array of values
}
```

So how do we reference elements in a 2-D array? Let's use our `houses` array for examples here. We can reference the whole of the first house using `houses[0]`, and we can reference Chris in this house using `houses[0][2]`. In other words, if we want to reference all of the occupants of the Mth house, we would use `houses[M]`, but if we wanted to be more specific and reference the Nth occupant of this house, we would need to add another index: `houses[M][N]`.

You should note that all of the arrays within an array do not need to be of the same size. For instance, if Craig moved into the first house too, we could create a new array:

```
String[][] newHouses = {
   {"Richard", "Dan", "Chris", "Craig"},
   {"Jeelani", "Stephen", "Romin"},
};
```

As you can see, each element of the first array dimension has an array, but the array length is different for each element. The first element is an array of length 4, and the second element is an array of length 3. In other words, `houses[0].length` = 4 and `houses[1].length` = 3.

As with 1-D arrays, we don't have to declare, define and initialize an array at the same time. For example, we might not know how many occupants there are in the houses:

```
String[][] newHouses  = new String[2][];
```

Here, we have told Java that the first dimension of the `newHouses` array will contain two elements which will both be arrays. When you declare a 2-D array, it important to declare at least the length of the first (primary) array dimension, although you are free to leave Java in the dark about the length of any arrays within the primary array until you actually use the array itself, as in the following example:

```
String[][] newHouses = new String[2][];

newHouses[0] = new String[4];

newHouses[0][0] = "Richard";
newHouses[0][1] = "Dan";
newHouses[0][2] = "Chris";
newHouses[0][3] = "Craig";

newHouses[1] = new String[3];

newHouses[1][0] = "Jeelani";
newHouses[1][1] = "Stephen";
newHouses[1][2] = "Romin";
```

Now, let's finish off the chapter by looking at another interesting feature of arrays, sorting them.

Sorting Arrays

The standard Java package `java.util` provides a class called `Arrays`. One of the methods of this class, called `Arrays.sort()`, provides a very convenient mechanism to sort the elements of the array. The `Arrays.sort()` method takes the contents of an array of data types and sorts it in ascending order numerically or alphabetically (depending on the data type).

For example, let's say we have an integer array called `ages` that holds the ages of five of your friends:

```
int[] ages = {25, 32, 19, 27, 24};
```

If we printed this array:

```
for(int i=0;i<ages.length;i++) System.out.println(ages[i]);
```

then we would expect to see:

```
25
32
19
27
24
```

Now, we could sort this array, and then print out the array again, using:

```
Arrays.sort(ages);
for(int i=0;i<ages.length;i++) System.out.println(ages[i]);
```

This time we should see:

```
19
24
25
27
32
```

In other words, the ages array has been sorted numerically, in ascending order.

Summary

In this chapter, we learned how to make decisions in our code, and then use this decision to direct the flow of execution to a particular point in our code, using control statements. We saw how to use relational operators to compare values, and we used examples to illustrate the use of the following control statements:

- ❏ Conditional Statements (if, if-else, and switch), where code execution depends upon whether an expression evaluates to true or false

- ❏ Iterative Statements (for, while, do-while), that allow us to loop through the same code block many times, so we don't need to write the same code again and again

- ❏ Branching Statements (break, continue, return) that direct execution to a user-defined point in code

We also covered arrays: collections of values of the same data type. Arrays allow us simplify the maintenance and processing of large numbers of variables. Using examples, we saw how to create arrays, and retrieve the values of array members (know as elements). We noted that using arrays and iterative statements together (iterating through an array) is a powerful programming tool. We finished by looking at how to create and use arrays of arrays, and why these two-dimensional arrays are useful, as well as how to sort array elements in ascending order.

The main reason for using arrays and control statements is to make our code simpler, easier to maintain, and more reusable. In the next chapter we are going to introduce you to tag libraries, which will allow us to simplify our JSP scripts still further.

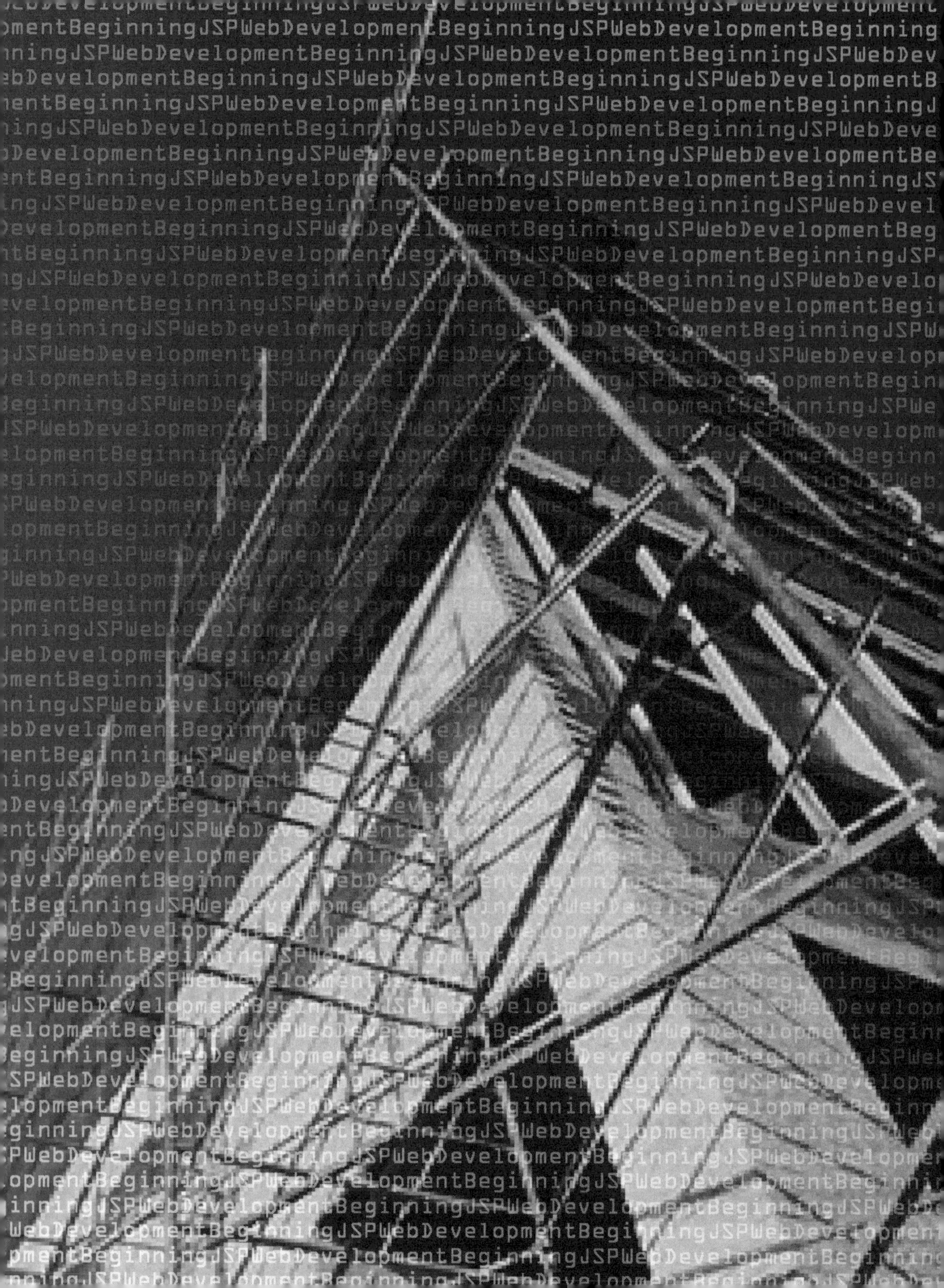
BeginningJSPWebDevelopment

Introducing Tag Libraries

In Chapter 4, we discussed the rationale behind separating applications into tiers and using components to provide efficient code reuse and ease of maintenance. You learned how to create a simple JavaBean and how to use it within a JSP page using bean tags. These tags were successful in removing Java code from the JSP tier.

In the last chapter we looked at conditional logic – how you make decisions in Java. You will often want to make decisions in a JSP page, perhaps based on the request that has been made by the client. The tags we saw in Chapter 4, though, do not have this functionality. These bean tags are also limited to interacting with the JavaBean; they cannot have any control over the JSP page. For instance, they have no access to the `request` and `response` objects. However, **custom tag libraries** can provide this functionality.

In this chapter, we will not be showing you how to create a tag library; instead, we will demonstrate how you can use one of the many custom tag libraries that are already written and freely available. You'll get a chance to create your own tag library in Chapter 10.

In this chapter we will:

- ❏   Look at why we need tag libraries
- ❏   Look at the components of a tag library
- ❏   Explain how to deploy and use the Request Tag Library provided by the Jakarta project, as an example
- ❏   Discuss what happens when we use a tag library from within a JSP page

Let's start then by looking at why we would want to use a tag library.

The Need for Tag Libraries

Let's consider an example of the type of scriptlet code that we would like to remove from the JSP page and place in a custom tag.

Many web sites need you to specify the country that you are located in when making an online purchase; often to ensure that correct shipping costs are calculated. If the countries of the world were stored in a database, along with the associated shipping costs, then we could write a JSP page that fetches the countries for us and displays them for the user to choose from them. A very simple version of this code is shown below. Don't try to run the code, just see if you can work out what it is trying to do.

```jsp
<%@ page import="java.util.*" %>
<%@ page import="java.awt.*" %>
<%@ page import="java.sql.*" %>

<html>
  <body>
    <%
      String url = "jdbc:odbc:countrydb";
      String user = "";
      String password = "";

      try {
        Class.forName("sun.jdbc.odbc.JdbcOdbcDriver");
        Connection con = DriverManager.getConnection(url, user, password);
        Statement stmt = con.createStatement();
        ResultSet rs = stmt.executeQuery("Select * from countries");

        while (rs.next()) {
          String result = rs.getString("name");
    %>

    <%= result %> <br />

    <%
        }
        rs.close();
      } catch (Exception e) {
        System.out.println(e);
      }
    %>
  </body>
</html>
```

How did you get on? While you might be able to make an educated guess as to what the code does, you probably won't be able to understand it completely. This is because the scriptlet accesses a database, and we don't cover database access until Chapter 15.

So just what does this code do? It makes a connection to a database, issues a request for data and prints out the results before closing the connection.

In comparison to the database code above, look at the following.

```jsp
<%@ taglib uri="getCountriesTag" prefix="countryTag" %>
<html>
  <body>
    <countryTag:getCountries />
  </body>
</html>
```

If we were to move the scriptlet code into a **custom tag** instead, then the equivalent custom tag-driven page would probably be no more complicated than the few lines above. Indeed the syntax we use in the tag made the functionality far clearer to anyone scanning through the script:

```
<countryTag:getCountries />
```

Clearly, it is easier for a JSP designer to work with this kind of transparent syntax, than to expect them to try to access a database using Java code with which they may be unfamiliar. Another major advantage is that the tag is easily reused – as we discussed in Chapter 4, scriptlet code is most definitely not.

If you consider what a tag can give you in terms of both reusability and the interaction they have with the implicit page objects, it soon becomes apparent that they are very useful. When you, as the developer, start to look at ways to reduce the complexity of a specific JSP page, you will see it makes sense for the page designer to have access to a set of tags that looks like the HTML markup they are used to working with.

Why Can't We Just Use JavaBeans?

You may be thinking, why can't we just do all this with a JavaBean? The answer is that a lot of the time JavaBeans *are* the approach you should take. You can use JavaBeans to group together pieces of similar functionality. However, JavaBeans cannot interact with the JSP page: they do not have access to the request and response objects and you cannot use them to perform the decision-making processes in you learnt about in Chapter 5.

Consider the arrays you learned about in Chapter 5. You might have some data in an array that the designer needs to use to produce a JSP page. For example, we could have an array of names of products that are displayed, according to whether the user has bought a similar product in the past. If we attempted to do this using bean tags we would end up incorporating presentation code into the bean – and one of the primary reasons for introducing beans was to avoid this mixing of presentation and business logic.

Custom **tag libraries** (tags with related functionality collected together) allow us to remove all the Java code from the JSP page. This means that a web designer who knows no Java can maintain a JSP based web site.

Now that you have an understanding of the advantages of what a tag library can do, let's take a look at the parts that make up a tag library.

Inside a Tag Library

Although we will not be building a custom tag library of our own in this chapter, it is still important that we understand what comprises a tag library, so that we are able to deploy and use one.

There are three important parts to understanding how to use a tag library:

- ❑ **Tag Handler Classes** – these provide the functionality of the tags.

- ❑ A **Tag Library Descriptor** (**TLD**) – this describes the tags and matches tags to tag handler classes.

❑ The **taglib Directive** – this is a directive placed at the top of your JSP, that allows you to make use of a particular tag library.

Let's investigate each of these components a little more closely.

Tag Handlers

A tag handler is a special type of class that contains the code that a tag executes; in other words, the functionality of the tag is contained in the tag handler. Unlike JavaBeans, which are collections of common functions, a tag handler has a very tightly-focused purpose – to support a single tag. A tag library has a tag handler for each custom tag.

You don't need to know how to implement a tag handler in order to use custom tag libraries, so we leave details of how to create tag handler classes until Chapter 10. At this stage, you do not need to know about the details of the tag handler code, only that steps are invoked on your behalf behind the scenes when you use a tag in a JSP page.

The JSP engine needs to know which tag handler classes correspond to particular tags in a JSP page, and what methods to call on those classes. This information is stored in a Tag Library Descriptor (TLD), which we cover next.

The Tag Library Descriptor

A Tag Library Descriptor (TLD) is an XML document that contains information about one or more custom tags. A TLD is a file that describes the custom tags and relates them to their tag handler classes.

> *Extensible Markup Language (XML) is a set of rules for marking up data (providing tags that describe the nature of the data) in a platform-neutral and language-independent way. For more information about XML see http://www.w3.org/XML., or refer to "Professional Java XML" by Kal Ahmed et al, Wrox Press, ISBN 186100401X.*

It is standard to name a TLD file after the tag handler class it refers to. It must be saved with a `.tld` extension and stored in the `WEB-INF` directory of the web application.

Existing tag libraries will come with a TLD file, so until you start writing your own tag libraries you do not need to understand the contents of a TLD file, only what it does.

The taglib Directive

To use the tags from a custom tag library in your JSP pages you must add a `taglib` directive at the top of each JSP page. For example:

```
<%@ taglib uri="http://jakarta.apache.org/taglibs/request-1.0"
           prefix="req" %>
```

The directive is required for each tag library you wish to use in your JSP page, and the `uri` and `prefix` attributes have values specific to each tag library.

The value of the `uri` attribute identifies the tag library. It often consists of the URL of the organization maintaining the tag library. The system does not actually try to access the URL; it exists to uniquely identify the tag library. It is simply that using a URL helps to document where the tag library originated and to ensure that it has a unique name. However, the URI can be a pathname with an appended file name. In this case, the system assumes that this file is your TLD file and attempts to load it. If the pathname does not map to the TLD file, the system will look elsewhere in the web application for the TLD file.

Whenever the JSP engine encounters a tag extension in a JSP, it looks at the value of the `uri` attribute in the `taglib` directive and then parses the tag library descriptor to find the required tag handler class. It then generates code to interact with the tag handler and enable your JSP to use the tags.

The value of the `prefix` attribute is used to identify a tag in a JSP page as part of a particular tag library. That way, if we have two tags with the same name, but from different tag libraries, it is possible to uniquely identify them. So, if we had a tag with a name `myTag` and a prefix of `myPrefix`, the tag would be written as:

```
<myPrefix:myTag />
```

There are no restrictions about what you can use as the value of `prefix`, except that you can't use `jsp`, `jspx`, `java`, `javax`, `servlet`, `sun`, or `sunw` as they are reserved words.

Now let's see how to deploy and use a tag library in a JSP web application.

Using a Tag Library

We are not going to create our own tag library in this chapter. Indeed, what we are trying to get across is that you can use libraries that other developers have created that fulfill your needs. We are going to use one of the tag libraries created by the people that previously brought you Tomcat – the Jakarta project.

The Jakarta project has created a large number of custom tag libraries. The one we will use is the Request Tab Library. The Request Tag Library contains tags that can be used to access all the information about the HTTP request for a JSP page. You used the `request` object in Chapter 3 to get this information. Now we will see how you can provide the same functionality in your JSP pages without having to know a single line of Java.

The Request Tag Library

You can download the latest release of the Request Tag Library from the Jakarta web site. At the time of writing, the latest builds could be found at:http://jakarta.apache.org/builds/jakarta-taglibs/nightly/projects/request/

If you have a choice of distributions simply download the latest version.

> *A new version of the Request Tag Library is made available every night. With this rate of release, it is possible that a version could be made available that does not work. If you find that you cannot run the examples in this chapter, you may have a corrupt version of the library. Under these circumstances, try downloading an older version from the Jakarta project.*

The file you download will be in a compressed format. Uncompress the file to a convenient location. You will have a directory named `jakarta-taglibs` that will contain another directory named `request`. The `request` directory contains everything we need to deploy and test the Request Tag Library.

Look inside the `request` directory. You should see four files:

❑   `request.jar` – this contains the tag handler classes

❑   `request.tld` – this is the TLD file for the Request tag library

❑   `request-doc.war` – this contains documentation for the tag library

❑   `request-examples.war`– this contains an example web application

The files with `.jar` and `.war` extensions are **archive** files. They are a compressed collection of files – much like `.zip` files. The contents of these files can be extracted using the **jar** tool that comes as part of the Java SDK you installed in Chapter 1.

The file `request-examples.war` contains a sample web application that demonstrates how to use the Request Tag Library. Let's set up and run this example.

Try It Out – Using the Request Tag Library

The sample web application that comes with the Request Tag Library contains everything we need, so in this example you're not going to have to write anything yourself. Once we have the example up and running, we will go through the structure of the web application and the contents of the various files.

Begin by creating a new web application directory under `%CATALINA_HOME%\webapps\`. Call it `begjsp-ch06`. Then place a copy of `request-examples.war` in the `begjsp-ch06` directory.

Open a command prompt and change the working directory to `%CATALINA_HOME%\webapps\begjsp-ch06\`. Then run the following command:

> **>jar xvf request-examples.war**

If successful, you should see several messages confirming the creation and extraction of directories and files. If you see a message warning you that `jar` is not recognized then check that you set up your `PATH` variable correctly, as set out in Chapter 1.

That is all you need to do to deploy the web application. The directories and files, including `WEB-INF`, are all set up for you.

Start up Tomcat and point your browser at http://localhost:8080/begjsp-ch06/. You should see something like this:

This page, `index.html`, contains a web form with a number of hidden input fields. These hidden input fields are present so that the form can be submitted with request parameters.

Click the SUBMIT button and you should see something similar to:

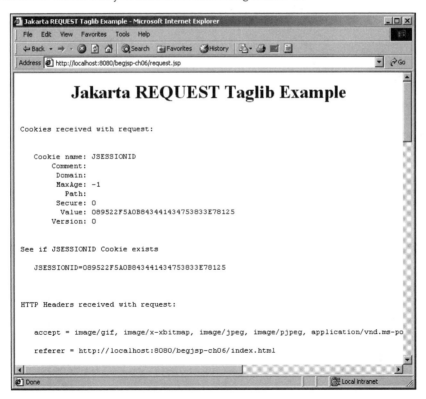

The page that you see may be different from that shown above, as the information displayed is dependent on the request made to the server by your browser. Look through this page; it contains a lot of information about the request made by your browser to the server. It includes details about your type of browser as well as the parameters from the form in index.html.

How It Works

The first page you saw was index.html, which invited you to click a SUBMIT button. When you clicked this, a form was submitted to response.jsp. Let's look at the code that makes up request.jsp. There is a large amount of code so we are only going to pick out the important and interesting parts.

The first piece of code to note is the taglib declaration, at about line 11:

```
<%@ taglib uri="http://jakarta.apache.org/taglibs/request-1.0"
            prefix="req" %>
```

The value of the uri attribute tells the JSP container what the unique identifier for the tag library is. The value of the prefix attribute tells the container that tags in the page with a prefix of req are part of this tag library.

When we introduced tag libraries we explained that they were required so that we could get the type of decision-making functionality we saw in Chapter 5 from tags. So, let's pick out two pieces of code from request.jsp that demonstrate this.

First, let's look at the tags that deal with request parameters: the code begins at about line 49.

```
GET or POST Parameters received with request:

<req:parameters id="param">
  <jsp:getProperty name="param" property="name"/> =
  <jsp:getProperty name="param" property="value"/>
</req:parameters>
```

There are two tags used in this code snippet, <req:parameters> and <jsp:getProperty>. You should recognize the <jsp:getProperty> tag from Chapter 4; it was used to get the value of a property from a JavaBean.

This code produces the following response when you submit the form in index.jsp.

138

This <req:parameters> tag loops through all the parameters received in the HTTP request. For each parameter the <jsp:getProperty> tag is used to get the name and value of the parameter. In other words, these tags are providing similar functionality to for or while loops.

Now, let's take a look at a tag that provides functionality similar to that of an if statement. Look at the code at about line 62:

```
See if test1 parameter exists
<req:existsparameter name="test1">
    test1=<req:parameter name="test1"/>
</req:existsparameter>
<req:existsparameter name="test1" value="false">
    Parameter test1 does not exist.
</req:existsparameter>
```

This code produces the following response when you submit the form in index.jsp.

This tag allows you to incorporate decision making into the JSP page without having to know any Java. It tests to see if a request parameter with the name test1 exists. If it does, then it includes the value in the page response. If the parameter does not exist it includes different text in the response.

The response.jsp page makes use of a number of other tags from the Request Tag Library. We are not going to explain them all, as this chapter is not intended to be a comprehensive reference for the Request Tag Library. What you should take away from this example is an understanding of how tags are inserted into a JSP page, and the type of dynamic functionality they can produce, not the specifics of using the Request Tag Library.

If you are interested in what the other tags in the Request Tag Library do, and how to use them, documentation is available at: http://jakarta.apache.org/taglibs/doc/request-doc/index.html#reference The documentation is also included in request-doc.war, which was part of the tag library download. You can extract the contents of this file using the jar tool as we did for request-examples.war.

We've seen some of the tags used in the response.jsp file. The next section deals with how the JSP container recongnises these tags and knows what to do when it encounters them.

Behind the Scenes

In the previous example, our tags had a prefix of req, but how does the JSP container know what to do when it encounters a tag with a req prefix? We saw earlier that the uri attribute in the taglib declaration uniquely identifies the tag library, but how does the JSP container use this identifier to match the tags with their tag handler classes? This is done in the web.xml file. You can find the web.xml file in the WEB-INF directory. Take a look at the contents of this file. We are interested in the code at about line 26.

```
<taglib>
  <taglib-uri>http://jakarta.apache.org/taglibs/request-1.0</taglib-uri>
  <taglib-location>/WEB-INF/request.tld</taglib-location>
</taglib>
```

This tells the JSP container that for a tag library identified by the uri, http://jakarta.apache.org/taglibs/request-1.0, the Tag Library Descriptor file is found at /WEB-INF/request.tld.

The JSP container can then read the correct TLD file, which will tell it which tag handler classes match which tags. Let's take a look at the TLD file for this web application. The section that deals with the parameters tag begins at about line 259.

```
<tag>
  <name>parameters</name>
  <tagclass>org.apache.taglibs.request.ParametersTag</tagclass>
```

The name of the tag is defined and then the tag handler class that implements the functionality of this tag is declared. Note that the fully qualified name of the class is given: the package that the class is part of must be specified.

```
<teiclass>org.apache.taglibs.request.ParametersTEI</teiclass>
<bodycontent>JSP</bodycontent>
<info>Loop through all parameters.</info>
<attribute>
  <name>id</name>
  <required>true</required>
  <rtexprvalue>false</rtexprvalue>
</attribute>
<attribute>
  <name>name</name>
  <required>false</required>
  <rtexprvalue>false</rtexprvalue>
</attribute>
</tag>
```

The other parts of the tag definition describe the content of the tag and what attributes it has. There is a similar tag element for each tag in the library. We will cover the contents of a TLD file in detail in Chapter 10.

The JSP container knows what tag handler class matches each tag so the only question now is: where are the tag handler classes stored? Do you remember how JavaBeans were stored in or below the `classes` directory under the `WEB-INF` directory? Similarly, the tag handler classes are stored in a `lib` directory under the `WEB-INF` directory. Look in this directory; you should see a file named `request.jar`. The tag handler classes have all been placed in an archive file for convenience, and the JSP container is capable of extracting the classes from this archive, as it needs them.

Summary

Custom tag libraries are a powerful extension to JSP, allowing non-Java developers to utilize the power of Java easily and transparently. Consequently, tag library repositories like those found at the Jakarta project are starting to appear, with developers eager to share the work that they have put into encapsulating a tricky set of activities into code.

Tag libraries also provide another means by which to reuse code. For example, by utilizing the Request Tag Library you can save yourself unnecessary coding, testing and debugging when you work with web forms.

The aim of this chapter was to enable you to use custom tag libraries, not to teach you how to write your own – that will be covered in Chapter 10. With this in mind, we covered the following:

❑ The reasons why you would want to use tag libraries and the benefits of code reuse and transparency that they bring

❑ How to use tags in JSP files, highlighting the importance of the `taglib` directive

❑ The different components of a tag library, such as tag handler classes and the Tag Library Descriptor file, and how the JSP container uses them

❑ How to deploy and use the Request Tag Library from the Jakarta project; these skills are transferable to other tab libraries too

In Chapter 10 you will learn how to create your own tag libraries, but even at this stage there are so many custom tag libraries available (and more on the way), that you can use tags to easily add a great deal of functionality to your applications.

In the next chapter we are going to expand your knowledge of Java classes, delving more deeply into issues that were mentioned briefly in Chapter 4, such as inheritance.

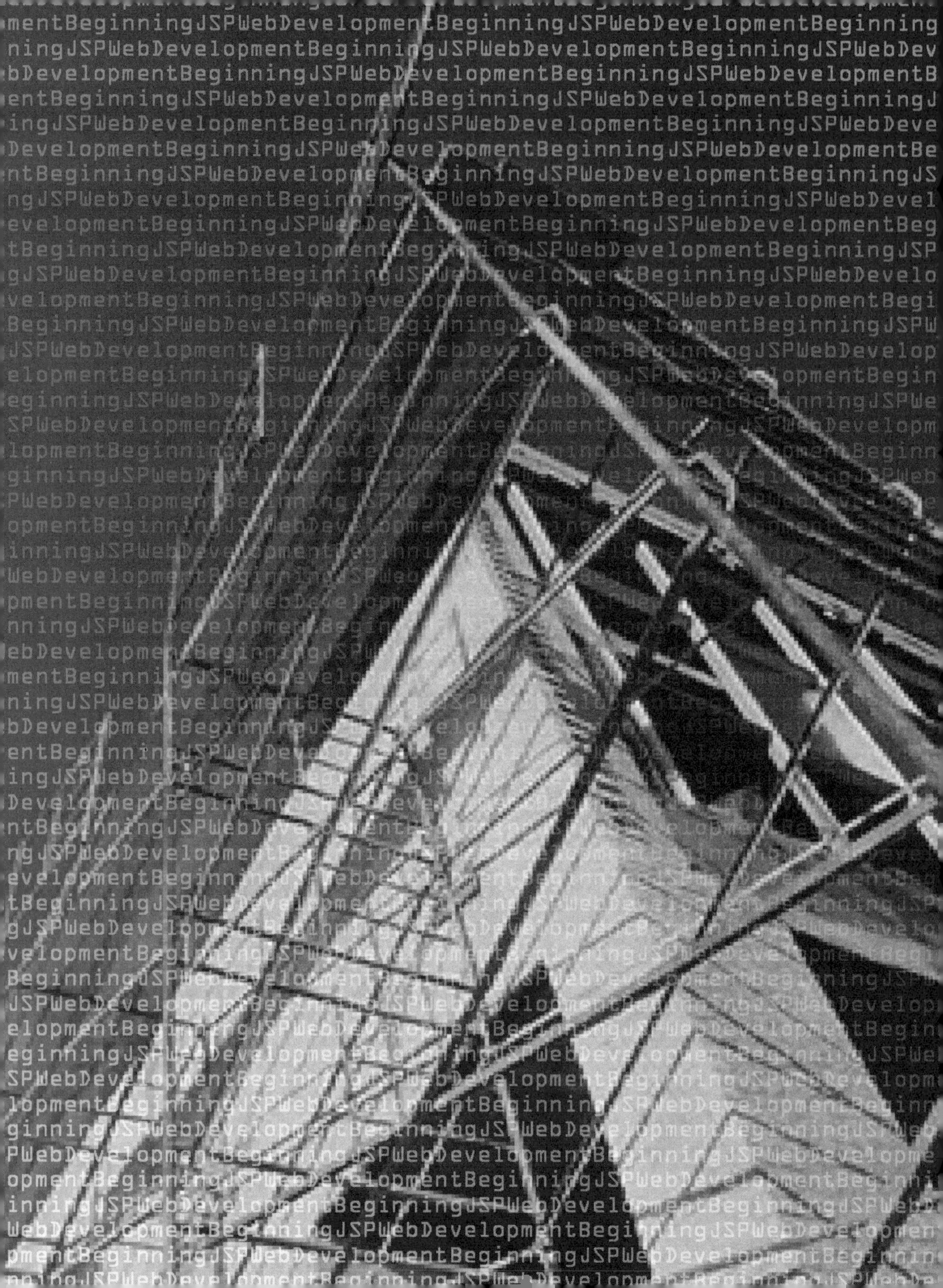

More On Objects

You were introduced to object orientation in Chapter 4. You saw how to create your own classes and then use instances of these classes as JavaBeans in JSP pages.

This chapter continues the theme of Chapters 4 and 6 of using objects in order to maximize code reuse, which leads to easier design and maintenance of applications.

With this in mind in this chapter we will:

❏   Review what you know about objects.

❏   Take a closer look at methods and constructors.

❏   Show how you can create classes based on existing classes, which will lead us into looking again at access modifiers.

❏   Show how you can define and implement classes and a closely related concept, interfaces.

Let's begin by quickly reviewing what you learned about objects in Chapter 4.

A Quick Review of Objects

Consider this code for a Book class that might be used as part of a library web application:

```
package com.wrox.library;

public class Book {

  private String title;

  public String getTitle() {
    return title;
  }

  public void setTitle(String title) {
```

```
      this.title = title;
   }

}
```

Let's quickly review what you understand about this code:

- ❑ The class is part of the `com.wrox.library` package.
- ❑ It has an attribute `title` that has `private` access. This means that `title` can only be accessed from within the class.
- ❑ It has two methods, `getTitle()` and `setTitle()`, that have `public` access. This means that they can be accessed from any class.
- ❑ The two methods, `getTitle()` and `setTitle()`, are known as getter and setter methods. They follow the JavaBean coding conventions, which mean that the class can be used as a JavaBean and accessed using the bean tags within a JSP page.

We will be using this `Book` class, and variations on it, throughout the chapter so let's create and test it.

Try It Out – A Simple Class

Create the web application we will be using in this chapter by creating the following directory structure, `%CATALINA_HOME%\webapps\begjsp-ch07\WEB-INF\classes`.

Open your editor and enter the following code.

```
package com.wrox.library;

public class Book {

  private String title;

  public String getTitle() {
    return title;
  }

  public void setTitle(String title) {
    this.title = title;
  }

  public Book() {
  }

}
```

Save this as `Book.java` in `%CATALINA_HOME%\webapps\begjsp-ch07\WEB-INF\classes\com\wrox\library\`.

Then enter the following code:

```
<html>
  <head>
    <title>A Simple Class</title>
  </head>

  <body>
    <jsp:useBean id="myBook" class="com.wrox.library.Book" />
    <jsp:setProperty name="myBook"
                     property="title"
                     value="Beginning JSP Web Development" />
    Book Title: <jsp:getProperty name="myBook" property="title" />
  </body>
</html>
```

Save this as `bookPage.jsp` in `%CATALINA_HOME%\webapps\begjsp-ch07\`.

Open a command prompt, change directory to `%CATALINA_HOME%\webapps\begjsp-ch07\WEB-INF\classes\` and run the following command:

javac com\wrox\library\Book.java

Start up Tomcat and navigate to http://localhost:8080/begjsp-ch07/bookPage.jsp. You should see something like:

How It Works

There isn't anything in this example that you didn't encounter in Chapter 4. The Book class we have created is just a simple JavaBean, with a single attribute `title`. Note the getter and setter methods that we introduced in Chapter 4, which allow us to use the class as a JavaBean and access the `title` property using the bean tags.

A Closer Look At Objects

Now that we have created our example `Book` class, we are ready to examine some of the advanced features of classes and objects.

Method Overloading

Method overloading is a fairly simple concept. To see how it works let's create an `Author` class to complement our `Book` class:

```
package com.wrox.library;

public class Author {

  private String lastName;
  private String firstName;
  private String otherNames;

  public void setName(String lastName,
                      String firstName,
                      String otherNames) {
    this.lastName = lastName;
    this.firstName = firstName;
    this.otherNames = otherNames;
  }

  public String getName() {
    return firstName + " " + otherNames + " " + lastName;
  }

}
```

Our author class is quite simple. It has private attributes that store the last name, first name and other names of an author, a method to set these attributes and a method to retrieve the full name of the author.

What would we do if an author did not have any other names; if for example, they were named William Shakespeare? We could use our setter method like this:

```
Author myAuthor = new Author();
myAuthor.setName("Shakespeare", "William", "");
```

But, wouldn't it be easier if we could just miss out the `otherNames` parameter? Well, we can as Java allows you to **overload** methods. This means that you can have several methods that have the same name, return the same type, but take different arguments.

Method overloading provides a convenient way for us to interact with our objects; instead of creating methods with names like `setFullName()` or `setShortName()` we can create a single, logical method name and keep the interaction simple.

So, we can have a second `setName()` method that takes the form:

```
    public setName(String lastName, String firstName) {
      this.lastName = lastName;
      this.firstName = firstName;
      this.otherNames = "";
    }
```

Or, if we wanted to be really efficient we can simply call the other form of the setName() method. In keeping with the aim of maximizing code reuse and easing maintenance, as we discussed in Chapter 4, we now only have to make changes to the original setName() method and the changes will be available to all the overloaded forms:

```
    public setName(String lastName, String firstName) {
      setName(lastName, firstName, "");
    }
```

Method overloading is especially useful with constructors.

Constructors

Recall from Chapter 4 that a constructor is a special method that is called when an object is instantiated. For example, we could have a constructor for our Author class like:

```
    public Author() {
    }
```

This isn't a particularly useful constructor, as it doesn't do anything. In fact the Java compiler will include a default constructor of this form if you don't declare any other constructor for a class.

There may be times when we want to set the name of an author at instantiation time. In this case we can use a constructor that takes the form:

```
    public Author(String lastName, String firstName, String otherNames) {
      this.lastName = lastName;
      this.firstName = firstName;
      this.otherNames = otherNames;
    }
```

Or, we may only want to set the lastName attribute at instantiation. In this case we can use a constructor that takes the form:

```
    public Author(String lastName) {
      this.lastName = lastName;
    }
```

As Java supports method overloading it is possible for a class to have all three of these constructors. This allows the creation of instances of the Author class in three different ways.

```
  Author author1 = new Author();
  Author author2 = new Author("Adams", "Douglas", "");
  Author author3 = new Author("Adams", "Douglas");
```

Let's extend our Book class to take advantage of multiple constructors. We will add the ability to set the title of a book at instantiation.

Try It Out – Method Overloading and Constructors

Make the following additions to Book.java. The additions are highlighted.

```java
package com.wrox.library;

public class Book {

  private String title;

  public String getTitle() {
    return title;
  }

  public void setTitle(String title) {
    this.title = title;
  }

  public Book() {
  }

  public Book(String title) {
    this.title = title;
  }

}
```

Create the following JSP page.

```jsp
<html>
  <head>
    <title>A Simple Class</title>
  </head>

  <body>
    <%
      com.wrox.library.Book myBook =
                new com.wrox.library.Book("Beginning JSP Web Development");
    %>
    Book Title:
    <%= myBook.getTitle() %>
  </body>
</html>
```

Save the JSP page as bookPage1.jsp.

We will need to recompile the Book class. Open a command prompt and change directory to %CATALINA_HOME%\webapps\begjsp-ch07\WEB-INF\classes\ and run the following command:

javac com\wrox\library\Book.java

Start Tomcat and navigate to http://localhost:8080/begjsp-ch07/bookPage1.jsp. You should see something like:

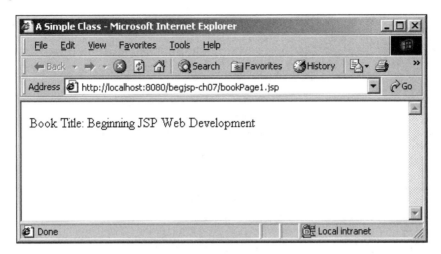

Note that this is the same as what we saw in the first example.

How It Works

We cannot use the Book class as a JavaBean in this example, as JavaBeans must use an empty constructor. Instead we use scriptlets to create and use our Book object.

We have introduced a constructor to our Book class that takes the title of the book as an argument. This is used to create a new instance of Book and set the title of the book at the same time.

```
<%
  com.wrox.library.Book myBook =
            new com.wrox.library.Book("Beginning JSP Web Development");
%>
```

We then use a standard scriptlet expression element to get the title of the book.

```
<%= myBook.getTitle() %>
```

You have seen how you can reuse code *within* your class by providing access to overloaded methods that in reality may perform very similar functions. The next section will show you how to reuse an entire object.

Inheritance

This is where we get to some of the really good stuff. Moving along with our library web application, let's introduce some additional requirements. Let's pretend that our project manager changed his mind (never happens, right?) and decided that simply creating a Book object isn't going to cut it. Instead, we need to create two different types of books: a children's book, and a technical book.

Each of these two book types is going to share functionality with the generic `Book` class. For example, they will both have a title, and will require methods to set and get the value of this attribute. In addition the two book types will have functionality not shared by other classes. This functionality will be:

❑   For the children's book, we need to record the minimum recommended age for the reader.

❑   For the technical book, we need to record a recommended skill level that will be something like "beginner".

So, how can we create two new classes that use the functionality of the `Book` class and also add new functionality to each class?

One way to do it would be to cut and paste the code from our `Book` object into two new class files called `ChildrenBook.java` and `TechnicalBook.java`, but this has the particularly gruesome disadvantage of putting the same code in two different places. If we had to change the shared behavior of the two objects we'd have to make the same changes to both files.

This does more than offend the laziness in all of us; it's just unwise. It makes it easy for errors to creep into the system; for example, as developers change one file and forget to change the other. We spent Chapters 4 and 6 maximizing code reuse for precisely these reasons.

Fortunately, Java objects supports **inheritance**, which means we don't have to duplicate our code at all. Instead, we'll create two new objects, `ChildrenBook` and `TechnicalBook`, and we'll have them **inherit** from the `Book` object, which means they both have the functionality of `Book`, but are able to extend it by providing new functionality on top of it.

This is what the code for our two new classes will look like. First, the listing for `ChildrenBook`.

```
public class ChildrenBook extends Book {

  private int minimumAge;

  public int getMinimumAge() {
    return minimumAge;
  }

  public void setMinimumAge(int a) {
    minimumAge = a;
  }

}
```

And here's the listing for `TechnicalBook`:

```
public class TechnicalBook extends Book {

  private String skillLevel;

  public String getSkillLevel() {
    return skillLevel;
  }
```

```
    public void setSkillLevel(String s) {
      skillLevel = s;
    }

}
```

These two classes are created in the same way we created our original `Book` object with one exception:

```
public class TechnicalBook extends Book {
```

The `extends` keyword tells Java that the `TechnicalBook` class is inheriting from the `Book` class, and thus has access to all of its functionality.

When a class inherits from another class, it is said to be the **subclass** of a **superclass**, or sometimes the child class of a parent class.

There are a couple of important caveats to inheritance that I need to mention.

❑   When a subclass inherits a superclass, it cannot access any of its private methods or variables; like a parent's bankbook, these remain off-limits to children.

❑   A subclass can only inherit one superclass, so no tricky writing children's technical books.

Constructors are not inherited although the subclass can call `public` and `protected` level constructors of a superclass. If you want to call a constructor of the superclass you use the `super()` method. This calls the constructor with a matching signature of the superclass.

For example, we can create a constructor for our `TechnicalBook` class that takes the title of the book as the argument as follows:

```
public TechnicalBook(String title) {
  super(title)
}
```

This will call the constructor in the `Book` class that takes a single `String` as an argument.

Let's see how inheritance works in practice.

Try It Out – Inheriting from Book

Create the following two classes, first `ChildrenBook`:

```
package com.wrox.library;

public class ChildrenBook extends Book {

  private int minimumAge;

  public int getMinimumAge() {
    return minimumAge;
  }
```

```
   public void setMinimumAge(int a) {
     minimumAge = a;
   }

   public ChildrenBook() {
     super();
   }

   public ChildrenBook(String title) {
     super(title);
   }
 }
```

and second `TechnicalBook`:

```
package com.wrox.library;

public class TechnicalBook extends Book {

  private String skillLevel;

  public String getSkillLevel() {
    return skillLevel;
  }

  public void setSkillLevel(String s) {
    skillLevel = s;
  }

  public TechnicalBook() {
    super();
  }

  public TechnicalBook(String title) {
    super(title);
  }

}
```

Save the `ChildrenBook` class as `ChildrenBook.java` and `TechnicalBook` class as
`TechnicalBook.java`, both under `%CATALINA_HOME%\webapps\begjsp-ch07\WEB-
INF\classes\com\wrox\library\`.

Then, save the JSP page below as `bookPage1.jsp` in `%CATALINA_HOME%\webapps\begjsp-
ch07\WEB-INF\classes\`:

```
<%@ page import="com.wrox.library.*" %>

<html>
  <head>
    <title>Inheritance</title>
```

```
  </head>

  <body>
    <%
      TechnicalBook techBook = new TechnicalBook("Car Mechanics");
      ChildrenBook childBook = new ChildrenBook("The Three Bears");
    %>

    Technical Book Title: <%= techBook.getTitle() %>
    <br />
    Childrens Book Title: <%= childBook.getTitle() %>

  </body>
</html>
```

Open a command prompt and change directory to %CATALINA_HOME%\webapps\begjsp-ch07\WEB-INF\classes\ and run the following commands:

javac com\wrox\library\TechnicalBook.java
javac com\wrox\library\ChildrenBook.java

Start up Tomcat and navigate to http://localhost:8080/begjsp-ch07/bookPage2.jsp; you should see something like:

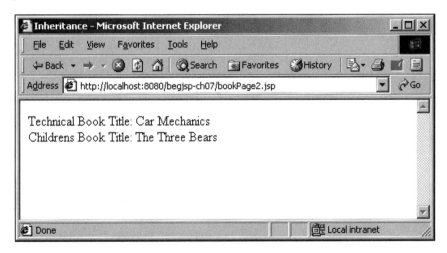

How it Works

Both the classes, ChildrenBook and TechnicalBook, extend and inherit from our Book class.

```
public class ChildrenBook extends Book {
```

They each have two constructors, which call the corresponding constructor in the superclass.

```
public ChildrenBook() {
  super();
}
```

153

```
    public ChildrenBook(String title) {
      super(title);
    }
  }
```

As before, the JSP page uses scriptlet elements in which instances of both `ChildrenBook` and `TechnicalBook` are created with a constructor that takes the title of the book as its only argument.

```
<%
  TechnicalBook techBook = new TechnicalBook("Car Mechanics");
  ChildrenBook childBook = new ChildrenBook("The Three Bears");
%>
```

The titles of the book are then retrieved using the `getTitle()` method that `ChildrenBook` and `TechnicalBook` inherit from `Book`.

```
Technical Book Title: <%= techBook.getTitle() %>
<br />
Childrens Book Title: <%= childBook.getTitle() %>
```

You've seen how to create classes that inherit from another class, but in fact you have been doing this every time you created a class – without even realizing it you've been extending the `Object` class.

The Object Class

All classes, including the `Book`, `TechnicalBook`, and `ChildrenBook` classes you created earlier extend the `java.lang.Object` class. Classes extend `Object` automatically so when you write:

```
public class Book {
```

the compiler understands this as:

```
public class Book extends Object {
```

(You'll note that we said `Object`, not `java.lang.Object`. The `java.lang` package is automatically available in any of your Java code.)

We said earlier that a class can only extend one class, and that's true; however, as you follow the "family tree" of any class back up through the superclasses you'll find that ultimately you get to a class that extends `Object`.

Your classes inherit several members from the `Object` class. These members are all methods, seven are `public`, and two are `protected`. There are two methods that you will use particularly; they are `toString()` and `equals()`, and both have `public` accessibility.

toString()

The `toString()` method is used to produce a string representation of an object. For instance the JSP code:

```
<%
  com.wrox.library.Book bk = new com.wrox.library.Book("The Three Bears");
%>
<%= bk.toString() %>
```

would produce output of the form:

com.wrox.library.Book@69c82e

As you can see the default behavior of `toString()` is to produce the fully qualified name of the class, followed by '@', and a hexadecimal representation of the object.

equals()

The `equals()` method is used to compare the object passed as an argument with the current object. If they are the same object (not just equal, they must be one and the same object) it returns `true`, else it returns `false`.

Overriding Methods

Inheritance is a great way to extend an object's functionality to do new things. But what happens if you want to inherit an object and then just slightly change its behavior? For instance, you might want your classes to do something other than the default when either `toString()` or `equals()` are called.

Java lets a subclass **override** a method; that is, provide a different implementation than the parent class. To illustrate overriding, let's override the `toString()` method that the `TechnicalBook` class inherits from `Object`. We will not override it in `ChildrenBook` in order to see the difference between the two implementations.

Try It Out – Overriding the toString() Method

Make the following additions to `TechnicalBook.java`; the additions are highlighted.

```
package com.wrox.library;

public class TechnicalBook extends Book {

  private String skillLevel;

  public String getSkillLevel() {
    return skillLevel;
  }

  public void setSkillLevel(String s) {
    skillLevel = s;
  }

  public String toString() {
    return getTitle();
  }

  public ChildrenBook() {
    super();
```

```
      }

      public ChildrenBook(String title) {
        super(title);
      }

    }
```

Create the following JSP page:

```
<%@ page import="com.wrox.library.*" %>

<html>
  <head>
    <title>Inheritance</title>
  </head>

  <body>
    <%
      TechnicalBook techBook = new TechnicalBook("Car Mechanics");
      ChildrenBook childBook = new ChildrenBook("The Three Bears");
    %>

    TechnicalBook toString(): <%= techBook.toString() %>
    <br />
    ChildrenBook toString(): <%= childBook.toString() %>

  </body>
</html>
```

Save this as `bookPage2.jsp` under `%CATALINA_HOME%\webapps\begjsp-ch07\`.

You will need to recompile the `TechnicalBook` class. Open a command prompt and change to the `%CATALINA_HOME%\webapps\begjsp-ch07\WEB-INF\classes\` directory. Then run the following command:

javac com\wrox\library\TechnicalBook.java

Start Tomcat and navigate to http://localhost:8080/begjsp-ch07/bookPage2.jsp. You should see something like:

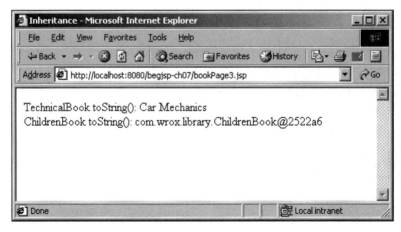

You won't see exactly the same output for the `toString()` method called on the `ChildrenBook` class: the hexadecimal representation is likely to be different.

How It Works

We have overriden the `toString()` method in the `TechnicalBook` class.

```
public String toString() {
  return getTitle();
}
```

Now, instead of returning the name of the class it calls the `getTitle()` inherited from `Book`, which returns the title of the book.

We didn't have to do anything special with the `toString()` method, we simply wrote it as we would any other method. The compiler will recognize that you are overriding the inherited method and act accordingly.

What Can You Override?

You may override the public members of a superclass, but you cannot override private members. This should make sense to you as we saw in Chapter 4 that access to private members was limited to within the class. In fact, it's time to look again at access modifiers.

Access Modifiers

The accessibility of the attributes and methods of a class are controlled by **access modifiers**. There are three access modifiers used to specify the accessibility of a class member, and when we discussed access modifiers in Chapter 4 we discussed two of these – `public` and `private`. The third access modifier is `protected`, which sits between the accessibility provided by `private` and `public`.

❑ `public` – allows access from any class.

❑ `private` – allows access from within the class only.

❑ `protected` – allows access to any class from within the same package, and from any sub-class. We'll look at subclasses later in the chapter.

Protected access functions just like private access except where inheritance is concerned. While subclasses may not access or override private members, subclasses may access and override protected members.

Protected access is best used when you want to hide your implementation from the world at large, but you do want to allow subclasses of your objects to be able to change that hidden implementation in varying ways.

Abstract Classes

Now that we've defined `ChildrenBook` and `TechnicalBook` as subclasses of `Book`, does it make any sense to actually instantiate a `Book` class? If our library consists of just children's books or technical books, it doesn't make sense. The `Book` class serves as a common parent to the two subclasses, but we would not need to use instances of the `Book` class. That is, all our objects will be either `ChildrenBook` or `TechnicalBook`.

In situations like these, Java uses the `abstract` keyword to define a class that cannot be instantiated. To make our `Book` class abstract, all we do is change the class declaration line from:

```
public class Book {
```

to:

```
public abstract class Book {
```

And voilà, `Book` can no longer be instantiated. Its subclasses can still be instantiated, which is of course the whole idea.

Methods in an abstract class can be marked as abstract, in which case you don't write the code for the method, just the signature that tells you its name, access modifier, parameters, and return type. In these situations, the abstract parent class indicates that any non-abstract (also called **concrete** because it can actually be instantiated) subclass must provide an implementation for its abstract methods.

We could have defined our `Book` class as `abstract` as follows, along with an abstract method `getType()`, that subclasses of `Book` must implement if they are to be non-abstract:

```
package com.wrox.library;

public abstract class Book {

   private String title;

   public String getTitle() {
     return title;
   }

   public void setTitle(String title) {
     this.title = title;
   }

   public abstract String getType();

   public Book() {
   }

   public Book(String title) {
     this.title = title;
   }

}
```

When you derive a class from an abstract base class, you don't have to define all the abstract methods in the subclass. However, if you don't then the subclass will also be abstract and you will be unable to declare any objects of it.

Abstract classes and methods provide an important mechanism to allow you to combine common code for multiple objects into a common parent even when subclasses must differ in their implementation of standard functionality.

Although you can no longer create an instance of the `Book` class, you can still declare a variable to be of type `Book`. This can have important uses, as we shall see in the next section.

Casting Objects

You encountered casting in Chapter 2 when you cast variables of one type to another. For example:

```
int i = 3;
double d = (double)i;
```

Here, a variable of type `int` is cast to a variable of type `double`.

In the same way, you can cast an object to another class type, but only if one is a superclass of the other. For example you can cast a `TechnicalBook` object to a `Book` object, as the `Book` class is the superclass of `TechnicalBook`.

```
TechnicalBook tb = new TechnicalBook();
Book b = (Book)tb;
```

This means that we can store instances of `TechnicalBook` and `ChildrenBook` in variables of type `Book`. For example:

```
Book myTechBook = (Book)(new TechnicalBook());
Book myChildrenBook = (Book)(new ChildrenBook());
```

In fact, we do not even need to include an explicit cast in this case as the compiler is always prepared to cast a subclass to a superclass. We can simply write:

```
Book myTechBook = new TechnicalBook();
Book myChildrenBook = new ChildrenBook();
```

We are now in a position to see the use of abstract methods, such as the abstract `getType()` method we introduced in the `Book` code.

Try It Out – Abstract Methods

Make the following changes to the `Book.java` file; the changes are highlighted.

```
package com.wrox.library;

public abstract class Book {

  private String title;

  public String getTitle() {
    return title;
  }

  public void setTitle(String title) {
    this.title = title;
```

```
      }

      public abstract String getType();

      public Book() {
      }

      public Book(String title) {
        this.title = title;
      }

}
```

Then, make the following changes to the `TechnicalBook.java` file; again the changes are highlighted:

```
package com.wrox.library;

public class TechnicalBook extends Book {

    private String skillLevel;

    public String getSkillLevel() {
      return skillLevel;
    }

    public void setSkillLevel(String s) {
      skillLevel = s;
    }

    public String toString() {
      return getTitle();
    }

    public String getType() {
      return "TECHNICAL";
    }

    public TechnicalBook() {
      super();
    }

    public TechnicalBook(String title) {
      super(title);
    }

}
```

Next, make the following changes to the `ChildrenBook.java` file; once more, the changes are highlighted:

```
package com.wrox.library;

public class ChildrenBook extends Book {

    private int minimumAge;

    public int getMinimumAge() {
```

```
      return minimumAge;
  }

  public void setMinimumAge(int a) {
    minimumAge = a;
  }

  public String getType() {
    return "CHILDREN";
  }

  public ChildrenBook() {
    super();
  }

  public ChildrenBook(String title) {
    super(title);
  }
}
```

Finally, create the following JSP page:

```
<%@ page import="com.wrox.library.*" %>

<html>
  <head>
    <title>Inheritance</title>
  </head>

  <body>
    <%
      Book techBook = new TechnicalBook("Car Mechanics");
      Book childBook = new ChildrenBook("The Three Bears");
    %>

    TechnicalBook Type: <%= techBook.getType() %>
    <br />
    ChildrenBook Type: <%= childBook.getType() %>

  </body>
</html>
```

Save the changes to `Book.java`, `ChildrenBook.java`, and `TechnicalBook.java`. Open a command prompt and change directory to `%CATALINA_HOME%\webapps\begjsp-ch07\WEB-INF\classes\`. Then run the following command:

javac com\wrox\library\Book.java
javac com\wrox\library\ChildrenBook.java
javac com\wrox\library\TechnicalBook.java

Save the JSP file as `bookPage4.jsp` in `%CATALINA_HOME%\webapps\begjsp-ch07\`. Start Tomcat and navigate to http://localhost:8080/begjsp-ch07/bookPage4.jsp. You should see something like the screenshot overleaf:

161

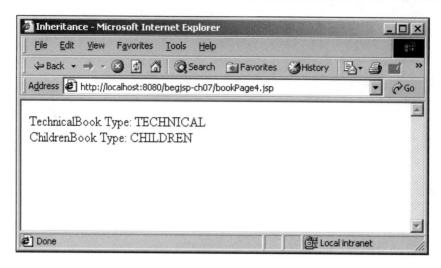

How It Works

Both the instance of `TechnicalBook` and `ChildrenBook` are stored in a variable of type `Book`.

```
<%
   Book techBook = new TechnicalBook("Car Mechanics");
   Book childBook = new ChildrenBook("The Three Bears");
%>
```

When we call the `getType()` method the output is different for `techBook` and `childBook`.

```
TechnicalBook Type: <%= techBook.getType() %>
<br />
ChildrenBook Type: <%= childBook.getType() %>
```

This shows that even though the objects were stored in a variable of type `Book`, the compiler remembers what the real type of the object is.

Using methods in this way is known as **polymorphism**.

Polymorphism

Polymorphism means the ability of a single variable of a given type to be used to reference objects of *different* types, and to automatically call the method that is specific to the particular type of the actual object the variable references. This allows a method call to behave differently, depending on the type of object to which the call applies.

When To Cast Objects

You can cast objects both ways through a class hierarchy. We've seen how and why you would cast upwards, for example casting a `TechnicalBook` object to a `Book`. When would you cast downwards?

If you had stored a collection of `TechnicalBook` and `ChildrenBook` objects in variables of type `Book`, you would be unable to call those methods specific to the `TechnicalBook` and `ChildrenBook` classes.

For example, if you wanted to call the `getMinimumAge()` method on a `Book` object that you knew to really be of type `ChildrenBook` you would cast downwards.

```
ChildrenBook childBook = (ChildrenBook)bk;
childBook.getMinimumAge();
```

You can shorten this to a single line of code:

```
((ChildrenBook)bk).getMinimumAge();
```

You should try to avoid explicitly casting objects like this as it increases the potential for an invalid cast, in which case an error will occur. (We'll return to the subject of errors in Chapter 9.) If you find that you have to explicitly cast objects often, it may be worth redesigning your classes.

Interfaces

All of this talk of abstract classes relates well to another mechanism in Java: interfaces. Interfaces are a lot like abstract classes with two important differences.

❑   An abstract class can define an implementation for some or all of its methods, but an interface cannot; it is like an abstract class with *all* of its methods declared abstract.

❑   A subclass can only descend from one superclass, but an object can implement multiple interfaces.

An **interface** is essentially a collection of constants and abstract methods. A class **implements** an interface. When a class implements an interface it is making a contract: it promises that all the constants and methods defined in the interface will be implemented in the class.

To illustrate the use of interfaces, let's leave our library application and imagine that we're creating a physics program that displays certain properties of particles and also certain properties of waves.

Try It Out – Implementing Interfaces

Create a `light` directory in `%CATALINA_HOME%\webapps\begjsp-ch07\WEB-INF\classes\com\wrox\`.

Enter the following code.

```
package com.wrox.physics;

interface Particle {

  long getMass();

  void setMass(long m);

}
```

```
package com.wrox.physics;

interface Wave {

  long getWavelength();

  void setWavelength(long w);

}
```

Save the `Particle` interface as `Particle.java` and the `Wave` interface as `Wave.java`, both in `%CATALINA_HOME%\webapps\begjsp-ch07\WEB-INF\classes\com\wrox\physics\`.

Finally, save the code below as `lightPage.jsp` in the `%CATALINA_HOME%\webapps\begjsp-ch07\` folder:

```
package com.wrox.physics;

public class Light implements Particle, Wave {

  private long mass;
  private long wavelength;

  public long getMass() {
    return mass;
  }

  public void setMass(long m) {
    this.mass = m;
  }

  public long getWavelength() {
    return wavelength;
  }

  public void setWavelength(long w) {
    this.wavelength = w;
  }

  public Light() {
    this.mass = 1;
    this.wavelength = 10;
  }

}
```

Save the `Light` class as `Light.java` in `%CATALINA_HOME%\webapps\begjsp-ch07\WEB-INF\classes\com\wrox\physics\`.

```
<%@ page import="com.wrox.physics.*" %>

<html>
  <head>
    <title> Light class - Implements Particle and Wave </title>
  </head>
```

```
<body>

<h2>Light class - Implements Particle and Wave</h2>

<% Light lightBeam = new Light(); %>
Mass: <%= lightBeam.getMass() %>
Wave Length: <% lightBeam.getWavelength() %>
<hr />
<% lightBeam.setMass(10); %>
Mass: <%= lightBeam.getMass() %>
Wave Length: <% lightBeam.getWavelength() %>


</body>
</html>
```

Open a command prompt and change directory to `%CATALINA_HOME%\webapps\begjsp-ch07\WEB-INF\classes\` and run the following command to compile the class:

javac com\wrox\physics\Light.java

Save the JSP file as `lightPage.jsp` in `%CATALINA_HOME%\webapps\begjsp-ch07\`. Start up Tomcat and navigate to `http://localhost:8080/begjsp-ch07/lightPage.jsp`. You should see something like:

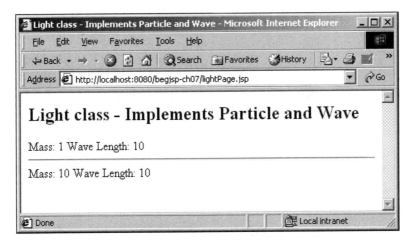

How It Works

Since light behaves as both a particle and a wave, we create a `Particle` interface, a `Wave` interface, and then a concrete `Light` class that implements both interfaces (apologies to any physicists who may be reading this chapter).

Note that methods in an interface don't have to be declared public; every method in an interface is public by default and it is conventional not to include the `public` modifier. The concrete class `Light` uses the keyword `implements` to indicate that it fulfills the contract specified by the interface.

Don't worry about the details of the methods; they are just to keep our physicist friends happy. The key point is the Light class has provided the four methods that it was contracted to do when it implemented the Particle and Wave interfaces.

Choosing Between Interfaces and Abstract Classes

While there are distinct situations in which you must use interfaces to achieve your desired effect, such as the Light example, there are many some situations in which you may employ either an interface or an abstract class.

In general, choose an abstract class when it makes sense to provide some measure of predefined functionality and the subclasses will only function as an extended version of their superclass.

Conversely, when it doesn't make any sense to provide any implementation details of a superclass or the subclasses may need to function as radically different objects, use an interface.

Static Members

The Book class cannot do anything until it is instantiated as an object. For example, the following code will not compile:

```
String title = Book.getTitle();
```

Instead, the Book class must first be instantiated as an object.

```
Book myBook = new Book();
String title = myBook.getTitle();
```

Static members are members of a class that can be used before a class is instantiated and are available across all instances of a class. For a member to be static the static keyword must be used when the member is declared in the source code of the class. Both attributes and methods of a class can be declared to be static.

Although this book is about JavaServer Pages, stand-alone Java applications are still useful for testing classes and if you are going to create a stand-alone Java application, you need to know about a special static method, main().

The main() Method

Every Java application contains a method called main(). This method is the **entry point** for an application; that is, it is the first method called.

The method has a particular form and if this form is not matched exactly then the application will not run. This form is:

```
public static void main(String[] args)
```

You need not be concerned with exactly why the method takes this form, but it must if your application is to run.

Open your editor and enter the following code:

```
public class BookApp {

  private String title;

  public String getTitle() {
    return title;
  }

  public void setTitle(String title) {
    this.title = title;
  }

  public static void main(String[] args) {
    BookApp myBook = new BookApp();
    myBook.setTitle("Beginning JSP Web Development");
    System.out.println(myBook.getTitle());
  }

}
```

Save the Book class as BookApp.java, and then compile the class by running the following command:

javac BookApp.java

Then run the Java application by executing the following command:

java BookApp

You should see the following output:

Beginning JSP Web Development

How It Works

The BookApp class contains the special static main() method:

```
public static void main(String[] args) {
```

The Java Runtime recognizes this method as the one to call to begin the application, and the method creates an instance of the BookApp class:

```
Book myBook = new BookApp();
```

Then it sets the title:

```
myBook.setTitle("Beginning JSP Web Development");
```

167

And finally it prints out the title of the book:

```
System.out.println(myBook.getTitle());
```

You don't need to worry about all the details of the code. Just understand that the `main()` method is recognized and called as the entry point of a Java application by the Java Runtime.

Summary

Java is an object-oriented language, and this provides significant benefits in the area of code reuse. We cannot provide a comprehensive coverage of object-orientated programming and design in one chapter: what we have done is introduce you to enough that you can confidently use classes and objects in JSP development.

These are the key points that you should take away with you.

❑   The access modifiers (public, protected, and private) enable developers to control what members of an object are visible and accessible and what are hidden. Hiding an object's members enables developers to revise the internal behavior at a future date. It also makes using objects simpler.

❑   Constructors allow objects to execute functionality at the moment they are instantiated.

❑   Method overloading enables objects to define multiple different methods with the same method name. The differing methods specify the same return type, the same name, but different parameters.

❑   Inheritance permits the creation of class hierarchies. Classes can have subclasses that inherit all of their functionality and add some of their own. Subclasses may also override the functionality of their superclass. A subclass may inherit from only one superclass.

❑   Abstract objects cannot be instantiated directly, but their subclasses may be instantiated, if the subclasses implement any abstract methods that the abstract object may have. Abstract classes are useful for sharing code amongst two different objects that share many members in common, but where the shared members don't make any sense on their own.

❑   Interfaces provide no functionality, but define the methods that an implementing class must provide. A subclass may inherit (that is, implement) multiple interfaces, and thus behave like many different objects.

❑   Static methods are shared amongst all instances of a class, and can be accessed without instantiating any instances of a class.

❑   There is a special static method, `main()`, that is used by the Java Runtime to determine the entry point for stand-alone applications.

You can find further coverage of objects in *Beginning Java 2* and *Beginning Java Objects*, both by Wrox Press.

In the next chapter we'll look at some of the useful classes that are provided as part of the Java environment.

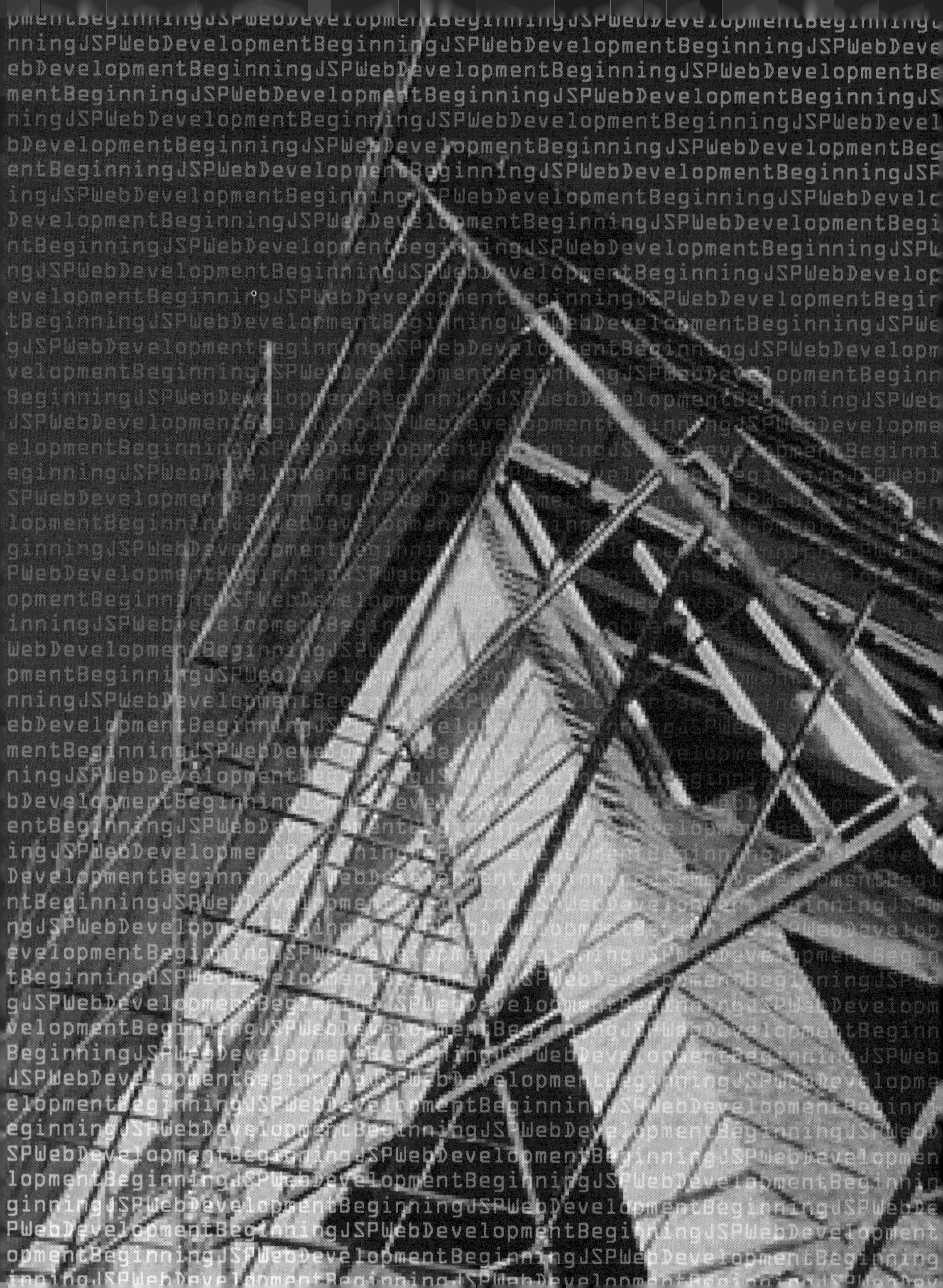

Utility Classes

In Chapter 5, we encountered arrays, and noted how they provide an efficient way of collecting together large numbers of variables of the same data type. However, we will often find that we need more sophisticated data-handling features than arrays can offer. Consider the following scenarios:

❑ A library holding a collection of books that is dynamic: its size changes over time.

❑ An organization keeps an employee list, and uses the employee ID to retrieve the appropriate information from the list.

In these situations, we could not use arrays. Since arrays have a fixed length (size), the first scenario precludes the use of an array to store book information. In the second scenario we would like to store the details for each employee in an array, and then reference each employee in the array using their ID. However, unless we can correlate the employee ID to the corresponding array index in some way, we can't use the ID to retrieve information from the array.

For these scenarios, we will not only need to design classes to hold information about the collections that interest us, but we also need routines that can sort and search through these collections. Fortunately, classes that do this have already been written and are available to us within the java.util package, which is often called the **utility classes** package.

In this chapter, we are going to look at:

❑ Types of collections: Lists, Sets and Maps.

❑ Utility classes that implement and manipulate these collection types (for example, classes that sort a collection, classes that allow fluctuation in collection size, and others that iterate through a collection).

We are going to finish off the chapter by discussing the date/time utility classes, which provide functionality for handling dates in our Java program.

Let's start by taking a closer look at collections.

Introducing Collections

A **collection** is simply an object that represents a group of other objects. To allow any collection to be manipulated by a class, regardless of the details of the collection itself, Java also includes a standard architecture for all classes that manipulate collections: this is known as the **collection framework**.

The collection framework provides us with a well-designed collection of interfaces, which classify the different types of collections:

❑   Sets (implemented by the interface `java.util.Set`)

❑   Lists (implemented by the interface `java.util.List`)

❑   Maps (implemented by interface `java.util.Map`)

The framework also provides us with a set of classes that implement the above interfaces, and allow us to manipulate the collections. These are the classes that you will use in your program; however it makes good sense to start with a discussion of the three types of collection.

Sets

A set is probably the simplest collection of all. It is simply a group of objects collected together, usually in no particular order. In other words, a set consisting of {object1, object2, object3, object4} is exactly the same as a set consisting of {object3, object2, object4, object1}, and any other variations on this theme. However, since there is no order to the objects, each object added to a set must be unique, or we would not be able to tell between objects inside the set.

You should note that there are variations on the basic set described above; for example, some sets may be ordered.

Lists

A list is a collection in which the objects are stored in a sequence, with a beginning and an end – in other words a list is an ordered collection. Because the list is ordered to some degree, the elements do not need to be unique, and we can also select the position at which we add new objects to the sequence.

Actually, we could say that an **array** is a fixed list, because it has all of the properties described above, except that once we have defined it we cannot add new elements to it, so its size is fixed. Ordinary lists on the other hand are free to expand (and decrease) in size. Like arrays, we can reference a particular object within a list using its index value.

Here's an example of a list, of employee names:

Employee Name	Index Value
Stephen	0
Romin	1
Jeelani	2
Stephen	3

Let's say that you wanted to add another employee, Richard, to this list. If we do not specify an index of where we want to insert a new element, it will be added by default at the end of the list. However, if we specify that we want to add the name Richard to the the second position (index = 1), the list becomes:

Employee Name	Index Value
Stephen	0
Richard	1
Romin	2
Jeelani	3
Stephen	4

Notice how the index values of all of the names occurring in the list after Richard have changed. When we used arrays, the value of a particular element did not change unless we manipulated the value of the element directly. With lists however, adding or removing objects from the list can also affect the values held by other objects. This is a consequence of the ability of lists to fluctuate in size.

Other types of lists include **stacks** and **queues**. Stacks are lists in which new objects are always added or removed from the end of the list (a "last in, first out" mechanism). Queues are "first in, first out" – new objects are added to the end of the list, while objects to be removed from the list are always taken from the start of the list.

Maps

In a map collection, objects are stored in pairs. One of the objects in the pair contains the information we wish to store in the collection, and the other object is a called a **key**. The value of the key uniquely identifies the pair, much as the index of an array element uniquely identifies the element. Unlike an index however, a key does not need to be an integer; it can be any type of object. Obviously, since the key is used to identify an object pair within the map collection, there cannot be duplicate key values in the map.

This means that when we wish to retrieve the information stored in an object pair, we locate the pair by looking up the appropriate key value. This becomes clearer when we use an example. Consider the employee directory shown below:

Employee ID	Employee Name
1001	Stephen
2003	Jeelani
3000	Romin

Every employee has a unique employee ID. It would be most convenient if we could get the employee name if we know the employee ID – in this case we want to use the employee ID as the key. So, if we know the key, we can also retrieve the employee information associated with the object pair.

Hashing

Cast your mind back to when we discussed arrays. Array elements are referenced using their index value, where the first element has an index value of 0, the second element has an index value of 1 and so on. Now, a map does not have an index feature like an array, but still it is still able to retrieve the value for you, given the key. How does it do this?

For every key present in the collection, the map uses the value of the key to generate a unique value called the **hashcode**; this process is known as hashing. Each hashcode generated is then placed in a hashtable associated with the map. Indeed, the terms "map" and "hashtable" are often used to mean the same thing.

Typically, the hashcode represents an offset from the start of the memory block that has been allocated to hold the map. The map key-value pairs are stored in this memory block as an array, so the hashcode also corresponds to the index of the key-value array. Therefore, when we want to find a particular key in the map, the hashcode is used to find the appropriate key-value pair.

Collection Classes

In the previous section you were introduced to three collection interfaces:

❑ `java.util.Set`

❑ `java.util.List`

❑ `java.util.Map`

Each of these three interfaces declare methods that you will use to work with each type of collection. However, we do not use any of these interfaces to represent a collection in Java. To create collection objects we need **collection classes**. Each collection class implements one of these interfaces, so that the collection object can make use of the interface's methods.

There are a total of nine collection classes in `java.util`; we can categorize them by the interfaces that they implement:

Interface	Collection Classes That Implement Interface
Set	HashSet, TreeSet
List	Vector, Stack, ArrayList, LinkedList
Map	Hashtable, TreeMap, HashMap, WeakHashMap

We can't go into detail about every one of these classes in this chapter. Instead we are going to pick a selection of the most commonly used collection classes and demonstrate their use, namely:

❑ `java.util.ArrayList`

❑ `java.util.Stack`

❑ `java.util.HashMap`

One final comment before we move on to look at `ArrayLists`: whenever you use a java.util class or interface in your code, remember to import it at the top of your program. For instance:

```
import java.util.ArrayList;
```

Now it's time to dive in and discuss our first collection class.

ArrayList Collections

We have already discussed the fixed nature of an array – the fact that it cannot fluctuate in length once it has been defined. Often though we encounter situations where we need more flexibility than this. For example, a shopping cart at an e-commerce site may contain anything from zero to dozens of items, and shoppers are welcome to purchase as many of these items as they want. They may then change their minds about their purchases and remove items from their shopping carts too. Since the capacity of the collection needed to store the items is unknown and liable to change anyway, we need to be able to dynamically size the collection as elements are added and removed. This capability is provided in Java by list collections.

In this section we are going to play with `java.util.ArrayList` objects, which represent typical examples of lists. An `ArrayList` is a dynamically-sized collection of objects of class `Object`. Since the `Object` class is the superclass of every Java object, you can store any class of object in an `ArrayList`.

You should note that another list collection class, `Vector`, is very similar to `ArrayList`, and is also widely used. However, `ArrayLists` are generally preferred to `Vectors` because they are more efficient, for reasons we will not touch on here.

Creating an ArrayList

The `java.util.ArrayList` class provides us with the `ArrayList()` constructor methods, that creates an empty `ArrayList`. For example:

```
ArrayList shoppingCart = new ArrayList();
```

This will create a new `ArrayList` object called `shoppingCart`. Note that we haven't defined the capacity of this collection. As we have mentioned, an `ArrayList` grows itself dynamically as you add elements to it. It does this by allocating an initial **capacity** when you create it. If you continually add elements to the `ArrayList`, it will fill all the space initially allocated. When this space is filled, the `ArrayList`, without any intervention on the part of the programmer, increases the capacity by a predetermined increment.

Alternatively, you might want to specify the initial capacity of the `ArrayList`. In this case we can use another form of the constructor, shown below:

```
ArrayList shoppingCart = new ArrayList(10);
```

This constructor will create an `ArrayList` with the capacity to hold the (integer) number of objects between the parentheses, which is declared to be 10 here.

Capacity and Size

Up to this point, we have been using the terms capacity and size interchangeably, to mean the number of objects that a collection can contain. However, this is not strictly true.

When an `ArrayList` is first created, it doesn't contain any objects – there is only a block of memory that will be used to hold the objects. The technical way of saying this is that the elements of `ArrayList` do not **reference** any objects. The amount of memory allocated to the new `ArrayList` object corresponds to the **capacity**, while the number of object references that `ArrayList` holds corresponds to the **size**. In other words, the capacity is the number of objects that an `ArrayList` *can* hold at any given moment, while the size is the number of objects that it is *currently* holding.

You should note that both the capacity and size of an `ArrayList` can change; we can add objects to `ArrayList` (increasing the size), until we exceed the memory allocation for `ArrayList` (the capacity). If more objects are added, the capacity of `ArrayList` is increased (by an amount defined by `incrementSize`).

The size of an `ArrayList` can be retrieved using the `size()` method:

```
int shoppingCart = shoppingCart.size();
```

This method returns an integer value of the number of objects referenced in `shoppingCart`.

Adding Objects To an ArrayList

To add objects to an `ArrayList`, we can use the `add()` method. Let's assume that we want to add instances of a `Product` class (representing products to buy on the e-commerce site). Then we can use the following code to add three more instances of product (`product1`, `product2`, `product3`) to our `shoppingCart` collection:

```
shoppingCart.add(product1);
shoppingCart.add(product2);
shoppingCart.add(product3);
```

You should note that this method appends an element to the *end* of the list. We can also add any Java object. The method returns `true` if the collection has changed as a result of the call. We can use another form of the `add()` method if we want to define the position at which the new object should be added too:

```
shoppingCart.add(2, product4);
```

Here, the first (integer) argument between the braces defines the position of the new addition: at index 2 for our example, so `product4` will be the third object in the `shoppingCart` list.

Retrieving Elements from an ArrayList

To retrieve an object from an `ArrayList`, we first need to know the index of the object that we wish to access. Once we know the index, we can retrieve that object using the `get()` method. By default the `get()` method returns an instance of the `Object` class which is the superclass of all objects. Therefore it is necessary to **cast** this to the correct class type (in other words we change the data type). Let's see an example:

```
Product prod = (Product) shoppingCart.get(2);
```

You can see that we are retrieving the third element (index 2) of shoppingCart, which we know corresponds to the product4 instance from the previous example. Since we want the get() method to return an object of type Product, we cast the value using (Product). In other words, the standard way to cast any object or variable is to use:

```
(ClassName) Instance
```

where Instance is the object instance that we want typecast, and ClassName is the class of object we want it cast to. The object returned after the cast is then placed in the Product instance prod. Therefore prod should contain the same information as contained in product4.

Removing Elements from an ArrayList

To remove a particular element from an ArrayList, we can use the remove() method. Again, you will need to specify the index of the element that you want to remove:

```
shoppingCart.remove(2);
```

Here we are completely removing the third object in the shoppingCart list (we saw before that this was product4). You should note that we can discard all of the objects referenced in an ArrayList, using the clear() method:

```
shoppingCart.clear();
```

Here we are removing every object from shoppingCart. Obviously this method should be used with care!

We've covered quite a few methods in this section so far, so now let's try them out.

Try It Out – Using an ArrayList

For this example, we will create a Java console program that will use an ArrayList and maintain a list of User objects.

We will first create a class called User as shown below. The User class defines a particular user in an organization. For this simple demonstration, let's assume that a user has only two attributes, a username and a phonenumber. Save the following file as User.java:

```
package com.wrox.utilities;

public class User {
   String username;
   String phonenumber;

   public User() {}

   public User(String uname, String pnum) {
      username = uname;
      phonenumber = pnum;
```

```
    }

    void setUsername(String uname) {
      this.username = uname;
    }

    String getUsername() {
      return username;
    }

    void setPhonenumber(String pnum) {
      this.phonenumber = pnum;
    }

    String getPhoneNumber() {
      return phonenumber;
    }
  }
```

Now, let's take a look at the main console program, `ArrayListDemo.java`, that will demonstrate the use of the `ArrayList` class:

```java
package com.wrox.utilities;
import java.util.ArrayList;

public class ArrayListDemo {
  public static void main(String[] args) {
    User usr1 = new User("J Smith","123-444-4444");
    User usr2 = new User("M Walker","123-555-5555");
    User usr3 = new User("R Johnson","123-666-6666");

    ArrayList userlist = new ArrayList();
    userlist.add(usr3);
    userlist.add(usr1);
    userlist.add(usr2);

    User usr = (User) userlist.get(1);
    System.out.println("Second user...");
    System.out.println("Username: " + usr.getUsername());
    System.out.println("User phone number: " + usr.getPhoneNumber());
    System.out.println("Userlist...");

    for(int i=0;i<userlist.size();i++) {
      usr = (User) userlist.get(i);
      System.out.println("Username: " + usr.getUsername());
      System.out.println("User phone number: " + usr.getPhoneNumber());
    }
  }
}
```

Running the Example

Save the above two Java source files, User.java and ArrayListDemo.java in a directory
%CATALINA_HOME%\webapps\begjsp-ch08\com\wrox\utilities. Place the files from the rest
of the examples in this folder too. Compile the above two Java source files from within the classes
folder, and run the program using the following command:

> java ArrayListDemo

You should see the following output in your console:

```
Second user...
Username:J Smith
User phone number: 123-444-4444
Userlist...
Username: R Johnson
User phone number: 123-666-6666
Username:J Smith
User phone number: 123-444-4444
Username: M Walker
User phone number: 123-555-5555
```

How It Works

We'll skim over the User class, because it is a simple bean class with two attributes (username and
phonenumber) and get/set methods for these attributes.

Let's turn our attention to ArrayListDemo.java. We first create the ArrayList and then add the
User objects to it, as shown below:

```
ArrayList userlist = new ArrayList();
userlist.add(usr3);
userlist.add(usr1);
userlist.add(usr2);
```

Then we retrieve the second object from the list, and print out its User attributes: the username
and phonenumber.

```
User usr = (User) userlist.get(1);
System.out.println("Second user...");
System.out.println("Username: " + usr.getUsername());
System.out.println("User phone number: " + usr.getPhoneNumber());
```

Finally, we use a for loop to iterate through the elements in the list. To be able to set the termination
expression, we need to know the number of elements in the list, so we use the size() method of the
ArrayList to determine that:

```
for(int i=0;i<userlist.size();i++) {
```

Then, for each index, we use the get() method to retrieve the element:

```
usr = (User) userlist.get(i);
```

179

Note the correct type casting of the object returned by the `get()` method to `User`. We finish by printing the attribute values for this particular instance:

```
        System.out.println("Username: " + usr.getUsername());
        System.out.println("User phone number = " + usr.getPhoneNumber());
    }
```

Iterating Through Collections

In Chapter 5 we noted that combining loops with arrays is a useful programming tool. The same is true of using loops with collections, as we demonstrated in the example above. However, there is an easier way than using a `for` loop to iterate through a collection. Any collection object can create another object called an **iterator**, implemented in an interface, `java.util.Iterator`. The `Iterator` object has references to all of the objects in the collection, and provides easy-to-use methods that enable us to walk through the collection selecting objects from it. Let's take a look at how to use them.

If we want to use an iterator, our first step is to make sure we have imported the `java.util.Iterator` class:

```
    import java.util.Iterator;
```

To retrieve an iterator, we call the `iterator()` method on the collection class. For instance, referring to the `userlist` collection we created in our previous Try-It-Out:

```
    Iterator userIter = userlist.iterator();
```

This creates an `Iterator` object called `userIter` that holds references to the objects in the `userlist` list.

Having created an iterator, we can now use its methods. There are three:

- ❏ `next()`
- ❏ `hasNext()`
- ❏ `remove()`

The `next()` method returns the next object in the list. The first call to `next()` will retrieve the first object, the second call to `next()` the second object, and so on; the iterator keeps track of where we are in the list. The `hasNext()` method peeks forward in the list to see if we have reached the end of it (it returns `false` if we have reached the end of the list, and `true` if not). As you can imagine, these two methods are often found together in code. For example, we could change the `for` loop from our `ArrayList` Try-It-Out to use an iterator instead:

```
    . . .
        while (userIter.hasNext()) {
            User usr = (User) userIter.next();
            System.out.println("Username: " + usr.getUsername());
            System.out.println("User phone number: " + usr.getPhoneNumber());
        }
    }
}
```

For each iteration, we first check if there are any more objects in the list by calling the `hasNext()` method on the iterator. If there are, then the expression evaluates to `true` and we can proceed with retrieving, and printing, the next object. You should take note that we again need to cast the object returned by the `next()` call to the correct type.

We have already seen how we can use the `remove()` method to remove a specific object from a collection, when we discussed `ArrayList`. For example:

```
userIter.remove(2);
```

This will remove the third element from `userlist`. We can also use `remove()` without including an index value as an argument to the method:

```
userIter.remove();
```

In this case it will remove the last object returned by `next()`, although if the `next()` method has not yet been called, or the `remove()` method has already been called for this object, we will get an error. You should note that not all iterators support this method.

You should also note that there is also a `java.util.ListIterator` interface that extends the `java.util.Iterator` class, but allows you to traverse a collection of objects forwards or backwards, and to add objects as well as remove them. However, for simplicity's sake, we will stick to using the `Iterator` class for this chapter.

Sorting an ArrayList

Consider the code snippet below that creates an `ArrayList` collection `names` and fills it (unsurprisingly) with names:

```
ArrayList names = new ArrayList();
names.add("James");
names.add("Robin");
names.add("Aaron");
```

If we use an iterator now to walk through the collection and print the objects, we find we get the following output:

James
Robin
Aaron.

At some point in the future we might envisage that these names would have to be sorted in alphabetical order:

Aaron
James
Robin.

So, it would be useful if we had a way to sort lists. Luckily, the collections framework provides a static `Collections.sort()` method to do this, which is available in the `java.util.Collections` class. This method usually sorts objects in ascending order, alphabetically or numerically. There are, however, exceptions to this rule for some classes, such as for the `Character` class (sorted numerically by Unicode value), and the `Date` class we will be meeting later in the chapter (which is sorted chronologically).

So, in order to sort the `names` list, we would use the following line of code:

```
Collections.sort(names);
```

Now we could use an iterator to print out the alphabetically-sorted `names` list. First we create an iterator:

```
nameIter = names.iterator();
```

And then we use the `hasNext()` and `next()` methods of the iterator to cycle through the list. For each iteration, we print out the `String` object representing the name:

```
while (nameIter.hasNext()) {
   String s = (String) nameIter.next();
   System.out.println(s);
}
```

Remember that to do this we would also need to have imported the `java.util.Collections` and `java.util.Iterator` classes at the top of our file.

Now, there is a proviso for using the `Collections.sort()` method in this simple way. This works just fine for pre-defined simple objects that you can fill your collection with, such as `Integers`, `Floats` and `Strings`. However, if we want to place user-defined objects in a list (like the `User` objects we defined earlier in the chapter), and then sort these, we need a little more work, because we must define how these objects should be sorted.

The Comparable Interface

To allow sorting of your own user-defined classes you will have to implement the `java.lang.Comparable` interface in your classes. The `Comparable` interface has a single method, `compareTo()`, which you will have to *overload* (write your own version of) if you want to make your class sortable. This method needs to return a positive value if `object1` is less than the object passed to the method (`object2`), and a negative value if the `object2` is the least. In other words, say we have the following call to the `compareTo()` method:

```
object1.compareTo(object2);
```

If `object1` is less than `object2`, then the call should return a positive value, but if `object2` is least, then we should get a negative value returned.

It is up to you to decide how your objects should sort. A common solution is to sort user-defined object instances by the values of one or more of their attributes. For example, let's say we had three instances of an `Employee` class. The class has two attributes, `ID` and `Name`. We might choose to sort on the basis of the value of `ID`; this scenario is shown below:

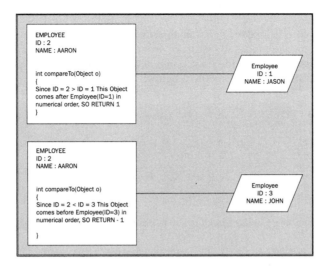

We first compare Aaron's ID to to Jason's and find Aaron's to be greater, so we place Aaron after Jason in the list. On the other hand, comparing Aaron's ID with John's, we find that John should come after Aaron.

In addition to the `compareTo()` method of the `Comparable` interface, we must also overload another two methods.

The first is the `equals()` method, that indicates if an object is equal to another, returning `true` if so, and `false` if not. For simple primitive data types, it is easy to determine if two values are equal or not. For user-defined object types it may be more tricky. Remember the `User` class from a Try-It-Out earlier in the chapter?

```
public class User {
  String username;
  String phonenumber;

  public User() {}

  void setUsername(String uname) {
    username = uname;
  }

  String getUsername() {
    return username;
  }

  void setPhonenumber(String pnum) {
    phonenumber = pnum;
  }

  String getPhoneNumber() {
    return phonenumber;
  }
}
```

As you can see, the class has two attributes and the get/set methods for these attributes too. Now, as with compareTo(), we must make a decision about which of these attribute(s) we wish to compare within the equals() method, to see if the User instances are identical. In this case, we make a decision that we need to check only the username of the two object instances. Take a look at how we might then implement the equals() method, below:

```
public boolean equals(Object obj) {
  if (!(obj instanceof User)) {
    return false;
  }
  User usr = (User)obj;
  return (usr.getUsername().equals(this.username));
}
```

We first check to see if the object being passed to the method is of class User, using the instanceof operator:

```
(obj instanceof User)
```

This expression will return true if obj is an instance of the User class, and false if not. If false is returned, the equals() method returns false too:

```
if (!(obj instanceof User)) {
  return false;
}
```

However, if the expression returns true, we then cast obj correctly to the User class and then use the equals() method to compare the two String username instances.

```
return (usr.getUsername().equals(this.username));
```

This comparison returns true or false, depending on whether the usernames of both instances are the same or not.

The final method we need to overload is the hashCode() method, which returns a hash value for the object. Again, for user-defined objects we need to define which object attribute(s) need to be hashed to give a hash value for the object. Here's a simple example of how we might do this for User:

```
public int hashCode() {
  return username.hashCode();
}
```

Here we have chosen to hash the username attribute of User, in order to obtain a hash value for the instance in question. We can use hashcode() with username because we don't need to overload the method for simple data types such as String.

Let's now use what we have learnt above to sort a list of names.

Try It Out – Sorting User-Defined Objects

Remember the `ArrayList` Try-It-Out that we created earlier? In this example, we are going to adapt this so that the `User` objects in the `ArrayList` can be sorted. First, open up your `User.java` file, and add the methods highlighted below. Then save the file into `%CATALINA_HOME%\webapps\begjsp-ch08\com\wrox\utilities` and recompile your new `User.java` file.

```java
package com.wrox.utilities;

public class User implements Comparable {
    String username;
    String phonenumber;

    public User() {}

    public User(String uname, String pnum) {
        username    = uname;
        phonenumber = pnum;
    }

    public boolean equals(Object obj) {
      if (!(obj instanceof User)) {
        return false;
      }
      User usr = (User)obj;
      return (usr.getUsername().equals(this.username));
    }

    public int hashCode() {
      return username.hashCode();
    }

    public int compareTo(Object element) {
      User usr = (User)element;
      String newusername = usr.getUsername();
      return (this.getUsername().compareTo(usr.getUsername()));
    }

    void setUsername(String uname) {
      username = uname;
    }

    String getUsername() {
      return username;
    }

    void setPhonenumber(String pnum) {
      phonenumber = pnum;
    }

    String getPhoneNumber() {
      return phonenumber;
    }
}
```

Next we need to modify the `ArrayListDemo.java` file we created earlier, so that we sort the `User` objects within the `ArrayList`. The changes are highlighted below; save the new file as `ArrayListSort.java` and compile it.

```java
package com.wrox.utilities;
import java.util.*;

public class ArrayListSort {
  public static void main(String[] args) {
    User usr1 = new User("J Smith","123-444-4444");
    User usr2 = new User("M Walker","123-555-5555");
    User usr3 = new User("R Johnson","123-666-6666");

    ArrayList userlist = new ArrayList();
    userlist.add(usr3);
    userlist.add(usr1);
    userlist.add(usr2);

    System.out.println("Before sorting...");
    iterateNames(userlist);
    Collections.sort(userlist);
    System.out.println("After sorting...");
    iterateNames(userlist);
  }

  public static void iterateNames(ArrayList usrlist) {
    Iterator iterator = usrlist.iterator();
    while (iterator.hasNext()) {
      User usr = (User) iterator.next();
      System.out.println(usr.getUsername());
    }
  }
}
```

Run the `ArrayListDemo.java` program in your command console. You should see:

```
Before sorting...
R Johnson
J Smith
M Walker
After sorting...
J Smith
M Walker
R Johnson
```

In other words we have sorted the names alphabetically.

How It Works

We have actually already introduced you to most of the new code in this modified version of the `ArrayList` example, so we won't go into it in much depth here.

First of all, we have the bean class `User.java`, to which we added three new methods:

```
public boolean equals(Object obj) {
...
}

public int hashCode() {
...
}

public int compareTo(Object element) {
...
}
```

We discussed the implementation of these methods in the section before this example, so we won't re-tread old ground here. Note that we also made sure that the `User` class was sortable by implementing the `Comparable` interface:

```
public class User implements Comparable {
```

Let's move on to the class that actually performs the sorting, `ArrayListDemo`. Here we create an `ArrayList` called `userlist` and fill it with names and phone numbers, as in our earlier `ArrayList` example. Now what we want to do is to iterate through all of the names, printing them out, sort the names, then print them out again. Since we want to iterate and print all of the names twice during the program, it makes sense to move this functionality into a method:

```
public static void iterateNames(ArrayList usrlist) {
    Iterator iterator = usrlist.iterator();
    while (iterator.hasNext()) {
        User usr = (User) iterator.next();
        System.out.println(usr.getUsername());
    }
}
```

The method takes an `ArrayList` as argument. The code inside the method should be familiar to you: we create an iterator for the list and then use the `hasNext()` and `next()` methods to iterate through the list. We print out each `username` we find to the console.

In the `main()` method of the program we make use of this method, by calling it to iterate through the `User` objects and print names before we sort the list:

```
System.out.println("Before sorting...");
iterateNames(userlist);
```

Then we sort the `userlist` collection:

```
Collections.sort(userlist);
```

Finally we print out the sorted list:

```
System.out.println("After sorting...");
iterateNames(userlist);
```

Stack Collections

Earlier in the chapter we introduced the idea of a stack: a list in which we use first-in, last-out (FILO) ordering. An example of a stack is a pack of cards laid face down on top of each other on a table. When we take cards from the pack, we take a card from the top of the pile, and place new cards on the top of the pile too. There are two fundamental operations that are used in accessing the items in a stack:

❑ **Push**: A push operation is used to place an item on the stack. The item that you push will always be present on the top (end) of the stack.

❑ **Pop**: A pop operation is used to remove an item from the stack. The item that will be popped out will always be the top item in the stack.

Let's reinforce your understanding of this push/pop mechanism via an example. In our example, we shall create a stack of Wrox books. Let's call the stack BOOKS and assume that it is empty initially. The only way that one can add elements to the stack and remove elements from the stack is via the push and pop operations. An example flow of operations with the current status of the stack is shown below:

1. First we push "Beginning JSP":

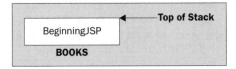

2. Pushing "Professional JSP" and "Beginning Java" too gives:

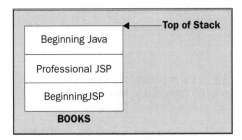

3. Now we pop the stack. This will retrieve the element "Beginning Java" from the top of the stack. The stack will then have only two elements as shown:

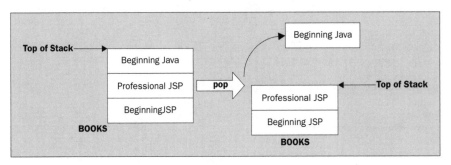

We implement stack collections in Java using the `java.util.Stack` interface. Pushing and popping objects is achieved using methods provided by the `Stack` object:

❑ `push()`

❑ `pop()`

Let's use our BOOKS stack as an example. First we'll create a new `Stack` object called books using the `Stack()` constructor:

```
Stack books = new Stack();
```

The books themselves will be represented by three String instances (`"Beginning JSP"`, `"Professional JSP"`, `"Beginning Java"`). Therefore, we can now repeat the pushing and popping in our example using Java code. First we push all of these `String` instances into the stack:

```
books.push("Beginning JSP");
books.push("Professional JSP");
books.push("Beginning Java");
```

Notice how the `push()` method takes the object as its argument. Now we pop the top book off the stack:

```
String book = (String) books.pop();
```

Here we pop books, cast the popped object to a `String`, and store it in a `String` instance called book. As usual, we must typecast the returned object because it will be returned as type Object.

There are three more useful `Stack` methods we are going to use:

Method	Description
`peek()`	Returns the object from the top of the stack without removing it.
`empty()`	Returns `true` if the stack is empty, returns `false` otherwise.
`search()`	Takes an object as an argument, and searches for it on the stack. If it finds the object, it returns the offset of the object from the top of the stack. If the object is not in the stack, it returns −1.

We will demonstrate the use of these methods in just a moment. Remember that any of the methods above that return an object must be cast to the correct type.

Let's now use all of these stack methods in an example that you can run.

Try It Out – Using a Stack

In this example, we are going to use our Wrox book stack scenario; building up a stack of three books and then playing around with the stack. Save the following file into `%CATALINA_HOME%\webapps\begjsp-ch08\com\wrox\utilities` as `StackDemo.java`:

```
package com.wrox.utilities;
import java.util.Stack;

public class StackDemo {

    static void printStack(Stack stack) {
      System.out.println("Stack consists of: " + stack);
    }

    public static void main(String[] args) {
      Stack books = new Stack();
      System.out.println("Stack is empty? " + books.empty());

      books.push("Beginning JSP");
      books.push("Professional JSP");
      books.push("Beginning Java");
      System.out.println("Pushed 3 books on the stack...");
      printStack(books);
      System.out.println("Stack is empty? " + books.empty());

      String book = (String) books.pop();
      System.out.println("Popped " + book + " off the stack...");
      printStack(books);

      book = (String) books.peek();
      System.out.println(book + " is at the top of the stack");
      int offset = books.search("Beginning JSP");
      System.out.println("Beginning JSP is " + offset + " books from the top
                                              of the stack");

    }
}
```

Compile the source code, and then run the above example in your command console using:

>java StackDemo

You should get the following output:

```
Stack is empty? true
Pushed 3 books on the stack...
Stack consists of: [Beginning JSP, Professional JSP, Beginning Java]
Stack is empty? false
Popped Beginning Java off the stack...
Stack consists of: [Beginning JSP, Professional JSP]
Professional JSP is at the top of the stack
Beginning JSP is 2 books from the top of the stack
```

How It Works

The example incorporates several lines that we have seen before. First we have the stack creation:

```
Stack books = new Stack();
```

Then we use the `empty()` method to check that the `books` stack is empty:

```
System.out.println("Stack is empty? " + books.empty());
```

We get an answer returned of `true`. Next we push three books onto the stack and print out a message to that effect:

```
books.push("Beginning JSP");
books.push("Professional JSP");
books.push("Beginning Java");
System.out.println("Pushed 3 books on the stack...");
```

Using a simple method we defined earlier in this class, `printStack()`, our next step is print out all of the books in the stack:

```
printStack(books);
System.out.println("Stack is empty? " + books.empty());
```

After we've checked to see if there are any objects in the stack (there are this time), we pop the book at the top of the stack, inform the user which book was popped, and then print out the contents of the stack again:

```
String book = (String) books.pop();
System.out.println("Popped " + book + " off the stack...");
printStack(books);
```

Next we use the `peek()` method to find the object at the top of the stack, and we place this book into the `book` object we created earlier when we popped. Note that this does not remove this object from the top of the stack. Then we print out the name of this book at the top of the stack:

```
book = (String) books.peek();
System.out.println(book + " is at the top of the stack");
```

Our final step is to use the `search()` method to find the offset of `"Beginning JSP"` from the top of the stack:

```
int offset = books.search("Beginning JSP");
System.out.println("Beginning JSP is " + offset + " books from the top
                                        of the stack");
```

We store the offset in `offset`, and then print out its value.

HashMap Collections

At the start of this chapter, we introduced the concept of a map as a way of storing data values with an associated key. Each key is unique, which enables us to use it to find and retrieve the data we want from the map collection quickly and efficiently.

All map classes implement the `java.util.Map` interface. In this section, we are going to look at the map collection class `java.util.HashMap`, which is a typical example of a map class.

Before we get into the methods of the HashMap class, let's throw together a scenario that we can use to demonstrate the use of a HashMap collection. In this scenario, we would like to store company employees' telephone numbers. Therefore, we want to create a key-value map in which the employee's name is the key, and the telephone number is the value we wish to retrieve. Here's a table of employees and their numbers:

Employee Name	Telephone Number
Ashish	111-222-3333
Archit	444-555-6666
Prashant	777-888-9999

We want to implement this map in a HashMap object, so our first step is to create a HashMap object. As you may have expected, we create a HashMap by invoking the HashMap() constructor:

```
HashMap empPhone = new HashMap();
```

Here we have named our new HashMap instance empPhone. Now we want to add the names and numbers to this map. To do this we need to use the put() method, as demonstrated below:

```
empPhone.put("Ashish","111-222-3333");
empPhone.put("Archit","444-555-6666");
empPhone.put("Prashant","777-888-9999");
```

The put() method takes two arguments: the first is the object to use as the key (a String representing the employee name here); the second is the object which will hold the data we want to retrieve (telephone numbers stored as Strings too).

So once the key-value pairs are in the map, how do we retrieve them? We use the get() method:

```
String phoneNum = (String) empPhone.get("Prashant");
```

The method requires that you know the key associated with the value you wish to retrieve, because this key object must be fed into the method as an argument. Here, the key is "Prashant". The method returns the value associated with this key, which must be typecast before we can save it to another object (phoneNum here).

The table below shows some other useful methods associated with HashMap that we will use in a moment:

Method	Description
remove()	Removes the value from the map for the key that you pass the method as argument, and returns the value that has been removed.
size()	Returns the number of key-value pairs in the map as an integer.
putAll()	Takes a map object as an argument; transfers all key-value pairs from this map object to the current map object.

You should note that we can use iterators with `HashMap` objects. To do this, we must first create a Set object which holds the keys from the key-value pairs, using the `keySet()` method. Let's do this for our `empPhone` object:

```
Set keys = empPhone.keySet();
```

The keys object now contains all of the key values from `empPhone`. Our next step is to create an `Iterator` object for the keys:

```
Iterator keyIter = keys.iterator();
```

Now that we have the iterator, we can do some iterating using the `hasNext()` and `next()` methods we have already seen. For instance, if we wanted to print out all of the employee names and telephone numbers present in the `empPhone` map, we could use:

```
while(keyIter.hasNext()) {
  String nextName = (String) keyIter.next();
  String phoneNum = (String) empPhone.get(nextName);
  System.out.println(nextName + ": " + phoneNum);
}
```

As always, remember to typecast objects returned from collection methods. Let's now tie all of the `HashMap` methods we have skimmed through so far into an example.

Try It Out – Using a HashMap

For this example we are going to use our employee phone directory scenario, playing around with the `empPhone` collection, and transferring some of its contents to another `HashMap`. Save the following files into `%CATALINA_HOME%\webapps\begjsp-ch08\com\wrox\utilities`. Here's the first, `HashMapDemo.java`:

```
import java.util.*;

public class HashMapDemo {

  public static void main(String[] args) {
    HashMap empPhone = new HashMap();

    empPhone.put("Ashish","111-222-3333");
    empPhone.put("Archit","444-555-6666");
    empPhone.put("Prashant","777-888-9999");

    Set keys = empPhone.keySet();
    Iterator keyIter = keys.iterator();
    while(keyIter.hasNext()) {
      String nextName = (String) keyIter.next();
      String phoneNum = (String) empPhone.get(nextName);
      System.out.println(nextName + ": " + phoneNum);
    }

    String phoneNum = (String) empPhone.remove("Ashish");
    System.out.println("Removed Ashish's number : " + phoneNum);
```

```
        HashMap newEmpPhone = new HashMap();
        newEmpPhone.putAll(empPhone);
        int dirSize = newEmpPhone.size();
        System.out.println("Created new phone directory with " + dirSize + "
                                                    numbers...");
        phoneNum = (String) newEmpPhone.get("Prashant");
        System.out.println("Prashant's number in new directory: " + phoneNum);
    }
}
```

Compile the example and then run it on your console using the `java` command. The output from the program is:

Prashant: 777-888-9999
Ashish: 111-222-3333
Archit: 444-555-6666
Removed Ashish's number: 111-222-3333
Created new phone directory with 2 numbers...
Prashant's number in new directory: 777-888-9999

How It Works

Let's walk through the class in the example. The first line of note is right at the start:

```
import java.util.*;
```

You should have expected us to import `java.util.HashMap`, since this is the class we are going to be using. However, we will need to use the `java.util.Set` and the `java.util.Iterator` classes too later in the example, so to keep things simple, we have imported all of the `java.util` classes here (the `*` character means "all classes" in this context).

Moving inside the `HashMapDemo` class we encounter a block of code that should be familiar: we create and fill the `empPhone` collection using the `HashMap()` and `put()` methods, and then iterate through the collection, printing out the key-value pairs. Remember that to iterate through the collection we need to make a `Set` of keys, and an iterator of this set:

```
        Set keys = empPhone.keySet();
        Iterator keyIter = keys.iterator();
```

This is why we needed to import the `java.util.Set` and `java.util.Iterator` classes earlier. After we have printed out the collection, we find out that Ashish has actually recently moved to a different company. This means we must remove the corresponding number from the collection:

```
        String phoneNum = (String) empPhone.remove("Ashish");
        System.out.println("Removed Aahish's number : " + phoneNum);
```

We use the `remove()` method with the key as an argument, to remove the number from `empPhone`, and then we print out the number we have removed.

We finish off the example by copying all of the data present in empPhone to another HashMap, newEmpPhone. We create the new map, and then we use the putAll() method to copy all of the key-value pairs across from empPhone to newEmpPhone:

```
HashMap newEmpPhone = new HashMap();
newEmpPhone.putAll(empPhone);
```

To check that the data has been copied across successfully, we do two thing check the number of key-value pairs in the newEmpPhone map, using the size() method, and retrieve a value from this map:

```
int dirSize = newEmpPhone.size();
System.out.println("Created new phone directory with " + dirSize + "
                                                   numbers...");
phoneNum = (String) newEmpPhone.get("Prashant");
System.out.println("Prashant's number in new directory: " + phoneNum);
```

The size() method returns an integer value for the number of key-value pairs, which we then print out. To retrieve a value (Prashant's phone number) from the new map, we use the get() method, as discussed earlier.

We now move on to discuss how to incorporate date and time objects into our Java code.

Date and Time Classes

Since dates and times are everyday considerations in our lives, it is inevitable that we will have to deal with them in our programs at some point. In this section, we will learn how to manipulate dates and times in our Java programs. Let's now take a look at the date/time classes which are available in the java.util package.

The Date Class

The java.util.Date class stores a date and time, with millisecond precision. To create a Date object we need to use the Date() constructor. There are two common ways of using this constructor. The first creates a Date instance that holds the current date, counted in milliseconds, from 00:00:00 January 1st 1970 GMT. For example, the following line will result in the creation of a Date instance called currentDate, which holds the current date:

```
Date currentDate = new Date();
```

We can also specify the date to be stored in a Date instance by telling the constructor the date we want it to hold:

```
Date myDate = new Date(992710981977);
```

Before you ask, the argument is supposed to be that big! Here we want to store the date of 18:03:01 June 16th 2001 GMT+01:00, but the argument to the method must be supplied in milliseconds. Obviously this is not particularly user-friendly, and we'll come back to this issue again in a moment.

Retrieving Dates

Retrieving the date from a `Date` instance is pretty easy. Printing out the date in calendar-style format is a matter of just printing out the instance itself:

```
System.out.println("Current Date: "  + currentDate);
```

This line would print:

Current Date: Sat Jun 16 18:03:01 GMT+01:00 2001

If you really want to retrieve the number of milliseconds stored in the instance too, you can use the `getTime()` method with the instance:

```
System.out.println("Current Date (ms): " + currentDate.getTime());
```

Comparing Dates

We will often want to compare two dates to see which one comes first. Since the `java.util.Date` class implements the `Comparable` interface that we covered in the previous section, we can use the `compareTo()` method, as shown below, to do this:

```
myDate.compareTo(currentDate);
```

It compares the value of the invoking instance (`myDate` here) to that of the argument passed (`currentDate`). If the values are equal it returns 0. If the invoking `Date` is later than the argument `Date` passed, then it returns a positive value. If the invoking `Date` is earlier than the argument, then it returns a negative value. So, assuming that the current date is later than the value in `myDate`, this call should return a negative value.

The GregorianCalendar Class

The Gregorian calendar is the most widely-used and therefore recognizable calendar in the western world. It provides the date and time in terms of years, days, hours, minutes, and seconds for different time zones instead of just milliseconds. Therefore, an object that represents this date format would be very useful. As you probably expect, Java provides such a class, `java.util.GregorianCalendar`, along with other calendar classes, which are found in `java.util.Calendar`. In this section we will focus on `GregorianCalendar`.

We use the constructor `GregorianCalendar()` to create an instance of this class. If we don't provide arguments to the constructor the current time will be placed in the instance.

```
GregorianCalendar gCalendar = new GregorianCalendar();
```

Here our instance is called `gCalendar`. There are another six variations of the constructor, where we can specify various different elements of a date (time zone, year, month...).

The `GregorianCalendar` class (and any other `Calendar` class in general) defines a set of constants, that make it easy for you not only to format the date stored in the `Calendar` instance, but also to retrieve specific information from the object like the month stored, the year stored, and so on. Here are examples of field constants (although there are many others, that deal with time zones for instance):

Constant	Example Value
gCalendar.YEAR	2001
gCalendar.MONTH	5 (0-11, 5 is June)
gCalendar.DATE	16 (1-31)
gCalendar.HOUR	6 (1-12)
gCalendar.MINUTE	3 (0-59)
gCalendar.SECOND	1 (0-59)
gCalendar.AM_PM	1 (AM is 0, PM is 1)
gCalendar.DAY_OF_WEEK	7 (1-7, 7 is Saturday)

These constants are all pretty self-explanatory (`DATE` is the day of the month). We can change the values of these constants using `get()` and `set()` methods. For example, let's use the `gCalendar` instance we made earlier, and reset the day of the month to the 25th:

```
gCalendar.set(gCalendar.DATE, 25);
```

You can see that we must specify the field constant and the new constant value as arguments. If we check the value of `gCalendar.DATE` now using `get()`:

```
System.out.println("Day of the month: " + gCalendar.get(gCalendar.DATE));
```

we will see the following output:

Day of the month: 25

Note that we need to provide the field constant as argument to `get()`. If we want, we can retrieve the full date using the `getTime()` method:

```
System.out.println("Date: " + gCalendar.getTime());
```

Date: Mon Jun 25 18:03:01 GMT+01:00 2001

The `getTime()` method needs no arguments; notice how the day of the week has been automatically changed to match the rest of the date. The full date returned includes the weekday, the local time zone, and the time down to a second. Now, chances are that you are not going to want to display all of this information to a user; you will want to be more selective because you have your own standard date format that you want to adhere to. So how can we specify a date format for our objects?

Formatting Dates

You may have noticed that the standard representation for the date and time varies from country to country. For example, the date format for the United States is:

```
MM/dd/yyyy
```

Here, `MM` is a number from 1-12 representing the month, `dd` is the day of the month, and `yyyy` is the year. For June 16th 2001, this would equate to 06/16/2001. The United Kingdom date format reverses the order of the month and day:

```
dd/MM/yyyy
```

There are lots more date/time format variations; here are some of the most common:

Format Pattern	Examples
dd-MM-yyyy	02-06-2001
dd MMMM yyyy	02 June 2001
EEE, dd MMMM yyyy	Sat, 02 June 2001
HH:mm:ss	06:36:33
hh:mm a	06:37 AM

Notice the use of `EEE` to represent the weekday, `a` for AM/PM, and `HH`, `mm`, `ss` to represent hours, minutes and seconds respectively.

Java provides a class, `java.text.SimpleDateFormat`, that allows us to format `Date` objects according to user-defined patterns like these. To do this, we must feed a date format to the `SimpleDateFormat()` constructor, like this:

```
SimpleDateFormat dateFormat = new SimpleDateFormat("EEE, dd MMMM yyyy");
```

In this case we have created a `SimpleDateFormat` object called `dateFormat` that will change the format of a `Date` object into `"EEE, dd MMMM yyyy"`. So if we have a `Date` object called `currentDate`, we can change it to this new format and print it out using:

```
System.out.println("Date: " + dateFormat.format(currentDate));
```

Notice how we invoked the method format() upon the dateFormat object to actually perform the formatting. The `Date` object we wish to format is fed into the method as an argument. We get a `String` containing the formatted date returned by the `format()` method.

If we want to format `Calendar` instances, including `GregorianCalendar` instances, we must first cast the instance into a `Date` instance using the `getTime()` method:

```
String gCalFormatted = dateFormat.format(gCalendar.getTime());
```

To finish off this section on Date/Time objects, we are now going to build an example that uses date/time classes, that you can try running for yourself. Since we've been concentrating on classes in this chapter far more than JSPs, let's build a proper JSP-based example that also makes use of a JavaBean, to remove as much scriptlet code from the JSP as possible.

Try It Out – Using Date/Time Classes

Remember the millenium counters that displayed the days until New Year's Eve 2000? This example does much the same thing – except that the year 2000 has passed us by, so we have the year 3000 to look forward to instead!

The example uses a JavaBean, `CounterBean.java`. This bean stores the current date and a target date (the new millenium for this example) as attributes, and allows us to get, set, and manipulate these dates. We also have a JSP that instantiates the bean and uses its methods to find out how many days there are to go until the year 3000. Then it displays the current date and the number of days to go until 3000 in the browser.

First, save the following file into a new directory `%CATALINA_HOME%\webapps\begjsp-ch08\com\wrox\counter` as `CounterBean.java`, and compile it using `javac`:

```
package com.wrox.counter;
import java.util.*;
import java.text.SimpleDateFormat;

public class CounterBean {

  private Date curDate;
  private SimpleDateFormat dateFormat;
  private GregorianCalendar targetDate;
  private String name;

  public CounterBean() {

    GregorianCalendar currentDate = new GregorianCalendar();
    curDate = (Date) currentDate.getTime();

    dateFormat = new SimpleDateFormat("EEE, dd MMMM yyyy");

    targetDate = new GregorianCalendar();
    targetDate.set(targetDate.YEAR, 3000);
    targetDate.set(targetDate.MONTH, 0);
    targetDate.set(targetDate.DATE, 1);
    targetDate.set(targetDate.AM_PM, 0);
    targetDate.set(targetDate.HOUR, 0);
    targetDate.set(targetDate.MINUTE, 0);
    targetDate.set(targetDate.SECOND, 0);

    name = "the new millennium";
  }

  public String getTodaysDate() {
    return dateFormat.format(curDate);
```

199

```
  }

  public void setTargetYear(int year) {
    targetDate.set(targetDate.YEAR, year);
  }

  public void setTargetMonth(int month) {
    targetDate.set(targetDate.MONTH, month);
  }

  public void setTargetDate(int date) {
    targetDate.set(targetDate.DATE, date);
  }

  public void setTargetAmPm(int ampm) {
    targetDate.set(targetDate.AM_PM, ampm);
  }

  public void setTargetHour(int hour) {
    targetDate.set(targetDate.HOUR, hour);
  }

  public void setTargetMinute(int minute) {
    targetDate.set(targetDate.MINUTE, minute);
  }

  public void setTargetSecond(int second) {
    targetDate.set(targetDate.SECOND, second);
  }

  public void setTargetEvent(String eventName) {
    name = eventName;
  }

  public String getTargetEvent() {
    return name;
  }


  public String getMessage() {
    Date millDate = (Date) targetDate.getTime();
    int dateTest = millDate.compareTo(curDate);

    switch(dateTest) {
      case 1:
        long millisecs = (millDate.getTime()) - (curDate.getTime());
        long msInDay = (1000*60*60*24);
        long daysToGo = (long) (millisecs/msInDay);
        return("Only " + daysToGo + " days to go until " + name + "!!!");
      case 0:
        return("Welcome to the new Millenium!!!");
      case -1:
        return("Sorry, counter has expired");
      default:
        return("Counter error");
    }
  }
}
```

Next, save the following file, `Counter.jsp`, into the `begjsp-ch08` folder:

```
<%@page contentType="text/html"%>   ,
<html>
<head><title>Counter</title></head>
<body>

<jsp:useBean id="counter" scope="page"
 class="com.wrox.counter.CounterBean"/>

<p>The current date is
    <jsp:getProperty name="counter" property="todaysDate"/></p>

<p><jsp:getProperty name="counter" property="message"/></p>

</body>
</html>
```

Running the Example

When both files are placed in the correct directories and compiled, start Tomcat and point your browser at http://localhost:8080/begjsp-ch08/Counter.jsp. You should see something like this (depending on the date of course):

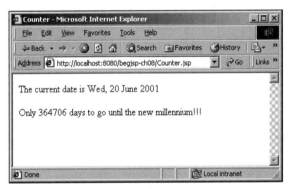

How It Works

Let's start with the bean. It's quite long, so it may look daunting at first, but be assured it's actually pretty simple. We start off by stating the package that the bean is in, and by importing the utility classes that we will need. The class itself has four attributes, a Date object to hold the current date, a SimpleDateFormat object to hold the date format, a GregorianCalendar object to hold the target date (the new millenium for this example), and a String that holds the name of the event we're counting down to:

```
private Date curDate;
private SimpleDateFormat dateFormat;
private GregorianCalendar targetDate;
private String name;
```

Next we initialize our attributes in the constructor. First of all we create a GregorianCalendar object that contains the current date and use the getTime() method to cast this instance to the Date class:

```
GregorianCalendar currentDate = new GregorianCalendar();
curDate = (Date) currentDate.getTime();
```

201

As you can see, we copy the contents of this `Date` instance (the current date) into our `curDate` attribute. Then we initialize the `SimpleDateFormat` object attribute with the format `"EEE, dd MMMM yyyy"`:

```
dateFormat = new SimpleDateFormat("EEE, dd MMMM yyyy");
```

The next attribute to initialize is the target date. We initialize this to the year 3000 by setting all of the field constants of the `targetDate` instance individually:

```
targetDate = new GregorianCalendar();
targetDate.set(targetDate.YEAR, 3000);
targetDate.set(targetDate.MONTH, 0);
targetDate.set(targetDate.DATE, 1);
targetDate.set(targetDate.AM_PM, 0);
targetDate.set(targetDate.HOUR, 0);
targetDate.set(targetDate.MINUTE, 0);
targetDate.set(targetDate.SECOND, 0);
```

We finish the initialization by setting the value of the `name` attribute:

```
name = "the new millennium";
```

After the constructor we encounter lots of get and set methods. The first retrieves today's date and returns it in the date format we want:

```
public String getTodaysDate() {
  return dateFormat.format(curDate);
}
```

The vast majority of the rest of the methods set one of the field constants of the target date. For example:

```
public void setTargetYear(int year) {
  targetDate.set(targetDate.YEAR, year);
}
```

This method sets the year of the target date to the input value (`year`).

We also have a method to set the name of the target date:

```
public void setTargetEvent(String eventName) {
  name = eventName;
}
```

The last method, `getMessage()`, in the bean class is the most interesting, because it does all the clever stuff. It computes the number of days to go until the target date, and prints out this number and the current date to the browser. Let's see how it does this.

Our first step is to check that the target date hasn't already passed us by! Therefore we cast the target date to the `Date` class, so that we can use the `compareTo()` method to compare this date to the current date:

```
Date millDate = (Date) targetDate.getTime();
int dateTest = millDate.compareTo(curDate);
```

There are three possible outcomes from this method. If the method returns 1, the current date is less than the target date. In other words the target date is still to come. If -1 is returned, the target date has passed us by already. The method can also return zero, in the extremely unlikely event that we run this program *exactly* on the target date specified. To deal with each of these possible results, we will use a `switch` statement:

```
switch(dateTest) {
```

Let's deal with the most likely case first. To find the number of days to go until the target date, we first use the `getTime()` method to extract both the current and target times in milliseconds. We then subtract the time for today from the time for the target:

```
case 1:
   long millisecs = (millDate.getTime()) - (curDate.getTime());
```

This gives us the time to go until the target date in milliseconds. Then we simply calculate the number of milliseconds in a day, and divide one figure by the other to get the number of days to go:

```
long msInDay = (1000*60*60*24);
long daysToGo = (long) (millisecs/msInDay);
```

Then we display a message telling the user the number of days to go:

```
return("Only " + daysToGo + " days to go until " + name + "!!!");
```

Next we deal with the other two scenarios; that we have happened to run the program on the exact target date:

```
case 0:
   return("Welcome to " + name + " !!!");
```

or that the target date has already passed:

```
case -1:
   return("Sorry, counter has expired");
```

Either way we print out a message to the browser informing the user. Now, we should also attempt to deal with any other situations that we haven't expected – errors. If the `dateTest` variable doesn't contain 1, 0, or -1 we know something's gone wrong so we display an error message:

```
default:
   return("Counter error");
}
```

Well, we've now walked through our bean. What about the JSP? Thankfully the JSP script is a lot shorter than the bean. Ignoring the HTML, we start by instantiating a `CounterBean` called `counter`:

```
<jsp:useBean id="counter" scope="page"
 class="com.wrox.counter.CounterBean"/>
```

Then we use `<jsp:getProperty>` tags to call bean methods. First we retrieve and display today's date by calling the `getTodaysDate()` method:

```
<p>The current date is
   <jsp:getProperty name="counter" property="todaysDate"/></p>
```

Finally we call the `getMessage()` method to display the number of days to go until the new millenium:

```
<p><jsp:getProperty name="counter" property="message"/></p>
```

And that's it! An incredibly clear and simple JSP script which avoids the need for any scriptlets. What's more, we haven't limited ourselves to counting down to any particular date; and the bean class is configurable and reusable. This illustrates why separating presentation from logic is such a great idea.

Summary

In this chapter, we discussed the Java utility classes present in `java.util`. Specifically:

❏   We introduced you to the concept of **collections** of user-defined objects. In Java, we find that there are three types of collection: **sets**, **lists**, and **maps**. We noted that each of these collection types is represented by an interface.

❏   We looked at **collection classes**, which we use to create objects that represent collections. Each of these objects can be classified as a type of set, list, or map, depending on the collection interface implemented by its class.

❏   We discussed and played with objects derived from three commonly-used collection classes: `ArrayList`, `Stack`, and `HashMap`.

❏   We also covered the use of the `Iterator` interface for iterating through a collection, and how to implement sorting of user-defined objects within a collection.

❏   We finished off the chapter by looking at `Date`, `Calendar`, and `GregorianCalendar` objects, which we can use for storing dates and times. We also learned how to change the format of the date stored in these objects, so that we can display the date in the way that we want. As a demonstration of how to use these classes we built a JSP that counts the number of days until the next millenium, taking the opportunity to show you how moving the logic for the counter into a bean makes the JSP much more simple and clear, and the logic code more reusable and maintainable.

In the final example of this chapter, you may have noticed that we attempted to account for possible errors by including a clause to cope with it in the `switch` statement. Surely there must be a neater way of dealing with possible errors than this? Well, in Java there is. In the next chapter, we will be discussing how to handle errors that occur when you attempt to run your code or JSPs, by using objects called Exceptions.

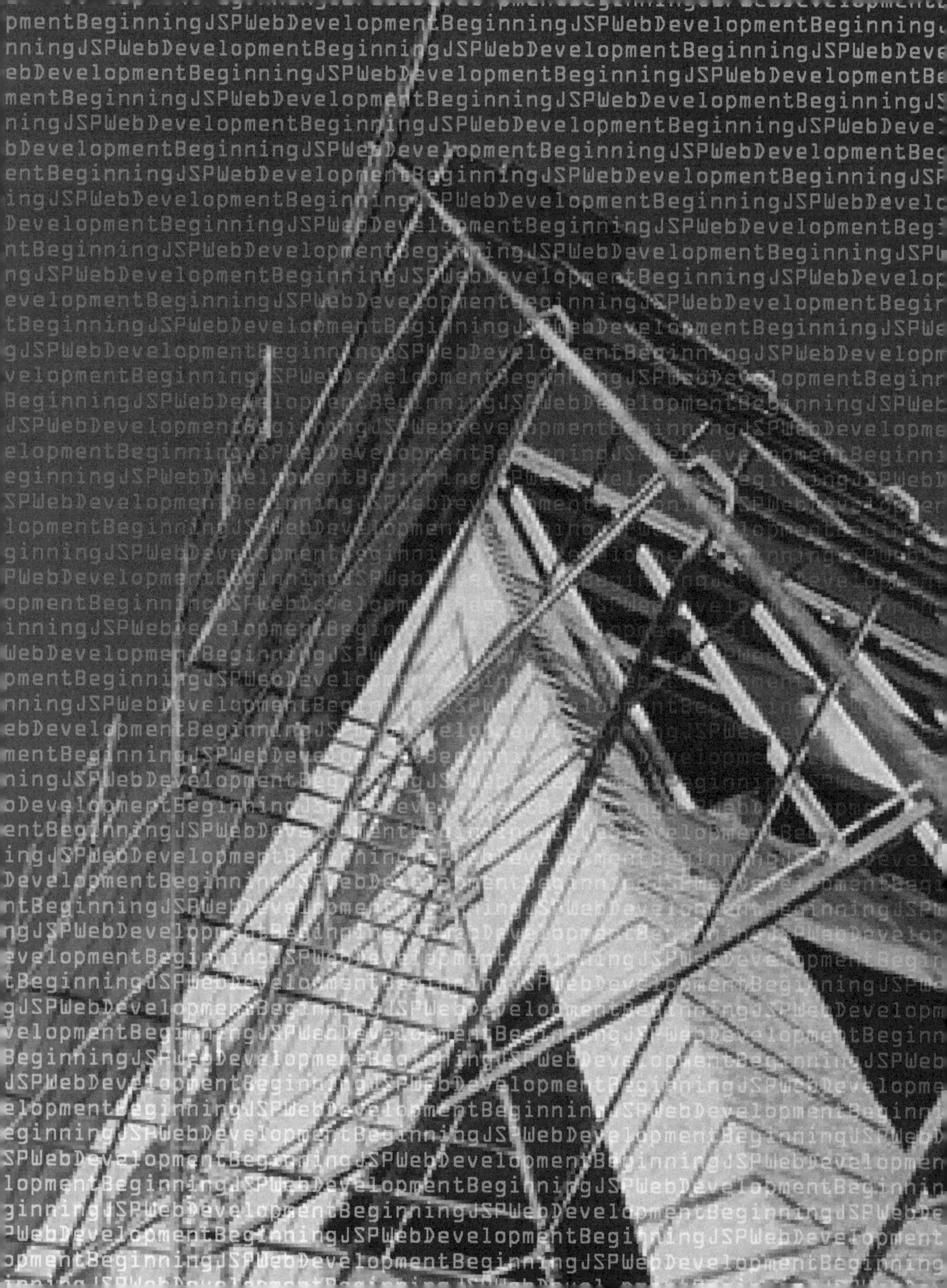
BeginningJSPWebDevelopment

When It All Goes Wrong

Errors are a fact of life in programming. The first step to reducing errors is simply to get into good programming habits; this book will help you to learn the basics in this respect. However, even the best programmer will still have errors to deal with in daily programming life. Therefore, Java steps in to help make the programmer's life easier!

Java takes an enlightened approach to error handling. Java starts with a simple but efficient error-handling model, which is known by the term **exception management**. This error model defines a set of classes that are built just to work with errors. The Java API then defines a simple methodology for handling errors. This means a framework is in place for us to use in capturing the errors (intervening when they occur) and handling them so a proper response can be generated for any given error. Finally, since the majority of errors a programmer encounters will be specific to their own programs, Java lets a programmer build and expand new error classes to represent errors that are specific to their code.

This chapter will walk you through the skills needed to be proficient in handling errors within the Java and JSP programming environments. The main push will be to cover how Java uses exceptions to handle events that need extra care and handling. However, JSP pushes Java into new areas, which even many Java programmers are not familiar with as programmers. This chapter will examine these features, which allow JSP to interface with the world outside of Java, and as a result we will examine areas which would not have been covered in a more traditional Java book. This means in addition to covering how Java handles errors, this book will take an especially close look at handling errors within the JSP environment. Because of this you will receive an overview of what types of problems face a server-side programmer and the tools to begin to safely untangle these problems to something more manageable.

We'll be looking in turn at:

- ❑ The different types of error that can occur in an application
- ❑ Java's exception-handling mechanism
- ❑ The specifics of using Java exception management in JSP
- ❑ How to diagnose and treat HTML and JavaScript-related errors in the JSP's output
- ❑ How to translating stack trace error messages
- ❑ Using log files for tracking exceptions over time
- ❑ Some resources that will help you to solve coding problems

Types of Error

When thinking about errors it turns out several different types of errors exist.

System Errors

System errors are errors that happen due to an unpredicted interaction of a Java program with the operating system it is running within. These errors are the ones that a programmer usually has the least control over; for example, such an error might be due to a bad software driver, low memory resources, or just trying to open a connection to a network that is down.

The good news is that these errors tend to be very visible. Handling a system error often means having to update a software driver or another piece of external software outside of your program's control: the bad news is that a programmer doesn't always have control or the authority to update the outside aspects of the system.

Application Errors

Most errors are due to something wrong within the application code itself. Generally speaking, coding errors can be found in two different styles:

- ❑ **Logic Error:** This is a problem that occurs due to faulty assumptions made in the code – for example, having an if statement that checks two possible conditions, when three conditions actually exist. This would mean that the code will work part of the time, but at other times the if statement will be wrong.

- ❑ **Syntax Error:** We all make spelling mistakes (typos) when we are typing code into a keyboard, which are sometimes overlooked. While these typos might seem to be easy to fix, don't underestimate their power to cause havoc. A common Java typo would be using a simple = within a logical comparison rather than ==.

When facing an error, determining what style of error you are up against is half the battle in solving it. Most programmers have a preferred method of scanning for an error. My own is when an error happens, I usually spend the first 3 minutes verifying the syntax is right; then I switch to reviewing the logic. The point is that the different styles of error require slightly different techniques to solve the problem.

When the error ends up being reported to the programmers it will generally be seen as one of two different formats:

- ❑ **Compilation Error:** Errors can occur during compilation, due to the code not following the necessary language syntax. Fortunately, since the Java compiler points out our error, these compilation errors are usually relatively easy to find and fix, often turning out to be syntax errors.

- ❑ **Run-time Error:** These are errors that occur because the code compiles but does not execute in the manner that was expected. Generally, run-time errors are logic errors. The logic error might be that the data being inputted into the system has changed, causing a breakdown of the system; or maybe, just maybe, we forgot a step while programming. These errors tend to be the hardest to track down since they require a programmer to closely examine the logic in the code. Since the execution of logic can vary depending on conditions within the code, it can be difficult to see all the possible logic conditions that exist.

So part of the confusion comes from the fact that the word error is used interchangeably for many different things. Java helps us by redefining the term **errors** and adding a new term called **exceptions**.

Introducing Exceptions

The heart of dealing with errors within Java is **exception handling**. An exception is when something of note happens which requires extra attention. While it is simple to think of an exception as an error, this is not the case; an exception is not necessarily an error. This is an important distinction as Java presents a methodology for tracking problems, or events, that require extra attention. On many occasions a problem might be something that was unanticipated by the programmer, or a reaction to something which occasionally requires extra work.

The goals of exception handling are:

❑   To provide a way of signaling an error or an unusual event when a program is executed

❑   To provide a mechanism which permits the program to recover, so that it doesn't crash

Java uses a special collection of classes to handle exceptions; these exception classes make it easy to handle problems within Java code. While exception handling makes handling application errors easy, it also allows us to do much more than dealing with a fixed number of possible system errors. In fact, the biggest advantage of Java exceptions is that they permit a programmer to create code that can handle both its own errors and **any** outstanding conditional processing.

Dealing with Exceptions

Now that we have had an introduction to the basic idea of an exception, let's take a quick look at how Java handles exceptions in the code. The goal of this first section is just to introduce the reader to the basic ideas and an example. After that, the chapter will explain in more detail what is happening behind the scenes. The first step is to look at one basic Java class and four Java keywords:

❑   `Exception`: A Java class built to store information about an `"exception"` or `"error"` that happens within the code.

❑   `throws`: When something needs attention then we **throw** an exception. Such an exception is then **caught** by special code that we build to handle the exception. In other words, by throwing an exception we are telling the code that something went wrong and as a result special logic should be called to deal with the problem.

❑   `try`: The `try` statement is used to wrap a block of code which may cause exceptions. This lets us tell Java to pay extra attention to our code block for possible exceptions.

❑   `catch`: Once an exception is thrown it then needs to get **caught**. The `catch` statement lets the programmer define a block of code to capture an exception.

❑   `finally`: At the end of the `try/catch` blocks the program may need to ensure that a block of code *always* get executed, whether an exception was thrown or not. The `finally` block lets us execute some code no matter what happens in the `try/catch` blocks; for example, we might need to make sure that a particular file is closed whatever happens.

Try It Out – Using a try/catch Block

In this example we are going to write a really simple JSP that attempts to display the result of dividing a number by zero. Of course, this is an invalid mathematical operation, so we expect an exception. We'll try it twice: in our first JSP we will just perform the arithmetic, attempt to display the result, and then see what happens. In the second, we will catch the exception and handle it using a `try/catch` block. Here's the first version; create a %CATALINA_HOME%\webapps\begjsp-ch09 folder (and a WEB-INF\classes and WEB-INF\lib folders within it) and save this code in it, as error_no_catch.jsp:

```
<%@page contentType="text/html"%>
<html>
<head><title>JSP Page</title></head>
<body>

<%
   int i = 10;
   int j = 0;
   i = i / j ;

%>

<p> The value of i is <%= i%> </p>

</body>
</html>
```

Here's the second JSP that is a modified version of the first, but with a `try/catch` block added. Save this as error_catch.jsp:

```
<%@page contentType="text/html"%>
<html>
<head><title>Error Introduction</title></head>
<body>

<%
   int i = 10;
   int j = 0;

   try {
      i = i / j ;
   } catch (Exception e) {
      out.print("An error just occurred of the following nature:<br>");
      out.print(e.toString());
   }
%>

<p> The value of i is <%= i%> </p>

</body>
</html>
```

Start Tomcat, then direct your browser to the first JSP, at http://localhost:8080/begjsp-ch09/error_no_catch.jsp. Running the first example reveals the following:

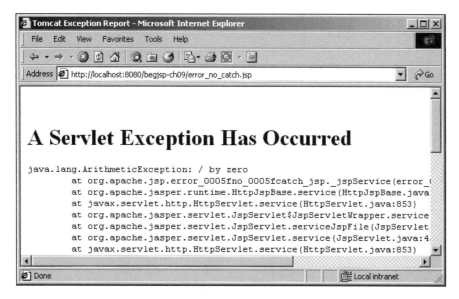

The JSP container will catch the error for us and report it in this rather unfriendly manner. The long message being shown at this point is known as a **stack trace**. This is Java's generic way to let us know something went wrong, and where the error happened within the code; later in the chapter we'll learn how to decipher it.

Now try navigating to the other JSP that includes a `try/catch` block, at http://localhost:8080/begjsp-ch09/error_catch.jsp:

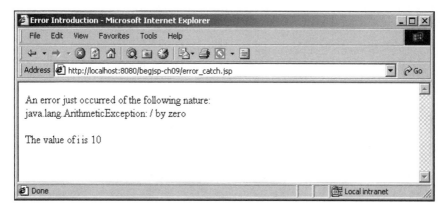

With this JSP, when the exception occurs the flow of execution moves to the `catch` block, where we have a line that prints out the problem to the screen in a much more user-friendly way.

How It Works

These JSP scripts are really simple to understand, so we won't spend a long time discussing them. Jumping straight to the scriptlet in the first JSP, we attempt to perform the invalid arithmetic:

```
int i = 10;
int j = 0;
i = i / j ;
```

At this point the execution of the program stops, and the exception name and stack trace is printed in the browser. We have no control over what is printed, though – this is entirely up to the web server. Turning to our second script, we see that we have placed the logic into a `try` block:

```
try {
  i = i / j ;
```

If an exception occurs (which it does, of course), execution jumps to the `catch` block:

```
} catch (Exception e) {
```

This just prints out a simple error message, and also retrieves the error message stored in the `Exception` object (e) using the `toString()` method, and prints that too:

```
out.print("An error just occurred of the following nature:<br>");
out.print(e.toString());
}
```

Therefore, the advantage of using `try/catch` blocks in this way is that we are able to control the output, and retrieve any messages placed specifically in the `Exception` object.

How Exception Handling Works

It's time to get into how it all works. In the previous section we introduced the `Exception` object and the `throws`, `try/catch`, and `finally` statements. Now let's look at each with a detailed examination of what is happening under the hood of Java.

The exception classes form the first part of the puzzle. These Java objects are the message carriers for keeping track of the problems that do occur within the Java code, and all of these classes have humble roots in the `Throwable` class.

The Throwable Class

All exception classes are subclassed from the `Throwable` class. When an exception is thrown, an object derived from the `Throwable` class is created, and handed to the Java run-time system (the **Java Virtual Machine**, or **JVM**) to handle. This act is known as **throwing an exception**, and is done using the `throw` keyword (not to be confused with `throws`). Only objects that are instances of `Throwable`, or a subclass of `Throwable`, can be thrown in this way.

`Throwable` has two main subclasses: `Exception` and `Error`. Any subclass based on `Error` should deal with non-recoverable errors – in other words, an error condition that would cause program termination. The `Exception` subclass is used to deal with conditions that the programmer can recover from, with the code continuing to execute safely. This chapter concentrates on `Exception`-based events, since `Error`-based exceptions are usually beyond the ability of the code to recover from and are usually handled by the JVM.

The `Throwable` class contains some useful methods that are inherited by all `Exception` classes:

```
public String getMessage()
```

`getMessage()` returns a message, which describes the exception that just occurred.

```
public String toString()
```

`toString()` returns a `String` with a short description of the error. This is the function that is used more than any other for reporting an exception. For example, if we had an `Exception` object e, we could print out the error that the exception represents by using:

```
out.print(e.toString());
```

There is also a `printStackTrace()` method that displays a stack trace of the error, similar to the output seen in the `error_no_catch.jsp` example above. Since generally a JSP programmer is looking to make error messages easy to understand, the `printStackTrace()` method won't be used very often.

Exception classes will usually have a minimum of two constructors: one standard constructor that takes no arguments, and one which takes a `String` argument for the error message used to describe the error. It is good practice to always associate an error message with the exception when possible. For example, we can create a new `Exception` object as follows:

```
Exception my_error = new Exception("On no it's trouble!");
```

This creates a new `Exception` object, called `my_error`, which will contain the descriptive message `"On no it's trouble!"`.

Java already has dozens of exception classes created for our convenience. This is important as it gives us access to many high-quality objects to help capture and deal with exceptions within the code. For example the `SQLException` object is built just to handle SQL (Structured Query Language, used to access data results – see Chapters 15 and 16) database exceptions. This exception object is expanded to deal with the specifics required for working with a SQL error. This means `SQLException` has specific functionality not found in other exceptions, such as the `getErrorCode()` method that returns the database error code. So it's a good idea when working with new Java code or parts of Java you are unfamiliar with, to also review what `Exception` objects are available for your use in the code.

Throwing and Catching an Exception

Throwing an exception in Java is very easy. First we create an `Exception` object (or, indeed, any descendent class of `Throwable`) to encapsulate the nature of the problem. Then we use the `throw` statement to "throw" the exception that was just created. Here's an example:

```
Exception trouble = new Exception("Bad things just happened!");
throw trouble;
```

This could also be written more concisely as:

```
throw new Exception("Bad things just happened!");
```

Catching an exception is just as easy. The code that could cause an exception to be thrown is enclosed in a `try` block; the `catch` statement comes after the `try` block, like this:

```
try {
  // Your code that could throw an exception
} catch(YourException e) {
  // Code to handle the Exception
}
```

Any exception that was just thrown needs to be handled by the code. Two ways exist to handle exception:

❑ **Internally**: Catch the thrown exception within a `try` block, and handle it in a `catch` block.

❑ **Externally**: The method that throws the exception declares that it can do so, using the `throws` clause that we'll see shortly. The exception is then passed back to the method that called this method. If this method doesn't want to deal with the exception either, it can throw it back to the method that called it, and so on.

With either method of handling an exception, Java has a very formal way to pass the exception through the code. We say that exceptions "bubble" up the **stack** at run-time. The stack is the list of method calls that were executed to get to the current code position; when an exception occurs in the one method the exception is able to automatically travel back up a chain of events, "bubbling up" or moving backwards through all the previous nested method calls until it finds some code that can handle the exception.

For example, let's imagine a situation where method a() calls method b(), which then calls method c().

An exception happens in method c(), but instead of dealing with the problem itself method c() throws the exception. So now method b() gets to handle the exception. However, method b() can also choose not to deal with the exception and can instead **rethrow** it. This means that the exception, which happened back in method c(), has been passed all the way back to method a().

In practice this means that when the programmer creates an exception they get the first chance at handling the exception at the time of the error. Once the exception is actually thrown Java transfers control to the first `try`/`catch` block within the code where the exception occurred. If the exception is not handled, it then gets passed back to the method that called the current method. The Java JVM steps backwards through the stack, until either some code handles the exception, or the JVM is forced to deal with the error itself. If the Java JVM is forced to deal with the exception it will terminate the program with a general exception in the form of a stack trace error. It is usually not a good idea to let the JVM handle an error this way, as it is both confusing and unhelpful to general users.

The nice thing about the way exception handling works its way up the chain of `catch` statements is that it lets us rethrow an exception to have an earlier `try`/`catch` block handle the error. This means it is possible to build generalized exception handlers at an early point of our code to handle exceptions in a generic fashion.

If you try to write code that throws an exception without either catching the error yourself, or declaring that the method can throw the exception, you will get a compiler error like the following:

Exception must be caught, or it must be declared in the throws clause of this method

Declaring a method that will throw an exception is a simple matter of using the `throws` keyword in the method declaration. So, for example, we might write:

```
public void validateUser(PageContext page) throws Exception
```

This function is capable of throwing an exception of class `Exception`. A function can however throw more than one type of exception. When this is the case, we just add a comma-separated list of exception classes to the method declaration:

```
public void validateUser(PageContext page) throws Exception, UserException
```

The most important thing about declaring a method in this manner is that this is the *only* indication to other programmers that a function may actually be throwing an exception they need to catch.

Try It Out – Throwing an Exception and Then Catching It

Let's see how this throwing and catching of exceptions works in practice. We'll create a simple HTML form containing fields for the user to enter a username and password; the form will be posted to a JSP that uses a JavaBean to check whether the supplied values are valid. If not, the bean will throw an exception for the JSP page to handle.

We'll start by creating the form page. Save this code as `%CATALINA_HOME%\webapps\begjsp-ch09\throwing_exception.html`:

```
<html>
<head><title>Throwing an Exception</title></head>
<body>
<p> This test page shows how to create a basic exception
    within a Javabean and how to use the exception.</p>


<form action="throwing_exception.jsp" method="post">
  <table>
    <tr>
      <td>Username:</td>
      <td><input name="username" type="text"></td>
    </tr>
    <tr>
      <td>Password:</td>
      <td><input name="password" type="password"></td>
    </tr>
    <tr>
      <td></td>
      <td><input name="submit" value="Log in!" type="submit"></td>
    </tr>
  </table>
</form>
</body>
</html>
```

Next, let's write the JavaBean. Save the code below as `%CATALINA_HOME%\webapps\begjsp-ch09\WEB-INF\classes\com\wrox\errors\User.java`:

```java
package com.wrox.errors;

import java.beans.*;
import javax.servlet.jsp.PageContext;
import javax.servlet.http.HttpSession;
import java.lang.Exception;

public class User extends Object implements java.io.Serializable {

  public User() {}

  private String username;
  private String password;

  public void setUsername(String name) {
    username = name;
  }

  public String getUsername() {
    return username;
  }

  public void setPassword(String pass) {
    password = pass;
  }

  public void validateUser() throws Exception {
    if (!(username.equals("Casey") && password.equals("Kochmer"))) {
      Exception trouble = new Exception("Couldn't validate your password!");
      throw trouble;
    }
  }
}
```

Finally, we create the JSP page that uses the `User` bean; save the code below as `%CATALINA_HOME%\webapps\begjsp-ch09\throwing_exception.jsp`:

```jsp
<%@ page contentType="text/html"%>
<html>
<head><title>Throwing an Exception</title></head>
<body>
<p> This test page shows how to create a basic exception
    within a Javabean and how to use the exception.</p>

<jsp:useBean id="myUser" class="com.wrox.errors.User" scope="page"/>
<jsp:setProperty name="myUser" property="*"/>

<%
   try {
     myUser.validateUser();
```

```
        out.print("The user: " + myUser.getUsername() + " is registered.");
    } catch (Exception e) {
        out.print("We encountered a problem: " + e.toString());
    }
%>
</body>
</html>
```

You will need to compile the `User` class by entering `javac com\wrox\errors\User.java` in the `WEB-INF\classes` directory, and then restart the JSP container. Direct the browser to the form page, http://localhost:8080/begjsp-ch09/throwing_exception.html:

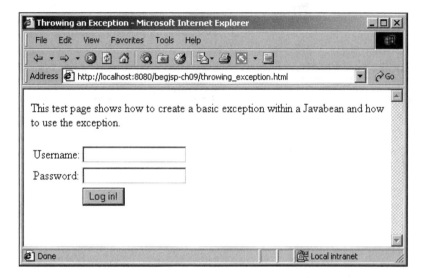

If you enter the username Casey and the password Kochmer (not very imaginative), and click Log in! you should see this screen:

In this case the code ran smoothly with no errors. If on the other hand you entered an incorrect password, you'd see the following:

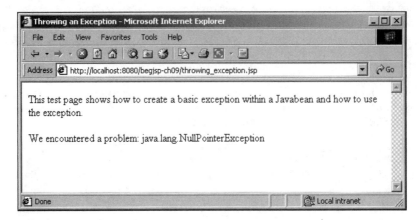

In this second case an exception was thrown by our bean, and is displayed on the screen.

How It Works

The bean is for the most part quite simple: it has setter and getter methods corresponding to the names of the form fields, and these properties will be filed in by the `<jsp:setProperty>` action in the JSP.

The action comes in the `validateUser()` method. If the username and password aren't recognized (and admittedly the password checking is a little primitive in this example) then we create an `Exception` object, with a suitably descriptive message, and throw it. Since `validateUser()` declares that it throws `Exception`, we pass the buck for handling the error condition to the code that calls the method – in other words, to the JSP:

```
public void validateUser() throws Exception {
  if (!(username.equals("Casey") && password.equals("Kochmer"))) {
    Exception trouble = new Exception("Couldn't validate your password!");
    throw trouble;
  }
}
```

The actual code of the JSP page is relatively simple also. First we create an instance of our `User` object using the `<jsp:useBean>` action, and populate its properties using `<jsp:setProperty>`. We then have to check the username and password were recognized, by calling `validateUser()`.

Since calling this method could cause an exception to be thrown, we use a `try/catch` block to capture any exceptions. If everything is fine we write which user was validated, otherwise we report the exception sent to us from the `User` object:

```
<%
  try {
    myUser.validateUser();
    out.print("The user: " + myUser.getUsername() + " is registered.");
  } catch (Exception e) {
    out.print("We encountered a problem: " + e.toString());
  }
%>
```

Catching Multiple Exceptions

So far we've only ever been interested in a single type of exception at a time; the examples were pretty simple, and a single `catch` block quickly captured the exception. However, it is possible that there might be several different types of exceptions requiring action within the code. It is possible to catch many different types of exceptions from a single `try` block. To do so is just a matter of creating a separate `catch` block for each exception you're interested in.

The catching order of multiple exceptions is important: the `catch(...)` clauses must be ordered from the most specific exception (the most distant subclasses of `Exception`) to the least (the `Exception` class). That is, you must catch subclasses of each exception type prior to the type itself. This is important as, if `Exception` was the first type of exception in the list of `catch` blocks, the `Exception` catch block would capture all exceptions because they are *all* subclasses of `Exception`. None of the other `catch` blocks would ever be executed, which is obviously not what we want!

The other fact to consider is once an exception occurs within the `try` block, the code within that block stops executing, and execution then jumps to one of the `catch` blocks to proceed with processing. So, even if you are testing for a hundred different exceptions, only one exception will be processed by a particular pass through a `try/catch` block.

Let's see an example of this.

Try It Out – Catching Multiple Exceptions

One problem with our earlier example occurs if we fail to enter any data in the username or password fields; the relevant JavaBean property value will then be `null`. Let's modify our `User` bean so that it checks for this problem as well.

Save the code below as `User2.java`, in the same folder as the earlier bean:

```
package com.wrox.errors;

import java.beans.*;
import javax.servlet.jsp.PageContext;
import javax.servlet.http.HttpSession;
import java.lang.Exception;

public class User2 extends Object implements java.io.Serializable {

  public User2() {}

  private String username;
  private String password;

  public void setUsername(String name) {
    username = name;
  }

  public String getUsername() {
    return username;
  }

  public void setPassword(String pass) {
```

```
        password = pass;
    }

    public void validateUser() throws Exception, NullPointerException {
        if ((username == null) || (password == null)) {
          NullPointerException trouble = new NullPointerException
                                        ("Must supply a username and password!");
          throw trouble;
        }

        if (!(username.equals("Casey") && password.equals("Kochmer"))) {
          Exception trouble = new Exception("Couldn't validate your password!");
          throw trouble;
        }
    }
}
```

Copy `throwing_exception.html` to `multi_catches_wrong.html` and change the line containing the `<form>` element:

```
<form action="multi_catches_wrong.jsp" method="post">
```

Then, save this file as `multi_catches_wrong.jsp`:

```
<%@ page contentType="text/html"%>
<html>
<head><title>Throwing an Exception</title></head>
<body>
<p> This test page shows how to create a basic exception
    within a Javabean and how to use the exception.</p>

<jsp:useBean id="myUser" class="com.wrox.errors.User" scope="page"/>
<jsp:setProperty name="myUser" property="*"/>

<%
   try {
     myUser.validateUser();
     out.print("The user: " + myUser.getUsername() + " is registered.");
   } catch (Exception e) {
     out.print("We encountered a problem: " + e.toString());
   } catch (NullPointerException e) {
     out.print("We encountered a NullPointerException: " + e.toString());
   }
%>
</body>
</html>
```

Compile the `User2` class, restart Tomcat, and browse to http://localhost:8080/begjsp-ch09/multi_catches_wrong.html. It doesn't work! You should see an error message like this:

org.apache.jasper.JasperException: Unable to compile class for JSPC:\jakarta-tomcat-4.0-
b5\work\localhost\begjsp-ch09\multi_0005fcatches_0005fwrong_jsp.java:99: catch not reached.
        } catch (NullPointerException e) {
        ^

How it Works

What went wrong? Well, when we wrote our code to check for either an `Exception` or a
`NullPointerException`, we put the catch block for `Exception` first:

```
} catch (Exception e) {
  out.print("We encountered a problem: " + e.toString());
} catch (NullPointerException e) {
  out.print("We encountered a NullPointerException: " + e.toString());
}
```

Since Java will always pick the first `catch` block that matches the class of exception that was thrown (that is,
the exception thrown is either that specified in the `catch` block or one of its subclasses), the second block
here (`NullPointerException`) will *never* be reached. `NullPointerException` is a subclass of
`Exception`, so the first `catch` block will always win. The Java environment realizes that this is the case
and prevents us from writing such code.

Try It Out – Catching Multiple Exceptions, Correctly

Let's try again with two new files, `multi_catches.html` and `multi_catches.jsp`.
`multi_catches.html` is virtually identical to `multi_catches_wrong.html`; only the `<form>`
element is different:

```
<form action="multi_catches.jsp" method="post">
```

In `multi_catches.jsp`, we swap the order of the two catch blocks from what we saw earlier:

```
<%@ page contentType="text/html"%>
<html>
<head><title>Throwing an Exception</title></head>
<body>
<p> This test page shows how to create a basic exception
    within a Javabean and how to use the exception.</p>

<jsp:useBean id="myUser" class="com.wrox.errors.User" scope="page"/>
<jsp:setProperty name="myUser" property="*"/>

<%
    try {
      myUser.validateUser();
      out.print("The user: " + myUser.getUsername() + " is registered.");
    } catch (NullPointerException e) {
      out.print("We encountered a NullPointerException: " + e.toString());
    } catch (Exception e) {
      out.print("We encountered a problem: " + e.toString());
    }

%>
</body>
</html>
```

If we request http://localhost:8080/begjsp-ch09/multi_catches.html, fail to enter any form data, and click the button, we should now get the error message as planned:

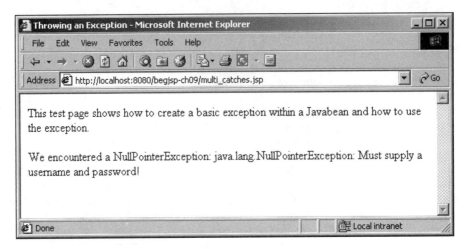

How it Works

Swapping the order of the catch blocks made all the difference:

```
} catch (NullPointerException e) {
  out.print("We encountered a NullPointerException: " + e.toString());
} catch (Exception e) {
  out.print("We encountered a problem: " + e.toString());
}
```

If the code in our `try` block throws a `NullPointerException` the first `catch` block will deal with it; if, on the other hand it threw an `Exception` or any of its other subclasses, the second `catch` block will take case of the consequences.

The finally Clause

The `finally` clause is an important corollary to the `try` and `catch` blocks. It permits Java to execute some code regardless of what happens within the `try/catch` blocks; this ability is critical because it is often necessary to shut down processes properly. For example, when performing database work it is good practice to close down the connection to the database no matter what happens within the code (since database connections tend to be resource intensive and can be limited due to licensing issues). Placing the database connection closing statement within a `finally` clause permits this.

Try It Out – Catching Multiple Exceptions

Let's look at an example. Save the code below as `finally.jsp`, in the `%CATALINA_HOME%\webapps\begjsp-ch09` folder:

```
<%@page contentType="text/html"%>
<html>
<head><title>Using the finally Statement</title></head>
<body>
```

```
<%
   int i = 10000;
   int j = 0;
   try {
     for (j = 5; j > -1  ; j--) {
       i = i / j ;
       out.print("Value of i=");
       out.print(i);
       out.print("<br>");
     }
   } catch (Exception e) {
     out.print("An error just occurred of the following nature:<br>");
     out.print(e.toString());
   } finally {
     /* Reset i to 10000 */
     i = 10000;
   }
%>

<p> The final value of i is <%= i %> </p>
</body>
</html>
```

Point your web browser to http://localhost:8080/begjsp-ch09/finally.jsp. You should see this output:

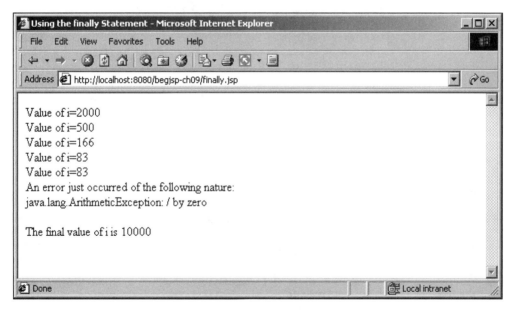

We can see that, despite the `ArithmeticException`, the `finally` clause is always executed and i set to 10000, no matter how or when the code exits the `try/catch` block.

How It Works

The new section of code here is the `finally` block, which comes immediately after the `catch` block:

```
    } catch (Exception e) {
        out.print("An error just occurred of the following nature:<br>");
        out.print(e.toString());
    } finally {
        /* Reset i to 10000 */
        i = 10000;
    }
```

Everything within the `finally` block is executed after the `try/catch` logic – in this case the code reinitializes the variable `i`.

Building New Exceptions

As we mentioned earlier, it is possible to create your own unique exceptions; in fact this is a common thing to do in Java as it permits the programmer to have a reusable and customized `Exception` type to use along with his own code. This is especially important for complicated business objects, which could interface with many different systems. A customized exception would make sure the object wouldn't crash the application when things didn't work right with the external systems.

The other advantage of having a unique `Exception` object is that it makes exception handling easier than using the generic `Exception` object, since the programmer has more control over which exceptions get caught and the error condition can be described in more detail.

Creating an exception is as easy as extending the `Throwable` class, or a subclass of `Throwable` such as `Exception`. The standard coding practice is to extend `java.lang.Exception`. Creating a new `Exception` class is a process with several steps:

1. First extend the `Exception` class.

2. Then, add any new properties. While many times this isn't required, it doesn't hurt to track additional information within the `Exception` object if it would be useful for solving a problem. This can give a `catch` block some additional information to work with when dealing with our exceptions.

3. Create the basic constructors – one with no arguments, and one with a `String` argument – and any additional constructors for special initialisation purposes.

4. Sometimes it is required to modify the new exception's methods that were inherited from the base class. For example, the `toString()` function can be expanded to report on additional properties and other features being tracked by the exception.

5. Add any unique processing or properties required to track and assist the programmer using the `Exception` object just created.

All in all it's pretty simple. Now let's modify our user class to make use of our new `Exception` class.

Try It Out – Building a New Exception Class

Let's create our own `Exception` class for our user object from the previous examples. Enter the code below and save it as `UserException.java`, in the `%CATALINA_HOME%\webapps\begjsp-ch09\WEB-INF/classes/com/wrox/errors` folder:

```
package com.wrox.errors;

public class UserException extends Exception {

  private String userValue = "null";

  public  String getUserValue() {
    return userValue;
  }

  public void setUserValue(String as_value) {
    if (as_value == null) {
      as_value="null";
    }
    userValue = as_value;
  }

  public String toString() {
    return (super.toString() + ": The User is " + this.getUserValue());
  }

  public UserException() {}

  public UserException(String msg) {
    super(msg);
  }

  public UserException(String msg, String as_user) {
    super(msg);
    setUserValue(as_user);
  }
}
```

Now we'll upgrade our user bean to use this new exception class. Save the code below as
`ImprovedUser.java` in the same folder as the `Exception` class:

```
package com.wrox.errors;

public class ImprovedUser extends Object implements java.io.Serializable {

  public ImprovedUser() {}

  private String username;
  private String password;

  public void setUsername(String name) {
    username = name;
  }

  public String getUsername() {
    return username;
  }
```

```
    public void setPassword(String pass) {
      password = pass;
    }

    public void validateUser() throws Exception, NullPointerException {
      if (username == null) {
        throw new UserException("Must supply a username!", null);
      }

      if (password == null) {
        throw new UserException("Must supply a password!", username);
      }

      if (!(username.equals("Casey") && password.equals("Kochmer"))) {
        throw new UserException("Couldn't validate password!", username);
      }
    }
}
```

Now let's pull it all together in the HTML and JSP pages. Our HTML form goes in `custom_error.html`, in the `%CATALINA_HOME%\webapps\begjsp-ch09` folder:

```
<html>
<head><title>Custom Exceptions</title></head>
<body>
<p>This test page shows how to create your own exception class.</p>

<form action="custom_error.jsp" method="post">
  <table>
    <tr>
      <td>Username:</td>
      <td><input name="username" type="text"></td>
    </tr>
    <tr>
      <td>Password:</td>
      <td><input name="password" type="password"></td>
    </tr>
    <tr>
      <td></td>
      <td><input name="submit" value="Log in!" type="submit"></td>
    </tr>
  </table>
</form>
</body>
</html>
```

The JSP that the form sends its data to is called `custom_error.jsp`, and should be saved in the same folder:

```
<%@ page contentType="text/html" %>
<%@ page import="com.wrox.errors.UserException" %>
<html>
<head><title>Custom Exceptions</title></head>
<body>
<p>This test page shows how to create a custom exception class</p>

<jsp:useBean id="myUser" class="com.wrox.errors.ImprovedUser" scope="page"/>
```

```
<jsp:setProperty name="myUser" property="*"/>

<%
   try {
      myUser.validateUser();
      out.print("The user: " + myUser.getUsername() + " is registered.");
   } catch( UserException e) {
      out.print("We had a Exception Problem: " + e.toString());
   }
%>
</body>
</html>
```

Compile these classes as we saw earlier, restart Tomcat, and direct your browser to the HTML page http://localhost:8080/begjsp-ch09/custom_error.html, and click the Log in button without entering anything into the form. You should get the following output:

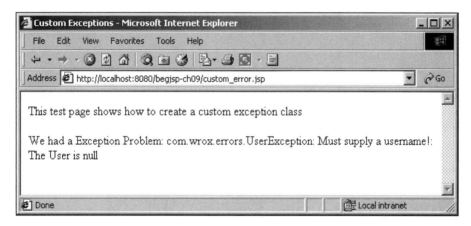

How It Works

The major changes for this example are the new `Exception` object itself. `UserException` extends `Exception`; the first feature of note in this class is the addition of a new property and the corresponding setter/getter methods:

```
private String userValue = "null";

public  String getUserValue() {
   return userValue;
}

public void setUserValue(String as_value) {
   if (as_value == null) {
      as_value="null";
   }
   userValue = as_value;
}
```

This property allows the exception to track information about the user. The second feature of note is that we expanded and added a new constructor method:

```
public UserException(String msg, String as_user) {
    super(msg);
    setUserValue(as_user);
}
```

Within this new constructor we call the parent constructor, and pass in the error string. That done, the second step is to set the new property we created with the user ID that is being passed in. The advantage of building a constructor like this is that it makes using the exception easier; instead of having to call both the constructor and the setter, we can now use one simple call to create the exception. For example, in the `ImprovedUser` class we used this code to create a new `UserException` object:

```
throw new UserException("Couldn't validate password!", username);
```

The last major part to the `UserException` is the overridden `toString()` method:

```
public String toString() {
    return (super.toString() + ": The User is " + this.getUserValue());
}
```

The `toString()` method of the base `Exception` class only reports basic information about the exception – its class and the message – but we would like to include the user value as well. So our version calls the superclass's version using `super.toString()` to get the basic error text, then appends the user value to the end of the error message.

The nice thing with these modifications is that the newly created `UserException` class is very easy to use, with almost no modification of the previous code examples.

Using Exceptions

Now that we've covered the basics of using exceptions, let's examine a number of issues that may not be immediately apparent.

What the Exception Object Tells the World About Itself

While exceptions are great, many `Exception` objects tend not to tell the world much about what just happened. Exceptions should always contain a message about the error they represent. However, many times this is all they have. This means the actual class of the `Exception` object being used can be as important to us as the error message contained within the exception.

As we saw, we can specify in our `catch` clause what particular class of `Exception` we're interested in; making intelligent use of this facility is the key to keeping track of what went wrong. For example when catching only an `Exception` object it is hard to know what the error is, as it can be any exception within Java. It is possible to parse the error message, but this is a bit tedious and not very effective for dealing with unknown types of errors.

However if we specify that we want to catch any `ArrayIndexOutOfBoundsException` that occurs, we know immediately that we've tried to read beyond the end of an array. Therefore, it's important to use the correct class of exception to handle a problem, rather than always using the generic `Exception` class to catch all of the errors. Using specific `Exception` classes makes the code modular, readable, and as a result more maintainable over the long run.

This also means that when creating an `Exception` class you should name it to clearly to identify what problem it is catching. This makes it easier for other programmers to use unique exceptions.

Checked and Unchecked Exceptions

A **checked** exception is an exception that forces the programmer to deal with the exception. In other words, we must either use a `try/catch` block to handle the exception, or declare that our own method can throw that exception. The compiler enforces this rule.

We will deal mainly with exceptions based on the `Exception` class, which are checked exceptions; however, there is a special subclass of `Exception` called `RuntimeException`. When using an exception that is a subclass of `RuntimeException`, the compiler doesn't enforce the normal rules of `Exception` management within the code (in other words, you're not forced to `catch` or `throw` the exception elsewhere). Sometimes this type of exception is also referred to as being an **unchecked** exception.

An example of an unchecked exception is the `ArithmeticException` class, which catches a division by zero error. However, when performing math on variables, a `try/catch` block is rarely used to double-check the math; a `try/catch` block isn't required because `ArithmeticException` is a subclass of `RuntimeException`. Some readers just might have noticed our original example was actually catching an `ArithmeticException` (while we were using the `Exception` class to catch the error, the actual exception generated was `ArithmeticException`). So it is fine to use `try/catch` blocks to capture unchecked exceptions, it just is not required.

Now, before thinking that this is the way to avoid the hassle of using `try/catch` blocks and exception management, please think again. Exception management is an important tool and short cuts around it shouldn't be taken lightly.

There are two cases when using a `RuntimeException` subclass is acceptable:

❑   When the operation being tested is very common indeed, and so the overhead of always performing checked exception management is too costly in terms of performance. Also, from a programming point of view this would be overly burdensome and tedious in coding time; for example, it would be terrible if you had to do a `try/catch` block for each division operation within the code.

❑   When a `RuntimeException` subclass is used for a system error that is not often handled by the programmer and normally wouldn't warrant the time to capture due to the rarity of its occurrence.

The other interesting fact is that when a method throws `RuntimeException` it doesn't have to declare itself as throwing that `RuntimeException`. This means that the function's users won't know from the method signature or documentation that a `RuntimeException` can be thrown.

> **Generally most exceptions you should consider building should be checked exceptions.**

Advantages and Disadvantages of Exceptions

So, in retrospect, here are some key points about exceptions in Java:

❑   Exception management should only be used for conditions that cannot easily be dealt with at the current level of code you are within. Exceptions should never be used just to replace simple conditional `if` logic, because throwing an exception requires creation of new objects and additional processing by the JVM. However, the act of using `try/catch` blocks doesn't adversely affect performance, it's the actual throwing of the exception that causes a performance hit.

❑   A perfect example of when to use an exception would be when connecting to outside resources such as database drivers. At the point of connection, if a driver doesn't exist the code cannot continue, and it doesn't know enough to try anything else. It is logical to throw an exception, so that we can jump back to the previous logical step and determine where to go now that the database connection could not be made.

❑   The nice thing about the Java exception model is that it helps to keep code clean. Exception management is a way to minimize how often a particular problem needs to be addressed within the code, because the error logic is encapsulated within controllable and distinct `try`, `catch`, and `finally` blocks.

❑   Don't overuse the `Exception` class to catch more specific exceptions. While using the `Exception` class to generically catch all possible exceptions is easy, it usually results in the code not having enough information to deal intelligently with more specific exceptions. The advantage of having specific exceptions is the code can be simple and each `catch` block can directly handle the one exception it is geared for.

❑   One advantage of using exceptions is that it gives us a chance to reset objects and roll data back to an original state if something does go wrong. Many programmers will forget to reset objects after an exception occurs.

Error Handling in JSP

Now that we have a basic understanding of how exceptions and errors are handled within Java we can look at how JSP expands the picture. JSP has some additional problems to deal with that a normal Java application doesn't need to worry about, and to this end JSP adds the ability to create an **error page** to centrally handle errors, and also has some methods to communicate status to browsers and other client tools.

JSP Error Pages

A JSP application isn't a single piece of Java code logic, but rather a collection of pages, loosely connected by URL links. While a Java application runs in a very linear fashion, a JSP application's life is a chaotic bouncing from page to page. In this environment we require a method to centralize the error handling, to simplify the programmer's life. To aid in this, JSP permits us to build specialized error pages to handle errors and exceptions.

Error pages are the same as any other JSP page, with one additional implicit object used in the tracking of errors. The big importance of an error page is that it gives JSP a way to define a central place to handle problems. What this means is that, instead of handling an exception *within* the JSP page where the error occurs, JSP permits us instead to go to a generic error-handling page. It is possible to create many different error pages for a single project.

There are four steps to making an error page:

1. Let a JSP page know which error page it should use if something goes wrong. This is done by using the page directive:

```
<%@ page errorPage="error.jsp" %>
```

This directive is set on the page where the error occurs. While this example references error.jsp, a programmer can substitute any JSP intended to be an error page.

2. Building an error page; this could be as simple as a notice saying something went wrong, or a complex analysis of the error. In real life it is common practice to make an error page send the system administrator an e-mail containing a report about the error.

3. On the error page, set the page directive's isErrorPage attribute to true. This attribute tells the JSP container to create the exception implicit object for the error page.

```
<%@ page isErrorPage="true" %>
```

4. Within the error page, the exception implicit object refers to the exception that occurred within the original JSP page and it is possible to query it for information on the error condition.

Try It Out – Creating a JSP Error Page

Let's start by creating a JSP page with an error in it. Save the code below as %CATALINA_HOME%\webapps\begjsp-ch09\simple_error.jsp:

```jsp
<%@ page contentType="text/html" errorPage="handle_errors.jsp" %>

<html>
<head><title>Building a simple error handling page.</title></head>
<body>
<%
  int i = 10;
  i = i / 0;
%>

</body>
</html>
```

Then create the error page; save this code as handle_errors.jsp, in the same folder:

```jsp
<%@ page contentType="text/html"%>
<%@ page isErrorPage="true" %>
<html>
<head><title>Our simple error handling page.</title></head>
<body>
You had an error:<br>
<%= exception.toString() %><br><br>
```

```
Please contact the System Administrator <br>

<p> This a simple error handler page. </p>

</body>
</html>
```

Make sure Tomcat is running, then browse to http://localhost:8080/begjsp-ch09/simple_error.jsp. The following error page gets generated:

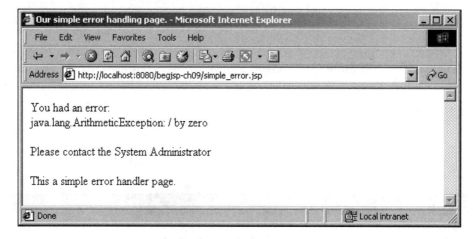

Notice that we are seeing the results of our handle_errors.jsp page while the URL shown is still for the simple_error.jsp example page. This is due to the fact that the JSP container **forwarded** the result to the handle_errors.jsp page – we'll see more about forwarding in Chapter 12.

How it works

On simple_error.jsp the only new thing for us to consider is the following line:

```
<%@ page contentType="text/html" errorPage="handle_errors.jsp" %>
```

The errorPage directive just tells the JSP container that if anything goes wrong it should forward the page to the handle_errors.jsp page.

Moving on to the error page itself, handle_errors.jsp, you should note two things:

❑ We use the page directive isErrorPage="true". This tells the JSP container to build up the exception implicit object for us to use.

❑ We use the exception implicit object to determine what problem did occur. The line of code where this happened was:

```
<%= exception.toString() %><br><br>
```

JSP and Client-Side Errors

Now it's time to take a deeper look into the client half of JavaServer Pages. JSP sits in the middle, converting your server-based logic into HTML and JavaScript code, which will in turn get executed on a remote client (for example, a web browser). This duality of JSP is the toughest part of the learning curve for most new JSP programmers. Part of the difficulty comes from the fact the errors can be from the client-side code, outside of the server-side code being tested, while the JSP page is executing on the server.

While this chapter won't spend a lot of time teaching client-side coding, it will touch upon some of the more important points. A basic problem that many JSP sites face is a mixture of bad client-side design and poor programmer attitude. As it is a server-side language, JSP developers tend to focus on the server side of the application; this results in a lack of understanding of the client side of the JSP project, and that in turn leads to a weakness of the final client-side output. Secondly, the way JSP can mix the logic of the server-side and the client-side code often produces gnarled code for the client. These two factors tend to combine to cause poorly designed HTML, which can cause serious site performance problems.

The other problem comes from the fact that JavaScript errors can just be tricky to track down. The basic truth is if the JSP page fails due to bad client-side code, it doesn't make a difference how good your server-side code was, the JSP page still failed! Keep in mind a JSP page fails right in front of your **customer's** eyes when the client side isn't right!

Make Sure the HTML is Well-Formed

It is important to ensure that the HTML generated by your JSP code is well formed; that is, it must be syntactically valid and use only tags that are implemented in the target browsers. Most importantly, make sure the HTML tags do not cross over each other. Keeping the client-side code well formed by using proper nesting of HTML tags is critical for program execution within the browser: when HTML is not well formed the browser will have unpredictable results, which usually results in the page not being displayed properly for the user. In the past I have seen everything from dropdown boxes not displaying correctly, to form elements appearing randomly at the wrong spot on the screen. The types of errors seen due to malformed HTML are varied and strange to say the least.

For example, here is a snippet of badly-formed HTML:

```
<table><form>
<tr><td>WROX</form>
</td></tr>
</table>
```

Note how the start and end `<form>` and `<table>` tags are improperly nested; that is, they cross over one another. Here is the same script that is rewritten to be well formed:

```
<form>
<table>
<tr><td>WROX</td></tr>
</table>
</form>
```

Two good tools exist to help a programmer validate their HTML output by double-checking the HTML to make sure it is formatted correctly:

❑   **HTML Tidy**, which can be found at http://tidy.sourceforge.net/

❑   The **HTML Validation Service** provided by the W3C organization, at http://validator.w3.org/

One problem with JSP comes from the fact that the client-side code is *dynamically* generated by Java code, making it difficult to check the validity of the HTML whilst viewing the JSP code. When checking client-side HTML, a good way around this problem is to use View | Source option in the browser, and if necessary run that HTML through an HTML checker such as HTML Tidy to spot problems.

Finding JavaScript Errors with Mozilla

JavaScript is an important part of almost any HTML-based JSP application. It permits the programmer to perform logical transactions *within the client machine*. With JavaScript it is possible to check form fields and dynamically change the page. But all this comes at a price: more bugs to fix! In other words, JavaScript errors are another potential source of frustration.

JavaScript can actually be tougher to debug than Java, due to its lack of serious exception handling. Also, JavaScript errors will lead to the page not functioning correctly on the client machine, but due to timing issues the page may actually *seem* like it worked just fine. The reason for this is that when a JavaScript error occurs, the browser stops executing the JavaScript. This will cause different kinds of problems, depending on where the script failed. The page will load the HTML, but only some of JavaScript may have been executed, leaving the page unfinished.

Several low-cost methods exist to help find JavaScript problems. The easiest way to track and solve JavaScript errors is to use the Mozilla browser (Netscape is based upon the Mozilla browser, and will also work in this example), which can be found at http://www.mozilla.org/releases/.

The Mozilla browser has a great JavaScript console window that will show a detailed list of all the JavaScript errors that have occurred on the page. Let's walk through an example showing how to use this feature.

Try It Out – Using Mozilla To Track Down JavaScript Errors

Save the code below as `error_javascript.jsp`, in the `%CATALINA_HOME%\webapps\begjsp-ch09` folder:

```
<%@page contentType="text/html"%>

<html>
<head><title>JavaScript Error</title></head>
<body>

<div id="test">
</div>

<script language="JavaScript">

    var l_doc = document.getElementById("test");
    l_doc.innerHTML = "First line to add  <br>";
    l_d0c.innerHTML = l_div.innerHTML + "Second line to add";
```

```
</script>
<br><br>
In this example there is a JavaScript error.
The error is a typo where l_doc is
spelled as l_d0c. Using the Mozilla JavaScript console
window it is possible to find the error quickly.

<p> Finding JavaScript Errors!</p>
</body>
</html>
```

With Tomcat running, direct the browser to http://localhost:8080/begjsp-ch09/error_javascript.jsp. The result will look like this:

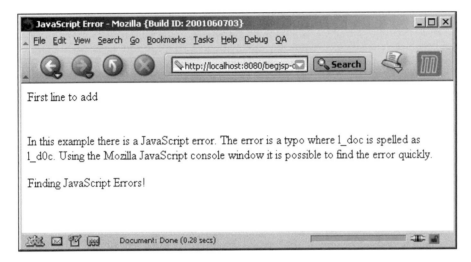

Looking at this, a programmer would be hard-pressed to even see that an error occurred. However, the error does happen, causing a line not to display.

So look for the JavaScript console window under the Tasks menu, under the Tools submenu, listed as JavaScript ConsoleWindow. Selecting this option will give us access to a window that lists all of the JavaScript errors that occurred within the page. It looks like this:

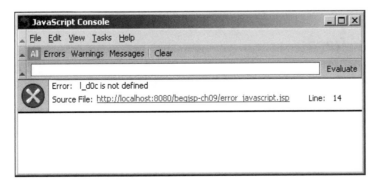

The tool gives us a description of the error itself and the line number of the error. In this case it tells us the code is trying to access a variable that doesn't exist, due to a mistyped variable name.

235

How It Works

The JSP page contains some simple JavaScript, which has one typo within it, mistyping a variable name as `l_d0c` rather than `l_doc`. This one typo isn't enough to stop the page from running, but is just enough to prevent one line of data from getting displayed to the user.

Before showing the output of this example, for programmers new to JavaScript we need to review two lines within this script in a little more detail. The `getElementById()` statement lets us get a handle on a HTML element within the page. Once the code has the handle on the element the JavaScript can then modify it dynamically at run-time:

```
document.getElementById("test");
```

The next line dynamically adds one line to the final page. It uses the `innerHTML()` statement, a powerful statement that lets us replace everything within the HTML tag in question with a new set of data. With this statement it becomes very easy to dynamically modify the HTML page with JavaScript:

```
l_doc.innerHTML = "First line to add  <br>";
```

Then the last line should add another part to the display, but the typo will cause the JavaScript to stop running:

```
l_d0c.innerHTML = l_div.innerHTML + "Second line to add";
```

> Both `innerHTML()` and `getElementById()` only work in the newer browsers.

You can see that it isn't hard to track the client-side errors with Mozilla. It should be mentioned that this method of tracking down JavaScript bugs does have one serious drawback: for developers building an application that is intended to work only in Internet Explorer, it is possible that the code will become incompatible with Mozilla.

Deciphering JSP Errors

When an unhandled JSP error occurs, the message output to the browser can be very confusing, and different JSP containers can handle the display and translation of the error differently. However, in the case of Tomcat, it is possible to walk you through how to translate the error into something more meaningful.

Using the Stack Trace

Earlier in the chapter, when executing the `error_no_catch.jsp` example, the JSP container produced a nice stack trace error. Let's rerun this example and take a closer look at the stack trace error for a moment:

```
java.lang.ArithmeticException: / by zero
    at org.apache.jsp.error_0005fno_0005fcatch_jsp._jspService
    (error_0005fno_0005fcatch_jsp.java:62)
        at org.apache.jasper.runtime.HttpJspBase.service(HttpJspBase.java:107)
        at javax.servlet.http.HttpServlet.service(HttpServlet.java:853)
```

```
at org.apache.jasper.servlet.JspServlet$JspServletWrapper.service(JspServlet.java:200)
at org.apache.jasper.servlet.JspServlet.serviceJspFile(JspServlet.java:379)
at org.apache.jasper.servlet.JspServlet.service(JspServlet.java:453)
at javax.servlet.http.HttpServlet.service(HttpServlet.java:853)
```

The first line tells us which exception was thrown; in this case it is an easy error to determine as it says that it is a "division by zero" error.

Now, the next question is: where did the error occur? As we'll see in Chapter 13, when you run a JSP it is converted into Java code (a servlet), and this is where the error occurred rather than in the JSP page itself. So, the second line is telling us which class the error occurred in: `error_0005fno_0005fcatch_jsp.java`; the line number where the problem happened is line 62.

You can find the compiled Java code in the `%CATALINA_HOME%\work\` folder, under a subfolder corresponding to the URL path of the JSP. So, for the URL http://localhost:8080/begjsp-ch09/error_no_catch.jsp, Java code can be found in `%CATALINA_HOME%\work\localhost\begjsp-ch09\error_0005fno_0005fcatch_jsp.java`. (Notice how the port number, 8080, was *not* included in the name.)

Opening this file and scanning down to line 62, we see the following line:

```
i = i / j ;
```

So, we have enough information to find the line of code causing the problem, and begin to solve it – it should be an easy matter to match the line of Java code to the original JSP file. Within the servlet, comments are embedded in the code indicating exactly which line number and JSP page to look for.

Using Log Files

Our JSP container keeps a log of any events, activities, or problems that occur when we use our JSPs, and this is especially useful when trying to figure out what went wrong for someone accessing the system. Often, users can only give a vague description of a problem, or they will not even alert the system administrator of problems. This makes the log file a very important tool while in pilot and production stages of a project, when users are using the system on a heavy daily basis. Reviewing the log file every once in a while, to keep track of errors that have happened over a period of time, is a good habit to get into for JSP programmers. With this in mind, let's now discuss the basics of a log file.

> **Our examples are all based upon Tomcat 4.0; a different JSP container may maintain the log file in a different directory, and there could be other differences as well.**

In the `%CATALINA_HOME%\conf\` there is the `server.xml` file, within which are the basic configuration settings for each of the web applications being hosted by Tomcat. Let's take a brief look at the section that deals with the `examples` web application (about half-way down `server.xml`):

```
<Context path="/examples" docBase="examples" debug="0"
         reloadable="true">
  <Logger className="org.apache.catalina.logger.FileLogger"
```

```
                   prefix="localhost_examples_log." suffix=".txt"
                   timestamp="true"/>
      <Ejb name="ejb/EmplRecord" type="Entity"
           home="com.wombat.empl.EmployeeRecordHome"
           remote="com.wombat.empl.EmployeeRecord"/>
      <Environment name="maxExemptions" type="java.lang.Integer"
                   value="15"/>
      <Parameter name="context.param.name" value="context.param.value"
                 override="false"/>
      <Resource name="jdbc/EmployeeAppDb" auth="SERVLET"
                type="javax.sql.DataSource"/>
      <ResourceParams name="jdbc/TestDB">
        <parameter><name>user</name><value>sa</value></parameter>
        <parameter><name>password</name><value></value></parameter>
        <parameter><name>driverClassName</name>
                   <value>org.hsql.jdbcDriver</value></parameter>
        <parameter><name>driverName</name>
                   <value>jdbc:HypersonicSQL:database</value></parameter>
      </ResourceParams>
      <Resource name="mail/session" auth="CONTAINER"
                type="javax.mail.Session"/>
      <ResourceParams name="mail/session">
        <parameter>
          <name>mail.smtp.host</name>
          <value>localhost</value>
        </parameter>
      </ResourceParams>
   </Context>
```

While there is quite a bit of information here, only the `<Logger>` element is of concern to us here. From this entry it can be seen that the log file is saved to `localhost_examples_log` with a `.txt` extension. In addition the log file will have a timestamp in the name (`timestamp="true"`). Tomcat maintains a local directory called `\logs\` to store the log files.

A quick peek at the errors stashed within the relevant log file reveals entries like this:

```
2001-06-04 21:52:08 jsp: init
2001-06-04 21:52:08 StandardWrapperValve[jsp]: Servlet.service() for servlet jsp threw exception
java.lang.ArithmeticException: / by zero
    at org.apache.jsp.ack_jsp._jspService(ack_jsp.java:62)
    at org.apache.jasper.runtime.HttpJspBase.service(HttpJspBase.java:107)
    at javax.servlet.http.HttpServlet.service(HttpServlet.java:853)
...
```

First of all we find the initialization and start-up information; for our purposes we can ignore this. The next part of the log file contains timestamp and stack trace of each error that happened within the web application. Note that exceptions that are handled by the code are not in the log file; only unhandled exceptions and errors make it in. Since we have a stack trace, it is possible to use the techniques discussed in the previous section to find the error within the servlet, and then trace back to the JSP.

If we don't set a `<Logger>` for our application, the errors go into a default log file called something like `localhost_log.<date>.txt`; alternatively, we can add a logger for our `begjsp-ch09` application by adding the following entry to the `server.xml` file, immediately after the closing `</Context>` shown above for the `examples` application:

```
      . . .
    </Context>

    <Context path="/begjsp-ch09" docBase="begjsp-ch09" debug="0"
            reloadable="true">
      <Logger className="org.apache.catalina.logger.FileLogger"
              prefix="localhost_wrox_log." suffix=".txt"
              timestamp="true"/>
    </Context>

  </Host>
  . . .
```

Old Fashioned Debugging

Before we end the chapter it is worth discussing several tried and true debugging techniques. Exceptions are a way to handle errors within the code; however, programmers *will* encounter general errors that need to be fixed before the code goes into production. This means some tricks are required to help solve problems that are outside the scope of exception handling:

❏ **Make a logic table:** Many programmers try to keep track of all the possible logic combinations of what the code will do within their head. It is useful at times to create a logic table, which lists all of the possibilities. A logic table is a simple matrix that consists of all the logical possible outcomes that you expect to happen within a block of code, and what data values trigger each logical possibility. Then, once the table is created, it becomes possible to verify each of the possibilities. Often we miss things, and the act of writing it down helps to catch all the possibilities.

❏ **Print the code out:** Looking at the code on the screen often hides errors, as the presentation is the same as when the code was entered into the computer. Looking at the code printed out on a piece of paper gives us a fresh perspective. This is often all it takes to spot an error within the code. When completely stuck this is a great technique, though many times it is used as a last-ditch effort in tracking a bug down.

❏ **Explain the code to someone else:** The simple truth is that we are blind to our own errors. Having someone else looking at the code is often the quickest way to solve a difficult problem. The other advantage to this technique is that it requires a programmer to explain out loud the logic of their code to the person helping solve the problem. Often the explanation of what is happening is enough to help spot the problems in the logic within the code. Some programmers go as far as to talk to inanimate objects when no other people are around; the simple act of talking through the logic and process is a tremendous help in solving problems.

❏ **Use a profiler or debugger:** Writing code is a static process; running code is a dynamic process. As a result, the logic of the code can be elusive when writing. A debugger lets the code run, and the programmer can watch what is happening in real time. A profiler is another piece of software that gathers performance statistics on how the code is running; in other words, it produces a profile of the history of the program as it runs. Using either or both of these tools will help a programmer to quickly spot where bad assumptions were made within the logic. Debuggers are often built into Java **IDEs (Integrated Developer Environment)** and you will have to check your particular tool to see if one is available for your use on your project. A profiler is a separate piece of software usually sold as a commercial product.

Be warned that it does take extra time to learn how to use either a debugger or a profiler properly. However, for professional programmers it is worth both the cost and the time to learn how to use these tools, since using one can save far more time and effort in solving problems.

❑ **Print statements within the code:** Often a snapshot of what is happening in your code is needed to help solve a problem. Debuggers are one way to see what is happening in real time. However, as a programmer it is also simple to add print statements in our own code. This gives the ability to get a better idea of where things stand in your code execution. While this solution won't offer the robustness of a debugger, it is easy to add print statements to the code to get snapshots of what is happening, for example:

```
<% System.out.println("The value of i is " + i); %>
```

Resources

In the quest to solve JSP/Java problems and errors, half of the battle is just knowing where to look. In this section we will provide a list of resources that can help. The following sites have forums or have extensive FAQ lists, which are searchable.

❑ For general questions about Java, try **JavaRanch** (http://www.JavaRanch.com/).

❑ For help on solving HTML problems, **SiteExperts** (http://www.siteexperts.com/) is a great place to ask questions.

❑ For help on tracking down JSP bugs two sites stand out: **JGuru** (http://www.jGuru.com/), which is a useful FAQ site for both Java and JSP, and the **Sun** JSP mailing list archive (http://archives.java.sun.com/archives/jsp-interest.html), which is an excellent place to search for answers.

❑ For help on solving JavaScript problems try **javascript.faqts**, which can be found at http://www.faqts.com/knowledge_base/index.phtml/fid/53/

❑ For general reference materials about JSP and building JSP applications, **JSPInsider** (http://www.jspinsider.com/) is one of the few JSP sites which concentrates on all aspects of building a JSP application.

❑ Finally, when needing additional information about exceptions, then check out **Sun**'s site. Part of the Java Trail has a nice review on exceptions called "Handling Errors with Exceptions", at http://java.sun.com/docs/books/tutorial/essential/exceptions/.

These sites should give a person a solid resource base to turn to when they are having problems debugging JSP and Java code.

Summary

There is a surprising amount to learn in dealing with errors in JSP. The biggest problem comes from the sheer number of types of errors that can exist. From system problems to Java coding errors, from typos in Java to typos in HTML, the variety of possible errors are mind-boggling.

Fortunately, part of JSP's strength is that it is based upon Java. Unlike many of the other server-side web solutions, Java provides JSP with a system of exception handling that allows a programmer to easily handle both errors and unexpected problems, so that we can avoid crashed web pages wherever possible. While this means some additional work during code implementation, the cost saving from using code that is reliable and able to cope intelligently with errors is important for building maintainable sites.

Error handling therefore requires a new way of thinking. Instead of just allowing errors to happen, Java permits us to be proactive and capture problems before they become out-of-control. It requires some time and practice to effectively build exception management into a web-application, but doing so builds a user-friendly and reliable system.

We saw how JSP inherits an elegant system with Java's exception management. It is surprisingly simple, with only five basic keywords: `throw`, `throws`, `try`, `catch`, and `finally`. However, with the addition of the `Throwable` class (and its subclasses) and the ability to add exceptions by creating user-based classes, Java's exception management is very flexible.

We also looked at the challenging environment JSP offers for error handling. With JSP code running on the server, but producing code which will run on a client machine, it presents many areas for things to go wrong. Understanding the nature of JSP is as important for solving problems as using solid exception management based on Java exception management.

Back in Chapter 6 we looked at the concept of JSP **tag libraries**, though there we only considered how we can make use of pre-existing libraries such as the request library from the Jakarta project. We've now learned enough to be able to start writing our very own tag libraries, and that's the subject for the next chapter.

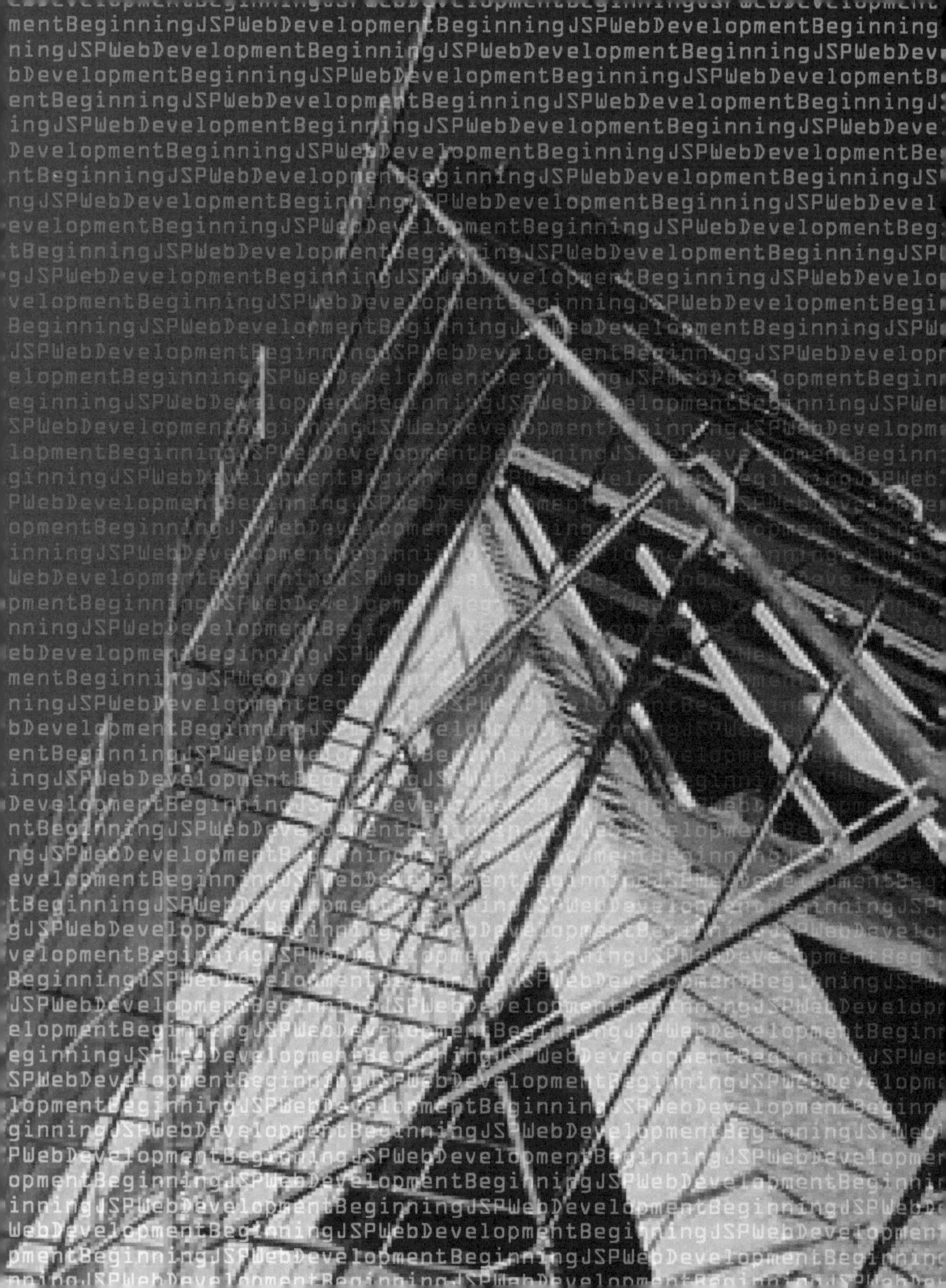

Writing Tag Libraries

We learned in Chapter 6 that custom tags are a great way to include powerful functionality in JSP pages, without littering them with complicated scriptlets. This makes your pages easier to maintain and can provide you with a library of reusable components, a basic tenet of object-oriented programming. An ever-growing range of tag libraries is being created and made freely available for your use but, inevitably, these only cover the most common functions. At some point, you will probably want to create new tags for the specific needs of your web application.

In this chapter we will:

❑   Learn how to create new custom tags

❑   Use cooperating tags

❑   Add attributes to our tags

❑   Create tags with scripting variables

❑   Access variables from the JSP using TEI helper classes

❑   Package a tag library into a JAR file

There will be lots of examples to aid your learning along the way. So let's get started!

Using a Custom Tag Library

Before we jump straight into coding a custom tag, let's have a quick review of what we already know about custom tag libraries. A custom tag library is a special set of tags that may be used within a JSP. Instead of directly being sent to the client, these tags link to some Java code and can perform various custom actions.

A tag library consists of two main components:

❑   A tag library descriptor file – this maps custom tags to their appropriate tag handler classes

❑   The tag handler classes – these contain the code that the tags execute.

Take, for example, the code in the following JSP:

```
<% @ taglib uri="exampleTags" prefix="example" %>
<html>
  <head></head>
  <body>
    Welcome to my web page. The current time is <example:time /> .
  </body>
</html>
```

The majority of this code is plain HTML, which will be sent to the client and ignored by the JSP container. The important things to the JSP container are the `taglib` directive and the custom tag `<example:time />`.

```
<% @ taglib uri="exampleTags" prefix="example" %>
```

The `taglib` directive contains two parts, a uniform resource indicator (`uri`) used to locate the tag library descriptor file, and the `prefix` that will be applied to all the custom tags in this JSP. The `prefix` can be any arbitrary string of characters except for a few reserved words (`jsp`, `jspx`, `java`, `javax`, `servlet`, `sun`, and `sunw`).

After the `taglib` directive we can still code as before, but now tags with the `example` prefix have a special meaning. Below is the line from the example code where the custom tag is used:

```
Welcome to my web page. The current time is <example:time /> .
```

The text will be sent directly to the client in the usual way; however, when the container reads a tag prefixed with `example` this is mapped to a **tag handler**. The tag handler will in turn execute your Java code, accomplishing some custom task. For the purposes of this mock example let us assume the custom tag time will return the current time to the container. A web browser that views this page will be sent the following HTML:

```
<html>
  <head></head>
  <body>
    Welcome to my web page. The current time is 13:06:00.
  </body>
</html>
```

The web browser will display the following:

Welcome to my web page. The current time is 13:06:00.

From this introduction, there are a few key points to remember about how custom tags work:

❑   A custom tag library is declared in a JSP by using the `taglib` directive. This directive must use a valid URI that points to the tag library descriptor. The tag library descriptor file links the tag handlers to each custom tag.

❑   After the `taglib` directive, custom tags can be used with the prefix supplied in the `taglib` directive. These tags all have the same prefix but different names. In our example the tag prefix was `example` and the tag name `time`. Each name will be mapped to a custom tag handler object provided by a tag developer.

❏   Custom tags are server-side, just like the rest of your JSP code. Clients don't see the custom tag itself, but instead see something produced by the tag, commonly HTML.

We will now start learning the steps needed to create the time tag we used in this introduction.

Building a Custom Tag

There are two stages to implementing a custom tag. A tag handler class must be created, and it is then mapped to its corresponding custom tag using a tag library descriptor file.

All tag handlers must support certain methods, the most important being doStartTag() and doEndTag(). When the starting tag (for instance <example:time>) is read, the container calls a tag handler's doStartTag() method. When the corresponding closing or end tag (</example:time>) is read, the container calls the doEndTag() method. In general creating a tag handler is nothing more than defining custom code to be executed for each of these methods.

To make sure the tag handler object contains all of the correct methods, it must implement a tag handler interface. The JSP 1.2 specification provides three tag handler interfaces:

❏   Tag

❏   IterationTag

❏   BodyTag

We'll create our first custom tag using the Tag interface.

The Tag Interface

The Tag interface is the base tag handler interface that defines the methods required by all tag handlers. The interface requires six methods: doStartTag(), doEndTag(), getParent(), setParent(), release(), and setPageContext(). Often though, you will only want to implement one or two of these methods in your tag handler class. Fortunately, there is a helper class, TagSupport, which already implements the Tag interface. If our tag handler class extends TagSupport, we only have to implement the methods we need to achieve our aim.

When we extend the TagSupport class, the two methods that we normally override relate to the JSP reading the custom tag.

When the starting tag is encountered, the doStartTag() method is called; the return value of this method determines what is done next. Valid return values include EVAL_BODY_INCLUDE or SKIP_BODY. Returning EVAL_BODY_INCLUDE will cause the tag body content to be evaluated and available for use in your tag handler. If SKIP_BODY is returned, the tag's body is skipped, so it should be used on tags that do not have a body, or tags where we don't want the body evaluated. We will see in later sections that the doStartTag() method can return other values too.

When the end tag is encountered, the `doEndTag()` method is called. If you have an empty tag, this method is still called, but will be called straight after `doStartTag()`. Valid return values for this method are `EVAL_PAGE` or `SKIP_PAGE`. If the `doEndTag()` method returns `EVAL_PAGE`, execution of the JSP continues as normal after the custom tag. However, if `doEndTag()` returns `EVAL_PAGE` the JSP will stop after evaluating the custom tag. This means the rest of your JSP will be completely skipped. Be cautious when returning this value, because code appearing after the tag will not be used.

The Tag Library Descriptor File

We know from the introduction to this chapter that tag handlers do not magically link to custom tags. The linking mechanism is a **Tag Library Descriptor** (TLD) file. A TLD file looks something like this:

```
<?xml version="1.0" encoding="ISO-8859-1"?>
<!DOCTYPE taglib PUBLIC
            "-//Sun Microsystems, Inc.//DTD JSP Tag Library 1.2//EN"
            "http://java.sun.com/dtd/web-jsptaglibrary_1_2.dtd">
<taglib>
...
</taglib>
```

A TLD is an XML document that describes your custom tag library. Don't worry if you have never used XML before. The parts of the TLD used throughout this chapter are introduced as they appear.

The first part of a TLD is always the same. To be compliant as an XML document the first line is always the XML declaration.

```
<?xml version="1.0" encoding="ISO-8859-1"?>
```

The next line starts the tag that links the XML document to a definition and validation mechanism for a TLD. It also will be the same for every JSP 1.2 TLD file.

```
<!DOCTYPE taglib PUBLIC
            "-//Sun Microsystems, Inc.//DTD JSP Tag Library 1.2//EN"
            "http://java.sun.com/dtd/web-jsptaglibrary_1_2.dtd">
```

The root element defined for a tag library descriptor is `<taglib>`. The `<taglib>` element must appear after the two default headers and must surround the rest of the elements describing our tag library.

```
<taglib>
...
</taglib>
```

You may find that the official DTD online, and the explanation of it in the JSP documentation are both pretty cryptic, so at this point we will discuss the elements that you will find in a typical TLD.

Inside the `<taglib>` element you must include a few more elements to describe your tag library. Here is a list of important `<taglib>` subelements that you must specify.

Element	Description
`<tlib-version>`	The version of the tag library implementation. This is arbitrary and set by the developers of the tag library.
`<jsp-version>`	The version of the JSP specification that the tag library depends upon.
`<short-name>`	A short, easy-to-remember name for this taglib.
`<uri>`	A URI that uniquely identifies this taglib.
`<display-name>`	A short name for the taglib, that is intended to be displayed by tools.
`<tag>`	Holds information about a single tag in this tag library. If you have more than one tag, use as many `<tag>` elements as needed.
`<description>`	A string describing the purpose of the tag library.

Let's now take a closer look at the information that is specified in the `<tag>` element.

The <tag> Element

Each custom tag must have a `<tag>` element linking it to a custom tag handler. All `<tag>` elements must at least contain the two subelements `<name>` and `<tag-class>`, and no two tags may have the same name. For example:

```
<taglib>
    ...
  <tag>
    <name>time</name>
    <tag-class>com.wrox.ch10.timeTag</tag-class>
  </tag>
</taglib>
```

The `<tag>` element has additional subelements for further information; again only the most important ones are listed.

Element	Required	Description
name	Yes	A unique name for the tag. This name corresponds directly to the element name of the custom tag in your JSP.
tag-class	Yes	The tag handler class that implements the `Tag`, `IterationTag`, or `BodyTag` interface.
tei-class	No	An optional Tag Extra Info class for the tag, that must be a subclass of `TagExtraInfo`. We will discuss the use of Tag Extra Info classes later in the chapter.

Table continued on following page

Element	Required	Description
display-name	Yes	A short name for the tag, that is intended to be displayed by tools.
description	No	A short description of this tag.
attribute	No	Information about an attribute used by the tag. We will be covering the use of attributes in tags later in the chapter. If the tag uses more than one attribute, use as many <attribute> elements as are needed.
variable	No	Creates a scripting variable that can be used by the tag. We will explain the use of scripting variables later in the chapter.

Now we know the basics of what we need to do, let's create a simple custom tag for ourselves.

Try It Out - Extending TagSupport To Create a Simple Tag

We'll create a simple tag, which can be used to print out the current time in a JSP. The first thing to create is the tag handler class.

Start your editor and enter the following code:

```
package com.wrox.ch10;

import javax.servlet.jsp.tagext.*;
import javax.servlet.jsp.*;
import java.text.SimpleDateFormat;

public class timeTag extends TagSupport {

  public int doEndTag() throws JspException {
    SimpleDateFormat sdf;
    sdf = new SimpleDateFormat("HH:mm:ss");
    String time = sdf.format(new java.util.Date());
    try {
      pageContext.getOut().print(time);
    } catch (Exception e) {
      throw new JspException(e.toString());
    }
    return EVAL_PAGE;
  }
}
```

Save this as timeTag.java in the webapps\begjsp-ch10\WEB-INF\classes\com\wrox\ch10\ directory of Tomcat.

Compile the timeTag class using the command below, from within the classes folder. You will need to include servlet.jar in your CLASSPATH when you are compiling tag handler classes. If you are using Tomcat, servlet.jar can be found at %CATALINA_HOME%\common\lib\servlet.jar.

```
> javac com\wrox\ch10\timeTag.java
```

Now we must create the tag library descriptor file:

```xml
<?xml version="1.0" encoding="ISO-8859-1"?>
<!DOCTYPE taglib PUBLIC
                "-//Sun Microsystems, Inc.//DTD JSP Tag Library 1.2//EN"
                "http://java.sun.com/dtd/web-jsptaglibrary_1_2.dtd">
<taglib>
  <tlib-version>1.0</tlib-version>
  <jsp-version>1.2</jsp-version>
  <short-name>ExampleTags</short-name>
  <description>A set of example tag handlers.</description>
  <tag>
    <name>time</name>
    <tag-class>com.wrox.ch10.timeTag</tag-class>
  </tag>
</taglib>
```

Save this as `exampleTags.tld` in the `webapps\begjsp-ch10\WEB-INF\` directory of Tomcat.

Now we'll create the JSP page that will use our new custom tag:

```jsp
<%@ taglib prefix="example" uri="WEB-INF/exampleTags.tld" %>
<html>
  <head></head>
  <body>
    Welcome to my web page. The current time is <example:time />
  </body>
</html>
```

Save the code above as `currentTime.jsp` in the `webapps\begjsp-ch10\` directory of Tomcat.

Start up Tomcat and navigate to http://localhost:8080/begjsp-ch10/currentTime.jsp. Your browser should display something similar to this:

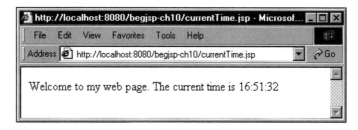

Try refreshing the browser, to see if the time updates, showing that the tag is working.

How It Works

We begin by writing a handler class, `timeTag`, that extends `TagSupport`. To implement your own code you must override the methods from `TagSupport`.

Recall that doEndTag() is called when the JSP container reaches the ending custom tag. For this class we override the doEndTag() method to have our custom code. The other methods will be left as is. For simple tags, TagSupport already does a great job implementing them.

```
public int doEndTag(){
  ...
  return EVAL_PAGE;
}
```

The code that outputs the current time is placed within the doEndTag() method. To generate the time we create a new instance of the java.text.SimpleDateFormat class, specifying the time format to be "hours:minutes:seconds".

```
SimpleDateFormat sdf;
sdf = new SimpleDateFormat("HH:mm:ss");
```

The current time is passed to SimpleDateFormat's format() method by creating a new instance of the java.util.Date object and the formatted date is stored in the string time.

```
String time = sdf.format(new java.util.Date());
```

Next, we print the current time:

```
pageContext.getOut().print(time);
```

Unlike in a JSP page, the out implicit object (used to send output to the client) is not directly available to our tag, so we can't just write out.print(). Instead, we use the PageContext object, which provides convenient access to implicit JSP objects. We can access the implicit out object via the PageContext object's getOut() method. You should note that inside a tag, access to any of the implicit objects is achieved by calling a similar getter method on pageContext.

Now let's look at the TLD file. The first two elements are required by all TLD files and specify that it is an XML document:

```
<?xml version="1.0" encoding="ISO-8859-1"?>
```

The next line specifies the document type; in this case a TLD, conforming to the JSP 1.2 specification. This is followed by the opening <taglib> element:

```
<!DOCTYPE taglib
          PUBLIC "-//Sun Microsystems, Inc.//DTD JSP Tag Library 1.2//EN"
          "http://java.sun.com/dtd/web-jsptaglibrary_1_2.dtd">
<taglib>
```

Each TLD must have the <tlib-version> and <jsp-version> elements. These correspond to the version of your tag library and the required JSP version to implement it respectively.

```
<tlib-version>1.0</tlib-version>
<jsp-version>1.2</jsp-version>
```

The `<short-name>` and `<description>` elements provide a little more information about your tags. These values are arbitrary and provide a unique name for your tag library along with a description of the tag's functionality.

```
<short-name>ExampleTags</short-name>
<description>A set of example tag handlers.</description>
```

The element of the most significance is `<tag>`. Each `<tag>` element appearing inside your TLD links a unique `name` to a tag handler class. The value of the `name` attribute will later be used by a JSP as the element in a custom tag. The `<tag-class>` element requires the value of your tag handler class.

```
<tag>
  <name>time</name>
  <tag-class>com.wrox.ch10.timeTag</tag-class>
</tag>
</taglib>
```

Now we have a complete TLD for our newly made custom tag. As the chapter progresses we will add new types of elements to the same TLD and extend the same custom tag library.

The code we used for our JSP is almost identical to the first mock example but with one thing modified, the `uri` attribute has been changed to the actual URI of our TLD file.

```
<%@ taglib prefix="example" uri="WEB-INF/exampleTags.tld" %>
<html>
  <head></head>
  <body>
    Welcome to my webpage. The current time is <example:time />
  </body>
</html>
```

The prefix attribute is arbitrary and may be changed. This being our example set of tags the `"example"` prefix seemed appropriate. The element name after the colon in our tag must match up with one of the tag entries in your TLD. The output from this JSP was the same as described in our original mock example.

Real Time/Date Tags

On a side note, this example was inspired by an actual set of commonly used JSP tags. Even though this first example is not the most complex of custom tags, it still simplifies a common task and aids a JSP developer. We will continue to improve on this tag in the next section, but if you are interested in seeing a fully-fledged time/date tag library the Jakarta DateTime Taglib can be found at: http://jakarta.apache.org/taglibs/doc/datetime-doc/intro.html.

The IterationTag Interface

The `IterationTag` interface is very similar to the `Tag` interface, but is used when a custom tag needs to repeatedly re-evaluate its body. Usually this functionality is used to loop (iterate) through a collection of objects without using a scriptlet. The `IterationTag` accomplishes the looping by extending the `Tag` interface and implementing a new method, `doAfterBody()`. This method is only called if `EVAL_BODY_INCLUDE` is returned from the `doStartTag()`.

This `doAfterBody()` method is called after the body of a tag is evaluated. The return value of this method will determine if the body should be evaluated again. If `doAfterBody()` returns the value `EVAL_BODY_AGAIN`, then the body should be evaluated again. After evaluation `doAfterBody()` is invoked again, and again, until `SKIP_BODY` or `EVAL_BODY_INCLUDE` is returned.

Creating a tag handler that implements `IterationTag` is done by extending `TagSupport` as we did with the `Tag` interface.

Try It Out – Iterating Over a Collection of Objects Using a Custom Tag

Demonstrating the `IterationTag` interface's functionality can best be accomplished with a small example. In it we will loop through a collection of objects and display some information about each one. For simplicity we will create our own static array of strings to loop through and in this sense the example is slightly contrived. In most practical uses involving JSP pages you would iterate over a dynamically generated collection, because a simple HTML web page can easily display static content.

The point to take away from this example is how the basic looping mechanism works with custom tags. Later on in the chapter we will improve the example to implement additional features of custom tags.

Save the following tag handler code as `iterateTag.java` in the `webapps/begjsp-ch10/WEB-INF/classes/com/wrox/ch10` directory of Tomcat.

```
package com.wrox.ch10;

import javax.servlet.jsp.*;
import javax.servlet.jsp.tagext.*;

public class iterateTag extends TagSupport{
  private int arrayCount = 0;
  private String[] strings = null;

  public int doStartTag(){
    strings = (String[]) pageContext.getAttribute("strings");
    return EVAL_BODY_INCLUDE;
  }

  public int doAfterBody() throws JspException{
    try{
      pageContext.getOut().print(" " + strings[arrayCount] + "<BR>");
    } catch(Exception e){
      throw new JspException(e.toString());
    }
    arrayCount++;
    if(arrayCount >= strings.length) {
      return SKIP_BODY;
    }
    return EVAL_BODY_AGAIN;
  }
}
```

Be sure to compile the new code.

Edit the `exampleTags.tld` file to include the new tag handler.

```
<taglib>
  <tlib-version>1.0</tlib-version>
  <jsp-version>1.2</jsp-version>
  <short-name>ExampleTags</short-name>
  <description>A set of example tag handlers.</description>
  <tag>
    <name>time</name>
    <tag-class>com.wrox.ch10.timeTag</tag-class>
  </tag>
  <tag>
    <name>iterate</name>
    <tag-class>com.wrox.ch10.iterateTag</tag-class>
  </tag>
</taglib>
```

Now we create a JSP that uses the new tag. Notice that the size of the static array can be as large as needed. The code is flexible enough to loop until the end of the array, and would work for any number of objects in the array.

Be sure to save `iterateTag.jsp` (below) in the `webapps/begjsp-ch10` directory of Tomcat.

```
<%@ taglib prefix="example" uri="WEB-INF/exampleTags.tld" %>
<html>
  <head></head>
  <body>
<%
  String[] strings = new String[]{ "Alpha", "Bruce Lee", "Omega" };
  pageContext.setAttribute("strings",strings);
%>
 <example:iterate>
   The string is:
 </example:iterate>
  </body>
</html>
```

Start or restart Tomcat and browse to http://localhost:8080/begjsp-ch10/iterateTag.jsp.

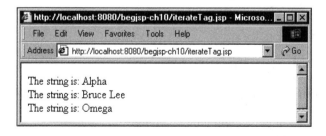

How It Works

The above example takes what we already know about tag handlers and demonstrates using the `doAfterBody()` method. The tag handler, `iterateTag.java`, was created in the same fashion as `timeTag.java` by extending the `TagSupport` object.

```
public class iterateTag extends TagSupport{
```

In this example our collection of objects is going to be an array of strings. Some variables are declared for the array, as well as an integer variable to track our position in the array.

```
private int arrayCount = 0;
private String[] strings = null;
```

The `doStartTag()` method is overridden to load an array of strings from the current `PageContext` object. This tag will depend on the array previously being set in the `PageContext` before being used. Later we will address this issue. For now notice the return value for the `doStartTag()` method. The value of `EVAL_BODY_INCLUDE` tells the custom tag to evaluate the contents of its body and send the results to the client. More importantly the custom tag will then invoke the `doAfterBody()` method to see what should be done next.

```
public int doStartTag(){
  strings = (String[]) pageContext.getAttribute("strings");
  return EVAL_BODY_INCLUDE;
}
```

The `doAfterBody()` method is where the magic happens. This method gives us the option of telling the tag to evaluate its body again. In this example we want to loop through each value of the array and print it out. The code inside the `doAfterBody()` method prints out the current item in the array and then increments the `count` value. If the `arrayCount` value is now larger than the array, the method returns `SKIP_BODY` and will not loop again. If the `arrayCount` value is smaller than the length of the array, the method returns `EVAL_BODY_AGAIN` and will loop through at least one more time.

```
public int doAfterBody() throws JspException{
  try{
    pageContext.getOut().print(" " + strings[arrayCount] + "<BR>");
  } catch(Exception e){
    throw new JspException(e.toString());
  }
  arrayCount++;
  if(arrayCount >= strings.length) {
    return SKIP_BODY;
  }
  return EVAL_BODY_AGAIN;
}
}
```

The logic behind the new tag handler is simple. All we are trying to accomplish is to use the newly-learned `doAfterBody()` method to loop through the tag a few times while evaluating the body.

The change in `exampleTags.tld` is nothing more than adding in a tag element to represent the new tag handler.

```
<tag>
  <name>iterate</name>
  <tag-class>com.wrox.ch10.iterateTag</tag-class>
</tag>
```

Once the tag handler and TLD are done the tag is ready for use in a JSP. In our example, we made a simple page that does two main things. First an array of strings is created for the custom tag, and then the `strings` property of the `pageContext` object is set to the value of the `strings` array.

```
<%@ taglib prefix="example" uri="WEB-INF/exampleTags.tld" %>
<html>
  <head></head>
  <body>
<%
  String[] strings = new String[]{ "Alpha", "Bruce Lee", "Omega" };
  pageContext.setAttribute("strings",strings);
%>
```

The second part of the JSP is using the new tag. The tag does not require a body, but we can optionally include some code to be evaluated with each item in the array. For this example we just display a little text before each array entry.

```
<example:iterate>
  The string is:
</example:iterate>
  </body>
</html>
```

The resulting page had the text repeated once per item along with each of the strings in the array.

The BodyTag Interface

`BodyTag` is the largest and most versatile of the three tag interfaces. The `BodyTag` interface extends `IterationTag` and provides functionality to manipulate its body contents. To fully understand the `BodyTag` interface we first need to introduce the `javax.servlet.jsp.tagext.BodyContent` object.

The `BodyContent` object holds the results from evaluating the body of our custom tag. `BodyContent` has methods for clearing its contents, reading its contents and converting the contents to a `String`. We can manipulate the `BodyContent` object each time we loop around and re-evaluate the body of your tag. This continues as long as needed and ends when `SKIP_BODY` is returned.

Do not imagine that `BodyTag` and `IterationTag` interfaces are identical. With `IterationTag`, you are restricted in the changes you can make to the content of the body. With `BodyTag`, there is no such restriction; changes can be stashed in a `BodyContent` object and used as you wish.

One new method is available in the `BodyTag` interface: `doInitBody()`.This method is invoked after the `doStartTag()` method is called, and only if the value `EVAL_BODY_BUFFERED` is returned by `doStartTag()`. In this case, a new `BodyContent` object will be created for storing the results of the tag's body. The `BodyContent` object will then be used and evaluated again.

Another pre-built object exists named `BodyTagSupport`. The `BodyTagSupport` class is used when coding a tag handler that implements the `BodyTag` interface. In a similar way to how we previously extended the `TagSupport` object, we can also extend the `BodyTagSupport` object to make a tag handler:

```
public class exampleTag extends BodyTagSupport{
  ...
}
```

255

Actually needing the flexibility of the `BodyTag` interface is another story. For most basic tags, and all of the examples in this chapter, extending the `TagSupport` object is fine. Implementing the more complex features of custom tag libraries can easily fill a book in itself. We will now finish this section with a small discussion of a possible use of the `BodyTag` interface and a link to code that matches.

Using the BodyTag Interface

Accessing the body content can be a very powerful tool for a JSP developer. Consider if you purchased software for an online forum. The software works well but you soon discover that the built-in profanity filtering doesn't work. Unfortunately the company you purchased from recently went bust so you are now stuck with a forum littered with profanities. A solution to this problem can be found in a small tag library.

The main tags of this library wrap an entire JSP page and implement the `BodyTag` interface. To accompany the tags you create a list of all the undesired words to filter. The tags work by processing their body once per word on the list. Whenever the current undesired word is encountered, it is replaced by a series of asterisks. After filtering the body content completely the results are saved and sent back to the client.

Because of the `BodyTag` interface you now have a simple solution to the problem. The profanity filter tags can also be reused on any JSP project with content that needs filtering. Manipulating the body of a tag is a powerful tool and a valuable advanced feature of custom tag libraries.

Below is an example of the type of code where you might use such a filter. In this case the filter searches for all occurrences of the word "Damn" and replaces it with "****". In this example the text to filter is hard-coded into the JSP but in principle the filter could be applied to text dynamically included.

```
<html>
<head>
  <title>Profanity Filter Example</title>
</head><body>
  <h1>Profanity Filter</h1>
  <%@ taglib uri="/exampleTags.tld" prefix="example" %>
  <example:profanityfilter>
    <p>
    Some text to filter: Damn!
    </p>
    <p>
    With a Damn and another Damn!
    </p>
  </example:profanityfilter>
</body></html>
<html>
```

The HTML passed to the client would look something like this:

```
<head>
  <title>Profanity Filter Example</title>
</head><body>
  <h1>Profanity Filter</h1>
    <p>
    Some text to filter: ****!
    </p>
```

```
      <p>
      With a **** and another ****!
      </p>
</body></html>
```

As you can see the content of the strings in the JSP has been modified.

Although the `BodyTag` interface is potentially very powerful, its implementation is a complicated subject, and the reader is referred to more advanced texts for further information. For instance, see Chapter 10 of "*Professional JSP 2nd Edition*", *Grant Palmer et al., Wrox Press, ISBN 1861004958.*

Simple Cooperating Tags

Creating a helper tag can be very beneficial for a JSP developer. Dumping all of the functionality inside one tag is not always good object-orientated programming and is not a limitation of custom tags. Also moving a commonly repeated scriptlet into a custom tag is generally desired for easy maintenance of the code. In our example, we can illustrate the above points by placing the script generating our static array into a custom tag. Should we later need to use this array across many pages, the custom tag would be an ideal option.

In general, when two or more tags function together they are referred to as **cooperating tags**. Our next example will illustrate one of the simplest cases where the two tags indirectly work together. The second tag will be the same iteration tag we just made. The first tag will handle the job of creating the array of strings.

Try It Out – Building a Set of Cooperating Tags

Here is the code for the new tag handler to replace the array-creating scriptlet we used in `IterationTag.jsp`. Save this code as `createArrayTag.java` in the `webapps/begjsp-ch10/WEB-INF/classes/com/wrox/ch10` directory of Tomcat.

```
package com.wrox.ch10;

import javax.servlet.jsp.tagext.*;

public class createArrayTag extends TagSupport {

  public int doStartTag() {
    String[] strings = new String[] {"Alpha", "Bruce Lee", "Omega"};
    pageContext.setAttribute("strings", strings);

    return SKIP_BODY;
  }
}
```

Be sure to compile the new code.

Now edit `exampleTags.tld` to now include the new tag handler. The tag handler will be linked to the `<createArray>` custom tag.

```
<?xml version="1.0" encoding="ISO-8859-1"?>
<!DOCTYPE taglib PUBLIC
```

257

```
                        "-//Sun Microsystems, Inc.//DTD JSP Tag Library
    1.2//EN"
                        "http://java.sun.com/dtd/web-jsptaglibrary_1_2.dtd">
    <taglib>
      <tlib-version>1.0</tlib-version>
      <jsp-version>1.2</jsp-version>
      <short-name>ExampleTags</short-name>
      <description>A set of example tag handlers.</description>
      <tag>
        <name>time</name>
        <tag-class>com.wrox.ch10.timeTag</tag-class>
      </tag>
      <tag>
        <name>iterate</name>
        <tag-class>com.wrox.ch10.iterateTag</tag-class>
      </tag>
      <tag>
        <name>createArray</name>
        <tag-class>com.wrox.ch10.createArrayTag</tag-class>
      </tag>
    </taglib>
```

Finally, modify `iterateTag.jsp` to use the new cooperating tags instead of the tag and scriptlet combination.

```
<%@ taglib prefix="example" uri="WEB-INF/exampleTags.tld" %>
<html>
  <head></head>
  <body>
  <example:createArray/>
  <example:iterate>
    The string is:
  </example:iterate>
  </body>
</html>
```

Browse to `iterateTag.jsp`. You will see we still get the same results, but the two tags now cooperate:

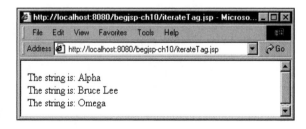

How It Works

No new concepts were needed in making the `<createArray>` tag. Instead we needed a tag for some functionality and knew exactly how to create the tag handler. In the tag handler code the only method overridden was `doStartTag()`.

The custom code does the same thing as the scriptlet used to. An array is created and stashed inside the current `PageContext` object.

```
public int doStartTag(){
   String[] strings = new String[]{ "Alpha", "Bruce Lee", "Omega" };
   pageContext.setAttribute("strings",strings);

   return SKIP_BODY;
   }
}
```

The modifications to `exampleTags.tld` should be easily recognized. The new tag handler code needs to have a new tag element in the TLD file. The TLD file maps the name to the `createArray` custom tag.

```
<tag>
  <name>createArray</name>
  <tag-class>com.wrox.ch10.createArrayTag</tag-class>
</tag>
```

The code for `iterateTag.jsp` does not change much either. Instead of the scriptlet we now have a set of cooperating tags.

```
<example:createArray/>
 <example:iterate>
   The string is:
 </example:iterate>
```

The results the client sees are no different than the results from the previous section's example. This example was not visual but rather geared to spark some thoughts on theoretical uses of custom tags.

The Benefits of Cooperating Tags

At this stage, we should point out some features of our previous example. The first is that two tags can cooperate and share functionality. For this example we used the two tags indirectly to pass information through the `PageContext` object. For more complex tag libraries tag handlers also provide a convenient mechanism for nesting and sharing information to the surrounding tags. We will not delve completely into this mechanism because it is not terribly helpful when creating a few simple tags. Some good resources to learn more about this functionality will be listed at the end of the chapter.

Another good point to note is that we now have all of the functionality consolidated inside the custom tags. Should the functionality be needed across many pages the custom tag can be included in each page. A practical example can be related to the `<createArray>` tag. Our `<createArray>` tag loads the array of strings into the `PageContext`. This same array could be reused across many pages and the array used for various tasks. One change to the tag handler's code and all of the implementing pages will be updated. Additionally imagine if the `<createArray>` tag provided some attributes for customizing and performed a more difficult task such as querying a database to generate the array. Then the `<createArray>` tag would become a powerful piece of cooperating logic inside an easy and reusable custom tag.

Do not let the simplicity of the example dilute the good concepts. This example's cooperating tags are simple because the concept is introduced with a contrived static array of strings. In practice, this is rarely the case and the cooperating tags provide a powerful tool for consolidating and reusing complex logic. In general, it is good to examine scriptlets and see if they would better suit a custom tag or work in cooperation with a custom tag. Custom tags work well and provide an easy interface for a JSP developer and those not terribly familiar with Java coding.

259

Later in this chapter, an additional benefit to custom tag libraries versus scriptlets will also be introduced to help enforce some of the above thoughts. Tag handler code and TLD files may be compressed and packaged into a single file called a JAR for easy use amongst many JSP projects.

Extending Custom Tag Functionality

In previous sections, we used only a small part of the functionality that custom tag libraries provide. There are three principal ways to extend the functionality of custom tags.

❑   Create Attributes

❑   Create Scripting Variables

❑   Use Tag Extra Info (TEI) classes

In this section we are going to take a close look at each of these. Let's start by discussing tag attributes.

Adding Attributes To Your Tags

The <time> custom tag we created earlier works fine but is not very flexible. What if we wanted to change the formatting of the date displayed? Right now the user is stuck with whatever we coded in to the tag. SimpleDateFormat has many options for how the formatting looks. We just need a mechanism to customize the output of the tag. We can solve this problem by adding a format attribute to the tag.

The concept of attributes used with tag handlers may be new to you, but from a coding standpoint, attributes will look very familiar. In Chapter 4, you learned about JavaBeans and implementing getter and setter methods for variables. The tag handler class implements an attribute using a setter method of the same name in your tag handler's code. These setter methods are no different from those seen with a JavaBean.

The <attribute> Element

Attributes for a tag must first be declared in the TLD file. The <attribute> element declared in the TLD file is a sub element of <tag>. There must be one <attribute> element for every attribute of a custom tag.

```
<tag>
  <attribute>
     ...
  </attribute>
</tag>
```

The <attribute> element has additional sub elements that contain more information about the attribute (note that only name below is a required attribute):

Element	Description
`<name>`	The name of the attribute.
`<required>`	Specifies if the attribute is required for the tag. You can specify either `true` or `yes` to make the attribute required. The value of `false` or `no` means the attribute is optional. The default value is `false`.
`<rtexprvalue>`	Specifies if the attribute can be created dynamically by a scriptlet at run-time. Values available for this element are `true` or `yes` to allow for a run-time scriptlet value, and `false` or `no` to disallow it.
`<description>`	A brief description of the attribute.

Let's now use this knowledge to add an attribute to the `time` tag we created earlier.

Try It Out – Adding an Attribute To a Tag Handler

Our objective for this section will be to add the following functionality to the time tag.

```
<example:time format="..."/>
```

The `format` attribute will let the user specify the format in which the time should be displayed from the tag.

First, add the following modifications to the tag handler `timeTag.java`.

```
package com.wrox.ch10;

import javax.servlet.jsp.tagext.*;
import javax.servlet.jsp.*;
import java.text.SimpleDateFormat;

public class timeTag extends TagSupport {
  String format = "HH:mm:ss";

  public void setFormat(String newFormat) {
    format = newFormat;
  }
  public int doEndTag() throws JspException {
    SimpleDateFormat sdf;
    sdf = new SimpleDateFormat(format);
    String time = sdf.format(new java.util.Date());
    try {
      pageContext.getOut().print(time);
    } catch (Exception e) {
      throw new JspException(e.toString());
    }
    return EVAL_PAGE;
  }
}
```

As usual, be sure to recompile the edited code.

Now we need to reflect the tag handler class changes in `exampleTags.tld` by adding the following highlighted lines.

```xml
<?xml version="1.0" encoding="ISO-8859-1"?>
<!DOCTYPE taglib PUBLIC
                 "-//Sun Microsystems, Inc.//DTD JSP Tag Library 1.2//EN"
                 "http://java.sun.com/dtd/web-jsptaglibrary_1_2.dtd">
<taglib>
  <tlib-version>1.0</tlib-version>
  <jsp-version>1.2</jsp-version>
  <short-name>ExampleTags</short-name>
  <description>A set of example tag handlers.</description>
  <tag>
    <name>time</name>
    <tag-class>com.wrox.ch10.timeTag</tag-class>
    <attribute>
      <name>format</name>
    </attribute>
  </tag>
  <tag>
    <name>iterate</name>
    <tag-class>com.wrox.ch10.iterateTag</tag-class>
  </tag>
  <tag>
    <name>createArray</name>
    <tag-class>com.wrox.ch10.createArrayTag</tag-class>
  </tag>
</taglib>
```

Finally, edit `currentTime.jsp` to use the new attribute.

```jsp
<%@ taglib prefix="example" uri="WEB-INF/exampleTags.tld" %>
<html>
  <head></head>
  <body>
    Hello, the current date and time is <example:time
                                       format="dd/MM/yy HH:mm:ss"/>
  </body>
</html>
```

Since we have changed the tag handler class, the TLD and the JSP, we need to make sure the container uses the current changes. Restart Tomcat to reload the changes and browse to `currentTime.jsp`. The new message and formatting will appear.

How It Works

Adding attributes to tag handlers is not a difficult task. Attributes are represented in a tag handler by a setter method of the same name. Our new attribute is named `format`. To reflect this in our tag handler code, a method is needed, called `setFormat()`. A new variable will also be created in the tag handler called `format`.

```
String format = "HH:mm:ss";

  public void setFormat(String newFormat){
    format = newFormat;
  }
```

The string passed to the `SimpleDateFormat` object is now changed to the (optionally) dynamic value of the `format` variable. If the user specifies special formatting it will be used, but by default the original formatting falls into place.

```
    sdf = new SimpleDateFormat(format);
```

Reflecting the custom tag's new attribute in the TLD is also an easy task. The new entry in `exampleTags.tld` is an `<attribute>` element between the `<tag>` element. The `<attribute>` element's value matches the name of the new attribute we wish to implement and also defines the setter method to call upon in the custom tag handler.

```
    <display-name>time</display-name>
    <attribute>
      <name>format</name>
    </attribute>
```

With the above changes the new tag is ready for use. Tomcat is restarted to ensure the new class file and TLD are read.

By default the original formatting remains "`HH:mm:ss`". If a new value for the `format` attribute is provided, the tag will change to display the new style. The possible values for the `format` attribute are the same as defined in the `SimpleDateFormat` object documentation. In the example we demonstrated this by adding in the date ahead of the current time.

Making Attributes Required

There is no restriction on the number of attributes for a custom tag. Adding additional attributes simply requires repeating the above steps for each attribute needed: add the appropriate setter method in your tag handler, and add the attribute to your TLD. By default, any attribute added will *not* be required by the tag. Sometimes it does not matter if an attribute is left optional; however other attributes might be critical to make the tag work. In these cases you will need to specify that the attribute is required in the TLD. Let's see how to do this.

The easiest method of requiring an attribute value is by inserting the `<required>` element as a child of the appropriate `<attribute>` element.

```
    <attribute>
      <name>format</name>
      <required>true</required>
    </attribute>
```

Using the `<required>` element and setting the body of this element to `true` will force the user to place information in the attribute before using the tag. If not an error will be thrown and presented to the user. By default a servlet exception is displayed, as below:

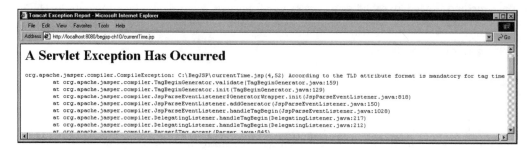

Displaying the error in such a crude manner is not a requirement. The point of mentioning the `<required>` attribute is to understand that restrictions may be placed on custom tag attributes. If the custom tag relies on a specific attribute this is the default mechanism for enforcing the validation. The error message does eventually say, "According to the TLD attribute format is mandatory for tag time", although a custom error page or a try/catch statement can easily pretty-up the servlet exception.

Evaluating Attribute Values at Runtime

The `<rtexprvalue>` element lets you control whether the attribute can accept scriptlet expressions evaluated at request time, or whether they must be static values instead. For better performance, custom tag attributes default to requiring static values. Additionally, the value of an attribute does not necessarily need to be a string. A more advanced feature of custom tag attributes is allowing any type of object to be passed in to the setter method. This feature is left for a more in-depth coverage of tag libraries, but it may only be used if the `<rtexprvalue>` element is set to `true`.

For an example, let us pretend `exampleTags.tld` had set the `rtexprvalue` element to `true`.

```
<attribute>
  <name>format</name>
  <rtexprvalue>true</rtexprvalue>
</attribute>
```

When using the `time` tag a scriptlet expression would be perfectly valid for our attribute value. It might look similar to below if the `format` value had been passed as a parameter in the `request` for the web page:

```
<%@ taglib prefix="example" uri="WEB-INF/exampleTags.tld" %>
<html>
  <head></head>
  <body>
    Welcome to my webpage. The current time is
    <% String format = request.getParameter("format"); %>
    <example:time format="<%= format %>"/>
  </body>
</html>
```

This would let the user specify the time format rather than having it statically coded into the JSP.

The Advantages of Using Tag Attributes

Using attributes with your custom tags provides a convenient method to customize your tags at run-time. Additionally the attribute values can also be generated at run-time. When adding in a new attribute only two changes are needed. First, a setter method is added to our tag handler code. Remember adding the setter is identical to what was previously seen with a JavaBean. Second, the TLD for the appropriate tag library must be updated to reflect the new attribute. Optionally additional elements may be used in the TLD to declare more information about the attribute.

Overall, it is very easy and beneficial to add in attributes for a custom tag. Therefore, in practice it is rare to see a custom tag that does not implement attributes for additional information. In general, all tag handlers can use attributes. The method of creating attributes and using them does not change between the three tag handler interfaces. Use attributes as needed with any custom tag.

Using Scripting Variables

One of the most popular uses for tag libraries is to remove scriptlets from your JSP, but tag libraries are not limited to this purpose. A tag handler can also create objects, set them in the `PageContext` object, and these can then be used by scriptlet code in your JSP. These objects created by the tag handler are known as **scripting variables**. In effect, they provide the same functionality as `<jsp:useBean>` action tags, but in a more flexible manner. We are also able to define the scripting variables scope within the JSP page too.

There are two ways that we can retrieve a scripting variable within a JSP:

❑ Declare the variable in the TLD

❑ Create a helper `TagExtraInfo` class

Let's look at each of these in turn.

Declaring Scripting Variables in the TLD File

If you want to create a variable in your tag handler which can be accessed by scriptlet code in your JSP, the simplest way is to declare it in the TLD file.

Recall from earlier the `<createArray>` tag creates an object and sets it within the `PageContext`. The `<createArray>` tag was originally designed to cooperate with the `<iterate>` tag, but we can also use `<createArray>` with a `scriptlet`. So, you may ask the question: why do we need to bother declaring a scripting variable in the TLD? After all, we could just retrieve the scripting variable using a scriptlet that calls the `PageContext.getAttribute()` method. To answer this question, let's do exactly that: we'll retrieve a scripting variable using a scriptlet.

Try It Out – Introducing a Scripting Variable into a JSP Using a Scriptlet

This first example may seem like a step backwards from the previous examples. Don't worry. We need to take a quick step back to introduce scripting variables before demonstrating their full potential.

In this example we remove the code from `iterateTag.java` and place it in a scriptlet.

Create a new JSP using the code below and save it as `scriptingVariables.jsp`. in the `webapps\begjsp-ch10` directory of Tomcat.

```
<%@ taglib prefix="example" uri="WEB-INF/exampleTags.tld" %>
<html>
  <head></head>
  <body>
  <example:createArray/>
<%
  String[] strings = (String [])pageContext.getAttribute("strings");
%>
There are <%= strings.length %> strings available.<BR>
<%
  for(int i = 0; i<strings.length; i++) {
    out.println("The value \"" + strings[i] + "\" is in slot #"
                            + i + " of the array.<BR>");
  }
%>
  </body>
</html>
```

Now browse to http://localhost:8080/begjsp-ch10/scriptingVariables.jsp:

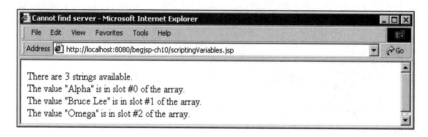

As you can see, the scriptlet can access the array of strings in the same fashion as the custom tag did.

How It Works

The example is quick and to the point. The JSP looks similar to `iterateTag.jsp` but instead of using the custom tag, we have placed a few scriptlets on the JSP.

```
<%@ taglib prefix="example" uri="WEB-INF/exampleTags.tld" %>
<html>
  <head></head>
  <body>
  <example:createArray/>
```

The first scriptlet takes the array stored in the `PageContext` object by the `<createArray>` tag and makes it into an array of strings available for the other scripts on the JSP.

```
<%
  String[] strings = (String [])pageContext.getAttribute("strings");
%>
```

The second section of code uses the new array of strings and shows a little information about them. The looping previously done by the `<iterate>` tag is now accomplished with a `for` loop for this single JSP.

```
There are <%= strings.length %> strings available.<BR>
<%
  for(int i = 0; i<strings.length; i++) {
    out.println("The value \"" + strings[i] + "\" is in slot #"
                                + i + " of the array.<BR>");
  }
%>
    </body>
</html>
```

On the plus side, with the new JSP we have seen that a cooperating tag need not always cooperate with other tags. Working with a scriptlet is perfectly valid. However, with the scriptlet there are two points we should look at and improve on. The first is how the scripting variable is introduced to the JSP. The first scriptlet is not actually needed at all: Consider the <jsp:useBean> action, where a scripting variable is directly created in our JSP. Custom tag libraries can also mimic this functionality and directly introduce scripting variables. The easiest method is by declaring the scripting variable in the TLD.

Another justification for eliminating the scriptlet is reusability and maintainability. When using scriptlets we have specific code on each JSP. As time progresses this code becomes more difficult to maintain because each page with a scriptlet needs to be modified. The custom tag puts all of our code in one place and leaves the custom tag syntax to be used on a JSP.

In the previous example we used a scriptlet specific to a custom tag. Now we are getting hit twice over because of using a scriptlet. If the script needs changing we must change it on each implementing JSP. Also if the custom tag's logic is changed it might modify the variable stored in the PageContext object. Should this be the case the tag will still work fine, but the scriptlet used to add the scripting variable will also need changing on every implementing JSP. We can solve this problem by letting the custom tag be responsible for both setting the variable in the PageContext and initializing a new scripting variable.

We already have the <createArray> tag setting our array in the PageContext. Adding a scripting variable via the TLD is accomplished by adding a <variable> element as a child to the appropriate <tag> element.

The <variable> Element

The (optional) <variable> element in the TLD is a subelement of <tag> and declares scripting variables for the custom tag:

```
...
<tag>
  <variable>
  </variable>
</tag>
...
```

The <variable> element has additional subelements for more information. All of the subelements below are required except for the <name-given> tag.

Element	Description
`<name-given>`	This contains the name of the scripting variable. You should note that another option exists for naming a scripting variable that we will not be covering in this chapter. As long as one of these appears, the TLD is valid.
`<variable-class>`	The value of this element represents the Java type of the scripting variable.
`<declared>`	The value of this element must be a boolean argument of `true` or `yes` if the scripting variable is new.
`<scope>`	Three values are available defining the scope of the scripting variable. If the value is `AT_BEGIN`, the scripting variable is in scope after the starting tag; `AT_END` after the ending tag, and `NESTED` between the start and end tags.

In the case of the `<createArray>` tag, we can add the `<variable>` element to remove the need for the first scriptlet in `scriptingVariables.jsp`. Let's see how.

Try It Out – Introducing a Scripting Variable into a JSP Using the TLD File

Edit `exampleTags.tld` to use the new variable element for the `<createArray>` tag.

```xml
<?xml version="1.0" encoding="ISO-8859-1"?>
<!DOCTYPE taglib PUBLIC
                "-//Sun Microsystems, Inc.//DTD JSP Tag Library 1.2//EN"
                "http://java.sun.com/dtd/web-jsptaglibrary_1_2.dtd">
<taglib>
  <tlib-version>1.0</tlib-version>
  <jsp-version>1.2</jsp-version>
  <short-name>ExampleTags</short-name>
  <description>A set of example tag handlers.</description>
  <tag>
    <name>time</name>
    <tag-class>com.wrox.ch10.timeTag</tag-class>
    <attribute>
      <name>format</name>
    </attribute>
  </tag>
  <tag>
    <name>iterate</name>
    <tag-class>com.wrox.ch10.iterateTag</tag-class>
  </tag>
  <tag>
    <name>createArray</name>
    <tag-class>com.wrox.ch10.createArrayTag</tag-class>
    <variable>
      <name-given>strings</name-given>
      <variable-class>java.lang.String []</variable-class>
      <declare>true</declare>
      <scope>AT_END</scope>
    </variable>
  </tag>
</taglib>
```

Now remove the unneeded scriptlet from `scriptingVariables.jsp`.

```
<%@ taglib prefix="example" uri="WEB-INF/exampleTags.tld" %>
<html>
  <head></head>
  <body>
  <example:createArray/>

There are <%= strings.length %> strings available.<BR>
<%
  for(int i = 0; i<strings.length; i++) {
    out.println("The value \"" + strings[i] + "\" is in slot #" + i +
      " of the array.<BR>");
  }
%>
  </body>
</html>
```

Restart Tomcat and browse to `scriptingVariables.jsp` to verify it now works without the removed scriptlet.

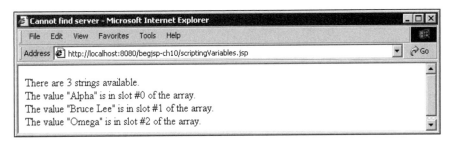

How It Works

Our previous example functions around the new `<variable>` element introduced to the `exampleTags.tld`.

The `<variable>` element is now responsible for introducing a new scripting variable. Notice the `<variable>` element is placed inside the `<tag>` element describing the `<createArray>` tag. Each of our custom tags may create scripting variables if needed and may create as many as needed. In this case we only want one and the `<createArray>` tag should create it. Should more variables be needed create additional `<variable>` elements.

```
<variable>
```

The `<variable>` element by itself does not do much. The element relies on some children to describe the scripting variable. Four subelements are used to describe different aspects of the new scripting variable. The first two are fairly straightforward. The `<name-given>` element describes the name to be given to our new scripting variable and also represents the name the object was stashed in `PageContext` with. In our example a scripting variable named `"strings"` is created from the object stored as `"strings"` in the `PageContext` object.

```
<name-given>strings</name-given>
```

269

The <variable-class> element defines the class type of the scripting variable's object. We know the variable stashed in the PageContext was an array of type java.lang.String. The value matches for our case, but may be changed as needed for other scripting variables.

```
<variable-class>java.lang.String []</variable-class>
```

The <declare> element determines if the scripting variable is being newly defined, or is already available. Give the value true if the scripting variable is new for the page, or false if the variable has previously been declared for the page.

```
<declare>true</declare>
```

The <scope> element defines when the new scripting variable can be used in the JSP. Three values exist: AT_BEGIN, AT_END and NESTED. Using a value of AT_BEGIN creates the scripting variable at the starting tag and keeps it around for the rest of the JSP. A value of AT_END creates the scripting variable at the ending tag and also keeps it around for the rest of the JSP. The NESTED value will only keep the scripting variable in scope between the starting and ending tags of the custom tag. For the <createArray> tag we want to make sure the variable is in scope after the custom tag so either the AT_BEGIN or AT_END values would work.

```
        <scope>AT_END</scope>
    </variable>
```

Cooperating Tags Using Scripting Variables

The first example of tags introducing scripting variables mentioned two points of improvement on the example. The first was demonstrated with the above example to remove the need of a scriptlet to create a scripting variable. The second point, that we will now examine, is how to use the extra functionality of the scripting variables with a custom tag.

The first example of the <iterate> tag iterated through an array of strings and sent appropriate values to the client along with a little description.

The example was given to demonstrate the basics of iteration using the doAfterBody() method. A restriction on the example was that the strings from the array would only appear after the text in the body of the tag. With the previous example of scripting variables we had the flexibility of placing the strings from the array anywhere we liked inside the results. Looking at the results of the JSP can show this. The values from the array appear in between filler text along with information about the location in the array.

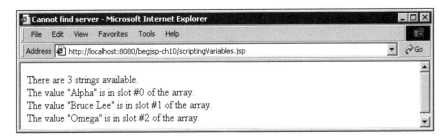

The extra flexibility in the second example is not restricted to scriptlets. Custom tag libraries can also take advantage of scripting variables.

Try It Out – Improving the Iterate Tag To Work With Scripting Variables

We are now stepping back to the idea of using custom tags to replace scriptlets. The previous two examples required scriptlets to demonstrate the basic functionality of introducing new scripting variables. Now we can use this knowledge to improve the <iterate> tag and give it much more flexibility.

First, add the following changes to the tag handler code iterateTag.java.

```java
import javax.servlet.jsp.*;
import javax.servlet.jsp.tagext.*;

public class iterateTag extends TagSupport {
  private int arrayCount = 0;
  private String[] strings = null;

  public int doStartTag() {
    strings = (String[]) pageContext.getAttribute("strings");
    pageContext.setAttribute("currentString", strings[arrayCount]);
    pageContext.setAttribute("arrayCount", new Integer(arrayCount));

    return EVAL_BODY_INCLUDE;
  }

  public int doAfterBody() throws JspException {
    arrayCount++;
    if (arrayCount >= strings.length) {
      return SKIP_BODY;
    }
    pageContext.setAttribute("currentString", strings[arrayCount]);
    pageContext.setAttribute("arrayCount", new Integer(arrayCount));

    return EVAL_BODY_AGAIN;
  }
}
```

Be sure to recompile the new code.

Now edit exampleTags.tld to have the iterate tag create two new scripting variables.

```xml
<?xml version="1.0" encoding="ISO-8859-1"?>
<!DOCTYPE taglib PUBLIC
                "-//Sun Microsystems, Inc.//DTD JSP Tag Library 1.2//EN"
                "http://java.sun.com/dtd/web-jsptaglibrary_1_2.dtd">
<taglib>
  <tlib-version>1.0</tlib-version>
  <jsp-version>1.2</jsp-version>
  <short-name>ExampleTags</short-name>
  <description>A set of example tag handlers.</description>
  <tag>
    <name>time</name>
    <tag-class>com.wrox.ch10.timeTag</tag-class>
    <attribute>
      <name>format</name>
    </attribute>
  </tag>
  <tag>
    <name>iterate</name>
    <tag-class>com.wrox.ch10.iterateTag</tag-class>
    <variable>
      <name-given>currentString</name-given>
      <variable-class>java.lang.String</variable-class>
      <declare>true</declare>
      <scope>NESTED</scope>
    </variable>
    <variable>
      <name-given>arrayCount</name-given>
      <variable-class>java.lang.Integer</variable-class>
      <declare>true</declare>
      <scope>NESTED</scope>
    </variable>
  </tag>

  <tag>
    <name>createArray</name>
    <tag-class>com.wrox.ch10.createArrayTag</tag-class>
    <variable>
      <name-given>strings</name-given>
      <variable-class>java.lang.String []</variable-class>
      <declare>true</declare>
      <scope>AT_END</scope>
    </variable>
  </tag>
</taglib>
```

Last, change `scriptingVariables.jsp` to avoid using any scriptlets, but instead use the new iterate tag.

```jsp
<%@ taglib prefix="example" uri="WEB-INF/exampleTags.tld" %>
<html>
  <head></head>
  <body>
 <example:createArray/>
There are <%= strings.length %> strings available.<BR>
<example:iterate>
```

```
     The value "<%= currentString %>" is in slot #<%= arrayCount %> of the
array.<BR>
</example:iterate>
   </body>
</html>
```

Be sure to restart Tomcat and then browse to the modified scriptingVariables.jsp. The page now creates the same results and consolidates all of the old script logic conveniently in custom tags.

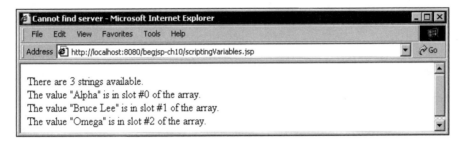

How It Works

This example leverages on our previous knowledge of scripting variables. Instead of just demonstrating how a single scripting variable works, we are modifying a previous example to provide more flexibility. The changes are nothing new to our skill set but rather more of a case study.

The first big change is to the code of the tag handler iterateTag.java. Two new values are placed in the PageContext to be used later as scripting variables. The tag handler sets the two new values in the PageContext at two different times. The first is done during the doStartTag() method to initialize the values. Notice when setting our int value into the PageContext object we create a new int object. This is done because int is a primitive type but the setAttribute() method of PageContext requires an object. We are forced to make an Integer object using the int to accomplish our goal:

```
public int doStartTag() {
   strings = (String[]) pageContext.getAttribute("strings");
   pageContext.setAttribute("currentString", strings[arrayCount]);
   pageContext.setAttribute("arrayCount", new Integer(arrayCount));
   return EVAL_BODY_INCLUDE;
}
```

The values are set a second time during the doAfterBody() method. These methods are called once for each item in the array we iterate through. The setter methods are needed this second time to make sure the scripting variable is current for each evaluation of the body.

```
public int doAfterBody() throws JspException {
   arrayCount++;
   if(arrayCount >= strings.length) {
     return SKIP_BODY;
   }
   pageContext.setAttribute("currentString", strings[arrayCount]);
   pageContext.setAttribute("arrayCount", new Integer(arrayCount));
   return EVAL_BODY_AGAIN;
}
```

The next change is to reflect the new scripting variables in the TLD. We added the two new <variable> elements under the <tag> element for the iterate tag in exampleTags.tld. These new elements will create the two scripting variables out of the two objects stashed in the PageContext object by the <iterate> tag.

The first variable represents the current string from our array of strings. The name used to set the object in PageContext was "currentString". The scripting variable is also named "currentString" for use by the JSP. The type of this object is java.lang.String, the scripting variable is newly declared to the JSP and only stays in scope for the body of the custom tag.

```
<variable>
  <name-given>currentString</name-given>
  <variable-class>java.lang.String</variable-class>
  <declare>true</declare>
  <scope>NESTED</scope>
</variable>
```

The second scripting variable is the current count of the array. The variable was set into the PageContext object as "arrayCount" and is initialized as a scripting variable with the same name. The object is of type java.lang.Integer. The variable is new to the JSP and the scripting variable will be in scope only for the body of the custom tag.

```
<variable>
  <name-given>arrayCount</name-given>
  <variable-class>java.lang.Integer</variable-class>
  <declare>true</declare>
  <scope>NESTED</scope>
</variable>
```

Advantages of Using Scripting Variables Within Iterating Tags

With the new <iterate> tag we overcome the limitations of the previous iterate tag with a few scripting variables. The previous <iterate> tag printed the current array string after the body of the tag was evaluated. With this example, we are now using the body of the tag to include our scripting variables. The values of these variables change and with each evaluation of the body the correct results are sent to the client. We can take a higher-level view and see the difference directly by comparing the code in iterateTag.jsp to the code in scriptingVariables.jsp.

Here is the code for iterateTag.jsp. It relies on printing out a static message and then appending a string from the array.

```
<%@ taglib prefix="example" uri="WEB-INF/exampleTags.tld" %>
<html>
  <head></head>
  <body>
 <example:createArray/>
 <example:iterate>
   The string is:
 </example:iterate>
   </body>
</html>
```

Compare it to the code we are now using for `scriptingVariables.jsp`. You should realize that this new code would not function if we had tried it back on the first example of the `<iterate>` tag, but the new `<iterate>` tag can easily print the results from the old `<iterate>` tag example if we desire.

```
<%@ taglib prefix="example" uri="WEB-INF/exampleTags.tld" %>
<html>
  <head></head>
  <body>
  <example:createArray/>
There are <%= strings.length %> strings available.<BR>
<example:iterate>
    The value "<%= currentString %>" is in slot #<%= arrayCount %> of the
array.<BR>
</example:iterate>
  </body>
</html>
```

In general the new improved `<iterate>` tag is a much more practical example of using the iteration ability of custom tags. Imagine if the array being iterated through was an array full of e-mail messages. The `<iterate>` tag might have a scripting variable for the address, subject and message of each e-mail that functions in the same method as `currentString` does in this example. The code in the body of the tag would need to be nothing more than the HTML for displaying each message along with the reference to the scripting variables as needed.

This imagined reference can actually be seen in a real-world tag library. Head to JSP Insider's Unofficial JavaMail tags:

http://www.jspinsider.com/jspkit/javamail/jspkit_javamail.html

Check out the tags for reading e-mail. The `<showMessage>` tag exists to perform the above functionality.

Declaring Scripting Variables Using TagExtraInfo Classes

Declaring a scripting variable by way of a TLD is simple and it works, but another method does exist. Each custom tag may have a `TagExtraInfo` (TEI) helper class declared to accompany it. The TEI class can create scripting variables in a similar fashion to the previous section. A bonus of using a TEI class is the ability to dynamically create scripting variables instead of relying on information coded in the TLD. In addition to creating scripting variables, a TEI class may also perform a validation of a custom tag.

Before we go into the details of how to declare a scripting variable using a TEI class, we need to understand two objects:

❑   `TagData` – holds information about tag attributes

❑   `VariableInfo` – describes a new scripting variable

Let's take a closer look at these objects.

The TagData Object

The `TagData` object provides information about a custom tag's attributes at translation time; it is generated automatically by the JSP container based on the corresponding custom tag. From a developer's view we only use the given `TagData` object to get information about the custom tag the TEI was declared for.

The `TagData` object has a few different methods we can use to get information about the custom tag's attributes. The first is the `getAttributes()` method, that returns an object called an **enumeration** (of class `java.util.Enumeration`). An enumeration object contains a collection of values, not unlike the `Iterator` object that we saw in Chapter 8. The enumeration returned by `getAttributes()` contains all of the attributes in the `TagData` object.

Another useful method is the `getAttributeString()` method, that takes a `String` representing the name of a particular attribute as argument, and returns another `String` representing the value of the attribute. The `getAttribute()` method is a variation on this theme, in that it takes a `String` attribute name argument, but returns the attribute value as an `Object`.

The VariableInfo Object

The `VariableInfo` object describes a new scripting variable. To make a `VariableInfo` object we need the same information previously used when declaring a scripting variable via TLD. Recall the following snippet from `exampleTags.tld` we have previously used:

```
<variable>
  <name-given>strings</name-given>
  <variable-class>java.lang.String []</variable-class>
  <declare>true</declare>
  <scope>AT_END</scope>
</variable>
```

This snippet is found in the body of the `<tag>` element for the `<createArray>` tag. The snippet creates a new scripting variable using the "strings" name, of type `java.lang.String` and with a scope starting after the end custom tag. When creating a `VariableInfo` object we use the same information as in the TLD, but as parameters in a constructor instead. For example:

```
VariableInfo vi =
        new VariableInfo(varName, className, true, VariableInfo.AT_END);
```

So what do all of the arguments in the constructor represent? The first, `varName` here, represents the name of the new scripting variable as a `String`. The second, `className`, is the full class name of the variable's type, represented as a `String`. The third, `true` here, is a boolean stating whether the scripting variable is new to the JSP and so must be declared. The final argument is an `integer` value representing the required scope of the scripting variable. The available values are shown in the table below:

Field	Description
`VariableInfo.AT_BEGIN`	The new scripting variable will be in scope after the starting custom tag.
`VariableInfo.AT_END`	The new scripting variable will be in scope after the ending custom tag.
`VariableInfo.NESTED`	The scripting variable will only be in scope inside the body of the custom tag.

Creating a Scripting Variable Using a TEI Class

New scripting variables are defined via TEI classes by using the getVariableInfo() method. The method takes a TagData object as argument, and returns an array of VariableInfo objects. A scripting variable is created for each VariableInfo object in the returned array. Each VariableInfo object is custom defined by the JSP developer when overriding this method in the TEI class.

Now that we have a general idea of what a TagExtraInfo class does, we can try using one with a custom tag. Luckily, we also already have some tag handlers requiring scripting variables. For this example, we will make the <createArray> tag use a TEI class. The <createArray> tag will also be modified to be more flexible with the scripting variable it creates.

Try It Out – Using a TEI Class To Declare a Scripting Variable in a JSP

First, modify the tag handler code createArrayTag.java to implement a new attribute called "name". The new attribute will determine the name of the scripting variable created.

```
package com.wrox.ch10;

import javax.servlet.jsp.tagext.*;

public class createArrayTag extends TagSupport {
   private String name = null;

   public int doStartTag() {
      String[] strings = new String[] {"Alpha", "Bruce Lee", "Omega"};
      pageContext.setAttribute(name, strings);

      return SKIP_BODY;
   }
   public void setName(String newName) {
      name = newName;
   }
}
```

Be sure to recompile the changed code.

Next, create a TagExtraInfo class to accompany the new tag handler. Extending the TagExtraInfo class is the preferred method for creating a TEI class. Save the following code as arrayExtraInfo.java in the webapps\begjsp-ch10\classes\com\wrox\ch10 directory of Tomcat.

```
package com.wrox.ch10;

import javax.servlet.jsp.tagext.*;

public class arrayExtraInfo extends TagExtraInfo {

   public VariableInfo[] getVariableInfo(TagData data) {

      String variableName = data.getAttributeString("name");

      VariableInfo vi =
         new VariableInfo(variableName,"String []", true, VariableInfo.AT_END);
      VariableInfo[] tagVariables = new VariableInfo[1];
```

```
        tagVariables[0] = vi;

        return tagVariables;
    }
}
```

Compile the new code.

Then modify exampleTags.tld so that we no longer use the <variable> element for the
<createArray> tag. Instead add in a new element named <tei-class>. The value of this element
will be the newly made TEI class. Also add in the new attribute added to the <createArray> tag.

```
<?xml version="1.0" encoding="ISO-8859-1"?>
<!DOCTYPE taglib PUBLIC
                "-//Sun Microsystems, Inc.//DTD JSP Tag Library 1.2//EN"
                "http://java.sun.com/dtd/web-jsptaglibrary_1_2.dtd">
<taglib>
  <tlib-version>1.0</tlib-version>
  <jsp-version>1.2</jsp-version>
  <short-name>ExampleTags</short-name>
  <description>A set of example tag handlers.</description>
  <tag>
    <name>time</name>
    <tag-class>com.wrox.ch10.timeTag</tag-class>
    <display-name>time</display-name>
    <attribute>
      <name>format</name>
    </attribute>
  </tag>
  <tag>
    <name>iterate</name>
    <tag-class>com.wrox.ch10.iterateTag</tag-class>
    <variable>
      <name-given>currentString</name-given>
      <variable-class>java.lang.String</variable-class>
      <declare>true</declare>
      <scope>NESTED</scope>
    </variable>
    <variable>
      <name-given>arrayCount</name-given>
      <variable-class>java.lang.Integer</variable-class>
      <declare>true</declare>
      <scope>NESTED</scope>
    </variable>
  </tag>
  <tag>
    <name>createArray</name>
    <tag-class>com.wrox.ch10.createArrayTag</tag-class>
    <tei-class>com.wrox.ch10.arrayExtraInfo</tei-class>
    <attribute>
      <name>name</name>
    </attribute>
  </tag>
</taglib>
```

Finally, create a JSP to demonstrate the dynamically named scripting variable created by the TEI class. Save the following code as `teiExample.jsp` in the `webapps\begjsp-ch10\` directory of Tomcat.

```
<%@ taglib prefix="example" uri="WEB-INF/exampleTags.tld" %>
<html>
   <head></head>
   <body>
   <example:createArray name="theArray"/>
   The array has <%= theArray.length %> items.
   </body>
</html>
```

Browse to `teiExample.jsp` to see the scripting variable does indeed work with the new `name` attribute.

How It Works

This example is focused upon the `name` attribute added to the `<createArray>` tag. The TEI class `arrayExtraInfo` dynamically names the new scripting variable to be the same as the value of the `name` attribute. The TEI class knows the value of the attribute because the JSP container passes in a current `TagData` object with the information.

The first change was to the tag handler code in `createArray.java`. We changed the tag handler to have a new attribute called "name". Adding this attribute requires no new information from this section. It involves adding a setter method for the name variable and an edit to the TLD. The process of adding attributes to our tag handlers was previously covered in the chapter.

```
private String name = null;
```

One line of previous code is also edited. This line sets the `name` variable in to the `PageContext` object. Instead of using the static value of `"strings"`, the `name` variable is now used.

```
pageContext.setAttribute(name ,strings);
```

To make the example TEI class the `TagExtraInfo` class provided in the Servlet/JSP API was subclassed. Similar to the `TagSupport` and `BodyTagSupport` objects and tag handlers, the `TagExtraInfo` class is provided for convenience.

```
package com.wrox.ch10;

import javax.servlet.jsp.tagext.*;

public class arrayExtraInfo extends TagExtraInfo {
```

Inside our custom TEI class `arrayExtraInfo.java` we can now start overriding methods. At the beginning of this section we mentioned the `getVariableInfo()` method determines if any scripting variables should be created. Since one scripting variable is to be created, we must override this method and return an array containing one `VariableInfo` object.

```
public VariableInfo[] getVariableInfo(TagData data) {
```

The name of the scripting variable is supposed to be the same value as the `name` attribute from the custom tag. To get the value of the `name` attribute we call the `getAttributeString()` method from the `TagData` object.

```
String variableName = data.getAttributeString("name");
```

The `VariableInfo` object is created representing the new scripting variable. For the constructor we give a few parameters. For the name of the scripting variable we use the `variableName` object previously matched to the `name` attribute's value. The class type of the scripting variable is kept as an array of strings. The scripting variable is declared new to the JSP, and it comes into scope after the ending custom tag.

```
VariableInfo vi =
    new VariableInfo(variableName,"String []", true, VariableInfo.AT_END);
```

Finally the `VariableInfo` object is placed in an array to be returned by the method. It is important to note that we could have returned as many `VariableInfo` objects as desired in this array. The purpose of returning an array is to allow for this sort of functionality.

```
VariableInfo[] tagVariables = new VariableInfo[1];
tagVariables[0] = vi;

return tagVariables;
  }
}
```

Two changes were made to `exampleTags.tld`. The first change was a declaration for the new attribute in the `<createArray>` tag. The second change was replacing the old `<variable>` element with a `<tei-class>` element for the `<createArray>` tag.

```
<tei-class>com.wrox.ch10.arrayExtraInfo</tei-class>
```

The `<tei-class>` element functions in the same manner as the `<tag-class>` element but for the `TagExtraInfo` class. Instead of defining the tag handler class the value of this new element defines our custom TEI class. In general if any custom tag is using a TEI class it will implement a `<tei-class>` element in a similar fashion.

The example JSP is nothing more than a simple demonstration of the new functionality the TEI class provides. In the new code we can dynamically name the scripting variable. For the example, we give a value of `"theArray"` to the name attribute of the `<createArray>` tag. Later a scripting variable is used of the same name.

```
<example:createArray name="theArray"/>
The array has <%= theArray.length %> items.<BR>
```

Here is where the point of the example can be seen. We can now name the new scripting variable anything we like. This little extra bit of flexibility is unavailable when declaring scripting variables with the TLD. Realistically this is one of the only advantages a TEI class offers over using the TLD to declare scripting variables. Theoretically any amount of code can be used when overriding the `getVariableInfo()` method of the custom TEI class. When declaring scripting variables much more custom logic can be used than the static method available with the TLD.

Using TEI Classes for Tag Validation

TEI classes also implement the `isValid()` method, that was one of the original mechanisms for validating the attributes of a custom tag. This method accepts a `TagData` object as argument. If the boolean value returned by the method is `true`, the tag will be used, but if it is `false` an error will be thrown.

The `isValid()` method will not be given a full example in this chapter, because this method of tag validation is not commonly used. The error message produced by the `isValid()` method is very crude and not customizable by a JSP developer. Here is a sample that can be added to `arrayExtraInfo.java` to see this error message.

```java
package com.wrox.ch10;
import javax.servlet.jsp.tagext.*;

public class arrayExtraInfo extends TagExtraInfo {

  public VariableInfo[] getVariableInfo(TagData data) {
    String variableName = data.getAttributeString("name");

    VariableInfo vi = new VariableInfo(variableName,"String []", true,
VariableInfo.AT_END);
    VariableInfo[] tagVariables = new VariableInfo[1];
    tagVariables[0] = vi;

    return tagVariables;
  }

  public boolean isValid(TagData data) {
    return false;
  }
}
```

In general, this is how the `isValid()` may be overridden to verify the tag. However, instead of immediately returning `false` the `TagData` object could be checked to see if tag values met any arbitrary requirements.

The resulting error message `teiExample.jsp` produces is as follows.

An error page can be used to catch and pretty up this screen, but that is usually not an adequate solution. The message of this error is, "`Attributes are invalid according to TagInfo.`" The error in no way says exactly what is wrong with the attribute or how to fix the problem. Since there is no convenient method to accomplish this flexibility using the `isValid()` method, it is rarely practical.

Additionally another good reason exists for the skimping on coverage of this TEI feature. Another customizable method exists for easy validation of custom tags. The `javax.servlet.jsp.tagext.TagLibraryValidator` class is an advanced feature of custom tag libraries. This class has a similar method to `isValid()` called `validate()`. The `validate()` method returns a string value that may describe any problems with the current attributes. The `TagLibraryValidator` class also has access to the entire JSP instead of just a specific custom tag. Because of these features, `TagLibraryValidator` is usually a better solution to validate custom tags. The `TagLibraryValidator` class is covered in "*Professional JSP 2nd Edition*", *Grant Palmer et al., Wrox Press, ISBN 1861004958.*

Locating a TLD File

When we use custom tags on a JSP, the TLD must be referenced so that the JSP container understands what the custom tags do. Up until now in the chapter, we have been using the real URI to the TLD file in the `taglib` directive. Recall that each example JSP had a similar start.

```
<%@ taglib prefix="example" uri="WEB-INF/exampleTags.tld" %>
```

The `uri` attribute's value is the real relative URI to the TLD. We are pointing directly to the actual TLD file. There is nothing wrong with this method, but two other methods also exist, that will be addressed in this section. The first of the other methods is creating a fictitious URI and linking it to the TLD via a configuration file for your JSP application.

Referencing the TLD Via the web.xml Deployment Descriptor

Using `web.xml` to map a custom tag library is the most commonly used method. While it is slightly less intuitive compared to the method we have been using, it allows for any URI to reference a TLD. This extra functionality comes from using `web.xml` as a middleman to the value given in the `taglib` directive's `uri` attribute. When the JSP container sees the URI given in the `taglib` directive, it will try to find the TLD using the URI as a path to the actual file. If this fails, the JSP container will then check `web.xml` and see if the URI is custom defined for the web application. If so, the `web.xml` file will also link the custom URI to the real location of the TLD file. We can demonstrate this with a small example.

Try It Out – Referencing a TLD using web.xml

The `web.xml` file is located in the `WEB-INF` directory of your JSP application. For this chapter, create a file named `web.xml` and place it in the `\webapps\begjsp-ch10\WEB-INF\` directory of Tomcat. Save the following code in this `web.xml` file:

```
<?xml version="1.0" encoding="ISO-8859-1"?>

<!DOCTYPE web-app PUBLIC
            "-//Sun Microsystems, Inc.//DTD Web Application 2.3//EN"
            "http://java.sun.com/j2ee/dtds/web-app_2_3.dtd">
```

```
<web-app>
  <taglib>
    <taglib-uri>exampleTags</taglib-uri>
    <taglib-location>/WEB-INF/exampleTags.tld</taglib-location>
  </taglib>
</web-app>
```

Now take `scriptingVariables.jsp` and edit the `taglib` directive to use a new URI.

```
<%@ taglib prefix="example" uri="exampleTags" %>
<html>
  <head></head>
  <body>
 <example:createArray/>
There are <%= strings.length %> strings available.<BR>
<example:iterate>
    The value "<%= currentString %>" is in slot #<%= arrayCount %> of the
array.<BR>
</example:iterate>
  </body>
</html>
```

Be sure to restart Tomcat and then browse to `scriptingVariables.jsp`. The page now works with the new URI given in the `taglib` directive.

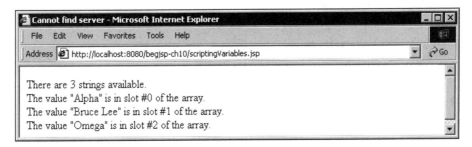

How It Works

This example relies on the addition we made to the newly introduced `web.xml` file. The `web.xml` file is an XML file and always starts with the same basic header and document element. The only optional element in our example is the `<taglib>` element with information about the tag library.

```
<?xml version="1.0" encoding="ISO-8859-1"?>
<!DOCTYPE web-app PUBLIC
              "-//Sun Microsystems, Inc.//DTD Web Application 2.3//EN"
              "http://java.sun.com/j2ee/dtds/web-app_2_3.dtd">

<web-app>
  <taglib>
    <taglib-uri>exampleTags</taglib-uri>
    <taglib-location>/WEB-INF/exampleTags.tld</taglib-location>
  </taglib>
</web-app>
```

The breakdown of the three highlighted lines is very straightforward.

❑ `<taglib>…</taglib>`
The `<taglib>` element informs your JSP container a new mapping for a tag library needs to be made. This entry may appear anywhere in between the `<webapps>` element. In our example it is the only element, however if you wish to add a tag library to a different web application's `web.xml` you may. Simply append the entry somewhere between the `<webapps>` elements but outside any other entry.

❑ `<taglib-uri>…</taglib-uri>`
This element must appear between your start and end `<taglib>` tags. The value is what you will give for the `uri` attribute in a `taglib` directive. If we wanted to use the same URI as we have been using in our examples, the value would be `WEB-INF/exampleTags.tld`. However, this would defeat the purpose of using `web.xml` to map our tag library. You have the freedom to use any value you like. Choose something simple and descriptive. For our example tags in this case `"exampleTags"` is the chosen value.

❑ `<taglib-location>…</taglib-location>`
The second element between the `<taglib>` tags must point to the actual location of your Tag Library Descriptor. If you list an incorrect value the JSP container will not be able to link the pseudo-URI to the real source.

You can now use the new URI in any of your `taglib` directives. The impact of this is potentially quite huge. Realize all of our previous examples are in the base directory of the web application. For this reason `"WEB-INF/exampleTags.tld"` is the correct relative URI to use; however, should we make a sub-directory this changes. In a sub-directory the relative URI would then be `"../WEB-INF/exampleTags.tld"`. For each sub-directory of the sub-directory we would have to add another set of double dots. With the URI mapped in `web.xml` we can go back to using the same URI for all of our `taglib` directives regardless of directory.

Remember our TLD file has not been changed. Creating a TLD for your tag library and referencing the TLD are distinctly different. These methods are all different ways to reference the same TLD. The final method for referencing a TLD is geared for tag libraries provided in a special package called a JAR.

Packaging Tag Libraries Into JAR Files

A Java Archive (JAR) is a convenient method of packaging together many class files into one main file. A JAR is a file using zip compression to combine many resources such as class files and tag library descriptors. In the case of custom tag libraries a JAR file is used to combine all the tag handler classes and the appropriate TLD files.

Packaging a custom tag library in a JAR is ideal for portability. Installing a JAR requires placing the JAR file in the `WEB-INF/lib` directory of the JSP application and rebooting Tomcat. Compared to copying various files and/or editing the `web.xml` file this method clearly is the winner.

Two ways currently exist for referencing TLD files inside a JAR file. The older JSP 1.1 specification supports the use of only one TLD file in a JAR. The TLD file must be called `taglib.tld` and be placed in the `META-INF` directory of your JAR.

This is then referenced in your JSPs using the following page directive:

```
<%@ taglib prefix="example" uri="WEB-INF/lib/example.jar" %>
```

where the `uri` must point to the location of your JAR file. This method has been superseded in the JSP 1.2 specification but must still be used if your web applications required backward compatibility with JSP 1.1 installations.

The JSP 1.2 specification provides a new method. Any number of tag libraries may be packaged in the same JAR as long as they each have all the appropriate tag handler class files and a TLD in the META-INF directory with the `.tld` extension. Additionally each TLD must specify different `uri` values. There may never be two tag libraries referenced with the same URI regardless of the method used to reference them. This method is demonstrated in the following example.

Try It Out – Packaging a Tag Library with JAR

As we saw in Chapter 1, the JDK comes with a tool named `jar` for creating a JAR file. Get to a command prompt and browse to the `JAVA_HOME/bin` directory. Execute the `jar` command and you will see help options appearing for the `jar` tool.

Before using the `jar` tool, we need to set up our files in a specific order. First, save all of the tag handler class files in the `JAVA_HOME/bin/com/wrox/ch10` directory. Next, copy `exampleTags.tld` into the `JAVA_HOME/bin/META-INF` directory.

Now open up the copy of `exampleTags.tld` and add the following entry:

```xml
<?xml version="1.0" encoding="ISO-8859-1"?>
<!DOCTYPE taglib PUBLIC
                "-//Sun Microsystems, Inc.//DTD JSP Tag Library 1.2//EN"
                "http://java.sun.com/dtd/web-jsptaglibrary_1_2.dtd">
<taglib>
  <tlib-version>1.0</tlib-version>
  <jsp-version>1.2</jsp-version>
  <short-name>ExampleTags</short-name>
  <uri>exampleURI</uri>
  <description>A set of example tag handlers.</description>
  <tag>
    <name>time</name>
    <tag-class>com.wrox.ch10.timeTag</tag-class>
    <display-name>time</display-name>
    <attribute>
      <name>format</name>
    </attribute>
  </tag>
  <tag>
    <name>iterate</name>
    <tag-class>com.wrox.ch10.iterateTag</tag-class>
    <variable>
      <name-given>currentString</name-given>
      <variable-class>java.lang.String</variable-class>
      <declare>true</declare>
      <scope>NESTED</scope>
    </variable>
    <variable>
      <name-given>arrayCount</name-given>
```

```
      <variable-class>java.lang.Integer</variable-class>
      <declare>true</declare>
      <scope>NESTED</scope>
    </variable>
  </tag>
  <tag>
    <name>createArray</name>
    <tag-class>com.wrox.ch10.createArrayTag</tag-class>
    <tei-class>com.wrox.ch10.arrayExtraInfo</tei-class>
    <attribute>
      <name>name</name>
    </attribute>
  </tag>
</taglib>
```

Use the `jar` utility with the following command, from the `%JAVA_HOME%/bin` directory:

```
> jar cvf example.jar com/wrox/ch10/*.class META-INF/exampleTags.tld
```

Output should appear describing the process of creating the JAR:

```
added manifest
adding: com/wrox/ch10/arrayExtraInfo.class(in = 744) (out= 410)(deflated 44%)
adding: com/wrox/ch10/createArrayTag.class(in = 694) (out= 442)(deflated 36%)
adding: com/wrox/ch10/iterateTag.class(in = 948) (out= 564)(deflated 40%)
adding: com/wrox/ch10/timeTag.class(in = 1011) (out= 595)(deflated 41%)
adding: META-INF/exampleTags.tld(in = 1326) (out= 498)(deflated 62%)
```

A new file will be created in the `JAVA_HOME/bin` directory called `example.jar`. This is the JAR file for the custom tag library. Place this file in the `webapps/begjsp-ch10/WEB-INF/lib` directory of Tomcat.

To test the new JAR edit `teiExample.jsp` to use a new URI. Notice this URI is not the real location of our TLD nor is it defined by `web.xml`.

```
<%@ taglib prefix="example" uri="exampleURI" %>
<html>
  <head></head>
  <body>
  <example:createArray name="theArray"/>
      We are now using a JAR File<br>
  The array has <%= theArray.length %> items.
  </body>
</html>
```

Restart Tomcat to load the new JAR and browse to `teiExample.jsp`. The example still works using the new URI.

Note: At the time of writing this example will not run on the latest version of Tomcat 4.0 (beta 5) due to a bug. This has been fixed in the latest nightly builds, and so this should work in future release versions of Tomcat.

How It Works

Although the example may seem complicated it is only making a small addition to `exampleTags.tld` and strategically placing it inside a JAR. The JAR works because it is using the third mechanism for linking a URI to a TLD of a custom tag library.

By default a JSP 1.2 compliant container will take any file placed in the `META-INF` folder of a JAR with a `.tld` extension and treat it as a TLD. The URI of a TLD read in this manner is defined by the `<uri>` element of the TLD. One of the steps in this example was adding the following `<uri>` element to `exampleTags.tld`:

```
<uri>exampleURI</uri>
```

The value of the `<uri>` element is `"exampleURI"`; this can be any arbitrary string. In a similar fashion to `web.xml` in the previous example, the JSP container now automatically acts as a middleman to resolve an unknown URI used by a `taglib` directive. In our case `scriptingVariables.jsp` uses `"exampleURI "` as a URI in its `taglib` directive. If our JAR file included multiple TLD files each must have a unique `<uri>` element

```
<%@ taglib prefix="example" uri="exampleTags.tld" %>
```

Tomcat remembers the URI `"exampleURI"` was contained in the `exampleTags.tld` file and links the prefix `example` to that tag library.

Resources

All of the official information for custom tags can be found in the current JSP specification:

http://java.sun.com/products/jsp/download.html

The JSP 1.2 specification plans for the future existence of a **Standard JSP tag library**. This is being handled by Java Specification Request 52. For more details, see:

http://jcp.org/jsr/detail/052.jsp

While the Standard tag library is still in the works, be aware that many free custom tag libraries do already exist. Checking around before diving into the code can save you time and effort. A few tag libraries were previously mentioned with examples. Here are more links to some of the larger current tag library resources.

❑ The **Jakarta Taglibs** project at http://jakarta.apache.org/taglibs/index.html is open-source and designed to be portable between any JSP container. Because of the large amount of support from the JSP developing community and a solid user base, the Jakarta Taglibs is arguably one of the best resources to find JSP custom tags.

❑ **JSPTags.com**, at http://www.jsptags.com, is a web site that provides current listings of the most popular tag libraries and provides a few of its own.

❑ **JSP Insider** at http://www.jspinsider.com is an extensive JSP information site with many tag library resources including articles and tutorials.

Finally, if you are interested in learning more about JAR files, **Sun** provides a free tutorial at http://java.sun.com/docs/books/tutorial/jar/index.html.

Summary

Throughout this chapter we have covered many aspects of writing tag libraries. In general the process of writing a tag library was broken down into two parts: creating tag handlers and linking your tag library with the JSP container.

When we create a tag handler there are three interfaces to choose from: `Tag`, `IterationTag`, and `BodyTag`. Implementing these interfaces can be tedious, especially when only one or two of the methods are of interest. Included in the JSP API are two helper classes called `TagSupport` and `BodyTagSupport`. Extending these helper classes is a quick and easy solution when creating a tag handler. Therefore, when you create a tag handler implementing the `Tag` or `IterationTag` interface, you should extend the `TagSupport` object. When creating a tag handler implementing the `BodyTag` interface, extend the `BodyTagSupport` object.

Mapping your tag library was further broken down into two main steps: creating a Tag Library Descriptor file (TLD) and linking this TLD with your JSP container.

The TLD can contain many elements that describe tags, and we discussed the most commonly used elements, and used them in our examples.

Linking your TLD with the JSP container can be accomplished by three different methods:

❑ Using the relative URI is an easy solution, and was used through the majority of our examples.

❑ Mapping through `web.xml` also exists, and allows for an arbitrary pseudo-URI.

❑ Finally when packaging your tag library in a JAR, automatic mapping is done on `.tld` files in the `META-INF` directory.

Using this last method provides the same functionality as mapping via `web.xml` does, but it also allows for your tag library to be easily ported between JSP projects.

Our introduction to tag libraries was enough to get you writing your own tags but was not a comprehensive look into everything the JSP 1.2 specification supports. Tag libraries are one of the most popular features of JSP and one chapter cannot do justice to the entire specification.

In the next chapter we will look at the techniques we can use to keep track of users in a web application.

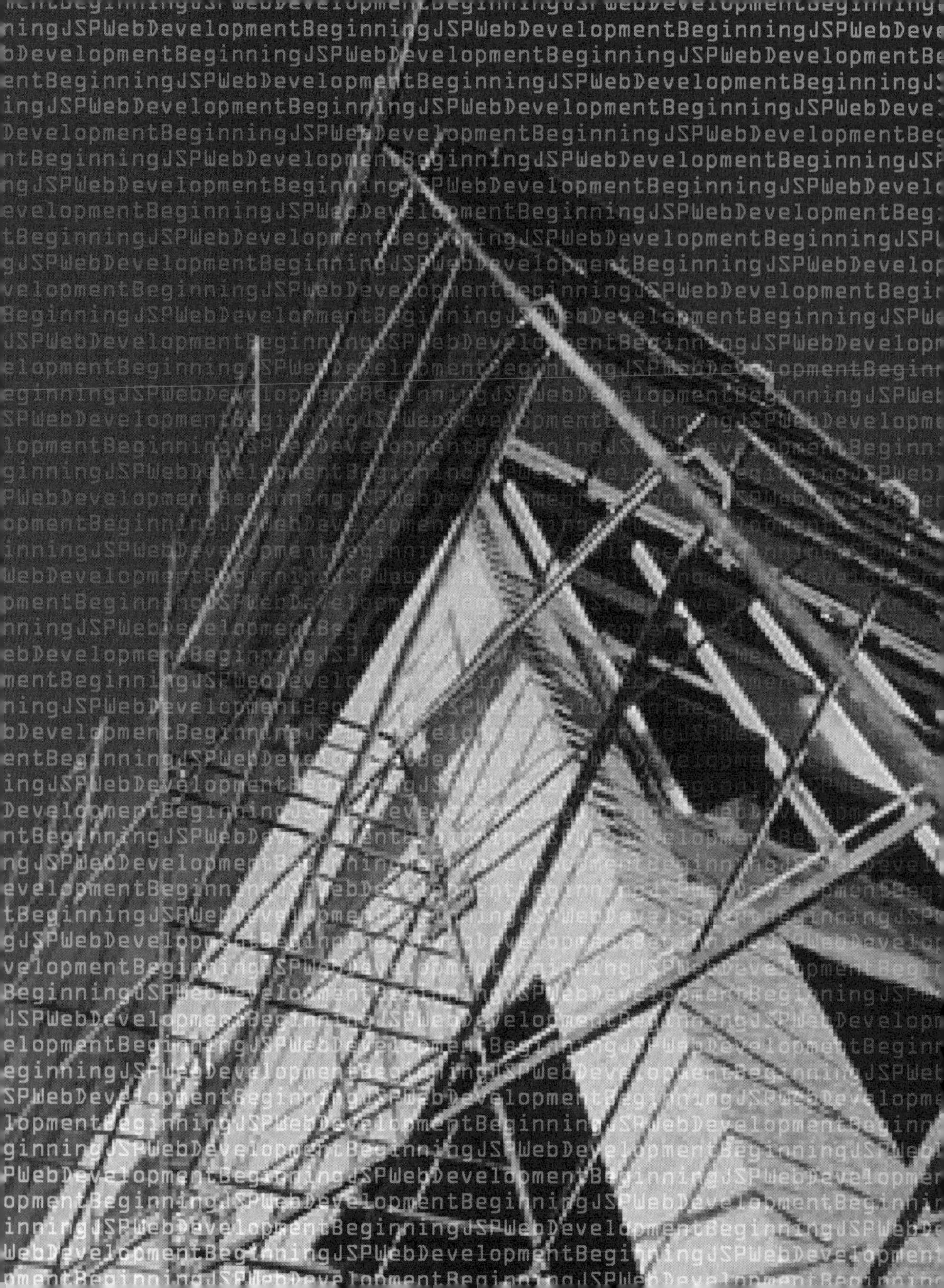
BeginningJSPWebDevelopment

Keeping Track of Users

Many successful web-sites depend on a personalized approach to attract and retain visitors. In order to create a personalized service the site must be able to remember the user across multiple visits. Take for example Amazon, which is a large online store visited by millions of returning customers each day. In order to increase sales Amazon need to highlight products that can provoke the customer's interest. So, like most web stores, Amazon will remember if the customer has visited before, what they are interested in, and what products they have bought in the past.

Sites also have to remember users during visits. For example, when a customer purchases products the site lets her purchase multiple products and allows her to pay for them all at the same time. We will be looking into the details of how the user is tracked in this type of application, where a user is tracked over a single visit. By the end of this chapter you will be able to explain how a user is tracked in, say, a mail application like Hotmail, from login to logout, and will know how to track users using several well-established methods. We will concentrate on using JSP for tracking users.

What Is a Session?

To build effective web applications, it is necessary that a series of different requests from a particular client be logically associated with each other. In shopping web sites, every purchase decision you make will be pushed into shopping cart, which collects your purchases so you can pay for them all together. The cart remembers all the items you decided to buy, even when you have surfed through hundreds of pages and bought tens of things. This is possible because these web applications are capable of tracking sessions.

> **The process of remembering a user for a specific length of time across different but logically related requests is called session tracking.**

Sessions can be tracked by uniquely identifying the client at each request made to the server. In the rest of the chapter, we will discuss in detail what session tracking is and how to achieve it. However, if session tracking is so important for web applications, then why isn't it built into the web server or browser? We'll learn the reason for this in the next section.

The HTTP Protocol

HTTP, the standard protocol that is used across the World Wide Web for file access is **stateless** by design. Internet communication protocols can be divided into two types: **stateful** and **stateless**. A protocol such as File Transfer Protocol (FTP), which is used to transfer files, remembers a client from login until logout. That is, it remembers the state of the connection with the client. So, you can perform several operations in a single session.

HTTP on the other hand is a stateless protocol. It is inherent in the HTTP protocol that there is no way to associate one request with another; they may come in at different times and on different ports. Therefore there is no association of requests by the server. If every time you added a new item to your shopping cart, it would forget all the previous items and it wouldn't even remember that it was your cart in the first place, it would be very difficult to build a successful online store!

How Does the HTTP Protocol Work?

The HTTP protocol was covered in Chapter 1, but here is a quick recap of the important points. Let's look at the sequence of events that take place when you request a web page; let's say http://www.wrox.com.

1. The browser opens an HTTP connection to the web server at Wrox.

2. Then it sends an HTTP request for a web page.

3. The web server responds to the request and sends an appropriate response (either the requested page or an error message).

4. Once the web server has fulfilled a browser's request for a web page, the connection between the web server and browser is closed.

Next time you send a request for another page to the same web server, a *new* connection is opened; the web server will not be able to tell that the request is coming from the same browser instance or the same user who accessed a page seconds ago.

Back to Sessions

A session can be viewed as an object associated with a single client, which helps to segregate and manage user specific data in a web application. Within our application, a session is treated like a unique object associated with a set of related data. A session can be created and destroyed as and when required. Also, a session can timeout and expire. Data like information about a current user can be associated with a session. For example, many web sites require you to log in to access their services and log out once you are finished. Here, once you log in, a session is created which will be filled with some information about you. This information can be read and written several times, as required by the application. When you log out, the data associated with your session is either stored on the server or destroyed. (Data stored on the server could be information about previous orders or preferences, so that the next time you log in to the site it will be just like you never left.)

Session tracking is important in today's e-commerce web applications. As we saw before, a shopping cart has to reflect accurately the choices made by the customer at every step of the shopping process.

Tracking Sessions

Three main mechanisms have been evolved to allow client tracking:

❑ Cookies

❑ URL rewriting

❑ Hidden form fields

Cookies

Cookies are the most widely used session tracking mechanism. A cookie is a text file stored on the client machine with the help of a web browser such as Netscape Navigator or Microsoft Internet Explorer. The cookie stores information using name-value pairs, and is returned to the server that created it on subsequent requests.

The server creates a cookie, fills it with relevant information, and sends it over to the client browser. The client stores this cookie on the hard disc and on each subsequent request it sends the cookie back to the server. All cookies have an expiry date set, so they are temporary, but this date can be set far in the future if needed.

However, there are drawbacks to using cookies. By convention, a cookie should not be more than 4KB in size, and no domain should have more than 20 cookies. Also, sensitive information like credit-card details should not be stored in a cookie. There has been much controversy regarding privacy concerns created by the use of cookies. For these reasons, some users disable cookies in their web browser, preventing cookies from being used as a session tracking mechanism. An application which depends on cookies to track sessions would then get's into trouble!

Even though JSPs have a high-level and easy-to-use interface for cookies, there are still a number of relatively tedious details that need to be handled:

❑ Extracting the cookie that stores the session identifier from the other cookies.

❑ Setting an appropriate expiration time for the cookie.

❑ Associating information on the server with the session identifier (there may be far too much information to actually store it in the cookie, plus sensitive data like credit card numbers should never go in cookies).

Try It Out – Using Cookies

This example contains two simple JSPs. `AddCookie.jsp` writes a cookie to the client browser, and `GetCookie.jsp` gets the cookies from the client then returns the value of the cookie that was set by `AddCookie.jsp`.

Create a folder named `begjsp-ch11` in Tomcat's `webapps` folder, and save the code overleaf in a file called `AddCookie.jsp` in that folder:

```
<!--AddCookie.jsp-->
<html>
<head><title>This page stores a cookie on your computer</title></head>
<body>
  <h1>Cookie is being stored on your computer!</h1>

  <%
    Cookie myCookie = new Cookie("user", "newUser");
    myCookie.setMaxAge(24*60*60);
    response.addCookie(myCookie);
  %>

  <a href="GetCookie.jsp"/>Read Cookie</a>

</body>
</html>
```

Create another file, GetCookie.jsp, containing this code:

```
<!--GetCookie.jsp-->
<html>
<head><title>This gets a cookie stored on your computer</title></head>
<body>
  <h1>The User's name will be displayed from the cookie stored.</h1>

  <%
    Cookie[] cookieList = request.getCookies();

    for(int I = 0; I< cookieList.length;I++) {
      Cookie myCookie = cookieList[I];
      if (myCookie.getName().equals("user")) {
        out.println("The Name of the user is: " + myCookie.getValue());
      }
    }
  %>

</body>
</html>
```

Direct your browser to http://localhost:8080/begjsp-ch11/AddCookie.jsp. After this page has loaded click on Read Cookie, and you should see the following result:

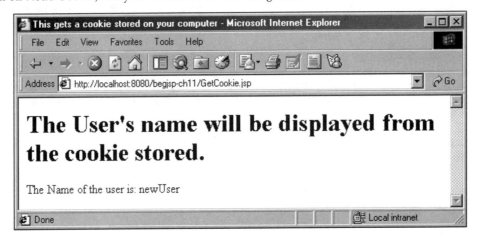

GetCookie.jsp has read the cookie data that was sent to the browser by AddCookie.jsp.

How It Works

AddCookie.jsp creates a new Cookie object, with the name "user" and the value "newUser":

```
Cookie myCookie = new Cookie("user", "newUser");
```

The maximum time the cookie will last is then set to be 24 hours:

```
myCookie.setMaxAge(24*60*60);
```

Finally, the cookie is sent to the client browser using the addCookie() method of the response object:

```
response.addCookie(myCookie);
```

GetCookie.jsp gets a list of all cookies stored in the request object and stores them in the Cookie[] array variable cookieList:

```
Cookie[] cookieList = request.getCookies();
```

It then iterates through the cookie array, looking for a cookie with the name "user". If a cookie with this name is found, its value is printed back to the browser:

```
for(int I = 0; I< cookieList.length;I++) {
  Cookie myCookie = cookieList[I];
  if (myCookie.getName().equals("user")) {
    out.println("The Name of the user is: " + myCookie.getValue());
  }
}
```

URL Rewriting

URL rewriting is used to append data that identifies the session to the end of each URL. The server associates the identifier with data it has stored about the session, so that on every subsequent request the ID can be used to associate the request with a particular client. A rewritten URL looks something like http://www.wrox.com/myApp/ShoppingCart.html;jsessionid=12345.

This solution has the advantage that it works with browsers that don't support cookies, or where the user has disabled cookies. However, it has most of the same problems as cookies, namely that the server-side program has a lot of straightforward but tedious processing to do:

❑   You have to be sure to append the information to every URL that references your site.

❑   Appending parameters brings up privacy issues; you may not want the actual data you are tracking to be visible.

❑   There is a loophole in that users can leave the session and come back using a bookmark, in which case your session information is lost.

This technique is rarely used because there are easier and less intrusive methods of tracking sessions.

Hidden Form Fields

HTML forms can have an entry that looks like the following:

```
<input type="hidden" name="session" value="12345">
```

Declaring its type as `"hidden"` can conceal a form field; nevertheless, when the form is submitted the specified name and value are included in the GET or POST data. This can be used to store information about the session. For example, as a user shops the product IDs of items a user has added to his shopping cart could be added as hidden form fields.

This technique is supported by all the major web browsers and doesn't require any form of user authorization; however, its usefulness is limited because it only works for a sequence of dynamically generated *forms*, and people can view the HTML source to see the stored data.

Many strategies like those described above have evolved over time for tracking user sessions. But most of them are difficult or troublesome for the programmer to directly apply.

Using Sessions in JavaServer Pages

JSPs provide a painless way to manage sessions, using the implicit object called `session`. This object internally uses one of the methods described above to track sessions under the hood, but the details are not exposed to the developer. For example, Tomcat uses cookies to identify the client if it can, otherwise it falls back on using URL rewriting.

Now we'll look at using the `session` object to track sessions, as defined in the JSP specification. It is pretty simple to use; the basic steps for using the object are:

❑   Declare that the page participates in a session.

❑   Read from or write to the `session` object.

❑   Either terminate the session by expiring it, or do nothing so it will eventually expire on its own.

As we have already seen, page properties in a JSP are declared using the `<%@page %>` directive. The directive shown below indicates that the scripting language is based on Java, that the classes declared in the package `java.util` are directly available to the scripting code, and that the page participates in sessions:

```
<%@page language="java " import="java.util.*" session="true "%>
```

If the `session` value is `"true"`, then an implicit script language variable (like the `request` object we're familiar with) of type `javax.servlet.http.HttpSession` is available for use in the page, with the name `session`. It will represent the existing session, or if there is no session existing already a new session will be created.

If the value of `session` above is `"false"` then the page cannot participate in sessions. If you try to write session-aware code in such a page, you will get a compilation error.

> By default, the value is **`"true"`**, so if you don't declare the value explicitly **`false`**, then it is assumed that the page is interested in tracking sessions.

You should note that there is one session for each web application on your server. This means that although JSPs in your `begjsp-ch11` folder (or its subfolders) can share session data with each other, they can't share it with JSPs in (for example) the `begjsp-ch10` folder.

The Session Object in Detail

As we've seen the `session` object is available to pages with the `session` attribute set to `"true"`. Now let's see what can we do with the `session` object.

Storing Data in the Session

The most obvious thing we want to do with the `session` object is to store information in it; this is done by calling its `setAttribute()` method:

```
Integer iFirstval = new Integer(1);
session.setAttribute("firstVal", iFirstval);
```

Here we are creating an `Integer` object, and storing it in the session under the name `"firstVal"`. Every object that you store in the session is associated with a unique name, a `String`, that identifies it. This is very similar to the way we specified a unique `id` attribute on the `<jsp:useBean>` action in Chapter 4.

But why are we storing an `Integer` object rather than using the primitive type `int`? Unfortunately, like the utility classes we saw in Chapter 8, the `session` object can only store objects rather than primitive values like `int`s. `Integer` is a **wrapper class**; that is to say, it provides a simple way of "wrapping up" an `int` value in an object, for use when we need an object rather than the primitive data type. The `Integer` constructor which we used above converts an `int` value into an `Integer` object, and `Integer`'s `intValue()` method converts it back into an `int`.

Once it is stored, an object bound to the session is available to any other JSP that is in the same session and context, by calling the session object's `getAttribute()` method and specifying the same name that was used when the object was stored:

```
Integer iPrevVal = (Integer) session.getAttribute("firstVal");
```

You may have noticed that while getting values back from the session, we have to cast our object back into its particular class. This is because the `getAttribute()` method's return type is declared as being `Object`. However, in this case we know that the object we stored is actually an `Integer`, and so we will be able to cast it to the right type. (If you get this wrong then a `ClassCastException` will be thrown.) You might want to get the names of all the objects in the session, and you can do this by calling the `getAttributeNames()` method, which returns an `Enumeration` of the attribute names. Finally, the `removeAttribute()` method removes a named object from the session.

Checking for a New Session

We can check whether the session is new by asking the `session` object the question:

```
if (session.isNew()) {
  // Yes it is
}
```

The session is considered new until a client joins the session. In other words, the session-related information given to the client has to be returned *back* to the server through a subsequent request, thus completing the circuit and saying that the session has been successfully established. Let's look at an example:

❑ A client sends an HTTP request to a web server, to access the application.

❑ The server generates a unique ID to identify the client, and passes it on to the client in a cookie sent along with the response.

❑ The client receives the response, and stores the ID.

❑ When the client sends the second request it forwards the cookie to the server, along with the request.

❑ Once the server receives this information along with the request, it assumes that the client is participating in the session.

The session continues to be new if the client fails to close the circuit. This might happen because the client might not know about the session yet, or the client might not support the session tracking mechanisms used by the server. For example, the server might support only cookie-based session tracking mechanism but cookies might have been disabled on the client. Then in this case the session.isNew() method will always return true.

Obtaining the Session Identifier

Every session is identified by a unique session ID, which is used to track multiple requests from the same client to the server and associate the client with its session data. We can get the session identifier, which is a unique string assigned to a specific session, by using the method getId():

```
String id = session.getId();
```

Removing the Session

We need to be able to "kill" the session when it is no longer needed, and this is done using the session.invalidate() method.

Session Timeouts

Unfortunately, the HTTP protocol doesn't tell us whether the client is still active or not, and if we didn't get rid of old sessions periodically we would eventually run out of storage space on our server. Since HTTP is stateless, the only mechanism that we can use to determine when a client has become inactive is by using a timeout period, and so to make sure that sessions are periodically flushed, servers allow us to define timeout periods for sessions.

Servers like Tomcat define the default timeout period for a session, which can be obtained via the session object's getMaxInactiveInterval() method. The developer can also change this timeout using the setMaxInactiveInterval() method; the timeout period used by these methods is defined in seconds. If the timeout period for a session is set to -1, the session will never expire.

When deploying your web application on Tomcat you can define the default session timeout by using the `<session-timeout>` tag in the web.xml file that specifies configuration information for the application. For example, the code below specifies that sessions in this application will by default not time out; to use this it should be saved as a file named web.xml in the WEB-INF folder within your application's folder:

```xml
<?xml version="1.0" encoding="ISO-8859-1"?>

<!DOCTYPE web-app
    PUBLIC "-//Sun Microsystems, Inc.//DTD Web Application 2.3//EN"
    "http://java.sun.com/j2ee/dtds/web-app_2_3.dtd">

<webapp>
  <session-config>
    <session-timeout>-1</session-timeout>
  </session-config>
</webapp>
```

Try It Out – Using the Session Object

Let's look at an example that demonstrates the usage of the session object in a JSP. This page will track the number of times a user accesses the page, storing the access count in the session. Every time the user accesses the page the access count is incremented and stored back in the session. Additionally, we will display other properties of the session like session ID, session creation time, and the time of last access.

Save the code below in a file named ShowSession.jsp, in the begjsp-ch11 folder:

```jsp
<!--ShowSession.jsp-->
<%@page import = "java.util.*"%>
<html> <head><title>Session Example</title></head>
  <body bgcolor="white">

  <%
    Integer accessCount =
      (Integer)session.getAttribute("accessCount");
    String heading = null;
    if (accessCount == null) {
      accessCount = new Integer(1);
      heading = "Welcome, this is your First Visit";
    } else {
      accessCount = new Integer(accessCount.intValue() + 1);
      heading = "Welcome, this is your visit # " + accessCount;
    }

    session.setAttribute("accessCount", accessCount);
  %>

  <h1 align=center>  <%=heading%>  </h1>
  <P>
  <h2 align=center>Information about Your Session</h2><br>

  <table border=1 align="center">
```

```
   <tr bgcolor="#F9AD00">
     <th>Info Type</th><th>Value</th></tr>
   <tr><td>ID</td>
     <td> <%=session.getId()%></td></tr>
   <tr><td>Creation Time</td>
     <td><%=new Date(session.getCreationTime())%></td></tr>
   <tr>
     <td>Time of Last Access</TD>
     <td><%=new Date(session.getLastAccessedTime())%></td></tr>
   <tr>
     <td>Number of Accesses</td>
     <td> <%=accessCount%> </td></tr>
   </table>
 </body> </html>
```

With Tomcat running, point your browser at http://localhost:8080/begjsp-ch11/ShowSession.jsp; you should see a screen like that shown below:

Hit your browser's Reload button; each time you do, you should see the access count increase:

How it Works

The exciting stuff happens in the scriptlet block near the top of `ShowSession.jsp`. We'll store the access count in the session under the name `"accessCount"` (well, it's logical), and the count itself will be represented as an `Integer` object. (Remember, we can't store primitive data types like `int` in the session.)

We start by trying to retrieve the access count from the session, casting it to type `Integer`, and assigning a `String` variable that we'll use to assemble the page header:

```
<%
   Integer accessCount =
      (Integer)session.getAttribute("accessCount");
   String heading = null;
```

Next, we check whether we actually found anything in the session. If `getAttribute()` returned `null`, there wasn't an object in the session under the name `"accessCount"`, meaning that it must be this user's first visit to the page. In that case, we create a new `Integer` object to represent the access count of 1:

```
   if (accessCount == null) {
     accessCount = new Integer(1);
     heading = "Welcome, this is your First Visit";
   }
```

On the other hand, if we did find an access count we add 1 to it and create a new `Integer` object containing the new access count:

```
   else {
     accessCount = new Integer(accessCount.intValue() + 1);
     heading = "Welcome, this is your visit # " + accessCount;
   }
```

Finally for this section, we store the *new* access count value back in the session:

```
      session.setAttribute("accessCount", accessCount);
   %>
```

The rest of the JSP is concerned with using the values of the `heading` and `accessCount` variables, together with other information obtained from the `session` object, to produce the page sent back to the user:

```
   <h1 align=center>  <%=heading%>    </h1>
   <P>
   <h2 align=center>Information about Your Session</h2><br>

   <table border=1 align="center">
   <tr bgcolor="#F9AD00">
     <th>Info Type</th><th>Value</th></tr>
   <tr><td>ID</td>
     <td> <%=session.getId()%></td></tr>
   <tr><td>Creation Time</td>
     <td><%=new Date(session.getCreationTime())%></td></tr>
   <tr>
     <td>Time of Last Access</TD>
     <td><%=new Date(session.getLastAccessedTime())%></td></tr>
```

```
  <tr>
    <td>Number of Accesses</td>
    <td> <%=accessCount%> </td></tr>
  </table>
</body> </html>
```

Session Scope

In Chapter 4 we looked at using the `<jsp:useBean>` action to instantiate JavaBeans components from a JSP, but always set the `scope` attribute to have the value `"page"`. In fact, an object declared in a JSP using the `<jsp:useBean>` action can be declared to be in one of the scopes `"page"`, `"request"`, `"session"`, or `"application"`, depending on where you want the bean to be stored. Using scopes other than `"page"` makes the bean available to other pages too, so that instead of always creating a new bean instance the action will first look to see if a bean matching the specified name and scope already exists. This allows us to share a single JavaBean between multiple pages.

You may think that this sounds rather like storing an object in, say, the session; you'd be right – in fact, if you use `"session"` scope for your beans they get stored in the `session` object just like objects that are put there using the `session` object's `setAttribute()` method.

The scope defines the availability of an object:

❑   `page` scope: Available to the handling page only.

❑   `request` scope: Available to the handling page and any page to which it passes control. (This will be covered in detail in Chapter 9.)

❑   `session` scope: Available to any JSP with in the same session.

❑   `application` scope: Available to any component of the same web application. (We'll look at this in a few pages.)

You cannot create objects with `session` scope in a JSP that doesn't participate in sessions. One other caveat, too: all the objects associated with a session are released once the session is destroyed, and if an attempt is made to use one an exception will be thrown.

In the following example we try to find an existing object that has the id `"ShoppingCart"` and is stored in the `session` object. If nothing is found, it will attempt to create one. The object is then available in all pages during the life of current session:

```
<jsp:useBean id="ShoppingCart" scope="session"
 class="JSPExample.ShoppingCart "/>
```

Try It Out – A Simple Shopping Cart

Now let's start building a simple shopping cart to demonstrate use of beans and sessions in JSPs. We'll provide the user with a list of books to purchase, and options to add books to the shopping cart and to remove them once added.

Enter the code below into a new file, called `Purchase.jsp`:

```
<%@ page import="java.util.Vector" %>
<html>
<head><title>Shopping Cart Example</title></head>
```

```
<body>
  <center>
    <form type=post action="Purchase.jsp">
      <h1>Shopping Cart Example</h1>
      <br>
      Please select a Product and add it to your Shopping Cart
      <br>
      <select name='product'>
        <option>Beginning Java 2 by Ivor Horton</option>
        <option>Professional Java Programming by Brett Spell</option>
        <option>Professional Jini by Sing Li</option>
        <option>Professional JSP by Sing Li et al</option>
        <option>Professional XSL by Andrew Watt et al</option>
        <option>XML Applications by Frank Boumphrey et al</option>
        <option>Beginning XML by Nikola Ozu et al</option>
        <option>Instant UML by Pierre-Alain Muller</option>
        <option>Beginning Java Objects by Jacquie Barker</option>
      </select>
      <input type=submit name="submit" value="add">
    </form>

<!-- Here goes the shopping cart display -->

<%
    String submit = request.getParameter("submit");
    if (submit != null) {
%>

    <hr>
    <h2 align="center">Your Shopping Cart</h2>
    <p>

    <jsp:useBean id="cart" scope="session"
     class="com.wrox.sessions.ShoppingCart"/>
    <jsp:setProperty name="cart" property="*" />

<%
    cart.processRequest(request);
%>

    <table width="75%" align="center" border="1">

<%
    Vector products = cart.getProducts();
    for(int i=0; i<products.size(); i++) {
%>

      <tr>
        <td><%= products.get(i) %></td>
        <td><a href="Purchase.jsp?product=<%= products.get(i)
            %>&submit=remove">Remove</a>
        </td>
      </tr>
<%
    }
    if (products.size() == 0) {
%>

      <tr><td>Your cart is currently empty</td></tr>
<%
    }
%>

    </table>
```

303

```
<%
   }
%>
   </center>
</body>
</html>
```

The processing of add and remove requests for this JSP is done by a `ShoppingCart` bean. Currently this represents a product simply by its name, so that the shopping cart will manage a list of `String` objects containing product names. This could be expanded further to include all of the details of the products by writing a simple product class.

Inside the `begjsp-ch11` folder create a `WEB-INF\classes\com\wrox\sessions` folder, and enter the Java code below into a new file there called `ShoppingCart.java`:

```java
package com.wrox.sessions;

import java.util.Vector;
import javax.servlet.http.HttpServletRequest;

public class ShoppingCart extends Object {

  private Vector cart = null;
  String product = null;
  String submit = null;

  public ShoppingCart() {
    cart = new Vector();
  }

  public void setProduct(String product) {
    this.product = product;
  }

  public void setSubmit(String submit) {
    this.submit = submit;
  }

  public Vector getProducts() {
    return cart;
  }

  public void addProduct(String product) {
    cart.add(product);
  }

  public void removeProduct(String product) {
    cart.remove(product);
  }

  public void processRequest(HttpServletRequest req) {
    if (submit != null) {
      if (submit.equals("add")) {
        addProduct(product);
      } else {
        removeProduct(product);
      }
      reset();
```

```
    }
  }

  public void reset() {
    submit = null;
    product = null;
  }
}
```

Compile the code by opening a command prompt in the `begjsp-ch11\WEB-INF\classes` folder and entering:

```
javac com\wrox\sessions\ShoppingCart.java
```

Restart Tomcat and browse to http://localhost:8080/begjsp-ch11/Purchase.jsp; you will get a screen containing the dropdown list of available products and an Add button:

Then try adding and removing items from the cart using the Add button and the Remove links:

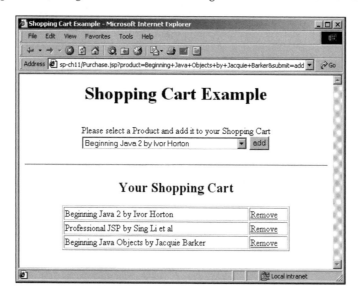

How It Works

The first part of the JSP presents the user with a series of books to choose from, in a dropdown box, together with an **Add** button that posts your selection to the server:

```
<%@ page import="java.util.Vector" %>
<html>
<head><title>Shopping Cart Example</title></head>
<body>
  <center>
    <form type=post action="Purchase.jsp">
      <h1>Shopping Cart Example</h1>
      <br>
      Please select a Product and add it to your Shopping Cart
      <br>
      <select name='product'>
        <option>Beginning Java 2 by Ivor Horton</option>
        <option>Professional Java Programming by Brett Spell</option>
        <option>Professional Jini by Sing Li</option>
        <option>Professional JSP by Sing Li et al</option>
        <option>Professional XSL by Andrew Watt et al</option>
        <option>XML Applications by Frank Boumphrey et al</option>
        <option>Beginning XML by Nikola Ozu et al</option>
        <option>Instant UML by Pierre-Alain Muller</option>
        <option>Beginning Java Objects by Jacquie Barker</option>
      </select>
      <input type=submit name="submit" value="add">
    </form>
```

If this is the user's first visit to the page, that's all we display (except for the HTML footer at the very end). If, on the other hand, the user has returned to the same page by clicking either on the **Add** button or on one of the **Remove** links, there will be a request parameter named `submit` present. If it's there, we also display the user's shopping cart in the bottom part of the screen:

```
<%
    String submit = request.getParameter("submit");
    if (submit != null) {
%>
    <hr>
    <h2 align="center">Your Shopping Cart</h2>
    <p>
```

. . .

```
<%
    }
%>
```

The shopping cart is represented by our `ShoppingCart` bean, so our next job is to make sure that a bean is instantiated and stored in `session` scope; this will mean that on subsequent requests the user can be reunited with their cart. We also set the bean properties to correspond to the request parameters, and call the bean's `processRequest()` method. We'll see what that does in a moment:

```
<jsp:useBean id="cart" scope="session"
 class="com.wrox.sessions.ShoppingCart"/>
<jsp:setProperty name="cart" property="*" />
```

```
<%
    cart.processRequest(request);
%>
```

The bean stores the current cart contents as a `Vector`; as we saw in Chapter 8, a `Vector` is very similar to an `ArrayList` object. To display the cart we retrieve the `Vector` and loop through each item in turn, creating a table with two columns, the first displaying the product name and the second a hyperlink that allows you to remove the book from the shopping cart. If the cart is empty we display a short message instead:

```
    <table width="75%" align="center" border="1">
<%
    Vector products = cart.getProducts();
    for(int i=0; i<products.size(); i++) {
%>
      <tr>
        <td><%= products.get(i) %></td>
        <td><a href="Purchase.jsp?product=<%= products.get(i)
            %>&submit=remove">Remove</a>
        </td>
      </tr>
<%
    }
    if (products.size() == 0) {
%>
        <tr><td>Your cart is currently empty</td></tr>
<%
    }
%>
    </table>
```

So, how does the `ShoppingCart` bean do its stuff? It's quite straightforward, in fact. Every request to add or remove a product from the cart will have two request parameters associated with it: `product`, containing the name of the item, and `submit`, which will either be `"add"` if we are to add the item to the cart or `"remove"` if we are to remove it. The bean has corresponding `setProduct()` and `setSubmit()` methods, so `<jsp:setProperty>` action in the JSP sets the property values to the corresponding request parameters:

```
String product = null;
String submit = null;

public void setProduct(String product) {
  this.product = product;
}

public void setSubmit(String submit) {
  this.submit = submit;
}
```

As we mentioned, the list of items in the cart is maintained in a `Vector`. This is instantiated when the bean itself is created, and there is a `getProducts()` method that the page uses to obtain the `Vector`:

```
private Vector cart = null;

public ShoppingCart() {
```

```
      cart = new Vector();
   }

   public Vector getProducts() {
      return cart;
   }
```

The `ShoppingCart` bean also defines a pair of methods for dealing with the shopping cart, `addProduct()` and `removeProduct()`:

```
   public void addProduct(String product) {
      cart.add(product);
   }

   public void removeProduct(String product) {
      cart.remove(product);
   }
```

Requests sent from the JSP are processed by the `processRequest()` method. Depending on whether the user wants to add or remove an item (as determined by the value of the `submit` request parameter), it calls either the `addProduct()` or `removeProduct()` method:

```
   public void processRequest(HttpServletRequest req) {
      if (submit != null) {
         if (submit.equals("add")) {
            addProduct(product);
         } else {
            removeProduct(product);
         }
         reset();
      }
   }
```

Finally, the `reset()` method tidies up the bean's `product` and `submit` properties ready for the next request:

```
   public void reset() {
      submit = null;
      product = null;
   }
```

The Application Object

Earlier we mentioned briefly that there are other places where your application can store data – other **scopes** – than the session. We'll round off this chapter with a brief look at the `application` implicit object, which is another useful facility for sharing data between the pages in your site.

The `application` object allows us to share information between *all* the JSPs in a site, irrespective of which user is accessing them; it is therefore useful for sharing objects that are widely needed in the application. For example, in an e-commerce application we might choose to store our product catalogue in the `application` object, so that it is readily accessible to all the JSPs.

Like `session`, the `application` object provides `getAttribute()`, `setAttribute()`, `getAttributeNames()`, and `removeAttribute()` methods; however, applications don't time out, can't be invalidated, and don't have unique identifiers.

We'll return to looking at the `application` object in Chapter 13.

Try It Out – Using the Application Object

Using the `application` implicit object is very similar to using the `session` object, with the obvious difference that values you store in it are available to *all* users not just the current session. Let's enhance our visitor counter JSP that we saw earlier to keep track not only of how many times a particular user has accessed the page, but also how many times it has been accessed in total by all users.

Create a new file, `ShowApplication.jsp`, in your `begjsp-ch11` folder and enter this code:

```
<!--ShowApplication.jsp-->
<%@page import = "java.util.*"%>
<html>
<head><title>Application Object Example</title></head>
<body bgcolor="white">

<%
    Integer accessCount =
       (Integer)session.getAttribute("accessCount");
    String heading = null;
    if (accessCount == null) {
      accessCount = new Integer(1);
      heading = "Welcome, this is your First Visit";
    } else {
      accessCount = new Integer(accessCount.intValue() + 1);
      heading = "Welcome, this is your visit # " + accessCount;
    }

    session.setAttribute("accessCount", accessCount);


    Integer totalAccessCount =
       (Integer)application.getAttribute("totalAccessCount");
    if (totalAccessCount == null) {
      totalAccessCount = new Integer(1);
    } else {
      totalAccessCount = new Integer(totalAccessCount.intValue() + 1);
    }

    application.setAttribute("totalAccessCount", totalAccessCount);
%>

  <h1 align=center><%=heading%></h1>
  <h2 align=center>Access Counts</h2>

  <table border=1 align="center">
    <tr bgcolor="#F9AD00">
      <th>Info Type</th><th>Value</th>
    </tr>
    <tr>
      <td>Your Accesses</td>
      <td> <%=accessCount%> </td>
    </tr>
```

```
      <tr>
        <td>Total Accesses</td>
        <td> <%=totalAccessCount%> </td>
      </tr>
   </table>

 </body>
 </html>
```

Then open several browser windows and point each of them to http://localhost:8080/begjsp-ch11/ShowApplication.jsp. You should see that the page shows both the number of times each user has accessed the page and the total number of accesses:

You may find that the server seems to think that all of your browser windows are in the same session; you can get around this by starting a new copy of the browser for each window, rather than using the File / New menu option.

How It Works

The scriptlet at the top of ShowApplication.jsp should look familiar – the first half of it is the same code we used in ShowSession.jsp. In the second half of the scriptlet we use very similar code to look up the "totalAccessCount" attribute in the application object; this is the object that will store the total number of people who have visited the page. Except that we are using the application rather than the session object, the code is familiar:

```
    Integer totalAccessCount =
      (Integer)application.getAttribute("totalAccessCount");
    if (totalAccessCount == null) {
      totalAccessCount = new Integer(1);
    } else {
      totalAccessCount = new Integer(totalAccessCount.intValue() + 1);
    }

    application.setAttribute("totalAccessCount", totalAccessCount);
```

In the second part of the JSP, which generates the HTML table, we use expression tags to display the values of the `accessCount` and `totalAccessCount` scripting variables.

```
<table border=1 align="center">
  <tr bgcolor="#F9AD00">
    <th>Info Type</th><th>Value</th>
  </tr>
  <tr>
    <td>Your Accesses</td>
    <td> <%=accessCount%> </td>
  </tr>
  <tr>
    <td>Total Accesses</td>
    <td> <%=totalAccessCount%> </td>
  </tr>
</table>
```

Summary

In this chapter, we have covered the reasons why users need to be tracked, the most popular ways to track users of web applications and some practical examples of user tracking.

The important concepts we learned in this chapter are:

❑   Session tracking is very important for current e-commerce web applications, among others. We need to use an appropriate session tracking mechanism to suit our application.

❑   HTTP is a stateless communication protocol, so we need to use special procedures to track users and sessions.

❑   Session can be tracked using methods like URL rewriting, hidden form fields, and cookies, but these procedures can create a lot of work for application developers.

❑   The `HttpSession` class provides a simple interface for implementing user tracking.

❑   Objects can be stored with different levels of "scope", so allowing us to determine which JSPs and users should be able to access them.

You'll have noticed that some of our JSPs are beginning to get a bit hard to follow, despite our use of JavaBeans and tag libraries. We need to apply some more thought to the best ways of arranging our applications' code to make them easier to write, read, and understand. We'll look at that in the next chapter.

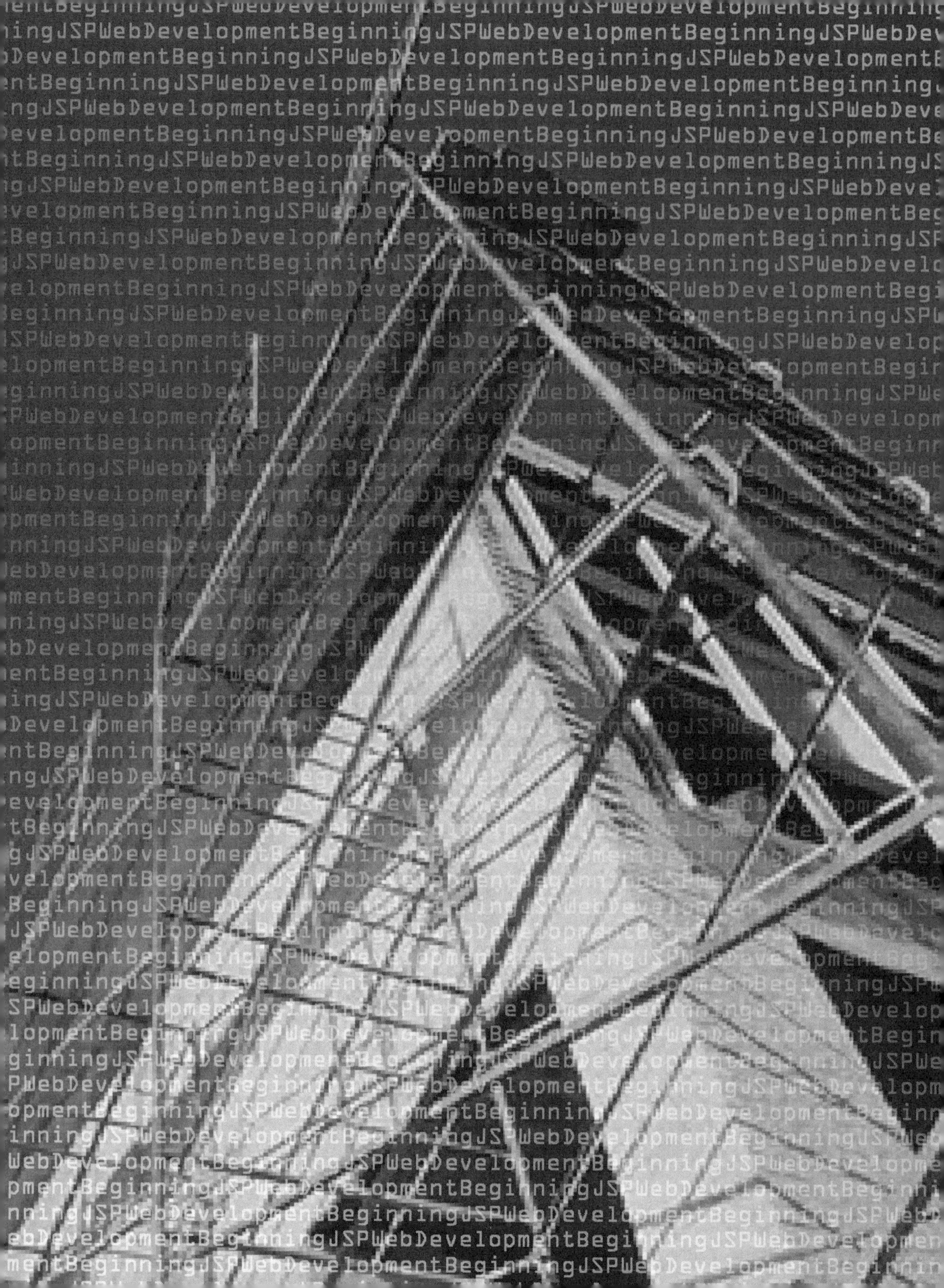
BeginningJSPWebDevelopment

Structuring Our Applications

One of the questions that have been preying on your mind up to now is: how do we approach planning out the structure of new JSP applications? One quick way is to gather up the requirements and quickly chalk out some JSPs and JavaBeans. Though this approach would probably work to some degree, you may end up overlooking things that may hinder you when you come to update or maintain your application. After all, we know that applications change over time; we need to add new functionality, and even sometimes drop some existing functionality. So it is very important that the application that we create is **maintainable**: we can change some functionality or introduce new functionality without breaking the other parts of the application. It is also important that we make as much code in our application **reusable**. If we need to introduce a new JSP or modify an existing JSP, we should be able to do that quickly if the application is structured correctly. By structuring our applications correctly, we will definitely go a long way towards achieving those goals.

In this chapter, we will look at several techniques that will help achieve the goals of maintainability and reusability in your applications.

We shall cover the following topics:

❑ Using the **include** mechanism, which helps you compose a JSP by including smaller JSPs

❑ JSP Model 1 Architecture, an example of an architecture used to structure JSP applications

❑ Using the request **forwarding** mechanism, which allows you to transfer control from one JSP page to another

❑ JSP Model 2 Architecture, which is an improvement over the Model 1 architecture

By the end of the chapter you should have a good understanding of how to separate your application out into an efficient but simple structure. But first, let's review why good maintainability and reusability is so important for our applications.

Maintaining and Reusing Code

Consider any real application. As our application grows larger, so will the number of JSP files in the application. And since the JSP files contain all of the functionality for flow control, business logic, data access, the maintenance and reusability of the code is going to get difficult.

For example, take a look at the page from a hypothetical **wrox.com** web site shown below:

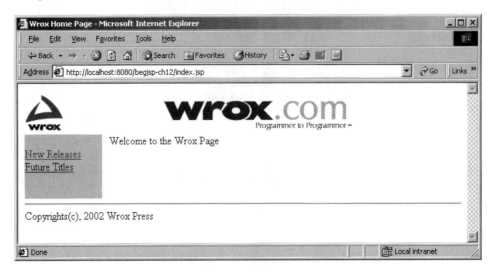

In the above page, we have a copyright message shown as Copyrights ©, 2001 Wrox Press. This copyright message is a standard footer message and is present in all the JSP files in the application. Say we wanted to change that to Copyrights ©, 2003 Wrox Press Ltd. The only way to do this would be to find each Copyrights © 2003 Wrox Press Ltd string in every JSP file in the application. For an application that has only a handful of pages, that might not seem like a big task. But imagine the situation if you have an application which has hundreds of JSP files! This system would obviously lead to poor code maintainability.

The same problem would occur if you had to do any of the following changes too:

❑   Changing the logo

❑   Adding a new menu option

Therefore this system would obviously lead to poor code **maintainability**.

So how could we get around this problem? Well, it would be more efficient if I could capture this copyright message in a separate JSP and include that in all the pages. Then we could use this same JSP page in lots of other pages: we only have to write the code to produce the footer once, and if we have to change the copyright message, all we need to do is change this footer JSP page. In other words, the key to making your applications more maintainable is to make your code **reusable**.

Including a File in a JSP

Since reusing JSPs in other JSPs is one way to make your code more reusable, we need a mechanism that will enable us to do this. This is achieved using the JSP `include` directive, which allows us to statically include the content of a resource into the current JSP at request time.

For example, if we wanted to include a file called `footer.jsp` into our JSP, we would write the following line in our JSP:

```
<%@ include file="footer.jsp" %>
```

And if we wanted to include `header.html`, we would use:

```
<%@ include file="header.html" %>
```

Given that we now have a mechanism to include file content in JSPs, let's now use this in our wrox.com home page scenario.

Try It Out – Using the include Directive

In this example, we will implement our idea of using the JSP `include` directive in the wrox.com home page shown earlier. We will separate out the copyright message into another file, and then include this file in our JSP page.

The first step therefore is to separate out the copyright message and move it into the `footer.jsp` file shown below:

```
<table border="0" cellpadding="0" cellspacing="0" width="100%">
  <tr>
    <td width="100%"><hr></td>
  </tr>
  <tr>
    <td width="100%">Copyrights(c), 2001 Wrox Press</td>
  </tr>
</table>
```

Then we modify the original home page, `index.jsp`, as shown below:

```
<html>

<head>
<title>Wrox Home Page</title>
</head>

<body>

<div align="right">
  <table border="0" cellpadding="0" cellspacing="0" width="100%">
    <tr>
      <td width="100%" colspan="2">
        <table border="0" cellpadding="0" cellspacing="0" width="100%">
          <tr>
            <td width="18%"><img border="0" src="wroxlogo.gif" width="60"
                                 height="60">
            </td>
            <td width="82%"><img border="0" src="wroxlogodetail.gif"
                                 width="385" height="50">
            </td>
          </tr>
        </table>
      </td>
```

315

```
      </tr>
      <tr>
        <td width="18%" valign="top">
          <table border="0" cellpadding="0" cellspacing="0" width="100%"
                                           bgcolor="#C0C0C0">
            <tr>
              <td width="100%"> </td>
            </tr>
            <tr>
              <td width="100%">
                <a href="newreleases.jsp">New Releases</a>
              </td>
            </tr>
            <tr>
              <td width="100%">
                <a href="futuretitles.jsp">Future Titles</a>
              </td>
            </tr>
            <tr>
              <td width="100%"> </td>
            </tr>
            <tr>
              <td width="100%"> </td>
            </tr>
          </table>
        </td>
        <td width="82%" valign="top">
          <table border="0" cellpadding="0" cellspacing="0" width="100%">
            <tr>
              <td width="2%"></td>
              <td width="98%">Welcome to the Wrox Page</td>
            </tr>
            <tr>
              <td width="2%"></td>
              <td width="98%"></td>
            </tr>
          </table>
        </td>
      </tr>
      <tr>
        <td width="100%" valign="top" colspan="2">
        <%@include file="footer.jsp"%>
        </td>
      </tr>
    </table>
  </div>
  </body>
  </html>
```

To run this and the other examples for this chapter, you will need to create a new folder under %CATALINA_HOME%\webapps\ called begjsp-ch12. Within this folder, create the basic directory structure needed for all JSP webapps, in other words:

%CATALINA_HOME%\webapps\begjsp-ch12\WEB-INF\classes

Now place your two JSPs in the `begjsp-ch12` folder, along with the following image files:

- ❏ `wroxlogodetail.gif`
- ❏ `wroxlogo.gif`

These image files come with the code download for this book, from http://www.wrox.com.

Now start up Tomcat and your browser, and navigate to: http://localhost:8080/begjsp-ch12/index.jsp. You should see the following:

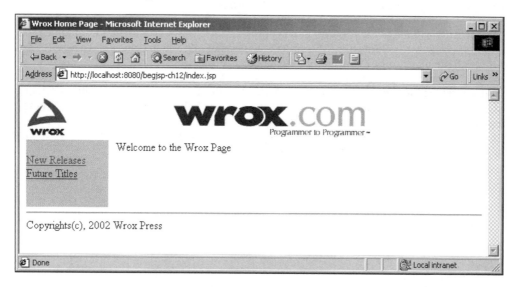

In other words, this home page is indistinguishable from the one we saw previously, but we are including the footer from a separate JSP instead.

How It Works

There is only one line we're really interested in, since both of our files are almost completely comprised of HTML. In the `index.jsp` file, we used the JSP `include` mechanism to include `footer.jsp`:

```
<%@include file="footer.jsp" %>
```

Now, when you navigate to the `index.jsp` page, the JSP engine includes the content of the `footer.jsp` into the `index.jsp` page.

In a similar fashion, we could also separate out the header, which contains the Wrox logo, into separate files, and include them too.

Dynamic Includes

As an experiment, change the `footer.jsp` file as shown below. Do not modify anything in the `index.jsp` file.

```
<table border="0" cellpadding="0" cellspacing="0" width="100%">
  <tr>
    <td width="100%"><hr></td>
  </tr>
  <tr>
    <td width="100%">Copyrights(c), 2003 Wrox Press Ltd</td>
  </tr>
</table>
```

Now, try viewing the index.jsp file again. You would expect that the copyright message would have changed to the new one above, but it does not. This is because the index.jsp file has not changed at all since it was first translated and compiled into a servlet, when it included the footer.jsp in it. The JSP engine will continue to use this servlet whenever index.jsp is requested, until it detects a change in index.jsp. In other words this JSP/servlet is buffered. Only when a change in index.jsp is detected will the new footer.jsp file get included.

What if we wanted the footer.jsp contents to be included in the index.jsp when we change footer.jsp content? In other words, we need the contents to be *dynamically included* whenever we change the footer.jsp, at request time. Luckily JSP provides us with a dynamic include mechanism too, the <jsp:include> action tag. For example, we could change our example above to dynamically include the footer.jsp file. We need to replace the line:

```
<%@include file="footer.jsp" %>
```

In its place, use the <jsp:include> action tag below to dynamically include the file instead:

```
<jsp:include page="footer.jsp" flush="true" />
```

You should note that we have specified the page to include, and we use flush="true" to specify that the buffer should be flushed prior to this include. Change the copyright date in footer.jsp and refresh your browser. You should see that this new footer is included.

Another version of the <jsp:include> tag allows you to pass one or more parameters to the included page using the <jsp:param> tag, which can then be retrieved in the included page via the request object. You can then use these parameters to generate dynamic content in the included page too. For instance, if we wanted to pass parameters menuitem1 and menuitem2 to an included page called menu.jsp, then we could use:

```
<jsp:include page="menu.jsp">
  <jsp:param name="menuitem1" value="News" />
  <jsp:param name="menuitem2" value="Sports" />
</jsp:include>
```

Here we pass the values "News" and "Sports" in the parameters. The parameters mentioned will be passed into the request object that will be available in the menu.jsp page. Then, in the menu.jsp page, you can use the getParameter() method of the request object to retrieve the values for the above parameters.

Now that we have covered the include mechanisms, it is easy to see how by including a JSP into another page, you are not only reusing that code in several pages but are also making it easier to maintain the pages.

Architecting Web Applications

In the next few sections, we shall take a look at architecting web applications. But just what is meant by "architecting a web application", and why do we need it? Let's answer these questions.

An **architecture** is used to structure or organize the various parts of an application. With reference to a web application, the different parts of the application mean the JSP pages, the Java classes, the HTML files, and so on. Therefore, defining your architecture will aid you in deciding how to go about partitioning your web application into JSP pages, JavaBeans, and so on. It would also provide you with guidelines for controlling the application so that all of these components work together to perform the functionality intended for the application. When we define the architecture, we will document what the benefits of using that architecture are, and any drawbacks to using it too. A particular architecture might be suited to solving a particular problem, while, in another case, it might not be suitable to use it.

There are a couple of JSP architectures that we shall discuss in this chapter. As we discuss them and illustrate them with examples, we will also cover in detail the benefits and drawbacks of each of the architectures.

JSP Model 1 Architecture

If you have been following all the examples in this book so far, you will notice that we have developed the JSP pages to present the view to the user. Along the way, we learned that JavaBeans provide a good mechanism to encapsulate some of your functionality into Java classes. We used these JavaBeans directly in our JSP pages via the `<jsp:useBean>` tags. You would have also noticed that most of our JSP pages not only displayed the data to the user (in other words the JSPs provide the presentation logic), but they were also responsible for controlling the flow of the application: for instance, they contained the logic to display the next page. This control logic was coded into the JSP pages as scriptlets. Such architecture is known as a page-centric architecture, and this particular page-centric architecture is known as the JSP Model 1 Architecture. This JSP Model 1 Architecture is shown below:

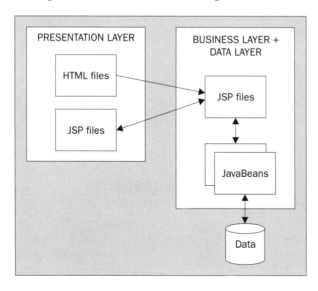

The main features of Model 1 Architecture are:

❑ The presentation layer is coded using HTML files or JSP files. The JSP files can use the JavaBeans for retrieving data if required.

❑ JSP files are also responsible for all the business and processing logic like receiving incoming requests, routing to the correct JSP, instantiating the correct JSP pages, and so on. This means that the Model 1 Architecture is a page-centric design – all the business and processing logic is present in the JSP pages itself.

❑ The data access is done either through JavaBeans, using the JavaBeans in your JSP pages, or you could write scriptlets in your JSP pages instead.

The JSP Model 1 Architecture is therefore called a page-centric architecture since the application logic and program flow are present in the pages itself. Therefore there is a tight coupling between the pages and the logic in the application. To control the flow of the application, we would need to go from one JSP page to another. This is done via an anchor link in your JSP or via the `action` attribute of your form. Let's take a look now at an example that uses the JSP Model 1 Architecture.

Try It Out – Using JSP Model 1 Architecture

In this example, we shall implement a simple login functionality, where a user enters his user ID and password, and clicks on the login button. The form is then submitted to a `ValidateLogin.jsp` page that will verify the user ID and password. If the user ID and password combination is correct, it displays the menu, otherwise it displays an error message.

For the purpose of demonstration, we will assume that the valid username and password for this example are "`wrox`" and "`wrox`" respectively.

The login form `LoginForm.html` is shown below. This is a simple HTML form that takes a user ID and password:

```
<HTML>
<HEAD>
<TITLE>Model 1 Architecture</TITLE>
</HEAD>
<BODY>
<form method="POST" action="ValidateLogin.jsp">
  <table border="0" cellpadding="0" cellspacing="0" width="100%"
                                                    height="69">
    <tr>
      <td width="1%" height="23">UserId</td>
      <td width="70%" height="23"><input type="text" name="userid"
                                             size="20"></td>
    </tr>
    <tr>
      <td width="1%" height="25">Password</td>
      <td width="70%" height="25"><input type="password" name="password"
                                             size="20">
      </td>
    </tr>
    <tr>
      <td width="1%" height="21"></td>
      <td width="70%" height="21"></td>
    </tr>
  </table>
```

```
    <p>
      <input type="submit" value="Submit" name="SubmitBtn">
      <input type="reset" value="Reset" name="B2">
    </p>
  </form>
</HTML>
```

When the user submits the above form, it is sent to the `ValidateLogin.jsp` page shown below:

```
<HTML>
<HEAD>
<TITLE>Model 1 Architecture</TITLE>
</HEAD>
<BODY>
<%
  String userid = request.getParameter("userid");
  String password = request.getParameter("password");

  if ((userid.equals("wrox")) && (password.equals("wrox"))) {
    out.println("Welcome !!! What do you want to do today?");
    out.println("<HR>");
    out.println("<A HREF=news.jsp>Read News</A><BR>");
    out.println("<A HREF=quotes.jsp>Get Stock Quotes</A><BR>");
    out.println("<A HREF=logout.jsp>Logout</A><BR>");
  } else {
    out.println("Invalid Login.
                  <A HREF=LoginForm.html>Please Try Again</A>");
  }
%>
</BODY>
</HTML>
```

Place your JSPs in the `begjsp-ch12` folder and navigate to: http://localhost:8080/begjsp-ch12/LoginForm.html

You should see the login screen displayed:

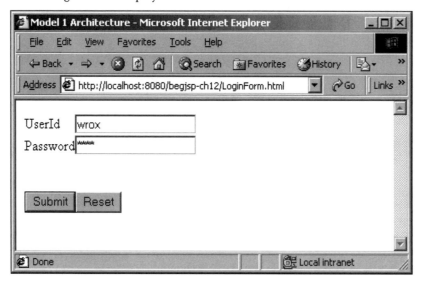

If you use the correct user ID and password (wrox, wrox) combination in this screen you will see the following output shown below:

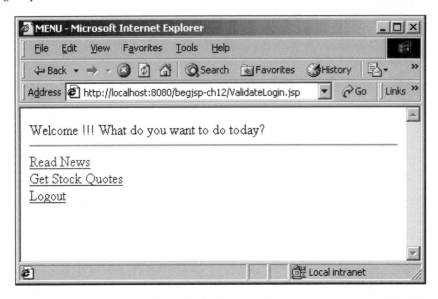

If you do not use the correct user ID/password combination then an error message will be shown as below:

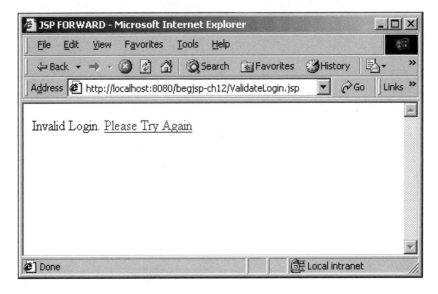

How It Works

In the LoginForm.html page, the user enters the user ID and password and clicks on Submit. This will submit the form to the ValidateLogin.jsp page because of the action attribute of the form present in the LoginForm.html page:

```
<form method="POST" action="ValidateLogin.jsp">
```

The `ValidateLogin.jsp` uses the `getParameter()` method of the `request` object to retrieve the user ID and password and compares them to "wrox" and "wrox" respectively:

```
String userid = request.getParameter("userid");
String password = request.getParameter("password");

if ((userid.equals("wrox")) && (password.equals("wrox"))) {
```

If they match then it means that the user has signed on successfully, and so he is presented with a list of options that lead him to different pages:

```
out.println("Welcome !!! What do you want to do today?");
out.println("<HR>");
out.println("<A HREF=news.jsp>Read News</A><BR>");
out.println("<A HREF=quotes.jsp>Get Stock Quotes</A><BR>");
out.println("<A HREF=logout.jsp>Logout</A><BR>");
```

If not, an error message is shown with a link that takes you back to the `LoginForm.html` page:

```
} else {
  out.println("Invalid Login.
            <A HREF=LoginForm.html>Please Try Again</A>");
}
```

Note that the `ValidateLogin.jsp` page not only has the control logic to determine whether the user ID and password combination is correct, it also has the presentation logic to display the links or an error message. If the user ID and password are correct, it displays the anchor links. If you click on the links then you are led to those respective pages. On the other hand, if the user ID and password are not correct, it displays the link back to the `LoginForm.html` so that you can try logging in again. Since all of the logic is embedded in the JSPs, this is an example of JSP Model 1 Architecture.

Drawbacks of JSP Model 1 Architecture

We saw in the previous section that in JSP Model 1 Architecture, the JSP pages are not only responsible for the control logic, but they also contain the presentation logic too. Therefore, in a JSP Model 1 Architecture, we have a number of JSP pages that need to be aware of each other.

In large applications this coupling of logic in pages, and the need to couple together pages, could cause problems. Large projects often involve teams of programmers working on different pages and in the Model 1 scenario, each team would have to have a detailed understanding of the pages all of the other teams were working on; otherwise modifying pages could break the flow of the application.

Another example of where the JSP Model 1 Architecture might not be suitable would be when we have to produce output for different devices. Let's say that we want to display the stock quotes on a browser, mobile phone or any other device. Since each of the devices has different capabilities in terms of its display area, we would need to format the data appropriately. This means that the JSP not only has to make the decision for the type of device but it also then needs to provide the correct presentation format for the kind of device.

Indeed, we noted in Chapter 4 that web sites often employ page designers and developers. The designer controls the layout (presentation) of the web page while the developers implement the logic that the web page uses to fulfill client requests. Packing both the presentation logic and the control logic into a JSP means that a page designer will have to wade through the (Java-based) control logic, as well as the presentation code that he is really interested in. Worse still, if he wanted to change the page, he would probably need to have an understanding of Java to make sure that his changes wouldn't be interfering with the control logic. Of course, the obvious way to get around this problem is to separate out the presentation code from the control logic. This leads us onto our next architecture, JSP Model 2.

JSP Model 2 Architecture

As we explained above, one of the major drawbacks of JSP Model 1 is the inclusion of both the presentation logic and the control logic into the JSP page itself. The JSP Model 2 Architecture avoids this problem by separating them. In the JSP Model 2 Architecture, the control flow (or the "application flow") is present in another module called the **controller**; this is illustrated in the diagram of the JSP Model 2 Architecture below:

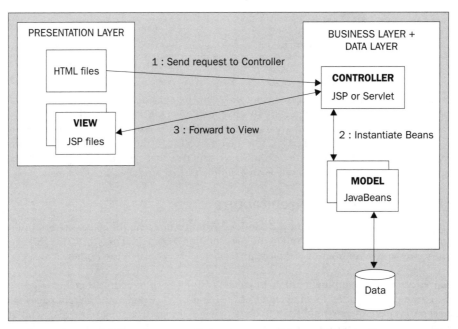

The controller is responsible for receiving all the requests of the application. For every request that it receives, the controller will make a choice depending on whether processing needs to be done, or data needs to displayed. If data needs to be displayed, it will delegate or forward the request to a JSP that contains the presentation logic (known as the **view**). If some processing needs to be done (like retrieving data from a database) then it will either perform that request itself by calling the appropriate JavaBean classes, or it may delegate or forward that request to a JSP containing the required processing logic.

In this way, we have individual JSPs that are responsible either for processing logic or display logic, and a central controller that coordinates the whole flow of the application – in other words, by introducing a central controlling mechanism, we have been able to cleanly separate both presentation logic and control flow. Because of the central nature of the controller, we can also use it as a mechanism to provide other useful features, like security.

Note that in our JSP Model 2 Architecture diagram we have labeled the **model**, which is another name for the part of the application that handles storing the data related to the application. In our example, the model is a set of JavaBeans that access a persistent store like a database. Once the controller receives the request, it instantiates the correct JavaBeans, which are populated accordingly.

So, you can see that we have three distinct roles within our application: the model, the view, and the controller. An architecture in which we delineate roles in this way is known as an **MVC** Architecture.

Now that we understand the advantages of the JSP Model 2 Architecture, our next question is: how do we write a controller?

Forwarding Using a Controller

In the example for the Model 1 JSP, we had seen how the `LoginForm.html` submitted a login request to the `ValidateForm.jsp` page. `ValidateForm.jsp` not only had the control logic in the page, but it also had the presentation logic.

Let's now restructure this application to fit the JSP Model 2 Architecture: to do this we will need to introduce a controller into the application, which transfers control (forwards) to appropriate pages. This controller will be responsible for validating the login request too.

But wait a moment... we don't know how to forward to a page yet! To do this we need to use the `<jsp:forward>` action tag, which is similar to the `<jsp:include>` tag, but control is passed to the target page and never returned to the forwarding page. So if we wanted to forward to a `page` called `menu.jsp`, we would use:

```
<jsp:forward page="menu.jsp"/>
```

We can forward to any web resource such as a JSP or a static HTML file. Additionally, as we saw with the `<jsp:include>` action, we can also add our own request parameters to the `request` object that will get passed to the forwarded page, as illustrated below.

```
<jsp:forward page="menu.jsp">
  <jsp:param name="userid" value="wrox" />
  <jsp:param name="password" value="wrox" />
</jsp:forward>
```

Here we are passing the `userid` and `password` parameters, both with the value "wrox". As usual, we can retrieve these parameters in the page we forward, by using the `getParameter()` method.

Now that we have the tool to be able to forward control between pages, let's implement our earlier example as JSP Model 2.

Try It Out – Writing a JSP Model 2 Controller

In this example, we will modify the `ValidateLogin.jsp` page to be a controller. If the controller determines that the login is valid, it will transfer control (forward) to a `menu.jsp` page, which will now contain (only) the presentation logic for the links. The `menu.jsp` will also display a personalised welcome message to the user. If the controller determines that the login is invalid, it will forward to an error page (`error.jsp`).

Let's look at the scripts. When the user submits the login form, it is sent to the modified version of the `ValidateLogin.jsp` page shown below:

```
<HTML>
<HEAD>
<TITLE>Model 1 Architecture</TITLE>
</HEAD>
<BODY>
<%
  String userid = request.getParameter("userid");
  String password = request.getParameter("password");

  if ((userid.equals("wrox")) && (password.equals("wrox"))) {
%>
    <jsp:forward page="menu.jsp">
      <jsp:param name="id" value="<%= userid %>" />
    </jsp:forward>
<%
  }
  else {
%>
    <jsp:forward page="error.jsp"/>
<%
  }
%>
</BODY>
</HTML>
```

Here's the `menu.jsp` page too:

```
<html>

<head>
<title>MENU</title>
</head>

<body>

Welcome <% out.println(request.getParameter("id")); %>!!!
What do you want to do today?
<HR>
<A HREF=news.jsp>Read News</A><BR>
<A HREF=quotes.jsp>Get Stock Quotes</A><BR>
<A HREF=logout.jsp>Logout</A><BR>

</body>

</html>
```

And here's the error page, `error.jsp`:

```
<html>

<head>
<title>JSP FORWARD</title>
</head>

<body>

Invalid Login. <A HREF=LoginForm.html>Please Try Again</A>

</body>

</html>
```

Place all of the above files into your `begjsp-ch12` folder below `webapps`. Then start up Tomcat and direct your URL to: http://localhost:8080/begjsp-ch12/LoginForm.html.

You should see the same login page that we saw for the previous example, and get the same response as before when you type in your user ID/password incorrectly. When you give a valid ID/password combination, you will see a personalized greeting and a set of links:

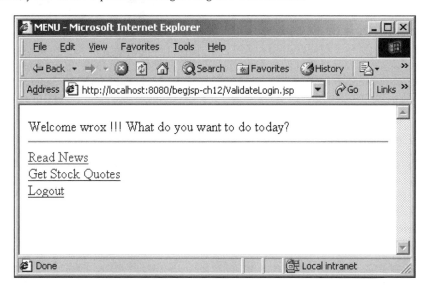

How It Works

Let's review what's new in the code. We'll skip over the login page though because we've seen that before and it hasn't changed.

The `ValidateLogin.jsp` page uses the `getParameter()` method of the `request` object to retrieve the user ID and password. Then it compares them to "wrox" and "wrox" respectively. If they match, then the control is forwarded to `menu.jsp`:

```
<jsp:forward page="menu.jsp"></jsp:forward>
   <jsp:param name="id" value="<%= userid %>" />
</jsp:forward>
```

327

Note that we also pass a parameter called `id` to `menu.jsp` via the `request` object. This parameter holds the name of the user, which is then retrieved using `getParameter()`, and displayed in the welcome message produced by `menu.jsp`:

```
Welcome <% out.println(request.getParameter("id")); %>!!!
What do you want to do today?
```

If the user ID/password combination passed to `ValidateLogin.jsp` is not correct, control is forwarded to the `error.jsp` page:

```
<jsp:forward page="error.jsp"></jsp:forward>
```

From this example, you can see that the `ValidateLogin.jsp` page now only acts as a controller: it determines what action to take depending on the user ID/password combination, and then it forwards control to the correct JSP page.

The `menu.jsp` page will now have only the presentation logic built into it. Similarly, the `error.jsp` page will have the appropriate presentation logic to display the correct error. So, by the introduction of this controller mechanism, you are able to achieve a cleaner separation of presentation and control logic.

Forwarding and Object Scope

When we forward control from one JSP page to another, it is important to note how forwarding would affect objects that we have created in our own scripts. In earlier chapters we noted that whenever we create an object via actions or through script, this object has a scope, which will determine where we can use it and where we cannot. Let summarize the object scopes again here for our benefit:

❑ **Page**: Objects declared with `page` scope are accessible only in the page where they were created.

❑ **Request**: Objects declared with `request` scope are accessible only in pages handling the same request. Once the request is processed, references to the objects are released, unless the request is forwarded to a resource in the same run-time. References to this object are stored in the `request` object.

❑ **Session**: Objects declared with `session` scope are accessible from all pages processing requests within the same session.

❑ **Application**: Objects declared with `application` scope are accessible from pages processing requests that are in the same application as the one in which they were created.

Therefore, when you forward parameters from a controller, you should bear in mind that the parameters will only be available to those scripts that are handling the same request as the controller. Consider a parameter `v1` passed in the `<jsp:forward>` action from `file1.jsp` to `file2.jsp`. Since this parameter has request scope only, you can only access this in `file2.jsp`. Trying to access this variable in any other page, even in the same session or application, will result in an exception.

Try It Out – Building a Sample Application Using JSP Model 2 Architecture

We will now look at a comprehensive example, which will demonstrate the JSP Model 2 Architecture. This example will also make use of the include and forward features of the JSP language.

In this example, we will assume our wrox.com site has branched out into online book shopping. The shopping application when fully developed will look like this:

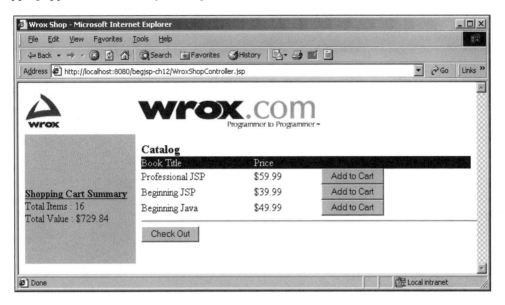

As you can see, on the opening page the shopper is shown a simplistic catalog of books. You can then click on the **Add to Cart** button to add a particular book to your shopping cart. The **Shopping Cart Summary** on the left shows the current state of the shopping cart: a count of the total items in the cart and the total value of the items. Once you have selected the books you wish to buy, you can hit the **Check Out** button. This will display the checkout screen shown below:

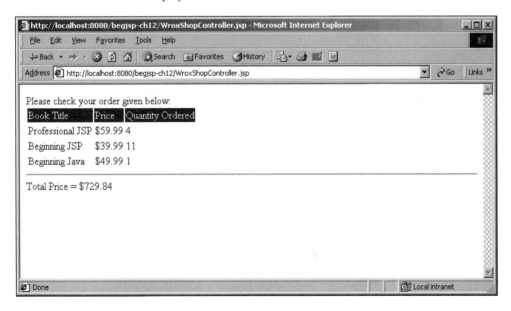

The checkout screen above will display the contents of your shopping cart in detail (Beginning JSP looks popular today!), and total up the books and the cost of your purchases.

Of course, this example does not provide all of the features of a fully comprehensive shopping cart site. For instance, there is no facility to delete items after adding them to the cart. However, since we will use this stripped-down application to illustrate how to implement JSP Model 2 Architecture, we do not need to make the example fully comprehensive. We will see how we can write the controller for the application and also look at the include and forward actions introduced earlier.

Implementing the Model

Let's discuss how we are going to implement the model. Since this is a site that sells books, which are selected and then placed in a shopping cart, this suggests that we need two objects:

- ❑   Book
- ❑   ShoppingCart

We should now consider how to implement these objects.

The Book JavaBean Class

Looking more closely at what we need from our Book object, obviously we will need attributes that include:

- ❑   Book Title
- ❑   Book Price (in dollars)
- ❑   Quantity of Books

We also need an attribute that will uniquely identify the book. Although we could use the book title, there is the possibility that two books could have the same title. A better choice for a unique book identifier would be the:

- ❑   ISBN Number

These attributes will be modeled as bookTitle, price, quantity, and ISBN respectively in the object. A book object will simply contain this data for each book, but we are also going to want to be able to change the values of these attributes when we need to: we will need simple getter and setter methods for these attributes. In other words, the best way to implement this object is as a JavaBean.

Let's now walk through the Book bean, Book.java.

```
package com.wrox.begjsp.model2;
```

We start off by defining the package in which the beans associated with the application will sit. Moving inside the class definition, we declare our attributes:

```
public class Book {
    String ISBN;
    String bookTitle;
    float price;
    int quantity;
```

Then we encounter the constructor. Here we initialize the values of all of our attributes:

```java
public Book() {
  ISBN="";
  bookTitle="";
  price =(float)0.0;
  quantity=0;
}
```

Finally, we have a series of simple getter and setter methods for our attributes:

```java
public void setISBN(String ISBN) {
  this.ISBN=ISBN;
}
public String getISBN() {
  return this.ISBN;
}
public void setBookTitle(String bookTitle) {
  this.bookTitle=bookTitle;
}
public String getBookTitle() {
  return this.bookTitle;
}
public void setPrice(float price) {
  this.price=price;
}
public float getPrice() {
  return this.price;
}
public void setQuantity(int quantity) {
  this.quantity=quantity;
}
public int getQuantity() {
  return this.quantity;
}
}
```

The ShoppingCart Class

As you shop for the books, you will need to hold the books that you want to shop for in a shopping cart. So, let's design a class called ShoppingCart.java. Since an object of this class will need to hold instances of the Book class, a ShoppingCart object will need to be a collection object. We will need two kinds of functionality from the ShoppingCart class:

❑   When the user clicks on the **Add To Cart** button, we need a method, addItem(), to add an instance of the Book class to the ShoppingCart.

❑   When the user clicks on the **Check Out** button, we need to retrieve and display the contents of the ShoppingCart. This functionality will also be used to display the **ShoppingCart Summary**, and will be implemented by the getContents() method.

We will implement the ShoppingCart object as an ArrayList. Let's now take a look at the ShoppingCart.java class.

```
package com.wrox.begjsp.model2;

import java.util.ArrayList;
import java.util.Iterator;

public class ShoppingCart {
```

When we want to display the contents of the `ArrayList` object, we are going to want to iterate through the list, so it makes sense to make use of an iterator here.

Our class has only one attribute, an `ArrayList` object called `items`, that represents the shopping cart:

```
private ArrayList items = new ArrayList();
```

Next we need to define the `addItem()` method. First we declare a `boolean` variable, that will tell us whether the book that we would like to add to our list is the same as any of the other books already present in the list. Then we check the size of the list, to see if there are any books in the list at all:

```
public void addItem(Book b) {
   boolean foundBook = false;
   if (items.size() == 0) {
     items.add(b);
```

If the list is empty, we will simply add the `Book` object to our list using the `add()` method. If the list already contains one or more objects, we iterate through the list, retrieving the contents of each `Book` object, and then check whether the ISBN of the book we wish to add is the same as any of the books already in the list:

```
} else {
        for(int i=0;i<items.size();i++) {
          Book book = (Book)items.get(i);
          if (book.getISBN().equals(b.getISBN())) {
```

If a book with the same ISBN is already present, we increment the `quantity` attribute of the `Book` object by one, and change the value of our `foundBook` variable to `true`. Then we break out of the loop:

```
            book.setQuantity(book.getQuantity()+1);
            foundBook = true;
            break;
          }
        }
```

If there are books in the list, but none have the same ISBN as the one we wish to add, we add this `Book` object to the list too:

```
        if (!foundBook) {
          items.add(b);
        }
```

```
      }
    }
```

Finally, our `getContents()` method displays how many items are in our cart at the moment, and returns an `Iterator` object that contains all of the items in the list. We will use this `Iterator` later.

```
    public Iterator getContents() {
      System.out.println(items.size());
      return items.iterator();
    }
  }
```

Implementing the View and the Controller

In the JSP Model 2 Architecture, a controller handles the application flow. This controller receives all of the requests. Once it gets a request, it determines from the request what action to perform next; it may do some pre-processing first, but it will then forward the control to the appropriate JSP.

Before we can consider how our controller, called `WroxShopController.jsp`, will forward requests, we must consider which pages it will be forwarding requests to. We will need three JSPs that implement the view:

❑ `Catalog.jsp`

❑ `ShoppingCartSummary.jsp`

❑ `CheckOut.jsp`

The `Catalog.jsp` page is our main page that displays the catalog of books and allows the user to place books from this list in his cart. This page includes another page, `ShoppingCartSummary.jsp`, that is responsible for displaying the number of books in the cart and the total price of these books at any given instant. Note that by separating out this functionality into another page and then including it in other pages, we are improving the reusability of our code significantly.

The `CheckOut.jsp` page is for displaying the contents of the cart in more detail, and providing a final summary of how much we are going to spend when we check out.

Where the controller forwards control on to depends upon the nature of the request. We can have two types of request:

❑ `AddToCart`. The user wishes to add a book to his cart. The controller needs to create a new `Book` instance and use it to update the contents of the `ShoppingCart` object, and then forward control back to `Catalog.jsp`.

❑ `CheckOut`: The user wishes to buy the books in his cart (check out). The controller needs to forward control to `CheckOut.jsp`.

These requests are obviously initiated by the user clicking on the **Add To Cart** and **Check Out** button on the `Catalog.jsp` page. This overall request scheme is illustrated in the diagram overleaf:

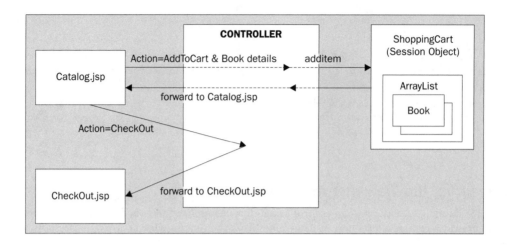

Now that we have unraveled the view pages that we need and the way the controller will handle requests, we can implement the relevant pages.

The Catalog Page

Here's the first, the main page that displays the catalog, `Catalog.jsp`:

```
<HTML>
<HEAD>
<TITLE> Wrox Shop </TITLE>
</HEAD>
<BODY>
<table border="0" cellpadding="0" cellspacing="0" width="100%">
  <tr>
    <td width="9%"><img border="0" src="wroxlogo.gif" width="60"
                                                      height="60">
            
    </td>
    <td width="91%"><img border="0" src="wroxlogodetail.gif" width="385"
                                                      height="50">
    </td>
  </tr>
  <tr>
    <td width="100%" colspan="2">
      <table border="0" cellpadding="0" cellspacing="0" width="100%">
        <tr>
          <td width="26%" valign="top">
            <table border="0" cellpadding="0" cellspacing="0" width="100%"
                                                      height="198">
            <tr>
              <td width="95%" bgcolor="#C0C0C0" height="21"> </td>
              <td width="6%" bgcolor="#FFFFFF" height="21"> </td>
            </tr>
            <tr>
              <td width="95%" bgcolor="#C0C0C0" height="177">
```

Most of the source code for this page is HTML that defines the layout. However, we are only really interested in the JSP-related code. The first line that makes use of JSP code in `Catalog.jsp` is the following one, where we use the `<jsp:include>` tag to dynamically include the ShoppingCartSummary JSP:

```
                    <jsp:include page="ShoppingCartSummary.jsp" flush="true">
                    </jsp:include>
                </td>
                <td width="6%" bgcolor="#FFFFFF" height="177"> </td>
            </tr>
        </table>
    </td>
    <td width="74%">
        <table border="0" cellpadding="0" cellspacing="0"
                                                    width="118%">
            <tr>
                <td width="100%" colspan="5">
                    <b><font size="4">Catalog</font></b></td>
            </tr>
            <tr>
                <td width="26%"></td>
                <td width="16%"></td>
                <td width="8%"></td>
                <td width="47%"></td>
                <td width="20%"></td>
            </tr>
            <tr>
                <td width="26%" bgcolor="#000080">
                    <font color="#FFFFFF">Book Title</font>
                </td>
                <td width="16%" bgcolor="#000080">
                    <font color="#FFFFFF">Price</font>
                </td>
                <td width="8%" bgcolor="#000080"> </td>
                <td width="47%" bgcolor="#000080"> </td>
                <td width="20%" bgcolor="#000080"> </td>
            </tr>
            <tr>
                <td width="26%" valign="middle">Professional JSP</td>
                <td width="16%" valign="middle">$59.99</td>
                <td width="8%" valign="middle">
```

When the user clicks an **Add to Cart** button, we need to use an HTML form containing hidden variables in order to POST the book details to the controller. Since there are three books in our catalog, we need to have three forms:

```
            <form method="POST" action="WroxShopController.jsp">
                <p>
                    <input type="submit" value="Add to Cart"
                                        name="AddToCartBtn">
                </p>
                <input type="hidden" name="ISBN" value="1861004958">
                <input type="hidden" name="Price" value="59.99">
```

```
                    <input type="hidden" name="Title"
                                    value="Professional JSP">
                    <input type="hidden" name="Action"
                                    value="AddToCart">
            </form>
        </td>
        <td width="47%"></td>
        <td width="20%"></td>
    </tr>
    <tr>
        <td width="26%" valign="middle">Beginning JSP</td>
        <td width="16%" valign="middle">$39.99</td>
        <td width="8%" valign="middle">
          <form method="POST" action="WroxShopController.jsp">
            <p>
              <input type="submit" value="Add to Cart"
                                name="AddToCartBtn">
            </p>
            <input type="hidden" name="ISBN" value="1861002092">
            <input type="hidden" name="Price" value="39.99">
            <input type="hidden" name="Title"
                                value="Beginning JSP">
            <input type="hidden" name="Action"
                                value="AddToCart">
          </form>
        </td>
        <td width="47%"></td>
        <td width="20%"></td>
    </tr>
    <tr>
        <td width="26%" valign="middle">Beginning Java</td>
        <td width="16%" valign="middle">$49.99</td>
        <td width="8%" valign="middle">
          <form method="POST" action="WroxShopController.jsp">
            <p>
              <input type="submit" value="Add to Cart"
                                name="AddToCartBtn">
            </p>
            <input type="hidden" name="ISBN" value="1861003668">
            <input type="hidden" name="Price" value="49.99">
            <input type="hidden" name="Title"
                                value="Beginning Java">
            <input type="hidden" name="Action" value="AddToCart">
          </form>
        </td>
        <td width="47%"></td>
        <td width="20%"></td>
    </tr>
</table>
<hr>
<table border="0" cellpadding="0" cellspacing="0"
                                    width="100%">
    <tr>
        <td width="15%" valign="top">
```

When the user clicks on **Check Out**, we need to inform the controller that the user has requested to be checked out. To do this we use another form:

```
                    <form method="POST" action="WroxShopController.jsp">
                      <p>
                        <input type="submit" value="Check Out"
                                            name="CheckOutBtn">
                      </p>
                      <input type="hidden" name="Action" value="CheckOut">
                    </form>
                  </td>
                  <td width="10%" valign="top"></td>
                  <td width="8%" valign="top"></td>
                  <td width="47%"></td>
                  <td width="20%"></td>
                </tr>
              </table>
            </td>
          </tr>
        </table>
      </td>
    </tr>
  </table>
</BODY>
</HTML>
```

The Controller

The `Catalog.jsp` page passes requests to our controller, `WroxShopController.jsp`. Let's take a look at this page.

```
<%@ page import="com.wrox.begjsp.model2.Book" %>
<%@ page import="com.wrox.begjsp.model2.ShoppingCart" %>
```

We start by importing the classes that we will need to use in order to add books to the cart. Then we instantiate a `ShoppingCart` instance, that has `session` scope (we want the instance to be available throughout the user's shopping session). If the instance already exists, this tag makes it available to the page.

```
<jsp:useBean id="cart"
            class="com.wrox.begjsp.model2.ShoppingCart"
            scope="session">
</jsp:useBean>
```

Next we declare a `String` variable called `URL`, that will hold the URL of the page we need to forward to:

```
<%!String URL="";%>
<%
```

Then we retrieve the `Action` parameter from the `request`:

```
    String action= request.getParameter("Action");
```

If we find that the user had clicked on **Add to Cart**, we retrieve the ISBN, title, and price of the book selected, and print these out on the command console:

```
if (action.equals("AddToCart")) {
  String ISBN  = (String)request.getParameter("ISBN");
  String title = (String)request.getParameter("Title");
  float  price = Float.parseFloat(request.getParameter("Price"));
  System.out.println(ISBN + "," + title + "," + price);
```

Next we create a new `Book` bean, and feed the values we just retrieved from the `request` object into the appropriate attributes using setter methods:

```
  Book b = new Book();
  b.setISBN(ISBN);
  b.setBookTitle(title);
  b.setPrice((float)price);
  b.setQuantity(1);
```

Obviously the user can only select one book at a time, so we set the `quantity` attribute to one. Then we add the `Book` instance to our `ShoppingCart` instance we created earlier. Then we make the URL variable equal to the Catalog page, because we will want to forward control back to this page::

```
  cart.addItem(b);
  URL = "Catalog.jsp";
```

If the user has selected **Check Out**, we will need to forward to `CheckOut.jsp` instead:

```
} else if (action.equals("CheckOut")) {
  URL = "CheckOut.jsp";
}

%>
```

Finally, we use the `<jsp:forward>` tag to actually forward control to the appropriate JSP:

```
<jsp:forward page="<%=URL%>" />
```

The Check Out Page

So what happens when we check out? Here's the `CheckOut.jsp` script:

```
<%@ page import="java.util.Iterator" %>
<%@ page import="com.wrox.begjsp.model2.Book" %>
<%@ page import="com.wrox.begjsp.model2.ShoppingCart" %>
```

First we import the classes that we are going to use, and then we make sure that the `ShoppingCart` instance that we have been using is available to the page:

```
<jsp:useBean id="cart"
             class="com.wrox.begjsp.model2.ShoppingCart"
             scope="session">
</jsp:useBean>

<%
```

Next we declare a variable that will hold the total value of the books in our cart, and we create an `Iterator` object that contains the contents of the cart:

```
float totalValue = (float)0.0;
Iterator contents = cart.getContents();
```

If there is nothing in the cart, we inform the user of this situation:

```
if (!contents.hasNext()) {
  out.println("You have no items to checkout !!");
```

If there are books in the cart, we display a message asking the user to check the order, and we create a table that will hold the title, price, and quantity ordered for each book:

```
} else {

%>

Please check your order given below:

<TABLE>
  <TR>
    <TD bgcolor="#000080">
      <font color="#FFFFFF">Book Title</font>
    </TD>
    <TD bgcolor="#000080">
      <font color="#FFFFFF">Price</font>
    </TD>
    <TD bgcolor="#000080">
      <font color="#FFFFFF">Quantity Ordered</font>
    </TD>
  </TR>

<%
```

We then use the `Iterator` object to walk through our shopping list. For each `Book` object, we use `getQuantity()` to retrieve the number of books with this ISBN in the cart, and multiply this figure by the value of a book obtained from `getPrice()`. This figure represents the total amount spend on books with this ISBN. We then add to this the `totalValue` variable, which means that when all of the iterations are done, the `totalValue` variable will contain the total amount spent on books in the cart.

```
  while (contents.hasNext()) {
    Book b = (Book)contents.next();
    totalValue = totalValue + b.getQuantity()*b.getPrice();

%>
```

Next, for each book, we display the book title, price and number of books bought in the table:

```
  <TR>
    <TD><%=b.getBookTitle()%></TD>
    <TD>$<%=b.getPrice()%></TD>
    <TD><%=b.getQuantity()%></TD>
  </TR>

<%

}

%>

</TABLE>
<HR>
```

When the iterations are finished, we then display the total amount spent:

```
Total Price = $<%=totalValue%>
<%

}

%>
```

The Shopping Cart Summary Page

The Catalog page includes the shopping cart summary page, which displays a summary of the number of books in the cart, and the total price of these books. As we mentioned before, the main purpose of separating out this presentation logic from the Catalog page is to emphasize reusability of code. Since we have separated this code out, we could include this page in all the pages constituting the shopping process. Let's now take a look at the code, ShoppingCartSummary.jsp:

```
<%@ page import="java.util.Iterator" %>
<%@ page import="com.wrox.begjsp.model2.Book" %>
<%@ page import="com.wrox.begjsp.model2.ShoppingCart" %>
```

As with the other view pages, we start by importing classes and making the ShoppingCart instance available to the page:

```
<jsp:useBean id="cart"
             class="com.wrox.begjsp.model2.ShoppingCart"
             scope="session">
</jsp:useBean>

<%
```

Next we create an `Iterator` object that contains the contents of the cart:

```
Iterator contents = cart.getContents();
```

Then we create new variables to hold the total value of the user's purchases, and the total number of books in the cart:

```
float totalValue = (float)0.0;
int   totalItems = 0;
```

We iterate through the contents of the cart, book by book. For each book, we use `getQuantity()` to retrieve how many books of this ISBN have been placed in the cart, and `getPrice()` to obtain the price of the book. As we iterate through the books we total up the number of books in the cart, and the total price of these books:

```
while (contents.hasNext()) {
  Book b = (Book)contents.next();
  totalItems = totalItems + b.getQuantity();
  totalValue = totalValue + b.getQuantity()*b.getPrice();
}
```

The variables `totalItems` and `totalValue` now contain the total number of books in the cart and their total cost respectively. We display this information to the user in the browser:

```
out.println("<B><U>Shopping Cart Summary</U></B>" + "<BR>");
out.println("Total Items : " + totalItems + "<BR>");
out.println("Total Value : $" + totalValue);
%>
```

And that's all of the code for the application. Let's see how to get it up and running.

Running the Example

Save the classes into:

```
...\begjsp-ch12\WEB-INF\classes\com\wrox\begjsp\model2
```

Compile them from the `classes` folder using the following command:

>javac com\wrox\begjsp\model2*.java

The * simply means "all files, whatever their name", so `*.java` means "all files with a `.java` filename extension in this directory".

Now place all of the JSPs in the `begjsp-ch12` folder. Make sure that you have the image files from an earlier example (`wroxlogodetail.gif`, `wroxlogo.gif`) in this folder too. Then start up Tomcat and point your browser to:

http://localhost:8080/begjsp-ch12/Catalog.jsp

You should see the Catalog page we showed earlier:

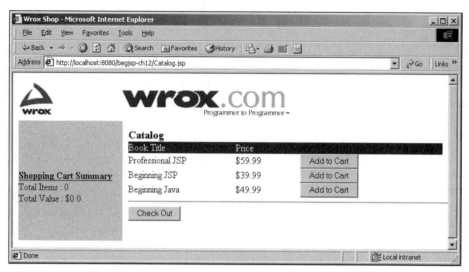

Try adding a few books to your cart and then checking out. Congratulations! You have successfully implemented a sample application based upon the JSP Model 2 Architecture.

Summary

In this chapter, we examined how we can optimize the structure, or **architecture**, of a JSP application. This is needed in order to make the application code as maintainable, and reusable as possible. We discussed the following common JSP-based architectures:

❑   JSP Model 1 Architecture, which is a page-centric architecture. We saw how in this architecture, the JSP pages contain both the presentation logic and the application logic. The major drawback of this architecture was that as the application becomes larger, the tight coupling between presentation and processing code in the JSPs leads to difficulty in maintaining and modifying your code.

❑   JSP Module 2 Architecture, which uses a **controller** to overcome the drawbacks of the JSP Model 1 Architecture. Here we place the application flow logic into a separate module called the controller. The controller then forwards control to the appropriate JSP that handles presentation (the view), or manipulates the data stored within the application (the **model**). The data storage in this **MVC**-based architecture may be provided by JavaBeans, or a database, for example.

We also learned about the include feature, which helps in improving code reusability by statically or dynamically including commonly used functionality present in smaller JSP files. We also saw how to forward control to JSP pages, and how it was crucial in implementing the controller in JSP Model 2 Architecture.

We finished off the chapter by building a sample on-line shopping application where we could "buy" Wrox books. This example was designed to show how we can implement JSP Model 2 Architecture in a simple yet effective way.

In the next chapter we will be delving much deeper into how JSPs really work. We mentioned in earlier chapters that a JSP is compiled into a class called a servlet; we will see how we can use a servlet in a JSP Model 2 Architecture.

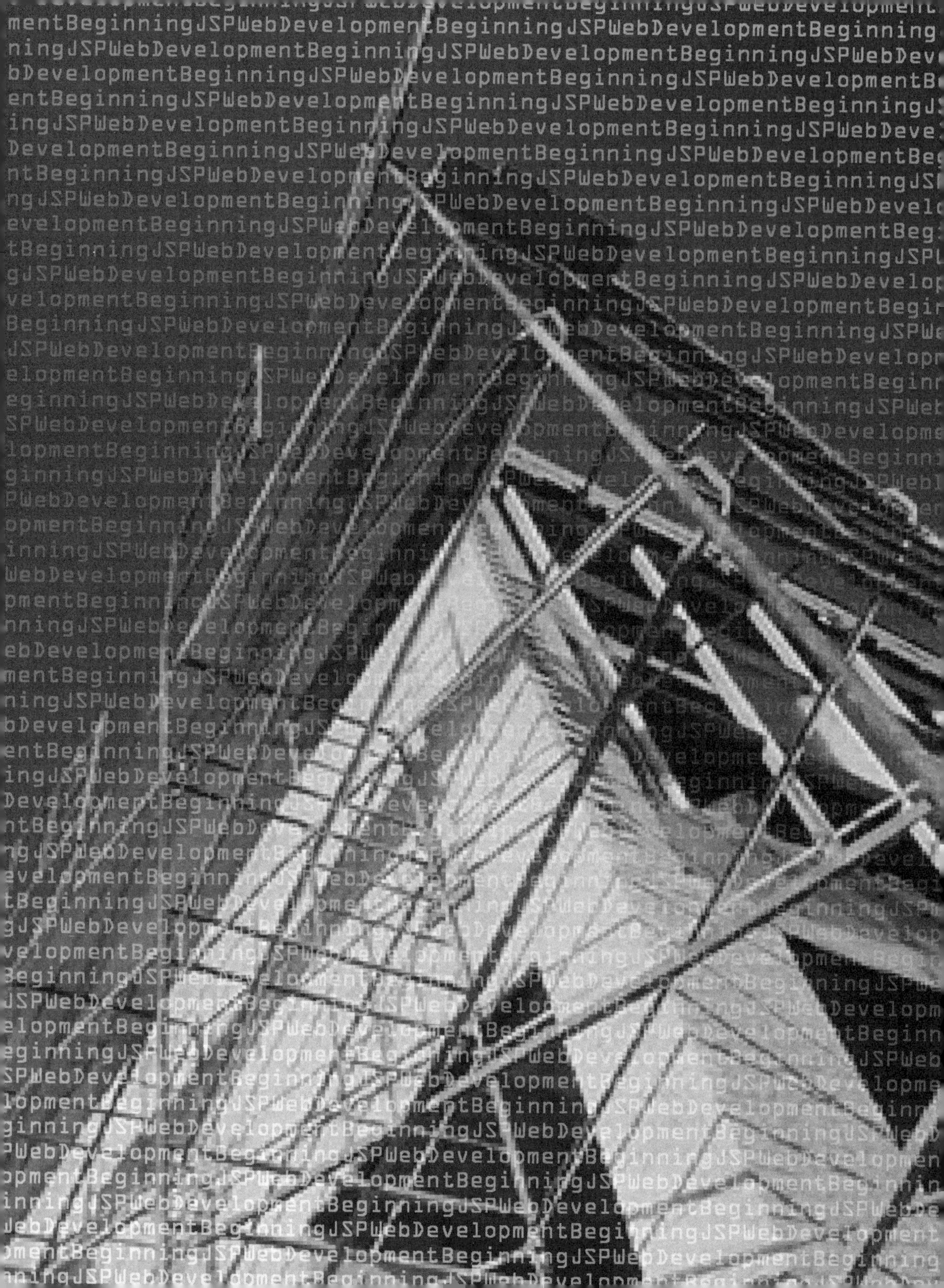
BeginningJSPWebDevelopment

Behind the Scenes

As a developer working with JSP technology, it is helpful to venture into its internals. Understanding what goes on behind the scenes will help us to use the technology effectively and aid debugging when things go wrong.

We will spend most of this chapter looking at the **Java Servlet API** since, under the covers, JSP technology and servlets have a lot in common. JSP technology derives most of its power and simplicity from the Java servlets, and in fact before it is run a JSP page is compiled into a servlet. The process is as follows:

❑   A programmer writes a JSP page using HTML template text, JSP tags, and JavaBeans, then deploys to a web container (a Java-enabled web server).

❑   The first time a request intended for a particular JSP arrives, the page is converted into a Java class that corresponds to the instructions in the JSP. The container is responsible for creating this object, which is actually a servlet.

❑   Requests from the clients are delivered to this object, and responses from the object are delivered to the client by the server.

❑   If the JSP is subsequently modified, the server will notice this and convert the new version into a fresh Java class.

So, servlet technology is clearly vital to JSP. This chapter will provide you with an overview of servlets, from a JSP programmer's point of view. We'll look at:

❑   The servlet architecture and how servlets work.

❑   What happens behind the scenes when you run a JSP.

❑   More about web applications, and the web.xml file that is used to configure them.

❑   Advanced servlet topics: session tracking, the servlet context, and how to forward and include requests.

You can find out more about Java servlets at http://java.sun.com/products/servlet/.

Introducing the Java Servlet Technology

A servlet is a web component or a program that generates dynamic web content; servlets are written using the **Java Servlet API** and are managed by a server or **container** like Tomcat. As we saw in Chapter 1, the HTTP protocol on which the web is built works using a request-response mechanism where a server receives requests, processes them, and sends out appropriate responses. The Java servlet API models this process in an object-oriented way to allow you to write code that can process client's requests and respond dynamically. For example, a servlet might be responsible for taking data from an HTML order-entry form and using it to update a company's order database.

As we've seen, servlets run inside a Java-enabled server (a **web container**) such as Tomcat, as illustrated below:

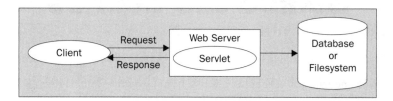

The web container loads, executes, and manages a servlet; the process is usually as follows:

❏   The client sends a request for a page to the container.

❏   If the servlet isn't already loaded, the container loads it. Once the servlet is loaded on the first request, it stays loaded until the container decides to unload it (typically, when the container itself shuts down).

❏   The container sends request information to the servlet, creating a new thread for each request to execute in. (Threading is a Java language feature that allows more than one task to be performed at a time. This allows a container to process several HTTP requests at once, which is important for busy sites.)

❏   The servlet processes the request, builds a response, and passes it to the container.

❏   The container sends the response back to the client.

You'll see that the container is a very important aspect of what's going on here: the container takes care of loading and initializing the servlet. It can manage multiple instances of a servlet, work out which servlet should be passed to any particular request, ensures that the servlet's response is sent back to the client, and finally destroys the servlet at the end of its useful life.

The Role of Servlets in Web Applications

In Chapter 12 we looked at how we can separate different parts of a web application using the `<jsp:forward>` and `<jsp:include>` actions, and saw how this leads us to the "Model 2" or "Model-View-Controller" architecture. One common use of servlets is as the controller or "application broker" in a web application. Servlets are ideal for the controller component as they have the full power of Java available unlike a JSP. A controller servlet takes action based on a client's request by coordinating or delegating among other servlets, shared objects, resource files, databases, and other resources available for its use.

Let's have a look at an example of a typical model-view-controller architecture:

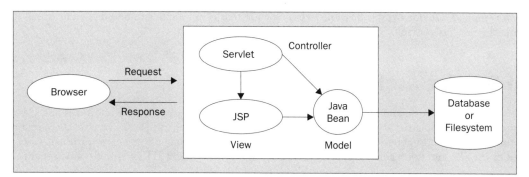

The processing is divided into information (model) and presentation (view) components, orchestrated by the controller. Here the role of the controller servlet is to process the requests, creating information components like JavaBeans or other objects used by the presentation (JSP) component. Commonly, the controller is also responsible for deciding which presentation component the request has to be forwarded to.

The MVC model makes the web application structured and modular, hence easier to develop and extend. Here the application is divided into three parts: **model**, **view**, and **controller**.

❏   **Model** – The model contains the core of the application's functionality. The model represents the state of the application. It knows nothing about the view or controller. A JavaBean fits into this role since it can be designed to hold most of the business logic for your application. It can interact with a database or file system and hence is responsible for maintaining the application data.

❏   **View** – The view provides the presentation of the model. That means, this component decides how the data is presented to the user. The view can access the model's data, but it may not change the data. In addition, it knows nothing about the controller. The view will be notified when changes to the model (data) occur. A web interface developer need not know or care about what happens in the database or what goes on in the business logic component. They are expected to have the knowledge of HTML but may not have an in-depth knowledge of Java or other programming languages. A JSP fits into this role since JSP is designed to have the least amount of non-HTML code.

❏   **Controller** – The controller reacts to the user input. It creates and provides input to the model. A servlet can contain both Java and HTML code. Hence it can take the HTTP requests from the client, take decisions on creating necessary JavaBeans and notifies the view about the changes to the model.

So, when is this architecture particularly suitable? You should consider using it when:

❏   The web page is based on information provided by the user at run-time. Examples are results pages from search engines, or applications that process orders for e-commerce sites.

❏   The data has to be frequently updated on the web site. The examples are weather report or news headlines pages.

❏   The web page has to use information from corporate/commercial databases. Examples are a web page at an online store that lists current prices and number of items in stock.

Servlets have the advantage over JSP in these sorts of high performance applications. It is generally best to avoid complicated Java code in JSP pages because they are automatically turned into servlets and then compiled. Obviously, it is possible to create code that is more efficient and less error prone if you write the servlets yourself.

The Servlet Architecture

Let's get down to work, and see how to actually write a servlet. All servlets use interfaces and classes defined in the packages `javax.servlet` and `javax.servlet.http`. The first package contains definitions to support generic servlets (servlets were originally designed to be cross-protocol, not only tied to HTTP), and the second supports servlets written for providing HTTP-specific functionality.

Every servlet must implement the `javax.servlet.Servlet` interface, which declares methods to manage the servlet and its communication with the client. The servlet programmer has to ensure that these methods are implemented when developing a new servlet; fortunately, a helper class `javax.servlet.http.HttpServlet` is provided which implements this interface. Therefore, most of the servlet classes we write in web applications actually extend `HttpServlet`. The inheritance for a typical servlet class is shown in the diagram below.

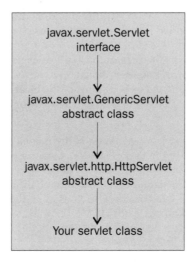

When a servlet accepts a call from a client, it receives two objects: one is an object that implements `javax.servlet.ServletRequest` and the other implements `javax.servlet.ServletResponse`. The `ServletRequest` class encapsulates the communication from the client to the server, while the `ServletResponse` class encapsulates the communication from the servlet back to the client.

In fact, since we're writing HTTP servlets, we get a `request` object that implements the `javax.servlet.http.HttpServletRequest` interface and a `response` object that implements `javax.servlet.http.HttpServletResponse`. (These interfaces extend `ServletRequest` and `ServletResponse` respectively.)

Handling Requests

As we have already seen, a servlet accepts a request from a client and processes it to create a response, which is passed back to the client. The basic `Servlet` interface defines a `service()` method for handling client requests; this method is called for each request that the servlet container passes on to the servlet.

The request is encapsulated by the `HttpServletRequest` object and the response by the `HttpServletResponse` object. We analyze the request using the methods provided by the `HttpServletRequest` class, and write the response into the `HttpServletResponse` object that is forwarded to the client by the container.

`HttpServlet` is an abstract class which implements the `Servlet` interface. It also adds additional methods, which means that you rarely have to provide your own `service()` method. Instead, the methods listed below are automatically called by the ready-made `service()` method, based on the type of request:

❏   `doGet()` is called for handling HTTP GET requests.

❏   `doPost()` is called for handling HTTP POST requests.

Typically, when developing HTTP based servlets, a servlet developer will only concern himself with the `doGet()` and `doPost()` methods. When a request for a page represented by the servlet is made, the container forwards it to the servlet by calling the `service()` method of the base class `javax.servlet.Servlet`. The implementation of the `HttpServlet`, depending on the type of request, calls either `doGet()` or `doPost()` method, so a servlet must normally override at least one of these methods.

However, there are five other similar methods that are less commonly used:

❏   `doHead()` is called for handling HTTP HEAD requests. The `doHead()` method in `HttpServlet` is a specialized method that will execute the `doGet()` method, but only return the headers produced by the `doGet()` method to the client.

❏   `doOptions()` is called for handling HTTP OPTIONS requests. The `doOptions()` method automatically determines which HTTP methods are directly supported by the servlet and returns that information to the client.

❏   `doTrace()` is called for handling HTTP TRACE requests. The `doTrace()` method causes a response with a message containing all of the headers sent in the TRACE request.

❏   `doPut()` is called for HTTP PUT requests.

❏   `doDelete()` is called for HTTP DELETE requests.

`HttpServlet` has a few extra methods of interest to us:

❏   `init()` and `destroy()`, which allow us to manage resources that are held for the life of the servlet

❏   `getServletInfo()`, which the servlet uses to provide information about itself

Try It Out – A Simple Servlet

Now let's start with a simple example, using some of the classes we just mentioned. Here `ExampleServlet` extends the `HttpServlet` class, which in turn implements the `Servlet` interface. It overrides the `doGet()` method, which is called when a client makes a GET request, and returns a simple HTML page to the client. We'll use this example as a reference when explaining the servlet life cycle.

Start by creating a new web application for this chapter by making a folder called `begjsp-ch13` in Tomcat's `webapps` folder. Inside that, we need to create rather a deep set of folders: inside your new `begjsp-ch13` folder create `WEB-INF\classes\com\wrox\servlets`.

Create a new file called `ExampleServlet.java` in the new `begjsp-ch13\WEB-INF\classes\com\wrox\servlets` folder and enter this code into it:

```
package com.wrox.servlets;

import java.io.*;
import javax.servlet.*;
import javax.servlet.http.*;

public class ExampleServlet extends HttpServlet {

  public void doGet(HttpServletRequest request,
                    HttpServletResponse response)
         throws ServletException, IOException {
    PrintWriter out;
    String title = "Servlet Example";
    response.setContentType("text/html");
    out = response.getWriter();
    out.println("<html><head><title>");
    out.println(title);
    out.println("</title></head><body>");
    out.println("<h1>This is an example servlet.</h1>");
    out.println("</body></html>");
    out.close();
  }

  public void doPost(HttpServletRequest request,
                     HttpServletResponse response)
         throws ServletException, IOException {
    doGet(request, response);
  }
}
```

Now we need to compile the servlet; you need to set the `classpath` as described in Chapter 1, then it is just a case of opening a command prompt, changing to the `begjsp-ch13\WEB-INF\classes` directory, and typing:

```
> javac com\wrox\servlets\ExampleServlet.java
```

Now start or restart Tomcat and navigate to http://localhost:8080/begjsp-ch13/servlet/com.wrox.servlets.ExampleServlet, and you should see the servlet's output shown below:

How It Works

The first parts of the code simply import the required resources and set up the class, which extends HttpServlet:

```
package com.wrox.servlets;

import java.io.*;
import javax.servlet.*;
import javax.servlet.http.*;

public class ExampleServlet extends HttpServlet {
```

The doGet() method first creates a PrintWriter object out, then the content type of the response is set to be HTML so the client knows how to render it. The writer is acquired from the response object and stored in out.

```
public void doGet(HttpServletRequest request,
                  HttpServletResponse response)
      throws ServletException, IOException {
   PrintWriter out;
   String title = "Servlet Example";
   response.setContentType("text/html");
   out = response.getWriter();
```

A series of HTML statements are printed to out then the close() method is called, which flushes then closes the output stream. The response is then returned to the client.

```
   out.println("<html><head><title>");
   out.println(title);
   out.println("</title></head><body>");
   out.println("<h1>This is an example servlet.</h1>");
   out.println("</body></html>");
   out.close();
}
```

As POST and GET requests are handled in the same way, so the doPost() method simply calls doGet().

```
   public void doPost(HttpServletRequest request,
                      HttpServletResponse response)
         throws ServletException, IOException {
  doGet(request, response);
}
```

The Servlet Lifecycle

Let's look next at the lifecycle of our servlet objects; as we've seen, the servlet container manages this for us, creating the servlet object and calling its methods as required. The figure below illustrates the servlet lifecycle in generic terms:

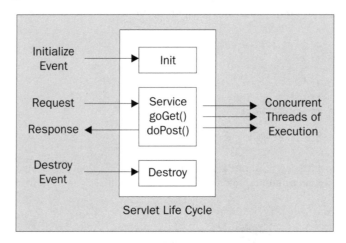

Servlet Life Cycle

Loading, Instantiation, and Initialization

A server loads and instantiates a servlet dynamically when its services are first requested. You can also configure the web server to load and instantiate specific servlets when the web server is initialized. This is done in cases where the initialization process involves time-consuming operations, like opening a database connection. This can greatly improving the response time for the first request. The servlet's init() method should perform any necessary initialization, and is called once for each servlet instance, before any requests are handled. An init() method is inherited from HttpServlet, so you only need to override this method in your servlet if a specific function should be accomplished at initialization. For example, we could use the init() method to load default data, or create database connections.

Handling Requests

Once the servlet is properly initialized, the container can use it to handle requests. For each request, the servlet's doPost() or doGet() method is passed a ServletRequest representing the request and a ServletResponse object that the servlet can use to create the response to the client.

In the case of an HTTP request, the container provides the `request` and `response` objects as implementations of `HttpServletRequest` and `HttpServletResponse`. When a request arrives at the container, it looks for an instance of the respective servlet; if one is not found it loads one and then creates a thread and calls the `doGet()` or `doPost()` method depending how the request was sent. This means that for each request, there is a separate thread executing the same `doGet()` or `doPost()` method. In this kind of a scenario, thread safety becomes very important. This topic is discussed in detail later in this chapter.

The Request Object

The `HttpServletRequest` interface allows the servlet to access information such as the request parameters passed in by the client. It also provides the servlet with access to the input stream object, `ServletInputStream`, through which the servlet can read data from clients that are using application protocols such as the HTTP `POST` method.

We actually met the `HttpServletRequest` object back in Chapter 3 – the built-in JSP `request` object is an instance of this class.

The `request` object encapsulates all the information from the client request. In the HTTP protocol, this information can be transmitted from the client to the server by the query string, in HTTP headers, and in the message body of the request.

The `HttpServletRequest` interface extends `ServletRequest` and contains the methods for accessing HTTP-specific header information, such as any cookies found in the request. It also allows us to access the parameters sent by the client with the request.

There are several methods provided to do this:

❑ The `getParameter()` method returns the value of a particular request parameter, given the parameter's name. If the parameter is expected to have more than one value, then you can use `getParameterValues()` instead, which returns an array of values. That is if the request contains three parameters, then an array three in length is returned.

❑ For HTTP `GET` requests, you can use the `getQueryString()` method, which returns a string of raw data from the client. In this case, you have to write the code that extracts the information you want yourself.

❑ For HTTP `POST` methods, you can either use `getReader()` method or `getInputStream()` method, depending on whether you are expecting text or binary data. `getReader()` returns a `BufferedReader` object and `getInputStream()` returns a `ServletInputStream` object.

The Response Object

The `HttpServletResponse` interface defines servlet methods for replying to the client. The purpose of a servlet is to process the request and generate an appropriate response; the `response` object encapsulates all the information to be returned from the server to the client. In the HTTP protocol, this information is transmitted from the server to the client in HTTP headers and the message body of the response.

An `HttpServletResponse` object provides two ways of returning data to the user, the `getWriter()` and `getOutputStream()` methods, which return a `Writer` object and a `ServletOutputStream` object respectively. You should use the first method when the output data is text, and the second when the output data is binary in nature. Closing the `Writer` or `ServletOutputStream` objects after sending the response allows the server to know when the response is complete.

There are also a number of other methods in `HttpServletResponse` provided for convenience:

❑ `sendRedirect()`
Redirects the client to a different URL. Here the URL needs to be an absolute URL.

❑ `sendError()`
Sends an error message (for example: `SC_METHOD_NOT_ALLOWED`) to the client using the current error code status; an optional descriptive message can be provided as well.

Try It Out – Using the Request and Response Objects

Let's write another servlet now, using more features of the `request` and `response` objects. Save the following Java code in a file called `DisplayServlet.java`, in the same folder as the previous servlet:

```
package com.wrox.servlets;

import java.io.*;
import java.util.*;
import javax.servlet.*;
import javax.servlet.http.*;

public class DisplayServlet extends HttpServlet {

  public void doGet(HttpServletRequest req, HttpServletResponse res)
        throws ServletException, IOException {
    res.setContentType("text/html");
    PrintWriter out = res.getWriter();
    out.println("<html><head><title>Example</title></head><body>");
    out.println("Query String being processed:<p>");
    out.println(req.getQueryString());
    out.println("<p>");
    out.println("Request Parameters:<p>");

    Enumeration enumParam = req.getParameterNames();
    while (enumParam.hasMoreElements()) {
      String paramName = (String) enumParam.nextElement();
      String paramValues[] = req.getParameterValues(paramName);
      if (paramValues != null) {
        for (int i = 0; i < paramValues.length; i++) {
          out.println(paramName + " (" + i + "): " + paramValues[i]
                + "<p>");
        }
      }
    }
    out.println("</body></html>");
    out.close();
  }
}
```

Compile the servlet by running:

```
> javac com\wrox\servlets\DisplayServlet.java
```

Restart Tomcat and browse to http://localhost:8080/begjsp-ch13/servlet/ com.wrox.servlets. DisplayServlet?firstname=Richard&lastname=Huss, and you should see the servlet's output shown below:

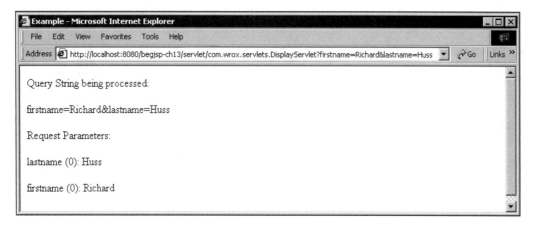

How It Works

In this example, we are reading all the request parameters and displaying them as an HTML page. This class only contains a doGet() method. The method getQueryString() returns the query string as a whole. Query string is the string that is displayed in the address bar in the above picture after the character "?".

```
out.println("Query String being processed:<p>");
out.println(req.getQueryString());
```

This is followed by a section of code that gets and prints out the parameters.

```
Enumeration enumParam = req.getParameterNames();
while (enumParam.hasMoreElements()) {
  String paramName = (String) enumParam.nextElement();
  String paramValues[] = req.getParameterValues(paramName);
  if (paramValues != null) {
    for (int i = 0; i < paramValues.length; i++) {
      out.println(paramName + " (" + i + "): " + paramValues[i]
                  + "<p>");
    }
  }
}
```

The `HttpServletRequest` object offers us a way to access all the parameter names by calling the `getParameterNames()` method, which returns a list of parameter values. These are stored in an `Enumeration enumParam`. The elements of the array contain all the parameter names stored in the request object. We iterate through the contents of `enumParam` storing each parameter name as `String`. Using this name, we can find out the associated value by calling the `getParameterValues()` method on the request object. The name-value pair is the printed out and we carry on looping through `enumParam` until we reach the end.

Unloading

A servlet is typically unloaded from memory once the container is asked to shut down. The container will call the servlet's `destroy()`. This method is inherited from the `GenericServlet` class and it is only necessary to override it in your servlet if there are some specific actions that need to be accomplished at shutdown. These could include closing any open files or database connections.

```
public void destroy() {
   // Close the database connection and any open files
}
```

Now that we have seen the full servlet lifecycle, let's go through the rest of the features.

What Happens To a JSP Behind the Scenes

As we indicated earlier, both JSP and servlet technology have their own advantages and disadvantages over each other. Servlets were introduced to make it easier for programmers to write code to generate dynamic HTML content based on business logic. However, here the code becomes cluttered with HTML and it is difficult to integrate a web interface designer's work with a Java programmer's work using servlets. The JSP approach was designed to make writing HTML code easy alongside clearly separated Java code containing business logic. In fact, a JavaServer Page goes through a translation phase very early in its life cycle (the first time it is requested by a user) to become a servlet, like a caterpillar transforming into a butterfly. Let's have an inside look at how this takes place.

Try It Out – A JSP Transformed into a Servlet

Save the code below as `transform.jsp`, in your `%CATALINA_HOME%\webapps\begjsp-ch13` folder:

```
<html>
<head><title>This is going to be transformed into a servlet</title></head>
<body>
<h1>
<%
  if (request.getParameter("username") == null) {
    out.println("Welcome!");
  } else {
    out.println("Hello " + request.getParameter("username") + ".");
    out.println("Welcome!");
  }
```

```
%>
</h1>
</body>
</html>
```

Make sure Tomcat is running, then navigate to http://localhost:8080/begjsp-ch13/transform.jsp. You should see the following cheerful message:

If you instead request http://localhost:8080/begjsp-ch13/transform.jsp?username=Richard, you'll get a more personal message because the JSP recognizes the request parameter username:

How It Works

You shouldn't have too much trouble understanding this JSP code – what's interesting is what's happening behind the scenes when it's run. Inside the folder where you installed Tomcat, you'll find a folder called work; have a look inside and you should find various further folders, including one called localhost\begjsp-ch13. Inside there will be a file called transform_jsp.java, this is the servlet that Tomcat created from our JSP.

Opening this file up, you'll find that the code is daunting, especially compared with our simple JSP page. We've tidied it up a bit here; let's go through it and see what's happening. You probably won't understand everything that's going on, in fact, you don't really need to; it's just helpful to have some idea what your JSP is turned into.

First, you'll see the package name shared by all JSP derived servlets and a list of import statements. If you recall various classes are implicit in a JSP and don't have to be declared; it should now be obvious why.

We can see that this class is called transform_jsp (which is fairly obviously derived from the JSP's name) and extends a special class provided by Tomcat called HttpJspBase, which extends HttpServlet:

```
package org.apache.jsp;

import javax.servlet.*;
import javax.servlet.http.*;
import javax.servlet.jsp.*;
import javax.servlet.jsp.tagext.*;
import org.apache.jasper.runtime.*;

public class transform_jsp extends HttpJspBase {
```

Next come various bits of special code to initialize the servlet:

```
static {}

public transform_jsp() {
}

private static boolean _jspx_inited = false;

public final void _jspx_init() throws org.apache.jasper.JasperException {
}
```

When the first request is delivered to a JSP page, a jspInit method is called to prepare the page. Similarly, a JSP container invokes the jspDestroy method to reclaim the resources used by the JSP page at any time when a request is not being serviced. This is the same life cycle as for servlets.

The interesting stuff happens in the next method, _jspService(). This is the JSP equivalent of the service() method for a servlet, and is called every time a user requests the page. It starts by doing various further initialization tasks like creating the implicit objects (page, session, application and out) that our JSPs can take advantage of:

```
public void _jspService(HttpServletRequest request,
                        HttpServletResponse response)
        throws java.io.IOException, ServletException {

    JspFactory _jspxFactory = null;
    PageContext pageContext = null;
    HttpSession session = null;
    ServletContext application = null;
    ServletConfig config = null;
    JspWriter out = null;
    Object page = this;
    String  _value = null;

    try {
        if (_jspx_inited == false) {
            synchronized (this) {
                if (_jspx_inited == false) {
                    _jspx_init();
                    _jspx_inited = true;
                }
            }
        }
```

```
        }

        _jspxFactory = JspFactory.getDefaultFactory();
        response.setContentType("text/html;charset=ISO-8859-1");
        pageContext = _jspxFactory.getPageContext(this, request, response,
                                            "", true, 8192, true);

        application = pageContext.getServletContext();
        config = pageContext.getServletConfig();
        session = pageContext.getSession();
        out = pageContext.getOut();
```

The previous parts of the code will appear pretty much the same for any JSP-derived servlet.

You should be able to see that the next line is based on the "template" text that was in our JSP file; it is sent straight back to the client:

```
        out.write("<html>\r\n<head><title>This is going to be transformed into a
  servlet</title></head>\r\n<body>\r\n<h1>\r\n");
```

The next extract from our JSP was a scriptlet, between <% and %>. This code is actually the same as in our JSP. So you can see the scriptlet code is inserted as is into the generated servlet.

```
        if (request.getParameter("username") == null) {
          out.println("Welcome!");
        } else {
          out.println("Hello " + request.getParameter("username") + ".");
          out.println("Welcome!");
        }
```

Finally, we have another piece of template text, then some error-handling code that is created by Tomcat for every generated servlet:

```
        out.write(" \r\n</h1>\r\n</body>\r\n</html>\r\n");

      } catch (Throwable t) {
        if (out != null && out.getBufferSize() != 0) {
          out.clearBuffer();
          if (pageContext != null) {
            pageContext.handlePageException(t);
          }
        }
      } finally {
        if (_jspxFactory != null) {
          _jspxFactory.releasePageContext(pageContext);
        }
      }
    }
  }
```

and that's it. Obviously, the particular servlet code that is generated will depend on the code you use in your JSP – if you use actions like <jsp:useBean> and <jsp:forward>, or tag libraries, Tomcat will create the necessary code to perform those operations.

Web Applications and web.xml

A web application can consist of various components:

❑   Servlets

❑   JavaServer Pages

❑   JavaBeans and utility classes

❑   Static documents (html, images, sounds, etc.)

❑   Descriptive meta-information that ties all of the above elements together

As we have seen, a web application exists as a structured hierarchy of folders (directories); the "root" of this hierarchy serves as the document root for serving files that are part of this application. For example, so far in this chapter we've been using the %CATALINA_HOME%\webapps\begjsp-ch13\ folder as the root of our web application, and this is accessed by URLs starting with http://localhost:8080/begjsp-ch13/. If a browser requested the file http://localhost:8080/begjsp-ch13/index.html, Tomcat would look for the file %CATALINA_HOME%\webapps\begjsp-ch13\index.html.

A special folder, named WEB-INF, exists within the web application folder; this folder contains:

❑   WEB-INF\web.xml
    The "deployment descriptor" file, providing the container with configuration information about the application.

❑   WEB-INF\classes\
    As we have already seen, this folder contains servlets, JavaBeans, and other utility classes, in the form of compiled .class files.

❑   WEB-INF\lib\
    Contains Java archive (.jar) files. JAR files are a special way of packaging sets of related Java classes, similar to a .zip file, and provide a convenient way of distributing packages such as the Struts framework that we'll be using in Chapters 18-20. All the classes – servlets, JavaBeans, or otherwise – in these .jar files will be available within the web application just like regular .class files in the WEB-INF\classes folder.

The deployment descriptor file conveys the configuration information about a web application to the container; it can contain various types of configuration, deployment, and custom tag library information: the web.xml could be described as the "glue" which holds a web application together. Throughout previous chapters we have encountered a few of its functions without going into detail. Here is a list of the most important functions it can provide:

❑   **ServletContext initialization parameters**
    A set of context initialization parameters can be associated with a web application. Initialization parameters can be used by an application developer to convey setup information, such as the name of a system that holds critical data. This data can be included under the tag <context-param> in the web.xml. It is different than servlet initialization parameters since it defines the initialization parameters, which are used by the whole application.

❑ **Session Configuration**
The `<session-config>` element defines the session parameters for the web application. For instance, we can define the session timeout parameter for the application.

❑ **Servlet/JSP Definitions**
We can define servlet and JSP related parameters like the name of the servlet and its class, the full path, and initialization parameters.

❑ **Servlet/JSP Mappings**
Under the `<servlet-mapping>` tag, mapping between a URL and the servlet, which has to be invoked, can be configured. This means that we can define which servlet handles which URLs.

❑ **Security Configuration**
We can configure security constraints for the web resources concerned with the web application.

All these features will be demonstrated in examples throughout in this chapter; a full listing of the format of the web.xml file can be found in Appendix C.

Try It Out – Mapping Servlets with web.xml

An example of a typical deployment descriptor is given below, in this case for a web application that contains the DisplayServlet we created earlier. The first two lines are mandatory in any web.xml file, and define the DTD (document type definition) for this class of XML:

```
<!DOCTYPE web-app PUBLIC "-//Sun Microsystems, Inc.//DTD Web Application
 2.3//EN" " http://java.sun.com/dtd/web-app_2_3.dtd">

<web-app>
  <display-name>A Simple Application</display-name>
  <servlet>
    <servlet-name>DisplayServlet</servlet-name>
    <servlet-class>com.wrox.DisplayServlet</servlet-class>
  </servlet>
  <servlet-mapping>
    <servlet-name>DisplayServlet</servlet-name>
    <url-pattern>/Display/*</url-pattern>
  </servlet-mapping>
  <session-config>
    <session-timeout>30</session-timeout>
  </session-config>
</web-app>
```

Put the web.xml file in the %CATALINA_HOME%/WEB-INF directory. Now restart Tomcat and navigate to http://localhost:8080/Display; your browser should display the same information as before, but with a bit less typing!

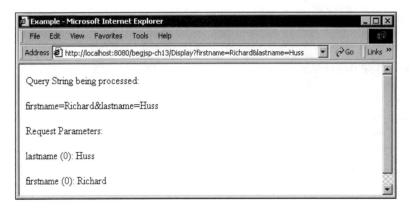

How It Works

The `<servlet>` element establishes a mapping between a servlet name and the full name (including the package name) of the servlet class:

```
<servlet>
  <servlet-name>DisplayServlet</servlet-name>
  <servlet-class>com.wrox.DisplayServlet</servlet-class>
..</servlet>
```

When Tomcat receives a request, it must determine which servlet should handle it. The `<servlet-mapping>` element can be used to designate that a certain set of URLs should be handled by a particular servlet. Here we specify that URLs starting with /Display/ should be handled by `DisplayServlet`. Note that this is relative to the root of the web application – for our `begjsp-ch13` application that means that we're mapping all URLs starting http://localhost:8080/begjsp-ch13/Display/ to the `Display` servlet:

```
<servlet-mapping>
  <servlet-name>DisplayServlet</servlet-name>
  <url-pattern>/Display/*</url-pattern>
</servlet-mapping>
```

We have to indicate to the Tomcat engine what should be the session timeout. We do it by defining the tag `<session-config>` in web.xml. In the `<session-config>` tag, we can define a tag `<session-timeout>`, which indicates the session timeout period in seconds to the container.

```
<session-config>
  <session-timeout>30</session-timeout>
</session-config>
```

Getting Initialization Information

The initialization information, such as database connection details, are passed to the servlet through a `ServletConfig` object that is passed to the servlet's `init()` method. We specify the initialization information in the deployment descriptor file, `web.xml`. The `ServletConfig` object represents this information to a running servlet. In the following example, we will get database login information from the `ServletConfig` object.

As we have already seen, the `ServletConfig` object contains servlet-specific initialization parameters, so each servlet has it's own. The parameters are stored as name-value pairs. Values can be accessed using the `getInitParameter()` method, which returns the value of the specified initialization parameter as a `String`.

```
String param = ServletConfig.getInitParameter("Name");
```

You can get the names of all of the initialization parameters using the `getInitParameterNames()` method:

```
Enumeration names = ServletConfig. getInitParameterNames();
```

This method returns an `enumeration` containing all the parameter names. These methods are inherited from the `GenericServlet` class, remember `HttpServlet` extends `GenericServlet`.

Context Initialization Parameters

A set of initialization parameters can be associated with a web application using the `<context-param>` element in the `web.xml` file. These can be accessed in the same way as for servlet parameters, calling the methods on the `ServletContext object`:

```
String contextParam = ServletContext.getInitParameter("Name");
```

Try It Out – Getting Initialization Information

This servlet will print out the database login information and port configuration, taken from the `web.xml` file. It even prints the password; this has been done for demonstration purposes only – it is strongly recommended never to display a password in any application:

```
package com.wrox.servlets;

import javax.servlet.*;
import javax.servlet.http.*;
import java.io.*;
import java.util.*;

public class InitParamServlet extends HttpServlet {

  public void doGet(HttpServletRequest req, HttpServletResponse res)
        throws IOException, ServletException {

    res.setContentType("text/plain");
    PrintWriter out = res.getWriter();

    String url = getInitParameter("URL");

    ServletConfig config = getServletConfig();
    ServletContext context = getServletContext();
    String uid = config.getInitParameter("UID");
    String pwd = config.getInitParameter("PWD");
    String port = context.getInitParameter("some-port");
```

```
      out.println("Values retrieved for the init parameters are: ");
      out.println("URL: " + url);
      out.println("UID: " + uid);
      out.println("PWD: " + pwd);
      out.println("some-port: " + port);
    }
}
```

Open up your existing web.xml file and add the highlighted lines below, which provide the initialization information and servlet mapping needed by this servlet:

```xml
<?xml version="1.0" encoding="ISO-8859-1"?>
<!DOCTYPE web-app PUBLIC "-//Sun Microsystems, Inc.//DTD Web Application 2.3//EN"
"http://java.sun.com/dtd/web-app_2_3.dtd">
<web-app>
  <display-name>A Simple Application</display-name>

  <context-param>
    <param-name>some-port</param-name>
    <param-value>5000</param-value>
  </context-param>

  <servlet>
    <servlet-name>DisplayServlet</servlet-name>
    <servlet-class>com.wrox.DisplayServlet</servlet-class>
  </servlet>
  <servlet>
    <servlet-name>init</servlet-name>
    <servlet-class>com.wrox.servlets.InitParamServlet</servlet-class>
    <init-param>
      <param-name>URL</param-name>
      <param-value>jdbc:odbc:testdb</param-value>
    </init-param>
    <init-param>
      <param-name>UID</param-name>
      <param-value>scott</param-value>
    </init-param>
    <init-param>
      <param-name>PWD</param-name>
      <param-value>tiger</param-value>
    </init-param>
  </servlet>

  <servlet-mapping>
    <servlet-name>DisplayServlet</servlet-name>
    <url-pattern>/Display/*</url-pattern>
  </servlet-mapping>
  <servlet-mapping>
    <servlet-name>init</servlet-name>
    <url-pattern>/init</url-pattern>
  </servlet-mapping>

  <session-config>
    <session-timeout>30</session-timeout>
  </session-config>
</web-app>
```

Compile the servlet as before:

```
> javac com\wrox\servlets\InitParamServlet.java
```

Restart Tomcat and navigate to the http://localhost:8080/beg-jsp/init; you should get the
following result:

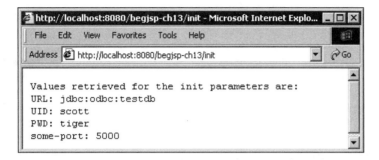

How It Works

Init parameters can be provided under <init-param> tags in web.xml; these parameters only apply
to the servlet they are declared for. Web application-wide parameters can be declared using the
<context-param> element. The web.xml also contains the servlet mapping information:

```
<web-app>
  <context-param>
    <param-name>some-port</param-name>
    <param-value>5000</param-value>
  </context-param>
  <servlet>
    ...
    <init-param>
      <param-name>URL</param-name>
      <param-value>jdbc:odbc:testdb</param-value>
    </init-param>
    ...
  </servlet>
</web-app>
```

The parameters declared in the web.xml file can be accessed from inside the servlet in several ways.

The InitParamServlet servlet implements just one method doGet(). First the method sets the
content type to be text and creates a PrintWriter object.

```
res.setContentType("text/plain");
PrintWriter out = res.getWriter();
```

The value of the attribute URL is stored in the string url simply by calling the getInitParameter()
method. The init() method, which this servlet inherits from the GenericServlet class, is called
when the servlet is created by the web container. This creates a ServletConfig object at
initialization; if no object is specified the getInitParameter() method is called on this object.

```
String url = getInitParameter("URL");
```

You can if needed get the `ServletConfig` and `ServletConfig` and store in them the appropriate objects, they can then be accessed in the same way.

```
ServletConfig config = getServletConfig();
ServletContext context = getServletContext();
String uid = config.getInitParameter("UID");
String pwd = config.getInitParameter("PWD");
```

The parameters declared using the `<context-param>` element can only be accessed from the `ServletContext` object.

```
String port = context.getInitParameter("some-port");
```

Collaboration Between Servlets

We've seen in earlier chapters how we can get JSPs to collaborate – how we can track user sessions and share information between JSPs in the same session. How we can use the `application` object to share information between all the JSPs in the same web application, and use the `<jsp:forward>` and `<jsp:include>` actions to involve several JSPs in processing a single user request. We can do all these things with servlets too, and that's what we'll look at next.

Session Tracking

We saw in Chapter 11 that the Hypertext Transfer Protocol (HTTP) is by design a stateless protocol. To build effective web applications, it is necessary that a series of different requests from a particular client should be logically associated with each other. Many strategies for session tracking have evolved over time, but all are difficult or troublesome for the programmer to use directly. So, the Java Servlet API provides a simple `javax.servlet.http.HttpSession` interface that allows a servlet container to track a user's session without involving the developer in the nuances of how this is done.

We encountered this interface in Chapter 11 – the `session` object in a JSP implements it.

Session tracking allows servlets to maintain state information about a series of requests from the same user across time. To make use of this mechanism we need to:

❑   Obtain the `HttpSession` object from the `HttpServletRequest`.

❑   Store and retrieve data from the `session` object.

❑   When you no longer need the data in the session, destroy the `session` object.

The `getSession()` method of the `HttpServletRequest` object returns the current session associated with the request; if there is no current session then one is created. While storing data in the session, we create name-value pairs. The `HttpSession` interface has methods allowing us to store, retrieve, and remove attributes:

- setAttribute()
- getAttribute()
- getAttributeNames()
- removeAttribute()

The invalidate() method invalidates the session, which means all the objects in the session are destroyed.

Try It Out – Session Tracking in a Servlet

Let's try writing a servlet that uses session tracking to keep track of how many times it has been accessed by a particular user, and to display some details of the current session.

Save the following Java code in a file called SessionDetails.java, in the same folder as before:

```
package com.wrox.servlets;

import java.io.*;
import javax.servlet.*;
import javax.servlet.http.*;

public class SessionDetails extends HttpServlet {

  public void doGet(HttpServletRequest req, HttpServletResponse res)
          throws ServletException, IOException {
    res.setContentType("text/html");
    PrintWriter out = res.getWriter();

    HttpSession session = req.getSession(true);

    Integer count = (Integer) session.getAttribute("count");

    if (count == null) {
      count = new Integer(1);
    } else {
      count = new Integer(count.intValue() + 1);
    }

    session.setAttribute("count", count);

    out.println("<html><head><title>SessionSnoop</title></head>");
    out.println("<body><h1>Session Details</h1>");
    out.println("<p>You've visited this page " + count
            + ((count.intValue() == 1) ? " time." : " times.</p>"));

    out.println("<h3>Details of this session:</h3>");
    out.println("<p>Session id: " + session.getId() + "</p>");
    out.println("<p>New session: " + session.isNew() + "</p>");
    out.println("<p>Timeout: " + session.getMaxInactiveInterval() + "</p>");
    out.println("<p>Creation time: " + session.getCreationTime() + "</p>");
    out.println("<p>Last access time: " + session.getLastAccessedTime()
            + "</p>");

    out.println("</body></html>");
  }
}
```

367

Add the following entry to the web.xml file next to the existing <servlet> entries:

```
<servlet>
  <servlet-name>SessionDetails</servlet-name>
  <servlet-class>com.wrox.servlets.SessionDetails</servlet-class>
</servlet>
```

and the following entry next to the existing <servlet-mapping> entries:

```
<servlet-mapping>
  <servlet-name>SessionDetails</servlet-name>
  <url-pattern>/Session</url-pattern>
</servlet-mapping>
```

Compile the servlet from the %CATALINA_HOME%\webapps\begjsp-ch13\WEB-INF\classes folder, by running the following command:

```
> javac com\wrox\servlets\SessionDetails.java
```

Restart Tomcat and browse to http://localhost:8080/begjsp-ch13/servlet/com.wrox.servlets. SessionDetails. You should see the servlet's output shown below:

Hit your browser's Reload button several times. You'll notice that the page shows how many times you've visited it, and also now says New session: false.

How It Works

First, we set the request content type to be HTML, create a PrintWriter object, and get the current session (a new one is created if needed):

```
res.setContentType("text/html");
PrintWriter out = res.getWriter();
HttpSession session = req.getSession(true);
```

Every time a page is accessed, we get the access count from the session by calling `getAttribute()`, which is incremented and stored back into the session. If null is returned from the `Session` object, meaning that no `count` attribute has been set yet, `count` is initialized with a value of one:

```
Integer count = (Integer) session.getAttribute("count");

if (count == null) {
  count = new Integer(1);
} else {
  count = new Integer(count.intValue() + 1);
}
```

In this servlet, we are using the `HttpServletSession` to store session specific information (access count). We store the access count by calling `setAttribute()` on the `session` object.

```
session.setAttribute("count", count);
```

In a `session`, we can store only objects and not any primitive data types. Hence, as you can see, we are storing objects of type `Integer` instead of primitive int type information. The rest of the servlet creates HTML output of the number of hits and other standard information stored by the session object.

The Servlet Context

The servlet context defines a servlet's view of the web application, for the servlet it is concerned with; it implements the `javax.servlet.ServletContext` interface. A servlet can use it to access all the resources available within the application, to log events, and to store attributes that other servlets belonging to context can use. (We encountered the `ServletContext` object in Chapter 11 – in a JSP it is known as the `application` object.)

For example, so far in this chapter we've placed several servlets in a web application that's based at http://localhost:8080/begjsp-ch13/. All the resources in our server that are in this application (in other words, that have request paths starting /begjsp-ch13/) share a single, common servlet context.

A servlet can set an object as an attribute into the context by name, just as it can with the `HttpSession`, providing a convenient place to store resources that need to be shared for general use in an application. Objects can be added, retrieved, or removed from the context using the following methods of `ServletContext`:

- ❑ `void setAttribute(String name, Object attribute)`
  Used to store an attribute in a context

- ❑ `Object getAttribute(String name)`
  Used to get an attribute from the context

- ❑ `Enumeration getAttributeNames()`
  Used to get the names of all the attributes currently stored in the context

❑   void removeAttribute(String name)
     Call this function to remove an attribute from the context

Try It Out – Getting Servlet Context Information

The following example shows a servlet accessing a shared resource, which keeps count of the total number of accesses to this page in the servlet context object. The previous example has been augmented with the extra details that are necessary to store the total count in the context. Observe the total number of visits in the example.

Add the following lines to SessionDetails, then save it as SessionDetails2 in the usual place:

```java
package com.wrox.servlets;

import java.io.*;
import java.util.*;
import javax.servlet.*;
import javax.servlet.http.*;

public class SessionDetails2 extends HttpServlet {

    public void doGet(HttpServletRequest req, HttpServletResponse res)
            throws ServletException, IOException {
    res.setContentType("text/html");
    PrintWriter out = res.getWriter();

    HttpSession session = req.getSession();

    Integer totalCount = (Integer) getServletContext().getAttribute
            ("com.wrox.SessionDetails.total");

    if (totalCount == null) {
      totalCount = new Integer(1);
    } else {
      totalCount = new Integer(totalCount.intValue() + 1);
    }

    Integer count = (Integer)session.getAttribute("count");

    if (count == null) {
      count = new Integer(1);
    } else {
      count = new Integer(count.intValue() + 1);
    }

    getServletContext().setAttribute
            ("com.wrox.SessionDetails.total",totalCount;

    out.println("<html><head><title>SessionSnoop</title></head>");
    out.println("<body><h1>Session Details</h1>");
    out.println("<p>You've visited this page " + count +
              ((count.intValue() == 1) ? " time." : " times.</p>"));
    out.println("<p>Total Number of visits:" + totalCount);
    out.println("<h3>Details of this session:</h3>");
```

```
        out.println("<p>Session id: " + session.getId() + "</p>");
        out.println("<p>New session: " + session.isNew()+ "</p>");
        out.println("<p>Timeout: " + session.getMaxInactiveInterval() + "</p>");
        out.println("<p>Creation time: " + new Date(session.getCreationTime()) +
                    "</p>");
        out.println("<p>Last access time: " +
                    new Date(session.getLastAccessedTime()) + "</p>");

        out.println("</body></html>");
    }
}
```

Add the following lines to your web.xml file, next to the other <servlet> entries:

```
<servlet>
    <servlet-name>SessionDetails2</servlet-name>
    <servlet-class>com.wrox.servlets.SessionDetails2</servlet-class>
</servlet>
```

and add these lines with the other <servlet-mapping> entries:

```
<servlet-mapping>
    <servlet-name>SessionDetails2</servlet-name>
    <url-pattern>/Session2</url-pattern>
</servlet-mapping>
```

Compile SessionDetails2:

> **javac com.wrox.servlets.SessionDetails2**

Restart Tomcat and navigate to http://localhost:8080/begjsp-ch13/Session2. If you open two browser windows and hit reload a few times you'll get a page looking something like this.

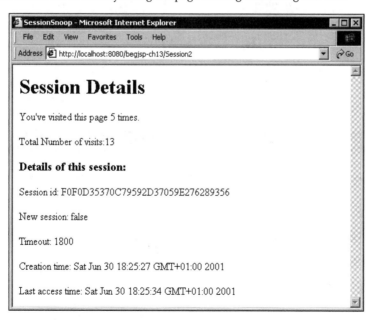

371

How It Works

After the title the first number records the total number of visits in this session which is the same as in the previous example and the second number records the total number of visits for all sessions.

We have just extended the previous example, to store some information in the `ServletContext` object so we can track the total number of hits.

```
Integer totalCount = (Integer)
getServletContext().getAttribute("com.wrox.SessionDetails.total");

    if (totalCount == null) {
      totalCount = new Integer(1);
    } else {
      totalCount = new Integer(totalCount.intValue() + 1);
    }
```

We can access the context by calling the method `getServletContext()` method, and we can get the attribute from the context by calling the method `getAttribute()`. We then take this value and increment it by one or if it has not yet been set it is initialized to one. We increment this count every time there is an access, irrespective of the session status. We can then store information in the context object by calling `setAttribute()`.

```
getServletContext().setAttribute("com.wrox.SessionDetails.total",totalCount;
```

Any servlet can remove an attribute from the context by calling the `removeAttribute()` method; therefore, care must be taken to ensure that other servlets are not using the same resource. This is the reason why it is recommended to use scoped names for context attributes, like `com.wrox.SessionDetails` instead of simple names like `SessionDetails`.

Forwarding and Including Requests

We saw in Chapter 12 that it is often convenient when building a web application to forward requests to some other resource for further processing, or to include the output of one servlet or JSP within another. In JSP we do this using the `<jsp:forward>` and `<jsp:include>` actions; a servlet can also forward to or include another resource, using the `javax.servlet.RequestDispatcher` interface.

Try It Out – Forwarding and Including Requests in a Servlet

Here we will create three new servlets, `Include`, `Forward`, and `Goto` to demonstrate forwarding and including requests. The code for the `Forward` servlet is shown below:

```
import java.io.*;
import javax.servlet.*;
import javax.servlet.http.*;

public class Forward extends HttpServlet {

  String forwardingAddress = "Goto";

  public void doGet(HttpServletRequest req, HttpServletResponse res)
```

```
          throws ServletException, IOException {
    req.setAttribute("option", "forward");
    RequestDispatcher dispatcher =
      req.getRequestDispatcher(forwardingAddress);
    dispatcher.forward(req, res);
  }
}
```

The code for the Include servlet is given below:

```
import java.io.*;
import javax.servlet.*;
import javax.servlet.http.*;

public class Include extends HttpServlet {

  String forwardingAddress = "Goto";

  public void doGet(HttpServletRequest req, HttpServletResponse res)
          throws ServletException, IOException {
    req.setAttribute("option", "include");
    RequestDispatcher dispatcher =
      req.getRequestDispatcher(forwardingAddress);
    dispatcher.include(req, res);
    PrintWriter out = res.getWriter();
    out.println("Response included successfully");
  }
}
```

Both of the above servlets use the Goto servlet shown below:

```
import java.io.*;
import javax.servlet.*;
import javax.servlet.http.*;

public class Goto extends HttpServlet {

  String forwardingAddress = "Goto";

  public void doGet(HttpServletRequest req, HttpServletResponse res)
          throws ServletException, IOException {
    String option = (String) req.getAttribute("option");
    PrintWriter out = res.getWriter();
    if (option != null) {
      if (option.equals("forward")) {
        out.println("You have been forwarded to this page");
      } else if (option.equals("include")) {
        out.println("This line will be included in the response");
      }
    }
  }
}
```

As before, we need to add some `<servlet>` entries to `web.xml`:

```
<servlet>
  <servlet-name>goto</servlet-name>
  <servlet-class>com.wrox.servlets.Goto</servlet-class>
</servlet>
<servlet>
  <servlet-name>forward</servlet-name>
  <servlet-class> com.wrox.servlets.Forward </servlet-class>
</servlet>
<servlet>
  <servlet-name>include</servlet-name>
  <servlet-class>com.wrox.servlets.Include</servlet-class>
</servlet>
```

We also need to provide `<servlet-mapping>` entries to map these to the correct URLs:

```
<servlet-mapping>
  <servlet-name>goto</servlet-name>
  <url-pattern>/Goto</url-pattern>
</servlet-mapping>
<servlet-mapping>
  <servlet-name>include</servlet-name>
  <url-pattern>/Include</url-pattern>
</servlet-mapping>
<servlet-mapping>
  <servlet-name>forward</servlet-name>
  <url-pattern>/Forward</url-pattern>
</servlet-mapping>
```

If you restart Tomcat and navigate to http://localhost:8080/begjsp-ch13/Forward, you should see the following result:

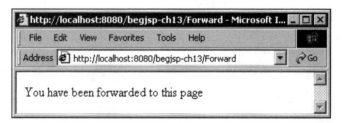

If you navigate to http://localhost:8080/begjsp-ch13/Include, on the other hand, you should see the following result:

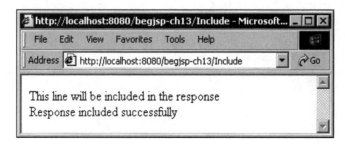

How It Works

As before, the `Forward` servlet just implements a `doGet()` method, this method is automatically called when you request the page using the `GET` method:

```
req.setAttribute("option", "forward");
RequestDispatcher dispatcher =
  req.getRequestDispatcher(forwardingAddress);
dispatcher.forward(req, res);
```

First, the request attribute `option` is given a value `"forward"`, and then a `RequestDispatcher` called "dispatcher" is created using the `getRequestDispatcher()` method of the `request` object. Finally, the `forward()` method is called on `dispatcher` which simply forwards the request to another servlet, in this case `Goto`. Here the forwarding path should be relative to the application root.

The `Include servlet`, also only implements a `doGet()` method, the contents of which is given below:

```
req.setAttribute("option", "include");
RequestDispatcher dispatcher =
  req.getRequestDispatcher(forwardingAddress);
dispatcher.include(req, res);
PrintWriter out = res.getWriter();
out.println("Response included successfully");
```

This is similar to the previous servlet, but the `option` attribute is set to `"Include"` and the `include()` method is called on `dispatcher`. This includes the response of the `Goto` servlet into the response of this servlet. After the response of the `Goto` servlet a writer object is created using the `getWriter()` method of the `request` object. Then a message **Response included successfully** is printed out.

The `Goto` servlet handles requests in much the same way as the other servlets by implementing a `doGet()` method.

```
String option = (String) req.getAttribute("option");
    PrintWriter out = res.getWriter();
    if (option != null) {
      if (option.equals("forward")) {
        out.println("You have been forwarded to this page");
      } else if (option.equals("include")) {
        out.println("This line will be included in the response");
      }
    }
  }
```

It finds out the origin of the request by querying for request attribute `option` and stores this as a String. A `PrintWriter` called "out" is created; finally, it prints out some text based on the value of `option`.

The `web.xml` file simply maps the servlets to the appropriate URLs.

User Authentication

A web application is expected to provide valuable services to its users. Therefore, you may want to restrict access to a limited set of users, for instance those that have paid a subscription. To do this the server needs to be able to **authenticate** the client – in other words, to make sure that the user is who they say they are. A simple but very effective way is to provide user identification and authentication through a password only known to the user.

In some web applications, only certain users are able to access particular resources – for example, it could be that only paid-up users will be able to use a particular servlet or JSP. With each user id-password pair there is associated one or more roles (for instance user, super-user and so on). It is possible to allow an authenticated user access to only the parts of the web application for which their assigned roles are valid.

Servlets technology provides several methods to implement these procedures in your web application. Four authentication methods are specified in the servlet 2.3 specification:

- ❑ HTTP Basic
- ❑ HTTP Digest
- ❑ Form based
- ❑ HTTPS client

We will cover the two most commonly used methods, HTTP Basic and Form based authentication in detail.

Of the other two methods, HTTP Digest is basically a more secure version of HTTP Basic and HTTPS client is the most secure method available, allowing encrypted communication between client and server. HTTPS client uses digital certificates and the secure sockets layer, which are beyond the scope of this book. A lot of insight can be gained on all these security concepts if you visit: http://developer.java.sun.com/developer/technicalArticles/Security/.

HTTP Basic Authentication

The HTTP protocol provides the Basic authentication mechanism based on the username/password model. When a user requests access to a protected resource, the server responds by popping up a dialog box for them to enter the user information, which is sent back to the server in plain text. If the submitted username and password match the data in the server's database, then access is granted to that user.

The authentication information can be retrieved by using the `HttpServletRequest` object's `getRemoteUser()` method, which returns the remote user's identification and `getAuthType()` method, which returns the authentication mechanism for a particular request. Typical return values are `"BASIC"` or `"SSL"`, or `null` if no authentication was used.

Try It Out – HTTP Basic Authentication

The example below demonstrates a simple servlet, which validates the authentication. The user provides the authentication by signing in to the application through a HTML page, which will be submitted to the `ProtectedServlet` for authentication.

```java
package com.wrox.servlets;

import javax.servlet.*;
import javax.servlet.http.*;
import java.io.*;
import java.util.*;
import java.security.*;

public class ProtectedServlet extends HttpServlet {
  public void init(ServletConfig cfg) throws ServletException {
    super.init(cfg);
  }

  public void doGet(HttpServletRequest req, HttpServletResponse res)
          throws IOException, ServletException {
    res.setContentType("text/plain");
    PrintWriter out = res.getWriter();
    String authType = req.getAuthType();
    out.println("You are authorized to view this page");
    out.println("You were authenticated using: " + authType
                + " method of authentication");
    Principal princ = req.getUserPrincipal();
    out.println("The user is: " + princ.getName());
  }
}
```

The `web.xml` file used to protect our servlet is given below; replace your existing file with the following:

```xml
<?xml version="1.0" encoding="ISO-8859-1"?>
<!DOCTYPE web-app PUBLIC "-//Sun Microsystems, Inc.//DTD Web Application 2.3//EN"
"http://java.sun.com/dtd/web-app_2_3.dtd">
<web-app>
  <servlet>
    <servlet-name>protected</servlet-name>
    <servlet-class>com.wrox.servlets.ProtectedServlet</servlet-class>
  </servlet>

  <servlet-mapping>
    <servlet-name>protected</servlet-name>
    <url-pattern>/protected</url-pattern>
  </servlet-mapping>

  <security-constraint>
    <web-resource-collection>
      <web-resource-name>Protected Area</web-resource-name>
      <url-pattern>/protected</url-pattern>
    </web-resource-collection>
    <auth-constraint>
      <role-name>begjsp</role-name>
    </auth-constraint>
  </security-constraint>

  <login-config>
    <auth-method>BASIC</auth-method>
    <realm-name>Wrox Area</realm-name>
  </login-config>
</web-app>
```

377

Finally we need to add an entry to the `tomcat-users.xml` file, this can be found in the `%CATALINA_HOME%/conf` directory. This is where all the password information for your web application is stored:

```
<tomcat-users>
  <user name="tomcat"  password="tomcat" roles="tomcat" />
  <user name="role1"   password="tomcat" roles="role1"  />
  <user name="both"    password="tomcat" roles="tomcat,role1" />
  <user name="newuser" password="tomcat" roles="begjsp" />
</tomcat-users>
```

Restart Tomcat and navigate to http://localhost:8080/begjsp-ch13/protected; you should be asked to enter your username and password. Enter the values you placed in the `tomcat-users.xml` file. When you are authenticated, the following page will be displayed:

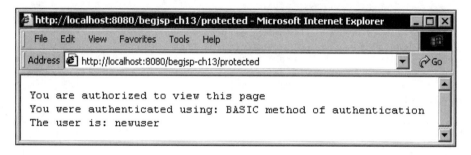

If you try one of the other passwords in the `tomcat-users.xml` file, you will see the authentication fails.

How It Works

The setup for all the security mechanism is contained in the web.xml file, the resource you are trying to access does not need to know how this works as it is all handled by the web container.

In the `web.xml` file we map the servlet to the path **/protected**. The information of the security setup for your web application is contained within the `<security-constraint>` element. This contains two subelements `<web-resource-collection>` and `<auth-constraint>`. `<url-pattern>` sets the path to the protected part of the web application and `<role-name>`, which roles can be authenticated.

```
<security-constraint>
  <web-resource-collection>
    <web-resource-name>Protected Area</web-resource-name>
    <url-pattern>/protected</url-pattern>
  </web-resource-collection>
  <auth-constraint>
    <role-name>begjsp</role-name>
  </auth-constraint>
</security-constraint>
```

The `<login-config>` element defines the configuration of the actual login. We select the BASIC method and the HTTP realm name; this name will be shown in the popup login box (on most browsers).

```
<login-config>
  <auth-method>BASIC</auth-method>
  <realm-name>Wrox Area</realm-name>
</login-config>
```

The authentication information for Tomcat is stored in the file %CATALINA_HOME%/conf/tomcat-users.xml. We add the following entry to create a new user:

```
<user name="newuser" password="tomcat" roles="begjsp" />
```

each <user> element has name, password, and roles attributes. The purpose of the name and password attributes is obvious; the roles attribute describes for which roles this user-password combination is effective for. Therefore, for each web application you only have to define the roles that are allowed to authenticate. If you recall from the web.xml file we set the acceptable roles to be role1 and tomcat, so all of the users listed in the above file would be able to authenticate our application.

When you try to access the /protected page the server responds with an "unauthorized" response as part of the response the server returns a WWW-Authenticate header, in this case

```
WWW-Authenticate: Basic realm="Wrox Area"
```

The browser then creates a popup dialogue box asking for a username and password, which are cached in memory and then returned to the server. If the values are authenticated, the server returns the requested page. As the values entered are cached the user is not prompted for them again when accessing pages with the same realm.

Form Based Authentication

The advantage of forms-based authentication is that it allows you to write custom login and error pages. The pages you create are responsible for transmitting the username and password to the web container. This is much more flexible than Basic authentication where this is all handled by the browser.

Try It Out – Form based Authentication

For this example, we need to create three JSP pages and modify the web.xml file. First, we create login.jsp, which will provide the actual login form:

```
<html>
  <head><title>Login Page</title></head>
<body>
<h2>Login page</h2>

<form method="POST" action="j_security_check" >
<input type="text" name="j_username">
<input type="password" name="j_password">
<input type="submit" value="Login Now">
</form>

</body>
</html>
```

We will also provide an error page to deal with users that enter incorrect details, `error.jsp`:

```
<html>
  <head><title>Authentication Error</title></head>
<body>
You have entered an invalid username/password.<br>
Please <a href="login.jsp">try again</a><br>
If you continue to experience difficulties please contact the site administrator
at webmaster@somesystem.com

</body>
</html>
```

Obviously, we try to access some resource if we are to be authenticated, so we provide `index.jsp`:

```
<html>
  <head><title>Protected Page</title></head>
<body>
<%
  out.println("<h2>Authentication mechanism "+ request.getAuthType()
    + "</h2>" );
%>
</body>
</html>
```

Finally we need to modify the `web.xml` file. It is not possible for a web application to have more then one authentication mechanism, so rather than modifying the previous file just replace it with this:

```
<?xml version="1.0" encoding="ISO-8859-1"?>
<!DOCTYPE web-app PUBLIC "-//Sun Microsystems, Inc.//DTD Web Application 2.3//EN"
"http://java.sun.com/dtd/web-app_2_3.dtd">

<web-app>
  <security-constraint>
    <web-resource-collection>
      <web-resource-name>Entire application</web-resource-name>
      <url-pattern>/*</url-pattern>
    </web-resource-collection>
    <auth-constraint>
      <role-name>begjsp</role-name>
    </auth-constraint>
  </security-constraint>

  <login-config>
    <auth-method>FORM</auth-method>
    <form-login-config>
      <form-login-page>/login.jsp</form-login-page>
      <form-error-page>/error.jsp</form-error-page>
    </form-login-config>
  </login-config>
</web-app>
```

Don't forget to restart Tomcat, then navigate to http://localhost:8080/begjsp-ch13/index.jsp and you should see the following page:

Enter the username and password. Click on the Login Button, and you will be redirected to login.jsp, which displays the authentication mechanism used:

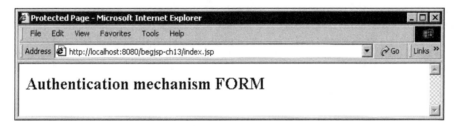

How It Works

If the user tries to access a page in a protected part of the application, a login form is returned instead of the requested resource. The login form contains fields for the user to specify their username and password. These *must* be called j_username and j_password, also the form action must be j_security_check:

```
<form method="POST" action="j_security_check" >
<input type="text" name="j_username">
<input type="password" name="j_password">
<input type="submit" value="Login Now">
</form>
```

The values entered for the username and password are then returned to the server via the POST method. These values are processed in the same way as for BASIC authentication. If the user is accepted, the page they wanted to access is returned, otherwise an error page is returned.

Making Servlets Thread Safe

Let's revisit a servlet's lifecycle. A servlet runs inside a web container, which first initializes the servlet by calling its init() method, and at the end of the servlet's life calls its destroy() method. While the servlet is alive, the container helps the servlet achieve its purpose, handling the client's requests, by calling the service() method of a particular instance of the servlet, in a separate thread for every client request.

> That means that multiple threads might be calling the **service()** method at the
> same time, and therefore we must write the code in the **service()** method (and, by
> extension, in **doGet()** or **doPost()**) so that it can safely be called by several threads
> simultaneously. This is called making the code thread safe.

There is a way you can save yourself from this grief of writing thread safe code by implementing the `SingleThreadModel` interface in your servlet.

```
public class ThreadSafeServlet extends HttpServlet
        implements SingleThreadModel {
  // Typical servlet code, with no threading concerns in the service method.
  // No extra code for the SingleThreadModel interface.
}
```

This action will ensure that no two threads will execute the same object's `service()` method concurrently. To achieve this, the servlet container will manage concurrent requests by either serializing requests on a single servlet object or by having a pool of servlet objects and assigning one object per request. In this case, since the container creating new instances of your servlet, there will be a performance hit. The best practice would be to synchronize and manage the shared resources effectively in the normal servlet code.

While implementing the `SingleThreadModel`, can simplify application development, this may ultimately be at the expense of your applications performance.

Summary

When a web browser accesses a web server and makes a HTTP request, the servlet container determines which servlet to invoke based on its configuration settings, and calls it with objects representing the request and response. The servlet processes the `request`, using the request object to obtain information about the request that the browser sent, and sends data back to the client using the `response` object.

In this chapter, we have learned:

❑ Features of the servlet technology, how servlets work, and their life cycle.

❑ How JSPs work behind the scenes: the relevance of servlet technology to JSP developers, and the fact that JSPs are compiled to servlets.

❑ The role of the web.xml file in a web application.

❑ How servlets can collaborate by means of session tracking, the servlet context, and how to forward and include requests when using servlets.

❑ How to ensure only authenticated users can access your web application.

One task we often want to perform in our JSPs and servlets is reading and writing files, and we'll look at that in the next chapter.

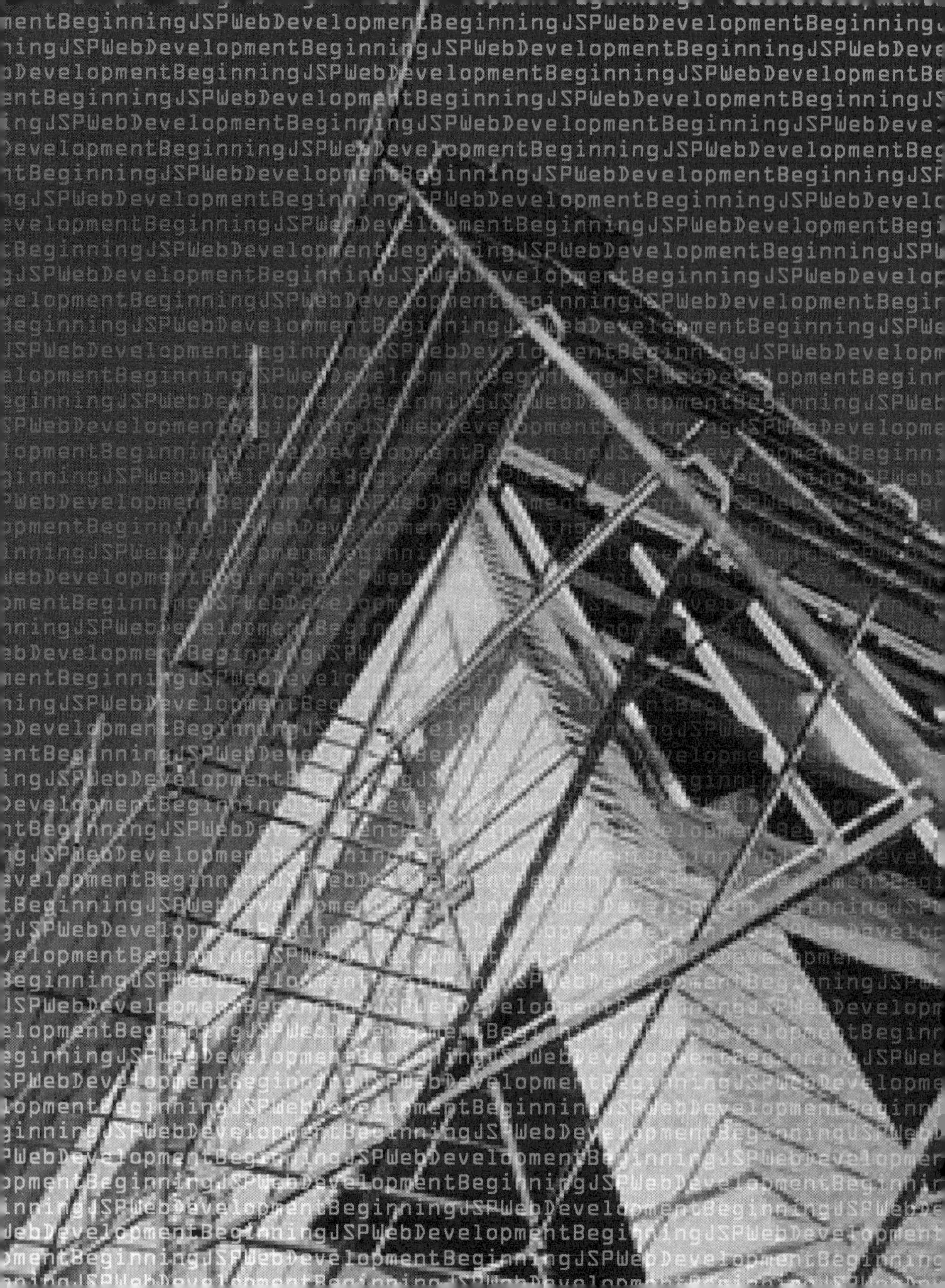
BeginningJSPWebDevelopment

Accessing Files

The Java language is the obvious choice for writing server-side applications, and almost any web application you see needs persistent storage of information (for example, storing a log of visitors), either as a flat file or in a database of some sort. Java contains a good number of classes to perform sophisticated input and output on files, the console, and the network.

The input and output (**I/O**) functionality in Java is based on **streams**; a stream is an abstract representation of a source and a destination. This means that an input stream can abstract many different kinds of input devices: a disk file, a keyboard, or a network socket. Likewise, an output stream may refer to the console, a disk file, or a network connection. Thus, the same I/O classes and methods can be applied to many types of device.

In this chapter we will:

❑   See how to access file attributes and use file paths and directories

❑   Learn about the different types of input and output operations in Java, and the differences between byte- and character-oriented I/O

❑   Look at the many different types of I/O stream classes provided in Java, and the features of each

Files and Streams

Java provides facilities both to read from and to write to streams; it also defines two types of streams: **byte** and **character**. Byte streams provide for handling input and output of streams, whereas character streams provide for handling input and output of characters.

The Java 1.0 version did not support character streams, and all I/O was byte-oriented. Java defines two major classes of byte streams: `InputStream` and `OutputStream`; these streams are subclassed to provide a variety of I/O capabilities such as reading from and writing to files. Java 1.1 introduced the `Reader` and `Writer` classes to provide for 16-bit **Unicode,** character-oriented I/O, though at the lowest level all I/O is still byte-oriented. These classes are also subclassed to provide additional capabilities.

Finally, but importantly, you should also understand the mechanism that Java has provided to interface with the file system in a machine-independent manner. The `File` class provides access to file and directory objects and supports a number of operations on them. `java.io` also supports random-access I/O using the `RandomAccessFile` class.

Overview of I/O Classes

The major components of Java I/O are the `InputStream`, `OutputStream`, `Reader`, and `Writer` classes. These higher-level classes have complementary subclasses, which we'll look at shortly. The diagram below shows the top-level classes of the `java.io` hierarchy:

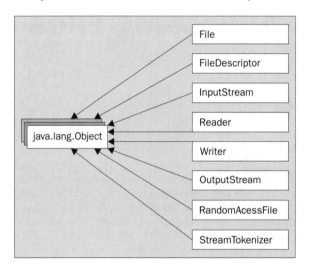

- ❑   `File` class – Manipulates information about the file system

- ❑   `FileDescriptor` class – Provides access to file descriptors maintained by the operating system.

- ❑   `InputStream` class – Abstract class providing for reading from byte streams

- ❑   `Reader` class – Abstract class providing for reading from character streams.

- ❑   `Writer` class – Abstract class providing for writing to character streams

- ❑   `OutputStream` class – Abstract class providing for writing to byte streams

- ❑   `RandomAccessFile` class – Implements direct (random) access for files

- ❑   `StreamTokenizer` class – Supports parsing of input streams

The `java.io` package provides a wide range of concrete subclasses of `InputStream`, `OutputStream`, `Reader`, and `Writer`, which we'll cover later. (There are additional classes that we are less likely to use, and which we won't cover in this chapter.)

Working with File Paths and Directories

Let's start our detailed exploration of these classes by looking at the `File` class, which is used to represent file paths and directories.

The File Class

The `java.io.File` class represents the pathname of a file or a directory. Note that it does not refer to the *contents* of a file: it deals directly with the underlying file system, and describes the properties of a file itself. The class has methods that allow us to query the file system, check for the existence of a file, manipulate the attributes of the file, and navigate directory hierarchies. However, an important point to remember is that:

> **When we instantiate a `File` object we do not create any file or directory; a `File` instance is only a representation of the pathname of a file or a directory. Similarly, throwing away the `File` object has no effect – it does not cause the file or directory to be deleted.**

The `File` class has various constructors that we can use to create a `File` object based on a file or directory:

```
File(String directoryPath)
File(String directoryPath, String fileName)
File(File dirObj, String fileName)
```

Here, `directoryPath` is the pathname of a directory, `fileName` is the name of the file, and `dirObj` is a `File` object that specifies a directory. The pathname can be an absolute pathname or a pathname relative to the current directory, but it must follow the conventions of the particular platform your application is running on.

On a Unix platform, a pathname is absolute if its first character is the separator character /, for example `/Wrox/docs`:

```
File dir = new File("/Wrox/docs");
```

On a Windows platform, a path is absolute either if the first character is a backslash (\), or if a backslash character follows the drive name (for instance, C:\Wrox\docs). On a Macintosh, a pathname is absolute if it begins with a name followed by a colon (for example HD:Wrox:docs).

However, the `File` class provides platform-independent constants that can be used to handle file and directory names in a portable way. These represent the character that separates the directory and file components in a pathname for different operating systems: / for Unix, \ for Windows, and : for Macintosh:

```
public static final char separatorChar
public static final String separator
```

For example, we can use the `File.separator` constant to help us construct a `File` object representing a file or directory, as follows:

```
File dir = new File(File.separator + "Wrox" + File.separator + "docs");
```

> **Even if you use a forward slash, /, on a Windows platform the path *will* resolve correctly.**

For example, the following code snippet, which uses the Unix convention, would work also on a Windows platform:

```
File dir = new File("/Wrox/docs");
```

You should note, however, that if you are using the Windows convention of a backslash, \, you will need to use the escape sequence \\ within a `String`. This is because the backslash character has a special meaning; it is used to help represent certain characters that cannot be entered directly, such as the newline character which is represented as \n. The double backslash, \\, represents a single backslash character.

So, to summarize, the key points that you should remember when you create an instance of the `File` class are:

❑ An instance of `File` describes a file or directory.

❑ The file or directory might or might not exist in the file system: the `File` class provides for a general machine-independent interface to the file system of the underlying platform, which can be used to query the file system for information about a file or directory.

❑ Creating or removing an instance of `File` has no effect on the file system.

File Attributes

The `File` class defines many methods that obtain the standard properties of a file, which are fairly self-explanatory. Many methods throw a `SecurityException` in the case of a security violation, for example if read or write access is denied. Some of the methods return a `boolean` value to indicate whether the operation was successful. The Java online documentation (see Appendix D for details of how to locate this) contains a detailed list of all the methods, but here are the most commonly used ones:

❑ `String getName()` – Returns the name of the file entry, excluding the directory in which it resides.

❑ `String getPath()` – Returns the absolute or relative pathname of the file represented by the `File` object.

❑ `String getAbsolutePath()` – Returns the absolute pathname. If the `File` object does not contain it, the pathname is constructed by concatenating the current directory pathname, the separator character, and the pathname of the `File` object.

❑ `String getParent()` – Returns the parent part of the pathname if one exists, otherwise `null` is returned.

- ❏ long lastModified() – Returns the time stamp, encoded as a long value.

- ❏ long length() – Returns the size of the file represented by the File object, in bytes.

- ❏ boolean exists() – Returns true if the File object denotes an entry that actually exists in the file system.

- ❏ boolean isFile() – Returns true if the File object represents a file.

- ❏ boolean isDirectory() – Returns true if the File object represents a directory.

- ❏ boolean canRead() – Returns true if the File object represents a file to which the application has read access.

- ❏ boolean setReadOnly() – Sets the file represented by the File object to read-only; returns true if successful.

- ❏ boolean canWrite() – Returns true if the File object represents a file to which the application has write access.

- ❏ boolean createNewFile() throws IOException – Returns true if it successfully creates a new empty file named by the pathname; returns false if the file already exists.

- ❏ boolean mkdir() – Returns true if it successfully creates the directory specified in the pathname.

- ❏ boolean mkdirs() – Returns true if the directory is successfully created. This method creates any missing intervening parent directories in the pathname of the directory to be created.

- ❏ boolean delete() – Returns true if the file or directory represented by the File object is successfully deleted. In the case of a directory, it must be empty before it can be deleted.

The File class lacks some features; for example on a Windows machine we might want to find out whether a file is a system, or an archived file. The reason for this is that the Java designers had to take the lowest common denominator when considering the file system of different platforms. So if Java tried to include features that aren't supported by all systems, it would jeopardize its universal compatibility across platforms.

We'll be seeing more methods that navigate directories in the next section, but we have already gained enough knowledge to try out a small example using the File object to access the characteristics of a file.

Try It Out – Accessing File Attributes

We'll create a simple command-line Java program that creates a directory and some files, displays the attributes of one of the files, renames the second file, and finally deletes the files and directory.

Save the following code as FileDemo.java:

```
/* FileDemo.java
   Code to demonstrate the File class */

import java.io.*;

public class FileDemo {
```

```
public static void main (String [] args) throws IOException {
  // Create instances of File objects for directory
  // and file entries
  File dir = new File(File.separator + "Wrox" + File.separator
                    + "docs");
  File f1 = new File(dir, "test1.txt");
  File f2 = new File(dir, "test2.doc");
  File f3 = new File(dir, "test3.txt");

  // Create directory and files
  dir.mkdirs();
  System.out.println("Directory \\Wrox\\docs created");
  f1.createNewFile();
  f2.createNewFile();
  System.out.println("Files \"test1.txt\" and \"test2.doc\" created");

  // Get file attributes
  System.out.println("\nAttributes of \"test1.txt\" \n" +
  "\n\"test1.txt\" exists: " + f1.exists() +
  "\n\"test1.txt\" is a file: " + f1.isFile() +
  "\n\"test1.txt\" is a directory: " + f1.isDirectory() +
  "\nCan read from \"test1.txt\": " + f1.canRead() +
  "\nCan write to \"test1.txt\": " + f1.canWrite() +
  "\nThe absolute path of \"test1.txt\": " + f1.getAbsolutePath());

  // Rename test2.doc to test3.txt
  System.out.println("\nThe name of the file object f2 is "
                    + f2.getName());
  System.out.println("Renaming :\"test2.doc\" to \"test3.txt\"");
  f2.renameTo(f3);
  System.out.println("The name of the file object f3 is "+f3.getName());

  // Delete all files and directory
  System.out.println("\nDeleting files and directory ");
  System.out.println("The file \"test1.txt\" is deleted: "
                    + f1.delete());
  System.out.println("The file \"test3.txt\" is deleted: "
                    + f3.delete());
  System.out.println("The directory docs is deleted: "
                    + dir.delete());
  }
}
```

Compile the code by opening a command prompt window, changing to the directory where you saved FileDemo.java, and typing:

> **javac FileDemo.java**

Then run the program by entering:

> **java FileDemo**

You should see the following output:

```
Directory \Wrox\docs created
Files "test1.txt" and "test2.doc" created

Attributes of "test1.txt"

"test1.txt" exists: true
"test1.txt" is a file: true
"test1.txt" is a directory: false
Can read from "test1.txt": true
Can write to "test1.txt": true
The absolute path of "test1.txt": C:\Wrox\docs\test1.txt

The name of the file object f2 is test2.doc
Renaming :"test2.doc" to "test3.txt"
The name of the file object f3 is test3.txt

Deleting files and directory
The file "test1.txt" is deleted: true
The file "test3.txt" is deleted: true
The directory docs is deleted: true
```

How It Works

Let's walk through how the methods of the File class are applied in this example. The source file
FileDemo.java is a stand alone Java application and contains only one class, FileDemo, with a
main() method. It imports the java.io package as the first statement. The main() method header
contains a throws clause. Many of the methods in the java.io package can throw an IOException,
but in this case we do not deal with IOExceptions but explicitly propagate them. In this case the
exception would end up with the default exception handler:

```
public static void main (String [] args) throws IOException {
```

Next we instantiate a File object, dir, which represents a directory \Wrox\docs, and also three
more File objects, f1, f2, and f3 that point to test1.txt, test2.doc, and test3.txt
respectively in that directory:

```
File dir = new File(File.separator + "Wrox" + File.separator
                    + "docs");
File f1 = new File(dir, "test1.txt");
File f2 = new File(dir, "test2.doc");
File f3 = new File(dir, "test3.txt");
```

The mkdirs() method is called to create the directory that is specified by dir; it automatically creates
the intervening parent directory also. We then created two empty files, test1.txt and test2.doc,
using the createNewFile() method:

```
dir.mkdirs();
```

The values returned from the different method calls made to the File object f1 (pointing to test1.txt)
are displayed. The method getAbsolutePath() returns a String, whereas the method calls
exists(), isFile(), isDirectory(), canRead(), and canWrite() return a boolean value.

The filename pointed to by the `File` object `f2` is displayed using the `getName()` method. This object is then renamed with the `rename()` method, so that it points to the `File` object `f3` (`test3.txt`):

```
f2.renameTo(f3);
```

To remove the directory created for the demo the `delete()` method is used. In the case of a directory it must be empty before it can be deleted, so using the same method we first delete the two newly created files before calling `delete()` on the object `dir`.

We have now covered the major part of the `File` class, covering how to manipulate files, but we have a few more methods to be seen that will help us to manipulate directories.

Listing Directory Contents

You'll recall that a `File` object can represent either a file or a directory pathname. If you have a `File` object representing a directory, you can call the `list()` method on that object to extract a list of the files and directories inside:

```
String[] list()
File[] listFiles()
```

As you can see, this method returns either an array of `String` objects or array of `File` objects. For example, you could use the following code snippet to extract a list of files and directories that are in the `"/Wrox/docs"` directory:

```
File dirtolist = new File("/adarsh/docs");
String[] files = dirtolist.list();
```

Filtering the List of Files

The `list()` and `listFiles()` methods are great, but you will often want to limit the list based on some criteria, and to do this you must use filters. A filter is an object of a class that implements either of the following two interfaces:

```
interface FilenameFilter {
    boolean accept(File currentDirectory, String fileName);
}
```

```
interface FileFilter {
    boolean accept(File pathname);
}
```

There are overloaded versions of `list()` and `listFiles()` that accept as a parameter a filter that determines whether an entry should be included in the list:

```
public String[] list(FilenameFilter filter)
public File[] listFiles(FilenameFilter filter)
public File[] listFiles(FileFilter filter)
```

These methods call the `accept()` method of the filter for each entry, to determine whether or not that entry should be included in the list. The following example demonstrates that we can list and filter the contents of a directory.

Try it out – Listing Directories

Save the following code as `Dir.java`:

```java
// Dir.java
import java.io.*;

public class Dir {

  public static void main(String [] args) {
    // create an instance of the File object with current
    //directory as the pathname
    File path = new File(".");
    String [] list;

    // use the command line argument if provided,
    // to filter the list of files in the current directory
    if (args.length == 0) {
      list = path.list();
    } else {
      list = path.list(new MyFilter(args[0]));
    }

    // display the list of files
    for (int i = 0; i < list.length; i++) {
      System.out.println(list[i]);
    }
  }
}

// Class implementing the FilenameFilter
class MyFilter implements FilenameFilter {

  String ext;

  MyFilter(String ext) {
    this.ext = ext;
  }

  // Returns true if the file name ends with the desired extension
  public boolean accept(File dir, String name) {
    return name.endsWith(ext);
  }
}
```

Compile the code by opening a command prompt window, changing to the directory where you saved `Dir.java`, and typing:

```
> javac Dir.java
```

Then run the program by entering:

> **java Dir java**

You should see a list of the files in the current directory whose names end in .java, for example:

```
Dir.java
FileDemo.java
```

Alternatively, run the command without the command-line parameter by typing:

> **java Dir**

You will get a list of all the files in the directory:

```
Dir.class
Dir.java
FileDemo.class
FileDemo.java
MyFilter.class
```

Of course the output will vary according to the contents of your directory, and the value of the command line argument you pass.

How It Works

The main() method of the Dir class has a String array parameter, args, which contains the command-line parameters used when running the Java program. (In the first case above the array will contain one element, "java".)

If no argument is provided, the program lists all of the files in the current directory and stores them in a String array, list:

```
if (args.length == 0) {
  list = path.list();
}
```

If, on the other hand, a command-line parameter was supplied we used the list() variant that takes a filter argument:

```
else {
  list = path.list(new MyFilter(args[0]));
}
```

The MyFilter class implements FilenameFilter by defining the accept() method; our implementation of this method returns true if the filename ends with the specified string and false otherwise. This is made possible by using the endsWith() method of the String class.

Finally, the list of files is displayed using a for loop to iterate through items.

Using the File Class in a JSP

To conclude our discussion on the `File` class, we'll see how we can apply what we know to a JSP. This page includes some declarations, expressions, and a little scripting code along with the HTML tags to list the available files in a directory, with links for the user to download them:

Try It Out – Using a JSP to List Files

Create a `%CATALINA_HOME%\webapps\begjsp-ch14\` folder, and save the following code in it as `filelist.jsp`:

```
<%@ page import="java.io.*, java.util.*, java.text.*" %>
<html>
<head>
  <title>A Page To List Files</title>
</head>
<body>

<%! String fpath; %>
<% fpath = application.getRealPath("/"); %>
<%!
    File [] fobj;
    String [] flist;

    public String [] getFileList() {
      String [] fl;
      File f = new File(fpath);
      fl = f.list();
      return fl;
    }

    public File [] getFileObjList() {
      File [] fl;
      File f = new File(fpath);
      fl = f.listFiles();
      return fl;
    }
%>
<% flist = getFileList(); %>
<% fobj = getFileObjList(); %>

<table border=3>
<caption><b>Download</b></caption>
<tr>
  <th>File Name</th>
  <th>Last Modified on</th>
  <th>Size</th>
</tr>

<%
```

```
      for (int i = 0; i < flist.length; i++) {
%>
    <tr>
      <td>
        <a href="<%= flist[i] %>"><%= flist[i] %></a>
      </td>
      <td>
        <%= DateFormat.getInstance().format
                  (new Date(fobj[i].lastModified())) %>
      </td>
      <td>
        <%= Long.toString(fobj[i].length()) %> Bytes
      </td>
    </tr>
<%
    }
%>

</table>
</body>
</html>
```

Start Tomcat, and direct your browser to http://localhost:8080/begjsp-ch14/filelist.jsp. You should see output similar to that below:

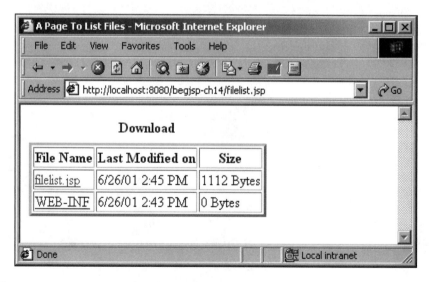

How It Works

We start by using the page directive to import the java.io, java.util, and java.text packages needed to compile the JSP.

We then use a declaration element to introduce the String variable fpath, which will hold the file path of the application, and use the application object's getRealPath() method to get the actual file path of the web application. The getRealPath() method takes a String argument; here we are asking it to return the real path of the web application's document root, "/":

```
<%! String fpath; %>
<% fpath = application.getRealPath("/"); %>
```

Next we declare two methods, getFileList() and getFileObjList(), which return arrays of String and File objects respectively listing the files in the directory. We assign these to the fobj and flist variables:

```
<%!
    File [] fobj;
    String [] flist;

    public String [] getFileList() {
      String [] fl;
      File f = new File(fpath);
      fl = f.list();
      return fl;
    }

    public File [] getFileObjList() {
      File [] fl;
      File f = new File(fpath);
      fl = f.listFiles();
      return fl;
    }
%>
<% flist = getFileList(); %>
<% fobj = getFileObjList(); %>
```

We use the File objects to retrieve the last modified date of each file and its size, using the lastModified() and length() methods. The date obtained from the lastModified() method is formatted using the format() method of the DateFormat class:

```
<%= DateFormat.getInstance().format
            (new Date(fobj[i].lastModified())) %>
```

The Stream Classes

As we saw at the start of this chapter, Java I/O is based on four abstract classes: InputStream, OutputStream, Reader, and Writer. These abstract classes provide the basic functionality, which are inherited and overridden by subclasses that provide specific functionality such as file access, buffered I/O, and so on.

In general you should use the concrete subclasses of the InputStream and OutputStream when working with bytes or binary objects, and the concrete subclasses of the Reader and Writer when working with characters and strings.

397

Byte I/O

The byte stream classes provide a number of methods for handling byte-oriented I/O, and can be used with any type of object; this versatility makes byte stream suitable to many types of programs.

The hierarchy below shows the sub classes under the `InputStream` class, which support input of byte streams:

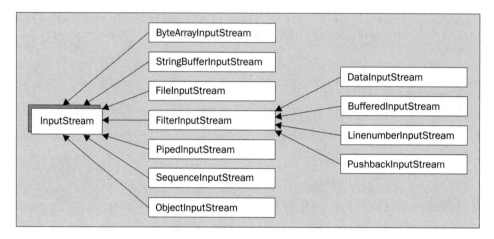

❑   `ByteArrayInputStream` class – Converts an array of bytes into an input stream

❑   `StringBufferInputStream` class – Converts a string into an input stream

❑   `FileInputStream` Class – Allows files to be used as input stream

❑   `PipedInputStream` class – Allows a "pipe" to be constructed allowing two different "threads" of execution in the program to communicate, and supports input from the pipe

❑   `SequenceInputStream` class – Allows two or more streams to be concatenated into a single stream

❑   `ObjectInputStream` Class – Used to read objects from a stream

❑   `FilterInputStream` class – Abstract class allowing its subclasses to filter an input stream

❑   `DataInputStream` Class – Subclass of `FilterInputStream` and allowing primitive data types to be read from a stream

❑   `BufferedInputStream` class – Subclass of `FilterInputStream` that maintains a buffer of the input data received, to improve performance

❑   `LineNumberInputStream` class – Subclass of `FilterInputStream` used to keep track of input line numbers

❑   `PushbackInputStream` class – Subclass of `FilterInputStream` that allows you to "push" characters back into the input stream after they have been read

The subclasses of `OutputStream` are shown below:

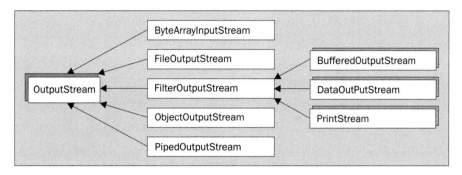

❏ `ByteArrayOutputStream` – Supports writing data to an array of bytes

❏ `FileOutputStream` class – Used for storing information to a file

❏ `PipedOutputStream` class – The data written here becomes input for an associated `PipedInputStream` object

❏ `ObjectOutputStream` class – Used to write objects to a stream

❏ `FilterOutputStream` class – Abstract class allowing its subclasses to filter an output stream

❏ `DataOutputStream` class – Subclass of `FilterOutputStream` used to write primitive data types to a stream

❏ `PrintStream` class – Subclass of `FilterOutputStream` used to produce formatted output

❏ `BufferedOutputStream` class – Subclass of `FilterOutputStream` used to buffer output data, which improves performance

Character I/O

Java programs represent characters internally in 16-bit **Unicode** character encoding. The byte stream classes provide sufficient functionality to handle any type of I/O operation, but they cannot work directly with Unicode characters. At the top of the character stream hierarchies are the `Reader` and `Writer` abstract classes, which do understand Unicode.

> *Unicode defines a fully international character set that can represent all of the characters in a wide range of human languages. It is a unification of character sets, such as Latin, Greek, Arabic, Cyrillic, Hebrew, and many more, and for this it requires 16 bits per character. More information on Unicode can be found at http://www.unicode.org/.*

Every platform has a default character encoding that can be used by `Readers` and `Writers` to convert between external encoding and internal Unicode characters. `Readers` and `Writers` can also explicitly specify which encoding schemes to use for reading and writing. Some common encoding schemes are:

Encoding Name	Character Set Name
8859-1	ISO-Latin-1
8859-2	ISO-Latin-2
8859-3	ISO-Latin-3
8859-4	ISO-Latin-/Cyrillic
UTF8	Standard UTF-8

Outside a Java program, Unicode characters are usually encoded using the UTF-8 encoding which has a multi-byte encoding format. It represents ASCII characters as one-byte characters, but uses several bytes for others. Readers and Writers can correctly and efficiently translate between UTF-8 and Unicode.

The classes of the Reader class hierarchy are shown below:

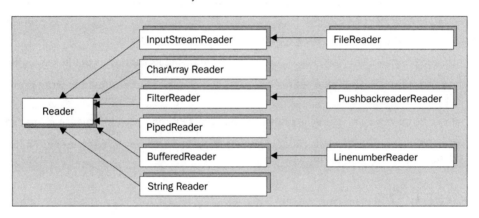

❑   CharArrayReader class – Converts a char array into a character input stream

❑   InputStreamReader class – Converts a byte input stream into a character input stream

❑   FileReader class – A subclass of InputStreamReader, used to read character files

❑   PipedReader class – Used to read characters from pipe

❑   FilterReader class – Abstract class allowing its subclasses to filter a character input stream

❑   PushbackReader class – Provides a filter that allows characters to be "pushed back" into the input stream after they have been read

❑   StringReader class – Used to read a character data from a String

❑   BufferedReader class – Supports buffered character input

❑   LineNumberReader class – Subclass of BufferedReader that supports buffered input and keeps track of line numbers

The classes of the `Writer` hierarchy are shown below:

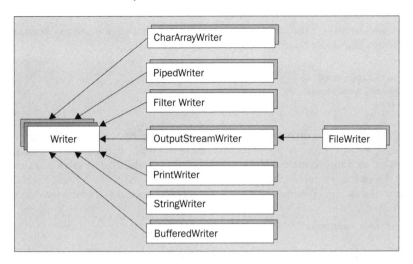

❑ `CharArrayWriter` class – Supports output to a `char` array

❑ `OutputStreamWriter` class – Allows a character output stream to be converted to a byte stream

❑ `FileWriter` class – Subclass of `OutputStreamWriter` that performs character output to a file

❑ `PipedWriter` class – Supports character output to a pipe

❑ `FilterWriter` class – Abstract class allowing its subclasses to filter a character output stream

❑ `StringWriter` class – Supports character output to a `String` object

❑ `PrintWriter` class – Supports platform-independent character printing

❑ `BufferedWriter` class – Supports buffered character output

Abstract Byte I/O Classes

The `InputStream` and `OutputStream` classes are abstract classes at the top of the Java input and output class hierarchy, and provide important methods that are inherited by all `InputStream` and `OutputStream` classes. All the methods in these classes will throw an `IOException` on error conditions, so a calling method must either catch the exception explicitly or specify it in a `throws` clause.

The InputStream Class

Let's look at the methods of `InputStream` first.

```
int read()
int read( byte barray[] )
int read( byte barray[], int offset, int numbytes)
```

The `read()` method has three overloaded forms. It can read a single byte, read an array of bytes into a buffer, or read part of an array of bytes starting at an offset. It returns the number of bytes read, or -1 if an end of stream was encountered.

```
int available()
```

This method is used to inspect the amount of data available on a stream; it returns the number of bytes that are currently available for reading.

```
boolean markSupported ()
void mark(int numBytes)
void reset()
```

The mark() method is used to remember where we are in the input stream; if we later use the reset() method we will return to the marked point in the input stream. The markSupported() method returns true if this particular stream provides the capability to mark a position in the stream and later reset the stream to the marked position. The marked position becomes invalid after a certain number of bytes of data, specified by the parameter mark() method's parameter, has been read.

```
long skip(long numBytes)
```

This method is used to skip over or ignore a specified number of bytes, and returns the actual number of bytes ignored or skipped.

```
void close()
```

This method closes the input stream and releases the system resources (such as any internal buffer) associated with it. If any read operation is attempted it will generate an IOException.

The OutputStream Class

Let's move on to look at the methods of the OutputStream class.

```
void write(int b)
void write(byte barray[])
void write(byte barray [],int offset, int numBytes)
```

As you can see, the write() method has three overloaded forms. It can write a single byte, an array of bytes, or a part of an array, when the number of bytes and the offset is specified.

```
void flush()
```

The flush() method causes any buffered data to be written to the output stream. That is, it flushes the output buffers.

```
void close()
```

This method is similar to the one we saw in the section on InputStream. It closes the output stream and releases the system resources associated with it. It is more important to close the OutputStream than the InputStream, because closing an output stream automatically flushes the stream, meaning that any data in its internal buffer is written out. So, if either the flush() method or the close() method is not called on an output buffer, the data remaining in the internal buffer is lost.

Abstract Character I/O Classes

The abstract classes `Reader` and `Writer` are the roots of the inheritance hierarchies for character input and output streams; the classes that extend `Reader` and `Writer` provide support for particular forms of character I/O. All the methods in these classes will throw an `IOException` on error conditions, and the calling method must either catch the exception explicitly or specify it in a `throws` clause.

The Reader Class

A `Reader` is an character input stream that reads a sequence of Unicode characters. All of the methods in this class will throw an `IOException` on error conditions.

```
int read()
int read(char buffer[])
int read(char buffer[], int offset, int numChars)
```

The `read()` method has three overloaded forms. In the first form it returns the integer representation of the next available character from the invoking input stream; in the second form it attempts to read into the buffer all the available characters and returns the actual number of characters that were successfully read; and in the third form it attempts to read a specified number of characters into the buffer, starting at a specified offset, and again returns the number of characters successfully read. It returns -1 when the end of file is encountered.

```
long skip(long numChars)
```

The `skip()` method skips or ignores the specified number of characters of input and returns the actual number of characters skipped.

```
void mark(int numChars)
```

The `mark()` method places an identifier at the current point in the input stream. This mark is valid until the specified numbers of characters given as the argument are read.

```
void reset()
```

The `reset()` method returns the stream to the point previously identified by the `mark()` method.

```
boolean markSupported()
```

The `marksupported()` method returns either `true` or `false` depending on whether the stream supports the `mark()` and `reset()` methods.

```
boolean ready()
```

The `ready()` method returns `true` if the next input request is ready, otherwise it returns `false`.

```
void close()
```

The `close()` method closes the input source. Any further attempt to read from the stream will generate an `IOException`.

The Writer Class

A `Writer` is an output character stream that writes a sequence of Unicode characters. All of the methods in this class return `void` and throw an `IOException` in the case of errors.

```
void write(int ch)
void write(char buffer[])
void write(char buffer[], int offsets, int numChars)
void write(String str)
void write(String str, int offsets , int numChars)
```

The `write()` method has five forms. The first form writes a single character to the output stream. The second form writes a complete array of characters to the output stream. The third form writes a part of the array, where the number of characters and the offset is specified. The fourth form writes a `String` to the output stream. The fifth form writes a part of the `String`, when the number of characters and offset is specified.

```
void flush()
```

The `flush()` method finalizes the output state so that the buffers are flushed (in other words, all the data is written to the file).

```
void close()
```

This method is similar to the one in the `Reader`, and closes the output stream. It is more important to close the `Writer` than the `Reader`, because the data written to the stream needs to be stored before the object is released.

Converting Between Character and Byte Streams

Having two types of I/O stream classes, for character and byte I/O, is all very well but we do sometimes need to bridge the gap between them. Fortunately there are two classes provided for this purpose, `InputStreamReader` and `OutputStreamWriter`.

The `InputStreamReader` class wraps an `InputStream` – a byte input stream – inside a character-oriented stream. `InputStreamReader` has two constructors:

```
InputStreamReader(InputStream in)
InputStreamReader(InputStream in, String encode)
```

The constructors each take an `InputStream` object as a parameter; the second constructor also takes a `String` parameter that identifies the character encoding to use in interpreting the input data. The `getEncoding()` method may be used to retrieve the encoding that is in effect.

The `OutputStreamWriter` class wraps an `OutputStream` – a character output stream – in a byte output stream. It too has has two constructors:

```
OutputStream Writer(OutputStream out)
OutputStream Writer(OutputStream out, String encode)
```

The constructors take an `OutputStream` object as a parameter. The translation is performed according to the default encoding unless the second constructor is used to specify a different encoding scheme.

File I/O

Let's do some real input and output, starting with file I/O. Input and output to a file is accomplished in Java through the classes:

❑   `File`

❑   `RandomAccessFile`

❑   `FileReader`

❑   `FileWriter`

❑   `FileInputStream`

❑   `FileOutputstream`

Of these, we have already covered the most commonly encountered, `File`. `RandomAccessFile` will have to wait until later in the chapter, but let's get stuck into using the various file input and output streams.

The FileInputStream Class

The `FileInputStream` class allows input to be read from a file as a sequence of bytes. An object of the `FileInputStream` can be created using the following constructors:

```
FileInputStream(String name) throws FileNotFoundException
FileInputStream(File file) throws FileNotFoundException
FileInputStream(FileDescriptor fdObj)
```

The first constructor is the most commonly used one, but the file can also be specified using a `File` or a `FileDescriptor` object. If the file does not exist, a `FileNotFoundException` is thrown.

`FileInputStream` overrides the methods of the `InputStream` class and provides two new methods, `finalize()` and `getFD()`. The `finalize()` method is used to close a stream when processed by the garbage collector; `getFD()` is used to obtain access to the `FileDescriptor` associated with the input stream.

The FileOutputStream Class

The `FileOutputStream` class allows output to be written to a file. A `FileOutputStream` object can be created using the following constructors:

```
FileOutputStream(String name) throws FileNotFoundException
FileOutputStream(String name, boolean append) throws FileNotFoundException
FileOutputStream(File file) throws IOException
FileOutputStream(FileDescriptor fdObj)
```

The file can be specified by its name, through a `File` object, or using a `FileDescriptor` object. If the file does not exist, it is created. Remember that if the file already exists at the time of creating an instance of the `FileOutputStream`, the original contents are deleted unless the second constructor is used with a boolean `true` value to indicate that the output should be appended.

`FileOutputStream` overrides the methods of the `OutputStream` class and in addition supports the `finalize()` and `getFD()` methods described for the `FileInputStream` class.

Let's see how we can use `FileInputStream` and `FileOutputStream` to write data to a file, and then read it back in again.

Try It Out – Basic File IO

Save the following code as `FileIO.java`:

```
/*FileIO.java*/
import java.io.*;

public class FileIO {
  public static void main(String [] args) throws IOException {

    // Declare a string
    String str = "When I was tapping away on my computer,"+
                 " my ten-year-old son sneaked up behind me.\n"+
                 "He turned and ran into the kitchen, squeaking"+
                 " to the rest of the family,\n\"I know Daddy's password!"+
                 " I know Daddy's password!\"\n"+
                 "\"What is it ?\" the others asked eagerly.\n"+
                 "Proudly he replied, \"asterisk, asterisk, asterisk,"+
                 " asterisk, asterisk!\"";

    // Convert the string into a byte array
    byte [] barray = str.getBytes();

    // Create an instance of FileOutputStream
    FileOutputStream fo = new FileOutputStream("humor.txt");

    // Write to the output stream and close it
    for(int i=0; i < barray.length; i++) {
      fo.write(barray[i]);
    }
    fo.close();

    // Create an instance of FileInputStream
    FileInputStream fi = new FileInputStream("humor.txt");

    // Read from the input stream, display it and close it
    int size = fi.available();
    for (int i = 0; i <= size; i++) {
      System.out.print((char)fi.read());
    }
    fi.close();
  }
}
```

Compile the code by opening a command prompt window, changing to the directory where you saved `FileIO.java`, and typing:

```
> javac FileIO.java
```

Then run the program by entering:

```
> java FileIO
```

You should see the following output:

```
When I was tapping away on my computer, my ten-year-old son sneaked up
behind me.
He turned and ran into the kitchen, squeaking to the rest of the family,
"I know Daddy's password! I know Daddy's password!"
"What is it ?" the others asked eagerly.
Proudly he replied, "asterisk, asterisk, asterisk, asterisk, asterisk!"?
```

How It Works

We started by declaring a `String` containing the data to be written to the file, and converted it to a `byte` array using the `getBytes()` method of the `String` class:

```
byte [] barray = str.getBytes();
```

Next, we created a `FileOutputStream` object using the filename `humor.txt`, and wrote the data to the file one byte at a time using the `write()` method. After doing so, we closed the file by calling the stream's close() method:

```
for(int i=0; i < barray.length; i++) {
  fo.write(barray[i]);
}
fo.close();
```

Finally, we created a `FileInputStream` to read the same file back in again, and read one byte at a time using the `read()` method:

```
FileInputStream fi = new FileInputStream("humor.txt");

// Read from the input stream, display it and close it
int size = fi.available();
for (int i = 0; i <= size; i++) {
  System.out.print((char)fi.read());
}
fi.close();
```

The FileReader Class

The `FileReader` class is a subclass of `InputStreamReader`, and is used to read the contents of a file. The two commonly used constructors are:

```
FileReader(String Filepath)
FileReader(File fObj)
```

`FileReader` does not override any of the methods of `InputStreamReader`.

The FileWriter Class

The `FileWriter` class is a subclass of `OutputStreamWriter` and is used to write to a file. The commonly used constructors are:

```
FileWriter(String filepath)
FileWriter(String filepath , boolean append)
FileWriter(file fObj)
```

If the file specified in the constructor does not exists, it is created; if the file already exists its contents are deleted, unless the second constructor is used with the second parameter set to `true` to indicate that the new output should be appended to the existing file.

Just as `FileReader` doesn't override any of `InputStreamReader`'s methods, neither does `FileWriter` override any of those from `OutputStreamWriter`.

Let's see an example of how we can use `FileWriter` and `FileReader` to do character-based I/O.

Try It Out – Reading and Writing Text Files

Save the following code as `TextIO.java`:

```java
/* TextIO.java */
import java.io.*;

public class TextIO{
  public static void main(String [] args) throws IOException {
    // Declare a String
    String str = "This is a test line\n";

    // Create a FileWriter to send the text to file
    FileWriter fw = new FileWriter("textio.txt");

    // Write one character at a time to the file
    for(int i = 0; i < str.length(); i++) {
      fw.write(str.charAt(i));
    }

    // Close the file
    fw.close();

    // Do the same again, appending to the same file
    str = "Another line of text";
    fw = new FileWriter("textio.txt", true);
    for(int i = 0; i < str.length(); i++) {
```

```
      fw.write(str.charAt(i));
    }
    fw.close();


    // Create a FileReader to read the text back in again
    FileReader fr = new FileReader("textio.txt");

    // Read one character at a time, and append to a StringBuffer
    StringBuffer sb = new StringBuffer("");
    int ch = 0;
    while((ch = fr.read()) != -1) {
      sb.append((char) ch);
    }

    // Display the text we just read in
    System.out.println(sb);
  }
}
```

Compile the code by opening a command prompt window, changing to the directory where you saved `TextIO.java`, and typing:

> **javac TextIO.java**

Then run the program by entering:

> **java TextIO**

You should see the following output:

```
This is a test line
Another line of text
```

How It Works

This example demonstrates the use of the `FileReader` and `FileWriter` classes. This is a rework of the example program `FileIO.java` but using the `FileReader` and `FileWriter` classes instead of `FileInputStream` and `FileOutputStream`. The characters are read into `StringBuffer` instead of a byte array.

Additionally, we demonstrated how to append to an existing file: after writing the initial line of text to the file we closed it, then reopened it using the `FileWriter` constructor that accepts a second, boolean parameter:

```
fw = new FileWriter("textio.txt", true);
```

This causes the second batch of output to be appended to the file rather than replacing its existing content.

I/O On Arrays and Strings

Whilst it may not be the first thing you'd have thought of, Java provides classes that let you perform I/O operations on arrays of `bytes` and `chars`, which can be useful if you have data in an array that you need to process. Let's start with the classes that deal with `byte` arrays.

Byte Array I/O

The classes that support input and output operations on byte arrays are `ByteArrayInputStream` and `ByteArrayOutputStream`, both of which use memory buffers to store the input or output data.

The ByteArrayInputStream Class

This class creates an input stream from an array of bytes, which must be passed to whichever of its two constructors is used:

```
ByteArrayInputStream(byte barray[])
ByteArrayInputStream(byte barray[], int offset, int numBytes)
```

Both of the constructors create a `ByteArrayInputStream` from an array of bytes; the second constructor allows us to use only a subset of the array. The class does not define any new methods, but overrides the abstract ones defined in the `InputStream` class.

The ByteArrayOutputStream Class

This class is an `OutputStream` that uses a byte array as the destination. It is complementary to the `ByteArrayInputStream`, and in addition provides capabilities to allow the output array to grow when new data is written to it. It has two constructors:

```
ByteArrayOutputStream()
ByteArrayOutputStream(int numBytes)
```

The first constructor creates a buffer of 32 bytes, and in the second a buffer is created with a size equal to that specified in the argument.

The class also defines some new methods in addition to those in `OutputStream`, including:

```
public void writeTo(OutputStream out)
```

The `writeTo()` method writes the `ByteArrayOutputStream`'s contents to the specified `OutputStream`.

```
public int size()
```

The `size()` method returns the number of bytes written to the buffer.

```
public void reset()
```

The `reset()` method clears the buffer.

```
public byte[] toByteArray()
```

`toByteArray()` returns the `ByteArrayOutputStream`'s contents as an array of `bytes`.

The following example demonstrates the use of the `ByteArrayOutputStream` and `ByteArrayInputStream` classes to write data into and read it from byte arrays. As the characters are read from the byte array they are converted to uppercase.

Try It Out – Implementing Byte Array Streams

Save the following code as `ByteArrayIO.java`:

```
/*ByteArrayIO.java */
import java.io.*;
public class ByteArrayIO {
  public static void main(String[] args)throws IOException {
    // Declare a string
    String str ="Demonstrating Byte Array IO";
    // Create an instance of ByteArrayOutputStream
    ByteArrayOutputStream bout=new ByteArrayOutputStream();

    // Write to the stream
    for(int i=0; i < str.length(); i++) {
      bout.write(str.charAt(i));
    }

    // Display the size of the output stream
    System.out.println("Size of the Output Stream : " + bout.size());

    // Convert string to a byte array
    byte barray [] = str.getBytes();

    // Create an instance of ByteArrayInputStream
    ByteArrayInputStream bin = new ByteArrayInputStream(barray);

    //Read and convert it to upper case
    int c;
    while((c = bin.read()) != -1) {
      System.out.print(Character.toUpperCase((char)c));
    }
  }
}
```

Compile the code by opening a command prompt window, changing to the directory where you saved `ByteArrayIO.java`, and typing:

```
> javac ByteArrayIO.java
```

Then run the program by entering:

```
> java ByteArrayIO
```

You should see the following output:

```
Size of the Output Stream : 27
DEMONSTRATING BYTE ARRAY IO
```

How It Works

We start by declaring a `String` variable, `str`, containing the text we will be writing and reading. Next, we create an instance of `ByteArrayOutputStream`, and use a `for` loop to write the characters from the `String` to the stream. We use the `charAt()` method of the `String` class to obtain the character at a specified index:

```
ByteArrayOutputStream bout=new ByteArrayOutputStream();
for(int i=0; i < str.length(); i++) {
  bout.write(str.charAt(i));
}
```

With the data safely inside the `ByteArrayOutputStream` we use its `size()` method to display the length of the byte array.

Next, we try reading from a byte array. We obtain such an array using the `String` class's `getBytes()` method. We then create an instance of `ByteArrayInputStream` using the byte array as its source. We read one character at a time and converted them into uppercase using the `toUpperCase()` method of the `Character` class:

```
byte barray [] = str.getBytes();
ByteArrayInputStream bin = new ByteArrayInputStream(barray);
int c;
while((c = bin.read()) != -1) {
  System.out.print(Character.toUpperCase((char)c));
}
```

Character Array I/O

The `CharArrayReader` class is similar to the `ByteArrayInputStream`, and `CharArrayWriter` is similar to `ByteArrayOutputStream`. The difference lies in the support of 8-bit and 16-bit character I/O.

The CharArrayReader Class

`CharArrayReader` is an implementation of an input stream that uses a character array as the source. This class has two constructors:

```
CharArrayReader(char array[])
CharArrayReader(char array [], int start, int numChars)
```

Both constructors require a character array as the input source; the second constructor creates a `Reader` from a subset of your character array that begins at the given location and is the specified number of characters long. The `CharArrayReader` class does not add any new methods beyond the ones provided by `Reader`.

The CharArrayWriter Class

`CharArrayWriter` is an implementation of an output stream that uses an array as the destination. This class has two constructors:

```
CharArrayWriter()
CharArrayWriter(int numChars)
```

The first constructor creates a buffer with a default size, whereas the second constructor allows you to specify the initial buffer size. The buffer size is increased automatically if needed.

Like `ByteArrayOutputStream`, `CharArrayWriter` provides some extra methods:

```
public int size()
public void reset()
```

These behave just like their `ByteArrayOutputStream` counterparts.

```
public char[] toCharArray()
```

`toCharArray()` returns the writer's contents as an array of `chars`.

The following example demonstrates reading and writing to an array using `CharArrayReader` and `CharArrayWriter`.

Try It Out – Implementing Character Array IO

Save the following code as `CharArrayIO.java`:

```java
/* CharArrayIO.java */
import java.io.*;

public class CharArrayIO {
  public static void main(String [] args) throws IOException {
    String str = "Demonstrating Character Array IO";
    int length = str.length();
    char [] c = new char[length];
    str.getChars(0, length, c, 0);

    System.out.println("Reading from an array using CharArrayReader");
    CharArrayReader car = new CharArrayReader(c);

    int i;
    while ((i = car.read()) != -1) {
      System.out.print((char)i);
    }

    System.out.println();
    System.out.println("Writing to an array using CharArrayWriter");

    CharArrayWriter caw = new CharArrayWriter();
    caw.write(c);
```

```
        char [] j = caw.toCharArray();
        for (int x = 0; x < j.length; x++) {
          System.out.print(j[x]);
        }
      }
    }
}
```

Compile the code by opening a command prompt window, changing to the directory where you saved `CharArrayIO.java`, and typing:

> **javac CharArrayIO.java**

Then run the program by entering:

> **java CharArrayIO**

You should see the following output:

```
Reading from an array using CharArrayReader
Demonstrating Character Array IO
Writing to an array using CharArrayWriter
Demonstrating Character Array IO
```

How It Works

The program starts by creating a `String` object, finding its length using the `length()` method, and declaring an array of characters of the requisite size:

```
int length = str.length();
char [] c = new char[length];
```

The characters are extracted into an character array from the `String` object using the `getChars()` method. This method takes the index of the beginning and end of the string that is to be extracted, the target character array, and the index within the target at which the string will be copied:

```
str.getChars(0, length, c, 0);
```

The array thus created is then used to create an instance of `CharArrayReader`. This character stream is read character by character:

```
CharArrayReader car = new CharArrayReader(c);
int i;
while ((i = car.read()) != -1) {
  System.out.print((char)i);
}
```

Lastly we create a `CharArrayWriter`, send it some data, extract the data using the `toCharArray()` method, and print the characters out one by one:

```
char [] j = caw.toCharArray();
for (int x = 0; x < j.length; x++) {
  System.out.print(j[x]);
}
```

String I/O

The `StringReader` class provides the capability to read character input from a `String`, and the `StringWriter` class is used to write character output to a `StringBuffer` object. Otherwise both the classes are functionally similar to the `CharArrayReader` and `CharArrayWriter`.

The `StringReader` class does not add any additional methods to those defined in `Reader`; the `StringWriter` class adds to `Writer` the `getBuffer()` method, which returns a `StringBuffer` containing the data that has been written to it, and overrides the `toString()` method to return a `String` version of the output buffer.

Sequential I/O

If you would like to combine two or more input streams into a single input stream, so that the individual streams are treated as a single logical stream, then `SequenceInputStream` is the answer. It provides methods for dealing with a sequence of related objects.

The SequenceInputStream Class

The `SequenceInputStream` allows you to concatenate multiple input streams into a single input stream. A `SequenceInputStream` constructor uses either a pair of `InputStream` objects, or an `Enumeration` containing `InputStreams`:

```
SequenceInputStream(InputStream first, InputStream second)
SequenceInputStream(Enumeration strms)
```

This class does not provide any new access methods, but when you read from a `SequenceInputStream` it fulfils the read requests from the first `InputStream` until it reaches the end of the stream, and then switches over to the second one. In case of the second constructor, this process continues till the end of the last `InputStream` in the `Enumeration`.

A typical case where you would use `SequenceInputStream` would be to combine two or more files, and the following example shows how to do this for two files specified as command line parameters.

Try It Out – Implementing SequenceInputStream

Save the following code as `SequenceIO.java`:

```
/*SequenceIO.java*/
import java.io.*;

public class SequenceIO{
  public static void main (String [] args) throws IOException {
```

```
      if (args.length < 2) {
        System.out.println("Specify two filenames to concatenate");
        return;
      }

      // Create instances of FileInputStream and SequenceInputStream
      FileInputStream f1 = new  FileInputStream(args[0]);
      FileInputStream f2 = new  FileInputStream(args[1]);
      SequenceInputStream s = new SequenceInputStream(f1,f2);

      // Read and display from SequenceInputStream
      int c;
      while ((c = s.read()) != -1) {
        System.out.print((char) c);
      }

      // Close all streams
      s.close();
      f1.close();
      f2.close();
    }
  }
```

Compile the code by opening a command prompt window, changing to the directory where you saved `SequenceIO.java`, and typing:

> **javac SequenceIO.java**

Then run the program by entering something like:

> **java SequenceIO hello.txt goodbye.txt**

You should see the contents of the two files you specified, one after another, for example:

```
"Hello" quipped Brian, as he walked into the crowded room.
Cedric, espying Brian entering the room, muttered "Goodbye" and slipped
out quietly.
```

How It Works

Two instances of `FileInputStream` are created, pointing to the two files:

```
FileInputStream f1 = new  FileInputStream(args[0]);
FileInputStream f2 = new  FileInputStream(args[1]);
```

Then we create an instance of `SequenceInputStream` connecting both of the `FileInputStream` objects:

```
SequenceInputStream s = new SequenceInputStream(f1,f2);
```

The resulting `SequenceInputStream` is then read and displayed.

Data I/O

When you begin using streams you'll quickly discover that byte streams and character streams are not always best suited for your needs. Often you'll want to read or write the primitive types of the Java language, and also Java objects, rather than dealing with bytes and characters.

The `DataInputStream`, `DataOutputStream`, `ObjectInputStream`, and `ObjectOutputStream` classes will help you to do this.

DataInput and DataOutput

The `DataInputStream` and `DataOutputStream` classes implement the `DataInput` and `DataOutput` interfaces respectively, and can be used to read and write binary representations of Java primitive values to and from an underlying stream. Methods for reading binary representations of Java primitive values are named `readX()`, and the methods for writing the Java primitive values are similarly named `writeX()`, where `X` is any Java primitive data type:

Data Type	DataInput Method	DataOutput Method
boolean	boolean readBoolean()	void writeBoolean(boolean v)
char	char readChar()	void writeChar(int v)
byte	byte readByte()	void writeByte(int v)
short	short readShort	void writeShort(int v)
int	int readInt()	void writeInt(int v)
long	long readLong()	void writeLong(long v)
float	float readFloat()	void writeFloat(float v)
double	double readDouble()	void writeDouble(double v)
String	String readLine()	void writeChars(String s)
String	String readUTF()	void writeUTF(String s)

Note the methods provided for reading and writing characters and strings. The methods `readChar()` and `writeChar()` handle a single character. The methods `readLine()` and `writeChars()` handle a string of characters, but use the UTF-8 character encoding. This `readLine()` method is deprecated, and the preferred method is the `readLine()` method of the `BufferedReader` class.

The `DataOutput` interface also defines the `write()` method in three overloaded forms:

```
void write(byte buffer [])
void write(byte buffer [] , int offset , int numBytes)
void write(int b)
```

Similarly, `DataInput` defines three overloaded forms of the `read()` method:

```
int read()
int read(byte buffer [])
int read(byte buffer [], int offfset, int numBytes)
```

The read() method with no arguments returns the next available byte represented as an integer, or returns -1 when the end of file is encountered. The other forms read into an array of bytes that is passed as an argument.

DataInputStream and DataOutputStream

The following constructors can be used to create DataInputStream and DataOutputStream objects that wrap an underlying stream:

```
DataInputStream(InputStream in)
DataOutputStream(OutputStream out)
```

The following example demonstrates some of the readX() and writeX() methods of the DataInputStream and DataOutputStream classes.

Try It Out – Implementing Data IO

Save the following code as DataIO.java:

```java
/* DataIO.java */
import java.io.*;
public class DataIO {
   public static void main (String [] args ) throws IOException {

      // Create a File OutputStream
      FileOutputStream fos = new FileOutputStream("test.dat");

      // Create a DataOutputStream and chain it to the FileOutputStream
      DataOutputStream dos = new DataOutputStream(fos);

      // Write values to the file
      dos.writeUTF("Sumatra, an Indonesian island, is called Java Minor: ");
      dos.writeBoolean(true);
      dos.writeUTF("The Square Root of 10 is: ");
      dos.writeDouble(Math.sqrt(10));

      // Close the output streams
      dos.close();
      fos.close();

      // Create a FileInput Stream
      FileInputStream fis = new FileInputStream("test.dat");

      // Create DataInputStream which is chained to the FileInputStream
      DataInputStream dis = new DataInputStream(fis);

      // Read values in the same order they were written
      System.out.println(dis.readUTF());
      System.out.println(dis.readBoolean());
      System.out.println(dis.readUTF());
      System.out.println(dis.readDouble());
```

```
        // Close the input streams
        dis.close();
        fis.close();
    }
}
```

Compile the code by opening a command prompt window, changing to the directory where you saved
DataIO.java, and typing:

> **javac DataIO.java**

Then run the program by entering:

> **java DataIO**

You should see the following output:

```
Sumatra, an Indonesian island, is called Java Minor:
true
The Square Root of 10 is:
3.1622776601683795
```

If you examine the test.dat file that was created, on the other hand, you'll find that its contents are
indeed in a binary rather than a textual form:

```
^@5Sumatra, an Indonesian island, is called Java Minor: ^A^@^ZThe Square
Root of 10 is: @       LX:Ú[S
```

How It Works

This example writes the binary representation of the Java primitive values to a file. We create a
FileOutputStream pointing to test.dat, which we then "wrap" in a DataOutputStream:

```
FileOutputStream fos = new FileOutputStream("test.dat");
DataOutputStream dos = new DataOutputStream(fos);
```

We can then use the DataInput methods to output primitive data values using the relevant write*X*()
methods:

```
dos.writeUTF("Sumatra, an Indonesian island, is called Java Minor: ");
dos.writeBoolean(true);
dos.writeUTF("The Square Root of 10 is: ");
dos.writeDouble(Math.sqrt(10));
```

Once we've finished writing to the file we close *both* the DataOutputStream *and* the
FileOutputStream that it wraps:

```
dos.close();
fos.close();
```

Similarly, to read the data back in we create a `FileInputStream`, which is wrapped in a `DataInputStream`. We read from the `DataInputStream` using the relevant `readX()` methods:

```
FileInputStream fis = new FileInputStream("test.dat");
DataInputStream dis = new DataInputStream(fis);
System.out.println(dis.readUTF());
System.out.println(dis.readBoolean());
System.out.println(dis.readUTF());
System.out.println(dis.readDouble());
dis.close();
fis.close();
```

Object I/O

Reading and writing primitive data types using `DataInputStream` and `DataOutputStream` is great, but it would be great to be able to read and write Java objects also. Well, the `ObjectOutputStream` and `ObjectInputStream` classes do just that, allowing objects to be written to and read from streams. These classes respectively implement the `ObjectOutput` and `ObjectInput` interfaces, which define methods that write and read objects that implement the `java.io.Serializable` interface.

Serialization

Serialization is the process of writing the state of an object to a byte stream. This allows you to store objects in files, communicate them across networks, and use them in distributed applications. The capability for an object to exist beyond the execution of the program, in an area such as a file, is known as **persistence**. Serialization is the key to implementing persistence, providing the capability to write an object to a stream and to read the object back. Not all classes will want to allow their instances to be persisted in this way, and so the `Serializable` interface is used to identify objects that *can* be written to a stream.

The Serializable Interface

Only an object that implements the `Serializable` interface can be saved and restored to a byte stream. The `Serializable` interface is easy to use, and it contains no methods; it is simply used to indicate that a class may be serialized. Before you do this you need to make sure that all the instance variables of your class are either of primitive types or of classes that are themselves `Serializable`; `Object` isn't, but many of the predefined classes such as `String` are. (You can find out which classes are `Serializable` using the online Java documentation, as described in Appendix D.) Making a class `Serializable` automatically makes all its subclasses `Serializable` too.

Once you have a `Serializable` class you can use an `ObjectOutputStream` to write objects to a stream – the `writeObject()` method automatically takes care of storing the correct information. Similarly, objects are read back using the `readObject()` method of the `ObjectInputSteam` class.

> **Variables that are declared as `transient` or `static` are not saved by the serialization facilities.**

The ObjectInput and ObjectOutput Interfaces

The `ObjectOutput` interface extends `DataOutput`, and in addition supports object serialization. The `writeObject()` method takes as its argument the object that is to be written to the stream:

```
void writeObject(Object obj)
```

The `flush()` method finalizes the output state so that the buffer is cleared:

```
void flush()
```

The `close()` method closes the invoking stream:

```
void close()
```

The `ObjectInput` interface extends `DataInput` and in addition supports object serialization. The `readObject()` method reads an object from the stream and returns it:

```
Object readObject()
```

The `available()` method returns the number of bytes that are now available in the input buffer:

```
int available()
```

The `skip()` method attempts to ignore the specified number of bytes in the invoking stream, and returns the number of bytes actually ignored:

```
long skip(long numBytes)
```

The `close()` method closes the invoking stream:

```
void close()
```

The ObjectOutputStream Class

The `ObjectOutputStream` class extends the `OutputStream` class and implements the `ObjectOutput` interface. It can write objects to any stream that is a subclass of the `OutputStream`, for example to a file.

An `ObjectOutputStream` wraps another `OutputStream`, and is created using the following constructor:

```
ObjectOutputStream(OutputStream OS) throws IOException
```

In order to create a persistent store for objects you need to store objects in a file. In this case, the `ObjectOutputStream` can wrap a `FileOutputStream`:

```
FileOutputStream fo = new FileOutputStream("obj.dat");
ObjectOutputStream os = new ObjectOutputStream(fo);
```

Any object that implements the `java.io.Serializable` interface can be written to the stream, using the `writeObject()` method:

final void writeObject(Object Obj) throws IOException

The ObjectInputStream Class

The `ObjectInputStream` class extends the `InputStream` class and implements the `ObjectInput` interface. It is used to de-serialize objects that have previously been serialized using an `ObjectOutputStream`.

An `ObjectInputStream` wraps another `InputStream`, and is created using the following constructor:

ObjectInputStream(InputStream in)
   throws IOException, StreamCorruptedException

For example, in order to restore objects from a file, an `ObjectInputStream` can wrap a `FileInputStream`:

```
FileInputStream if = new FileInputStream ("obj.dat");
ObjectInputstream is = new ObjectInputStream (if);
```

The method `readObject()` of the `ObjectInputStream` class is used to read an object from the stream:

final Object readObject()
   throws OptionalDataException, ClassNotFoundException, IOException

Note that the reference returned is of type `Object` regardless of the actual class of the retrieved object, but can be cast to the desired type.

The following example defines a class that has a `String` as its only instance variable. The class overrides the `toString()` method to display the value of this `String` variable. An instance of this class is created, and written to a file using the `ObjectOutputStream`. The same object is again read back, and displayed.

Try It Out – Implementing Object IO

Save the following code as `TestSerialize.java`:

```
/*TestSerialize.java*/
import java.io.*;

public class TestSerialize {
  public static void main (String [] args) throws Exception {

    // Create an instance of TestClass
```

```java
        TestClass tc1 = new TestClass();

        // Create an instance of FileOutputStream and ObjectOutputStream
        FileOutputStream fos = new FileOutputStream("obj.dat");
        ObjectOutputStream oos = new ObjectOutputStream(fos);
        System.out.println("TestClass: "+tc1);

        // Write the object to the file and close the stream
        oos.writeObject(tc1);
        oos.flush();
        oos.close();

        // Declare another TestClass variable, but *don't* instantiate an
        // actual object instance
        TestClass tc2;

        // Create an instance of FileInputStream and ObjectInputStream
        FileInputStream fis = new FileInputStream("obj.dat");
        ObjectInputStream ois = new ObjectInputStream (fis);

        // Recreate the object from file
        tc2 = (TestClass)ois.readObject();
        ois.close();
        System.out.println("Deserialized the object");
        System.out.println(tc2);
    }
}


// A test class that can be serialized
class TestClass implements Serializable {

  String str;

  public TestClass() {
    this.str ="This is the Test class";
  }

  public String toString() {
    return str;
  }
}
```

Compile the code by opening a command prompt window, changing to the directory where you saved
`TestSerialize.java`, and typing:

> **javac TestSerialize.java**

Then run the program by entering:

> **java TestSerialize**

You should see the following output:

```
TestClass: This is the Test class
Deserialized the object
This is the Test class
```

If you look at the `obj.dat` file that was written, you'll see that, like the file produced by `DataOutputStream`, it is a binary file not intended for human reading or editing.

How It Works

In this example we created a simple class, `TestClass`, which contains a `String` variable and a `toString()` method. This class implements the `Serializable` interface.

An instance of the `TestClass` is created, so that we can serialize it. A `FileOutputStream` is created and wrapped in an `ObjectOutputStream`:

```
TestClass tc1 = new TestClass();
FileOutputStream fos = new FileOutputStream("obj.dat");
ObjectOutputStream oos = new ObjectOutputStream(fos);
```

The `ObjectOutputStream` is then used to write the object to the file, using the `writeObject()` method; the output stream is then flushed and closed:

```
oos.writeObject(tc1);
oos.flush();
oos.close();
```

To read back the object from the file, a `FileInputStream` is created and wrapped in an `ObjectInputStream`:

```
FileInputStream fis = new FileInputStream("obj.dat");
ObjectInputStream ois = new ObjectInputStream (fis);
```

The object is read back from the file using the `ObjectInputStream`'s `readObject()` method; note that since `readObject()` returns a reference to an `Object` we have to cast the returned value to `TestClass`:

```
tc2 = (TestClass)ois.readObject();
ois.close();
```

Finally, we display the object we read from the file.

Custom Serialization: The Externalizable Interface

The `Serializable` interface and the `writeObject()` and `readObject()` methods of the `ObjectOutputStream` and `ObjectInputStream` provide the most convenient way to save objects to a stream and restore them.

However, there are cases in which the programmer may need to have control over these processes. The `Externalizable` interface extends `Serializable` to provide you with additional control. Because `Externalizable` extends `Serializable`, you can use `Externalizable` objects with `ObjectOutputStream` and `ObjectInputStream` in the same manner that you could use the `Serializable` object. In addition you must implement the `writeExternal()` and `readExternal()` methods defined by the `Externalizable` interfaces:

```
void readExternal(ObjectInput oi) throws IOException, ClassNotFoundException
void writeExternal(ObjectOutput oo) throws IOException
```

The `Externalizable` interface gives you complete control over the way that objects are written to and read from streams, but this control comes at the expense of having to implement your own methods for reading and writing the objects. You would use the `Externalizable` interface if you need such control, for example, you would like to compress the object before writing it, and decompress after reading it.

Using Externalizable is an advanced topic, and we won't look at it further in this book.

Filtered I/O

Filtered streams are simply wrappers around input or output streams, and are used to adapt the streams to specific program needs. For example, filters are used for buffering data, and for data translation. The filters sit between your program code and a source of input data to perform the special processing. A number of filters can also be combined, with one filter acting on the output of another.

FilterInputStream, FilterOutputStream, FilterReader, and FilterWriter

The filtered byte streams are `FilterInputStream` and `FilterOutputStream`. Their constructors are:

```
protected FilterInputStream(InputStream in)
protected FilterOutputStream(OutputStream out)
```

The `FilterInputStream` class is an abstract class, and provides the design for the basic capability to create one stream from another. This is accomplished with the help of the in parameter. This is specified to be an `InputStream`, so any type of `InputStream` object can be chained together with another, each subsequent object accessing the output of the previous one.

`FilterOutputStream` complements `FilterInputStream` and is the parent class of all filtered output classes. There is an out parameter, which is an object of class `OutputStream`, so arbitrary output streams can be filtered. Data written to a `FilterOutputStream` can be modified as needed to perform filtering operations and then forwarded to the out object.The `FilterReader` and `FilterWriter` classes are similar to `FilterInputStream` and `FilterOutputStream`. The `FilterReader` class uses the in parameter for input filtering and `FilterWriter` uses the out parameter for output filtering:

```
protected FilterReader(Reader in)
protected FilterWriter(Writer out)
```

The PrintStream Class

The PrintStream class is not new to you: you have been using an instance of the PrintStream class for some time, to write output to the Java console window using the System.out object. The PrintStream class has two constructors:

```
PrintStream(Outputstream)
PrintStream(Outputstream os, boolean flushOnNewLine)
```

Because PrintStream is a filter, it takes an instance of OutputStream as an argument to its constructors. The second constructor takes an additional boolean value to determine whether Java flushes the output stream every time a new line (\n) character is sent.

PrintStream provides two methods, print() and println(), that are overloaded to print any primitive data types or objects. The difference is that println() additionally prints a new line (\n) character after producing its output. (Objects are printed by first converting them into a String using their toString() method, inherited from the Object class.)

```
public void print(boolean b)
public void print(char c)
public void print(int i)
public void print(long l)
public void print(float f)
public void print(double d)
public void print(char[] s)
public void print(String s)
public void print(Object obj)
public void println()
public void println(boolean x)
public void println(char x)
public void println(int x)
public void println(long x)
public void println(float x)
public void println(double x)
public void println(char[] x)
public void println(String x)
public void println(Object x)
```

The PrintStream constructors are deprecated, because PrintStreams do not handle Unicode characters correctly. The preferred class is PrintWriter, which we will see in a moment. But note that the methods defined by PrintStream are not deprecated, which indicates that it is OK to use a PrintStream but not to create one. This might seem odd, but the reason is that the widely used System.out object is a PrintStream.

However for new programs, it is best to restrict your use of System.out to simple debugging and example programs. Any real-world programs that display console output should do so through a PrintWriter.

The PrintWriter Class

The `PrintWriter` class is the character-oriented replacement for the `PrintStream` class, and can wrap either a `Writer` or an `OutputStream` using one of the following constructors:

```
PrintWriter(Writer out)
PrintWriter(Writer out, boolean autoFlush)
PrintWriter(OutputStream out)
PrintWriter(OutputStream out, boolean autoFlush)
```

The `autoFlush()` argument specifies whether the `PrintWriter` should be flushed when any `println()` method is called.

`PrintWriter` provides the same wide variety of `print()` and `println()` methods as `PrintStream`. However, these methods do not throw `IOExceptions`; instead the `boolean checkError()` method must be called to check for any errors.

The PushbackInputStream Class

`PushbackInputStream` is a filter, used on an input stream, that allows you to read a byte and then return it back to the stream, so that it can be re-read later. This type of filter is normally used when the incoming data needs to be parsed in complicated ways, when it is useful to be able to peek at what is coming from an input stream without disturbing it.

`PushbackInputStream` has two constructors:

```
PushbackInputStream(InputStream is)
PushbackInputStream(InputStream is, int numBytes)
```

The first constructor allows one byte to be unread, but the second constructor creates a buffer of the size specified in the constructor, allowing multiple bytes to be returned to the input stream. Aside from the other normal `InputStream` methods, `PushbackInputStream` introduces the `unread()` method, used to push back the character(s) that were read:

```
void unread(int ch)
void unread(byte buffer[])
void unread(byte buffer[], int offset, int numChars)
```

The `unread()` method provides for pushing back either a single byte or a byte array (if the stream was created using the second constructor). You can also specify an offset and number of bytes if pushing back an arrray.

The following example demonstrates the use of `PushbackInputStream` on an array of bytes. After reading each character from the stream we peek ahead at the next character, then push it back into the stream.

Try It Out – Implementing PushbackInputStream

Save the following code as `Pushback.java`:

```java
/* Pushback.java */
import java.io.*;

public class Pushback {
  public static void main(String [] args) throws IOException {
    // Declare a string and convert it into a byte array
    String str = "Hello";
    byte [] buf = str.getBytes();
    System.out.println("The array to read is: "+str);

    // Open a ByteArrayInputStream pointing to the byte array and
    // wrap this stream within a PushBackInputStream
    ByteArrayInputStream bain = new ByteArrayInputStream(buf);
    PushbackInputStream pin = new PushbackInputStream(bain);
    int c;

    // Read - display - read ahead - display - unread
    while ((c = pin.read()) != -1) {
      System.out.println("The character read is: "+ (char)c);
      if ((c = pin.read()) != -1) {
        System.out.println(" The next character is: "+ (char) c);
        pin.unread(c);
      }
    }
  }
}
```

Compile the code by opening a command prompt window, changing to the directory where you saved `Pushback.java`, and typing:

> **javac Pushback.java**

Then run the program by entering:

> **java Pushback**

You should see the following output:

```
The array to read is: Hello
The character read is: H
 The next character is: e
The character read is: e
 The next character is: l
The character read is: l
 The next character is: l
The character read is: l
 The next character is: o
The character read is: o
```

How It Works

This example creates a `String` object and converts it into an array of bytes using the `getBytes()` method:

```
String str = "Hello";
byte [] buf = str.getBytes();
```

A `ByteArrayInputStream` is created from the byte array, and wrapped in a `PushbackInputStream`:

```
ByteArrayInputStream bain = new ByteArrayInputStream(buf);
PushbackInputStream pin = new PushbackInputStream(bain);
```

We read each character from the `PushbackInputStream` and display it, until the end of the stream is reached. After every read we look at the next byte, display it, and push it back into the stream using the `unread()` method:

```
int c;
while ((c = pin.read()) != -1) {
  System.out.println("The character read is: "+ (char)c);
  if ((c = pin.read()) != -1) {
    System.out.println(" The next character is: "+ (char) c);
    pin.unread(c);
  }
}
```

The PushbackReader Class

The `PushbackReader` class is a subclass of `FilterReader` that allows one or more characters to be pushed back to the input stream, very much like `PushbackInputStream`. The constructors are:

```
PushbackReader(Reader inputStream)
PushbackReader(Reader inputStream, int bufSize)
```

The first constructor allows one character to be pushed back, whereas the second constructor allows the size of the pushback buffer to be specified.

```
void unread(int ch)
void unread(char buffer[])
void unread(char buffer[], int offset, int numChars)
```

The various forms of the `unread()` method provides for pushing back a single character, or returning an array of characters to the buffer.

Buffered I/O

The buffered streams extend the filter streams by using a temporary cache for data that is read from or written to a stream. This allows programs to read or write large number of bytes of data, increasing the performance. The buffer also helps in skipping, marking, and resetting the stream. `BufferedInputStream` and `BufferedOutputStream` implement buffered streams.

Similarly, readers and writers can buffer their input and output using a `BufferedWriter` or a `BufferedReader` to wrap the underlying writer or reader.

BufferedInputStream and BufferedOutputStream

`BufferedInputStream` creates and maintains a buffer and wraps an `InputStream` within it. You can construct a `BufferedInputStream` object using the two constructors:

```
BufferedInputStream(InputStream is)
BufferedInputStream(InputStream is, int bufsize)
```

The first constructor uses the default buffer size. In the second, the size of the buffer is passed as an argument. The optimal buffer size is dependent on many factors such as the host operating system, the amount of memory available, and the configuration of the machine. You need not get into such complex calculations to make a good use of buffering. A good guess for a size is around 8KB.

`BufferedInputStream` does not introduce any new methods of its own in addition to those provided by `InputStream`, though it does provide implementations of `mark()` and `reset()`.

`BufferedOutputStream` performs output buffering, in a similar way to `BufferedInputStream`. The methods are the same as in any `OutputStream`, but in addition it has a `flush()` method which ensures that the data is physically written to the output device. `BufferedOutputStream` has two constructors:

```
BufferedOutputStream(OutputStream os)
BufferedOutputStream(OutputStream os, int bufsize)
```

The first constructor creates a buffered stream using the default buffer size of 512 bytes, while the second allows you to specify the buffer size.

The following example demonstrates the `mark()`, `skip()`, and `reset()` methods with buffered streams. It reads characters from a `ByteArrayInputStream` one at a time and prints them out, but once it encounters the letter a it marks the current location and skips forward 5 characters; afterwards, it returns to the marked position and prints from there to the end of the stream.

Try It Out – Implementing Buffered Streams

Save the following code as `BufferedIO.java`:

```
/* BufferedIO.java */
import java.io.*;
public class BufferedIO {
  public static void main(String [] args) throws IOException {
```

```
// Create a string and convert it to an array
String str = "This is a test line";
System.out.println("Test line: "+str);
byte buf [] = str.getBytes();

// Create a BufferedInputStrean and wrap it round a ByteArrayInputStream
// Create a BufferedOutputStream and wrap System.out
ByteArrayInputStream bain = new ByteArrayInputStream(buf);
BufferedInputStream bufin = new BufferedInputStream(bain);
BufferedOutputStream bufout = new BufferedOutputStream(System.out);

// Demonstrating skip(), mark() and reset()
int c;
while((c = bufin.read()) != -1) {
  bufout.write ((char)c);
  System.out.print((char) c);
  if (c == 'a') {
    bufin.mark(15);
    bufin.skip(5);
  }
}

System.out.println("\nA mark has been placed and 5 bytes skipped.");
bufin.reset();
while ((c = bufin.read()) != -1) {
  bufout.write((char)c);
  System.out.print((char) c);
}
System.out.println("\nThat is the output after a reset");
  }
}
```

Compile the code by opening a command prompt window, changing to the directory where you saved BufferedIO.java, and typing:

> **javac BufferedIO.java**

Then run the program by entering:

> **java BufferedIO**

You should see the following output:

```
Test line: This is a test line
This is a line
A mark has been placed and 5 bytes skipped
 test line
That is the output after a reset
```

How It Works

We start by creating a `String` object converting it into an array of bytes using the `getBytes()` method. An instance of the `ByteArrayInputStream` class is created from the byte array, and wrapped in a `BufferedInputStream`. A `BufferedOutputStream` is also created wrapping `System.out`:

```
String str = "This is a test line";
byte buf [] = str.getBytes();
ByteArrayInputStream bain = new ByteArrayInputStream(buf);
BufferedInputStream bufin = new BufferedInputStream(bain);
BufferedOutputStream bufout = new BufferedOutputStream(System.out);
```

The `BufferedInputStream` is read one character at a time, and displayed using the `BufferedOutputStream`, until the end of the stream is reached. If the `read()` method encounters character a, it marks the place. The `mark()` method takes an integer as its argument, in this case, the value 15, meaning that 15 bytes can be read before the mark becomes invalid. It then skips 5 bytes, and continues to read.

```
int c;
while((c = bufin.read()) != -1) {
  bufout.write ((char)c);
  System.out.print((char) c);
  if (c == 'a') {
    bufin.mark(15);
    bufin.skip(5);
  }
}
```

On reaching the end of the stream, the pointer is reset to the previously marked position, and we continue to read again until the end of the stream is reached:

```
bufin.reset();
while ((c = bufin.read()) != -1) {
  bufout.write((char)c);
  System.out.print((char) c);
}
```

BufferedReader and BufferedWriter

The `BufferedReader` and `BufferedWriter` classes support buffered character I/O, and are the character-based equivalents of `BufferedInputStream` and `BufferedOutputStream`.

`BufferedReader` improves performance by buffering input. It has two constructors:

```
BufferedReader(Reader inputStream)
BufferedReader(Reader inputStream, int bufsize)
```

The default buffer size is used unless the buffer size is explicitly specified as a second parameter. The `BufferedReader` class also provides the `readLine()` method to read a line of text from the underlying reader:

```
String readLine() throws IOException;
```

This method returns `null` when the end of the stream is reached.

`BufferedWriter` can increase performance by reducing the number of times data is physically written to the output stream. It has two constructors:

```
BufferedWriter (Writer outputStream)
BufferedWriter (Writer outputStream, int bufSize)
```

Again, the default buffer size is used unless the buffer size is explicitly specified. `BufferedWriter` also provides the `newLine()` method for writing the platform-dependent line separator, and a `flush()` method that can be used to ensure that the data buffers are physically written to the actual output stream.

Try It Out – A JSP Using BufferedWriter and FileWriter

In this example we'll create an HTML form requesting comments on this book, *Beginning JSP Web Development*, which submits the details to another JSP for processing. The data will be stored in a file for later viewing.

Enter the following code and save it as `Feedback.jsp` in your `%CATALINA_HOME%\webapps\begjsp-ch14` folder:

```
<html>
<head>
<title>COMMENT BOX</title>
<style>
<!--
body {font-family : "Times New Roman";
      font-style : normal;
      font-weight : bold;
      background-color : "FF0000";
      color : yellow}
h1,h2,h3 {font-family : "sans-serif";
      color : white}
-->
</style>
</head>
<body>
<h1 align=center>Tell Us What You Think About</h1>
<h3 align=center>Beginning JSP Web Development</h2>
<form action="Comment.jsp" method="post">
<p>
Name:
<input type="text" name="name"  size="25" maxlength="25">
Email address:
<input type="text" name="email" size="32" maxlength="32"><br>
Comments and Suggestions:<br>
<textarea name="feedback" rows="8" cols="72"></textarea><br>
<input type="submit" value="Submit"><input type="reset" value="Reset">
</p>
</form>
</body>
</html>
```

Then save the following code as `Comment.jsp`, in the same folder:

```
<%@ page import="java.io.*" %>

<html>
<head> <title> Thank you </title>
<style>
<!--
body {font-family : "Times New Roman";
      font-style : normal;
      font-weight : bold;
      background-color : "ff0000";
      color : black}
h1,h2,h3 {font-family : "sans-serif";
      color : white}
-->
</style>

</head>
<body>
<center>
<h1>Thank you.</h1>
Have a look at the feedback from others - <br>

<%
    String tname = request.getParameter("name");
    String temail = request.getParameter("email");
    String tfeedback = request.getParameter("feedback");
    String tfilepath = application.getRealPath("/")+"feedback.txt";

    BufferedWriter bw = new BufferedWriter(new FileWriter(tfilepath,true));
    bw.write("<tr> <td>");
    bw.write("<em>Name: </em>"+tname+"<br>");
    bw.write("<em>Email address: </em>"+temail);
    bw.write("</tr> </td>");
    bw.newLine();
    bw.write("<tr> <td>");
    bw.write("<em>Says - </em><br>");
    bw.newLine();
    bw.write(tfeedback);
    bw.write("</tr> </td>");
    bw.newLine();
    bw.write("<hr>");
    bw.write("</tr> </td>");

    bw.newLine();
    bw.close();
%>

<table frame=box border=3 bgcolor="white">
<jsp:include page="feedback.txt" flush="true" />
</table>
</center>
</body>
</html>
```

Ensure that Tomcat is running and direct your browser to http://localhost:8080/begjsp-ch14/Feedback.jsp. You should see the following screen:

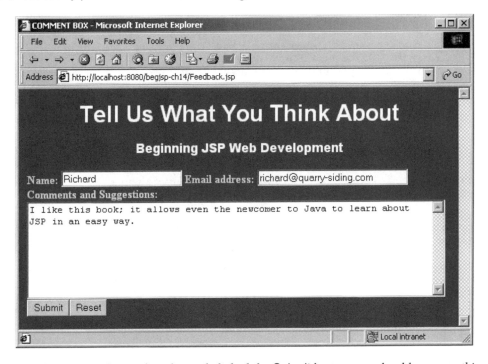

When you have entered your thoughts and clicked the Submit button, you should see something similar to this:

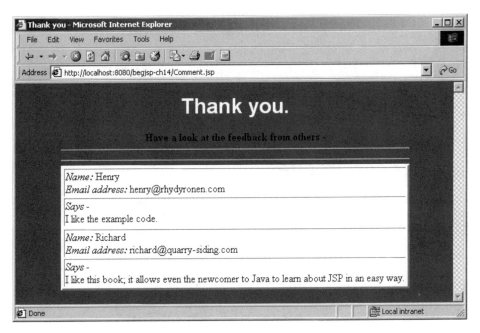

How it Works

Feedback.jsp simply creates the HTML form that posts to Comment.jsp, which is where the action is. We start by reading in the relevant request parameters containing the data from the form:

```
String tname = request.getParameter("name");
String temail = request.getParameter("email");
String tfeedback = request.getParameter("feedback");
```

Next, we use the application object's getRealPath() method to get the web application's document root directory, where we will create the file where we store the feedback:

```
String tfilepath = application.getRealPath("/")+"feedback.txt";
```

We then create a BufferedWriter, which wraps a FileWriter pointing to the feedback.txt file. The write() method is used to store the data, and the stream is closed.

```
BufferedWriter bw = new BufferedWriter(new FileWriter(tfilepath,true));
bw.write("<tr> <td>");
bw.write("<em>Name: </em>"+tname+"<br>");
bw.write("<em>Email address: </em>"+temail);
bw.write("</tr> </td>");
bw.newLine();
bw.write("<tr> <td>");
bw.write("<em>Says - </em><br>");
bw.newLine();
bw.write(tfeedback);
bw.write("</tr> </td>");
bw.newLine();
bw.write("<hr>");
bw.write("</tr> </td>");
bw.newLine();
bw.close();
```

Finally, we use the <jsp:include> action to include the feedback.txt file within the response to the browser:

```
<jsp:include page="feedback.txt" flush="true" />
```

Random Access To Files

The RandomAccessFile class has the capability of reading and writing binary data to random locations within a file, rather than simply treating the file as a continuous stream of information. This class is unique among the stream-related classes in that it is not derived from InputStream or OutputStream, but it implements the DataInput and DataOutput interfaces meaning that Java primitive values can be written and read from a random access file.

The following are the constructors for RandomAccessFile objects:

```
RandomAccessFile(String name, String mode)
RandomAccessFile(File file, String mode)
```

The file is specified by a filename or by a `File` object, and the `mode` argument must be equal to either `"r"` (for reading) or `"rw"` (for both reading and writing).

`RandomAccessFile` introduces several new methods besides those implemented from `DataInput` and `DataOutput`, including:

```
void seek(long offset) throws IOException
long getFilePointer() throws IOException
long length() throws IOException
```

The `seek()` method sets the `RandomAccessFile` object to a particular location within the file, the `getFilePointer()` method returns the current location in the file, and `length()` returns the current length of the file.

When the random access file is no longer needed, it should be closed to free the resources:

```
void close() throws IOException
```

The following example creates a file with a set of `int` values, and uses `RandomAccessFile` to display numbers from various positions within the file.

Try It Out – Implementing Random Access

Save the following code as `RandomIO.java`:

```java
/* RandomIO.java */
import java.io.*;

public class RandomIO {
  public static void main (String [] args) throws IOException {

    // Create an instance of the RandomAccessFile class
    RandomAccessFile raf = new RandomAccessFile("number.txt","rw");

    // Store numbers 100 to 110
    for(int i = 100; i <= 110; i++) {
      raf.writeInt(i);
    }

    // Seek the beginning of the file and display the entire list
    raf.seek(0);
    for (int c = 0; c <= 10; c++) {
      System.out.print(raf.readInt() + " ");
    }

    // Read the first, sixth, and fourth numbers in the list
    raf.seek(0);
    System.out.println("\nThe first number in the list is :" +
                    raf.readInt());
```

```
    // Seek position = (size of int * position) ie. 4 * 5 = 20
    raf.seek(12);
    System.out.println("The sixth number in the list is:" +
                       raf.readInt());

    // Seek position = (size of int * position) ie. 4 * 53 = 12
    raf.seek(20);
    System.out.println("The fourth number in the list is :" +
                       raf.readInt());
    // close the stream before exiting
    raf.close();
  }
}
```

Compile the code by opening a command prompt window, changing to the directory where you saved RandomIO.java, and typing:

> **javac RandomIO.java**

Then run the program by entering:

> **java RandomIO**

You should see the following output:

```
100 101 102 103 104 105 106 107 108 109 110
The first number in the list is: 100
The sixth number in the list is: 105
The fourth number in the list is: 103
```

How It Works

This example demonstrates how to use the RandomAccessFile class. We start by constructing a RandomAccessFile object in read/write mode, and store 11 numbers (100 to 110) in it using the writeInt() method:

```
RandomAccessFile raf = new RandomAccessFile("number.txt","rw");
for(int i = 100; i <= 110; i++) {
  raf.writeInt(i);
}
```

We seek the beginning of the file using the seek() method and read back the numbers using the readInt() method:

```
raf.seek(0);
for (int c = 0; c <= 10; c++) {
  System.out.print(raf.readInt() + " ");
}
```

We then seek the first, third and fifth number by calculating the number of bytes from the beginning of the file. Note that the size of an `int` is four bytes, so the nth int will be at position $(n-1)*4$; for example, the fourth number will be at byte position 12. We use the `seek()` method to go to that position in the file, and read and print out the number, for example:

```
raf.seek(20);
System.out.println("The fourth number in the list is :" +
                    raf.readInt());
```

Note how we can move about within the file at will.

Summary

In this chapter you saw:

- ❑ How to work with Java streams, which provide an abstraction that simplifyies the complex and cumbersome task of file I/O
- ❑ The Java stream class hierarchy
- ❑ How to use filters to customize I/O proccessing
- ❑ Java's support for character-oriented I/O
- ❑ How to perform random-access I/O
- ❑ How to integrate file access into JSP pages

This chapter was about I/O on plain, ordinary files, which can be hard work as they lack structure. In the next chapter we will learn about the fundamentals of databases, which overcome the shortcomings of the flat files.

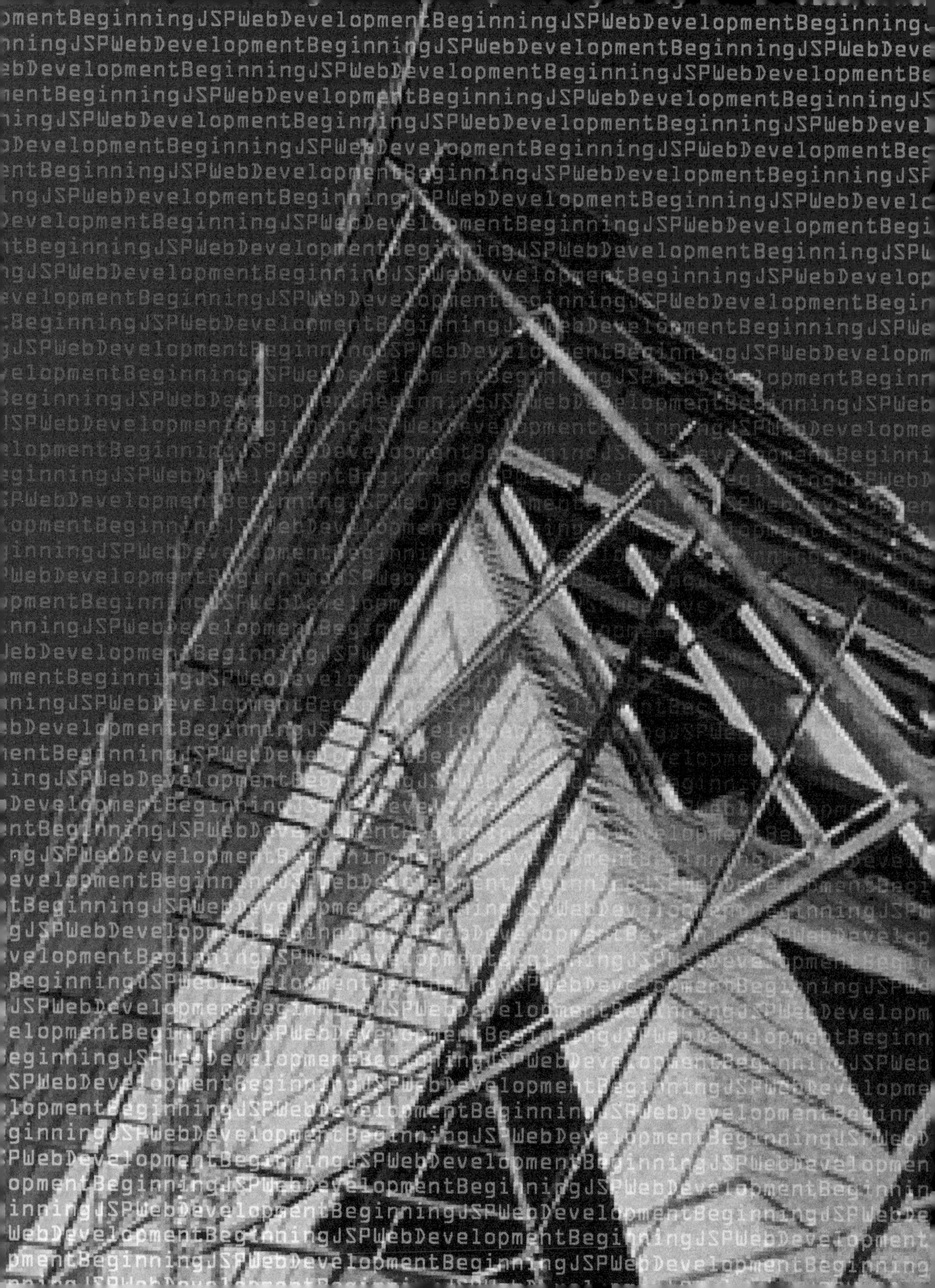

Creating Databases with Java

This chapter is the first of two that will introduce you to databases, how to store and manage data within them, and how to connect to databases using Java and JSP.

In this chapter you will learn:

- ❑ What a database is.
- ❑ What a relational database is, and the concepts associated with it, such as normalization.
- ❑ How to install a database management system, MySQL.
- ❑ The basics of Structured Query Language (SQL), so that we can create and modify the contents of a database.
- ❑ How to connect to a database from a Java program, in order to create database tables and populate them with data.

Let's start by establishing what databases are, and why we would want to use them.

Introducing Databases

In the previous chapter you saw how files could be used to manage data in applications. For simple data, such as a list of e-mail addresses, these simple files are adequate. However, if you want to store large amounts of complex structured data, simple files are inadequate. Instead, you need to use a **database**. Many web applications, from online shopping sites to message-boards, integrate with a database.

> A database is a collection of data that is organized in such a way that its contents can be easily accessed and manipulated.

To understand this definition better, consider an example of an unsorted pile of papers. How do you find a particular paper within the pile? You would probably start from the top of the pile and work your way down until you find the paper you want, which would be a time-consuming process if you had a large pile and your paper was near the bottom of it. This unorganized environment is analogous to a situation where data is stored in no particular order in a normal "flat" file on a computer – it is difficult to locate the information you want.

Now consider a library or bookshop. When you need a particular book, you search through the card catalog or the book index. This is an example of a (non-electronic) database. It is a well-organized database in which data is stored in specific locations; and because of its structure and organization, any data can be retrieved quickly and easily.

A software program that helps you create and modify a database is called a **database management system (DBMS)**. The DBMS removes the complexities of storing the database information in specific locations, within the particular files, directories and disk volumes used by the server. The server keeps track of where the data is stored, so that the database user doesn't have to worry about it.

Using Tables

When we wish to organize data, one of the most common ways to do so is to arrange the data into **tables**. For instance, referring back to our bookshop analogy, we could make a table of books. Each book's data (author(s), title, category, price, and so on) would fill a **row** (or **record**) of the table. Since we would want to use the table to compare data from different books, we would arrange the data we wish to compare (the price, say) into a **column** (or **field**). Assuming our wise bookshop owner stocks Wrox books, a portion of the Book table might look something like this:

Title	Category	Author(s)	Price
Professional Java Data	Java	Danny Ayers, John Bell, Carl Calvert Bettis, Thomas Bishop, Mike Bogovich, Matthew Ferris, Rick Grehan, Bjarki Holm, Tony Loton, Glen E. Mitchell II, Nitin Nanda, Kelly Lin Poon, Sean Rhody, Mark Wilcox.	$59.99
Professional Java Security	Java	Jess Garms, Daniel Somerfield	$49.99
Beginning SQL Programming	SQL	John Kauffman, Brian Matsik, Kevin Spencer, Tom Walsh	$49.99

As you can see, this groups data about each book into rows, and data about each **attribute** of a book into columns.

Now, if we were to construct a database to contain this data, we would do exactly the same thing – organize the data into a table. In fact, a database will probably contain more than one table, each holding data about a different **entity** – books, computers, movies, whatever.

Of course, the fact that we create tables to hold information about a particular entity implies that the records within the table share common attributes – in other words, the records within a table are related. After all, it makes no sense to store unrelated information, like mixing up the information related to your movie collection with the information about the books in your bookstore.

Relational Databases

Let's go back to our Book table. While it is perfectly logical to store related data about books in a table, this table is not as efficient at storing this data as it may first appear.

First, you can see that we have several similar entries in the category column. Why is this a problem? Well, imagine if we wanted to change the name of a particular category. If we stocked just two Wrox Java titles, this wouldn't be too much of a problem. However, if we stocked twenty, then having to go through the table modifying all of the appropriate entries is going to be a time-consuming task, and the chance of a data entry error occurring will increase too. For a much bigger book category than this, the time needed to update the database will quickly become unacceptable, and data entry errors will become very likely, leading to inconsistencies between records. Therefore, we would eliminate data repetition where possible.

Another obvious problem lies in the way we store authors. We are storing them in the table as a list in a single column. This will makes things difficult if we want to use this data meaningfully. What if we wanted to add another column to the table that listed any other books written by a particular author? This would mean that each author associated with a particular record would need a table cell that may hold many book titles. How would we arrange the table to hold data like this?

Relationships Between Data

This second problem arises due to the nature of the relationships between attributes within the table. We have no problem storing data within a table when all of the attributes map **one-to-one** (1:1) or **one to many** (1:M). What we mean by a one-to-one relationship is that each column involved in the relationship contains unique values. This scenario might arise if we decided, for some reason, to stock only single-author books by authors that had only written one book. In this case each book title is only associated with one author, and each author is only associated with one book title. You should note that one-to-one relationships are pretty rare.

On the other hand, we already have several one-to-many relationships in our table. An example is between title and price: a book can only have one price in the store, but we can have more than one book selling at the same price. We don't have a problem organizing 1:M relationships within a table, although we can encounter the data repetition problem discussed earlier.

The big problem comes when we encounter **many-to-many** (M:M) relationships. The example of this in our table is between titles and authors. A book can have more than one author, but an author may have written more than one book too. Organizing many-to-many relationships into a table is a difficult task, as we have seen, and one that reduces our ability to modify the table later.

The Relational Model

One common way to solve the problems discussed above is to break up a big table into smaller ones that together hold the same data. This multi-table approach is called the **relational model**, because there are relationships between the data in different tables. Obviously we need a way to preserve these relationships even though the data is now in separate tables. To do this, we share one attribute per table with another table; these attributes that are shared between tables are called **keys**.

For instance, we might choose to place information about Authors in one table, and data about Books in another, and link the two tables using the author name attribute as a key. In this case, if we looked up information on a particular book title in the Book table, and then wanted to find out about the authors of that book, we would note the names of the book authors and scan down the Authors table until we found the correct records. Note that in this case, the author name column of the Author table would have to contain unique values; otherwise we would get confused when we try to track down the record for a particular author. A key column like this, that is only allowed to contain unique values, is called a **primary key**. The corresponding author name column in the Book table is called a **foreign key**, because it refers to values from a key column in another table.

But which attributes do we choose to be keys? We need a process to follow that will enable us to optimize our database table split. Luckily, this process exists, and is called **normalization**.

Normalization

The process towards database normalization progresses through a series of steps, typically known as **normal forms**. E.F.Codd introduced this concept during the 1970s. When you normalize a database, we have seen that you should have these goals in mind:

- Arrange data into logical groupings such that each group describes a small part of the whole
- Minimize the amount of duplicate data stored in a database
- Organize the data such that, when you modify it, you make the change in only one place
- Build a database in which you can access and manipulate the data quickly and efficiently without compromising the integrity of the data in storage

There are three sets of rules that are listed below for database normalization. If the first set of rules as presented below is observed, the database is said to be in **first normal form.** Likewise if all three sets of rules are observed, the database is considered to be in **third normal form.**

The rules that you should follow for converting the database to its first normal form are:

- Eliminate repeating groups in individual tables
- Create a separate table for each set of related data
- Identify each set of related data with a primary key

The rules to convert the database to its second normal form are (the database should be in its first normal form):

- Create separate tables for sets of values that apply to multiple records
- Relate these tables with a foreign key

Continuing on the quest for complete normalization of the database, the next step in the process would be to satisfy the rule of the third normal form

- Eliminate transitive dependencies (where a non-key attribute is dependent on another non-key attribute).

Adhering to the third normal form, while theoretically desirable, is not always practical. For instance, if you wanted to create a database of friends' addresses, you would need to eliminate all possible inter-field dependencies, creating separate tables for cities, ZIP codes, and so on. In theory, full normalization is worth pursuing. However, many small tables may degrade performance or exceed open file and memory capacities. It may be more feasible to apply third normal form only to data that changes frequently. If some dependent fields remain, design your application to require the user to verify all related fields when any one is changed.

Although other levels of normalization are possible, third normal form is considered the highest level necessary for most applications. As with many formal rules and specifications, real-world scenarios do not always allow for perfect compliance. If you decide to violate one of the first three rules of normalization, make sure that your application anticipates any problems that could occur, such as redundant data and inconsistent dependencies.

Given the guidance from the normalization process, let's now split our Books table into the most efficient set of relational tables. Before, we mentioned that we could split the table into Book and Author tables, but this still presents us with inefficiencies:

❑ The category column in the Book table still contains data repetition.

❑ Although this is not the case at the moment, as we add new books to the table, we might encounter different authors with the same name, and different books with the same title – so it would not be wise to use either of these columns as primary keys.

❑ Each title in the Book table can still have many authors, which makes it difficult to match entries in the author name column of the Title table with corresponding entries in the author name column in the Author table. Obviously, you are going to want to use software (a relational database management system, or **RDBMS**) to perform record matching between tables when you come to implement the database on your machine. If the author name column can contain lots of data values for each record, as well as the software having problems matching records, it would also be difficult to know how much memory to assign to store entries in the author name column; after all, there is no limit to the number of authors a book could have.

However, we can solve these problems. To get around the first problem, we create another table to hold categories. This Category table will contain a category name column, and another column that consists of unique ID values, with each category assigned one of these ID values. This category ID column can then be used as the primary key for this table. Since category ID values, not category names, will be used by other tables, we are then free to modify a category name without having to modify every record that belongs in this category. We can use the same idea to solve the second problem too, by creating author ID and title ID primary key columns.

Solving the last problem takes a bit more effort. We will get around the problem of multi-author entries by creating the concept of an author *contribution*. The Contribution table will simply consist of the author's ID, the ID of a book associated with the author, and a contribution ID (the primary key).

Here's a summary of our database model now:

Table	Column	Identifier
Book	Title_ID	Primary Key
	Title	–
	Price	–
	Category_ID	Foreign Key
Author	Author_ID	Primary Key
	Author_Name	–
Category	Category_ID	Primary Key
	Category_Description	–
Contribution	Contribution_ID	Primary Key
	Title_ID	Foreign Key
	Author_ID	Foreign Key

We are now almost ready to implement this database structure (or **schema**) on our machines. However, there is one last aspect of relational databases we should consider before we do: integrity of data.

Referential Integrity

Let's consider what happens when you start manipulating the records in our tables. You can edit the book information at will without any ill effects, but what would happen if you needed to delete a title? The entries in the Contribution table will be orphaned. Clearly you can't have a contribution detail without the associated book title being present. So you must have a means in place to enforce a corresponding book title for each contribution. This is the basis of enforcing **referential integrity**. There are two ways that you can enforce the validity of the data in this situation. One is by cascading deletions through the related tables; the other is by preventing deletions when related records exist.

Database applications have several choices available for enforcing referential integrity, but if possible, you should let the database engine do its job and handle this for you. Database engines allow you to use declarative referential integrity. You specify a relationship between tables at design time, indicating if updates and deletes will cascade through related tables. If cascading updates are enabled, changes to the primary key in a table are propagated through related tables. If cascading deletes are enabled, deletions from a table are propagated through related tables.

Before you go ahead and enable cascading deletes on all your relationships, keep in mind that this can be a dangerous practice. If you define a relationship between the Category table and the Title table with cascading deletes enabled, and then delete a record from Category, you will delete all Title table records that come under this category. Be cautious, or you may accidentally lose important data.

Introducing SQL

In a moment, we are going to install a RDBMS so that we can create and manipulate databases. First, however, let's introduce you to the language we use to communicate with relational databases: **Structured Query Language**, or **SQL** for short. A **query** is simply a statement that we send to an RDBMS in order to get it to retrieve data.

There are actually three languages within SQL itself:

❑   **Data Definition Language (DDL)** – used to create databases and tables

❑   **Data Maintenance Language (DML)** – for adding, removing, and changing the data contained in tables

❑   **Data Query Language (DQL)** – for retrieving data from a table

As we will see later, SQL resembles a human language, and reads almost like a form of a broken English. SQL itself is platform independent, although the implementation of SQL varies with the relational database management system used. There are many options to choose from the numerous RDBMS. They come in different levels of capability, from simple ones with limited features, to sophisticated databases capable of handling large number of concurrent users and support for additional features like distributed transactions and powerful search algorithms. But, they all use SQL as the data access language. Examples of common RDBMS include:

❑   Oracle

❑   Sybase

❑   Informix

❑   Microsoft SQL Server

❑   Access

❑   MySQL

As well as being easy to use and having great performance and reliability, the last RDBMS on that list, MySQL, has a popular feature: it is freely available. It has been released under GNU Public License.

> *GNU stands for "GNU's Not UNIX", and applies to useful free software packages that are being distributed by the GNU project at MIT, largely through the efforts of Richard Stallman. The circular acronym name ("GNU" contains the acronym GNU as one of the words it stands for) is a joke on Richard Stallman's part. GNU General Public License is intended to guarantee your freedom to share and use free software, to make sure the software is free for all its users.*

Because of these features, we will be using MySQL for our database examples. Let's now show you how to download and install it.

Installing MySQL

You can download the latest zipped binary version of MySQL from http://www.mysql.com. You should download version 3.23.38 or higher, because it will then have binaries for both normal MySQL and for MySQL-Max (which supports *transactions*, that we will be looking at in Chapter 16).

Here's how to install MySQL on Windows 2000:

1. Download MySQL.

2. Unzip it in some empty directory and run the `setup.exe` program. By default, MySQL will be installed in `C:\mysql`.

3. To start MySQL as a service (which means that MySQL runs when your machine starts up), you will need to open a command console and move to the folder `C:\mysql\bin`, where all of the MySQL programs are kept. Now type:

   ```
   > mysqld-nt --install
   ```

   This will install MySQL as a service.

4. You should also start up the extremely useful `winmysqladmin` tool, by double clicking on its icon in the `C:\mysql\bin` folder. This tool allows you to control the MySQL server program. You should see a traffic signal icon representing the tool on the right hand side of your Start menu; right clicking on this icon brings up a menu that allows you to start and stop the server. Clicking on the **Show me** option brings up the tool's administrative window. Open this up, and select the **my.ini Setup** tab. You will see a set of options labeled **mysqld file** on the left; select the **mysqld-max** option.

To install MySQL on Windows 98, you will need to follow the same instructions as above, but you should note that MySQL can only be installed as a service on Windows 2000, so skip this step.

Troubleshooting

Here are some handy tips if you encounter problems during installation.

- ❑ Check the `C:\mysql\mysql.err` file for debugging information.

- ❑ Move to the `C:\mysql\bin` folder and start up MySQL by typing in `mysqld --standalone`. In this case you may get some useful information on the screen that may help solve your problem.

- ❑ Start `mysqld` with the `--standalone --debug` options. In this case `mysqld` will write a log file in `C:\mysqld.trace` that should indicate why `mysqld` won't start.

You can test whether MySQL is working by moving to the `C:\mysql\bin` folder and executing the following command:

```
> mysqlshow
+-----------+
| Databases |
+-----------+
| mysql     |
| test      |
+-----------+
```

This will list out the default MySQL databases.

Using MySQL

Now that we have MySQL installed, let's have a little play with it. To do this, we must first invoke the `mysql` command line tool, of which there are two versions. In your command console, move to the folder `C:\MySQL\bin\`, then execute either:

```
> mysql
```

or:

```
> mysqld
```

The first command invokes the `mysql` tool compiled on native Windows, which offers very limited text editing capabilities. The second invokes the tool compiled with the Cygnus GNU compiler and libraries, which offers `readline` editing (to use this you must also copy `C:\MySQL\lib\cygwinb19.dll` to `C:\windows\system`).

Extra care should be taken when MySQL is installed on Windows, because the default privileges on Windows give all local users full privileges to all databases. To make MySQL more secure, you should set a password for all users of MySQL, and remove the default record in the `mysql.user` table that has `Host='localhost'` and `User=''`, using the following command:

```
mysql> DELETE FROM user WHERE Host='localhost' AND User='';
mysql> QUIT
```

The first command removes the appropriate record, and the second quits from the `mysql` tool.

> *You should have noted the mix of cases in the MySQL command lines we have used so far. SQL commands such as DELETE, WHERE, and QUIT are not actually case-sensitive, but table and column names as well as values are case-sensitive, so be careful. The convention is to write all SQL commands as uppercase to distinguish them from the table data, and we have followed this convention in this book.*

Now, you should also add a password for the root user. To do this, make sure that you are in the `C:\MySQL\bin\` folder, where you can use another command line tool, `mysqladmin`:

```
> mysqladmin reload
> mysqladmin -u root password your_password
```

Obviously substitute `your_password` for a password that is a little more secure. After you've set the password, if you want to shut down the `mysql` server, you can do so using this command:

```
> mysqladmin --user=root --password=your_password shutdown
```

Now that you can get the MySQL server up and running securely, you can experiment with some basic database administration issues.

Connecting and Disconnecting to the MySQL Server

To connect to the server, you'll usually need to provide your MySQL username when you invoke mysql and, most likely, a password (don't worry about creating a new user account yet – we'll come back to that in a little while). If the server runs on a machine other than the one where you log in, you'll also need to specify a hostname.

```
> mysql -h hostname -u username -p
```

Pressing *Enter*, you should see:

```
Enter password: ********
```

The ******** represents your password. When you have entered it, you should see some introductory information followed by a mysql> prompt. After you have connected successfully, you can disconnect at any time by typing QUIT at the prompt (in which case you will receive a farewell message):

```
mysql> QUIT
Bye
```

You can also disconnect by pressing *Control-D*. Most examples in the following sections assume you are connected to the server, indicated the presence of the mysql> prompt.

Issuing SQL Commands At the Command Prompt

It is very important to know how to issue commands and understand the basic principles of entering commands. Here's a simple command that asks the server to tell you the current date. Try it yourself:

```
mysql> SELECT CURRENT_DATE;
+--------------+
| CURRENT_DATE |
+--------------+
| 2001-06-27   |
+--------------+
```

Note how we end a SQL statement with a semicolon. This query illustrates several things about the mysql tool:

❑ A command normally consists of a SQL statement followed by a semicolon. But there are some exceptions where a semicolon is not needed. QUIT, mentioned earlier, is one of them.

❑ When you issue a command, mysql sends it to the server for execution and displays any results in a **result set**, then prints another mysql to indicate that it is ready for another command.

❑ mysql displays query output as a table (rows and columns). The first row contains labels for the columns. The rows following are the query results. Normally, column labels are the names of the columns you fetch from database tables.

❑ mysql shows how many rows were returned and how long the query took to execute, which gives you a rough idea of server performance.

The command we just entered is a relatively short, single-line statement. However, you can enter multiple statements on a single line, as long as each statement ends with a semicolon. When you press *Enter*, the statements will be executed one after another. You can also carriage return within a statement, as long as you don't break up a word – until you write a semicolon and then press *Enter*, the statement will not be executed. The following table shows each of the prompts you may see and summarizes what they mean about the state that mysql is in:

Prompt	Meaning
mysql>	Ready for new command.
->	Waiting for next line of multiple-line command.
'>	Waiting for next line, collecting a string that begins with a single quote.
">	Waiting for next line, collecting a string that begins with a double quote.

SQL Data Types

When we create a database table in our database, we will need to define the data type and the size of the entries in each column. MySQL supports a number of column types, which may be grouped into three categories:

❑ Numeric

❑ Date and Time

❑ String

Here's a table of the MySQL data types:

Numeric Data Types

Data Types	Description	Range/Format
INT	Normal-sized integer	$(-2^{31}$ to $2^{31}-1)$, or $(0$ to $2^{32}-1)$ if UNSIGNED
TINYINT	Very small integer	$(-2^7$ to $2^7-1)$, or $(0$ to $2^8-1)$ if UNSIGNED
SMALLINT	Small integer	$(-2^{15}$ to $2^{15}-1)$, or $(0$ to $2^8-1)$ if UNSIGNED
MEDIUMINT	Medium-sized integer	$(-2^{23}$ to $2^{23}-1)$, or $(0$ to $2^{24}-1)$ if UNSIGNED
BIGINT	Large integer	$(-2^{63}$ to $2^{63}-1)$, or $(0$ to $2^{64}-1)$ if UNSIGNED
FLOAT	Single-precision floating-point number	Minimum non-zero $\pm1.176\times10^{-38}$; maximum non-zero $\pm3.403\times10^{+38}$
DOUBLE/REAL	Double-precision floating-point number	Minimum non-zero $\pm2.225\times10^{-308}$; maximum non-zero $\pm1.798\times10^{+308}$
DECIMAL	Float stored as string	Maximum range same as DOUBLE

Data/Time Data Types

Data Types	Description	Range/Format
DATE	A Date	YYYY-MM-DD format. Range 1000-01-01 to 9999-12-31
DATETIME	A Date and Time	YYYY-MM-DD hh:mm:ss format. Range 1000-01-01 00:00:00 to 9999-12-31 23:59:59
TIMESTAMP	A Timestamp	YYYYMMDDhhmmss format. Range 19700101000000 to sometime in 2037
TIME	A Time	hh:mm:ss format. Range −838:59:59 to 838:59:59
YEAR	A Year	YYYY format. Range 1900 to 2155

Character Data Types

Data Types	Description	Range/Format
CHAR	Fixed-length string	0–255 characters
VARCHAR	Variable-length string	0–255 characters
BLOB	Binary Large OBject	Binary data 0–65535 bytes long
TINYBLOB	Small BLOB value	Binary data 0–255 bytes long
MEDIUMBLOB	Medium-sized BLOB	Binary data 0–16777215 bytes long
LONGBLOB	Large BLOB value	Binary data 0–4294967295 bytes long
TEXT	Normal-sized text field	0–65535 bytes
TINYTEXT	Small text field	0–255 bytes
MEDIUMTEXT	Medium-sized text	0–16777215 bytes
LONGTEXT	Large text field	0–4294967295 bytes
ENUM	Enumeration	Column values are assigned one value from a set list
SET	Set value(s)	Column values are assigned zero or more values from a set list

Aside from the types listed above, there are other modifiers that can define the properties of a column. A few of them are unique to MySQL. The most common ones are:

Modifier	Description
AUTO_INCREMENT	Allows a numeric column to be automatically updated when records are modified. Useful for creating a unique identification number for rows.
DEFAULT *value*	Assigns a default value to a column.
NULL	A column is allowed to contain NULL values.
NOT NULL	Guarantees that every entry in the column will have some non NULL value.
PRIMARY KEY	Makes the column the primary key. It must also contain a NOT NULL modifier.

Our next task is to use this information to create a MySQL database and tables. Let's first get familiar with the SQL statements that help us do these.

Creating Databases and Tables Using SQL

In this section we are going to review the SQL commands we would use to create, delete, and alter databases and database tables.

The CREATE DATABASE statement creates an entirely new empty database. You must be the administrative user for MySQL to be able to use this statement. You are already familiar with getting connected to the server, and working with the mysql tool. Fire up the prompt and let us create our sample database, that we will call "Wrox":

```
mysql> CREATE DATABASE Wrox;
```

To check that we created the database successfully, we can use the SHOW DATABASES command, which lists all of the databases in MySQL:

```
mysql> SHOW DATABASES;
+----------+
| Database |
+----------+
| Wrox     |
| mysql    |
+----------+
```

Now try removing the Wrox database, using the DROP DATABASE command:

```
mysql> DROP DATABASE Wrox;
```

Of course, we actually want to use the Wrox database, because we want to add our tables to it, so recreate it using the CREATE DATABASE command again. Now, in order to make it clear to mysql which database we wish to work with when we add tables, we must use the USE command:

```
mysql> USE Wrox;
Database changed
```

Now we can use the CREATE TABLE statement to define the structure of a table within the database. This statement consists of the name of the new table followed by any number of field (column) definitions in parentheses. The syntax of the field definition is the name of the field, followed by its data type, followed by any modifiers as described in the previous section. Each field definition is separated by a comma. Let's see how we can create the Book table using this syntax:

```
mysql> CREATE TABLE Book (
    -> Title_ID INTEGER NOT NULL PRIMARY KEY,
    -> Title CHAR(50),
    -> Category_ID INTEGER);
```

This statement gives the table name, and tells the RDBMS about each column in the table. We created a Title_ID integer field that cannot contain any null values, and is automatically updated when records are added or removed, and is the primary key for the table. We also added a Title field of 50 characters in length, and an integer Category ID field. You have probably noted that we haven't added the Price field yet. We'll come to that in just a moment.

Let's now use the SHOW TABLES command to check that our Book table is in our database:

```
mysql> SHOW TABLES;
+----------------+
| Tables_in_Wrox |
+----------------+
| book           |
+----------------+
```

Everything looks fine. Let's now play around with this table a little.

Altering Tables

Having created a table, the chances are that we will want to modify it at some point in the future. This can be achieved using the ALTER TABLE statement, used to add, change, rename, or remove columns from an existing table. Here are a few examples. First we will add our Price field to the table, using the ADD command, and specifying the properties of the field:

```
mysql> ALTER TABLE Book ADD (Price INTEGER);
```

So here we've added a field called Price that contains integer values...ah, a mistake. We should have made the field a decimal because it will hold a price. Let's remove this field using the DROP command and try again:

```
mysql> ALTER TABLE Book DROP Price;
mysql> ALTER TABLE Book ADD (Prize DECIMAL(8,2));
```

Well, we've done it again; we've made another mistake. This time, the data type of the field is correct (a decimal field with maximum 8 characters, 2 of which are after the decimal point) but the name of the field is wrong. This time, let's modify the field we created using the CHANGE command, instead of deleting it and creating a new one:

```
mysql> ALTER TABLE Book CHANGE Prize Price DECIMAL(8,2);
```

Finally our field is just how we want it. Note that we had to specify all of the properties of the new field when we used the `CHANGE` command, even though we just wanted to change the field name.

There is another couple of SQL commands used with `ALTER TABLE` that you should be aware of. The first is the `ALTER` command that we can use to change field definitions. For instance, if we wanted to set the `Category_ID` field to a default value of zero, we could use:

```
mysql> ALTER TABLE Book ALTER Category_ID SET DEFAULT 0;
```

The other command is the `MODIFY` command, that we would use to modify the whole definition of a particular field. Let's say, to be awkward, we wanted to change the `Price` field back into an integer field. Then we could use:

```
mysql> ALTER TABLE Book MODIFY Price INTEGER;
```

If you've just tried this command, change the field back to a decimal; we'll need it in the right type when we come to insert data into the table.

Our logical next step is to learn how to execute SQL statements like these on a database using Java. However, before we can do this, we need to take a step back and learn how to connect to a database from a Java program, using the JDBC API.

Java Database Connectivity

The API used to execute SQL statements is different for each database engine. Java programmers, however, are lucky and are freed from such database portability issues. They have a single API, the **Java Database Connectivity API (JDBC)**, that's portable between database engines.

The JDBC library provides an interface for executing SQL statements. It provides the basic functionality for data access. The classes and interfaces that make up the JDBC API are abstractions from concepts common to database access for any kind of database. The JDBC API makes it easy to send SQL statements to relational database systems and supports all dialects of SQL. But the JDBC 2.0 API goes beyond SQL, also making it possible to interact with other kinds of data sources, such as files containing tables of data. In other words, with the JDBC library, it isn't necessary to write one program to access a MySQL database, another program to access an Oracle database, and so on. You can write a single Java program that uses the JDBC library, and the program will be able to send SQL or other statements to the appropriate data source. This is, of course, in keeping with the *write once, run anywhere* Java approach.

Drivers

Although we can use the JDBC API to access virtually any data source from a Java application, there is a proviso: we need access to the specific **driver** for the database. A driver is an implementation of the JDBC interface that is suited to a specific database. It is a middleware layer that translates Java method calls into proprietary database API calls, which are then used to manipulate the database. The exact details of how the driver enables this communication between Java application and database API depends upon the driver.

A JDBC driver makes it possible to do three things:

❑ Establish a connection with a data source

❑ Send queries and UPDATE statements to the data source

❑ Retrieve result sets

A number of drivers are available for MySQL, and information about this can be obtained at the MySQL homepage at http://www.mysql.com/downloads, under JDBC. For our purpose, we will use the MM.MySQL driver. MM.MySQL is a Type-4 JDBC driver that is under the GNU Library License. It allows Java developers to make connections to MySQL servers from both Java applications and applets. You should download the binary for this driver, and place it somewhere appropriate (we suggest the Tomcat common\lib folder), and then make sure your CLASSPATH environmental variable points to it. A complete listing of available JDBC drivers is available at http://industry.java.sun.com/products/jdbc/drivers.

Data Access Models

The JDBC API supports both two-tier and three-tier models for database access. In the two-tier model, a Java applet or application talks directly to the data source. This requires a JDBC driver that can communicate with the particular data source being accessed. An application's commands are delivered to the database, and the results of those statements are sent back to the user. This is illustrated in this diagram:

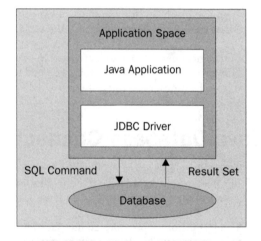

In the three-tier model, commands are sent to a "middle tier" of services, which then sends the commands to the data source. The data source processes the commands and sends the results back to the middle tier, which then sends them to the user. This is illustrated as shown:

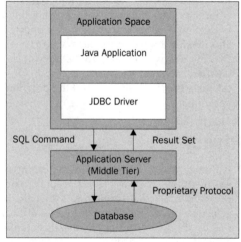

Here a JDBC driver links the application with the middle tier, and the middle tier uses another driver to communicate with the database. With enterprises increasingly using the Java programming language for writing server code, the JDBC API is being used more and more in the middle tier of a three-tier architecture too. Some of the features that make JDBC a server technology are its support for advanced database handling features, such as connection pooling (that we will meet in Chapter 16).

JDBC Driver Types

JDBC drivers are classified into four categories:

❑ **Type 1: JDBC-ODBC Bridge Driver:** The JDBC-ODBC bridge provides JDBC access through drivers written to the ODBC standard. The **ODBC** (Open Database Connectivity) standard is a predecessor to JDBC that is similar to it in many ways. It was originally used for Windows platforms but was later enhanced so that it would work on other platforms too. This driver is included in the Java Development Kit. The bridge is useful when a pure JDBC driver doesn't exist for the database you want to access. It is also good for prototyping and development, but is not recommended for use in production servers, because the three-tier approach is less optimized for performance.

❑ **Type 2: Native API-Partly Java Driver:** This kind of driver converts JDBC calls into calls on native methods in the database API for Oracle, Sybase, Informix, IBM DB2, or other DBMS. Note that, like the bridge driver, this style of driver requires that some operating system-specific binary code be loaded on each client machine, so it isn't very portable across platforms. However, the two-tier model is faster than the Type 1 driver.

❑ **Type 3: JDBC-Net Protocol Pure Java Driver:** This driver translates JDBC calls into a DBMS-independent net protocol (for example HTTP), which is then translated to a DBMS protocol by a custom middleware server. This net server middleware is able to connect its pure Java clients to many different databases. The specific protocol used depends on the vendor. In general, this is the most flexible JDBC alternative.

❑ **Type 4: Native-protocol pure Java driver:** This driver converts JDBC calls directly into the network protocol used by a DBMS. This allows a direct call from the client machine running Java to the DBMS server, which is similar to the Type 2 driver but bypassing the need to make a database API method call. The directness of this approach results in considerable performance improvement. If this class of driver is available to you, then it is the one you should use.

Driver types 3 and 4 are the preferred way to access databases using the JDBC API. Driver types 1 and 2 are interim solutions where direct pure Java drivers are not yet available.

Mapping SQL Data To Java

One tricky subject that you need to be aware of when accessing databases using JDBC is that data types in SQL do not correspond exactly to Java data types.

Indeed there are also significant variations between the SQL types supported by different database products. Even when different databases support SQL types with the same semantics, they may give those types different names. For example, most of the major databases support a SQL data type for large binary values, but Oracle calls this type LONG RAW, Sybase calls it IMAGE, Informix calls it BYTE, and DB2 calls it LONG VARCHAR FOR BIT DATA. Fortunately, you will normally not need to concern yourselves with the actual SQL type names used by a target database. You will be programming against existing database tables, and need be not concerned with the exact SQL type names that were used to create these tables.

JDBC defines a set of generic SQL type identifiers in the class `java.sql.Types`. These types have been designed to represent the most commonly-used SQL types. While programming with the JDBC API, you will be able to use these JDBC types to reference generic SQL types, without having to concern yourself with the exact SQL type name used by the target database. But one major place where you may need to use SQL type names is in the SQL CREATE TABLE statement. If you want to write portable JDBC programs that can create tables on a variety of different databases, you are faced with two choices:

❑ First, you can restrict yourself to using only very widely accepted SQL type names such as INTEGER, FLOAT, or VARCHAR, which are likely to work for all databases.

❑ Second, you can use the `java.sql.DatabaseMetaData.getTypeInfo()` method to discover which SQL types are actually supported by a given database, and select a database-specific SQL type name that matches a given JDBC type.

JDBC defines a standard mapping from the JDBC database types to Java types. The Java types do not need to be *exactly* the same as the JDBC types; they just need to be able to represent them with enough type information to correctly store and retrieve parameters, and recover results from SQL statements. For example, a Java `String` object does not precisely match any of the JDBC CHAR types, but it gives enough type information to represent CHAR, VARCHAR, or LONGVARCHAR types successfully.

The following table illustrates the general correspondence between Java data types and SQL types:

Java Type	SQL Type
String	CHAR, VARCHAR, or LONGVARCHAR
java.math.BigDecimal	NUMERIC
boolean	BIT
byte	TINYINT
short	SMALLINT
int	INTEGER
long	BIGINT
float	REAL
double	DOUBLE
byte[]	BINARY, VARBINARY, or LONGVARBINARY
java.sql.Date	DATE
java.sql.Time	TIME
java.sql.Timestamp	TIMESTAMP
Clob	CLOB
Blob	BLOB
Array	ARRAY
Struct	STRUCT
Ref	REF
Java class	JAVA_OBJECT

Accessing a Database Using JDBC

There are several steps you will need to go through, if you want to use JDBC to access a database:

1. Load and register the appropriate JDBC driver with the DriverManager

2. Define the link between the driver and the datasource using a JDBC URL

3. Create a connection object using the JDBC URL

4. Feed a SQL statement into an execute method, which executes the statement

Let's now walk you through these steps, finishing with an example of how we can use JDBC to create the tables we defined earlier.

Loading the JDBC Driver

The `DriverManager` class is the traditional management layer of JDBC, working between the user and the drivers. It keeps track of the drivers that are available on your system, and handles establishing a connection to a database using the appropriate driver.

The first step toward using a driver to make a database connection is obviously to **load** the appropriate driver. To do this, we need to add the driver class to the system property `jdbc.drivers`. Then, as the `DriverManager` class is initialized, it looks for the value of this system property, and if it finds the names of one or more drivers, the `DriverManager` class will attempt to load them.

So how do we add the names of driver classes to the `jdbc.drivers` system property? To do this, we must use the `System.setProperty()` method, like this:

```
System.setProperty("jdbc.drivers","org.gjt.mm.mysql.Driver");
```

Here we are adding the class name of the MM.MySQL driver to the `jdbc.drivers` system property. Note that we can add more than one driver to the property at a time, simply by separating the driver names with commas:

```
System.setProperty("jdbc.drivers",
                   "org.gjt.mm.mysql.Driver"
                   "jdbc.odbc.JdbcOdbcDriver");
```

We added the JDBC-ODBC bridge driver this time too. Now, it may be that you are not allowed to modify this system property in this way, due to the security policy on your system. In this case you need to use a more direct approach, loading the driver explicitly using the `Class.forName()` method:

```
Class.forName("org.gjt.mm.mysql.Driver");
```

When it is loaded, a driver class will usually instantiate a driver object, and register this instance with the `DriverManager` class by calling its `DriverManager.registerDriver()` method automatically. You shouldn't have to call the `registerDriver()` method directly to register a driver class.

JDBC URLs

Our next step on the road to a database connection is to define a JDBC URL that links a driver to a datasource.

Now, you will be used to seeing URLs referring to web sites. For example, the Wrox home page:

http://www.wrox.com

The first part of the URL specifies the protocol used to access information, and a colon always follows it. The rest of a URL gives information about where the data source is located. A JDBC URL is similar, but it provides a way of identifying both a datasource and the JDBC driver we wish to use to connect to it. The standard syntax for a JDBC URL is:

```
jdbc:<subprotocol>:<data source identifier>
```

These three parts of this JDBC URL are:

❑   jdbc – the protocol

❑   `<subprotocol>` – the name of the driver

❑   `<data source identifier>` – the name of the datasource

For example, the JDBC-ODBC bridge driver uses the driver identifier `odbc`. If we have a local data source called `Wrox`, we could create a JDBC URL with the format:

```
jdbc:odbc:wrox
```

A data source on a remote server requires more information than this. If the data source is to be accessed over the Internet, the network address must be included in the JDBC URL as part of the data source identifier.

We can also specify configuration parameters for the connection, by tagging a query string onto the end of the URL, like this:

```
jdbc:odbc:wrox?user=username&password=user_password
```

As with other URL query strings, we start the query string with a question mark, and then we have name-value pairs separated with & characters. You will have guessed that we specified a MySQL username and password here. These and other configurable connection parameters are shown in the table below:

Parameter	Description	Default
user	The username	none
password	The password to be used when connecting	none
autoReconnect	Whether the driver attempts to reconnect if the connection fails first time (true/false)	false

Parameter	Description	Default
maxReconnects	If `autoReconnect` is enabled, the number of reconnect attempts	3
initialTimeout	If `autoReconnect` is enabled, the initial time to wait between reconnects (in seconds)	2
maxRows	The maximum number of rows to return (0 means return all rows)	0
useUnicode	Should the driver use Unicode character encoding when handling strings? (`true`/`false`)	false
characterEncoding	If `useUnicode` is `true`, the character encoding that the driver should use when dealing with strings	none

Making the Connection

Now that we have loaded our driver, and constructed a JDBC URL to link the driver to a data source, we can actually make the connection using the `DriverManager.getConnection()` method. Here's a simple example:

```
String url = "jdbc:odbc:wrox";
Connection con = DriverManager.getConnection(url);
```

Here, we created a JDBC URL `String`, and then fed it into the `getConnection()` method. The `DriverManager` tests each registered driver in turn to see if it can establish a connection. It may sometimes be the case that more than one JDBC driver is capable of connecting to a given URL. The `DriverManager` tries to use each driver in the order it was registered. It tests the drivers by calling the method `Driver.connect()` on each one in turn, passing them the URL that the user originally passed to the method `DriverManager.getConnection()`. The first driver that recognizes the URL makes the connection.

The method returns a connection, or more specifically it returns an object `con` that implements the `java.sql.Connection` interface. The connection object provides a way for you to create and execute SQL commands.

Creating Statements

Once a connection to a particular database is established, then that connection can be used to send SQL statements. To do this, we need to create a statement object that will allow us to create a SQL command and execute it.

There are three kinds of statement object, and all of them are used for executing SQL statements on a given connection:

- ❑ `Statement` objects
- ❑ `PreparedStatement` objects
- ❑ `CallableStatement` objects

Statement objects are objects of a class that implements the `java.sql.Statement` interface, while `PreparedStatement` objects implement the `java.sql.PreparedStatement` interface, and `CallableStatement` objects implement the `java.sql.CallableStatement` interface. You should note that the `PreparedStatement` interface extends the `Statement` interface, and the `CallableStatement` interface extends the `PreparedStatement` interface.

However, we won't be dealing with `PreparedStatement` and `CallableStatement` objects in this chapter; we'll save those for the next chapter. In this chapter we will focus on how to use `Statement` objects to execute statements.

A `Statement` object is created by the `Connection.createStatement()` method. Here's an example:

```
Statement stmt = con.createStatement();
```

Here we have created a `Statement` object called `stmt`, by calling the `createStatement()` method on the `Connection` object called `con`.

Executing Statements

Once we have created a `Statement` object, we can execute a SQL command by calling a variety of execute methods on the object. The correct method to use is determined by what you expect back when the SQL statement is executed. The SQL statement to be sent to the database is supplied as the argument of the execute method.

The `java.sql.Statement` interface provides three different methods for executing SQL statements:

❑   executeUpdate()

The method `executeUpdate()` is used to execute SQL DDL statements such as CREATE TABLE, DROP TABLE, and ALTER TABLE. The return value of the `executeUpdate()` method is an integer (referred to as the update count) that indicates the number of rows that were affected. For statements such as CREATE TABLE or DROP TABLE, which do not operate on rows, the return value of `executeUpdate()` is always zero.

❑   executeQuery()

❑   execute()

The `executeQuery()` method is designed for statements that return a single result set, such as SELECT statements that we will meet in the next chapter. The method `execute()` is used to execute statements that return more than one result set, more than one update count, or a combination of the two. We will see more about these two methods in the next chapter.

Now that we know how to create a database connection using JDBC, and how to execute a SQL command, let's use our knowledge to create the tables we need for our database.

Try It Out – Creating Database Tables Using JDBC

This example demonstrates the use of a `Statement` object that executes an SQL statement. We will use the database `Wrox`, that we created in the previous chapter. The SQL statement in this example creates the `Author`, `Category`, and `Contribution` tables that we designed earlier (we are assuming you created the `Book` table while we played with SQL earlier). We had already created the `Book` table while working on the MySQL prompt. Save the following file as `createTable.java`.

```java
import java.sql.*;

public class CreateTable {
  public static void main(String args[]) {
    Connection con = null;
    try {

      Class.forName("org.gjt.mm.mysql.Driver").newInstance();
      System.out.println("JDBC driver loaded");
      con = DriverManager.getConnection(
      "jdbc:mysql://localhost/wrox ?user=username&password=user_password");
      System.out.println("Database connection established");

      Statement stmt = con.createStatement();
      String upd = "CREATE TABLE Author (
                  Author_ID INTEGER NOT NULL PRIMARY KEY,
                  Author_Name CHAR(50));";
      stmt.executeUpdate(upd);
      System.out.println("Table - Author created");

      upd = "CREATE TABLE Category (
          Category_ID INTEGER NOT NULL PRIMARY KEY,
          Category_Description CHAR(50));";
      stmt.executeUpdate(upd);
      System.out.println("Table - Category created");

      upd = "CREATE TABLE Contribution (
          Contribution_ID INTEGER NOT NULL PRIMARY KEY,
          Title_ID INTEGER,
          Author_ID INTEGER);";
      stmt.executeUpdate(upd);
      System.out.println("Table - Contribution created");

    } catch (ClassNotFoundException cnfe) {
      System.out.println("ClassNotFoundException: Could not locate driver");

    } catch (SQLException cnfe) {
      System.out.println("SQLException: "+cnfe);
    } catch (Exception e) {
      System.out.println("An unknown error occurred while connecting to
                                          the database");
    }finally {
      try {
        if ( con != null )
        con.close();
```

```
        } catch(SQLException sqle) {
          System.out.println("Unable to close database connection.");
        }
      }
    }
  }
```

Remember to change the values of the username and password for accessing your database to suit your system. Place the code in a folder ...\webapps\begjsp-ch15\WEB-INF\classes, and compile the code from this folder. This is what you will see in the command console when you execute this code:

```
> java CreateTable
JDBC driver loaded
Database connection established
Table - Author created
Table - Category created
Table - Contribution created
```

How It Works

We started by loading a JDBC driver and making a connection. We then created an instance of the driver and registered it with the DriverManager.

With JDBC, the DriverManager manages the establishment of connections. The DriverManager needs to be told which JDBC drivers it should try to make connections with. The easiest way to do this is to use Class.forName() on the class that implements the java.sql.Driver interface. With the MM.MySQL driver, the name of this class is org.gjt.mm.mysql.Driver.

Some virtual machines don't properly call some static class initializers. This causes the driver registration to fail when using the Class.forName() method. The work-around is to add the newInstance() call, to assure that their applications will run on all virtual machines:

```
Class.forName("org.gjt.mm.mysql.Driver").newInstance();
```

Then we called the static method DriverManager.getConnection(), which returns the java.sql.Connection object. Obtaining a connection requires a URL for the database.

```
con = DriverManager.getConnection(
"jdbc:mysql://localhost/wrox ?user=username&password=user_password");
```

Note that the JDBC URL has a query string ?user=username&password=user_password at the end. Remember to substitute in your MySQL username and password here.

After obtaining a connection, we use it to create and execute SQL statements that create tables in our database, using the executeUpdate() method. For instance, we first create a Statement object:

```
Statement stmt = con.createStatement();
```

Then we create a String that contains our SQL command:

```
String upd = "CREATE TABLE Author (
                Author_ID INTEGER NOT NULL PRIMARY KEY,
                Author_name CHAR(50), Title_ID INTEGER)";
```

Finally we use `executeUpdate()` to execute the command via JDBC:

```
stmt.executeUpdate(upd);
```

Care should be taken here because the JDBC API is not database-specific, and has been written to provide abstraction for database-application programming; it does not put any restrictions on the kinds of SQL statements that can be sent. Therefore, it is up to you to ensure the underlying database can process the SQL statements being sent. We then repeated the process for the other tables, and finally closed the connection:

```
}finally {
  try {
    if ( con != null )
    con.close();
```

The next thing we would like to do is to populate our tables with data, but we don't yet have the know-how. Let's now dive back into SQL, and learn how to construct statements that will enable us to fill tables with data.

Populating Tables

We are going to finish this chapter by showing you how to insert data into your database, using the `mysql` tool first, and then using JDBC.

Inserting Data Into Tables Using SQL

Let's insert two rows into the `Book` table. To do this, we need to use the `INSERT INTO...VALUES` command. For example, to insert the data for the "Professional Java Data" book, we need to use the following line:

```
mysql> INSERT INTO Book (Title_ID, Category_ID, Title, Price) VALUES
    -> (1,1,'Professional Java Data',59.99);
```

Note how we have specified the fields to place the data in, and then listed the values to go in these fields in the same order. All fields and values are separated by commas.

Let's check that the data has been placed in our table correctly, by using the following command:

```
mysql> SELECT * FROM Book;
+----------+------------------------+-------------+-------+
| Title_ID | Title                  | Category_ID | Price |
+----------+------------------------+-------------+-------+
|        1 | Professional Java Data |           1 | 59.99 |
+----------+------------------------+-------------+-------+
```

This `SELECT * FROM` command summarizes and displays the data in the specified table. The `SELECT` command, used for retrieving data, is very versatile and we will see a lot more of it in Chapter 16.

You should note that we can insert more than one record at a time by using more than one set of values separated by commas, as in the following example:

```
mysql> INSERT INTO Book (Title_ID, Category_ID, Title, Price) VALUES
    -> (1,1,'Professional Java Data',59.99),
    -> (2,1,'Professional Java Security',49.99);
```

Escaping Quotes

You should have noticed that when we insert character data, it must be placed in quotes (single or double). But what happens when there are quotes within the string? The answer is that we must escape the quotes using a \ character, otherwise the string will not be accepted by MySQL. For example, we could use `'I\'m a JSP developer'` or `"I\'m a JSP developer"`, but not `'I'm a JSP developer'`. Actually, we can also use `"I'm a JSP Developer"` too, because as long as the type of quotes (single or double) surrounding the string are different to those inside the string, the string will be accepted.

Modifying Data

Just like how we might want to modify the structure of our tables, we will almost certainly want to modify the data within them at some point. This is achieved using the `UPDATE... SET` command. Let's have an example. To update the price of our first book in the table, we would need to use the following command:

```
mysql> UPDATE Book SET Price = 50.00 WHERE Title_ID = 1;
```

This would change the price of this book to be $50.00.

Deleting Data from Tables

To delete the recently added row, we would use the `DELETE FROM... WHERE` command:

```
mysql> DELETE FROM Book
    -> WHERE Title_ID = 1;
```

Try using the `SELECT` command now:

```
mysql> SELECT * FROM Book;
+----------+----------------------------+-------------+-------+
| Title_ID | Title                      | Category_ID | Price |
+----------+----------------------------+-------------+-------+
|        2 | Professional Java Security |           1 | 49.99 |
+----------+----------------------------+-------------+-------+
```

Since `Title_ID` is a primary key (with unique values), we know that by specifying only records `WHERE Title_ID = 1` will delete only one record. However, this may not always be the case. Let us say we are deleting rows based on `WHERE Category_ID = 1`. In this case all records that contain the value 1 in the `Category_ID` column will also be deleted, which may be several since `Category_ID` is not a uniquely-valued field.

Now that we know the SQL syntax for adding data to our database tables, it's time to learn how to do the same thing from a Java program, using JDBC.

Inserting Data Into Tables Using JDBC

Earlier in the chapter, we saw that we can use the `executeQuery()` method on the `Statement` object to create tables. What we didn't mention was that we can use this same method to insert, delete or modify data too. For example, we can use the following lines to add the first data record to our `Book` table:

```
String upd = "INSERT INTO Book (Title_ID, Category_ID, Title, Price)
              VALUES (1,1,'Professional Java Data',59.99)";
stmt.executeUpdate(upd);
```

This is exactly the same as the code we used to execute a `CREATE TABLE` statement in our example earlier, except that we feed a `String` containing an `INSERT` statement into the `executeUpdate()` method, instead of a `String` containing a `CREATE TABLE` statement. And that's all there is to it, for inserting, deleting, and updating data: we simply substitute the appropriate SQL command into the `String`.

Given that this is all we need to know to insert data using JDBC, let's now populate our tables.

Try It Out – Populating Database Tables Using JDBC

In this example we are going to insert some data into the database tables we created earlier, using JDBC. Open up the earlier `CreateTable.java` file, and modify the lines highlighted below. Then save this new file as `PopulateTable.java`. Note that we are assuming that you are populating the tables from scratch, so if you have anything in them, remove the data using the `DELETE` command described above.

```
import java.sql.*;

public class PopulateTable {
  public static void main(String args[]) {
    Connection con = null;
    try {

      Class.forName("org.gjt.mm.mysql.Driver").newInstance();
      System.out.println("JDBC driver loaded");
      con = DriverManager.getConnection(
      "jdbc:mysql://localhost/wrox ?user=username&password=user_password");
      System.out.println("Database connection established");

      Statement stmt = con.createStatement();
      String upd = "INSERT INTO Book (Title_ID, Category_ID, Title, Price)
                    VALUES (1,1,'Professional Java Data',59.99),
                           (2,1,'Professional Java Security',49.99),
                           (3,1,'Beginning SQL Programming',49.99)";
      stmt.executeUpdate(upd);
      System.out.println("Table - Book populated");

      upd = "INSERT INTO Author (Author_ID, Author_Name) VALUES
            (1,'Danny Ayers'), (2,'John Bell'), (3,'Carl Calvert Bettis'),
```

```
                        (4,'Thomas Bishop'), (5,'Mike Bogovich'), (6,'Matthew Ferris'),
                        (7,'Rick Grehan'), (8,'Bjarki Holm'), (9,'Tony Loton'),
                        (10,'Glen E. Mitchell II'), (11,'Nitin Nanda'),
                        (12,'Kelly Lin Poon'), (13,'Sean Rhody'), (14,'Mark Wilcox'),
                        (15,'Jess Garms'), (16,'Daniel Somerfield'),
                        (17,'John Kauffman'), (18,'Brian Matsik'),
                        (19,'Kevin Spencer'), (20,'Tom Walsh');";
            stmt.executeUpdate(upd);
            System.out.println("Table - Author populated");

            upd = "INSERT INTO Category (Category_ID, Category_Description)
                        VALUES (1,'Java'), (2,'SQL');";
            stmt.executeUpdate(upd);
            System.out.println("Table - Author populated");

        } catch (ClassNotFoundException cnfe) {
            System.out.println("ClassNotFoundException: Could not locate driver");

        } catch (SQLException cnfe) {
            System.out.println("SQLException: "+cnfe);
        } catch (Exception e) {
            System.out.println("An unknown error occurred while connecting to
                                                    the database");
        }finally {
            try {
                if ( con != null )
                con.close();
            } catch(SQLException sqle) {
                System.out.println("Unable to close database connection.");
            }
        }
    }
}
```

As with the previous example, remember to change the values of the username and password to suit your system. Place the code in the ...\webapps\begjsp-ch15\WEB-INF\classes folder and compile it. When you execute this code, you should see this:

```
> java PopulateTable
JDBC driver loaded
Database connection established
Table - Book populated
Table - Author populated
Table - Category populated
```

You can check the contents of each table using the SELECT * FROM command at the mysql prompt. As an example, here's what you get if you use this command on the Category table:

```
mysql> SELECT * FROM Category
+-------------+----------------------+
| Category_ID | Category_Description |
+-------------+----------------------+
|           1 | Java                 |
|           2 | SQL                  |
+-------------+----------------------+
```

How It Works

We aren't going to spend long looking over the script, because we use the same commands over and over but for different tables. As with our previous example we loaded a driver and then created a connection to the `Wrox` database. Then we created a `Statement` object, and a `String` containing our SQL `INSERT` command that we will use to populate a table:

```
String upd = "INSERT INTO Book (Title_ID, Category_ID, Title, Price)
                VALUES (1,1,'Professional Java Data',59.99),
                       (2,1,'Professional Java Security',49.99),
                       (3,1,'Beginning SQL Programming',49.99)";
```

Here we are going to populate the `Book` table. Then we feed this `String` to the `executeUpdate()` method, which initiates the data insertion. Finally we display a message informing the user that the table has been populated:

```
stmt.executeUpdate(upd);
System.out.println("Table - Book populated");
```

Then we do the same kind of thing for the `Author` and `Category` tables too. You probably noticed that we didn't insert data into the `Contribution` table; we leave that as an exercise for you if you wish.

Summary

By now you should have a basic understanding of what a **database** is, and why its high degree of internal organization is preferred over the use of flat files for storing data.

We have also explained what a **relational** database is, and its advantages, and we installed a freely-available relational database management system, MySQL. This led us onto creating commands to manipulate databases, using the SQL language, and we sent SQL commands directly to the database using the `mysql` command-line tool.

However, remembering that our interest was in accessing databases from Java and JSP pages, we then discussed:

- ❑ The different database access models available to Java programmers
- ❑ The Java Database Connectivity API, and its characteristics
- ❑ JDBC drivers
- ❑ Using JDBC in a Java program in order to access a database, adding and populating database tables

In the chapter we ran two Java programs, one that created some database tables, and another that populated the tables. We can now build upon this, working on the database with more advanced features in the next chapter, with more real-life examples. We will also see how JDBC can be used not just with Java programs, but with JSP pages, which was our aim all along.

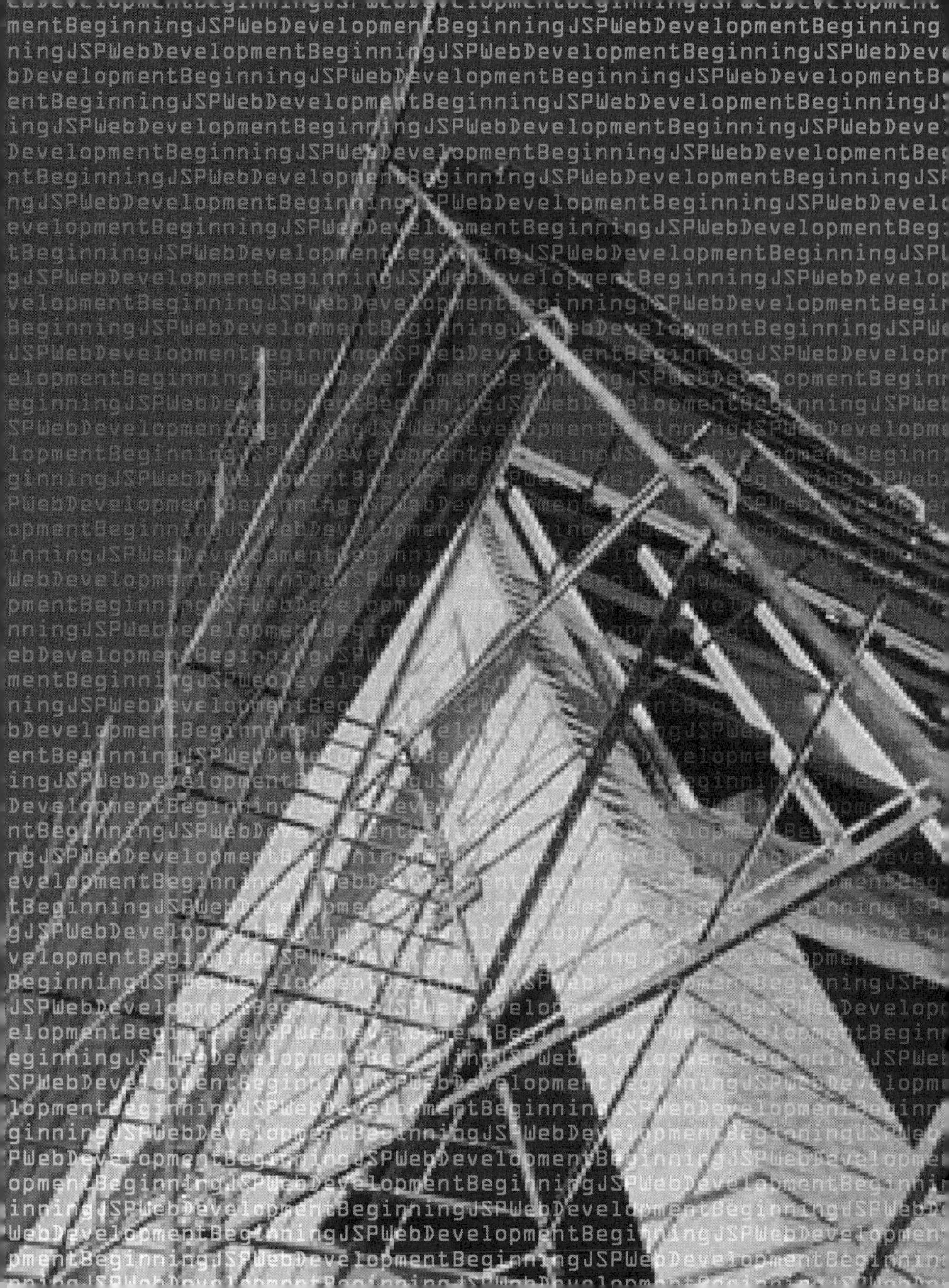

Querying Databases with Java

In the previous chapter we learned a lot about databases: how they store data, how to create and alter tables in a database, and how to insert and update the actual data itself. We also saw how Java provides an API, **JDBC**, to facilitate talking to databases from our applications.

What we didn't see in any detail was how we get the data back *out* of the database, and that's what this chapter will teach you to do. We'll learn both the SQL commands for querying the database and how we can use JDBC to interpret those results and use them in our own Java and JSP applications.

We'll look in turn at:

❑   How to query the database using MySQL's command line interface.

❑   How to do the same using JDBC, from a Java program.

❑   Lots of the hard detail of the SQL code for querying the database, including selecting only certain rows from the database and combining the data from several tables.

❑   Some of the advanced JDBC features that you'll encounter from time to time, including different ways to connect to databases and transactions, an important feature for real-world applications that don't want to let their data get muddled up.

❑   Finally, we'll see how this all fits into web applications with JSP, looking at where we should write our JDBC code and at a freely-available tag library that takes a lot of the hard work out of it.

So, let's get stuck straight in by seeing how we can query our existing Wrox database.

Querying the Database

As we said, you've learned a lot about SQL and databases, but could use some means of getting the data back out of the database again! That's where the SQL SELECT statement comes in. We'll start by looking at the SQL syntax itself, then jump back to Java and see how we can use JDBC to query the database and interpret the results.

SELECT Statement Basics

Continuing with our example from the previous chapter, let's say you have added two more records to the `Book` table and now you want to see the list of all the books in the database. We use the `SELECT` statement to retrieve data – it is probably the SQL statement you will use most often.

For example, let's extract the titles and prices of all the books in the database. The SQL command for this is:

```
mysql> SELECT Title, Price
    -> FROM Book;
+----------------------------+-------+
| Title                      | Price |
+----------------------------+-------+
| Professional Java Data     | 59.99 |
| Professional Java Security | 49.99 |
| Beginning SQL Programming  | 49.99 |
+----------------------------+-------+
3 rows in set (0.04 sec)
```

So what did we do there? We asked to see all the rows from the `Book` table, but only to see the columns called `Title` and `Price`, and we got back a set of rows containing just the data we asked for. Note that the statement, like all the previous SQL statements we've seen, ends with a semicolon (`;`). The general form for a `SELECT` statement that retrieves all of the rows in the table is:

```
SELECT ColumnName, ColumnName, FROM TableName;
```

As we saw in Chapter 15, there is also a special form we can use to get *all* the columns from a table, without having to type all column names:

```
SELECT * FROM TableName;
```

For example we could extract all the data from the `Book` table like this:

```
mysql> SELECT * FROM Book;
+----------+----------------------------+-------------+-------+
| Title_ID | Title                      | Category_ID | Price |
+----------+----------------------------+-------------+-------+
|        1 | Professional Java Data     |           1 | 59.99 |
|        2 | Professional Java Security |           1 | 49.99 |
|        3 | Beginning SQL Programming  |           2 | 49.99 |
+----------+----------------------------+-------------+-------+
3 rows in set (0.00 sec)
```

Note however that using this SELECT * FROM is generally not good practice, as it may return data that we're not actually interested in.

Querying with JDBC

OK, so we know the basic SQL for querying the database. Now how do we do this from Java? We've seen the `Statement` interface's `executeUpdate()` method, used to perform SQL statements like `INSERT`, `UPDATE`, and `DELETE`. That method just returned an `int` value to tell us how things went; to perform a `SELECT` statement from our Java code we'll need to use `Statement`'s `executeQuery()` method, which returns us our query results in the form of an object that implements the `ResultSet` interface.

The ResultSet Interface

So, a `ResultSet` contains the results of executing a SQL query (`SELECT` statement) – in other words, it contains the rows that satisfy the conditions of the query. Whilst there are many methods in the `ResultSet` interface, the basic facilities that you'll use most often are:

❑   The `getXXX()` methods, which allow you to access the various columns of the current row. There are different methods available depending on the data type of the column (for example, `getString()` and `getFloat()`); you can specify which column you're interested in by either its name or, as we'll see later, by its position.

❑   The `next()` method, which is used to move to the next row of the `ResultSet` (if there is a next row).

Try It Out – Querying the Database Using JDBC

Let's see how we can use what we've learned to query our `Wrox` database. Enter this code and save it as `Result.java`:

```
// Result.java

import java.sql.*;

public class Result {
  public static void main(String args[]) {
    Connection con = null;
    try {
      Class.forName("org.gjt.mm.mysql.Driver").newInstance();
      System.out.println("JDBC driver loaded");

      con = DriverManager.getConnection
              ("jdbc:mysql://localhost/wrox?user=root&password=adarsh");
      System.out.println("Database connection established");

      Statement stmt = con.createStatement();

      ResultSet rs = stmt.executeQuery("SELECT Title, Price FROM Book");
      while (rs.next()) {
        String title = rs.getString("Title");
        float price = rs.getFloat("Price");
        System.out.println(title + " " + price);
      }
    } catch (ClassNotFoundException cnfe) {
      System.out.println("ClassNotFoundException: Could not locate driver");
```

```
      } catch (SQLException cnfe) {
        System.out.println("SQLException: Could not connect to database");
      } catch (Exception e) {
        System.out.println
              ("An unknown error occurred while connecting to database");
      } finally {
        try {
          if (con != null) {
            con.close();
          }
        } catch(SQLException sqle) {
          System.out.println("Unable to close database connection.");
        }
      }
    }
  }
}
```

Compile the code by typing javac Result.java, and run it making sure that the MySQL JDBC driver is in your CLASSPATH (as in the previous chapter). The output from the program should be something like the following:

```
JDBC driver loaded
Database connection established
Professional Java Data 59.99
Professional Java Security 49.99
Beginning SQL Programming 49.99
```

How It Works

Just like before, we start by loading the JDBC driver, and creating a Connection object by specifying the JDBC URL to use:

```
Class.forName("org.gjt.mm.mysql.Driver").newInstance();
con = DriverManager.getConnection
          ("jdbc:mysql://localhost/wrox?user=root&password=adarsh");
```

After obtaining the connection we created a Statement object, which we will use to execute the SQL command:

```
Statement stmt = con.createStatement();
```

Now for the new bit: we use the Statement object's executeUpdate() method to perform the query, passing it the SQL code for the query:

```
ResultSet rs = stmt.executeQuery("SELECT Title, Price FROM Book");
```

executeQuery() returns us a ResultSet containing the output from the query. We saw earlier that the SELECT statement returns a set of rows, and so the ResultSet too contains a set of rows of data. It remembers which is its "current row" in the data, and the next() method is used to move it on to the next row.

`next()` returns a `boolean` value, indicating whether there are any more results, and we use this to loop through all the rows of data that were returned:

```
while (rs.next()) {
```

You might think that this code would always skip the first row of results as `next()` is the first thing that gets called; however this isn't the case, as when the `ResultSet` is created it is positioned before the first row. The first time `next()` is called it moves onto the first row.

Finally, for each row we use the `getString()` and `getFloat()` methods to retrieve the values from the `Title` and `Price` columns, and print them out:

```
String title = rs.getString("Title");
float price = rs.getFloat("Price");
System.out.println(title + " " + price);
}
```

ResultSet – The Details

Let's look in some more detail at the `ResultSet` interface and its facilities.

A `ResultSet` maintains a **cursor**, which points to its current row, and moves down one row each time the method `next()` is called. When a `ResultSet` object is first created, the cursor is positioned before the first row, so that as we saw the first call to the `next()` method puts the cursor on the first row. `ResultSet` rows can be retrieved in sequence from top to bottom as the cursor moves down one row with each successive call to the method `next()`.

By default this forward movement is the only way you can move a `ResultSet`'s cursor, and it is the *only* cursor movement possible with drivers that implement the JDBC 1.0 API. This kind of result set returns the value `ResultSet.TYPE_FORWARD_ONLY` from its `getType()` method and is referred to as a **forward-only result set**.

If a driver implements the cursor movement methods in the JDBC 2.0 core API, however, its result sets can be **scrollable**. A scrollable result set's cursor can move both forwards and backwards, as well as to a particular row, using the `previous()`, `first()`, `last()`, `absolute()`, `relative()`, `afterLast()`, and `beforeFirst()` methods.

The previous example demonstrated moving the cursor forward. It is also possible to iterate through a result set backwards, for example by replacing the `while` loop in the previous code with the following:

```
rs.afterLast();
while (rs.previous()) {
  System.out.println(rs.getString("Title") +" " + rs.getFloat("Price"));
}
```

The cursor is first moved to the very end of the result set (with the method `afterLast()`), and then the method `previous()` is invoked within a `while` loop to iterate through the contents of the result set by moving to the previous row with each iteration. The method `previous()` returns `false` when there are no more rows, so the loop ends after all the rows have been visited.

We have already used the `ResultSet.getXXX()` methods for retrieving column values from the current row in the above code fragment. It is always advisable with the forward-only result sets to retrieve the column values in order from left to right, but with scrollable result setsthere are no such restrictions.

Either the column name or the column number can be used to designate the column from which to retrieve data. For example, if the second column of a `ResultSet` object `rs` is named `Title`, and it stores values as strings, either of the following will retrieve the value stored in that column:

```
String s = rs.getString(2);
String s = rs.getString("TITLE");
```

Note that columns are numbered from left to right, starting with column 1. Also, column names used as input to `getXXX()` methods are case insensitive.

If the name of a column is known but not its index, the method `findColumn()` can be used to find the column number. Information about the columns in a `ResultSet` is available by calling the method `ResultSet.getMetaData()`, which returns a `ResultSetMetaData` object giving the number, types, and properties of the `ResultSet` object's columns.

Advanced Queries

Having seen how to manipulate the results of our queries, let's return to the SQL syntax for a bit and see how we can create more complicated queries that do more than just return all the rows from a single table.

Conditional Selection

The first step to enhancing our queries is to be able to restrict ourselves to retrieving only certain rows from a table. To help us explore this conditional selection of rows, let's add some more data to the `Book` table, so that it looks like this:

```
mysql> SELECT * FROM Book;
+----------+----------------------------------+-------------+-------+
| Title_ID | Title                            | Category_ID | Price |
+----------+----------------------------------+-------------+-------+
|        1 | Professional Java Data           |           1 | 59.99 |
|        2 | Professional Java Security       |           1 | 49.99 |
|        3 | Beginning SQL Programming        |           2 | 49.99 |
|        4 | Beginning Java Objects           |           1 | 39.99 |
|        5 | Beginning Java 2 - JDK 1.3 Edition |         1 | 49.99 |
|        6 | Java Programmer's Reference       |          1 | 34.99 |
|        7 | Professional ASP.NET             |           3 | 59.99 |
+----------+----------------------------------+-------------+-------+
7 rows in set (0.00 sec)
```

Relational Operators

There are six relational operators in SQL, which behave very much like the Java operators:

Symbol	Meaning
=	Equal to
<>	Not equal to
<	Less than
>	Greater than
<=	Less than or equal to
>=	Greater than or equal to

The WHERE clause is used to specify that only certain rows of the table are to be retrieved, based on criteria described in that WHERE clause. It is most easily understood by looking at a couple of examples.

Firstly, looking at the above data you'll see that Java books all have the value 1 in their Category_ID column. To retrieve only the Java books we could use the "equal to" operator:

```
mysql> SELECT Title, Price FROM Book
    -> WHERE Category_ID = 1;
+------------------------------------+-------+
| Title                              | Price |
+------------------------------------+-------+
| Professional Java Data             | 59.99 |
| Professional Java Security         | 49.99 |
| Beginning Java Objects             | 39.99 |
| Beginning Java 2 - JDK 1.3 Edition | 49.99 |
| Java Programmer's Reference        | 34.99 |
+------------------------------------+-------+
5 rows in set (0.04 sec)
```

Note that the equal to operator in SQL is a *single* =, not == like in Java. The = operator works just as well on text columns; for example if we wanted to know the price of *Beginning Java Objects* we could use the following SQL:

```
mysql> SELECT Price FROM Book
    -> WHERE Title = 'Beginning Java Objects';
+-------+
| Price |
+-------+
| 39.99 |
+-------+
1 row in set (0.00 sec)
```

We can also, of course, use the other relational operators. For example, to see those books that cost $49.99 or more we can use:

477

```
mysql> SELECT Title, Price FROM Book
    -> WHERE Price >= 49.99;
+------------------------------------+-------+
| Title                              | Price |
+------------------------------------+-------+
| Professional Java Data             | 59.99 |
| Professional Java Security         | 49.99 |
| Beginning SQL Programming          | 49.99 |
| Beginning Java 2 - JDK 1.3 Edition | 49.99 |
| Professional ASP.NET               | 59.99 |
+------------------------------------+-------+
5 rows in set (0.00 sec)
```

Logical Operators

In addition to the relational operators we've just seen, there are various logical operators that allow us to combine conditions: AND, OR, and NOT.

The AND operator joins two or more conditions, and displays a row only if that row's data satisfies all the conditions. For example, to list the Java books (in other words, having a Category_ID of 1) that cost $49.99 or more we would use:

```
mysql> SELECT Title FROM Book
    -> WHERE Price >= 49.99
    -> AND Category_ID = 1;
+------------------------------------+
| Title                              |
+------------------------------------+
| Professional Java Data             |
| Professional Java Security         |
| Beginning Java 2 - JDK 1.3 Edition |
+------------------------------------+
3 rows in set (0.02 sec)
```

The OR operator joins two or more conditions, but returns a row if *any* of the conditions listed hold true. To see books that cost less than $40 or are on SQL (a Category_ID of 2) we should use the following query:

```
mysql> SELECT Title FROM Book
    -> WHERE Price < 40.00
    -> OR Category_ID = 2;
+----------------------------+
| Title                      |
+----------------------------+
| Beginning SQL Programming  |
| Beginning Java Objects     |
| Java Programmer's Reference |
+----------------------------+
3 rows in set (0.00 sec)
```

Note that this list includes *Beginning SQL Programming* even though it costs $49.99.

The NOT operator displays a row only if that row's data does not satisfy the condition. To display all books that are not about SQL, use:

```
mysql> SELECT Title FROM Book
    -> WHERE NOT (Category_ID = 2);
+-----------------------------------+
| Title                             |
+-----------------------------------+
| Professional Java Data            |
| Professional Java Security        |
| Beginning Java Objects            |
| Beginning Java 2 - JDK 1.3 Edition |
| Java Programmer's Reference       |
| Professional ASP.NET              |
+-----------------------------------+
6 rows in set (0.00 sec)
```

Operators can be combined, for example:

```
mysql> SELECT Title FROM Book
    -> WHERE Category_ID = 1 AND Price < 40 OR Price > 45;
+-----------------------------------+
| Title                             |
+-----------------------------------+
| Professional Java Data            |
| Professional Java Security        |
| Beginning SQL Programming         |
| Beginning Java Objects            |
| Beginning Java 2 - JDK 1.3 Edition |
| Java Programmer's Reference       |
| Professional ASP.NET              |
+-----------------------------------+
7 rows in set (0.00 sec)
```

The SQL engine selects the list of rows that satisfy the condition where the Category_ID is 1 and the Price is less than $40. Then, this new list is tested for the OR condition (that is, Price greater than $45), and the resultant list is displayed. SQL evaluates all of the individual conditions, then applies the NOT operator, then evaluates the AND "pairs", and finally evaluates the OR pairs (where both operators evaluate left to right).

To perform ORs before ANDs, use parentheses:

```
mysql> SELECT Title FROM Book
    -> WHERE Category_ID = 1 AND (Price < 40 OR Price > 45);
+-----------------------------------+
| Title                             |
+-----------------------------------+
| Professional Java Data            |
| Professional Java Security        |
| Beginning Java Objects            |
| Beginning Java 2 - JDK 1.3 Edition |
| Java Programmer's Reference       |
+-----------------------------------+
5 rows in set (0.00 sec)
```

Using IN and BETWEEN

An easier method of using compound conditions uses the IN and BETWEEN keywords. To select books that have a Category_ID of either 1 or 2 (Java or SQL), you can use the IN operator:

```
mysql> SELECT Title FROM Book
    -> WHERE Category_ID IN (1,2);
+-----------------------------------+
| Title                             |
+-----------------------------------+
| Professional Java Data            |
| Professional Java Security        |
| Beginning SQL Programming         |
| Beginning Java Objects            |
| Beginning Java 2 - JDK 1.3 Edition |
| Java Programmer's Reference       |
+-----------------------------------+
6 rows in set (0.02 sec)
```

The BETWEEN operator allows you to check for a range of values; if you wanted to list all books costing between $40 and $50, use:

```
mysql> SELECT Title FROM Book
    -> WHERE Price BETWEEN 40 and 50;
+-----------------------------------+
| Title                             |
+-----------------------------------+
| Professional Java Security        |
| Beginning SQL Programming         |
| Beginning Java 2 - JDK 1.3 Edition |
+-----------------------------------+
3 rows in set (0.00 sec)
```

To list the books that are not in this range:

```
mysql> SELECT Title FROM Book
    -> WHERE Price NOT BETWEEN 40 and 50;
+----------------------------+
| Title                      |
+----------------------------+
| Professional Java Data     |
| Beginning Java Objects     |
| Java Programmer's Reference |
| Professional ASP.NET       |
+----------------------------+
4 rows in set (0.00 sec)
```

Similarly, NOT IN lists all rows excluded from the IN list.

Using LIKE

The LIKE operator allows us to perform inexact textual comparisons. Let's see how we can select all the Wrox *Beginning ...* books from our database:

```
mysql> SELECT Title FROM Book
    -> WHERE Title LIKE 'Beginning %';
+----------------------------------+
| Title                            |
+----------------------------------+
| Beginning SQL Programming        |
| Beginning Java Objects           |
| Beginning Java 2 - JDK 1.3 Edition |
+----------------------------------+
3 rows in set (0.01 sec)
```

The percent sign (%) is used to represent any possible character (number, letter, or punctuation) or set of characters that might appear after the word Beginning.

The % character can occur in any position you like within the string of characters to be matched; for example, to find all the books whose titles contain the word Java, use '%Java%'. NOT LIKE displays rows that do *not* fit the given description. There is also a second special character, the question mark (?), which matches any single character in the column being matched. For example, '?SP' would match JSP or ASP.

Joining Tables

A **join** enables you to match a row from one table up with a row in another table. As we saw in the previous chapter, good database design suggests that each table contains data only about a single entity; in a relational database we can use several tables and a join to represent more complex data.

The basic form of join is what is called as the **inner join**; there is also an **outer join**, which is less commonly used and which we will not explore further.

Let's look again at our sample database, this time having added some values into the Category table:

```
mysql> SELECT * FROM Book;
+----------+------------------------------+-------------+-------+
| Title_ID | Title                        | Category_ID | Price |
+----------+------------------------------+-------------+-------+
|        1 | Professional Java Data       |           1 | 59.99 |
|        2 | Professional Java Security   |           1 | 49.99 |
|        3 | Beginning SQL Programming    |           2 | 49.99 |
|        4 | Beginning Java Objects       |           1 | 39.99 |
|        5 | Beginning Java 2 - JDK 1.3 Edition |     1 | 49.99 |
|        6 | Java Programmer's Reference  |           1 | 34.99 |
|        7 | Professional ASP.NET         |           3 | 59.99 |
+----------+------------------------------+-------------+-------+
7 rows in set (0.00 sec)

mysql> SELECT * FROM Category;
+-------------+----------------------+
| Category_ID | Category_Description |
+-------------+----------------------+
|           1 | Java                 |
|           2 | SQL                  |
|           3 | ASP                  |
+-------------+----------------------+
3 rows in set (0.00 sec)
```

You can see here that these two tables are related to each other; the `Book` table has a column, `Category_ID`, which relates each book to one of the categories listed in the `Category` table. The `Category` table's `Category_ID` column is its **primary key**; the column of the same name in the `Book` table is a **foreign key** as it refers to one of the primary key values in a different ("foreign") table.

The primary and foreign keys help us to create the relationship of data across tables, without having to repeat the same data in every table; this is the power of relational databases. For example, you can find the category description of a book without having to list the full description of the category in the `Book` table. Instead, you can use the `Category_ID` column to relate the data in the two tables.

For example, the query below lists all books and their category descriptions:

```
mysql> SELECT Book.Title, Category.Category_Description, Book.Price
    -> FROM Book, Category
    -> WHERE Book.Category_ID = Category.Category_ID;
+------------------------------------+----------------------+-------+
| Title                              | Category_Description | Price |
+------------------------------------+----------------------+-------+
| Professional Java Data             | Java                 | 59.99 |
| Professional Java Security         | Java                 | 49.99 |
| Beginning Java Objects             | Java                 | 39.99 |
| Beginning Java 2 - JDK 1.3 Edition | Java                 | 49.99 |
| Java Programmer's Reference        | Java                 | 34.99 |
| Beginning SQL Programming          | SQL                  | 49.99 |
| Professional ASP.NET               | ASP                  | 59.99 |
+------------------------------------+----------------------+-------+
7 rows in set (0.00 sec)
```

Note that both tables involved in the relation are listed in the `FROM` clause of the statement. Secondly, note how the ID columns are related from one table to the next by use of the `WHERE` `Book.Category_ID = Category.Category_ID` clause. Only where IDs match across tables will the descriptions from the `Category` table be listed. Because the joining condition used an equal sign, this join is called an equi-join. (Other types of join are possible, but are outside the scope of this book.)

We used the 'dot' notation, prefixing the table names to the column names to avoid ambiguity. If the column names are different in each table, however, this will not be necessary.

Aliases

As we saw in the previous example, when you use column names that are fully qualified with their table and column name the names can grow to be quite unwieldy. SQL allows you to use an **aliased name**, usually shorter and more descriptive, in place of the longer name. This is done using the `AS` keyword:

```
SELECT Book.Title AS Title, Category.Category_Description AS Category, Book.Price
AS Price,
Book.Category_ID, Category.Category_ID
FROM Book, Category
WHERE Book.Category_ID = Category.Category_ID;
```

What we have done is provided aliases for column names; likewise, table aliasing is also permitted.

Miscellaneous SQL Features

SELECT also supports the concept of functions. There are several built-in functions that can operate upon the table, returning the computed value or values. With some functions, the value returned depends on whether you want to receive a numerical or string value. This is regarded as the context of the function. When selecting values to be displayed to you, only text context is used, but when selecting data to be inserted into a field or to be used as the argument of another function, the context depends upon what the receiver is expecting. For instance, selecting data to be inserted into a numerical field will place the function into a numerical context, but when returning values from a query the SUM() function returns a string, rather than a number.

Aggregate Functions

There are five important aggregate functions: SUM(), AVG(), MAX(), MIN(), and COUNT(). They are called aggregate functions because they summarize the results of a query, rather than listing all of the rows.

Function	Description
SUM()	Gives the total value of the given column's values that match any condition that was specified
AVG()	Gives the average value of the given column's rows that match any condition that was specified
MAX()	Gives the largest figure in the given column that matches any condition that was specified
MIN()	Gives the smallest figure in the given column that matches any condition that was specified
COUNT(*)	Gives the number of rows satisfying any condition that was specified

Let's see how we can use these functions on the tables in our Wrox database:

```
mysql> SELECT SUM(Price), AVG(Price)
    -> FROM Book;
+------------+------------+
| SUM(Price) | AVG(Price) |
+------------+------------+
|     344.93 |  49.275714 |
+------------+------------+
1 row in set (0.04 sec)
```

This query shows the total price of one copy of each title, and the average price of all of the books in the table.

```
mysql> SELECT MIN(Price) FROM Book
    -> WHERE Category_ID = 1;
+------------+
| MIN(Price) |
+------------+
|      34.99 |
+------------+
1 row in set (0.00 sec)
```

This query returns the price of the cheapest Java book.

```
mysql> SELECT COUNT(*)
    -> FROM Book
    -> WHERE Category_ID = 1;
+----------+
| COUNT(*) |
+----------+
|        5 |
+----------+
1 row in set (0.00 sec)
```

This query tells you how many Wrox Java books are in the database.

You may be wondering what these functions gain you: if we want to find out how many Java books there are, why not just returns a list of all of them and then write some Java code that counts how many times next() return true? The answer comes when you consider what would happen if, instead of having 7 rows, our Book table had tens of thousands of rows. Then, transferring all that data across the network from the database to our Java program, only for it to be counted and then discarded, would be wasteful in the extreme. These functions allow you to improve performance by moving some of the processor-intensive operations into the database itself.

In addition to the above listed aggregate functions, some DBMS's allow more functions to be used in SELECT lists. You should consult your database documentation for details of these.

GROUP BY

There are a few other SQL keywords that we ought to mention before we leave the subject of queries. One is the GROUP BY keyword, used to associate an aggregate function (especially COUNT(*)) with groups of rows, so that COUNT(*) counts the number of rows in each group rather than in total.

Our Book table has a column named Price, containing the price of each title. The GROUP BY clause allows us to find out the price of the most expensive book in each category. To do this we tell it to group the books together based on their Category_ID, then find the maximum price in each group:

```
mysql> SELECT Category_ID, MAX(Price)
    -> FROM Book
    -> GROUP BY Category_ID;
+-------------+------------+
| Category_ID | MAX(Price) |
+-------------+------------+
|           1 |      59.99 |
|           2 |      49.99 |
|           3 |      59.99 |
+-------------+------------+
3 rows in set (0.05 sec)
```

ORDER BY

The ORDER BY clause allows us to change the order in which results are returned. For example, let's return the books, sorted by price:

```
mysql> SELECT Title, Price FROM Book
    -> ORDER BY Price;
+-----------------------------------+-------+
| Title                             | Price |
+-----------------------------------+-------+
| Java Programmer's Reference       | 34.99 |
| Beginning Java Objects            | 39.99 |
| Professional Java Security        | 49.99 |
| Beginning SQL Programming         | 49.99 |
| Beginning Java 2 - JDK 1.3 Edition| 49.99 |
| Professional Java Data            | 59.99 |
| Professional ASP.NET              | 59.99 |
+-----------------------------------+-------+
7 rows in set (0.00 sec)
```

We can also sort them in descending order of price, by adding the DESC keyword:

```
mysql> SELECT Title, Price FROM Book
    -> ORDER BY Price DESC;
+-----------------------------------+-------+
| Title                             | Price |
+-----------------------------------+-------+
| Professional Java Data            | 59.99 |
| Professional ASP.NET              | 59.99 |
| Professional Java Security        | 49.99 |
| Beginning SQL Programming         | 49.99 |
| Beginning Java 2 - JDK 1.3 Edition| 49.99 |
| Beginning Java Objects            | 39.99 |
| Java Programmer's Reference       | 34.99 |
+-----------------------------------+-------+
7 rows in set (0.00 sec)
```

Finally, let's see how we can sort by more than one column. Here we're printing out the title, price, and category description of every book; they are ordered first by the category they're in, then in descending order of price:

```
mysql> SELECT Book.Title, Book.Price,
    -> Category.Category_Description AS Category
    -> FROM Book, Category
    -> WHERE Book.Category_ID = Category.Category_ID
    -> ORDER BY Category, Book.Price DESC;
+-----------------------------------+-------+----------+
| Title                             | Price | Category |
+-----------------------------------+-------+----------+
| Professional ASP.NET              | 59.99 | ASP      |
| Professional Java Data            | 59.99 | Java     |
| Beginning Java 2 - JDK 1.3 Edition| 49.99 | Java     |
| Professional Java Security        | 49.99 | Java     |
| Beginning Java Objects            | 39.99 | Java     |
| Java Programmer's Reference       | 34.99 | Java     |
| Beginning SQL Programming         | 49.99 | SQL      |
+-----------------------------------+-------+----------+
7 rows in set (0.01 sec)
```

Try It Out – Using Advanced SQL Queries with JDBC

It's been a while since we saw some Java, but in fact any of the SELECT statements we've seen could be called from Java, using JDBC. Let's see how that would work for this last example; enter the following code and save it as ComplexQuery.java:

```java
// ComplexQuery.java

import java.sql.*;

public class ComplexQuery {
  public static void main(String args[]) {
    Connection con = null;
    try {
      Class.forName("org.gjt.mm.mysql.Driver").newInstance();
      System.out.println("JDBC driver loaded");

      con = DriverManager.getConnection
              ("jdbc:mysql://localhost/wrox?user=admin&password=admin");
      System.out.println("Database connection established");

      Statement stmt = con.createStatement();

      ResultSet rs = stmt.executeQuery
              ("SELECT Book.Title, Book.Price," +
                "Category.Category_Description AS Category " +
                "FROM Book, Category " +
                "WHERE Book.Category_ID = Category.Category_ID " +
                "ORDER BY Category, Book.Price DESC;");
      while (rs.next()) {
        String title = rs.getString("Book.Title");
        float price = rs.getFloat("Book.Price");
        String category = rs.getString("Category");
        System.out.println(title + " costs $" + price +
                          " and is in category " + category);
      }
    } catch (ClassNotFoundException cnfe) {
      System.out.println("ClassNotFoundException: Could not locate driver");
    } catch (SQLException cnfe) {
      System.out.println("SQLException: Could not connect to database");
    } catch (Exception e) {
      System.out.println
              ("An unknown error occurred while connecting to database");
    } finally {
      try {
        if (con != null) {
          con.close();
        }
      } catch(SQLException sqle) {
        System.out.println("Unable to close database connection.");
      }
    }
  }
}
```

Compile the code by typing javac ComplexQuery.java and run it, again making sure that the MySQL JDBC driver is in your CLASSPATH. The output from the program should be something like the following:

```
JDBC driver loaded
Database connection established
Professional ASP.NET costs $59.99 and is in category ASP
Professional Java Data costs $59.99 and is in category Java
Beginning Java 2 - JDK 1.3 Edition costs $49.99 and is in category Java
Professional Java Security costs $49.99 and is in category Java
Beginning Java Objects costs $39.99 and is in category Java
Java Programmer's Reference costs $34.99 and is in category Java
Beginning SQL Programming costs $49.99 and is in category SQL
```

How It Works

This example works just like the previous one! The only things we changed were the actual text of the SQL query, and which columns we retrieve within the while loop. Other than that, this complex query works just the same under JDBC as our first SELECT Title, Price FROM Book query!

Views, Indices, and Subqueries

It's not feasible to give you full coverage of SQL syntax in the space of one chapter, and so some less-used features will of necessity by omitted. Notable among these are **views**, **indices**, and **subqueries**.

❑ A **view** allows you to assign the results of a query to a new, "virtual" table that you can use in other queries and specify in their FROM clauses like any other table. Views can be used to restrict database access, as well as to simplify a complex query. MySQL does not currently support views, but if it did we could create and use a view Titles like this:

```
CREATE VIEW Titles AS SELECT Title FROM Book;
SELECT title FROM Titles;
```

❑ **Indices** help the database store data in a way that makes for quicker searches and makes data access quicker. The index is a special data structure in the database that tells the DBMS where a certain row is in the table, given the value of an indexed column; this is much like the way a book index tells you what page a given word appears. Unfortunately, you sacrifice disk space and modification speed for the benefit of quicker searches.

The most efficient use of indices is to create an index for columns on which you tend to search the most. Let's create an index for the title in the Book table:

```
CREATE INDEX TITLE_IDX ON Book (Title);
```

❑ **Subqueries** involve the use of operators to allow a WHERE condition to include the output from a second query (the "subquery"). The query below lists the buyers who purchased an expensive item (an item costing at least $50 more than the average price of all the items purchased):

```
SELECT Buyer_ID FROM Buyer
WHERE Price >
(SELECT AVG(Price) + 50 FROM Book);
```

Deleting Tables, Indexes, and Databases

The DROP command is used when we want to delete tables, indexes, and even entire databases. To delete an index, we simply type:

```
DROP INDEX TITLE_IDX;
```

It's just as easy to get rid of a table, or a database:

```
DROP TABLE Author;
DROP DATABASE Wrox;
```

SQL in Retrospect

We've seen a lot of SQL in the last section, particularly the SELECT statement. Using SQL you can search for data, enter new data, modify data, or delete data. SQL is simply the most fundamental tool you will need for your interaction with the database.

Whilst we've seen a lot of use of the MySQL command-line interface, all of these SQL commands can equally well be called by a Java program using JDBC, and the Statement and ResultSet interfaces. Let's move back to the Java side, and look at more JDBC features.

More On JDBC

JDBC is a trademarked name and is not an acronym, but it is often thought of as standing for **Java DataBase Connectivity**. The **JDBC API** is an application-programming interface for the Java programming language. It provides the basic functionality for data access and provides a standard way to access the latest object-relational features being supported by today's relational database management systems. In addition, the latest version provides advanced features such as scrolling updateable result sets, connection pooling, and distributed transactions. These advanced features will be covered later in the chapter.

The complete JDBC API includes both the java.sql package (the **Core API**) and the javax.sql package (the **Optional Package**, formerly called the **Standard Extension**). The core API is part of the Java 2 Platform, Standard Edition and the optional package can be downloaded from http://java.sun.com/products/jdbc/download.html – look for the JDBC 2.0 Optional Package Binary section on the page.

Apart from the core functionality of JDBC, we have a few other classes and interfaces that support it. The SQLException class extends java.lang.Exception with added functionality to provide information about the database error; its SQLState property describes the error as defined by the SQL specification. The vendor error code, returned by the getErrorCode() method, is an integer which has meaning only with reference to the database vendor manual.

JDBC provides an extension to the SQLException class called SQLWarning, which deals with any non-fatal errors that should not halt application processing.

Let's recap what we have learned about JDBC so far:

- ❑ It consists of a set of classes and interfaces written in the Java programming language that provide a standard API for developers to write industrial-strength database applications. One can write a single program using the JDBC API, and the program will be able to send SQL or other statements to the appropriate data source.

- ❑ In simple terms the JDBC API, with the appropriate driver, makes it possible to do three things:

  - ❑ Establish a connection with a data source.

  - ❑ Send queries and update statements to the data source.

  - ❑ Process the results.

- ❑ The JDBC API supports both two-tier and three-tier models for database access, depending on the driver type.

- ❑ JDBC defines a standard mapping from the JDBC database types to Java types. The Java types do not need to be exactly equivalent to the JDBC types; they just need to be able to represent them with enough type information to correctly store and recover data.

- ❑ The DriverManager class is the traditional management layer of JDBC, working between the user and the drivers. It keeps track of the drivers that are available and handles establishing a connection between a database and the appropriate driver.

Now let us look again at some aspects of how an application uses JDBC as the interface through which it passes all its requests to the database.

Database Connections

The main classes and interfaces traditionally involved in making a connection to the database are:

- ❑ The java.sql.Driver interface – Responds to connection requests from the DriverManager and provides information about its implementation.

- ❑ The java.sql.DriverManager class – Maintains a list of Driver implementations.

- ❑ The java.sql.Connection interface – Represents a single logical database connection.

The only driver-specific information JDBC requires from your application is the database URL. Using the database URL, a user ID, and a password, your application requests a Connection from the DriverManager. The DriverManager searches through the known Driver implementations; all being well, one of them recognizes your URL and provides the DriverManager with an instance of a class that implements Connection, which in turn is passed back to the application.

For simple applications, the only method in the DriverManager class that you need to use directly is DriverManager.getConnection(). As its name implies, this method establishes a connection to a database. As we saw in the last chapter, drivers are loaded either by setting the jdbc.drivers system property or by using the Class.forName() method call.

This process of passing a driver name and the URL for obtaining a connection seems to be unnecessarily complex when you are trying to write database independent code. Details like registering-drivers should be abstracted away from the application, and this is made possible with the **Java Naming and Directory Interface** (**JNDI**) and the JDBC Optional Package.

Naming and Directory Services

So just what is this JNDI? A **naming service** is used to map logical names to things like files, servers, and even Java objects; a **directory service** is an extension of a naming service that allows naming service entries to have attributes. The most common directory services are NIS, Microsoft Active Directory, and LDAP. JNDI is the Java API that allows you to access naming and directory services in a transparent way.

The standard JDBC connection procedure requires that you provide a URL, and register a JDBC driver – however, this requires your code to be aware of the name of the driver, and its URL. The JDBC 2.0 Optional Package contains a new interface, `javax.sql.DataSource`, that encapsulates all the information necessary to create a JDBC connection. A `DataSource` implementation can be stored in a JNDI naming service, from where your application can retrieve it. Then, simply changing the directory entry can change the details of database connectivity, and the application is never aware of it.

Connection Pooling

`DataSources` are also closely associated with **connection pooling**. Connection pooling is a mechanism whereby, when an application closes a connection, the connection is recycled rather than being destroyed. Because establishing a connection to the database can be a time-consuming operation, reusing connections can improve performance dramatically by cutting down on the number of new connections that need to be created. A connection pool is a repository of database connections that can be shared, as required, between all components of an application.

In a standalone application (an application that is started using the `main()` method), a connection is typically created once and kept open until the application is shut-down, because a standalone application serves only one user at a time. But this does no good in real-world server applications, which may have many concurrent connections to the database because they may have many concurrent users.

The interfaces that implement Java's connection pooling mechanism are:

- ❑ `javax.sql.DataSource` – This is an alternative to the `DriverManager` facility. A `DataSource` object represents a database, and is a preferred way to get a `Connection`. The class that implements the interface can provide connection-pooling capabilities.

- ❑ `javax.sql.ConnectionPoolDataSource` – This interface extends `DataSource` and is a factory for `PooledConnection` objects. An object that implements this interface will typically be registered with a naming service that is based on JNDI.

- ❑ `javax.sql.PooledConnection` (Interface) – A `PooledConnection` object represents a physical connection to a data source. When the application asks the `DataSource` for a `Connection` it creates a `PooledConnection` object, or gets a new one from its `ConnectionPoolDataSource`.

Using a DataSource

Using a `DataSource` implementation is better than using `DriverManager`, for two important reasons:

- ❑ It makes code more portable
- ❑ It makes code easier to maintain

You can use a `Connection` object produced by a `DataSource` object in just the same way you use one produced by the `DriverManager`; as the application developer, all you need to know about how a `PooledConnection` differs from a regular `Connection` object is that, when the application calls the `close()` method, the physical connection to the database is not closed; instead, the pooled connection is returned to the pool.

A `DataSource` object represents a real world data source, which can be anything from a relational database to a spreadsheet or a file in tabular format. When a `DataSource` object has been registered with a JNDI naming service, you can retrieve it from the naming service and use it to make a connection to the data source it represents.

The information about the `DataSource` is stored in the form of properties within the object, making the application more portable because it does not need to hard-code the driver and URL name. It also makes maintaining the code easier because if, for example, the data source is moved to a different server, all that needs to be done is to update the relevant property: the code using that data source need not be altered.

A systems administrator will normally register the data source with a JNDI naming service and set its properties. As part of the registration process, the systems administrator will associate the `DataSource` object with a logical name, which can be almost anything – usually, it's a name that describes the data source and that is easy to remember. In the example that follows, the logical name for the data source is `WroxDB`. By convention, logical names for `DataSource` objects are preceded by `jdbc/`, so the full logical name in this example is `jdbc/WroxDB`.

So, how do we connect to this data source? The first two highlighted lines below use the JNDI API to get the `DataSource` object; the third line uses JDBC API to get the connection:

```
import javax.naming.*;
import java.sql.*;
import javax.sql.*;

try {
  Context ctx = new InitialContext();
  DataSource ds = (DataSource) ctx.lookup("jdbc/WroxDB");
  Connection con = ds.getConnection("Userid", "Password");
} catch (NamingException e) {
  System.out.println("Oops, the lookup didn't work");
} catch (SQLException e) {
  System.out.println("Oops, we got a SQL Exception");
}
```

Because of the advantages it offers, using a `DataSource` object is the recommended way to obtain a connection. Also, there is virtually no difference in the code for using a pooled connection. The only change is that the connection should be closed in a `finally` block because, even if a method throws an exception, the connection will be closed and put back into the connection pool. The code for the `finally` block should look like this:

```
finally {
  try {
    if (con != null) {
      con.close();
```

```
    }
  } catch(SQLException sqle) {
    System.out.println("Unable to close database connection.");
  }
}
```

Notice that Connection's close() method can itself throw a SQLException, which we have to handle too.

Accessing the Database

We saw in the previous chapter that a Statement object is used to send SQL statements to a database once a connection is obtained. And there are in fact three kinds of Statement object in JDBC:

❑   java.sql.Statement – The most fundamental of the three JDBC interfaces representing SQL statements. It will run all of the basic SQL statements.

❑   java.sql.PreparedStatement – This interface extends Statement and enables our SQL statements to contain parameters, so we can execute a single statement repeatedly with different values for those parameters.

❑   java.sql.CallableStatement – This interface extends PreparedStatement and is similar to it, but allows us to access **stored procedures** in our database. (These are a special way of embedding bits of program code in the database, for speed.) Stored procedures are an advanced database concept and we won't be exploring them any further in this book.

The PreparedStatement Interface

The PreparedStatement interface extends Statement, and an instance of PreparedStatement contains an SQL statement that has already been compiled. The SQL statement contained in a PreparedStatement object may have one or more parameters, so that the application can dynamically assign values to it.

The value is not specified when the SQL statement is created. Instead, the statement has a question mark (?) as a placeholder for each parameter. An application must set a value for each parameter in a prepared statement before executing the statement. Execution of PreparedStatement objects is faster than that of Statement objects, so a PreparedStatement is often used when a particular SQL statement needs to be executed many times.

When creating a Statement we don't have to supply the actual SQL statement to be run; that's done when calling the executeUpdate(), executeQuery(), or execute() methods. With PreparedStatement, on the other hand, the SQL code must be supplied when the object is first created, by passing it to the Connection.prepareStatement() method. The statement-execution methods for a PreparedStatement don't require any parameters.

The following code fragment creates a PreparedStatement object containing an SQL UPDATE statement, with two placeholders for IN parameters:

```
PreparedStatement pstmt = con.prepareStatement
        ("UPDATE Book SET Price = ? WHERE Title = ?");
```

(Note that a `PreparedStatement` object can contain either a query or an update statement.)

Before we execute the `PreparedStatement` we must set an actual value for each of its parameters, represented in the SQL code by the ? placeholder. This is done using a range of set*XXX*() methods which are analogous to the get*XXX*() methods we used earlier on the `ResultSet` interface.

For example, if the parameter is of type `float` the method to be used is `setFloat()`. This takes two parameters; the first is the **position** of the parameter within the statement. (Remember that there may be more than one parameter; the numbering starts at 1.) The second method parameter is the **value** to which the parameter is to be set. For example, the following code sets the first parameter to 123.45:

```
pstmt.setFloat(1, 123.45);
```

Each set*XXX*() method corresponds to a type in the Java language; it is the programmer's responsibility to make sure that this type maps to a JDBC type that is compatible with the data type expected by the database.

There are a few methods in the set*XXX*() category that need a special mention. A programmer can explicitly convert an input parameter to a particular JDBC type by using the method `setObject()`. This method can take a third argument, which specifies the target JDBC type. The driver will convert the instance of `Object` to the specified JDBC type before sending it to the database. The `setNull()` method allows a programmer to send a SQL NULL value to the database.

Try It Out – Using a PreparedStatement

This example demonstrates the advantage of using the parameterized `PreparedStatement` object for populating the `Category` table of our database. Save the code below as `PopulateTable.java`:

```
// PopulateTable.java

import java.sql.*;

public class PopulateTable {
  public static void main(String args[]) {
    Connection con = null;
    try {
      Class.forName("org.gjt.mm.mysql.Driver").newInstance();
      System.out.println("JDBC driver loaded");

      con = DriverManager.getConnection(
          "jdbc:mysql://localhost/wrox?user=admin&password=admin");
      System.out.println("Database connection established");

      int id[] = {4,5,6};
      String desc[] = {"XML", ".NET", "Oracle"};
      String upd = "INSERT INTO Category VALUES(?,?);";

      PreparedStatement ps = con.prepareStatement(upd);
```

```
          for (int i=0; i < id.length; i++) {
            ps.setInt(1, id[i]);
            ps.setString(2, desc[i]);
            ps.executeUpdate();
            System.out.println(desc[i]+" added to the table");
          }
        } catch (ClassNotFoundException cnfe) {
          System.out.println("ClassNotFoundException: Could not locate driver");
        } catch (SQLException se) {
          System.out.println("SQLException: " + se);
        } catch (Exception e) {
          System.out.println
                  ("An unknown error occurred while connecting to database");
        } finally {
          try {
            if ( con != null ) {
              con.close();
            }
          } catch(SQLException sqle) {
            System.out.println("Unable to close database connection.");
          }
        }

    }
}
```

Compile the code by typing javac PopulateTable.java and run it, again making sure that the MySQL JDBC driver is in your CLASSPATH. The output from the program should be something like the following:

```
JDBC driver loaded
Database connection established
XML added to the table
.NET added to the table
Oracle added to the table
```

How It Works

The JDBC driver is loaded and a connection object is obtained as in our previous example; the excitement starts when we store the parameterized SQL code necessary for the example, and create a PreparedStatement using it:

```
String upd = "INSERT INTO Category VALUES(?,?);";
PreparedStatement ps = con.prepareStatement(upd);
```

In our example, instead of creating three separate update statements, we created one prepared statement, with placeholders for the data that changes each time.

We then loop through the set of categories we want to add to the database; for each, we use setXXX() methods (in this case, setInt() and setString()) to tell the PreparedStatement the actual values we want to use, then execute the statement:

```
for (int i=0; i < id.length; i++) {
  ps.setInt(1, id[i]);
  ps.setString(2, desc[i]);
  ps.executeUpdate();
  System.out.println(desc[i]+" added to the table");
}
```

Advanced ResultSet Use

Just like there are several types of statement in JDBC, there are also various different types of result sets. These may be classified into different types, based on their different capabilities:

❑ TYPE_FORWARD_ONLY – This result set is non-scrollable, and its cursor can move forward only.

❑ TYPE_SCROLL_INSENSITIVE – The result set is scrollable, so its cursor can move forward or backward and can be moved to a particular row or to a row whose position is relative to its current position. The result set generally does *not* show changes to the underlying database that are made while the result set is open. The order and column values of rows are typically fixed when the result set is created.

❑ TYPE_SCROLL_SENSITIVE – The result set is scrollable; its cursor can move forward or backward, and can be moved to a particular row or to a row whose position is relative to its current position. The result set *is* sensitive to changes made while it is open, so if the underlying column values are modified the new values are visible in the ResultSet, thus providing a dynamic view of the underlying data.

Result sets can also have different **concurrency levels**:

❑ CONCUR_READ_ONLY – Indicates a result set that *cannot* be updated programmatically. This allows you to read data but not to change it.

❑ CONCUR_UPDATABLE – Indicates a result set that *can* be updated programmatically, with the changes being transferred to the underlying database.

With the JDBC 2.0 API, it is possible to create statements that will produce result sets that are scrollable and updateable. This is done by using new versions of the createStatement() and prepareStatement() methods that take additional parameters for specifying the type of result set and the concurrency level of the result set being created.

For example, the following code fragment creates a PreparedStatement object that will produce a ResultSet object that is scrollable and updatable:

```
PreparedStatement pstmt = con.prepareStatement
      ("SELECT Title_ID, Title, Price FROM Book WHERE Category_ID = ?",
       ResultSet.TYPE_SCROLL_SENSITIVE,
       ResultSet.CONCUR_UPDATABLE);
pstmt.setFetchSize(25);
pstmt.setInt(1, 6);
ResultSet rs = pstmt.executeQuery();
```

The ResultSet object rs will be scrollable, updatable, and sensitive to changes to its data. We also specified that the driver should fetch 25 rows at a time from the database.

Updatable ResultSets

We saw that a `ResultSet` object may be updated programmatically if its concurrency type is `CONCUR_UPDATABLE`; however, to be able to do this the query should select the primary key, and should reference only a single table. The `updateXXX()` methods make it possible to update values in a result set without using SQL commands. (As with the `getXXX()` and `setXXX()` methods we saw earlier, there is an update method for each data type.)

The `updateXXX()` methods take two parameters, the first to indicate which column is to be updated, and the second to give the value to assign to the specified column. The column to be updated can be specified by giving either its name or its index; note that it is the column number in the result set, rather than that in the database table, that is used.

In the following code fragment, the value in the second column of the `ResultSet` object `rs` is retrieved using the method `getInt()`, and the method `updateInt()` is used to update that column value with an `int` value of 60:

```
int n = rs.getInt(2);
rs.updateInt(2, 60);
```

These `updateXXX()` methods update a value in the current row of the result set, but they do not automatically update the value in the underlying database table. The method `updateRow()` is used to do this, and so it is very important that the `updateRow()` method should be called while the cursor is still on the current row (the row to be updated). You can explicitly cancel the updates to a row by calling the method `cancelRowUpdates()`.

The JDBC 2.0 API provides the method `deleteRow()` to delete the current row from a `ResultSet` object; before calling `deleteRow()` you must position the cursor on the row you want to delete. Unlike the `updateXXX()` methods, which affect only the data in the result set, this method affects both the result set data *and* the underlying row in the database.

The following two lines of code remove the first row of the `ResultSet` object `rs` *and* delete the underlying row from the database (which may or may not be the first row of the database table, depending on the `SELECT` statement used):

```
rs.first();
rs.deleteRow();
```

New rows may be inserted into a result set table, and into the underlying database table. For this purpose, the API defines the concept of an **insert row**. This is a special row used for building the row to be inserted, and to access it you call `moveToInsertRow()`, which positions the cursor on the insert row. Then you should call the appropriate `updateXXX()` methods to add column values to the insert row.

When all of the columns of the row to be inserted have been set, you should call the `insertRow()` method. This method adds the insert row to both the result set and the underlying database, simultaneously. The following code fragment demonstrates these steps for inserting a row:

```
rs.moveToInsertRow();
rs.updateInt(1, 60);
rs.updateString(2, "Book1");
rs.updateFloat(3, 49.99f);
rs.insertRow();
rs.moveToCurrentRow();
```

The call to `moveToCurrentRow()` returns you to the row you were on before you called `moveToInsertRow()`.

Transactions

Transactions are crucial for safe database programming. Often we will have a set of operations that must stand and fall together – the classic example is a transfer of funds between two bank accounts. We have two operations here: withdrawing the funds from one account, and crediting them to the other. If the first fails (perhaps because the account doesn't have sufficient funds) then we shouldn't proceed with the second; on the other hand, if the second fails (perhaps because there is a limit on the amount that account can hold) then the first operation should be undone so that money is not lost.

So, a transaction consisting of one or more statements are to be executed as a single unit, and then either **committed** or **rolled back** by calling the connection's `commit()` or `rollback()` methods; the current transaction then ends.

A new `Connection` object is in **auto-commit** mode by default, which means that when a statement is completed the `commit()` method will be called on that statement automatically. In this case, a transaction consists of only one statement. If auto-commit mode has been disabled, a transaction will not terminate until the method commit or rollback is called explicitly, so it will include all the statements that have been executed since the last call of either `commit()` or `rollback()` is made. In this case, all the statements in the transaction are committed or rolled back as a group.

Most JDBC drivers support transactions; the JDBC 2.0 Standard Extension API also makes it possible for a `Connection` to be part of a distributed transaction.

> *Distributed transactions are transactions that span two or more data sources. This becomes more relevant as more businesses move towards an enterprise model, where different types of information of the same business is maintained in different databases and environments.*

Transaction Isolation Levels

There can be conflicts when two transactions are operating on a database at the same time, and we can specify a **transaction isolation level** to indicate how the conflict should be resolved. For example, when one transaction changes a value and a second transaction reads that value before the change has been committed or rolled back, the changed value read by the second transaction will be invalid if the first transaction is subsequently rolled back.

The transaction isolation levels in JDBC allow you to prevent three different types of problems:

❑ A **dirty read** is when a value is read before it has been committed.

❑ A **non-repeatable read** prevents a situation where reading a row two times within a transaction gives different results since a second transaction has changed the database in the meantime.

❑ A **phantom read** occurs if a `SELECT` statement is performed twice within a transaction, but another transaction has updated the database in the meantime causing different data to match the `WHERE` clause.

The `Connection` interface defines five transaction isolation levels, summarized in this table:

Isolation level	Transactions supported?	Dirty reads?	Non repeat. reads?	Phantom reads?
TRANSACTION_NONE	No	Yes	Yes	Yes
TRANSACTION_READ_UNCOMMITTED	Yes	Yes	Yes	Yes
TRANSACTION_READ_COMMITTED	Yes	No	Yes	Yes
TRANSACTION_REPEATABLE_READ	Yes	No	No	Yes
TRANSACTION_SERIALIZABLE	Yes	No	No	No

As you can see, as we move down the table the number of possible data consistency problems that are prevented is reduced; however, this may well be at the expense of performance as concurrent transactions have to queue for access to database resources.

> **The transaction isolation level that can actually be supported depends on the capabilities of the underlying DBMS.**

When a new `Connection` object is created its transaction isolation level depends on the driver, but normally it is the default for the underlying data source. You can call the method `setTransactionIsolation()` to change the transaction isolation level, passing it one of the constants mentioned above, and the new level will be in effect for the rest of the connection session.

Transactions not only let us group work on data, but also help us to maintain the integrity of our data. Applications should apply the **ACID** transaction concept to make more robust use of transaction concepts. ACID is an acronym, which stands for **Atomicity, Consistency, Isolation, Durability**:

❑ **Atomicity** – A transaction allows for the grouping of one or more changes to tables and rows in the database to form an atomic or indivisible operation. That is, either all of the changes occur or none of them do. If for any reason the transaction cannot be completed, it can be restored to the state it was in prior to the start of the transaction via a rollback operation.

❑ **Consistency** – Data can be said to be consistent as long as it conforms to a set of conditions, such as no two rows in the customer table having the same customer ID, or all orders have an associated customer row. While a transaction executes these invariants may be violated, but no other transaction will be allowed to see these inconsistencies, and all such inconsistencies will have been eliminated by the time the transaction ends.

❑ **Isolation** – A given transaction should be able to think that it is running all by itself on the database. The effects of other concurrent transactions should be invisible to this transaction, and the effects of this transaction should be invisible to others until the transaction is committed.

❑ **Durability** – Once a transaction is committed, its effects should be guaranteed to remain even in the event of subsequent system failures. Until the transaction commits, the changes made by that transaction are not durable, but are guaranteed not to persist in the face of a system failures, as crash recovery will rollback their effects.

Transaction Support in MySQL

Whilst old versions of MySQL did not support transactions, the latest versions do so by supporting additional table types (BDB, InnoDB, and GEMINI) that support transactions. To create a table in the BDB format you must specify TYPE = BDB in the CREATE TABLE statement, for example:

```
mysql> CREATE TABLE CUSTOMER (A INT, B CHAR (20)) TYPE = BDB;
Query OK, 0 rows affected (0.71 sec)
```

You also need to be running the "MySQL Max" version of the database, rather than the "normal" version, to be able to use BDB tables.

When a connection is created, it is in auto-commit mode; as we saw earlier, this means that each individual SQL statement is treated as a transaction and will be automatically committed right after it is executed. The way to allow two or more statements to be grouped into a transaction is to disable auto-commit mode:

```
con.setAutoCommit(false);
```

Once auto-commit mode is disabled, no SQL statements will be committed until you call the method commit() explicitly. All statements executed after the previous call to the method commit will be included in the current transaction and will be committed together as a unit. The following code snippet, in which con is an active connection, illustrates a transaction:

```
con.setAutoCommit(false);

PreparedStatement updateSales = con.prepareStatement
        ("UPDATE Book SET SALES = ? WHERE Title LIKE ?");
updateSales.setInt(1, 50);
updateSales.setString(2, "Beginning JSP Web Development");
updateSales.executeUpdate();

PreparedStatement updateInvoice = con.prepareStatement(
    "UPDATE Bill SET Amount = ? WHERE Title LIKE ?");
updateTotal.setInt(1, 2500);
updateTotal.setString(2, "Beginning JSP Web Development");
updateTotal.executeUpdate();

con.commit();
con.setAutoCommit(true);
```

In this example, auto-commit mode is disabled for the connection con, which means that the two prepared statements updateSales and updateBill will be committed together when the method commit() is called. Whenever the commit() method is called (either automatically when auto-commit mode is enabled or explicitly when it is disabled), all changes resulting from statements in the transaction are made permanent.

The final line of this example enables auto-commit mode, so that each statement will once again be committed automatically when it is completed. You will then be back to the default state where you do not have to call commit() yourself. It is advisable to disable auto-commit mode only while you want to be in transaction mode. This way, you avoid holding database locks for multiple statements, which increases the likelihood of conflicts with other users.

Calling the method `rollback()` aborts a transaction and returns any values that were modified to their previous values. If you are trying to execute one or more statements in a transaction and get an `SQLException`, you should call the method `rollback()` to abort the transaction.

Batch Updates

The JDBC 2.0 core API provides a batch update facility, which allows a `Statement` to submit multiple update commands together as a single unit, to improve performance over performing several such commands one at a time. The following code fragment demonstrates how to send a batch update to a database:

```
con.setAutoCommit(false);
Statement stmt = con.createStatement();
stmt.addBatch(
  "INSERT INTO Order VALUES ('Beginning JSP Web Development', 49.99)");
stmt.addBatch(
  "INSERT INTO Stock VALUES ('Beginning JSP Web Development', 'C100', 60)");
int[] updateCounts = stmt.executeBatch();
```

In this example, a new row is inserted into two different tables, `Order` and `Stock`. We start by disabling the `Connection`'s auto-commit mode in order to allow multiple statements to be sent together as one transaction. After creating the `Statement` object we add two SQL `INSERT` commands to the batch with the `addBatch()` method, then send the batch of updates to the database with the `executeBatch()` method.

Because the connection's auto-commit mode is disabled, the application is free to decide whether or not to commit the transaction if an error occurs or if some of the commands in the batch fail to execute. For example, the application may decide not to commit the changes if any of the insertions fail, thereby avoiding the situation where the `Stock` table is updated without the `Order` table being updated.

The `PreparedStatement` interface has its own version of the `addBatch()` method, which adds a set of parameters to the batch, as shown in the following code fragment:

```
PreparedStatement pstmt = con.prepareStatement(
        "UPDATE Book SET Price = ? WHERE Title = ?");

pstmt.setString(1, "Book 1");
pstmt.setFloat(2, 55.99f);
pstmt.addBatch();

pstmt.setString(1, "Book 2");
pstmt.setFloat(2, 45.99f);
pstmt.addBatch();

int[] updateCounts = pstmt.executeBatch();
```

When we call the `PreparedStatement`'s `executeBatch()` method it will execute the `UPDATE` statement twice, once with each set of parameters that we specified.

Database Access and JSP

To round up our discussion of JDBC, we will see how it can be employed in a JSP web application. First, we will implement a JavaBean to connect and interact with our `Wrox` database. Then we will show how a custom tag library can be used to achieve the same result – but with a lot less code.

Using a JavaBean

First of all, let's place the functionality for connecting and interacting with a database into a JavaBean that we can then use from within a JSP page.

Open your editor and save the following as `Books.java` in `%CATALINA_HOME%\webapps\begjsp-ch16\WEB-INF\classes\com\wrox\databases`:

```
package com.wrox.databases;

import java.sql.*;
import java.util.*;

public class Books {

  String error;
  Connection con;

  public Books()    { }

  public void connect() throws ClassNotFoundException,
                               SQLException,
                               Exception {
    try {
      Class.forName("org.gjt.mm.mysql.Driver").newInstance();
      con = DriverManager.getConnection(
        "jdbc:mysql://localhost/Wrox ?user=root&password=adarsh ");
    } catch (ClassNotFoundException cnfe) {
      error = "ClassNotFoundException: Could not locate DB driver.";
      throw new ClassNotFoundException(error);
    } catch (SQLException cnfe) {
      error = "SQLException: Could not connect to database.";
      throw new SQLException(error);
    } catch (Exception e) {
      error = "Exception: An unknown error occurred while connecting " +
              "to database.";
      throw new Exception(error);
    }
  }

  public void disconnect() throws SQLException {
    try {
      if ( con != null ) {
        con.close();
      }
    } catch (SQLException sqle) {
      error = ("SQLException: Unable to close the database connection.");
      throw new SQLException(error);
    }
  }
```

```
public ResultSet viewBooks() throws SQLException, Exception {
  ResultSet rs = null;
  try {
    String queryString = ("SELECT * FROM Book;");
    Statement stmt = con.createStatement();
    rs = stmt.executeQuery(queryString);
  } catch (SQLException sqle) {
    error = "SQLException: Could not execute the query.";
    throw new SQLException(error);
  } catch (Exception e) {
    error = "An exception occured while retrieving books.";
    throw new Exception(error);
  }
  return rs;
}

public void addBooks(int id, String title, float price, int cid)
                    throws SQLException, Exception {
  if (con != null) {
    try {
      PreparedStatement updatebooks;
      updatebooks = con.prepareStatement(
                    "insert into Book values(?, ?, ?, ?);");
      updatebooks.setInt(1, id);
      updatebooks.setString(2, title);
      updatebooks.setInt(3, cid);
      updatebooks.setFloat(4, price);
      updatebooks.execute();
    } catch (SQLException sqle) {
      error = "SQLException: update failed, possible duplicate entry";
      throw new SQLException(error);
    }
  } else {
    error = "Exception: Connection to database was lost.";
    throw new Exception(error);
  }
}

public void removeBooks(String [] pkeys) throws SQLException, Exception {
  if (con != null) {
    try {
      PreparedStatement delete;
      delete = con.prepareStatement("DELETE FROM Book WHERE Title_ID=?;");
      for (int i = 0; i < pkeys.length; i++) {
        delete.setInt(1, Integer.parseInt(pkeys[i]));
        delete.execute();
      }
    } catch (SQLException sqle) {
      error = "SQLException: update failed, possible duplicate entry";
      throw new SQLException(error);
    } catch (Exception e) {
      error = "An exception occured while deleting books.";
      throw new Exception(error);
    }
  } else {
    error = "Exception: Connection to database was lost.";
    throw new Exception(error);
  }
}
}
```

We need to compile this class so it can be used as a JavaBean in a JSP page. Open a command prompt and change the working directory to `%CATALINA_HOME%\webapps\begjsp-ch16\WEB-INF\classes\`, then run the following command:

```
> javac com\wrox\databases\Books.java
```

Then, enter the following code and save it as `booklist.jsp` in `%CATALINA_HOME%\webapps\begjsp-ch16\`:

```
<%@ page language="java"
    import="java.sql.*, java.io.*, java.util.*, com.wrox.databases.*"
    errorPage="error.jsp" %>

<jsp:useBean id="book" class="com.wrox.databases.Books" />

<html>
  <head>
    <title> Wrox Press Ltd. </title>
  </head>

  <body>
    <h1> Wrox Press Ltd.</h1>
    <h2> List of Books </h2>

    <a href="newbook.jsp"><b>Add More Books</b></a>

    <form action="delete.jsp" method="post">
      <table border="1">
        <tr>
          <td><b>ID:</b></td>
          <td><B>Title:</b></td>
          <td><B>Price:</b></td>
        </tr>

        <%
          book.connect();
          ResultSet rs = book.viewBooks();
          while (rs.next()) {
        %>

        <tr>
          <td>
            <input type="checkbox" name="pkey"
                   value="<%= rs.getString("Title_ID") %>" />
          </td>
          <td><%= rs.getString("Title") %></td>
          <td><%= rs.getString("Price") %></td>
        </tr>

        <%
          }
        %>

      </table><br />

      Check books for deletion.<BR>
      <input type="submit" value="Delete All Checked Books">
    </form>
```

```
        <% book.disconnect(); %>
      </body>
  </html>
```

Now, let's create our error handling page. Enter the following and save it as `error.jsp` in `%CATLALINA_HOME%\webapps\begjsp-ch16\`:

```
<%@ page language="java" isErrorPage="true"%>

<html>
  <head>
    <title>Error Page</title>
  </head>

  <body>
    <h2>An error has occurred.</h2>
    <h4>Error:</h4>
    <%= exception.toString() %><br />
  </body>
</html>
```

Enter the following and save it as `newbook.jsp` in `%CATALINA_HOME%\webapps\begjsp-ch16\`:

```
<html>
  <head>
    <title>Add a new book.</title>
  </head>

  <body>
    <h1> Add a new book.</h1>
    <form action="add.jsp" method="POST">
      <table>
        <tr>
          <td align="RIGHT">ID:</td>
          <td><input type="text" name="Title_ID" size="5" /></td>
        </tr>

        <tr>
          <td align="RIGHT">Title:</td>
          <td> <input type="text" name="Title" size="30" /></td>
        </tr>

        <tr>
          <td align="RIGHT">Price:</td>
          <td> <input type="text" name="Price" size="10" /></td>
        </tr>

        <tr>
          <td>Category ID:</td>
          <td> <input type="text" name="Category_ID" size="5" /></TD>
        </tr>

      </table><br />

      <input type="submit" value="Add to book list" />

    </form>

  </body>
</html>
```

Now, enter the following and save it as `add.jsp` in `%CATLALINA_HOME%\webapps\begjsp-ch16\`:

```jsp
<%@ page language="java"
    import="java.sql.*, java.io.*, java.util.*"
    errorPage="error.jsp" %>

<jsp:useBean id="book" class="com.wrox.databases.Books"/>

<html>
  <head>
    <title>Add Books</title>
  </head>

  <body>

    <%
      int id = Integer.parseInt(request.getParameter("Title_ID"));
      String title =  request.getParameter("Title");
      float price =  Float.parseFloat(request.getParameter("Price"));
      int cid = Integer.parseInt(request.getParameter("Category_ID"));
      book.connect();
      book.addBooks(id, title, price, cid);
      book.disconnect();
    %>


    The new book has been added. <br />
    Click <a href="booklist.jsp">Here</a> To Go Back.

  </body>
</html>
```

Finally, enter the following and save it as `delete.jsp` in `%CATLALINA_HOME%\webapps\begjsp-ch16\`:

```jsp
<%@ page language="java"
    import="java.sql.*, java.io.*, java.util.*"
    errorPage="error.jsp" %>

<jsp:useBean id="book" class="com.wrox.databasesBooks"/>

<html>
  <head>
    <title>Delete Books</title>
  </head>

  <body>

    <%
      String [] kys = request.getParameterValues("pkey");
      book.connect();
      book.removeBooks(kys);
      book.disconnect();
    %>

    The marked books have been deleted. <br />
    Click <a href="booklist.jsp">Here</a> To Go Back.

  </body>
</html>
```

Start up Tomcat and navigate to http://localhost:8080/begjsp-ch16/booklist.jsp; you should see something like this:

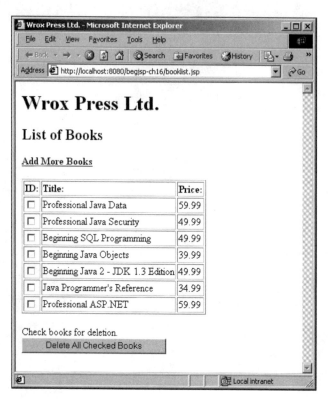

If you click on the Add More Books link you will see the following page:

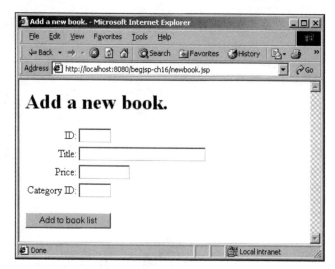

Enter the details of a new book and click the Add to book list button. (Be careful not to enter a duplicate ID.) You should see a message confirming that a new book has been added to the database:

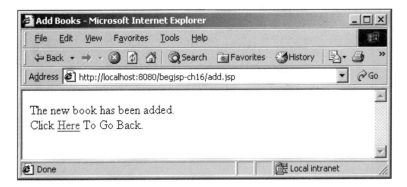

If you return to `booklist.jsp` you will find that your new book is listed. Now try deleting the new book. Check the box next to the name of the book:

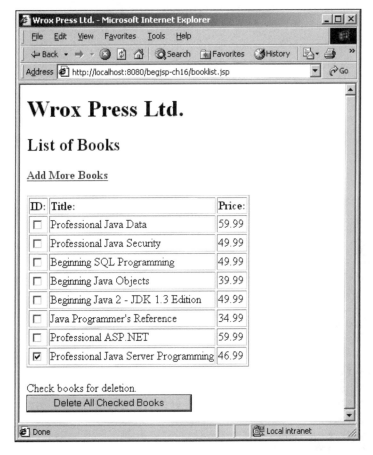

Then click the Delete All Checked Books button and you will see a message confirming that the book has been deleted:

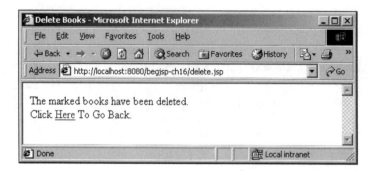

Go back to `booklist.jsp` to see for yourself that the book is no longer listed.

How It Works

The Book class contains the functionality of this application; it is responsible for making the connection to the database, retrieving, updating, and deleting records.

It begins with a standard `package` declaration and imports two packages:

```
package com.wrox.databases;

import java.sql.*;
import java.util.*;

public class Books {
```

String and Connection members are declared:

```
String error;
Connection con;
```

And a default constructor is declared, so that the class can be used as a JavaBean from within a JSP page:

```
public Books()    { }
```

Now we come to five methods that this class exposes. The first is connect(), which creates the connection to the database:

```
public void connect() throws ClassNotFoundException,
                             SQLException,
                             Exception {
    try {
      Class.forName("org.gjt.mm.mysql.Driver").newInstance();
```

The connection is stored in the con member so that it will be available to other methods:

```
    con = DriverManager.getConnection(
      "jdbc:mysql://localhost/Wrox ?user=root&password=adarsh ");
    }
```

If any errors occur a message is stored in the `error` member for inspection later and the exception is then re-thrown. This methodology is used throughout this class:

```
    catch (ClassNotFoundException cnfe) {
    error = "ClassNotFoundException: Could not locate DB driver.";
    throw new ClassNotFoundException(error);
  } catch (SQLException cnfe) {
    error = "SQLException: Could not connect to database.";
    throw new SQLException(error);
  } catch (Exception e) {
    error = "Exception: An unknown error occurred while connecting " +
            "to database.";
    throw new Exception(error);
  }
}
```

Next, we have the `disconnect()` method, which closes an open connection to the database:

```
public void disconnect() throws SQLException {
  try {
    if ( con != null ) {
      con.close();
    }
  } catch (SQLException sqle) {
    error = ("SQLException: Unable to close the database connection.");
    throw new SQLException(error);
  }
}
```

The `viewBooks()` method returns a `ResultSet` to the caller that contains the results of a `SELECT` query on the `Book` table. All fields from the table are included in the `ResultSet`:

```
public ResultSet viewBooks() throws SQLException, Exception {
  ResultSet rs = null;
  try {
    String queryString = ("SELECT * FROM Book;");
    Statement stmt = con.createStatement();
    rs = stmt.executeQuery(queryString);
  } catch (SQLException sqle) {
    error = "SQLException: Could not execute the query.";
    throw new SQLException(error);
  } catch (Exception e) {
    error = "An exception occured while retrieving books.";
    throw new Exception(error);
  }
  return rs;
}
```

The addBooks() method is used to add a book to the Book table. It takes the ID, title, price and category ID as arguments, creates a statement to insert the new record into the table and executes it.

```
public void addBooks(int id, String title, float price, int cid)
                    throws SQLException, Exception {
  if (con != null) {
    try {
      PreparedStatement updatebooks;
      updatebooks = con.prepareStatement(
                    "insert into Book values(?, ?, ?, ?);");
      updatebooks.setInt(1, id);
      updatebooks.setString(2, title);
      updatebooks.setInt(3, cid);
      updatebooks.setFloat(4, price);
      updatebooks.execute();
    } catch (SQLException sqle) {
      error = "SQLException: update failed, possible duplicate entry";
      throw new SQLException(error);
    }
  } else {
    error = "Exception: Connection to database was lost.";
    throw new Exception(error);
  }
}
```

Finally, the removeBooks() method removes one or more records from the table. It takes an array of String objects as its argument. This is an array of the ID field of the Book table and for each key in turn, a matching record is deleted:

```
public void removeBooks(String [] pkeys) throws SQLException, Exception {
  if (con != null) {
    try {
      PreparedStatement delete;
      delete = con.prepareStatement("DELETE FROM Book WHERE Title_ID=?;");
      for (int i = 0; i < pkeys.length; i++) {
        delete.setInt(1, Integer.parseInt(pkeys[i]));
        delete.execute();
      }
    } catch (SQLException sqle) {
      error = "SQLException: update failed, possible duplicate entry";
      throw new SQLException(error);
    } catch (Exception e) {
      error = "An exception occured while deleting books.";
      throw new Exception(error);
    }
  } else {
    error = "Exception: Connection to database was lost.";
    throw new Exception(error);
  }
}
```

The JSP pages `booklist.jsp`, `add.jsp`, and `delete.jsp` use the Book class to display a list of all books, create a new book, add a new book, and delete one or more books from the database, by calling the respective method on Book.

`booklist.jsp` calls the `viewBooks()` method on a `Books` object and loops through each record in the `RecordSet` in turn:

```
<%
   book.connect();
   ResultSet rs = book.viewBooks();
   while (rs.next()) {
%>

<tr>
  <td>
     <input type="checkbox" name="pkey"
```

The value of the `Title_ID` column is used to set the value of the checkbox:

```
         value="<%= rs.getString("Title_ID") %>" />
   </td>
```

And the values of the `Title` and `Price` columns are included in the HTML.

```
   <td><%= rs.getString("Title") %></td>
   <td><%= rs.getString("Price") %></td>
</tr>

<%
   }
%>
```

If the **Add new book** link is followed from `booklist.jsp`, we are sent to a page to fill in the details of a new book. When the form on this page is submitted the details are sent to `add.jsp`. The request parameters are passed to the `addBooks()` method, which as we saw earlier will insert a new record into the database.

```
<%
   int id = Integer.parseInt(request.getParameter("Title_ID"));
   String title =  request.getParameter("Title");
   float price =  Float.parseFloat(request.getParameter("Price"));
   int cid = Integer.parseInt(request.getParameter("Category_ID"));
   book.connect();
   book.addBooks(id, title, price, cid);
   book.disconnect();
%>
```

If one or more books are selected in `booklist.jsp` and the **Delete All Checked Books** button is clicked we are sent to `delete.jsp`. This page extracts the ID of each book that has been selected for deletion and calls the `delete()` method to remove them from the database:

```
<%
  String [] kys = request.getParameterValues("pkey");
  book.connect();
  book.removeBooks(kys);
  book.disconnect();
%>
```

You saw in Chapter 6 how custom tag libraries could be used to remove scriptlets from your JSP pages so that they are more readable and easier to maintain. We are going to see how we can use a tag library to access, and retrieve data from, a database – without using a single line of Java code.

Using a Tag Library

In this section we are going to use the DBTags tag library; like the request tag library we saw in Chapter 6, it is from the Jakarta project. The steps to download and install this tag library for use with our web application are outlined here. If you are unsure of what the files do you should review Chapter 6.

Download and Installation

Go to http://jakarta.apache.org/builds/jakarta-taglibs/nightly/projects/dbtags/ and download the latest distribution. The downloaded files will be in a compressed format so extract the files to a convenient location. You should have the following files:

- ❏   dbtags.tld
- ❏   dbtags.jar
- ❏   dbtags-doc.war
- ❏   dbtags-examples.war

You should copy dbtags.jar to %CATALINA_HOME%\webapps\begjsp-ch16\WEB-INF\lib\ and dbtags.tld to %CATALINA_HOME%\webapps\begjsp-ch16\WEB-INF\.

The archive file dbtags-examples.war contains a sample web.xml file that you can use with your web application. You can copy that file to %CATALINA_HOME%\webapps\begjsp-ch16\WEB-INF\. If you want to create it yourself then enter the following XML and save it as web.xml in %CATALINA_HOME%\webapps\begjsp-ch16\WEB-INF\:

```
<?xml version="1.0" encoding="ISO-8859-1"?>

<!DOCTYPE web-app
    PUBLIC "-//Sun Microsystems, Inc.//DTD Web Application 2.2//EN"
    "http://java.sun.com/j2ee/dtds/web-app_2.2.dtd">

<web-app>

  <description>
  Example web application illustrating the use of tags in the
  DBTags custom tag library, from the JAKARTA-TAGLIBS project.
  </description>
```

```
  <taglib>
    <taglib-uri>http://jakarta.apache.org/taglibs/dbtags</taglib-uri>
    <taglib-location>/WEB-INF/dbtags.tld</taglib-location>
  </taglib>
  <security-role>
    <role-name>admin</role-name>
  </security-role>

</web-app>
```

Now you are ready to use the DBTags Tag Library with your web application. So, let's use it to display the list of books from our Wrox database.

Try It Out – Using the DBTags Tag Library

Enter the following and save it as customlist.jsp in %CATALINA_HOME%\webapps\ begjsp-ch16\:

```
<%@ taglib uri="http://jakarta.apache.org/taglibs/dbtags" prefix="sql" %>

<sql:connection id="con">
  <sql:url>jdbc:mysql://localhost/Wrox</sql:url>
  <sql:driver>org.gjt.mm.mysql.Driver</sql:driver>
  <sql:userId>root</sql:userId>
  <sql:password>adarsh</sql:password>
</sql:connection>

<html>
  <head>
    <title></title>
  </head>
  <body>
    <table>
      <sql:statement id="stmt" conn="con">
        <sql:query>
          select Title_ID, Title from Book
        </sql:query>
        <sql:resultSet id="rset">
          <tr>
            <td><sql:getColumn position="1"/></td>
            <td><sql:getColumn position="2"/></td>
          </tr>
        </sql:resultSet>
      </sql:statement>
    </table>
  </body>
</html>

<sql:closeConnection conn="con"/>
```

Start up Tomcat and navigate to http://localhost:8080/begjsp-ch16/customlist.jsp, and you should see this screen:

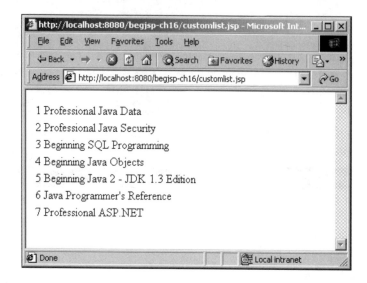

How It Works

To use the tags from the DBTags Tag Library in our JSP page we must add a taglib directive at the top of the page. We associate it with the prefix sql:

```
<%@ taglib uri="http://jakarta.apache.org/taglibs/dbtags" prefix="sql" %>
```

Next, we use the <sql:connection> tag. This tag accepts a database URL that can obtain a Connection through Driver Manager:

```
<sql:connection id="con">
  <sql:url>jdbc:mysql://localhost/Wrox</sql:url>
  <sql:driver>org.gjt.mm.mysql.Driver</sql:driver>
  <sql:userId>root</sql:userId>
  <sql:password>adarsh</sql:password>
</sql:connection>
```

Every connection tag requires the id attribute. After the end tag, a java.sql.Connection object will be added as a page scope bean, and can then be referenced by other tags, including <sql:statement>, <sql:preparedStatement>, and <sql:closeConnection>.

In order to query the database, we open a <sql:statement> tag, pass it an SQL query, and then either execute the statement for inserts, updates, and deletes, or call the <sql:resultSet> tag to iterate over the results from a SELECT statement:

```
<sql:statement id="stmt" conn="con">
  <sql:query>
    select Title_ID, Title from Book
  </sql:query>
```

Result sets are the product of a `SELECT` statement, and so the `<sql:resultSet>` tag automatically loops, once per row, through the result set:

```
<sql:resultSet id="rset">
  <tr>
```

The `<sql:getColumn>` tag grabs values from each row and can either display them, or store them as a `String`. Here we use it to write the column value directly to the user:

```
    <td><sql:getColumn position="1"/></td>
    <td><sql:getColumn position="2"/></td>
  </tr>
</sql:resultSet>
</sql:statement>
```

Finally, we close the connection by passing its reference to the `<sql:closeConnection>` tag:

```
<sql:closeConnection conn="con"/>
```

A complete list of tags and its configurable aspects can be found in the documentation files contained in `dbtags-doc.war`. Take a look through the documentation to discover the power and versatility of this tag library. We will return to this tag library in Chapter 18.

You should note that, although it is possible to use these tags to insert data into a database in general, you should limit their use to data queries. Good architecture design demands that data insertion is placed into the business logic, rather than the presentation, of your application.

Summary

In this chapter we covered most of the aspects of the JDBC API in depth, and provided practical examples of its use in database programming. We saw:

❑ How to use the SQL `SELECT` statement to query the database.

❑ Using a `Statement` object to perform a query from Java code, and how the `ResultSet` interface makes the query data available to us.

❑ Advanced JDBC topics including connection pooling, `PreparedStatement`, transactions, and batch updates.

❑ How to make a JSP talk to a database by employing JavaBeans and custom tag libraries.

We'll return to databases when we start constructing our case study application in Chapters 19 and 20; however, the next chapter takes a look at a rather different kind of data your application may need to deal with: e-mail.

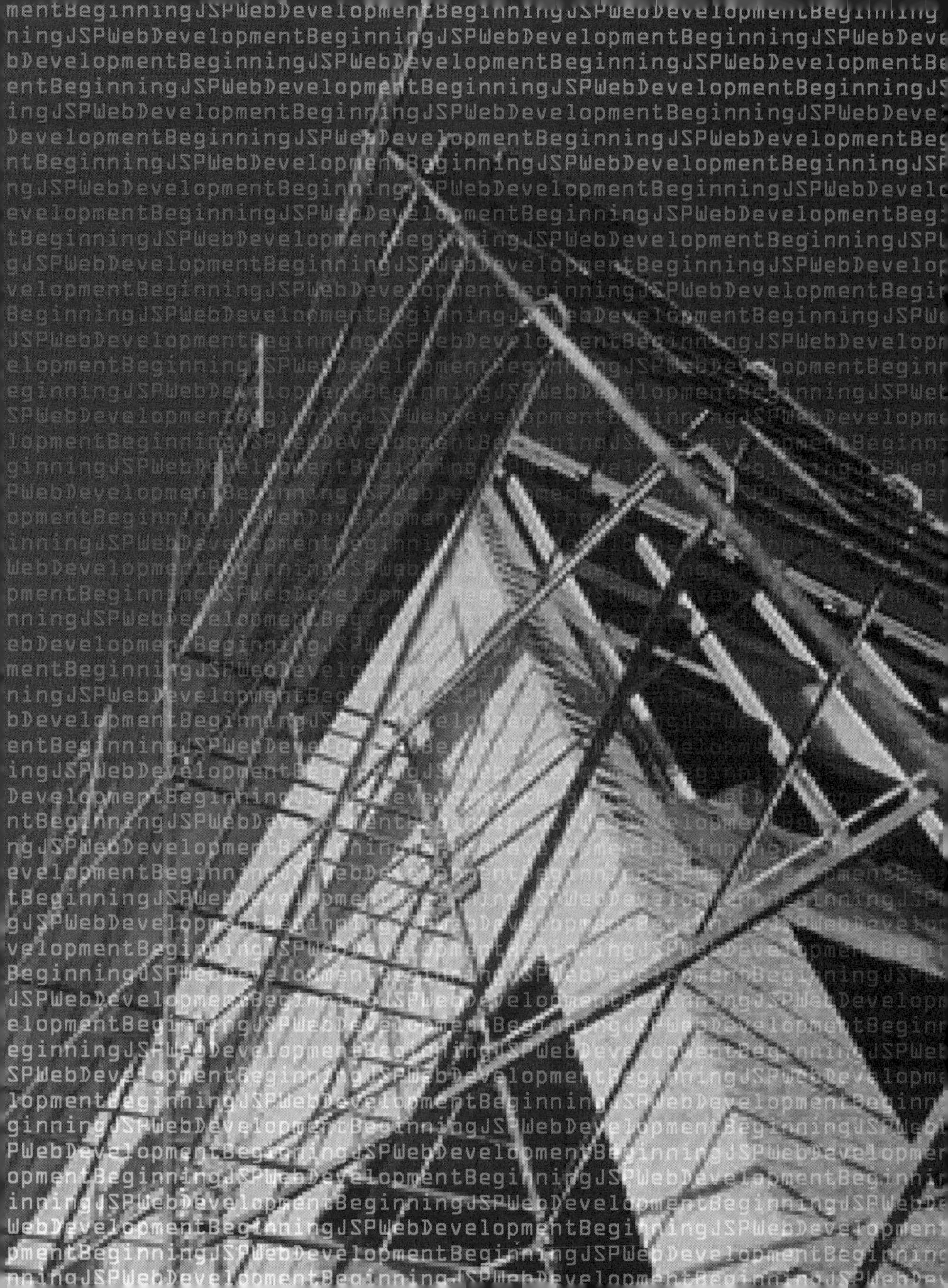

Handling E-mail

E-mail is one of the most popular and widely used services on the internet, so the chances are that any web site you create, is going to need to use e-mail in one form or another. Perhaps you will send out automated responses to customer orders, or a weekly newsletter.

The protocols involved in sending and receiving e-mail are complicated, so in this chapter we will explore how to use the **JavaMail** Application Programming Interface (API) to easily create, send and retrieve e-mail on the server. The JavaMail API allows us to manipulate e-mail using relatively simple classes that hide the complexity from the developer.

We will be looking at:

❏   What JavaMail is and why it is useful

❏   How to install JavaMail for use with Tomcat

❏   The classes that make up the JavaMail API

❏   How to send plain text and HTML-formatted e-mail

❏   How to send attachments with e-mail

❏   How to retrieve e-mail from a mailbox

So, let's start off by explaining what JavaMail is and why you should learn about it.

What is JavaMail and Why Should I Use It?

Web applications often need to manipulate e-mail on the server, and the JavaMail API makes this simple for a JSP web developer to achieve. The JavaMail API makes it so simple because it hides the detailed implementation of e-mail standards from the developer.

Applications that need to send or receive e-mail must be built to support standardized **Requests For Comments** (**RFCs**). RFCs are the standards on which much of the internet is built and there are RFCs that specify how hosts should communicate with each other to send e-mail. These RFCs are often long, complicated documents and all of the guidelines in a RFC must be followed in order to build a correct implementation. If you are interested you can find a copy of the RFC for SMTP, a popular e-mail protocol, at http://www.imc.org/rfc2821.

As developers, when we create a JSP web application to send or receive e-mail we don't want to have to figure out how to implement all the guidelines. Fortunately, Sun Microsystems provide the JavaMail API for dealing with e-mail in Java applications, which implements the most popular e-mail protocols.

So, with JavaMail we do not have to worry about implementing RFCs, but rather can focus on building an application that manipulates e-mail.

But, before we can use the JavaMail API in our applications we need to download and install it.

Installing JavaMail with Tomcat

To download JavaMail, visit http://java.sun.com/products/javamail/ and follow the instructions on screen. In this chapter we will be using version 1.2 of JavaMail and this is the version you should download. Save the downloaded file to a convenient location. It will be in a compressed format and you will need to extract the contents using a file compression tool, such as WinZip.

We will also be using the **JavaBeans Activation Framework** (**JAF**) in this chapter and now is a convenient time to download it. The JAF provides a mechanism for taking an arbitrary piece of data, encapsulating access to it and figuring out what JavaBean should be used to manipulate it. JavaMail requires JAF to enable file handling with e-mail attachments.

You can download version 1.0.1 of JAF from http://java.sun.com/products/javabeans/glasgow/jaf.html. Again, follow the instructions, save the compressed file to a convenient location and extract the contents.

Next, let's set up the web application we will use in this chapter. Create the directory structure `%CATALINA_HOME%\webapps\begjsp-ch17\WEB-INF\lib\`.

We need to make the JavaMail API and JAF available for use with our web application. To do this, we place the Java classes that the web application needs access to in the `lib` directory.

Copy both the `mail.jar` file from the JavaMail download and the `activation.jar` file from the JAF download to the `lib` directory. Both of these files are Java archives that contain the class files our web applications require.

Reality Check

Before we start to use the JavaMail API and JAF we should check that the relevant files have been installed correctly.

Open your editor and enter the following code:

```
<%@ page import="javax.mail.*,javax.mail.event.*,javax.mail.internet.*" %>
<h1>Installation is successful.</h1>
```

Save this in a file named `testJavaMail.jsp` in the `%CATALINA_HOME%\webapps\begjsp-17\` directory.

You should now have the following file and directory structure:

```
%CATALINA_HOME%\webapps\begjsp-ch17\testJavaMail.jsp
%CATALINA_HOME%\webapps\begjsp-ch17\WEB-INF\lib\mail.jar
%CATALINA_HOME%\webapps\begjsp-ch17\WEB-INF\lib\activation.jar
```

Start Tomcat and navigate to http://localhost:8080/begjsp-ch17/testJavaMail.jsp. If everything is working correctly you should see:

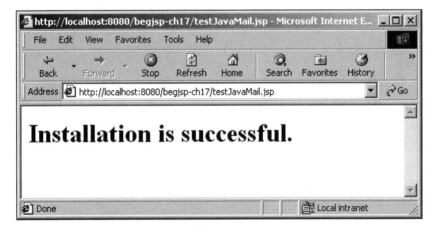

If you receive an error message, go back and check that you have added `mail.jar` and `activation.jar` to the correct directories, then restart Tomcat.

Once everything is working correctly we are ready to write applications that can send and receive e-mail, but where are we going to send our e-mail to? We will need an account with an e-mail service provider and the next section will explain how to set one up.

Setting Up an E-mail Account

JavaMail does not provide you with an e-mail server. The JavaMail API abstracts *client-side* e-mail operations, and installing it on your machine will not provide you with all the tools required to send and retrieve e-mail.

For this you will need an e-mail server with which you have an account. This section introduces a free e-mail service from Yahoo that you can use with your JSP applications; if you already have access to an e-mail server you can use that, but please bear in mind that the example code will be aimed at users of this free service. So, if you use your own e-mail server you may have to make changes to the example code to get it to run.

There are many free web-based e-mail services available but the service provided by Yahoo has everything we need for this chapter. All the examples in this chapter will be written to work with a Yahoo e-mail account.

To sign up for an account with Yahoo go to http://mail.yahoo.com. A login page should appear:

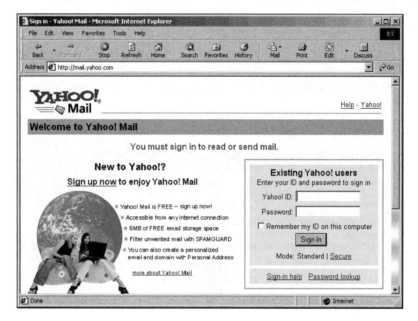

Click on the Sign up now link and follow the instructions to set up an account.

Once you have completed the sign up, try logging in to your Yahoo! mail account. We will be sending our e-mail here so remember how to get back to it.

One further step is required before we can use this account in our examples. You need to tell Yahoo to allow other applications to access the Yahoo e-mail server to use your account.

Make sure you are logged into your account and click on the Options link in the navigation frame on the left-hand side of the screen. Then ensure that POP Access and Forwarding are turned on. You will be asked to confirm your choices, so accept the changes to the mail forwarding and POP access options:

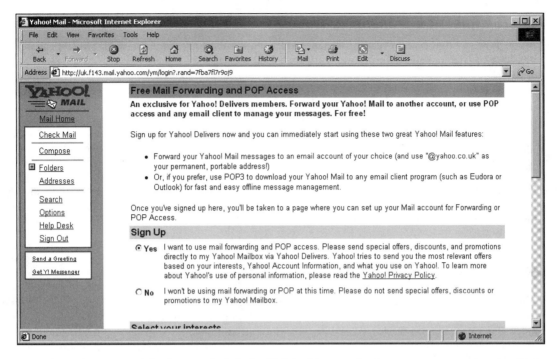

Read through the rest of the form and click the Finished button. In the next screen, ensure that Web and POP Access is selected, and click Submit. POP access is now turned on, which means that we can access the account with our own applications.

The final screen that appears tells us about two very important pieces of information. First is the name of the POP e-mail server, typically pop.mail.yahoo.com. The second is the name of the SMTP server, typically smtp.mail.yahoo.com. Make a note of these two addresses, as we will be using them later in order to read and write e-mail to this account.

We have casually introduced two new terms here: **POP** and **SMTP**. They are both e-mail protocols that describe how e-mail should be sent and read; you don't need to understand them in great depth, but some background is useful so let's take a closer look at them.

POP (Post Office Protocol)

POP is a protocol designed for computers with limited resources to receive e-mail. After all, not every computer can be constantly connected to the internet. Using POP, such computers can rely on a dedicated server to manage e-mail for them. E-mail can then be retrieved from this server and read or deleted as required.

This protocol is one of the most popular methods for reading e-mail and the current implementation, POP3, is officially defined at http://www.ietf.org/rfc/rfc1939.txt.

The pop.mail.yahoo.com address we noted earlier is the name of our dedicated e-mail server provided by Yahoo.

SMTP (Simple Mail Transfer Protocol)

Just as POP is a standard for reading e-mail, SMTP is a standard for sending e-mail. SMTP provides a flexible and effective method of transporting an e-mail message.

SMTP is not the only method to send e-mail, but it does have almost universal support. The official specification for SMTP is defined at http://www.imc.org/rfc2821.

Most of the examples in this chapter will focus on sending e-mail and our applications will send e-mail through a server using SMTP. The `smtp.mail.yahoo.com` address we noted earlier is the server we will send e-mail to in our examples.

With JavaMail installed and an e-mail account set up for our use, we are almost ready to start using the JavaMail API to create web applications that can manipulate e-mail; but before we do, let's take a closer look at some of the classes that make up the JavaMail API.

Key Parts of the JavaMail API

The JavaMail API models an e-mail system by breaking down each significant part into objects. We say that a part of an e-mail system is **abstracted** to a class. An understanding of these abstracted classes is all a developer needs to use the JavaMail API. This is useful as it means, for example, that the developer does not need to know how an e-mail is transported from the client to the server – only how to use the class that abstracts the concept. As long as we understand the abstract idea, we don't need to understand the specifics.

The JavaMail API breaks down an e-mail system as follows:

- ❑ The e-mail message is abstracted to the `Message` class.

- ❑ The process of sending e-mail is abstracted away from protocols to the `Transport` class.

- ❑ Receiving e-mail is also abstracted from protocols, to the `Store` class.

- ❑ Finally to link them all together the `Session` class contains generic information about the whole package, including the username, password, and e-mail server address.

With these abstractions in mind let's look at two objects that will be needed in any JavaMail application: `Session` and `Message`.

The javax.mail.Session Class

The `javax.mail.Session` class manages a user's e-mail configuration – including username, password, and server name – for the services used during the session. Don't confuse it with `javax.servlet.http.HttpSession`, which we introduced in Chapter 11, as no state information is saved in `javax.mail.Session`. If you want to store that type of information you will need to store the JavaMail session in the servlet's session.

Every operation you perform with the JavaMail API requires a `Session` object to provide information about the entire system.

`Session` objects rely on a `java.util.Properties` object to provide information such as name of the mail server, the account username, and the account password. The `Properties` class is used to store a list of keys and their associated values. For example, you might store a username property with a key `mail.user` and a value of `johndoe`.

You can create a new `Properties` object with an empty constructor:

```
Properties props = new Properties();
```

And information can be stored in a `Properties` object using the `put()` method. For example this stores a property with a key of `mail.smtp.host` and a value of `smtp.mail.yahoo.com`:

```
props.put("mail.smtp.host", "smtp.mail.yahoo.com");
```

We can create a `Session` object by calling the static `Session.getInstance()` method and passing it a `Properties` object:

```
Session session = Session.getInstance(props);
```

A `Session` object is not usually passed an empty `Properties` object; depending on what you are doing with the JavaMail API, the `Properties` object will need to have some values set. Here are some of the properties that can be set in a `Properties` object passed into `Session.getInstance()`:

Property	Description
`mail.host`	The mail server to be used by your JavaMail application. By default, this is the local computer.
`mail.user`	The username for the e-mail account.
`mail.store.protocol`	The default protocol to be used for *retrieving* e-mail.
`mail.transport.protocol`	The default protocol to be used for *sending* e-mail.
`mail.`*protocol*`.host`	The specific host for a given protocol; change *protocol* to the correct protocol being used. For example, if SMTP was being used the property name would be `mail.smtp.host`.
`mail.`*protocol*`.user`	The specific username to be used with a given protocol; change *protocol* to the correct protocol being used. For example, if SMTP was being used the property name would be `mail.smtp.user`.
`mail.from`	The user's return e-mail address.
`mail.debug`	A `boolean` value representing whether debugging information should be displayed about an e-mail transaction. By default, this is `false`.

The javax.mail.Message Class

The `javax.mail.Message` class is an abstraction of a mail message sent or received by the JavaMail API.

The `Message` class implements the `Part` interface, which defines a content structure common to most messages, and has attributes containing all the information required to describe the message. Subclasses of `Part` and `Message` define specific types of messages for use with the JavaMail API.

The most commonly used subclass is `javax.mail.internet.MimeMessage`, which represents a **Multipurpose Internet Mail Extensions** (**MIME**) e-mail. MIME types are used to represent the type of content in an e-mail, for example `text/plain` or `text/html`. A MIME e-mail can contain one or more of these types of content.

`Message` objects rely on a `Session` object. If we had created a `Session` object as we did in the previous section a new `MimeMessage` object could be created as follows:

```
MimeMessage message = new MimeMessage(session);
```

Once we have a message object we can start modifying its attributes to describe our particular e-mail. If we wanted to create a simple e-mail saying hello, we could set the subject and body content of the e-mail as follows:

```
message.setSubject("This is displayed as the subject of my message.");
message.setText("Testing the JavaMail API...");
```

We have created an e-mail message, but before we can send it we need to know how to address it. For this, we use the `Address` class.

The javax.mail.Address Class

The `Address` class represents an e-mail address used in a message. Multiple addresses may be used in a message, but at the very least we must provide an address for the sender and an address for the recipient of each message.

`Address` is, like `Message`, an abstract class, and requires a concrete sub-class for specific implementations. In this chapter we will use the `InternetAddress` class provided by the JavaMail API.

The `InternetAddress` class has two constructors that we will use. One takes a single argument, a `String` representation of the address:

```
InternetAddress address = new InternetAddress("you@example.com");
```

The second constructor allows you to include information about a personal name for the addressee. This name may be anything you like, and can be used by applications when displaying the address:

```
InternetAddress address = new InternetAddress("you@example.com",
                                              "John Smith");
```

Adding addresses to a `Message` object is easy, and involves using the appropriate setter method for the address. The address of the sender is set using the `setFrom()` method:

```
InternetAddress from = new InternetAddress("me@example.com");
message.setFrom(from);
```

Setting the address of the receiver requires a little more work. Instead of just passing an `InternetAddress` object to the `Message` object, we must also specify the type of the recipient:

```
InternetAddress to = new InternetAddress("you@example.com");
message.setRecipient(MessageRecipient.TO, to);
```

The different message recipient types are available as static values from the `javax.mail.Message.RecipientType` class. By default there are three types of recipients supported by the `Message` object:

❑ First is an address the e-mail should be sent to. The `Message.RecipientType.TO` value is used for this case.

❑ One or more copies of the message might, optionally, be required for other purposes. The simplest copy of a message is called a Carbon Copy (CC). The `Message.RecipientType.CC` value represents a CC address.

❑ Additionally another type of CC exists called Blind Carbon Copy (BCC). The difference between CC and BCC is whether the recipient in the `TO` address should be aware of the copied e-mail. Other recipients will not be aware about a BCC, but will see if a normal CC is sent. For a BCC address the `Message.RecipientType.BCC` value is used.

More than one address may be set for an e-mail at a time. This is possible as the `MimeMessage` object includes methods that take an array of recipients of a specific type as their argument. For example:

```
message.setRecipients(MessageRecipient.CC, addresses);
```

where `addresses` is an array of `InternetAddress` objects.

Since all your messages will often be sent from the same address the JavaMail API provides a convenience property, with a key of `mail.from`. If this property is set, all messages will, by default, have the sender's address set as required. For example:

```
Properties properties = new Properties();
properties.setProperty("mail.from", "you@example.com");
Session session = Session.getInstance(properties);
```

All messages sent from this session will have the sender's address set to `you@example.com`.

The `Message` class will be used throughout this chapter, along with the `Session` class. Now that you understand how to create a message and set the relevant properties you are ready to start sending, or transporting, your messages.

Transporting Messages

All of the logic behind sending a message with the JavaMail API is handled by the `javax.mail.Transport` class. `Transport` is independent of a specific protocol or message type: the message and protocol are provided at the time of sending, and the `Transport` class handles the rest.

There are two possible ways to use `Transport` to send a message. Firstly, we can call the static `send()` method of the `Transport` class. This will immediately try to send the message:

```
Transport.send(message);
```

Alternatively, a protocol-specific instance of `Transport` may be retrieved from the current `Session` object:

```
Transport transport = session.getTransport("SMTP");
```

This new `Transport` object can then be used to send a message:

```
transport.connect();
transport.send(message);
transport.close()
```

The two different methods are useful for different circumstances. The first method creates a separate connection to the mail server for each message, but the second allows for multiple messages to be sent from one connection. Therefore, the first method is usually more convenient when only a single e-mail is to be sent.

We now have all the parts required for a simple mail application, so let's build one.

Try it Out – Sending a Message

If you have a Yahoo mail account set up then try the following example. If you are using a different mail server then you may need to make some changes to this code. The changes you need to make are explained in the *How It Works* section.

Open your favorite text editor and create the following JSP page:

```jsp
<%@ page import="java.util.*, javax.mail.*, javax.mail.internet.*" %>
<%
  Properties props = new Properties();
  props.put("mail.smtp.host", "smtp.mail.yahoo.com");
  Session s = Session.getInstance(props);

  MimeMessage message = new MimeMessage(s);

  InternetAddress from = new InternetAddress("yahooUsername@yahoo.com");
  message.setFrom(from);
  InternetAddress to = new InternetAddress("yahooUsername@yahoo.com");
  message.addRecipient(Message.RecipientType.TO, to);

  message.setSubject("Test from JavaMail.");
  message.setText("Hello from JavaMail!");
```

```
    // Next two lines are specific to Yahoo
    Store store = s.getStore("pop3");
    store.connect("pop.mail.yahoo.com", "yahooUsername", "yahooPassword");

    Transport.send(message);

    // Next line is specific to Yahoo
    store.close();

%>

<html>
  <body>
    <p align="center">
      Mail has been sent.
        <a href="http://mail.yahoo.com/">Check your Inbox</a>.
    </p>
    <p align="center">
      <a href="sendmail.jsp">Click here to send another!</a>
    </p>
  </body>
</html>
```

Save this file as `sendmail.jsp` in `%CATALINA_HOME%\webapps\begjsp-ch17\`.

Before you can use this JSP page you will need to make some changes to the code to tailor it to your specific e-mail account. The string `yahooUsername` appears three times and should be replaced with your actual Yahoo mail account name. Where `yahooPassword` appears it should be replaced with your account password.

Make sure you're connected to the internet, start up Tomcat and navigate to http://localhost:8080/begjsp-ch17/sendmail.jsp. You should see something like:

Check the inbox for your e-mail account and you should find a new message, sent by your web application.

How it Works

First we import the required libraries:

```
<%@ page import="java.util.*, javax.mail.*, javax.mail.internet.*" %>
```

Next, a `Properties` object is created so we can create a `Session` object.

```
Properties props = new Properties();.
```

The Yahoo mail server provides a SMTP service for sending e-mail, and so we set the `mail.smtp.host` property accordingly:

```
props.put("mail.smtp.host", "smtp.mail.yahoo.com");
```

If you are using a different mail provider you will need to change this line of code accordingly. With that, the properties are set and a `Session` object can be created:

```
Session s = Session.getDefaultInstance(props);
```

We can now create a `Message` object from the `Session` object. `MimeMessage` is the subclass of `Message` that we use:

```
MimeMessage message = new MimeMessage(s);
```

Now the `Message` object is customized, setting the "`from`" and "`to`" address fields for the message to your own e-mail account; you'll need to change these to more appropriate values:

```
InternetAddress from = new InternetAddress("yahooUsername@yahoo.com");
message.setFrom(from);
InternetAddress to = new InternetAddress("yahooUsername@yahoo.com");
message.addRecipient(Message.RecipientType.TO, to);
```

The message content is manipulated next. This code could have appeared before or after the address code: it doesn't matter, as long as you finish editing the message before sending it off. The subject of our message will be a simple phrase saying we are testing out JavaMail; the message body will be a simple message to say hello:

```
message.setSubject("Testing out JavaMail");
message.setText("Hello from JavaMail!");
```

Finally, the message is sent. Since we only have one message, there is no difference between using the static `send()` method or creating a new `Transport` object for sending our message. Here is where code appears for our specific Yahoo mail server. Don't worry about the specifics of this code; it is fully covered in a later section. Basically, the Yahoo mail server requires us to log in and authenticate ourselves via the POP3 protocol before sending e-mail. The extra step ensures Yahoo knows who is sending the e-mail. On most SMTP servers you can completely omit these lines and the code will work perfectly fine:

```
// Next two lines are specific to Yahoo
Store store = s.getStore("pop3");
store.connect("pop.mail.yahoo.com", "yahooUsername", "yahooPassword");
```

```
Transport.send(message);

// Next line is specific to Yahoo
store.close();
```

At the end we have some HTML to inform the user that the message has been sent:

```
<html>
<p align="center">Mail has been sent.
<a href="http://mail.yahoo.com/">Check your Inbox</a>.</p>
<p align="center"><a href="sendmail.jsp">Click here to send
another!</a></p>
</html>
```

This example is somewhat idealized, as we make no effort to deal with exceptions that may arise. Rest assured that later examples will deal with this issue.

A JSP Mail Sending Utility

In the previous example the text of the message was restricted to what is hard-coded in the scriptlet. For most practical purposes the message will be dynamic. With a few tweaks and a simple HTML form we can create a JSP that allows for custom text e-mail to be created and sent.

Let's create a new JSP, sendDynamicMail.jsp, based on our existing sendmail.jsp. The changes to sendmail.jsp are highlighted:

```
<%@ page import="java.util.*, javax.mail.*, javax.mail.internet.*" %>
<%
  Properties props = new Properties();
  props.put("mail.smtp.host", "smtp.mail.yahoo.com");
  Session s = Session.getInstance (props);

  MimeMessage message = new MimeMessage(s);

  InternetAddress from = new InternetAddress("yahooUsername@yahoo.com");
  message.setFrom(from);
  InternetAddress to = new InternetAddress(request.getParameter("to"));
  message.addRecipient(Message.RecipientType.TO, to);

  message.setSubject(request.getParameter("subject"));
  message.setText(request.getParameter("text"));

  // Next two lines are specific to Yahoo
  Store store = s.getStore("pop3");
  store.connect("pop.mail.yahoo.com", "yahooUsername", "yahooPassword");

  Transport.send(message);

  // Next line is specific to Yahoo
  store.close();
```

```
%>

<html>
<p align="center">Mail has been sent. Check your Inbox.</p>
<p align="center"><a href="sendDynamicMail.html">Click here to send
another!</a></p>
</html>
```

Save this as `sendDynamicMail.jsp` in `%CATALINA_HOME%\webapps\begjsp-ch17\`. This JSP page relies on another resource to POST it the required parameters, which is provided by the following HTML page:

```
<html>
<form action="sendDynamicMail.jsp" method="post">
<table>
   <tr><td>to:</td><td><input name="to" size="40"></td></tr>
   <tr><td>subject:</td><td><input name="subject" size="40"></td></tr>
   <tr>
     <td colspan="2"><textarea name="text" cols="45"
     rows="5"></textarea></td>
   </tr>
</table>
<input type="submit" value="Submit">
</form>
</html>
```

Save this as `sendDynamicMail.html` in `%CATALINA_HOME%\webapps\begjsp-ch17\`, start up Tomcat and navigate to http://localhost:8080/begjsp-ch17/sendDynamicMail.html. You should see something like:

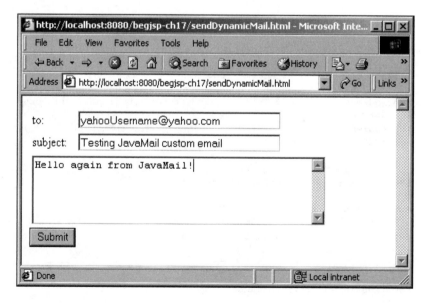

Fill in each of the fields of the form as you like, but be sure the mail address is one you will be able to check! After filling in all of the fields press the Submit button and the e-mail will be sent. You should see something like:

Your e-mail has been successfully sent.

How it Works

The functionality of sendDynamicMail.jsp is much the same as sendmail.jsp. However, instead of using static values we are using dynamic values for the to, subject, and text fields. These dynamic values are found in the request object – if it does not contain the needed values sendDynamicMail.jsp will throw an exception. These values are set in the form we fill in and submit from sendDynamicMail.html.

sendDynamicMail.html contains a form with fields corresponding to our JSP request parameters. The form is sent to sendDynamicMail.jsp. The values used in the form are then be available to our JSP, via the request object:

```
<html>
<form action="sendDynamicMail.jsp" method="post">
<table>
  <tr><td>to:</td><td><input name="to" size="40"></td></tr>
  <tr><td>subject:</td><td><input name="subject" size="40"></td></tr>
  <tr>
    <td colspan="2"><textarea name="text" cols="45"
    rows="5"></textarea></td>
  </tr>
</table>
<input type="submit" value="Submit">
</form>
</html>
```

What happens if a user forgets to fill in one of the fields on the form? On submission of the form, `sendDynamicMail.jsp` will not work and an error message will be displayed:

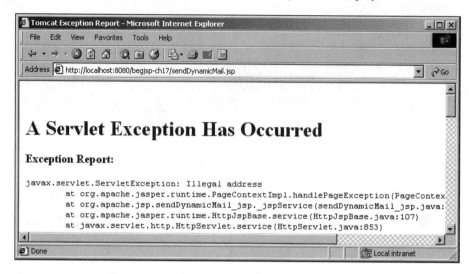

Now would be a good time to implement some of the error-handling techniques we learned about in Chapter 9.

Error Handling for sendDynamicMail.jsp

There are many ways to provide error handling for `sendDynamicMail.jsp`. Solutions range from simply ignoring the error to highlighting the problem and redisplaying the incomplete form.

For our application we will choose a solution right in the middle: a simple error page will be displayed informing the user what is wrong, but we will rely on the user pressing the **Back** button on their browser if they wish to reuse the previous information in the form.

Let's see how we can add error handling to our e-mail application.

Try it Out – Building Error Handling

Let's create another new JSP, called `safeSendMail.jsp`. As before, additions to `sendDynamicMail.jsp` are highlighted. Save `safeSendMail.jsp` in `%CATALINA_HOME%\webapps\begjsp-ch17\`.

```
<%@ page
   import="java.util.*, javax.mail.*, javax.mail.internet.*"
   errorPage="errorpage.jsp" %>
<%
   Properties props = new Properties();
   props.put("mail.smtp.host", "smtp.mail.yahoo.com");
   Session s = Session.getDefaultInstance(props);

   MimeMessage message = new MimeMessage(s);

   InternetAddress from = new InternetAddress("yahooUserName@yahoo.com");
```

```
message.setFrom(from);

  try {
    String toValue = request.getParameter("to");
    if(!toValue.equals("")) {
      InternetAddress to = new InternetAddress(toValue);
      message.addRecipient(Message.RecipientType.TO, to);
    } else {
      throw new MessagingException
              ("You must fill in a value for the \"to\" field.");
    }

    String subject = request.getParameter("subject");
    if(!subject.equals("")) {
      message.setSubject(subject);
    } else {
      throw new MessagingException
              ("You must fill in a value for the \"subject\" field.");
    }

    String text = request.getParameter("text");
    if(!text.equals("")) {
      message.setText(text);
    } else {
      throw new MessagingException
              ("You must fill in a value for the body of the message.");
    }
  } catch(MessagingException e) {
    throw new MessagingException("Error getting form values: " +
                                 e.toString());
  }

  // Next line is specific to Yahoo
  Store store = s.getStore("pop3");

  try {
    // Next line is specific to Yahoo
    store.connect("pop.mail.yahoo.com", "yahooUsername", "yahooPassword");
    Transport.send(message);
  } catch(MessagingException e) {
    throw new MessagingException("Cannot send mail. Please contact the " +
            "<a href=\"mailto:admin@example.com\">administrator</a>.");
  } finally {
    // Next line is specific to Yahoo
    store.close();
  }
%>
<html>
<p align="center">Mail has been sent. Check your Inbox.</p>
<p align="center"><a href="safeSendMail.html">Click here to send
another!</a></p>
</html>
```

This JSP references an error page, `errorpage.jsp`, so we also need to create that file:

```
<%@ page isErrorPage="true" %>
<html>
<h2 align="center">An Error has Occurred.</h2>
<p align="center"><%= exception.getMessage() %></p>
</html>
```

Save this as `errorpage.jsp` in `%CATALINA_HOME%\webapps\begjsp-ch17\`.

Finally, copy `sendDynamicMail.html` to `safeSendMail.html` and update it so that the form is posted to `safeSendMail.jsp`:

```
<html>
<form action="safeSendMail.jsp" method="post">
<table>
...
```

Start Tomcat and navigate to http://localhost:8080/begjsp-ch17/safeSendMail.html. Fill out the displayed form but purposely leave the "to" field blank and press Submit.

A helpful message is now displayed reminding the user what they have forgotten to do:

Try leaving different fields blank and check that the correct message is displayed.

How it Works

The new code for `safeSendMail.jsp` should not be surprising: the code is an example of the type of error-handling code we saw in Chapter 9.

First, an error page was specified to handle any errors that arise in the page:

```
<%@ page
   import="java.util.*, javax.mail.*, javax.mail.internet.*"
   errorPage="errorpage.jsp" %>
```

Next, all of the `request.getParameter()` calls were placed inside a `try/catch` statement:

```
try {
  String toValue = request.getParameter("to");
  if(!toValue.equals("")) {
    InternetAddress to = new InternetAddress(toValue);
    message.addRecipient(Message.RecipientType.TO, to);
  } else {
    throw new MessagingException
            ("You must fill in a value for the \"to\" field.");
  }

  String subject = request.getParameter("subject");
  if(!subject.equals("")) {
    message.setSubject(subject);
  } else {
    throw new MessagingException
            ("You must fill in a value for the \"subject\" field.");
  }

  String text = request.getParameter("text");
  if(!text.equals("")) {
    message.setText(text);
  } else {
    throw new MessagingException
            ("You must fill in a value for the body of the message.");
  }
} catch(MessagingException e) {
  throw new MessagingException("Error getting form values: " +
                               e.toString());
}
```

Because of the `try/catch` statement and the individual checks for the parameters, we then had control to throw our own error.

If one of the parameters is not available a very specific error is thrown. This is very beneficial because a user might have forgotten to fill in a field when submitting the form, or perhaps the user browsed directly to `safeSendMail.jsp` instead of the HTML counterpart. In these cases the new error handling would have detected the problem and thrown an error explaining what was wrong.

If more fields are added to the form, then we can easily add more error handling by putting in additional `if/then` statements inside the `try` statement.

One last `try/catch/finally` block was added around the code responsible for sending the message. The `try` block opens a connection and attempts to send the message:

```
try {
  // Next line is specific to Yahoo
  store.connect("pop.mail.yahoo.com", "yahooUsername", "yahooPassword");
  Transport.send(message);
} catch(MessagingException e) {
  throw new MessagingException("Cannot send mail. Please contact the " +
          "<a href=\"mailto:admin@example.com\">administrator</a>.");
}
```

If an error occurs the user will be notified that the message cannot be sent, but the most important thing to notice in the code is in the `finally` block:

```
finally {
  // Next line is specific to Yahoo
  store.close();
}
```

Whether or not the message is sent correctly, the connection to the e-mail server is closed. Leaving the connection open will keep the current user logged on to the e-mail server, but to avoid any problems with the e-mail server it is good practice to make sure the connection is closed when the code is finished.

Finally, `errorpage.jsp` provides a simple error page that displays the error message and provides some HTML for formatting.

Expanding Beyond Plain Text E-mail

We now have a fully functional JSP web application for sending e-mail. The only limitation is that the content of this e-mail is always plain text. For many purposes this is perfectly fine, but the JavaMail API is not limited to text content.

The `MimeMessage` class we have been using is designed to support **Multipurpose Internet Mail Extensions** (**MIME**), and thus allows for many different types of content to be sent in an e-mail. There are many types of MIME content, but these are the two we will be using:

MIME Type	Description
text/plain	Content under this type will be displayed as plain text. This is the most common form of e-mail content.
text/html	Content of this type is also plain text, however the client should render the content as HTML before displaying the message.

The content of our `MimeMessage` is actually a `Multipart` object, which may have many content parts if required. So far we have been using the convenient `setText()` method for e-mails; the downside is that this method hides what is going on in the background when creating a message.

Calling `setText()` actually does a few different things. Principally, a new `MimeBodyPart` object is created for the e-mail and is set with a MIME type of `text/plain`. Because the default MIME type is `text/plain`, all messages created by using `setText()` will be displayed only as plain text.

If we want to create and use different MIME types we need to learn a little about the `Multipart` and `BodyPart` e-mail classes.

Introducing javax.mail.internet.MimeMultipart

The general container that holds the content of an e-mail is the abstract `Multipart` class, which defines methods for adding, removing, and getting the content of the different parts of an e-mail.

Since, like `Message`, `Multipart` is an abstract class, we must use a concrete subclass for it and the JavaMail API provides the `javax.mail.internet.MimeMultipart` class for use with `MimeMessage` objects. There are many constructors for the `MimeMultipart` class, and many additional methods for manipulating the object. For our utility we only need to use the default constructor and one method.

So far when creating the content of our messages, we have been relying on `setText()` to create the `Multipart` object for our message. From now on we will create and customize our own `MimeMultipart` object by starting with the default constructor:

```
MimeMultipart multipart = new MimeMultipart();
```

The one method of the `MimeMultipart` object we will be using is `addBodyPart()`, which adds `BodyPart` objects to our e-mail content. A message can have many parts, and a `BodyPart` is needed to represent each one.

Like many JavaMail classes, `BodyPart` is an abstract class and the concrete subclass used for a `MimeMessage` is the `MimeBodyPart` class.

The javax.mail.internet.MimeBodyPart Class

A `MimeBodyPart` object represents a piece of content in a `MimeMessage` object. Each `MimeBodyPart` can be thought of as having two parts:

- ❏ A MIME type
- ❏ The content to match the type

When creating a `MimeBodyPart` object we start by using the default constructor:

```
MimeBodyPart mbp = new MimeBodyPart();
```

Next, define a MIME type and set the `MimeBodyPart`'s content, specifying the MIME type. For text messages the MIME type is `text/plain` and the content is just a `String` representing the body of your message:

```
String text = "Hello I am text.";
mbp.setContent(text, "text/plain");
```

Now we have one piece of content for a message. If we stopped and added only this to our message it would be the equivalent of using the `setText()` method.

Here is `safeSendMail.jsp` modified to use what we have just learned instead of using the `setText()` method:

```
<%@ page
  import="java.util.*, javax.mail.*, javax.mail.internet.*"
  errorPage="errorpage.jsp" %>
<%
  Properties props = new Properties();
  props.put("mail.smtp.host", "smtp.mail.yahoo.com");
```

```
Session s = Session.getDefaultInstance(props);

MimeMessage message = new MimeMessage(s);

InternetAddress from = new InternetAddress("yahooUserName@yahoo.com");
message.setFrom(from);

try {
  String toValue = request.getParameter("to");
  if(!toValue.equals("")) {
    InternetAddress to = new InternetAddress(toValue);
    message.addRecipient(Message.RecipientType.TO, to);
  } else {
    throw new MessagingException
            ("You must fill in a value for the \"to\" field.");
  }

  String subject = request.getParameter("subject");
  if(!subject.equals("")) {
    message.setSubject(subject);
  } else {
    throw new MessagingException
            ("You must fill in a value for the \"subject\" field.");
  }

  String text = request.getParameter("text");
  if(!text.equals("")) {
    MimeMultipart mm = new MimeMultipart();
    MimeBodyPart mbp = new MimeBodyPart();
    mbp.setContent(text,"text/plain");
    mm.addBodyPart(mbp);
    message.setContent(mm);
  } else {
    throw new MessagingException
            ("You must fill in a value for the body of the message.");
  }
} catch(MessagingException e) {
  throw new MessagingException("Error getting form values: " +
                                e.toString());
}

// Next line is specific to Yahoo
Store store = s.getStore("pop3");

try {
  // Next line is specific to Yahoo
  store.connect("pop.mail.yahoo.com", "yahooUsername", "yahooPassword");
  Transport.send(message);
} catch(MessagingException e) {
  throw new MessagingException("Cannot send mail. Please contact the " +
          "<a href=\"mailto:admin@example.com\">administrator</a>.");
} finally {
  // Next line is specific to Yahoo
  store.close();
}
```

538

```
%>
<html>
<p align="center">Mail has been sent. Check your Inbox.</p>
<p align="center"><a href="safeSendMail.html">Click here to send
another!</a></p>
</html>
```

The above code would have the exact same effect as our previous `safeSendMail.jsp`.

The benefit of this code is that we can now customize the `MimeBodyPart` object to be of other MIME formats than `text/plain`. Take, for instance, HTML, which has the MIME type `text/html`. If the user wished to send the message as HTML the MIME type can now simply be changed accordingly.

Try it Yourself –Sending HTML Mail

Let's add to our example the option of sending HTML mail in place of plain text. Our HTML and JSP pages will now be called `sendHTMLMail.html` and `sendHTMLMail.jsp` respectively. As before, save these files in `%CATALINA_HOME%\webapps\begjsp-ch17\`.

This is the modified `sendHTMLMail.html`, to which we've added a new field named `"type"`:

```
<html>
<form action="sendHTMLMail.jsp" method="post">
<table>
  <tr><td>to:</td><td><input name="to" size="40"></td></tr>
  <tr><td>subject:</td><td><input name="subject" size="40"></td></tr>
  <tr><td>Type:</td>
      <td>
        <select name="type" size="1">
          <option value="text/plain">Text</option>
          <option value="text/html">HTML</option>
        </select>
      </td>
  </tr>
  <tr>
    <td colspan="2"><textarea name="text" cols="45"
    rows="5"></textarea></td>
  </tr>
</table>
<input type="submit" value="Submit">
</form>
</html>
```

`sendHTMLMail.jsp` is only slightly different from the code used in the previous example:

```
<%@ page
  import="java.util.*, javax.mail.*, javax.mail.internet.*"
  errorPage="errorpage.jsp" %>
<%
  Properties props = new Properties();
  props.put("mail.smtp.host", "smtp.mail.yahoo.com");
  Session s = Session.getDefaultInstance(props);

  MimeMessage message = new MimeMessage(s);
```

```
InternetAddress from = new InternetAddress("yahooUsername@yahoo.com");
message.setFrom(from);

try {
  String toValue = request.getParameter("to");
  if(!toValue.equals("")) {
    InternetAddress to = new InternetAddress(toValue);
    message.addRecipient(Message.RecipientType.TO, to);
  } else {
    throw new MessagingException
            ("You must fill in a value for the \"to\" field.");
  }

  String subject = request.getParameter("subject");
  if(!subject.equals("")) {
    message.setSubject(subject);
  } else {
    throw new MessagingException
            ("You must fill in a value for the \"subject\" field.");
  }

  String text = request.getParameter("text");
  if(!text.equals("")) {
    MimeMultipart mm = new MimeMultipart();
    MimeBodyPart mbp = new MimeBodyPart();
    String type = request.getParameter("type");
    mbp.setContent(text, type);
    mm.addBodyPart(mbp);
    message.setContent(mm);
  } else {
    throw new MessagingException
            ("You must fill in a value for the body of the message.");
  }
} catch(MessagingException e) {
  throw new MessagingException("Error getting form values: " +
                                  e.toString());
}

// Next line is specific to Yahoo
Store store = s.getStore("pop3");

try {
  // Next line is specific to Yahoo
  store.connect("pop.mail.yahoo.com", "yahooUsername", "yahoopassword");
  Transport.send(message);
} catch(MessagingException e) {
  throw new MessagingException("Cannot send mail. Please contact " +
          "the <a href=\"mailto:admin@example.com\">administrator</a>.");
} finally {
  // Next line is specific to Yahoo
  store.close();
}
%>
```

```
<html>
<p align="center">Mail has been sent. Check your Inbox.</p>
<p align="center"><a href="safeSendMail.html">Click here to send
another!</a></p>
</html>
```

Save your changes, start Tomcat and navigate to http://localhost:8080/begjsp-ch17/sendHTMLMail.html:

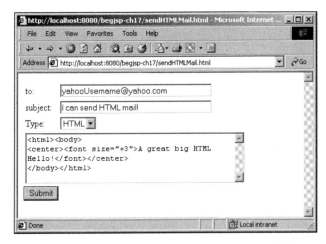

Select the type HTML in the drop down box. Be sure to type in some HTML code in the message of the e-mail, for example:

```
<html>
  <body>
    <center><font size="+3">A great big HTML Hello!</font></center>
  </body>
</html>
```

And press the Submit button. You should see something like:

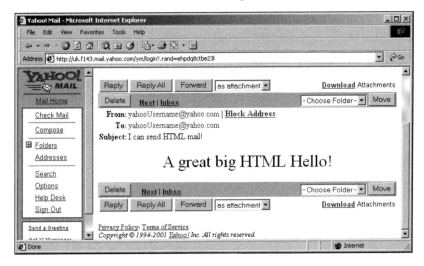

Now go back to the HTML page and select the type **Text**. Be sure to type the same HTML code in as the message of the e-mail, then hit the **Submit** button and check the inbox the mail was sent to. You should see something like this:

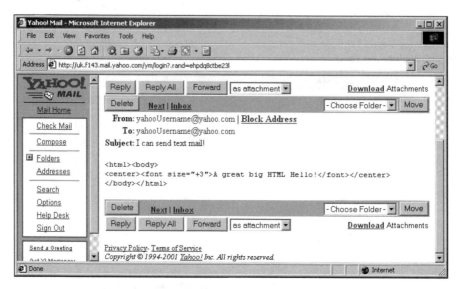

Notice the e-mail does not display the HTML. Instead the HTML code is dumped on the screen. Only when the type is set as **HTML** on the form does the e-mail client display the HTML properly.

How it Works

This example works by changing the content's MIME type. A MIME type tells the e-mail client what type of content a specific part of the e-mail contains. If the e-mail client understands what the MIME type is, it might handle the content specially instead of just showing it as an attachment. Just about every e-mail client understands the `text/plain` MIME type.

In our case, the Yahoo mail client understands exactly what `text/plain` is, and the text of the message is displayed exactly as it would appear in a simple text editor. The Yahoo mail client also understands that `text/html` represents HTML, and that instead of directly showing the text making up the HTML it should format the HTML accordingly. Since we sent two similar messages with different MIME types they were displayed differently.

In the code changes it should be easy to spot where the MIME types come from. In `sendHTMLMail.html` the select box links the value `text/plain` to the **Text** option and the value `text/html` to the **HTML** option:

```
<select name="type" size="1">
  <option value="text/plain">Text</option>
  <option value="text/html">HTML</option>
</select>
```

When the user clicks **Submit**, the appropriate MIME type is sent as a request parameter, based on what the user selected. In `sendHTMLMail.jsp` there is now a fourth parameter, `"type"`, used to determine the MIME type of the message:

```
String type = request.getParameter("type");
mbp.setContent(request.getParameter("text"), type);
```

Instead of using the `setText()` method for setting the content of the e-mail, we are now creating the actual `MimeMultipart` object and `MimeBodyPart` objects needed. Different MIME types can then be used for e-mail sent via `sendHTMLMail.jsp`.

File and URL Attachments

By now you should understand the effect of a MIME type on the content of an e-mail. This naturally leads us to ask what are the different MIME types available. In this chapter we have seen two MIME types, for the most common e-mail message formats: plain text and HTML. These are the only two MIME types we will look at in detail in this chapter.

> *For a quick link to all the official MIME types and corresponding RFCs go to* http://www.isi.edu/in-notes/iana/assignments/media-types/media-types. *Information about MIME types can also be found in the RFCs previously mentioned, at* http://www.imc.org.

Text and HTML messages are usually all that is required for an e-mail application. There is, however, a need to sometimes attach additional non text-based resources to an e-mail, and this chapter will not leave you in the dark on this matter.

The JavaMail API conveniently provides a method of attaching any other file or URL resource to an e-mail message, via a `DataHandler` object.

javax.activation.DataHandler and Non-Text Attachments

The JavaMail API does not restrict a message to text only; any form of information may be used as part of a `MimeMessage`. It is common for file attachments to be included as part of an e-mail message, in addition to a text message. The JavaMail API provides an easy mechanism allowing us to include non-text `BodyPart` objects, by using a `DataHandler` object.

The JavaMail API does not have any `DataHandler` classes bundled with it. Instead JavaMail relies on the common data handling functionality available in the **JavaBeans Activation Framework** (**JAF**) that we downloaded earlier. The JAF can identify arbitrary types of data and expose the operations that are performable on those types via an appropriate JavaBean.

The JAF contains the two `DataHandler` classes we will be covering, as well as documentation for them.

So far we have been using the `setText()` and `setContent()` methods to set the MIME type and text for a part of our e-mail messages. There is another method, `setDataHandler()`, that takes a `DataHandler` object as a parameter and accomplishes the same task.

These `DataHandler` objects automatically handle some arbitrary data and let the JavaMail API use it for the content of a `MimeBodyPart`.

Here is a JSP page that uses the `setDataHandler()` method instead of `setContent()` or `setText()`. It is identical in functionality to the previous `sendHTMLMail.jsp`, apart from the use of `setDataHandler()`:

543

```
<%@ page import="java.util.*,
                 javax.mail.*,
                 javax.mail.internet.*,
                 javax.activation.*"
         errorPage="errorpage.jsp" %>
<%
  Properties props = new Properties();
  props.put("mail.smtp.host", "smtp.mail.yahoo.com");
  Session s = Session.getDefaultInstance(props);

  MimeMessage message = new MimeMessage(s);

  InternetAddress from = new InternetAddress("yahooUser@yahoo.com");
  message.setFrom(from);

  try {
    String toValue = request.getParameter("to");
    if(!toValue.equals("")) {
      InternetAddress to = new InternetAddress(toValue);
      message.addRecipient(Message.RecipientType.TO, to);
    } else {
      throw new
      MessagingException
             ("You must fill in a value for the \"to\" field.");
    }

    String subject = request.getParameter("subject");
    if(!subject.equals("")) {
      message.setSubject(subject);
    } else {
      throw new MessagingException
             ("You must fill in a value for the \"subject\" field.");
    }

    String text = request.getParameter("text");
    if(!text.equals("")) {
      MimeMultipart mm = new MimeMultipart();
      MimeBodyPart mbp = new MimeBodyPart();
      String type = request.getParameter("type");
      DataHandler dh = new DataHandler(text, type);
      mbp.setDataHandler(dh);
      mm.addBodyPart(mbp);
      message.setContent(mm);
    } else {
      throw new MessagingException
             ("You must fill in a value for the body of the message.");
    }
  } catch(MessagingException e) {
    throw new MessagingException("Error getting form values: " +
                                 e.toString());
  }

  // Next line is specific to Yahoo
  Store store = s.getStore("pop3");
```

```
      try {
        // Next line is specific to Yahoo
        store.connect("pop.mail.yahoo.com", "yahooUser", "yahooPassword");
        Transport.send(message);
      } catch(MessagingException e) {
        throw new MessagingException("Cannot send mail. Please contact the " +
                "<a href=\"mailto:admin@example.com\">administrator</a>.");
      } finally {
        // Next line is specific to Yahoo
        store.close();
      }
%>
<html>
<p align="center">Mail has been sent. Check your Inbox.</p>
<p align="center"><a href="safeSendMail.html">Click here to send
another!</a></p>
</html>
```

The above code would function identically to the previous `sendHTMLMail.jsp`. Since the constructor for the `DataHandler` takes the same parameters as the `setContent()` method, it may appear as if we have not gained any benefit.

To see the value of the new code we need to look at another constructor for the `DataHandler` object:

public DataHandler(DataSource ds)

This constructor requires one parameter, a `javax.activation.DataSource` object.

`DataSource` objects provide a way to link resources, such as files, with your `DataHandler`. The JAF provides two pre-built `DataSource` objects, `FileDataSource` and `URLDataSource`.

The javax.activation.FileDataSource Class

A `FileDataSource` object may represent local files, and anything your server has direct access to. So, a local file may be attached to a `MimeMessage` object by creating a new `MimeBodyPart`:

```
MimeMultipart mm = new MimeMulipart();
MimeBodyPart mbp = new MimeBodyPart();
```

setting the correct `DataSource` for the file:

```
FileDataSource fds = new FileDataSource("c:/example.txt");
mbp.setDataHandler(new DataHandler(fds));
```

and then adding the `MimeBodyPart` to the `MimeMultipart` object for the current message:

```
mm.addBodyPart(mbp);
```

The javax.activation.URLDataSource Class

Remote resources, not a URL pointing to them, are represented by an `URLDataSource` object. A remote resource may be attached to a `MimeMessage` object by creating a new `MimeBodyPart` object:

```
MimeMultipart mm = new MimeMulipart();
MimeBodyPart mbp = new MimeBodyPart();
```

setting the correct `DataSource` for the URL:

```
URLDataSource uds = new URLDataSource("http://www.jspinsider.com/logo.jpg");
mbp.setDataHandler(new DataHandler(uds));
```

and then adding the `MimeBodyPart` to the `MimeMultipart` object for the current message:

```
mm.addBodyPart(mbp);
```

Between the two `DataSource` objects, just about any resource can be added to a `MimeMessage`. Let's look at an example to see how this works.

Try it out – Include a File and a URL Resource in an E-mail

Save the following code as `sendDataSources.jsp`:

```
<%@ page import="
    java.util.*,
    javax.mail.*,
    javax.mail.internet.*,
    javax.activation.*,
    java.net.*" %>
<%
  Properties props = new Properties();
  props.put("mail.smtp.host", "smtp.mail.yahoo.com");
  Session s = Session.getDefaultInstance(props);

  MimeMessage message = new MimeMessage(s);

  InternetAddress from = new InternetAddress("yahooUsername@yahoo.com");
  message.setFrom(from);

  InternetAddress to = new InternetAddress("yahooUsername@yahoo.com");
  message.addRecipient(Message.RecipientType.TO, to);
  message.setSubject("Trying out DataHandlers.");

  MimeMultipart mm = new MimeMultipart();
  MimeBodyPart mbp = new MimeBodyPart();

  DataHandler dh = new DataHandler("Trying out a datahandler",
                                   "text/plain");
  mbp.setFileName("message.txt");
  mbp.setDataHandler(dh);
  mm.addBodyPart(mbp);
```

```
  mbp = new MimeBodyPart();
  URLDataSource uds = new URLDataSource(
                          new URL("http://www.jspinsider.com/logo.jpg"));
  dh = new DataHandler(uds);
  mbp.setDataHandler(dh);
  mbp.setFileName("url.txt");
  mm.addBodyPart(mbp);

  mbp = new MimeBodyPart();
  FileDataSource fds = new FileDataSource("C:/test.txt");
  dh = new DataHandler(fds);
  mbp.setDataHandler(dh);
  mbp.setFileName("test.txt");
  mm.addBodyPart(mbp);

  message.setContent(mm);

  // Next two lines are specific to Yahoo
  Store store = s.getStore("pop3");
  store.connect("pop.mail.yahoo.com", "yahooUsername", "yahooPassword");

  Transport.send(message);

  // Next line is specific to Yahoo
  store.close();
%>
<html>
<p align="center">Mail has been sent. Check your Inbox.</p>
</html>
```

As before, you will need to change the username and password accordingly.

Save the following file as `test.txt` on the `c:` drive of your computer:

```
Sample file. While this is text it could just have easily been any other text or
non-text file on the local computer.
```

If there is no `c:` drive save it in a convenient location and make sure you change the following line of `sendDataSources.jsp` to refer to the correct location:

```
FileDataSource fds = new FileDataSource("C:/test.txt");
```

Start up Tomcat and navigate to http://localhost:8080/begjsp-ch17/sendDataSources.jsp. You should see a message confirming that your message has been sent.

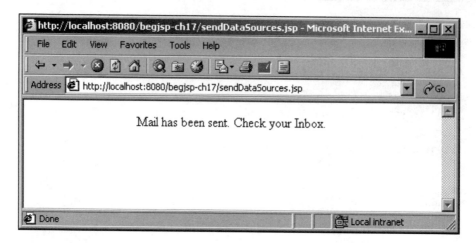

Now, open the message in your inbox:

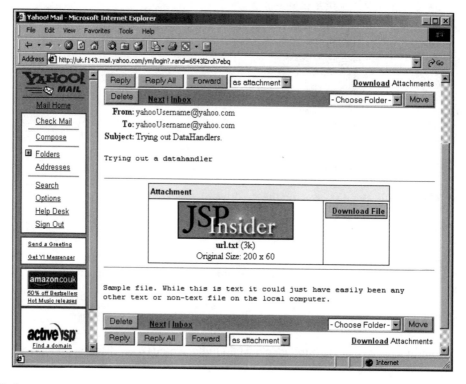

How It Works

The example works same as the earlier examples, except that we're now using `DataHandler` objects for each part of the e-mail.

First all of the needed libraries are imported. A new package appears here named `java.net.*`. This is a standard Java package that contains the `URL` class. We need this class for use with the `URLDataSource` object:

```
<%@ page import="java.util.*,
                 javax.mail.*,
                 javax.mail.internet.*,
                 javax.activation.*,
                 java.net.*" %>
```

As before, a `Session` and a `Message` object are created:

```
Properties props = new Properties();
props.put("mail.smtp.host", "smtp.mail.yahoo.com");
Session s = Session.getDefaultInstance(props);

MimeMessage message = new MimeMessage(s);
```

The message is addressed:

```
InternetAddress from = new InternetAddress("yahooUsername@yahoo.com");
message.setFrom(from);

InternetAddress to = new InternetAddress("yahooUsername@yahoo.com");
message.addRecipient(Message.RecipientType.TO, to);
```

And we set a descriptive subject:

```
message.setSubject("Trying out DataHandlers.");
```

The new code comes next, and demonstrates what we just learned about `DataHandler` objects, `DataSource` objects, and the `setDataHandler()` method. Three different `DataHandler` objects are created and set as part of the e-mail content.

The first `DataHandler` is for a text message, like the ones we've been sending all along. A new piece of code is the `setFileName()` method.

```
DataHandler dh = new DataHandler("Trying out a datahandler",
                                 "text/plain");
mbp.setFileName("message.txt");
```

This method lets us set the name of the file, as an e-mail client should display it. Look back on the screen shot showing the attachment names. They all match up with these values.

The second `DataHandler` is created using an `URLDataSource` object, which relies on a `URL` object for linking to a resource online. In this case we link to a web site about JSP, and link the site's logo.

```
mbp = new MimeBodyPart();
URLDataSource uds = new URLDataSource(
                        new URL("http://www.jspinsider.com/logo.jpg"));
dh = new DataHandler(uds);
mbp.setDataHandler(dh);
mbp.setFileName("url.txt");
mm.addBodyPart(mbp);
```

The attachment will be the same information that would be returned to a browser visiting http://www.jspinsider.com/logo.jpg. Optionally we could have attached full pages of the site too. Just change the URL to your favorite web page.

The third `DataHandler` uses the `FileDataSource` object to include a file from the local computer sending the e-mail. A `File` object does not need to be created for the `FileDataSource` object's constructor; we only need a `String` containing the file's location:

```
mbp = new MimeBodyPart();
FileDataSource fds = new FileDataSource("C:/test.txt");
dh = new DataHandler(fds);
mbp.setDataHandler(dh);
mbp.setFileName("test.txt");
mm.addBodyPart(mbp);
```

Once we've added all the `MimeBodyPart` objects to the message's `MimeMultipart` object, we set the `MimeMultipart` as the content for the message:

```
message.setContent(mm);
```

Finally the message is sent off and a confirmation is displayed for the user:

```
    // Next two lines are specific to Yahoo
    Store store = s.getStore("pop3");
    store.connect("pop.mail.yahoo.com", "yahooUsername", "yahooPassword");

    Transport.send(message);

    // Next line is specific to Yahoo
    store.close();
%>
<html>
<p align="center">Mail has been sent. Check your Inbox.</p>
</html>
```

Sending More E-mail

The previous examples have shown you how to create and send just about any type of e-mail. Much of the time, plain text messages may be sufficient for your application; but if you require more than text support. You now know how to change content types and include local or remote resources.

The previous example also demonstrated how to send several "parts" in a single e-mail. In general, you can attach as many parts as you require to a single `MimeMessage` object. Simply create as many `MimeBodyPart` objects as required, and add them all to the same `MimeMultipart` object.

As you have seen, the JavaMail API provides an excellent mechanism for sending e-mail. Often your JSP web applications will only need to send e-mail, but sometimes it is necessary to also retrieve and manipulate messages from an e-mail server. The JavaMail API also provides support for this functionality.

Receiving and Handling Messages

The JavaMail API complements the `javax.mail.Transport` object, used for sending messages, with the `javax.mail.Store` object for retrieving messages. Creating a `Store` object relies on the current session but is still done in a protocol-specific way. Once the `Store` object's `connect()` method has been called e-mail can be retrieved from the hosting server.

You should recognize this first snippet from previous examples in this chapter. We had to use this code with our Yahoo mail account, as Yahoo requires us to log in this way before allowing direct SMTP access for sending mail:

```
Store store = session.getStore("POP3");
store.connect("your.mail.server", "username", "password");
```

This code was all we needed to make our mail-sending examples work with the Yahoo mail server. What we did not cover was what else could be accomplished once the `Store` object successfully connected to the server. Once connected, a `Store` object can also read e-mail from the server by asking for an e-mail folder and creating a new object to represent it.

A `javax.mail.Folder` object represents a particular folder of mail on the server. Once a `Store` object is connected we can call the `getFolder()` method. This method takes a argument of type `String` to get an e-mail folder on the server. For the POP3 protocol the only folder available should be `"INBOX"`, and this is the string value we pass to the `getFolder()` method.

After we have a folder object we can open it for reading e-mail. The `open()` method accomplishes this:

```
Folder folder = store.getFolder("INBOX");
folder.open(Folder.READ_ONLY);
```

A few options exist for reading messages from a `Folder` object. In general, a `Folder` object can be opened and read to retrieve an array of messages. Then we are right back to the familiar `MimeMessage` object we learned about earlier.

```
MimeMessage[] messages = (MimeMessage[])folder.getMessages();
```

Finally, after all the operations on the e-mail server are finished the `Store` and `Folder` connections should be terminated with the `close()` method. If this is not done the server might continue keeping the connection alive and the user logged on, which can cause problems as the e-mail server may only allow one connection per user.

As good practice you should always call the `close()` method when done retrieving e-mail. The `Folder` object's `close()` method takes an additional argument specifying if e-mail marked for deletion should be permanently removed:

```
folder.close(true);
store.close();
```

`close()` was the other method we had to use when sending mail to the Yahoo mail server. In those examples we never actually retrieved any messages using the `Store` object; instead the connection was

551

needed simply to verify our identity before we could send e-mail using the `Transport` object. After every message was sent we called the `close()` method on the `Store` object.

In general, the above code will be repeated in all of the examples of retrieving e-mail; the only thing that changes is what is done with the retrieved messages. Let's build an example application to complement our earlier examples.

Building the above code into a JSP is not much work at all: we'll build a simple JSP that connects to our POP mail server and displays a list of messages along with their bodies.

Try it Out – Make a JSP E-mail Reading Utility

As when we created our mail-sending application, we'll split the code down into two separate pages: an HTML form for us to input our server, username, and password, and a JSP page that performs the actual operations on the mail server. Let's start with the HTML form. Save the following code as `readmail.html` in `%CATALINA_HOME%\webapps\begjsp-ch17\`:

```html
<html>
<form action="readmail.jsp" method="post">
<table>
  <tr>
    <td>user:</td>
    <td><input name="username" size="40"></td>
  </tr>
  <tr>
    <td>password:</td>
    <td><input type="password" name="password" size="40"></td>
  </tr>
  <tr>
    <td>server:</td>
    <td><input name="server" size="40"></td>
  </tr>
</table>
<input type="submit" value="Submit">
</form>
</html>
```

The other page we need is the JSP page that will connect to the POP server and read the messages. Save the following code as `readmail.jsp`, in `%CATALINA_HOME%\webapps\begjsp-ch17\`:

```jsp
<%@ page import="java.util.*, javax.mail.*, javax.mail.internet.*"
  errorPage="errorpage.jsp" %>
<%
  Properties props = new Properties();
  Session s = Session.getInstance(props);

  Store store = s.getStore("pop3");
  try {
    String username = request.getParameter("username");
    String password = request.getParameter("password");
```

```
      String server = request.getParameter("server");
      store.connect(server, username, password);
   } catch (MessagingException e){
      throw new Exception("Cannot log on to e-mail server. Please verify " +
            "the username and password are correct for the given server.");
}


   try {
      Folder folder = store.getFolder("INBOX");
      folder.open(Folder.READ_ONLY);

      Message[] messages = folder.getMessages();

      for (int i=0; i<messages.length; i++) {
        InternetAddress[] from = (InternetAddress[])messages[i].getFrom();
        InternetAddress[] to = (InternetAddress[])messages[i]
                                    .getRecipients(Message.RecipientType.TO);
%>

      <p>To <%= to[0].getAddress() %>, from <%= from[0].getAddress() %>,
        subject <%= messages[i].getSubject() %></p>

      <p>
<%
      if(messages[i].getContentType().indexOf("text/plain") != -1) {
        out.print(messages[i].getContent().toString());
      } else {
        MimeMultipart mm = (MimeMultipart)messages[i].getContent();
        MimeBodyPart mbp = (MimeBodyPart)mm.getBodyPart(0);
        out.print(mbp.getContent().toString());
      }
 %>
      </p>

<%  }     // End of for loop
    }     // End of try block
  catch (MessagingException e) {
    throw new Exception("Cannot read messages. Please verify your e-mail " +
                      "server has a valid INBOX");
  } finally {
    store.close();
  }
%>
```

Start Tomcat and navigate to http://localhost:8080/begjsp-ch17/readmail.html. You should see something like:

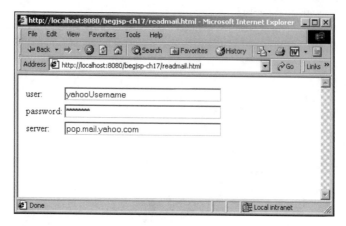

Fill in the form with the appropriate information and press the Submit button. A screen should appear that displays some information about each of the messages in the inbox. You should see something like:

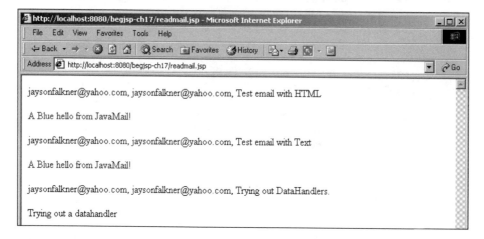

How it Works

First all of the needed libraries are imported, along with an error page set to errorpage.jsp. Should the user mistype some information the same friendly error message page we created earlier will be displayed:

```
<%@ page import="java.util.*, javax.mail.*, javax.mail.internet.*"
    errorPage="errorpage.jsp" %>
```

A Properties and Session object are then created:

```
Properties props = new Properties();
Session s = Session.getInstance(props);
```

From the `Session` object we can get a `Store` object, which we use to connect to an e-mail server. The code is the same as we previously used in the mail sending examples, but now we are using dynamic values as the arguments for the username, password and server, which are retrieved from the submitted form.

```
Store store = s.getStore("pop3");
try {
  String username = request.getParameter("username");
  String password = request.getParameter("password");
  String server = request.getParameter("server");
  store.connect(server, username, password);
} catch (MessagingException e){
  throw new Exception("Cannot log on to e-mail server. Please verify " +
        "the username and password are correct for the given server.");
}
```

Once we have connected to the server we want to access the inbox. There are two possible options we can use when opening a folder:

❑   `Folder.READ_ONLY`

❑   `Folder.READ_WRITE`

Either of the two will provide access to a folder's resources, but only `Folder.READ_WRITE` will allow for messages to be changed. The appropriate value should be passed in to the `open()` method of the `Folder` object. In this sense the `Folder.READ_ONLY` value should be used if you are only interested in reading e-mail. The `Folder.READ_WRITE` value should be used if you would like to also edit or delete messages.

For this page we only want to read the messages:

```
try {
  Folder folder = store.getFolder("INBOX");
  folder.open(Folder.READ_ONLY);
```

We can start working with the messages in the folder by calling the `getMessages()` method on the `Folder` object:

```
Message[] messages = folder.getMessages();
```

Finally, we can start manipulating the array of messages. Each message object has 'getter' methods to compliment the 'setters' we were using previously. We use a small loop that will call the getters and display some information about each message.

The first two 'getter' methods return the first FROM and TO address of the e-mail. An array of `InternetAddress` objects is returned for each of the 'getters' because many addresses may be included. This example uses the zero indexes of the arrays for the first `InternetAddress` objects; a more robust tool would have to loop through the entire array from start to end:

```
for (int i=0; i<messages.length; i++) {
  InternetAddress[] from = (InternetAddress[])messages[i].getFrom();
  InternetAddress[] to = (InternetAddress[])messages[i]
```

```
                                     .getRecipients(Message.RecipientType.TO);
    %>

        <p>To <%= to[0].getAddress() %>, from <%= from[0].getAddress() %>,
```

The final 'getter' method displays the one and only subject of the e-mail:

```
        subject <%= messages[i].getSubject() %></p>

    <p>
```

For each message the content type is quickly checked. If the content is only a string it is displayed directly. If the content is anything else the first MimeBodyPart object is retrieved and displayed as a String. This sample page is assuming that each message is a String; for a more robust application you should use the getContentType() method to handle individual MIME types accordingly:

```
    <%
        if(messages[i].getContentType().indexOf("text/plain") != -1) {
            out.print(messages[i].getContent().toString());
        } else {
            MimeMultipart mm = (MimeMultipart)messages[i].getContent();
            MimeBodyPart mbp = (MimeBodyPart)mm.getBodyPart(0);
            out.print(mbp.getContent().toString());
        }
    %>
        </p>

    <%  }     // End of for loop
        }         // End of try block
      catch (MessagingException e) {
        throw new Exception("Cannot read messages. Please verify your e-mail " +
                            "server has a valid INBOX");
      }
```

Once we have finished accessing the folder and finished with the Store object the close() methods should be called to end the connection with the e-mail server. We could also pass the true value as an argument to the Folder object's close() method to expunge any deleted e-mails. Again this statement appears inside a finally block to ensure the connection is always closed:

```
        finally {
        store.close();
      }
    %>
```

The resulting web page will differ depending on how many messages are in the inbox. Running this on the Yahoo account you have been using for the earlier examples would result in a page looking similar to that shown above.

Notice the contents of the e-mails are displayed without regard to the MIME type. While the Yahoo mail client displayed both plain text and HTML correctly, our utility did not. If we wanted to correctly display the text we would have to check for specific MIME types and deal with the HTML markup.

Reading More E-mail

Here is where we will finish our look at receiving e-mail. The coverage was somewhat brief, but should give you a good start on reading e-mail.

Once the `Message` objects are retrieved from the e-mail server it is only a matter of using the getter methods to retrieve the message's content. Pretty up the display, and you too can have a mail client like Yahoo.

In general the code we have made for the mail reader utility will be the same for any e-mail server JavaMail supports. Remember that as the JavaMail API abstracts the process of receiving e-mail, there was only one place in our code that required the protocol for our e-mail server.

```
Store store = s.getStore("pop3");
```

The `readmail.html` form could easily be modified to have another field allowing the user to choose between mail protocols. The JavaMail API currently supports both the POP3 and IMAP protocols, and using `imap` in place of `pop3` would create a `Store` object that uses the IMAP protocol. The rest of the code would stay the same.

Keep in mind we have only seen how to display messages with only one, text-based, body part; manipulating and dealing with multipart e-mails and file attachments is beyond the scope of this chapter. However, you should be aware that not all messages will be text based and you need to be prepared to deal with them.

Links of Interest

In most cases you will only need to send e-mail from your applications and support for such functionality is widely available. In fact many open-source projects provide pre-built custom tag libraries, which were covered in Chapters 6 and 10.

Taking advantage of these tag libraries is a great way to use the JavaMail API with JSP. Here are a few of the current most popular tag libraries.

❑ **JSP Insider Unofficial JavaMail Tag Library**
http://www.jspinsider.com/jspkit/javamail

JSP Insider provides a set of custom tags built to support the JavaMail API. These unofficial JavaMail tags are complemented with tutorials and articles on the site. In fact many of the examples from this chapter can be found at JSP Insider.

❑ **Jakarta Mailer Tag Library**
http://jakarta.apache.org/taglibs/doc/mailer-doc/intro.html

The Jakarta project also has a set of e-mail tags called the mailer taglib. These tags currently provide the functionality to send e-mail using the JavaMail API.

For those situations where a tag library is not desired having a good FAQ is critical, and arguably the best JavaMail FAQ is available from JGuru:

❑ **JGuru JavaMail FAQ**
http://jguru.com/faq/home.jsp?topic=JavaMail

Sun Microsystems also provides the official JavaMail FAQ:

❑ **Official JavaMail FAQ**
http://java.sun.com/products/javamail/FAQ.html

Summary

In this chapter we learned about combining JavaMail API functionality with JSP pages. We learned that the JavaMail API is provided by Sun Microsystems for dealing with e-mail. What makes the JavaMail API so useful is that it allows developers to build Java e-mail utilities without worrying about the tedious task of implementing the standard e-mail RFCs.

The rest of the chapter looked at the specifics of sending and receiving e-mail using JavaMail:

❑ First, we looked at sending e-mail. Sending plain text e-mail was the simplest task, and even had a convenience method, setText() available to call on MimeMessage objects.

❑ To enhance our e-mail messages we introduced MIME types, and the MimeMultipart and MimeBodyPart classes. By manually setting the parts of an e-mail message we learned how to remove the restrictions of plain text e-mail.

❑ We saw how to create attachments to our e-mail messages, from both files and URL sources.

❑ Lastly, we introduced the Store and Folder objects, which connect to and read e-mail from an e-mail server. We also saw how to retrieve information about the messages on the server.

Combining JSP and JavaMail together provides a great tool to add useful functionality to your web applications and can be made even easier by using some of the widely available custom tag libraries.

Back in Chapter 12 we looked at different ways of structuring our web applications, to make them easier to understand, extend, and maintain. One way of easing this a lot is to use a ready-made **framework** to provide a lot of the "infrastructure" code. In the next chapter we'll look at one such framework, known as **Struts**, which is becoming very popular as a basis for JSP web application development.

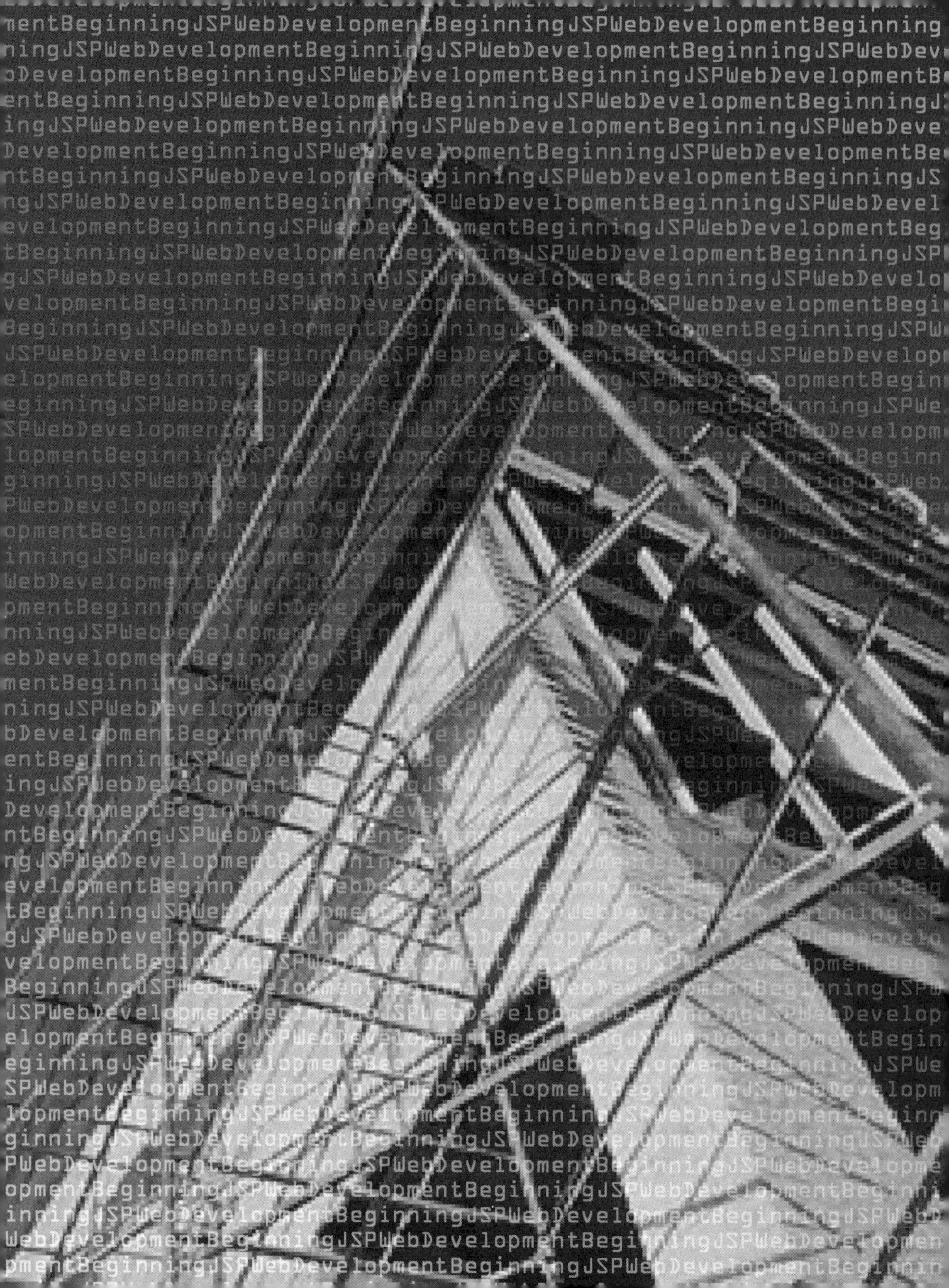
BeginningJSPWebDevelopment

The Struts Framework

In the previous chapters we have seen how to write JSPs, use custom tags, and access relational databases. We've discussed how to track users, and looked at the architectural options for developing JSP-based web applications. We have also introduced you to the concept of J2EE web applications, and the use of web containers for utilizing system level services (for instance security).

There seem to be a lot of issues to consider when building an application from scratch. And there appears to be a lot of code to write if we want to incorporate these basic features in our own applications. Surely there must be an easier way? After all, there must be lots of well-designed JSP web applications out there that have already implemented these features, so why can't we reuse some of this pre-existing functionality?

The answer is that we can, and we should. Instead of reinventing the wheel every time you develop a JSP-based web application, it makes sense to reuse a pre-existing **framework** that will take care of common architectural issues, and provide a library of components for tasks that are performed repeatedly. On top of this you can then build the components that are unique to your application. These frameworks can be developed within your organization and then reused, or you can use third-party off-the-shelf frameworks. However, it's a good idea to reuse third-party software wherever possible, as there is no point to go through the tedious cycles of analysis, design, development and testing if there is already tried-and-tested third-party software available that can be easily integrated into the system.

In this chapter we will be looking at an off-the-shelf JSP-based web application framework, the **Apache Struts Framework**. We will focus on the following aspects of Struts:

- ❑ Building and installing Struts
- ❑ Struts Architecture
- ❑ Controller and configuration
- ❑ Actions, mappings and forwards
- ❑ Action form beans
- ❑ Tag library
- ❑ Internationalization

We'll finish the chapter by creating an application that uses the Struts framework.

Why Do We Need Web Frameworks?

If you study almost any real-world application, you will find that its components can be broadly classified into two types:

❑   Business components

❑   Application services

In most scenarios, it is difficult to reuse the business components across different applications, since the functionality provided by the business components may not be needed in other applications: it may be unique to your application. However, application services can be reused across applications within an organization, as well as across organizations, because they provide services that are useful to many different types of application. These application services might include request routing (for an MVC architecture), error handling, generating client-side scripts in a generic manner, and ready-made tag libraries.

Any piece of software that can provide these types of services, and be used to build your application by incorporating your business components, can be termed a web application **framework**.

Many big organizations develop in-house frameworks that can be reused by different applications developed within the organization. However, some large companies, as well as smaller organizations that can't afford enough time and resources for developing an in-house framework, can use third-party off-the-shelf frameworks instead: either commercial software or open-source freeware. The advantage of this route is that you get a package that is already developed and tested, and therefore ready for use – saving time, money and resources.

In this chapter we will be covering one of the most popular third-party web application frameworks, the **Apache Struts Framework**. In the next two chapters we build on our knowledge, designing and developing a real application using Struts.

Introducing the Struts Framework

Struts (`org.apache.struts`) is an open-source web application framework, based on the MVC design pattern, and built using the servlet and JSP APIs that can be used for building complex web applications. It allows us to decouple the business logic, control logic, and presentation code of an application, making it more reusable and maintainable. The Struts framework is a part of the Jakarta Project managed by the Apache Software Foundation. Struts can be downloaded from http://jakarta.apache.org/struts.

The Struts framework provides the following services.

❑   A servlet that acts as the controller in the MVC paradigm.

❑   JSP tag libraries for bean management, HTML and JavaScript generation, template handling, and flow control in a JSP.

❑   A framework for **internationalizing** messages. Internationalizing your webapp means making sure that any user messages that occur when your webapp is being used are written in the preferred spoken language of the user. This means that you need to create an *application resources* file containing the messages for each language.

❑   An implementation of JDBC to define datasources and a database connection pool.

❑   A generic error and exception handling mechanism, which involves retrieving error messages from an application resources file.

❑   XML parsing.

❑   File upload utilities.

❑   Logging utilities.

For the rest of this chapter, we will explain how to use many (although not all) of these features, and we will finish with a case study that uses them too.

The Struts Architecture

Let's start off at the top. Struts is built using the MVC paradigm; the diagram below depicts the high-level architecture for this framework.

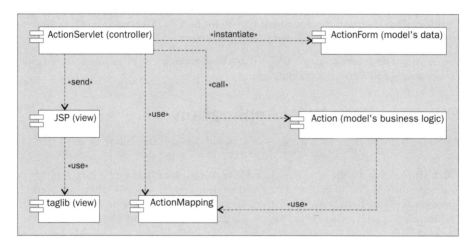

We will now review each of the elements of this diagram.

The presentation tier (the *view*) of a Struts-based application is built using the **Struts tag libraries** (taglibs). Requests from the client are passed to a servlet called the `ActionServlet`, which acts as the *controller*. In an application that uses Struts, all the requests that need to go through the framework pass through the `ActionServlet`. This `ActionServlet` passes data from the request into an `ActionForm` JavaBean.

An `ActionForm` is a JavaBean that represents the input data from a form view component. These forms are generated by JSPs using the Struts `html` tag library. The bean is populated with `request` parameters by the `ActionServlet`, which may also ask the `ActionForm` to validate the form data that the user submitted.

The `ActionServlet` is configured by defining a set of `ActionMappings`. An `ActionMapping` is an object that maps the URL in a request to components provided by the application developer to process the request. Configuration of the `ActionServlet` and `ActionMappings` are performed in XML configuration files.

The application-specific components used to process the request are known as `Action` classes; they represent the *model* in the MVC architecture. It may be used to validate the information entered by the users, and if an application error occurs during information processing the `Action` class can create instances of `error` objects that are then stored in the HTTP `request` object. If the logic within the `Action` class is been executed successfully, the class passes an `ActionForward` object, representing the JSP needed to render the response, to the controller. These `ActionForwards` come in two kinds: forwards specific to a particular `Action` class, or a global forward (any `Action` class can pass these `ActionForwards` to the controller).

Installing and Configuring Struts

The latest version of the Struts source files or binaries can be downloaded from the Jakarta web site http://jakarta.apache.org/struts. At the time of press, the final release of Struts 1.0 had just been released, and we recommend that you download the zipped binary distribution of this. Once you have downloaded this zipped archive extract the contents to a folder in your local file system. The unpacked folder will contain the following two folders.

❏   `lib`: This folder includes the `struts.jar` file, the tag library descriptors (`tlds`) for the Struts custom tags, and the document-type definition (DTD) for the Struts configuration file `struts-config.xml` mentioned in the last section.

❏   `webapps`: This folder contains the web application archive (WAR) files for the example applications and Struts documentation.

Using Struts in Your Web Application

To use the Struts framework in your webapp you should perform the following steps.

1. Make sure you have the `struts.jar` file that is present in the `lib` directory of your Struts software distribution in your `CLASSPATH` environmental variable when you compile your Java classes, especially your `Action` classes. Whenever you create a new webapp that uses Struts, place a copy of `struts.jar` in a `lib` folder below the `WEB-INF` folder.

2. Copy all of the tag library descriptors present in the `lib` directory of your Struts directory to the `WEB-INF` folder of your webapp.

3. Modify the web application deployment descriptor (`web.xml`) to declare the Struts `ActionServlet`, and map the required requests to the `ActionServlet` as shown below:

```
<servlet>
  <servlet-name>action</servlet-name>
  <servlet-class>
    org.apache.struts.action.ActionServlet
  </servlet-class>
  <load-on-startup>2</load-on-startup>
</servlet>

<servlet-mapping>
```

```
    <servlet-name>action</servlet-name>
    <url-pattern>*.do</url-pattern>
  </servlet-mapping>
```

The above excerpt from the `web.xml` file declares the `ActionServlet` by name, and maps the request URIs ending with `.do` to the `ActionServlet`. The (optional) contents of the `<load-on-startup>` element must be a positive integer indicating the priority of this servlet. Lower integers are loaded before higher integers, so this servlet should be loaded second. The `ActionServlet` takes a host of initialization parameters. All of these parameters have default values if not specified. You should refer to the Struts documentation (http://jakarta.apache.org/struts/userGuide/) for further details.

4. Modify `web.xml` to declare logical names for the Struts tag library location to be used in the JSPs, as shown below:

```
<taglib>
  <taglib-uri>/bean</taglib-uri>
  <taglib-location>/WEB-INF/struts-bean.tld</taglib-location>
</taglib>

<taglib>
  <taglib-uri>/form</taglib-uri>
  <taglib-location>/WEB-INF/struts-form.tld</taglib-location>
</taglib>

<taglib>
  <taglib-uri>/logic</taglib-uri>
  <taglib-location>/WEB-INF/struts-logic.tld</taglib-location>
</taglib>

<taglib>
  <taglib-uri>/template</taglib-uri>
  <taglib-location>/WEB-INF/struts-template.tld</taglib-location>
</taglib>
```

The excerpt shown above maps the tag library descriptor files for Struts `bean`, `form`, `logic` and `template` tags to the logical URIs `/bean`, `/form`, `/logic` and `/template` respectively. This means that within a JSP file these tag libraries can be used as:

```
<@ taglib uri="/bean" prefix="bean" %>
<@ taglib uri="/form" prefix="form" %>
<@ taglib uri="/logic" prefix="logic" %>
<@ taglib uri="/template" prefix="template" %>
```

5. You will need to create a Struts configuration file `struts-config.xml` that will contain the `ActionMapping` information, JDBC datasource information, `ActionForm` beans information, and global forwards for your webapp. Copy it to the `WEB-INF` directory of your webapp. We are going to discuss the contents of this configuration file next, and we will create one later too for our example application based upon Struts.

The Struts Configuration File

The controller element in the Struts MVC model comprises the components:

- ☐ `ActionServlet` (the main controller component)
- ☐ `ActionMapping` objects

The `ActionServlet` is the main component of the controller element, responsible for delegating requests. To do this, it needs a guide to which requests need to go to which components; in other words it needs to understand the *mapping* of a particular request, based on its URL, to the component that will process the request. This mapping information is contained in `ActionMapping` objects.

`ActionMappings` are defined in a Struts configuration XML file, provided by the application developer, and loaded by the `ActionServlet` on startup. The name and location of the configuration file can be defined as an initialization parameter to the `ActionServlet`. If not specified it defaults to the `.../WEB-INF/struts-config.xml` file. This file also defines JDBC datasources, `ActionForm` beans and global forwards. The `ActionServlet` can also be forced to reload this configuration information programmatically.

The root element for the configuration file is `<struts-config>`. The configuration file is used to define the following information.

- ☐ `ActionForm` beans. Each bean is defined within `<form-bean>` element, and these elements are grouped together inside the `<form-beans>` element.
- ☐ `ActionMappings`. Action definitions are placed inside `<action>` elements, and these elements are placed within the `<action-mappings>` element.
- ☐ Global Forwards. We can define global forwards for JSP pages that will be used a lot in our application. Each global forward is defined within a `<forward>` element, and these elements are grouped together under `<global-forwards>`.
- ☐ JDBC Data sources. We can also configure connections to external databases in this configuration file. Each datasource is defined under a `<data-source>` element, and these elements are in turn grouped together under the element `<data-sources>` in the Struts configuration file.

We will now take a look at how to configure each of these in turn, by building up an example `struts-config.xml` file.

Walking Through a Sample Struts Configuration File

We start off with the top-level `<struts-config>` element:

```
<struts-config>
```

Now let's configure a form bean.

Configuring ActionForm Beans

As we have noted, `ActionForm` beans are used by the `ActionServlet` to hold `request` parameters. These beans have attribute names that correspond to the names of the HTTP `request` parameters. The controller populates the `ActionForm` bean instances from the `request` parameters, and then passes the instances to `Action` classes.

`ActionForm` beans are declared globally within the configuration file using `<form-bean>` elements. Here are the attributes of this element:

Element Attribute	Description
`className`	This is the fully qualified name of the class used by Struts to create the `ActionForm` bean. The default `org.apache.struts.action.ActionFormBean` is normally assumed, although we can define our own bean class if we wish.
`name`	The name of the form bean in its associated scope (in other words, the name of the attribute of the `request/session` object that will store the bean). This attribute is used to associate the bean to an `ActionMapping`.
`type`	The fully qualified name of the class (including the package name).

The excerpt from our sample configuration file below shows how a form bean can be declared:

```
<form-beans>
  <form-bean
    name="sqrtForm"
    type="com.example.SqrtForm"/>
</form-beans>
```

Here a form bean of type `com.example.SqrtForm` is declared to use the name `sqrtForm` in its associated scope. In the next section we will see how this bean can be mapped to an `ActionMapping`.

Configuring ActionMappings

`ActionMapping` objects are used for mapping incoming request URIs to `Action` classes, and to associate `Action` classes with `ActionForms`. The `ActionServlet` stores this mapping internally, and transfers the control to an instance of the correct `Action` class by looking at the request URI when a request arrives. All `Action` classes use a `perform()` method to implement the application-specific code. This method returns an instance of the `ActionForward` class that contains the name of the target resource to which the response has to be forwarded.

`ActionMappings` are defined using the `<action-mappings>` element, which may include zero or more `<action>` elements. The `<action>` element has a number of attributes and subelements. The attributes defined for the `<action>` element are listed below (the first three attributes are required):

Element Attribute	Description
path	The relative path to the Action class.
name	This attribute defines the name of the ActionForm bean associated with this action, as used by the Action class. This is the same name used to define the form bean in a <form-bean> element.
type	The fully qualified name of the Action class linked to by this mapping.
scope	The value can be either request or session to indicate the scope of the ActionForm bean.
prefix	Prefix used to match request parameters to bean properties.
suffix	Suffix used to match request parameters to bean properties.
attribute	This is the name of the request or session scope attribute under which the ActionForm bean is stored, if it is different from the name attribute explained above.
className	The fully qualified name of the class used by Struts to create the ActionMapping object. The default class org.apache.struts.action.ActionMapping is assumed, but we can extend this class if we wish, and define our own class to create these ActionMapping objects.
input	Relative path to the input form, to which the control must be returned if a bean validation error is encountered.
unknown	If the value of this attribute is set to true, this action is used as the default action for request URIs for which no ActionMapping is defined.
validate	If the value of this attribute is set to true, the ActionServlet will call the validate() method on the ActionForm bean to perform input validation, before the perform() method is called on the Action class instance.

One of the vital subelements of the <action> element is the <forward> element. The <forward> element is a convenient way to configure local forwards. We define logical names to resources to which responses from the Action class are to be forwarded.

The Action classes can access the forwards by name using the findForward() method defined in the ActionMapping class. This method takes a String representing the name of the forward as an argument, and returns an instance of the ActionForward class to the ActionServlet.

The `<forward>` element contains the following attributes:

Attribute	Description
className	The fully qualified classname of the `ActionForward`. This is an implied attribute and defaults to the value of the `forward` initialization parameter value passed to the `ActionServlet`. If not specified, the value defaults to `org.apache.struts.action.ActionForward`. In normal cases the default implementation class is always used.
name	The logical name by which an `Action` class can access this `ActionForward`.
path	A relative path to the resource to which the response should be forwarded.
redirect	If set to `true`, the `ActionServlet` uses the `sendRedirect()` method to forward the resource, otherwise it uses the `forward()` method on the request dispatcher.

The excerpt below shows a typical `<action-mapping>` element.

```
<action-mappings>
  <action path="/sqrt"
    type="com.example.SqrtAction"
    name="sqrtForm"
    scope="request"
    input="/input.jsp">
    <forward name="success" path="/output.jsp"/>
  </action>
</action-mappings>
```

This mapping matches to a path `/sqrt`, and uses an `Action` class of type `com.example.SqrtAction`. A request-scoped form bean with logical name `sqrtForm` is associated with this mapping. The relative path to the form page that originated the request is `/input.jsp`, while a local forward is defined called `success`, that forwards responses from the `Action` class to `/output.jsp`.

Configuring Global Forwards

Global forwards are defined using the `<global-forwards>` element, that contains `<forward>` elements for each global forward. These forwards can be accessed by name using the `findForward()` method on the `ActionMapping`. The excerpt below shows a global forward declaration:

```
<global-forwards>
  <forward name="logon" path="/logon.jsp"/>
</global-forwards>
```

The `name` attribute simply defines the name of the global forward, while `path` gives the relative path to the target URL.

Configuring JDBC Datasources

JDBC datasources can be defined in the configuration file under the element `<data-sources>`. Multiple datasources can be defined within the datasources element using the `<data-source>` element. The `<data-source>` element defines different attributes for specifying the datasource properties that are listed below.

Element Attribute	Description
type	The name of the class that implements the JDBC extension API interface
description	A description of this datasource
autoCommit	Default auto commit mode for connections created using this datasource
driverClass	A class used by the datasource that implements the JDBC driver interface
key	A name used by `Action` classes for looking up this connection
loginTimeout	The value for database login timeout
maxCount	Maximum number of connections that may be made to this datasource
minCount	Minimum number of connections that need to be created
password	The password for accessing the database
readOnly	Read only state for the connections created
user	The username for accessing the database
url	The value for the JDBC URL

The excerpt below illustrates how we can use these attributes to define a data source in the Struts configuration file.

```
<data-sources>
  <data-source
    autoCommit="false"
    description="My datasource"
    driverClass="com.sybase.jdbc2.jdbc.SybDriver"
    maxCount="10"
    minCount="1"
    password="xxxxxx"
    url="jdbc:sybase:Tds:localhost:6000/mydata"
    user="meeraj"
    key="myPool"
  />
</data-sources>
```

The data source can be accessed from an `Action` class, using a method defined in the `ActionServlet`, by specifying the `key` name. The code snippet below shows how the datasource could be accessed from an `Action` class:

```
javax.sql.Datasource ds = servlet.findDataSource("myPool");
java.sql.Connection con = ds.getConnection();
```

Here `servlet` is an instance of the `ActionServlet` class, and this instance is passed to the `Action` class after the `ActionServlet` instantiates the `Action` class.

Finally, with all of the configuration done in our `struts-config.xml` file, we need to close the top-level element:

```
</struts-config>
```

Now that we have sorted out our Struts configuration, let's take look a little more deeply at how the components of Struts fit together.

A Closer Look At Struts Components

In this section, we are going to discuss the relationships between the main Struts components, namely:

❑   The `ActionServlet` controller

❑   `Action` classes

❑   `ActionForm` beans

❑   `ActionMapping` objects

❑   `ActionForward` objects

We will also explain how errors are handled within Struts. Let's start by examining the main controller component, the `ActionServlet`.

ActionServlet

The `ActionServlet` is the main controller component, and it is implemented by the Struts class `org.apache.struts.action.ActionServlet` (this class inherits the standard `javax.servlet.http.HttpServlet` class). The controller performs the following tasks while handling a request:

1. Find the request URI for the incoming request.

2. Match the URI to the appropriate `ActionMapping`.

3. Create/find the `ActionMapping` instance that encapsulates all the information defined for the current mapping.

4. Create/find an `ActionForm` bean instance if one is declared in the mapping, and try to populate the properties of the bean from the `request` parameter.

5. Call the appropriate `perform()` method on the `Action` class instance declared in the `ActionMapping`, and pass it the `ActionForm` bean (if declared in the mapping), the `ActionMapping` object, and the `request` and `response` objects.

6. Accept the returned `ActionForward` from the `perform()` method and forward the response to the resource specified by the `ActionForward`.

ActionServlet Configuration

Earlier, when we installed Struts, we saw that we needed to declare the `ActionServlet` in the `web.xml` file, and configure it to load on startup. We mentioned that the servlet may take a host of configuration information as initialization parameters. In this section we will discuss these configuration parameters in more depth; they are explained in the table below:

Parameter [Default]	Description
application [null]	Application resource bundle class (provides tools for supporting messages in multiple languages).
bufferSize [4096]	Buffer size for file upload.
config [/WEB-INF/struts-config.xml]	The location and name of the configuration file.
content [text/html]	Default content type.
debug [0]	Debug level.
detail [0]	Debug detail level.
factory [null]	Message resources factory. Message resources are explained in the section on internationalization.
formBean [org.apache.struts.action. ActionFormBean]	The name of the class that encapsulates information on `ActionForm` beans.
forward [org.apache.struts.action. ActionForward]	The name of the class that encapsulates information on `ActionForwards`.
locale [true]	If set to `true` this stores a `locale` object in the user's session.
mapping [org.apache.struts.action. ActionMapping]	The name of the class that encapsulates information on `ActionMappings`.
maxFileSize [250M]	Maximum size for file upload.
multipartClass [org.apache.struts. upload.DiskMultipartRequestHandler]	The name of the class for handling multipart requests.
nocache [False]	Whether the required HTTP headers are to be set to disable caching.
null [True]	If set to `true`, a null is returned for an invalid message key.
tempDir [The working directory provided to this web application as a servlet context attribute]	Temporary working directory to use when processing file downloads.

Parameter [Default]	Description
validate [True]	Whether the new form of configuration file is used (old versions of Struts used a different form of configuration file).
validating [True]	Whether to use a validating parser for the configuration file.

Specialized subclasses of `ActionServlet` provided by application developers may take extra parameters as well, although for most cases the standard servlet is sufficient to meet all requirements. Many of the initialization parameters above are configurable using getter and setter methods.

The `ActionServlet` instantiates the `Action` class when the request URI mapped to the `Action` class is received for the first time, and the `ActionServlet` stores a handle to itself in the `Action` class instance in a variable named `servlet`. After it has been instantiated, the `Action` instance is cached for reuse. The `ActionServlet` provides various methods that can be used by `Action` classes for accessing datasources, global forwards, and so on, through the use of the `servlet` instance variable.

ActionServlet Methods

The `ActionServlet` provides a host of public methods that can be used by the `Action` class instances. In this section we will briefly discuss some of those methods. For more in-depth information about `ActionServlet` methods, refer to the Struts documentation at http://jakarta.apache.org/struts.

The `ActionServlet` has methods that allow us to add or remove `ActionForm` beans, `ActionForwards`, and `ActionMappings`. The **signatures** for these methods are shown below:

```
public void addFormBean(ActionFormBean formBean)
public void removeBean(ActionFormBean formBean)
public void addForward(ActionForward forward)
public void removeForward(ActionForward forward)
public void addMapping(ActionMapping mapping)
public void removeMapping(ActionMapping mapping)
```

Each signature shows the scope of the method (all `public`), the object returned by the method (all `void`), and the arguments taken by the method. The following methods find these objects by name:

```
public ActionFormBean findFormBean(String name)
public ActionForward findForward(String name)
public ActionMapping findMapping(String name)
```

The next two methods are used to handle datasources:

```
public void addDataSource(String key,DataSource ds)
public Datasource findDataSource(String key) - returns a DataSource instance
```

The `findDataSource()` method finds a datasource by name. The datasource may be the one statically defined in the Struts configuration file, or one added dynamically, by the `addDataSource()` method.

573

Finally, we can use the following `destroy()` method to gracefully shut down the `ActionServlet`, and the `reload()` method to reload the information from the Struts configuration file into the `ActionServlet`.

Action Classes

The `Action` classes provided by the application developers are responsible for processing the users' requests. If the `ActionServlet` can't find a valid mapping for a particular action it will invoke the default `Action` class if there is one defined in the configuration file.

The `ActionServlet` passes the `Action` class an `ActionMapping` class associated with the current action. This can be used for a variety of tasks like finding local forwards, getting and setting `ActionMapping` attributes, and so on. It also passes the `ServletRequest` or `HttpServletRequest` object (which one depends on the servlet environment) the version of the `perform()` method that is overridden. `Action` classes can use this for getting and setting `request` attributes, getting request parameters and so on.

All `Action` classes are required to extend the Struts class `org.apache.struts.action.Action` and override one of the `perform()` methods defined in the class. The class defines two overloaded `perform()` methods:

```
perform(ActionMapping action,
        ActionForm form,
        ServletRequest request,
        ServletResponse response)
        throws IOException, ServletException

perform(ActionMapping action,
        ActionForm form,
        HttpServletRequest request,
        HttpServletResponse response)
        throws IOException, ServletException
```

The `Action` classes provide the required business logic for request processing in this `perform()` method. The method returns an `ActionForward` object to the `ActionServlet`; this `ActionForward` contains the path to the resource to which the response should be forwarded.

The `Action` class provides a set of protected access methods that can be used by `Action` subclasses; these are covered in the next section.

Action Class Methods

In this section we will discuss the various protected access methods defined by the `Action` class that can be used by the specialized subclasses provided by the application developers.

The following methods get or set the locale (a representation of the language that messages associated with the application should be displayed in) associated with a specified request:

```
protected Locale getLocale(HttpServletRequest request)
protected void setLocale(HttpServletRequest request,Locale locale)
```

The following method gets the message resources for the application:

```
protected MessageResource getResources()
```

This method returns `true` if the cancel button on the form associated with the action was pressed:

```
protected boolean isCancelled(HttpServletRequest request)
```

`Action` classes can use this `saveErrors()` method to store error messages when application errors occur:

```
protected void saveErrors(HttpServletRequest request, ActionErrors errors)
```

The `ActionErrors` instance is used to store error messages. This method stores the `ActionErrors` object in the request attribute list under an error key. JSPs can display these error messages using custom tags defined in the HTML tag library. The `ActionErrors` object is explained in detail in the next section, and the Struts tag for displaying error messages `<html:errors>` is explained later in the section on the Struts tag libraries.

Error Handling in Struts

The Struts framework provides two classes and a custom tag for error handling. In this section we will cover the two classes provided by Struts for error handling:

❑   `org.apache.struts.action.ActionErrors`

❑   `org.apache.struts.action.ActionError`

An `ActionErrors` instance holds a collection of `ActionError` instances. The `ActionError` instances represent individual error messages. These instances contain `key` values that can be mapped to the actual error messages stored in the application resources file, specified as an initialization parameter to the `ActionServlet`. `ActionError` instances can be added to the `ActionErrors` instance under the `ActionErrors.GLOBAL_ERROR` property, or any user-defined property.

The ActionError Class

The `ActionError` class defines a set of overloaded constructors for creating error messages. The first constructor method takes a `String` as argument. For instance:

```
ActionError error = new ActionError("error.invalid");
```

Here the instance `error` maps to an error message in the application resources file:

```
error.invalid=<b>Invalid Number</b>
```

Therefore, the message displayed in the JSP using the `<html:error>` custom tag (covered later in the chapter) would be as follows.

Invalid Number

Another form of the constructor can be used for specifying replacement strings within messages using the `MessageFormat` class in the `java.text` package. Say, for example, the following line is present in the resources file:

```
error.invalid=<b>Invalid Number {0}</b>
```

then if you created an error message as follows:

```
ActionError error = new ActionError("error.invalid",new Double(-1.2));
```

the message displayed in the JSP using the `<html:error>` tag would be:

Invalid Number –1.2

An extension of this is to specify more than one replacement string in the constructor, as shown below:

```
ActionError(String key, Object value0, Object value1, Object value2)
```

The `ActionError` class also provides a method for getting the (`String`) error key for a particular message, `getKey()`, and a method to get a `String` array of replacement values for the error message, `getValues()`.

ActionErrors Class

`ActionError` classes are never used alone for error handling. They are always stored in `ActionErrors` class instances that each hold a collection of `ActionError` class instances against specified property values. You can either use your own property values, or `ActionErrors.GLOBAL_ERROR`. The code snippet below illustrates a typical error-handling scenario in the `perform()` method of an `Action` class.

```
SqrtForm sqrtForm = (SqrtForm)form;
double num = sqrtForm.getNumber();
if(num < 0) {
  ActionErrors errors = new ActionErrors();
  ActionError error =
            new ActionError("error.negativeNumber",new Double(num));
```

The `ActionForm` bean `form` is first cast to the specific `ActionForm`. If the number entered by the user is negative, an instance of the `ActionErrors` class is created and an `ActionError` instance is added under the global `error` property, using the `add()` method:

```
errors.add(ActionErrors.GLOBAL_ERROR,error);
saveErrors(req,errors);
String input = mapping.getInput();
return new ActionForward(input);
}
```

Note how the add() method takes two arguments: a String representing a property, and an ActionError object. The ActionError passes a replacement string as a double object containing the number entered by the user. Finally the input JSP that instigated the Action class is retrieved from the ActionMapping object (mapping) and an ActionForward is returned back to the ActionServlet asking it to display the input JSP.

If the input JSP uses the custom tag for rendering error messages, and the application resource file contains the following entry:

```
error.negativeNumber=
          <b>Square roots cannot be computed for negative numbers ({0})<b>
```

the JSP will display the following message, for example, if the user entered –2.1:

Square roots cannot be computed for negative numbers (-2.1)

Here are some more of the ActionErrors class' useful methods:

Method	Description
clear()	Clears all error messages.
empty()	Returns true if ActionErrors object is empty.
get()	Returns error messages: if no argument is supplied, all messages will be returned as an Iterator object; if a String of a particular property is supplied, the set of error messages related to this particular property will be returned as an Iterator.
properties()	Returns an Iterator containing the property names which have at least one error.
size()	Returns the (integer) number of errors: if no argument is supplied the total number of errors for all properties is returned; if a String property name is supplied as argument, the number of errors for this property is returned.

ActionForm

The ActionForm classes provided by application developers must extend the Struts class org.apache.struts.action.ActionForm. When the ActionServlet invokes the Action class, it creates and populates the relevant ActionForm bean instance, and then passes it to the Action class. The beans provided by application developers may contain extra properties with getter and setter methods that are accessed by the ActionServlet using **reflection** (a package of resources – java.lang.reflect – that allows any Java program to get information about loaded classes/objects).

In this section we will have a look at the common methods provided by the ActionForm class.

```
public void setMultipartRequestHandler(MultipartRequestHandler
                                       multipartRequestHandler)
public MultipartRequestHandler getMultipartRequestHandler()
```

The methods above are used for getting and setting the multipart request handlers for file upload.

```
public ActionErrors validate(ActionMapping mapping,
                             ServletRequest request)
public ActionErrors validate(ActionMapping mapping,
                             HttpServletRequest request)
```

These methods are an alternative way of doing error handling. For this to work you need to override the validate() method in the specific ActionForm bean, and set the validate attribute to true in the <action> element in the configuration file. Then the ActionServlet calls the validate() method before it invokes an Action class, and if the size of the returned ActionErrors instance is greater than zero, it will save the instance in the request attribute list by the error key name. The ActionServlet then forwards the response to the input attribute value specified for the <action> element in the configuration file.

The code snippet below shows how all this can be done:

```
public class SqrtForm extends ActionForm {

  private double number;
  ..
  ..

  public ActionErrors validate(ActionMapping mp,HttpServletRequest rq) {

    ActionErrors errors = new ActionErrors();
    if(number < 0) {
      ActionError error = new ActionError("error.negativeNumber",
                                          new Double(num));
      error.add(ActionErrors.GLOBAL_ERROR,error);
      String input = mp.getInput();
    }
    return errors;
  }
}
```

It is recommended to do the validation in the Action class.

```
public void reset(ActionMapping mapping,HttpServletRequest request)
public void reset(ActionMapping mapping,ServletRequest request)
```

These methods reset the bean properties to their default values.

ActionForward

An Action class creates a response to a user request, and then forwards it to a specific resource using an ActionForward class, which is defined in a <forward> element of the configuration file. To remind you, the attributes of this element are the following:

❑ name: The logical name of the resource.

❑ path: A relative path to the resource.

❑ redirect: Whether to redirect the response or to use the request dispatcher forward() method.

The class provides getter and setter methods for all these attributes. `Action` classes can get a handle to an `ActionForward` instance in three ways, and then return them back to the `ActionServlet`.

❑ Use the `findForward()` method on the `ActionServlet` to get a global forward by name.

❑ Use the `findForward()` method on the `ActionMapping` instance passed in the `perform()` method, to find a local forward by name.

❑ Create a new `ActionForward` instance using one of the constructors provided.

Three overloaded constructors are provided for creating `ActionForward` objects:

```
public ActionForward()
```

This creates a new instance with default values.

```
public ActionForward(String path)
```

This creates a new instance with the specified path.

```
ActionForward(String path, boolean redirect)
```

This creates a new instance with the specified path and redirect flag.

ActionMapping

An instance of the class `org.apache.struts.action.ActionMapping` is passed to the `perform()` method of an `Action` class instance by the `ActionServlet`. This object encapsulates all the information defined in the `<action>` element of the configuration file for the `Action` class to which the object is passed; the various attributes for the `<action>` element have been discussed in detail in the section on Struts configuration. The `ActionMapping` class defines getter and setter methods for these attributes.

When they have processed the `request`, `Action` classes can use `ActionMapping` objects to find local forwards too, using the `findForward()` method:

```
public ActionForward findForward(String name)
```

The name argument is the name of the local forward. A variation on this theme is the `findForwards()` method:

```
public ActionForward[] findForwards()
```

This method finds all local forwards associated with this action. Finally, the following method adds an `ActionForward` dynamically to the mapping:

```
public void addForward(ActionForward forward)
```

Now that we have discussed the most important classes of the Struts Framework, let's move on to look at the Struts tag library.

Introducing the Struts Tag Library

The Struts tag library, used by JSP view components, is comprised of four sets of tags. Here's a brief description of what these tags are for:

- ❑ `bean` – manipulate beans within the JSP
- ❑ `logic` – flow control within the JSP
- ❑ `html` – generate HTML, display values in forms, and encode URLs with the session ID
- ❑ `template` – can construct pages that use a common format, using dynamic templates

Now let's take a detailed look at each of these sets of tags in turn, starting with `bean` tags.

Bean Tags

The Struts framework provides a variety of custom tags for handling JavaBeans within JSPs. These tags are packaged into a common tag library, whose tag library descriptor is defined in the file `struts-bean.tld`. The `bean` tag library defines tags that fall into four subcategories:

- ❑ Bean copying tags
- ❑ Tags for defining scripting variables
- ❑ Bean rendering tags
- ❑ Message internationalization tags

Let's review each of these.

Bean Copying

The `bean` tag library defines a powerful tag for performing actions such as defining new beans, copying existing beans, and copying properties from existing beans: the `<bean:define>` tag. In this section we will have a look at this tag in detail.

The `define` tag is mainly used to:

- ❑ Define new `String` constants
- ❑ Copy existing bean objects to newly defined bean objects
- ❑ Copy properties of existing bean objects in order to create new beans

Here are the attributes for the `<bean:define>` tag (all of these attributes are dynamic; they can take run-time expressions):

Attribute	Description
id	The name of the scripting variable by which the newly defined bean will be available. This attribute is required
type	Defines the class for the scripting variable introduced
value	Assigns a new object to the scripting variable defined by the id attribute
name	The name of the target bean. This is a required attribute if the value attribute is not specified
property	The property name of the bean defined by the name attribute, that is used to define the new bean. If not specified, the bean specified by the name attribute is assigned to the scripting variable specified by the id attribute
scope	The scope of the source bean. If not defined it is searched from page scope to application scope
toScope	The scope of the target bean. If not specified this defaults to page scope

Here are some examples. The tag below defines a bean named foo that is a java.lang.String object of value "This is a new String":

```
<bean:define id="foo"
            value="This is a new String"/>
```

In the example below, we have a bean named sourceBean in the page scope, and this is copied to a bean named targetBean in the request scope:

```
<bean:define id="targetBean"
            name="sourceBean"
            scope="page"
            toScope="request"/>
```

Tags for Defining Scripting Variables

The bean tag library defines various tags for defining and populating scripting variables from a variety of sources like cookies, request parameters, HTTP headers, and so on. In this section we will have a look at some of these tags.

Cookie, Header and Parameter Tags

These tags will retrieve a cookie, a HTTP header from the request, or a parameter from the request, and introduce a scripting variable and page scope attribute of type Cookie, or type String (for request headers or parameters). The attributes of these tags are explained below; all of the attributes can take run-time expressions.

Attribute	Description
id	The name of the scripting variable and page scope attribute to be defined
name	The name of the cookie/header/parameter

Table continued on following page

581

Attribute	Description
multiple	Whether to define an array of Cookies/Strings if multiple cookies/headers/parameters are found by the same name. If there are multiple cookies/headers/parameters with the same name, and the multiple attribute is set to true, the scripting variable is defined to be a Cookie/String array
value	A default cookie or value to return if no match is found

An example for the `<bean:cookie>` tag is shown below.

```
<bean:cookie id="myCookie"
             name="userName"/>
```

Here the name of the scripting variable is myCookie, and the name of the cookie used to create this attribute is userName. Here's an example of the `<bean:header>` tag:

```
<bean:header id="myHeader"
             name="Accept-Language"/>
```

In this case the name of the scripting variable is myHeader, and the name of the request header is Accept-Language. Finally, an example for the `<bean:parameter>` tag is shown below:

```
<bean:parameter id="myParameter"
                name="myParameter"/>
```

Here the scripting variable is called myParameter, and it holds the value of a request parameter also called myParameter.

Include Tag

This `<bean:include>` tag will retrieve the response of a resource and introduce a scripting variable and page scope attribute of type String. The resource can be a page, Struts ActionForward, or an external URL. This is very similar to the `<jsp:include>` action, but the response of the resource is stored in a page scope bean instead of being written to the output stream. Here are some of the attributes for this tag. All of the attributes can take run-time expressions.

Attribute	Description
id	The name of the scripting variable and page scope attribute to be defined
page	An internal resource
forward	A Struts ActionForward
href	Fully qualified URL of the resource to be included.

An example for the include tag is shown below.

```
<bean:include id="myInclude"
              page="MyJsp?x=1"/>
```

Here the name of the scripting variable is myInclude, and the response to retrieve is from the resource MyJsp?x=1.

Resource Tag

This tag will retrieve a web application resource, and introduce a scripting variable and page scope attribute of type InputStream or String. If there is a problem retrieving the resource a request time exception is thrown. The attributes of this tag are explained below. All of the attributes can take run-time expressions:

Attribute	Description
id	The name of the scripting variable and page scope attribute to be defined.
name	Relative path to the resource.
input	If this attribute is not present the resource is made available as a String.

An example for the <bean:resource> tag is shown below:

```
<bean:resource id="myResource"
               name="/WEB-INF/images/myResource.xml"/>
```

Here the name of the scripting variable is myResource, and the name of the resource to retrieve is myResource.xml.

Rendering Bean Properties

The bean tag library defines the <bean:write> tag for writing bean properties to the enclosing JSP writer. This tag is similar to the standard <jsp:getProperty> tag. The attributes of this tag are explained below. As before, all of these attributes can take run-time expressions.

Attribute	Description
name	The name of the bean whose properties are to be rendered
property	The name of the property to be rendered. If the property class has a java.beans.PropertyEditor the getAsText() method will be called or the toString() method will be called
scope	The scope of the bean. If not specified the bean will be searched from page to application scope
filter	If set to true any HTML special characters in the property values will be changed to their corresponding entity references
ignore	If set to false a request time exception is thrown if the property is not found, otherwise a null value is returned

Here's an example of using the `<bean:write>` tag:

```
<bean:write name="myBean"
            property="myProperty"
            scope="request"
            filter="true"/>
```

Here we see that the property `myProperty` of the bean `myBean` should be rendered. The bean has `request` scope, and if any HTML special characters are found they should be changed to their corresponding entity references.

Message Tag and Internationalization

The Struts framework supports **internationalization** and **localization**. We noted earlier that internationalizing your webapp means that messages displayed by your webapp are written in the preferred spoken language of the user. In effect this means that the user defines his locale on his machine, and then when the webapp needs to print a message, it refers to a resources file containing all of the messages written in the correct language. The webapp may provide many resource files, each of which provides messages written in a different language.

Struts supports internationalization using the `<bean:message>` tag, along with the Java 2 Platform's inbuilt support for these tasks using the `Locale` and `ResourceBundle` classes defined in the `java.util` package. Message formatting is also supported using the techniques defined by the `java.text.MessageFormat` class. The power of Struts is that the application developers need not know about the intricacies of these classes to use internationalized and formatted messages. In this section we will have a look at how internationalization and localization can be achieved using Struts.

The first step is to define a name for the application resources file that will contain all the messages for the application in the default language for the server. The messages need to be stored as **key-value** pairs as shown below:

```
error.validation.location=The entered location is invalid
```

Here `error.validation.location` is the key, while `The entered location is invalid` is the value.

This file needs to be stored in the `CLASSPATH`, and the location of this file needs to be passed to the `ActionServlet` as the value of the initialization parameter `application`. The value passed should follow the standard naming scheme for fully-qualified Java classes. For example, if the resources file is stored in the directory `/WEB-INF/classes` and the file is called `Resources.properties`, the value that needs to be passed is simply `Resources`. If the file is stored in the directory `/WEB-INF/classes/com/example` then it should be `com.example.Resources` instead.

To enable internationalization, all resource files must be stored in the same directory as the one in which the *base* resources file (the resources file which contains messages written in the *default locale* – the local language) is stored. If the base resource file is called `Resources.properties` then the resources files containing messages in other specific languages are called `Resources_xx.properties` where xx is the ISO code for the particular language (for instance, English is en, while Spanish is es). These files should therefore contain the same message keys, but messages in the specific languages.

The locale initialization parameter for the `ActionServlet` needs to be passed with a value `true`. This will enable the `ActionServlet` to store a locale object specific to the user's client machine in the user session under the key `Action.LOCALE_KEY`. Now everything is set up to run a truly internationalized web site which will automatically serve web pages in the language set for the locale on the user's client machine.

If you need to replace portions of your messages by specific strings you can define placeholders in the messages in the same way as you use `java.text.MessageFormat`.

```
Error.invalid.number=The number {0} is invalid
```

You can use the Struts `<bean:message>` tag to replace the string {0} in the above message with any number you want. This tag allows you to write internationalized messages, labels, prompts, and so on in your JSP. The attributes for the `<bean:message>` tag are explained below; all of these attributes can take run-time expressions:

Attribute	Description
key	The key of the message as defined in the resource file.
locale	The name of the attribute under which the `locale` object is stored in the user's session. If not specified, the value of `Action.LOCALE_KEY` is used.
bundle	The name of the attribute under which the `resources` object is stored in the application context. If not specified, the value of `Action.MESSAGES_KEY` is used.
arg0	First parametric replacement value.
arg1	Second parametric replacement value.
arg2	Third parametric replacement value.
arg3	Fourth parametric replacement value.
arg4	Fifth parametric replacement value.

the example below illustrates the use of the `<bean:message>` tag. Suppose there is a message defined in the resources file as follows:

```
info.myKey=The numbers entered are {0},{1},{2},{3}
```

then if we use the following message tag:

```
<bean:message key="info.myKey" arg0="5" arg1="6" arg2="7" arg3="8"/>
```

the output written to the JSP by the `message` tag will be:

The numbers entered are 5,6,7,8

Logic Tags

The Struts tag library provides a set of tags for handling flow control within a JSP; for instance, iteration or conditional evaluation of the tag body. These tags are packaged into a common tag library with a TLD file `struts-logic.tld`. The logic tag library defines tags that perform three functions:

❑   Conditional logic

❑   Iteration

❑   Forwarding/redirecting response

Let's take a closer look at these tags now.

Conditional Tags Based On Comparison

There are three categories of Struts conditional tags. The first category of tags compares the value of one of the following entities to a specified constant:

❑   A cookie

❑   A request parameter

❑   A bean or a bean property

❑   A request header

The tags defined in this category are the following:

Tag	Functionality
`<equal>`	Returns `true` if the constant value is equal to that of the defined entity
`<notEqual>`	Returns `true` if the constant value is not equal to that of the defined entity
`<greaterEqual>`	Returns `true` if the constant value is equal to or greater than that of the defined entity
`<lessEqual>`	Returns `true` if the constant value is equal to or less than that of the defined entity
`<lessThan>`	Returns `true` if the constant value is less than that of the defined entity
`<greaterThan>`	Returns `true` if the constant value is greater than that of the defined entity

All of the tags belonging to this category have the same attributes, described on the next page. Note that all of these attributes can take run-time expressions.

Attribute	Description
value	The constant value that is to be compared
cookie	The name of the HTTP cookie to be compared against
header	The name of the HTTP request header to be compared against
parameter	The name of the HTTP request parameter to be compared against
name	The name of the bean if the value is to be compared against a bean or a bean property
property	The bean property that is to be compared against
scope	The scope of the bean; if the scope is not specified it is searched from page to application scope

Now let's have a look at a few examples using these logic tags. Here's the first, that uses the `<logic:equal>` tag:

```
<logic:equal parameter="name" value="Meeraj">
   The entered name is Meeraj
</logic:equal>
```

This tag evaluates the body if there is a `request` parameter called `name` and the value equals `Meeraj`. Here's another, that uses the `<logic:greaterThan>` tag:

```
<logic:greaterThan name="bean" property="prop" scope="page" value="7">
   The value of myBean.myProp is greater than 7
</logic:greaterThan>
```

This tag evaluates the body if there is a bean named `bean` in the `page` scope, which has a property named `prop` – but only if the value of the property is greater than 7. If the property can be converted to a numeric value a numeric comparison is performed, otherwise a string comparison is made.

The second category of conditional tags defines two tags:

❑   `<logic:present>`

❑   `<logic:notPresent>`

As their name suggests, these tags check whether a particular item is present or not before evaluating the tag body. The `<logic:present>` tag evaluates the body if a particular item *is* present, while the `<logic:notPresent>` tag only evaluates the body if the item *is not* present. The item checked for is governed by the attributes of the tag, and the values of these attributes. Here's a table of these attributes (all of them can take run-time expressions):

Attribute	Description
value	The constant value that is to be compared
cookie	The presence of the cookie specified by the attribute is checked
header	The presence of the request header specified by the attribute is checked
parameter	The presence of the request parameter specified by the attribute is checked
name	The presence of the bean specified by the attribute is checked, if the property attribute is not specified. If the property attribute is specified, the existence of the bean as well as that of the property within the bean is checked
property	The presence of the bean property specified by the attribute is checked for the bean specified by the attribute name
scope	If the bean name is specified, this is the scope of the bean; if the scope is not specified it is searched from page to application scope
role	Checks whether the currently-authenticated user belongs to the specified role
user	Checks whether the currently-authenticated user has the specified name

Now let's have a look at a few examples using these tags. First, we have an example of how to use the <logic:notPresent> tag:

```
<logic:notPresent parameter="name">
   Parameter name is not present
</logic:notPresent >
```

This tag evaluates the body if the request parameter called name is not present. Next, here's an example of how you would use the <logic:present> tag:

```
<logic:present name="bean" property="prop" scope="page">
   The bean property bean.prop is present
</logic:present>
```

In this case, the tag evaluates the body if there is a bean named bean in the page scope, and this bean has a property named prop.

A third type of conditional tag is a bit more complicated to understand than those above. These tags evaluate the body content based on the result of pattern matching; in other words, the tags evaluate whether the value of a particular item is a substring of a specified constant. There are two of these tags:

❑   <logic:match>

❑   <logic:noMatch>

The tags allow the JSP engine to evaluate the body of the tag if a match is found (for <logic:match>) or not found (for <logic:noMatch>). Both of the tags belonging to this category have the same set of attributes: All these attributes can take run-time expressions:

Attribute	Description
value	The constant value that is to be compared
cookie	The name of the HTTP cookie to be compared against
header	The name of the HTTP request header to be compared against
parameter	The name of the HTTP request parameter compared against
location	If a value for this attribute is specified, the match should occur at this specified location (index value)
name	The name of the bean if the value is to be compared against a bean or a bean property
property	The bean property that is compared against the value
scope	If the bean name is specified, the bean scope; if the scope is not specified it is searched from page to application scope

Now we will have a look at a few examples that use the tags explained above:

```
<logic:noMatch parameter="name" value="xyz">
  The parameter name is not a substring of the string xyz
</logic: noMatch>
```

This `<logic:noMatch>` tag above only evaluates the body if there is a request parameter called name whose value is *not* a substring of the string xyz. Here's another example:

```
<logic:match parameter="name" value="xyz" location="1">
  The parameter name is a substring of the string xyz from the index 1
</logic:match>
```

This tag only evaluates the body if there is a request parameter called name whose value *is* a substring of the string xyz, but this substring must start from the index 1 of xyz (in other words the substring must be y or yz).

The Iterate Tag

The logic tag library defines the `<logic:iterate>` tag, that evaluates the body content of the tag multiple times, depending on the number of elements in a particular collection. The collection can be of type java.util.Iterator, java.util.Collection, java.util.Map, or an array. There are three ways of defining the collection.

- ❑ Use a run-time expression that returns a collection for the attribute collection.

- ❑ Define the collection as a bean, and specify the name under which the attribute is stored using the name attribute.

- ❑ Use the name attribute to define a bean, and the property attribute to define a bean property that would return a collection.

589

The current element of the collection will be defined as a page scope bean. The attributes of the tag are explained below. All the attributes can take run-time expressions:

Attribute	Description
length	The maximum number of iterations.
offset	An index from where the iteration has to be started.
collection	The collection to be iterated if the name attribute is not specified.
name	The name of the bean that is the collection, or the name of the bean whose property defined by the property attribute is a collection.
property	The name of the bean property that is a collection.
id	The name of the page scope bean and the scripting variable that holds the handle to the current element in the collection.
type	The type of the page scope bean defined for the current element.
scope	If the bean name is specified, the bean scope; if the scope is not specified it is searched from page to application scope.

Now we will see an example for the <logic:iterate> tag:

```
<%
  List myList = new ArrayList();
  myList.add(new Integer(0));
  myList.add(new Integer(1));
  myList.add(new Integer(2));
  myList.add(new Integer(3));
  myList.add(new Integer(4));
%>

<logic:iterate id="currentInt"
             collection="<%= myList %>"
             type="java.lang.Integer"
             offset="1"
             length="2">
  <%= currentInt %>
</logic:iterate>
```

The code above will iterate two elements from the list starting from the second element, and it will make the current element available as a page scope bean and scripting variable of type java.lang.Integer. In other words, the code will print 1 and 2.

Forwarding and Redirecting Tags

The Struts logic tag library defines a tag for forwarding the response, and another for redirecting to a URL.

Forward Tag

The `<logic:forward>` tag will either forward or redirect the response to the specified global `ActionForward`. The type of the global `ActionForward` decides whether the response is forwarded using the `PageContext` or redirected using `sendRedirect`. The only attribute defined for the tag is the name attribute that contains the name of the global `ActionForward`. An example is shown below.

```
<logic:forward name="MyGlobalForward"/>
```

Redirect Tag

The `<logic:redirect>` tag is a powerful mechanism for performing a HTTP redirect. The redirect can be achieved in different ways, depending on the attributes specified. It also lets the developers specify query arguments for the redirected URL. The attributes for the tag are explained below; all of these attributes can take run-time expressions.

Attribute	Description
forward	The logical name of the global `ActionForward` that maps to the relative path of the resource.
href	The fully qualified URL of the resource.
page	The relative path of the resource.
name	Either: the name of a `page`, `request`, `session` or `application` attribute of type `Map` that contains the name-value pairs of the query arguments to be attached to the redirected URL (if the `property` attribute is not specified); or the name of a bean which has a property of type `Map` that contains the same information (if the `property` attribute is specified).
property	The name of the bean property that is a `Map`. The bean's name is given by the `name` attribute above.
scope	If the bean name is specified, this is the scope in which the bean is searched for. If the scope is not specified it is searched from `page` to `application` scope.
paramId	Defines the name of a particular query argument.
paramName	Either: the name of a bean of type `String` that contains the value of the query argument (if the attribute `paramProperty` is not specified); or a bean that has a property (specified by the name `paramProperty`) that contains the query argument value.
paramProperty	The name of the `String` bean property that contains the query argument value.
paramScope	The scope in which the bean defined by the `paramName` attribute is searched for.

The tag should specify either one of the `forward`, `href` or `page` attributes to identify the resource to which the response should be redirected. A couple of examples are shown below.

```
<%
  request.setAttribute("manager","Ranieri");
%>
<logic:redirect href="http://www.myClub.co.uk"
                paramId="manager"
                paramName="manager"
                paramScope="request"/>
```

This will redirect the response to http://www.myClub.co.uk?manager=Ranieri. Here we have a bean that contains the value from the name-value pair that is used in the URL query argument. Now take a look at this example:

```
<%
  HashMap queryMap = new HashMap();
  queryMap.put("manager","Ranieri");
  request.setAttribute("manager",queryMap);
%>
<%logic:redirect href="http://www.myClub.co.uk"
                 name="manager"
                 scope="request"/>
```

This will redirect the response to the same URL as before. Here, however, we have a `request` attribute that is of type `Map`, and this contains the query name-value pair.

HTML Tags

The Struts `html` tag library defines a variety of custom tags. These tags can be broadly classified into the following functionalities:

❑   Rendering form elements and input controls

❑   Displaying error messages.

❑   Rendering other HTML elements

Let's start by looking at tags that render forms and form controls.

Tags for Rendering Form and Input Elements

Struts tightly couples an HTML form to the corresponding `ActionForm` bean defined for the action of the form. The name of the form input fields should correspond to the property names defined in the `ActionForm` bean. The first time the form is rendered, the form input fields are populated from the `ActionForm` bean, and when the form is submitted the `ActionForm` bean instance is populated from the `request` parameters.

All of the nested tags for rendering HTML input elements that can be used within the `<form>` tag have the following attributes for defining JavaScript event handlers:

Attribute	Description
onblur	For when the field loses focus
onchange	For when the field loses focus and its value has changed
onclick	For when the field receives a mouse click
ondblclick	For when the field receives a mouse double click
onfocus	For when the field receives input focus
onkeydown	For when the field has focus and a key is pressed.
onkeypress	For when the field has focus and a key is pressed and released
onkeyup	For when the field has focus and a key is released
onmousedown	For when the field is under the mouse pointer and a mouse button is pressed
onmousemove	For when the field is under the mouse pointer and the pointer is moved
onmouseout	For when the control was under the mouse pointer, but the pointer was moved outside the element
onmouseover	For when the field was not under the mouse pointer, but the pointer is moved inside the element
onmouseup	For when the field is under the mouse pointer, and a mouse button is released

The other common attributes that can be defined against the `<form>` elements are the following.

❑   `accessKey`: Defines the shortcut key for accessing the input field.

❑   `style`: Defines the styles for the input field.

❑   `styleClass`: Defines the style sheet class for the input field.

❑   `tabIndex`: The tab order for the input field.

Form Tag

The `<html:form>` tag is used for rendering an HTML tag. The name and class name of the `ActionForm` bean can be specified with the tag. If these attributes are not specified, the configuration file is queried for the `ActionMapping` for which the current JSP is the input, and the bean name and class are retrieved from this mapping. If a bean of the specified name is not found in the scope specified in the `ActionMapping`, a new bean is created and stored.

The `<form>` tag may contain other child tags corresponding to the different HTML input fields; these tags are explained later in this section. The attributes for the `<html:form>` tag are explained below.

Attribute	Description
name	Name of the `ActionForm` bean associated with the form. If not specified the name is retrieved from the configuration information.
type	The fully qualified name of the action form bean. If not specified the name is retrieved from the configuration information.
action	The action associated with the form. This action will also be used to identify the `ActionForm` bean associated with the form, from the configuration file.
scope	The scope within which the `ActionForm` bean has to be searched. If not specified the name is retrieved from the configuration information.
method	The HTTP method used for the form.
enctype	The encoding type used for the form HTTP method.
focus	The field within the form that needs initial focus.
onreset	Javascript event handler when the form is reset.
onsubmit	Javascript event handler when the form is submitted.
style	The styles to be applied.
styleClass	The style sheet class for this element.
target	The target frame or window for this form.

A simple example for the `<html:form>` tag is shown below.

```
<html:form action="validateEmployee.do" method="post">
...
</html:form>
```

We see that the action path associated with the form is `validateEmployee`, and the form data is passed via the `post` method. For this form, all the `ActionForm` bean information like the bean name, type, scope, and so on are retrieved from the `ActionMapping` for the action specified for the form:

```
<form-beans>
  <form-bean name="empForm" type="com.example.EmployeeForm"/>
</form-beans>

<action-mappings>
  <action path="/validateEmployee"
    type="com.example.ValidateEmployeeAction"
    name="empForm"
    scope="request"
    input="/employeeInput.jsp">
    <forward name="success" path="/employeeOutput.jsp"/>
  </action>
</action-mappings>
```

If the configuration file containing the information listed above and the request URIs *.do are mapped to the Struts `ActionServlet`, the name, type and scope of the action form bean associated with the form will be empForm, com.example.EmployeeForm and request respectively. These properties can also be explicitly defined using the <html:form> tag attributes.

Button and Cancel Tags

The <html:button> is used for rendering an HTML button control, while the <html:cancel> tag is used for rendering an HTML cancel button. These tags must be nested within an <html:form> tag. The attributes of the tags, both of which can take run-time expressions, are property and value. The property attribute defines the request parameter name sent back to the server when the form is submitted, and the value attribute is the value of the label to be placed on the button.

Reset and Submit Tags

The <html:reset> and <html:submit> tags can be used for rendering HTML reset and submit buttons respectively. These tags must be nested within a <html:form> tag.

Text and Textarea Tags

The <html:text> and <html:textarea> tags are nested inside an <html:form> tag, and are used for rendering HTML textboxes and textareas respectively. Here are the attributes of these tags:

❑ name: The name of the bean whose property is queried to decide the current value of the textbox or textarea. If this attribute is not specified, the name of the ActionForm bean associated with the enclosing form is used.

❑ property: This attribute defines the request parameter name sent back to the server when the form is submitted, and the bean property name that is queried to decide the current value of the text element.

The <html:text> tag also has the following attributes:

❑ maxlength: The maximum number of characters that can be entered.

❑ size: The size of the textbox (in characters).

The attributes below are specific to the <html:textarea> tag:

❑ rows: The number of rows in the textarea.

❑ cols: The number of cols in the textarea.

All of the attributes above can take run-time expressions.

Checkbox and Multibox Tags

The <html:checkbox> tag can be used for rendering a checkbox control. This tag must be nested within a form tag.

The <html:multibox> tag nested in an <html:form> tag can be used for rendering an HTML checkbox control. This tag is preferred to the <html:checkbox> tag if you wish to render multiple checkboxes with the same name, so that a getParameterValues() call on the request object passing the checkbox name would give back an array of Strings.

The attributes of these tags are explained below. All of the attributes can take run-time expressions:

❑ name: The name of the bean whose property is queried to decide whether the checkbox is rendered as checked or not. If this attribute is not specified the name of the `ActionForm` bean associated with the enclosing form is used.

❑ property: The name of the checkbox, as well as the name of the bean property which decides whether the checkbox is rendered as checked or not. In the case of a multibox, the property needs to be an indexed property defined as an array.

❑ value: The value of the `request` parameter that will be sent back to the server if the checkbox is checked.

An example of the use of `<html:checkbox>` is shown below.

```
<html:checkbox property="married" value="Y"/>
```

Here we have a checkbox called `married`, that will send a value of `Y` back to the server on form submission.

File Tag

The `<html:file>` tag can be used for rendering an HTML file control; this tag must be nested within an `<html:form>` tag. The attributes of this tag are explained below. All the attributes can take run-time expressions:

Attribute	Description
name	The name of the bean whose property is queried to decide the contents to be rendered in the file control. If this attribute is not specified, the name of the `ActionForm` bean associated with the enclosing form is used.
property	This attribute defines the `request` parameter name sent back to the server when the form is submitted, as well as the bean property name that is queried to decide the contents to be rendered in the file control.
accept	Set of content types that the server can process. This also filters the file types available for selection in the dialog box on the client browser.
value	Value of the label to be placed on the button for browsing the file on the local file system.

Handling multipart requests using Struts is covered in detail in a later section.

Hidden Tag

The `<html:hidden>` tag, when nested within a `<form>` tag, can be used for rendering an HTML hidden input element. The attributes of this tag are explained below:

❑ name: The name of the bean whose property is queried to decide the current value of the hidden element. If this attribute is not specified the name of the action form bean associated with the enclosing form is used.

❑ property: This attribute defines the request parameter name sent back to the server when the form is submitted, as well as the bean property name that is queried to decide the current value of the hidden element.

❑ value: The value that needs to be initialized for the hidden input element.

All of these attributes can take run-time expressions.

Password Tag

The <html:password> tag can be used for rendering an HTML password control. This tag has to be nested within an <html:form> tag. The attributes of this tag are explained below.

Attributes	Description
name	The name of the bean whose property is queried to decide the current value of the password element. If this attribute is not specified the name of the ActionForm bean associated with the enclosing form is used.
property	This attribute defines the request parameter name sent back to the server when the form is submitted, as well as the bean property name that is queried to decide the current value of the password element.
maxlength	The maximum number of characters that can be entered.
redisplay	Whether to display the password contents if the corresponding bean property is already populated when the field is rendered.
size	The size of the field.

All of these attributes can take run-time expressions.

Radio Tag

We can use the <html:radio> tag nested within an <html:form> tag for rendering an HTML radio button control. The attributes of this tag are explained below.

❑ name: The name of the bean whose property is queried to decide whether the radio button should be rendered as checked or not. If this attribute is not specified the name of the action form bean associated with the enclosing form is used.

❑ property: The request parameter name sent back to the server when the form is submitted, as well as the bean property name that is queried to decide whether the radio button should be rendered as checked or not.

❑ value: The value sent back to the server if the radio button is checked.

All of the attributes can take run-time expressions.

Select Tag

The `<html:select>` tag, when nested inside an `<html:form>` control, can be used for rendering an HTML select control. The attributes of this tag are explained below.

- ❑ name: The name of the bean whose property is queried to decide which one of the options needs to be selected. If this attribute is not specified the name of the `ActionForm` bean associated with the enclosing form is used.

- ❑ property: This attribute defines the `request` parameter name sent back to the server when the form is submitted, as well as the bean property name that is queried as to which one of the options need to be selected.

- ❑ value: Can be used to indicate the option that needs to be selected.

- ❑ multiple: Indicates whether the select control allows multiple selections.

- ❑ size: The number of options that can be displayed at one time.

All the attributes above can take run-time expressions.

Options Tag

The `<html:options>` tag can be used for rendering a collection of HTML option elements. This element should be nested within the `<html:select>` tag. The attributes of this tag are explained below, all of which can take run-time expressions:

- ❑ collection: The name of a collection that is stored as an attribute in some scope that contains a collection of beans. The number of options is the same as the number of elements in the collection. The `property` attribute can be used to define the bean property used for the option's value and the `labelProperty` attribute can be used to define the bean property used for the option's label.

- ❑ labelName: This attribute can be used to specify a bean stored in some scope, which is a collection of `Strings` that can be used to define the labels for the `<html:option>` elements if they are different from the values.

- ❑ labelProperty: Defines the bean property used to write the option's label when used with the `collection` attribute.

- ❑ name: If only this attribute is specified, this identifies a bean stored in some scope, which would return a collection of `Strings` used to write the `value` attribute for `<html:option>` elements.

- ❑ property: The `property` attribute, when used with the `collection` attribute, defines the name of the property in each individual bean that will render the value of the option. If used without the `collection` attribute, this defines the property of the bean defined by the `name` attribute (if the `name` attribute is present) or the `ActionForm` bean that would return a collection to write the values for the options.

Now we will see a few examples for this tag. Here's the first:

```
<html:options collection="optionCollection"
              property="optionValue"
              labelProperty="optionLabel"/>
```

This tag assumes that there is a collection called `optionCollection` stored in some scope, that contains individual beans each with a property called `optionValue` that is used as the value of an option. Each option's label is defined by a bean's `optionLabel` property.

```
<html:options name="optionValues" labelName="optionLabels"/>
```

In this case `optionValues` represents a bean stored in some scope which is a collection of `Strings` that can be used to write the values of the option, and `optionLabels` represents a bean stored in some scope which is a collection of `Strings` that can be used to write the option labels.

```
<html:options name="optionValues"/>
```

In this case `optionValues` represents a bean stored in some scope that is a collection of `Strings` that can be used to write the values of the options, and the option labels are left empty.

Tags for Rendering Error Messages

The `<html:errors>` tag can be used in conjunction with `ActionErrors` for displaying error messages. The tag first reads the message key `error.header` from the resources file for the current locale, and then renders the message text. Next it loops through the `ActionErrors` object generally stored as a `request` attribute under the key `Action.ERROR_KEY`, reads the message key for individual `ActionError` objects, reads and formats the corresponding messages from the resources file for the current locale, and renders them. Then it reads the message corresponding to the key `error.footer` and renders it too.

Defining the `property` attribute can filter the error messages that are displayed. The value of this attribute should correspond to the key under which the `ActionError` object was stored in the `ActionErrors` object. The attributes of this tag are explained below. All of the attributes below can take run-time expressions.

- ❏ `bundle`: The name of the application scope attribute that contains the message resources. The default value is `Action.MESSAGE_KEY`.

- ❏ `locale`: The name of the `session` scope attribute that stores the locale for the user currently logged on. The default value is `Action.LOCALE_KEY`.

- ❏ `name`: The name of the `request` attribute that stores the `ActionErrors` object. The default value is `Action.ERROR_KEY`.

- ❏ `property`: This can be used for specifying the keys under which individual `ActionError` objects are stored within the `ActionErrors` object, for filtering messages.

A few examples are shown below:

```
<html:errors/>
```

This will display all the errors. Here's another:

```
<html:errors property="missing.name"/>
```

This will display only those errors stored against the key `missing.name`.

599

Other HTML Tags

The Struts HTML tags also define the following tags for rendering other HTML elements.

- ❑ `<html:html>`: Renders the html element.

- ❑ `<html:img>`: Renders the HTML image tag.

- ❑ `<html:link>`: Renders a HTML link or an anchor.

- ❑ `<html:rewrite>`: Generates a URI without the anchor tag.

Template Tags

Dynamic templates are a powerful way of modularizing web page layout. Assume your web application has got hundreds of web pages using the same layout with a header section, footer section and the main content section. The simplistic way of implementing a common layout is to use HTML tables and JSP includes as shown below.

```
<html>
  <head>
    <title></title>
  </head>
  <body>
    <table width=100% height=100%>
      <tr height="10%">
        <td>
          <jsp:include page="header.html"/>
        </td>
      </tr>
      <tr height="80%">
        <td>
          <jsp:include page="employeeList.jsp"/>
        </td>
      </tr>
      <tr height="10%">
        <td>
          <jsp:include page="employeeFooter.jsp"/>
        </td>
      </tr>
    </table>
  </body>
</html>
```

The problem with the code above is that the template is hard-coded into the JSP. If you decide to change the height of the header to 15% and you have hundreds of JSPs it will become a massive change. This is where dynamic templates come into their own. Dynamic templates encapsulate the layout, and the template page is included in all your JSPs rather than hard-coding the details. So if you decide to change the template, the only place you need to make changes is the template JSP.

The Struts template tag library defines custom tags for implementing dynamic templates. In this section we will cover those tags in detail.

Insert Tag

The `<template:insert>` tag can be used within your JSP pages to insert a dynamic template. The only attribute the tag takes is the `template` attribute that is used to define the template JSP. The pages to be inserted into the template are specified using multiple `<template:put>` tags defined as the body content for the `<template:insert>` tag.

Put Tag

The `<template:put>` tags are used within the `<template:insert>` tag for specifying the resources to be inserted in the template. The attributes for the tag are explained below.

❑ `name`: The name of the content to be inserted.

❑ `role`: If this attribute is specified, the content is inserted only if the currently authenticated user has the specified role.

❑ `content`: Defines the content to be inserted, like a JSP file or a HTML file.

❑ `direct`: If set to `true` the string specified by the `content` attribute is printed directly rather than being included in the JSP.

Get Tag

The `<template:get>` tag is used within the template JSP to get the resources inserted by the `<template:put>` tags into the content JSPs. The attributes of the tag are the following.

❑ `name`: The name of the content that was inserted by the `<template:put>` tag.

❑ `role`: If this attribute is specified, the content is inserted only if the currently authenticated user has the specified role.

Using Template Tags

Now we will see how the Struts template tags can be used to create dynamic templates. First we will write a template JSP that will be used by all our web pages. That JSP may look as listed below.

```
<html>
  <%@ taglib uri="/template" prefix="/template" %>
  <head>
    <title></title>
  </head>
  <body>
    <table width=100% height=100%>
      <tr height="10%">
        <td>
          <template:get name="header"/>
        </td>
      </tr>
      <tr height="80%">
        <td>
          <template:get name="content"/>
        </td>
      </tr>
      <tr height="10%">
```

```
        <td>
          <template:get name="footer"/>
        </td>
      </tr>
    </table>
  </body>
</html>
```

Let's call this file `template.jsp`. This JSP uses the `<template:get>` tag to get the contents put by our content JSPs using the `<template:put>` tag, and lays out the contents in an HTML table. The three content types expected are `header`, `content` and `footer`. A typical content JSP may look as shown below.

```
<%@ taglib uri="/template" prefix="/template" %>
<template:insert template="template.jsp">
  <template:put name="header" content="header.html"/>
  <template:put name="content" content="employeeList.jsp"/>
  <template:put name="footer" content="footer.html"/>
</template:insert>
```

This application JSP uses the `<template:insert>` tag to define the template, and then uses the `<template:put>` tag to push three resources identified by unique `content` names to the template JSP. If we have hundreds of JSPs using the same scheme, and we suddenly decide to change the template, the only place we will have to make a change now is the `template.jsp` file.

A Sample Web Application Based On Struts

In this section we will develop a simple web application that uses most of the concepts we have discussed so far in the chapter, including:

❑ Struts configuration file

❑ `ActionForm` beans and `Action` classes

❑ `ActionErrors`, `ActionMappings` and `ActionForwards`

❑ Struts bean, `logic`, and `html` tags

We will also be implementing an application-specific tag library. Our application will provide an HTML form for the user to enter the following employee information:

❑ `Name`: A text field.

❑ `Department`: A list of departments.

❑ `Skills`: A series of checkboxes, allowing multiple selections.

When the form is submitted the information entered by the user is validated. If there is any missing information the user is re-presented with the input form retaining all the data he entered. Otherwise the information entered by the user is displayed in a read-only mode. The employee information will be stored in a simple JavaBean, `EmployeeForm`.

The EmployeeForm JavaBean

Our previous discussion of the employee information provided by the user leads us naturally to the properties we need to expose in the `EmployeeForm` bean.

❑   name (a `String`)

❑   department (a `String`)

❑   skills (a `String` array)

All of these properties will have associated getter and setter methods for retrieving or modifying their values.

The source code for the file `EmployeeForm.java` is shown below.

```
package com.example;
import org.apache.struts.action.ActionForm;

public class EmployeeForm extends ActionForm {
```

Note how our bean class extends the Struts base `org.apache.struts.action.ActionForm` class, and belongs to the package `com.example`. All of our classes will belong to this package. Next we define the `name`, `department`, and `skills` attributes and their associated getter and setter methods:

```
private String name = "";
private String department = "";
private String[] skills;

public String getName() {
  return name;
}

public void setName(String name) {
  this. name = name;
}

public String getDepartment() {
  return department;
}

public void setDepartment(String department) {
  this.department = department;
}

public String[] getSkills() {
  return skills;
}

public void setSkills(String[] skills) {
  this.skills = skills;
}
}
```

The Employee Action Class

The next step is to write the `Action` class that will validate the information entered by the user. We will call this class `ValidateEmployeeAction` and we will inherit it from the Struts class `org.apache.struts.action.Action` and override the `perform()` method.

Here's the sequence of events that take place in the `Action` class:

1. The `ActionServlet` calls the `perform()` method on our `Action` class, passing it the instances of the `EmployeeForm` bean, the `ActionMapping`, the HTTP `request` and the HTTP `response`.

2. The `Action` class creates an instance of the `ActionErrors` class.

3. It first checks whether the employee name is empty, in which case it creates a new `ActionError` object and stores this in the `ActionErrors` object.

4. The `Action` class does the same check for `department` and `skills`.

5. It checks the size of the `ActionErrors` object.

❑ If the size of `ActionErrors` is greater than zero, it saves the object in the `request` attribute list under the key `Action.ERROR_KEY`, creates an `ActionForward` by getting the input resource name from the `ActionMapping` class instance, and returns it to the `ActionServlet`.

❑ Otherwise, if no validation error occurs, the `Action` class retrieves the `ActionForward` defined by the logical name `success` from the `ActionMapping` instance, and returns it to the `ActionServlet`.

Let's now step through the source code for the `Action` class `ValidateEmployeeAction.java`:

```
package com.example;
import org.apache.struts.action.ActionForm;
import org.apache.struts.action.ActionForward;
import org.apache.struts.action.Action;
import org.apache.struts.action.ActionMapping;
import org.apache.struts.action.ActionErrors;
import org.apache.struts.action.ActionError;
import org.apache.struts.action.ActionServlet;

import javax.servlet.http.HttpServletRequest;
import javax.servlet.http.HttpServletResponse;
import javax.servlet.ServletException;

import java.io.IOException;
import java.util.List;
```

After we have imported all of the classes we need, we define our `ValidateEmployeeAction` class as extending the `org.apache.struts.action.Action` base class:

```
public class ValidateEmployeeAction extends Action {

  public ActionForward perform(ActionMapping mapping,
                               ActionForm form,
                               HttpServletRequest request,
                               HttpServletResponse response)
                               throws IOException,ServletException {
```

Next we move on to define the `perform()` method of our `Action` class. First we create a new instance of the `ActionErrors` class, and cast the passed `ActionForm` to our `EmployeeForm` bean class:

```
ActionErrors errors = new ActionErrors();
EmployeeForm empForm = (EmployeeForm)form;
```

If the employee name is empty we create an error, with the error key as `error.missing.name`. This key should be mapped to a valid message in the application resources file. The `html:errors` tag will read this key and render the appropriate message.

```
String name = empForm.getName();
if(name.trim().equals("")) {
  ActionError error = new ActionError("error.missing.name");
  errors.add(ActionErrors.GLOBAL_ERROR,error);
}
```

Note that we use the `trim()` method to remove any whitespace from the beginning or end of the `name` `String`. Then we perform a similar check for empty `department` name and `skills` attributes:

```
String department = empForm.getDepartment();
if(department.trim().equals("")) {
  ActionError error = new ActionError("error.missing.department");
  errors.add("ActionErrors.GLOBAL_ERROR",error);
}

String[] skills = empForm.getSkills();
if(skills == null) {
  ActionError error = new ActionError("error.missing.skills");
  errors.add("ActionErrors.GLOBAL_ERROR",error);
}
```

If the number of errors is greater than zero, we save the errors into the `ActionErrors` instance and return the control back to the input JSP:

```
if(errors.size() > 0) {
  saveErrors(request,errors);
  return new ActionForward(mapping.getInput());
}
```

Otherwise we forward the control to the output JSP:

```
  return mapping.findForward("success");
 }
}
```

Sample Application-Specific Custom Tags

In the form for entering employee information we will have a list of departments and a collection of checkboxes for different skills. This data doesn't come from the employee form bean. One easy way to populate this data is to hard code them in the JSP. But there are two potential problems to this approach:

❑   If we write more JSPs that have department and skills information in the future, we will have to replicate the same code over and over. Hard coding this data into a JSP will therefore lower the reusability of the code.

❑   If we hard code them we may find it difficult to use the Struts `html` and `logic` tags, because the data won't be available in `page`-scoped variables at run-time.

Therefore we will define the `departments` and `skills` as lists of `Strings`, and these will be stored in the `page` scope so that Struts tags can access them. To make it more elegant, and avoid the use of scriplets, we will define two custom tags, one for creating the `department` list and storing it in the `page` scope, and another that does the same for the `skills` list.

DepartmentTag

The `DepartmentTag` is a simple empty tag that extends `TagSupport`. The source code for the tag handler class, `DepartmentTag.java`, is shown below:

```
package com.example;

import java.util.List;
import java.util.ArrayList;
import javax.servlet.jsp.tagext.TagSupport;

public class DepartmentTag extends TagSupport {

  public int doStartTag() {
```

First we create an `ArrayList` collection, which is then used to store the departments:

```
    List department = new ArrayList();
    department.add("");
    department.add("Client Server");
    department.add("E-Commerce");
    department.add("Legacy Integration");
```

Then we store this `ArrayList` in the `page` scope under the name `departmentList`:

```
    pageContext.setAttribute("departmentList",department);

    return SKIP_BODY;
  }
}
```

SkillsTag

The `SkillsTag` tag handler class is very similar to that of the `DepartmentTag`, but we have a list of `skills` instead of a list of `departments`. Here's the code for `SkillsTag.java`:

```java
package com.example;

import java.util.List;
import java.util.ArrayList;
import javax.servlet.jsp.tagext.TagSupport;

public class SkillsTag extends TagSupport {

  public int doStartTag() {

    List skills = new ArrayList();
    skills.add("EJB");
    skills.add("Java Mail");
    skills.add("JDBC");
    skills.add("JMS");
    skills.add("JNDI");
    skills.add("JSP");
    skills.add("JTA");
    skills.add("Servlets");

    pageContext.setAttribute("skillsList",skills);

    return SKIP_BODY;
  }
}
```

Tag Library Descriptor

The tag library descriptor `app.tld` defines both of these tags, and specifies the `<bodycontent>` of both of the tags as empty.

```xml
<?xml version="1.0"  ?>
<!DOCTYPE taglib PUBLIC
                "-//Sun Microsystems, Inc.//DTD JSP Tag Library 1.1//EN"
                "http://java.sun.com/j2ee/dtds/web-jsptaglibrary_1_1.dtd">

<taglib>

  <tlibversion>1.0</tlibversion>
  <jspversion>1.1</jspversion>
  <shortname>User</shortname>
  <info>
    This tag library contains employee tag extensions
  </info>

  <tag>
    <name>departmentList</name>
    <tagclass>com.example.DepartmentTag</tagclass>
    <bodycontent>empty</bodycontent>
```

```
    </tag>

    <tag>
      <name>skillsList</name>
      <tagclass>com.example.SkillsTag</tagclass>
      <bodycontent>empty</bodycontent>
    </tag>

  </taglib>
```

The JSPs for the Sample Application

Our sample web application contains two JSP files:

❑ inputContent.jsp

❑ outputContent.jsp

The inputContent JSP displays the form for entering the employee information. If the information is incomplete when the form is submitted, the same JSP is send back to the user, and the form retains all of the information previously entered by the user plus the relevant error messages about missing data. On successful validation of the information entered by the user, outputContent.jsp is displayed, with the employee information displayed in read-only mode.

The JSP pages use <bean:message> tags to retrieve messages from the application resources file; we will review this file after we have walked through the JSPs.

inputContent.jsp

This JSP uses the standard Struts bean, HTML, and logic tags, as well as our application-specific tag library. The error messages and HTML form elements are rendered using the Struts HTML tags, the internationalized prompts and labels are rendered using the Struts bean tags, iteration and control flow are implemented using Struts logic tags, while the application tags are used for populating the list of departments and skills in the page scope.

Now let's scan through the source code for the JSP. The first thing we do is to import all the tag libraries used within the JSP:

```
<%@ taglib uri="/bean" prefix="bean" %>
<%@ taglib uri="/html" prefix="html" %>
<%@ taglib uri="/logic" prefix="logic" %>
<%@ taglib uri="/app" prefix="app" %>

<html>
  <head>
    <title></title>
  </head>

  <body>
```

Now we use the Struts <html:errors/> tag to display the validation errors, if the JSP is sent back to the user because of bad input. Note that the first time the JSP is displayed this tag doesn't render any messages.

```
<html:errors/>
```

Next we populate the list of departments in a bean in the page scope, using our application-specific tags. This data will be used to populate the items in the pick-list of departments.

```
<app:departmentList/>
```

Then we populate the list of employee skills in a similar way:

```
<app:skillsList/>
```

Rendering the form is achieved by using the <html:form> tag. This form is associated with the relevant ActionForm by querying the ActionMapping for the correct Action:

```
<html:form action="validateEmployee.do">

  <table>
    <tr>
      <td align="right">
```

Now we use the <bean:message> tag to read the resources file for the user's locale, and render the message corresponding to the key prompt.employee.name:

```
        <bean:message key="prompt.employee.name"/>
      </td>
```

Using the Struts <html:text> tag, our next step is to render the HTML text control corresponding to the name of the employee. The name of the input text control that is rendered is (strangely enough!) name. The value of this control is found by consulting the name attribute of the ActionForm bean:

```
      <td>
        <html:text property="name"/>
      </td>
    </tr>

    <tr>
      <td align="right">
```

Next, as we did for name, we use the <bean:message> tag to read the resources file for the user's locale, and then render the message corresponding to the key for the department:

```
        <bean:message key="prompt.employee.department"/>
      </td>
```

Again, as we did with name, we now render the HTML control for department (a drop-down select control instead of a text one this time). The select tag will consult the department attribute from the ActionForm bean, to decide on the options that should be displayed as selected.

```
      <td>
        <html:select property="department">
          <html:options name="departmentList"/>
        </html:select>
      </td>
    </tr>

    <tr>
      <td align="right" valign="top">
```

Then we go through the same routine for a third time, but using the `skills` attribute instead, and producing a checkbox. We start by retrieving the appropriate message from the resources file:

```
        <bean:message key="prompt.employee.skills"/>
      </td>
      <td>
```

We use the `<logic:iterate>` tag to loop through the `skillsList` bean (a collection of `Strings` populated by the `skillsList` custom tag). This `iterate` tag exposes the current item in the list as a page scope bean called `currentSkill`, and the value of this `currentSkill` bean is used to render the checkbox label and value. The `multibox` tag will consult with the indexed property `skills` of the `ActionForm` bean as to whether the checkbox should be rendered as checked or not. The name of all the checkboxes that are rendered is `skills`.

```
        <logic:iterate id="currentSkill" name="skillsList">
          <html:multibox property="skills">
            <%= currentSkill %>
          </html:multibox>
          <%= currentSkill %>
          <br/>
        </logic:iterate>
      </td>
    </tr>
```

Finally, the submit control, labeled **Validate**, is rendered using the Struts `<html:submit>` tag.

```
    <tr>
      <td colspan="2" align="center">
        <html:submit value="Validate"/>
      </td>
    </tr>
  </table>
</html:form>
</body>
</html>
```

outputContent.jsp

This JSP uses the Struts `bean` and `logic` tags. The internationalized prompts, labels, and bean properties are rendered using the Struts bean tags and iteration and control flow are implemented using Struts `logic` tags.

Let's have a look at the source code for the JSP. First we need to import the required custom tag libraries:

```
<%@ taglib uri="/bean" prefix="bean" %>
<%@ taglib uri="/logic" prefix="logic" %>

<html>
  <head>
    <title></title>
  </head>

  <body>
    <table>
      <tr>
        <td align="right">
```

Then we use the `<bean:message>` tag to read the resources file for the user's locale and render the message corresponding to the key `prompt.employee.name`, as we saw in the `inputContent` JSP:

```
        <bean:message key="prompt.employee.name"/>
      </td>
      <td>
```

Now we use the Struts `<bean:write>` tag to render the `name` property of the `empForm` bean:

```
        <bean:write name="empForm" property="name"/>
      </td>
    </tr>

    <tr>
      <td align="right">
```

Next the `<bean:message>` tag is used to read the resources file for the user's locale, and render the message corresponding to the key `prompt.employee.department`.

```
        <bean:message key="prompt.employee.department"/>
      </td>
      <td>
```

Then, as before with `name`, we use the Struts `<bean:write>` tag to render the `department` property of the `empForm` bean:

```
        <bean:write name="empForm" property="department"/>
      </td>
    </tr>

    <tr>
      <td align="right" valign="top">
```

We finish by retrieving the key `prompt.employee.skills`, and using the Struts `<logic:iterate>` tag to loop through the employee skills defined for the employee:

```
          <bean:message key="prompt.employee.skills"/>
        </td>
        <td>
          <logic:iterate id="currentSkill" name="empForm" property="skills">
            <%= currentSkill %>
            <br/>
          </logic:iterate>
        </td>
      </tr>

    </table>

  </body>
</html>
```

Application Resources File

The application resources file is called `ApplicationResources.properties` and this value is passed to the `ActionServlet` as the value of the initialization parameter `application`. The file contains keys for all of the error messages, prompts, labels and so on, used in the application. A message is associated with each key. If the client's preferred locale is different from the default locale, you can create new resources files as described in the section on internationalization. The listing for the resources file for the default locale on the server is shown below:

```
error.missing.name=<li><font color="red">Please enter the first name</font></li>
error.missing.department=<li><font color="red">Please pick a
department</font></li>
error.missing.skills=<li><font color="red">Please select the relevant
skills</font></li>

prompt.employee.name=<b>First Name:</b>
prompt.employee.department=<b>Department:</b>
prompt.employee.skills=<b>Skills:</b>
```

Web Deployment Descriptor for the Application

In this section we will create the deployment descriptor for the web application, as a final step for deploying the web application in the Struts framework. The main items defined in this `web.xml` file are the `ActionServlet` declaration, the mapping, and the declaration of logical names for the tag library URIs for both Struts and application-specific tags. The source listing for the deployment descriptor is shown below:

```
<?xml version="1.0" encoding="ISO-8859-1"?>

<!DOCTYPE web-app PUBLIC
              "-//Sun Microsystems, Inc.//DTD Web Application 2.2//EN"
              "http://java.sun.com/j2ee/dtds/web-app_2_2.dtd">

<web-app>
```

We start by declaring the `ActionServlet` instance, and then configure it to load on startup, and pass the name of the application resources file as an initialization parameter:

```
<servlet>
  <servlet-name>action</servlet-name>
  <servlet-class>org.apache.struts.action.ActionServlet</servlet-class>
  <init-param>
    <param-name>application</param-name>
    <param-value>ApplicationResources</param-value>
  </init-param>
  <load-on-startup>2</load-on-startup>
</servlet>
```

Next we map all of the requests ending with `*.do` within the web context to the `ActionServlet`:

```
<servlet-mapping>
  <servlet-name>action</servlet-name>
  <url-pattern>*.do</url-pattern>
</servlet-mapping>
```

We finish by mapping various tag libraries to their URIs (for instance the Struts bean tag library is mapped to the URI /bean, while the application tag library is mapped to the URI /app):

```
<taglib>
  <taglib-uri>/bean</taglib-uri>
  <taglib-location>/WEB-INF/struts-bean.tld</taglib-location>
</taglib>

<taglib>
  <taglib-uri>/html</taglib-uri>
  <taglib-location>/WEB-INF/struts-html.tld</taglib-location>
</taglib>

<taglib>
  <taglib-uri>/logic</taglib-uri>
  <taglib-location>/WEB-INF/struts-logic.tld</taglib-location>
</taglib>

<taglib>
  <taglib-uri>/template</taglib-uri>
  <taglib-location>/WEB-INF/struts-template.tld</taglib-location>
</taglib>

<taglib>
  <taglib-uri>/app</taglib-uri>
  <taglib-location>/WEB-INF/app.tld</taglib-location>
</taglib>

</web-app>
```

Struts Configuration for the Sample Application

Let's now take a look at the Struts configuration file (`struts-config.xml`) for the web application. The application will present the user with a form for entering the employee information, and when the user submits the form the `request` parameters are sent to the server for validation. So, in the Struts configuration file we need to define the `ActionForm` bean for the employee form, as well as the Struts `Action` associated with it.

Here's the listing for the Struts configuration file:

```xml
<?xml version="1.0" encoding="ISO-8859-1" ?>

<!DOCTYPE struts-config PUBLIC
          "-//Apache Software Foundation//DTD Struts Configuration 1.0//EN"
          "http://jakarta.apache.org/struts/dtds/struts-config_1_0.dtd">

<struts-config>
```

First we declare our form bean, `com.example.EmployeeForm`, and give it the logical name `empForm`. This value will be used to link our `ActionForm` to its `ActionMapping`:

```xml
<form-beans>
  <form-bean name="empForm" type="com.example.EmployeeForm"/>
</form-beans>

<action-mappings>
```

Next we must declare the `ActionMapping` for the action instigated when the user submits the employee form.

Think back to the `web.xml` file. Remember that we mapped the request URI pattern `*.do` to the `ActionServlet`? The path we are mapping here is `/validateEmployee` so the action we need to define for the HTML form should be `/validateEmployee.do`. We will encounter this action later, when we look at the JSP pages for our application.

```xml
<action path="/validateEmployee"
```

The Struts `Action` class used for handling the request is defined as `com.example.ValidateEmployeeAction`. The bean defined by the logical name `empForm` is also attached to this `ActionMapping`. This means that when the `ActionServlet` forwards the control to the `Action` class it will pass an instance of the class `com.example.EmployeeForm` populated with the information entered by the user. The scope for the `ActionForm` is defined as request scope.

```xml
type="com.example.ValidateEmployeeAction"
name="empForm"
scope="request"
```

The input resource that instigates this action is defined as `inputContent.jsp`. This JSP contains the employee form, and this is the JSP first displayed to the user. The first time this JSP is displayed it will have an empty instance of the `ActionForm` class. After that, whenever a validation error occurs the JSP will be associated with an `ActionForm` instance populated with the data entered by the user; in this case the JSP is displayed back to the user, and the data previously entered by the user is retained in the form.

```
input="/inputContent.jsp">
```

We finish by defining a local forward that maps to the resource `outputContent.jsp`. This forward is given the logical name `success`. The `Action` class returns this `ActionForward` to the `ActionServlet` on successful validation, and the JSP retrieves the `ActionForm` from the `request` scope, displaying the data entered by the user in read-only mode.

```
        <forward name="success" path="/outputContent.jsp"/>
      </action>
    </action-mappings>

  </struts-config>
```

Deploying the Application

To deploy the application, follow the following steps.

1. Create a directory `...\begjsp-ch18\WEB-INF\classes\com\example` under your `%TOMCAT_HOME%\webapps` folder, and place your classes in the `example` folder.

2. Place your JSP pages in the `begjsp-ch18` folder.

3. Put your application-specific `tld` file in with the other Struts `tld` files in the `WEB-INF` folder, and place your `web.xml` file in here too.

4. Your application resources file should be placed in the `classes` folder.

5. Create a new folder under `WEB-INF` called `lib`, and place your `struts.jar` file in there.

6. Open a command console and move to the `...\begjsp-ch18\WEB-INF\classes` folder. Compile all of your classes from this folder using the command:

>javac com\example*.java

Your deployment should now be complete.

Running the Application

Restart Tomcat, and access the URL http://localhost/begjsp-ch18/inputContent.jsp using your browser. This will display the window shown below:

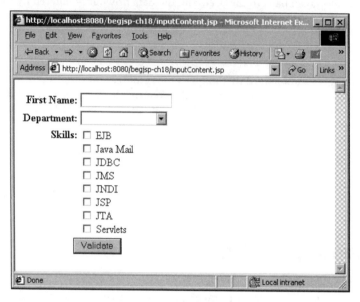

We are going to fill in the info for an employee called Johnny Wrox. Enter a value for the First Name, then click on the Validate button. This will display the window shown below:

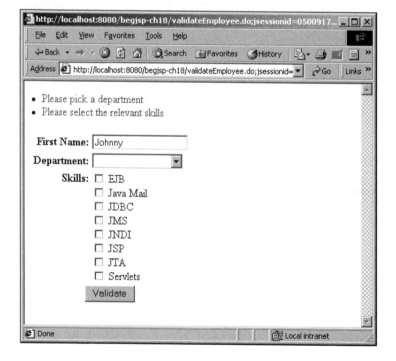

We get a message saying we've forgotten to pick Johnny's Department or select his Skills. Fill these in, and then click the Validate button again. This will display the summary window shown below.

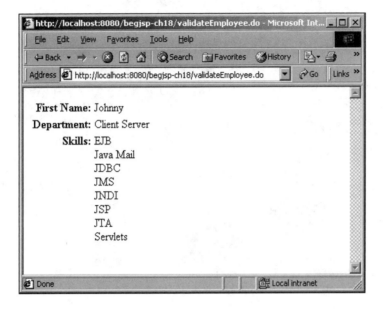

Summary

In this chapter we have covered almost all aspects of Struts. The key aspects we have covered in this chapter include:

- ❑ Importance of using third-party web application frameworks.

- ❑ The Struts architecture, including a close look at the roles and methods of the main Struts components: the `ActionServlet`, `ActionForm`, `ActionMapping`, `ActionForward`, and `Action` classes.

- ❑ Struts configuration and application deployment.

- ❑ The functionality of the Struts `bean`, `html`, `template` and `logic` tag libraries.

- ❑ A simple web application that uses most of Strut's features.

In the next two chapters we will be covering a detailed case study on developing a real web application using Struts.

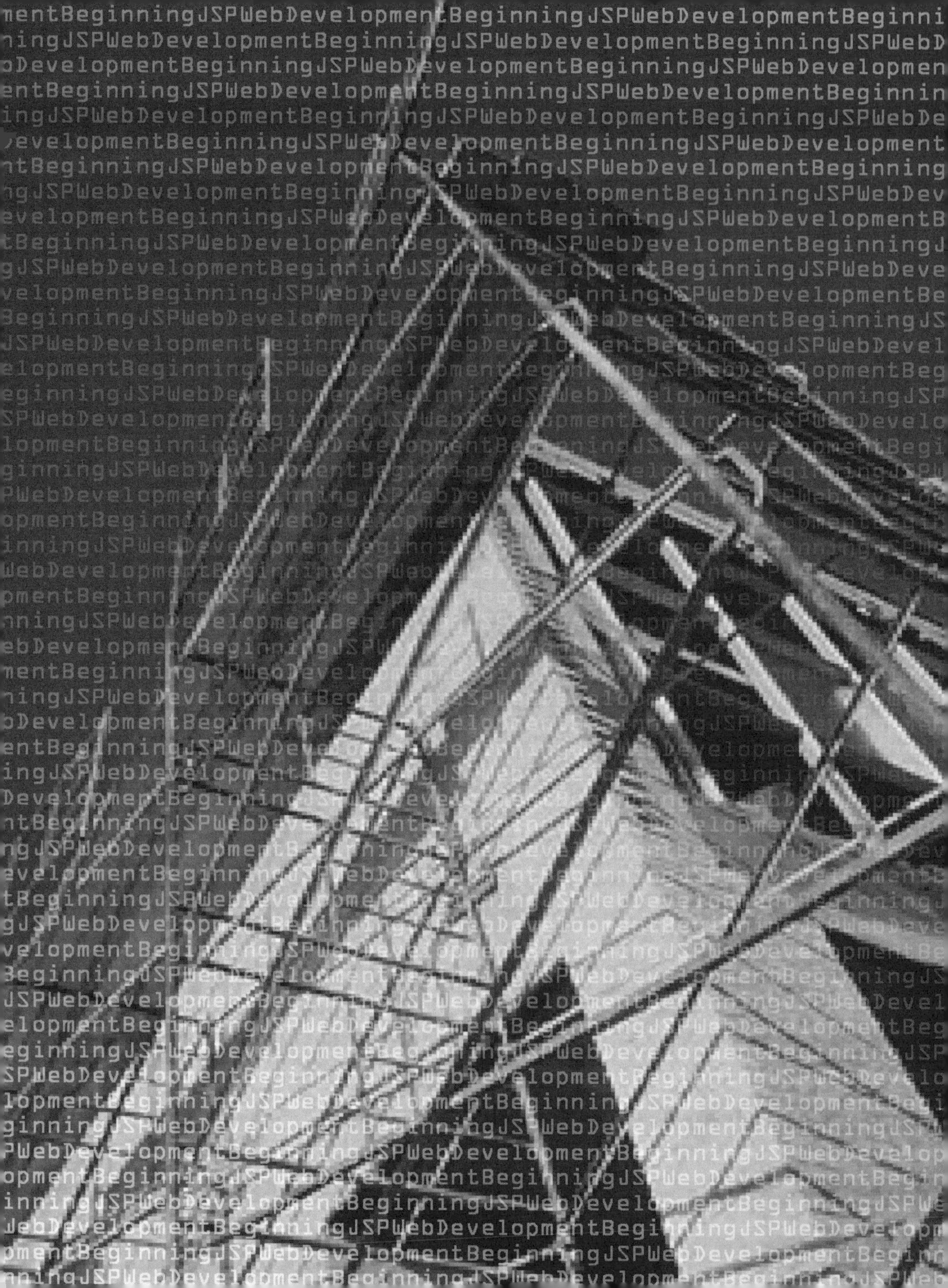
BeginningJSPWebDevelopment

Case Study:
Design and Data Access

In the last chapter we discussed the Apache Struts web framework in detail; in these final two chapters we will be designing and developing a real-world web application on top of the Struts framework. This application is a web site for the local tourism authority, which can be used by tourists who want to browse local attractions and associated events. In addition, the local attractions will be able to register themselves with the web site so that their information is made available to the tourists visiting the web site.

In the course of these chapters, the topics we'll be covering in these chapters include:

❑   All aspects of the analysis, design, development and deployment phases of the project

❑   Extensive use of **UML** (the **Unified Modeling Language**) for modeling both the dynamic and static aspects of the system

❑   Almost all aspects of the Struts framework explained in the last chapter

❑   Different aspects of security like authentication, authorization, custom security realms etc.

❑   Use of Model 2 architecture for partitioning the components of the application

❑   Use of business and data access objects

❑   Database connection pooling

❑   Dynamic template management

❑   And of course JSPs, JSPs, and more JSPs

Because this is a fairly substantial application, we've split it into two chapters. In this first chapter we'll be looking at what the application is required to do, its overall structure, security, and how we represent the data that it needs to maintain. In the second chapter we'll move on to create the Struts objects and JSPs that form the web interface to the system.

Requirements Analysis

Let's get down to business. Once we've decided that it's feasible to go ahead with the project, our first step is to do a detailed **requirements analysis** to identify the list of functionality the system is expected to provide. What this means, in effect, is that we're going to make sure we've got a clear idea of what we need the application to do *before* we actually start work on creating it.

As we work through the case study we'll be using a variety of diagrams to help us clarify our requirements, and later on to illustrate the application design and the steps it will have to take to perform each of its actions. To do this we'll be using a notation called **UML**, the **Unified Modeling Language**. If you've not used UML before don't panic – the diagrams are there to help you understand the system, not to confuse matters. As we introduce each type of diagram we'll walk through what it's showing us, and in fact you'll find that the diagrams are a really helpful way to explain what the system will be doing before we write the actual code.

As we have already seen in the introductory section, the system will have two different kinds of users:

- ❑ Normal users – members of the public – who are tourists accessing the web site to browse the details about local attractions and the associated events

- ❑ The managers of local attractions who can register the attractions with the system so that their information is made available to the web site's public users.

In this section, we will be identifying all of the operations that the system's users (of both types) can perform as they interact with the system – these are known in UML terminology as **use cases**. We will also be drawing up a **use case diagram** to model the external view of the system and illustrate its interactions with the outside world.

The public users accessing the system should be able to access various resources without any security authentication; they should be able to:

- ❑ View the list of local attractions available

- ❑ Drill down to any selected attraction and view its details

- ❑ View the list of events associated with each attraction

- ❑ Register a new local attraction

Attraction managers, on the other hand, should be able to:

- ❑ Perform all the tasks that can be performed by public users

- ❑ Provide security authentication to log on to the system before they can access and modify the attraction details

- ❑ Update the attraction details

- ❑ Edit and modify the list of events associated with the attraction

- ❑ Add new events to the attraction

- ❑ Remove existing events from the attraction

- ❑ Deregister the attraction

- ❑ Log off from the application

These requirements are modeled in the use case diagram shown below:

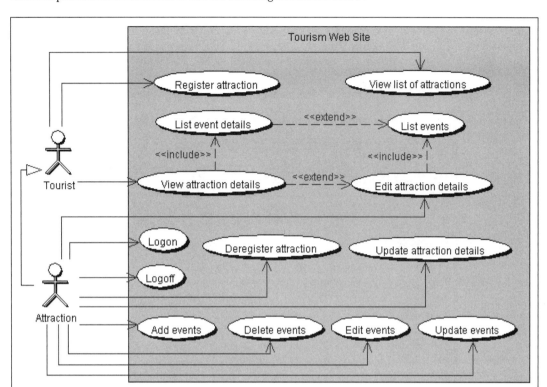

The figure may look rather complicated, but don't panic, it's actually fairly straightforward. The two stick figures on the left – labeled Tourist and Attraction – represent the different types of user the system has; in UML terminology these are called **actors**. Each actor points to a number of ovals within the gray box representing the system; each oval represents a use case that the actor can perform.

You'll note that there is a triangular-headed arrow pointing from the Attraction to the Tourist actor; this is how we indicate in the diagram that, as we mentioned earlier, an Attraction can perform any of the actions that a Tourist can.

There are also a number of dashed lines within the system; these allow us to depict ways in which one use case is a specialized version of another, or in which a number of use cases incorporate the same or similar functionality. For example, in the diagram you can see that the "Edit attraction details" use case is a specialized version of "View attraction details", and that "Edit attraction details" includes the "List events" function.

You may be wondering what the difference is between "Edit attraction details" and "Update attraction details", or between "Edit events" and "Update events". Put simply, in each case the former (the "Edit" use case) is the action the user performs to get a form with the relevant details for them to edit, whereas the latter ("Update") is what they do once they have amended the details in the form and want to store the new details in the database.

When users access the website they will be presented with a list of registered attractions and will be able to select each of the listed attractions and view the details; as we saw earlier, the details will include attraction address, web site URL etc., as well as a list of the events associated with the attraction. The users will also be presented with a menu allowing them to:

❑ Register a new attraction

❑ Log on to the system, if they are the manager of a registered attraction

The screenshot below shows the initial screen of the system, when the users first access the web site:

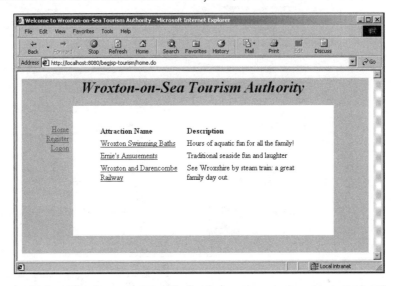

Clicks on the name of a particular attraction will take the user to a screen with more details about that attraction, including the list of its special events:

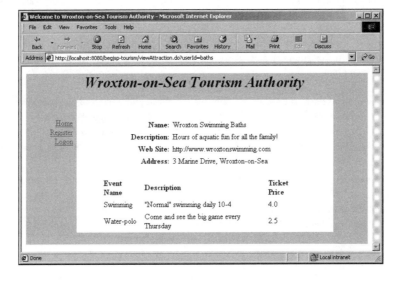

Clicking on the **Register** link takes the user to a form for registering a new attraction, where the various attraction details can be entered:

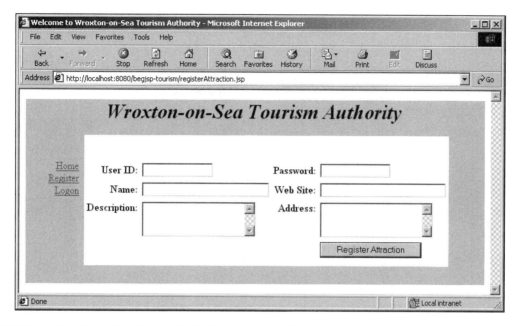

Clicking on **Register Attraction** will add the attraction to the database, so that it will now be included in the list of attractions on the home page.

Once an attraction is registered, the attraction manager can log on using the password he/she supplied by clicking on the **Logon** link. Once they are successfully authenticated, the system will present a screen for modifying the attraction details like password, address, description, web site etc. A menu will also be available for:

❑   Listing the events

❑   Adding new events

❑   Logging out

❑   Deregistering the attraction.

From the list of events, the attractions will be able to edit or delete individual events. The screenshot below shows the first screen after a local attraction has logged on to the system:

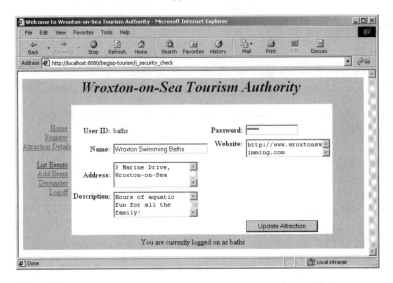

There will need to be further screens for attraction managers to list, update, and add special events – we'll see these later when we come to create them. But this walkthrough should have given you a good idea of what the application we're creating will do, and what it will look like when it's finished.

Choosing the Right Technology

Once we have consolidated the requirements, the next step is to choose the technology we will use for developing and implementing the system. The important factors we need to consider in choosing the right technology include:

- ❑ Standards-based technology
- ❑ Support for rapid development
- ❑ Extensibility
- ❑ Proven web application development paradigm
- ❑ Good quality tool support
- ❑ Vendor-neutral and low-cost implementation
- ❑ Proper division of roles during application design and development: keeping Java development separate from development of the look of the finished web pages

Taking all these factors into consideration, it's an obvious choice to use Java Servlets and JSPs to implement the web application. The next step is to identify the datastore in which we will store our persistent data like attraction and event details; as we've seen earlier in the book, the best solution for storing inter-related persistent entities is a relational database, which can be accessed from Java language programs using the JDBC API.

Finally, we'll take a brief look at the tools we'll use for developing and implementing the system; so far in this book we've used **Tomcat 4.0** to host our JSPs and Servlets, and **MySQL** as our relational datastore. Since both are open-source, free-of-charge products they are ideal for our current purposes.

Application Architecture

So now we know what we want the system to do; the next step is to try to come up with an appropriate architectural model for developing the web application. In Chapter 12 we saw the different web application paradigms that we might use. The important factors that we need to consider in formulating the architectural solution for the system include:

❑ Proper **partitioning** of the application, with a modular, component-based design so that individual parts of the system are simple, easy to understand, and don't interact with each other in complicated ways. (We call this **decoupling** the application components.)

❑ **Maintainability**: the "cleaner" the design, the easier it will be to maintain the system as it will be easier to understand and we will be less likely to introduce subtle mistakes.

❑ **Separating presentation from content**, so that each can be worked on separately.

Keeping all these factors in mind, we will use the MVC/Model 2 paradigm for implementing the system, because it allows us to divide the system up neatly into separate layers which deal with logic and presentation, and to further divide the logic layer into components that deal with each individual use case.

The application views will be implemented using JSPs; for the controller element, rather than reinventing the wheel, we will use a third party off-the-shelf framework. The Apache Struts framework is an excellent choice because it provides a good infrastructure for our logic classes, rich tag libraries for building our JSP views, and a variety of utilities. It is becoming overwhelmingly popular and, like Tomcat and MySQL, is free of charge.

The next step is to identify the components that will build the "model" part of our application – the part that stores data and lets the web components access and update it easily. The model components can be broadly classified into:

❑ **Business logic components**
These components are responsible for implementing the business logic for maintaining the various entities in the system like attractions, events etc. We will call these components **Business Objects**.

❑ **System state components**
These components provide the object incarnations for the system state stored in the underlying relational model. We will call these components **Entities**. In our scenario, the entities will also function as the Struts action form beans.

❑ **Database access logic components**
Finally, we also need components that will implement the data access logic for transforming the records in the underlying relational database to our system state components, and storing the state of our system state components back to the database. We will call these components **Data Access Objects**.

The requests coming from the browser can be broadly classified into data *retrieval* and data *modification* requests; these requests will be routed to the appropriate action classes by the Struts action servlet, depending on the mapping information provided in the Struts configuration file.

❏ Data modification requests will be handled by the business objects, which will in turn use the data access objects to modify the underlying relational data.

❏ For data retrieval requests, the action classes will use the data access objects directly to get an entity or a collection of entities, which will be stored in a request attribute. We then forward the request to the relevant JSP, which will use the appropriate Struts tags to retrieve and render the information.

The diagram below depicts the high-level structure of the system we are going to develop:

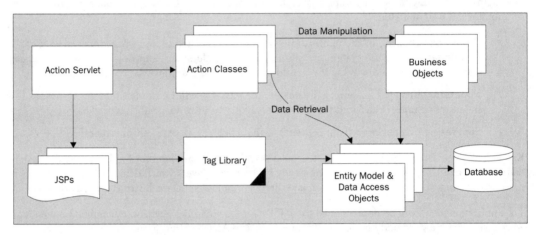

Out of these components, the action servlet and the tag libraries are provided by the Struts framework. We get to create the database schema, the entity model and data access objects, the business objects, the action classes, and the JSPs.

That may look like a very complex structure for our application, but in fact it'll be *easier* to write things this way. That's because, although there are many components to write, each individual component has a very specific purpose: it does only one set of related operations, and its role within the application as a whole is clear. Stepping back at this stage and seeing the whole application in context is *much* easier than leaping in and starting to write before we've got it clear how the different pieces will fit together.

With our overall structure sorted, we can start on the specifics. The application has a fundamental split into the parts that are accessible to anyone, and those that only attraction managers can access after having logged in. Let's start by looking at the security model and how we're going to differentiate between these types of user.

Security

We have already seen the details of web application security in Chapter 13, but let's just have a quick recap of those concepts and produce a security model for our web application. The main four aspects of web application security are:

❏ **Authentication**
The different parties communicating with each other prove their credentials (prove that they are who they say they are) using authentication.

❑ **Authorization**

Once the users are authenticated, we need to determine which resources within the web application they are allowed to access. This is controlled using **ACLs** (**Access Control Lists**) that list the specific "permissions" that are needed to access each resource.

❑ **Data Integrity**

Data integrity ensures that the data sent by one party is not tampered with by a third party before it reaches its destination.

❑ **Data Privacy**

Data privacy ensures that the data sent by one party is not read by someone else before it reaches its destination.

In this section, we will be concentrating on authentication and authorization; by its nature, this application does not handle sensitive data such as credit card numbers and data integrity and privacy need not concern us here.

Authentication

The Servlet API provides us with four different mechanisms for authenticating users:

❑ **Basic Authentication**

If the web application is using HTTP Basic authentication, the browser prompts the user with a window to enter the security credentials. The user's credentials are transmitted to the server in a simple encoding known as base64.

❑ **Digest Authentication**

Digest authentication is similar to Basic authentication, but the only difference is that the username and password are transmitted back to the server in an encrypted form.

❑ **Form Based Authentication**

In Basic and Digest authentication the web application developers have no control over the look and feel of the window used by the browsers to gather the user credentials. In Form Based authentication, on the other hand, the developers can specify an HTML or JSP page to be used for gathering the user credentials. This page can then resemble the appearance of the rest of our application.

This page needs to have a HTML form that posts to the URL j_security_check; the form should have two fields for entering the username and password, called j_username and j_password respectively. When the users try to access secure resources, the web container will send the login page to the user before access for the requested resource is granted. Once the user is successfully authenticated, the server checks whether the user has the required role for accessing the resource.

❑ **HTTPS Client Authentication**

HTTPS client authentication is based on Public Key Certificates. This is a very strong authentication mechanism, but isn't commonly used.

Defining the Authentication Scheme

The authentication to be used within the web application is specified in the web.xml deployment descriptor file. In our web application we will use HTTP Form Based authentication, and the snippet from the web application deployment descriptor shows how the authentication scheme is specified:

```
   . . .
   <login-config>
     <auth-method>FORM</auth-method>
     <form-login-config>
       <form-login-page>/login.jsp</form-login-page>
       <form-error-page>/login.jsp</form-error-page>
     </form-login-config>
   </login-config>
   . . .
```

(We'll see the full text of this file later in the case study.) This defines the logon page as `login.jsp`; if the user is not successfully logged in, they will be sent to an error page which in this case is also `login.jsp`.

Authorization

J2EE promotes resource authorization using **roles** – a user can have a number of different roles, for example in a financial system a counter clerk might have the role `clerk`, while the bank manager might have the roles `clerk` and `manager`. This means that the bank manager can do everything that the counter clerk can do, but additionally can perform operations that require the role `manager`.

For J2EE web applications, the resources may be secured by defining the security constraints in the deployment descriptor, as shown below:

```
   . . .
   <security-constraint>

     <web-resource-collection>
       <web-resource-name>Delete event</web-resource-name>
       <url-pattern>deleteEvent.do</url-pattern>
     </web-resource-collection>

     <auth-constraint>
       <role-name>attraction</role-name>
     </auth-constraint>

   </security-constraint>
   . . .
```

This states that the web resource collection accessed by the request URL `deleteEvent.do` can be accessed only by users having the role `attraction`. What's interesting about this is that it is **declarative**, in other words we specify the authorization requirement purely by saying in the `web.xml` file that users need to be logged in with a certain role to access that resource. This is much easier than **programmatic** security – where the web resource itself has to check whether the user can access it.

In our application, we have two different types of resources:

❑ Resources that can be accessed by public users: listing the available attractions, viewing the attraction and event details and registering a new attraction

❑ Resources that can be accessed only by attraction managers: editing and modifying the attraction details, adding, editing, deleting and modifying events and deregistering the attraction

The first set of resources is not protected and can be accessed by all the users. However, the second set of resources can be accessed only by authenticated users. For this we define a logical role called `attraction`, and define a security constraint in the deployment descriptor to restrict access to resources falling in the second category to only those users who have the `attraction` role.

Security Realms

What we haven't looked at yet is how the specific users and roles are actually defined; it turns out that this very much depends on the particular web server (Tomcat, for example) that we use to deploy the application. This is where **security realms** come into the picture. A security realm may be defined as a logical group of users, roles, and access control lists. In the web application the access control and the roles are defined within the web application deployment descriptor, but mapping the physical users and groups to these roles is done using the web container specific facilities.

Most Java-based web servers let you specify a custom realm for performing authentication and authorization. The basic tasks the container needs to perform when a user accesses a secure resource are:

1. Check whether the user is already authenticated

2. If not, prompt for the credentials

3. Check whether the credentials supplied exist in the security realm the container is using

4. Check whether the authenticated user belongs to a group authorized to access the requested resource

A very simple security realm could just use a text file, or an XML file, containing the security credentials and access control lists, which is read by the server when it starts up. The drawback of this scheme is that whenever a new user or group is added you will have to restart the server before the newly added users can start using the system. Most of the modern servers let the users specify alternative realms like LDAP, JDBC sources, UNIX/NT security realms etc.

Since we are going to deploy our web application with Tomcat, we need to look at the different schemes available with Tomcat. As attraction managers can register with the system and will need to be able to start using the system immediately, we need to use a dynamic realm for our application. Luckily, Tomcat provides a realm based on JDBC database access.

This realm uses two database tables for performing authentication and authorization: the first table needs to store the usernames and passwords, and the second defines the roles each user has been assigned. To specify that we want to use this realm, we add an entry to Tomcat's `server.xml file` (which can be found in the `conf` directory under Tomcat installation). The entry also specifies the names of the tables and the columns holding the relevant data:

```
...
<Realm className="org.apache.catalina.realm.JDBCRealm"
    driverName="org.gjt.mm.mysql.Driver"
    connectionURL="jdbc:mysql://localhost:3306/tourism_db"
    userTable="attraction"
    userNameCol="user_id"
    userCredCol="password"
    userRoleTable="user_role"
    roleNameCol="role_name" />
...
```

629

This defines the following information:

- ❑ The `className` is the name of the class that performs the tasks for authentication and authorization. This class is provided by Tomcat, but we could write our own if we enjoyed hard work.

- ❑ The `driverName` is the name of the JDBC driver used for accessing the database.

- ❑ The `connectionURL` is the JDBC URL for the database.

- ❑ The `userTable`, `userNameCol`, and `userCredCol` are the names of the database table and columns that store usernames and passwords. For this we will be using the table in which we store the attraction details; whenever a new attraction is registered we will be adding a row to this table containing (among other things) the user id and password. The realm class can then use this information to authenticate the users if they decide to logon to the system after registration.

- ❑ The `userRoleTable` and `roleNameCol` entries specify the name of the table and column that store user roles. When an attraction registers itself, a record is inserted into this table with the attraction's username and the role name `attraction`. The realm class can then use this information to authorize the users when they try to access secure resources within the system.

This may all seem a bit complex, and it is – the JDBC realm is designed to be very flexible and can be configured in many different ways; in particular, many applications will have more roles than the one, `attraction`, that we have defined. The `attraction` and `user_role` database tables are discussed in detail in the next section.

Identifying the Entities

The next thing we will do is identify the items of data (**entities**) that model the state of the application, representing the persistent data that is stored in the underlying database. The entities map to relational tables in the database. From the initial requirements analysis, and the discussion on security realms, we can identify three major entities that will be used within the system:

- ❑ `Attraction`: This entity represents the local attractions that are registered with the system.

- ❑ `Event`: This entity represents the events associated with each attraction.

- ❑ `UserRole`: This entity models the roles assigned to each user.

Attractions have a one-to-many bi-directional relation with events and roles: each attraction can have many events associated with it, and similarly each attraction may have many roles (though in the present application each attraction will have precisely one role). Now we need to identify the attributes – the individual data items – associated with each entity.

The `Attraction` entity has the following attributes:

- ❑ The `userId` uniquely identifies an attraction.

- ❑ The `password` attribute defines the security credential used by the user to log on to the system. In our case, the password is stored as plain text, though you might want to encrypt it for security.

- ❏ The `name` attribute defines the name of the attraction.

- ❏ `description` contains a description of the attraction.

- ❏ `website` contains the web site URL of the attraction.

- ❏ `address` contains the address of the attraction.

The `Event` entity has the following attributes:

- ❏ The `eventId` uniquely identifies an event.

- ❏ The `userId` attribute relates the event to the attraction: its value will be the value of an `Attraction`'s `userId`.

- ❏ `name` defines the name of the event.

- ❏ `description` contains a description of the event.

- ❏ `ticketPrice` contains the ticket price for the event.

The `UserRole` entity has the following attributes:

- ❏ The `userId` attribute defines the user for which the role is defined: its value will be the value of an `Attraction`'s `userId`.

- ❏ The `roleName` attribute defines a role for the user. In our case, the value for this attribute will always be `"attraction"`.

The **class diagram** below depicts the entity model for our system. A class diagram is another type of UML diagram, representing individual Java classes within the system. Each box represents a particular class: `Event`, `Attraction`, and `UserRole`. Below the name of each class is a list of its attributes, together with the type of each; for example, `Event` has an `int` property called `eventId` and a `String` property called `userId`. The `-` in front of each attribute name indicates that the attribute itself is `private`.

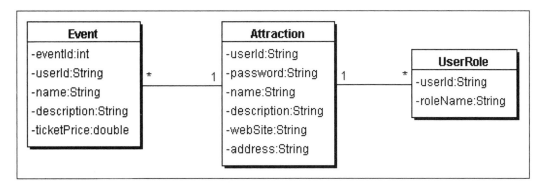

Implementing the Entities

We need to implement the entities as both database tables that will store the data in the long term, and Java classes that will let us access them easily within the application.

Database Scripts

Let's start by creating the database itself. You should already have MySQL installed from Chapter 15; start up the `mysql` command-line utility and enter:

```
create database tourism_db;
use tourism_db;
```

> *Note that the database scripts defined in this section are specific to MySQL; if you want to use different database software you will need to amend the scripts to suit your chosen system.*

Attraction

We'll store the attraction information in a table called `attraction`; the primary key is `user_id`. All the columns in the table are defined as `not null`, so it's not possible to leave that field blank. The snippet of SQL below defines the data definition script for the `attraction` table:

```
create table attraction (
   user_id varchar(15) not null primary key,
   password varchar(15) not null,
   name varchar(30) not null,
   description varchar(60) not null,
   web_site varchar(30) not null,
   address varchar(60) not null)
   type=BDB;
```

> *The `type=BDB` line at the end makes MySQL create the table in such a way that it will work correctly with JDBC transactions; you must be using MySQL Max for this.*

Event

The primary key identified for the `event` table is `event_id`; this column is defined to have values that are automatically incremented by MySQL when records are inserted:

```
create table event (
   event_id int not null primary key auto_increment,
   user_id varchar(15) not null,
   name varchar(30) not null,
   description varchar(60) not null,
   ticket_price double not null)
   type=BDB;
```

UserRole

The `user_role` table defines a composite primary key comprising of `user_id` and `role_name`:

```
create table user_role (
   user_id varchar(15) not null,
   role_name varchar(15) not null,
   primary key (user_id,role_name))
   type=BDB;
```

632

Java Classes

Now we will define the Java classes that will model our entities; later, we'll move on to the data access and logic classes. The classes for attraction and event entities can also serve as Struts action form beans that can be associated with the forms for entering the attraction and event details. Therefore, these two classes extend the Struts class org.apache.struts.action.ActionForm. All these classes are defined in the Java package com.wrox.tourism.entity.

Attraction

This class models the attraction table and defines the attributes that represent the columns in the table. The class also defines get and set methods for all the attributes:

```
package com.wrox.tourism.entity;

import org.apache.struts.action.ActionForm;

public class Attraction extends ActionForm {

  private String userId;
  private String password;
  private String name;
  private String description;
  private String webSite;
  private String address;

  public String getUserId() {
    return userId;
  }

  public void setUserId(String userId) {
    this.userId = userId;
  }

  public String getPassword() {
    return password;
  }

  public void setPassword(String password) {
    this.password = password;
  }

  public String getName() {
    return name;
  }

  public void setName(String name) {
    this.name = name;
  }

  public String getDescription() {
    return description;
  }

  public void setDescription(String description) {
```

```
      this.description = description;
    }

    public String getWebSite() {
      return webSite;
    }

    public void setWebSite(String webSite) {
      this.webSite = webSite;
    }

    public String getAddress() {
      return address;
    }

    public void setAddress(String address) {
      this.address = address;
    }

}
```

Event

This class models the event table and defines the attributes that represent the columns in the table, together with their get and set methods:

```
package com.wrox.tourism.entity;

import org.apache.struts.action.ActionForm;

public class Event extends ActionForm {

  private int eventId;
  private String userId;
  private String name;
  private String description;
  private double ticketPrice;

  public int getEventId() {
    return eventId;
  }

  public void setEventId(int eventId) {
    this.eventId = eventId;
  }

  public String getUserId() {
    return userId;
  }

  public void setUserId(String userId) {
    this.userId = userId;
  }
```

```
      public String getName() {
        return name;
      }

      public void setName(String name) {
        this.name = name;
      }

      public String getDescription() {
        return description;
      }

      public void setDescription(String description) {
        this.description = description;
      }

      public double getTicketPrice() {
        return ticketPrice;
      }

      public void setTicketPrice(double ticketPrice) {
        this.ticketPrice = ticketPrice;
      }

    }
```

UserRole

This class models the `user_role` table and, again, defines the attributes that represent the columns in the table along with their get and set methods:

```
    package com.wrox.tourism.entity;

    public class UserRole {

      private String userId;
      private String roleName;

      public String getUserId() {
        return userId;
      }

      public void setUserId(String userId) {
        this.userId = userId;
      }

      public String getRoleName() {
        return roleName;
      }

      public void setRoleName(String roleName) {
        this.roleName = roleName;
      }

    }
```

So that's the basic database schema and entity model completed; the next step is to consider how we're going to tie them together with JDBC code. First, however, we will need to take a detour and think about how we get hold of database connections in our web application.

Pooling Database Connections

In a properly designed enterprise application, connections to external resource managers are always pooled for improving performance and enhancing efficiency, rather than opening a connection each time the resource manager is accessed. Classes using the pool can request a connection from the pool when they need to use one, and return it back to the pool after use.

Resources that are commonly pooled include network sockets, connections to the Java Message Service, and of course JDBC connections. Since we are going to use a relational database in our web application, it will be a good idea to come up with a scheme for pooling JDBC connections. Connection pools normally maintain a pool of connections to the underlying resource manager.

In Chapters 15 and 16 we have seen there are two ways of getting a database connection using the JDBC API:

❑ Using the `java.sql.DriverManager` class in the JDBC core API.

❑ Using the `javax.sql.DataSource` interface in the JDBC extension API, which can be used as a factory for creating connections.

We have also seen in Chapter 18 that Struts provides an implementation of the `DataSource` interface. Therefore, the obvious choice to implement the connection pool is simply to declare the datasource in the Struts configuration file.

One downside of doing this is that datasources declared in the Struts configuration file are accessed through the action servlet, and only the action classes have direct access to the action servlet. However, we may need to access the datasource from our business objects, or elsewhere, and we therefore need to have an instance of the connection pool accessible from anywhere within the application.

Our solution is to create an instance of the `org.apache.struts.util.GenericDataSource` class (the Struts class that implements `DataSource`) and wrap it in a class that can be accessed from anywhere within the application, which we'll call `ConnectionPool`. The `ConnectionPool` class can expose methods for retrieving connections from the datasource, and pass these calls on to the underlying datasource. There needs to be only one instance of this class; this way of designing a class is known as a **Singleton**. Singleton is a pattern that ensures there is only one instance of the class available within the application.

The last design issue is to consider where we should initialize this single instance of the `ConnectionPool` class, and we have a couple of options:

❑ The Servlet 2.3 specification allows us to create a listener class that gets told when the application starts up and is shut down. However, since we may ultimately want to run the application on a server other than Tomcat 4.0, we will pass this option by for now.

❑ The second option, which we will use, is to use a servlet which is loaded when the application starts up.

The diagram below shows the classes we use for implementing the connection pool:

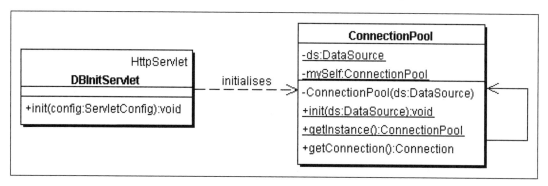

Again, we've introduced some more UML notation in this diagram, but again it's all fairly straightforward. The `DBInitServlet` class extends `HttpServlet`, hence the text in the top right hand corner of that box. The bottom section of each class lists its constructors and methods. The rather cryptic `+init(config:ServletConfig):void` means that there is a `public` (+) method called `init` which takes one parameter, `config`, of type `ServletConfig`, and whose return type is `void`. You'll notice again the – sign indicating that `ConnectionPool`'s constructor is private, and the underlining means that the same class's `init()` and `getInstance()` methods are `static`.

Implementing the Pool

As illustrated in the class diagram above, we need to implement two classes:

❑   The class that implements the connection pool

❑   The servlet that initializes the connection pool class

ConnectionPool

As we have already discussed we want to implement this class as a singleton, so that only one instance of the class will exist. One simple way to implement a singleton class is:

❑   Provide a private constructor so that the class may not be initialized from anywhere outside the class

❑   Define a static variable of type as the same class itself

❑   Provide a static method that initializes the static variable explained in the previous step

❑   Provide a static method to access the static variable

In addition to the above steps, when our singleton instance is initialized we need to pass it an instance of a `DataSource` object; we also need to provide a method that can be used by client classes to retrieve a connection to the database. This method simply asks the `DataSource` object itself for a connection, and passes the returned connection to the client class that requested the connection:

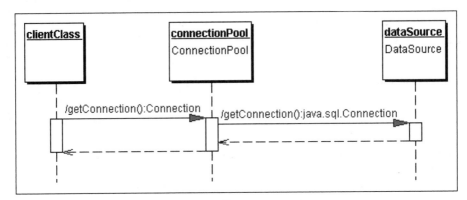

Another new type of diagram! Fortunately we've almost covered them all now. This is a UML **sequence diagram**, and shows how different objects are calling methods on each other. On the left is the client class, which calls the `ConnectionPool`'s `getConnection()` method, which in turn calls the `DataSource`'s `getConnection()` method. Each column represents one object, and the boxes on the vertical lines represent the time during which that object is performing an operation. The underlined name at the top of each box is the object's name; below it is shown the object's class.

Let's have a look at the source file for the implementation class:

```
package com.wrox.tourism.db.util;

import java.sql.SQLException;
import java.sql.Connection;
import javax.sql.DataSource;

public class ConnectionPool {
```

We define an instance of `DataSource`, which we will use to handle the calls for retrieving JDBC connections:

```
    private DataSource ds;
```

We also define the static singleton instance of the `ConnectionPool` class itself:

```
    private static ConnectionPool mySelf;
```

The constructor is private, and is used for initializing the datasource: it takes an instance of the datasource and assigns it to the instance variable:

```
    private ConnectionPool(DataSource ds) {
      this.ds = ds;
    }
```

The `init()` method initializes both the singleton instance and the datasource, calling the private constructor and passing it the datasource instance. It also initializes the static singleton instance:

```
public static void init(DataSource ds) {
  mySelf = new ConnectionPool(ds);
}
```

Things start to come together now as we provide a static method to access the singleton instance; this is the method that the rest of our application can call when it wants to get hold of a connection pool. It returns the `ConnectionPool` instance that we created in the `init()` method, or throws `IllegalStateException` if the pool has not been initialized:

```
public static ConnectionPool getInstance() {

  if (mySelf == null) {
    throw new IllegalStateException("Pool not initialized.");
  }
  return mySelf;

}
```

Finally, we provide an instance method to retrieve a JDBC connection, as we discussed earlier. This method delegates the task of retrieving the JDBC connection to the underlying datasource object:

```
public Connection getConnection() throws SQLException {
  return ds.getConnection();
}

}
```

That's it for the connection pool class; next up is the servlet that initializes it for us.

DBInitServlet

This is a standard HTTP servlet with the `init()` method overridden, and will be configured to be loaded when the web application starts up. In the `init()` method, an instance of the Struts datasource implementation class will be initialized and passed to the connection pool initialization method explained in the last section. To configure the datasource object we define some initialization parameters in the deployment descriptor:

Let's start by looking at the relevant excerpt from the deployment descriptor:

```
. . .
<servlet>
  <servlet-name>dbInit</servlet-name>
  <servlet-class>com.wrox.tourism.db.util.DBInitServlet</servlet-class>
  <init-param>
    <param-name>driverClass</param-name>
    <param-value>org.gjt.mm.mysql.Driver</param-value>
  </init-param>
  <init-param>
    <param-name>jdbcURL</param-name>
    <param-value>jdbc:mysql://localhost:3306/tourism_db</param-value>
```

```
      </init-param>
      <init-param>
        <param-name>minCount</param-name>
        <param-value>1</param-value>
      </init-param>
      <init-param>
        <param-name>maxCount</param-name>
        <param-value>10</param-value>
      </init-param>
      <load-on-startup>1</load-on-startup>
    </servlet>

    ...
```

The `<load-on-startup>` element tells Tomcat that the servlet should be loaded on startup; we also provide an integer value that is used to define the order in which servlets start. This excerpt from `web.xml` also defines the following initialization parameters that will be used to configure the datasource object:

- ❑   `driverClass`: The name of the JDBC driver class to use.

- ❑   `jdbcURL`: The JDBC URL to the database to which the connections are to be created.

- ❑   `minCount`: The minimum number of connections in the pool.

- ❑   `maxCount`: The maximum number of connections the pool may have.

Now we will have a look at the source code for the servlet:

```
package com.wrox.tourism.db.util;

import javax.servlet.http.HttpServlet;
import javax.servlet.ServletConfig;
import javax.servlet.ServletException;

import java.sql.SQLException;
import java.sql.Connection;
import javax.sql.DataSource;

import org.apache.struts.util.GenericDataSource;

public class DBInitServlet extends HttpServlet {
```

The `init()` method is where the work happens. We start, as normal, by calling the superclass's `init()` method:

```
  public void init(ServletConfig config) throws ServletException {

    super.init(config);

    try {
```

Next we create an instance of the class `GenericDataSource`:

```
      GenericDataSource ds = new GenericDataSource();
```

and set its properties from the init parameters passed to the servlet:

```
ds.setDriverClass(getInitParameter("driverClass"));
ds.setUrl(getInitParameter("jdbcURL"));
ds.setMinCount(Integer.parseInt(getInitParameter("minCount")));
ds.setMaxCount(Integer.parseInt(getInitParameter("maxCount")));
ds.setAutoCommit(false);
```

With that done, we open the `DataSource`:

```
ds.open();
```

and initialize the connection pool by passing it the datasource object:

```
      ConnectionPool.init(ds);

   } catch (SQLException e) {
      e.printStackTrace();
      throw new ServletException("Unable to open datasource.");
   }

  }

}
```

And that's it. You'll notice that we didn't do anything in the `doGet()` or `doPost()` methods, because we're not using this servlet to process any actual client requests: it's just there to initialize the connection pool when the server starts up.

Data Access Objects

Now we'll move on to have a look at the data access objects that we will use for accessing the relational database. These objects will be used to transform the database records to entity class instances, and viceversa, encapsulating the database calls and isolating other parts of the application from SQL statements.

There will be a one-to-one correspondence between the entity objects and data access objects, with each entity object having a corresponding data access object that encapsulates the database calls for that entity, one each corresponding to the `Attraction`, `Event`, and `UserRole` entities.

Each class will have:

❑   A method for creating the entity in the database

❑   A method for removing the entity from the database

❑   A method for updating the information regarding an existing entity

❑   One or more methods for finding entities from the database based on specific criteria. (Each data access object will at least have a method to find a single entity from its primary key.)

When we create an instance of a data access object, we will pass its constructor a JDBC connection that it should use for sending SQL statements to the relational database.

Exception Handling in Data Access Objects

Before we look at the data access objects itself, we need to create a specialized set of exception classes to deal with problems that might occur when accesssing the database. If we want our database access objects to be able to handle error conditions robustly, we need to have a range of exception types available so that we can signal to the rest of the application what went wrong, and (more importantly) what that means in terms of the entity it was trying to manipulate. The code is very similar for each exception.

CreateException

A CreateException will be thrown if, for some reason, we fail to create the entity in the database:

```
package com.wrox.tourism.db;

public class CreateException extends Exception {

  public CreateException(String message) {
    super(message);
  }

}
```

DuplicateKeyException

This exception is a specialized subclass of the CreateException and is thrown if we fail to create the entity because another entity already exists in the database with the specified primary key:

```
package com.wrox.tourism.db;

public class DuplicateKeyException extends CreateException {

  public DuplicateKeyException(String message) {
    super(message);
  }

}
```

FinderException

A FinderException is thrown if, for some reason, we fail to find an entity or collection of entities in the database:

```
package com.wrox.tourism.db;

public class FinderException extends Exception {

  public FinderException(String message) {
    super(message);
  }

}
```

ObjectNotFoundException

This is a specialized subclass of `FinderException`, which is thrown if we were searching for a specific entity but it was not found in the database:

```
package com.wrox.tourism.db;

public class ObjectNotFoundException extends FinderException {

  public ObjectNotFoundException(String message) {
    super(message);
  }

}
```

NoSuchEntityException

This unexpected exception is thrown in cases where we are trying to remove or update an entity, but the specified entity is not found in the database. This exception extends the system exception `java.lang.RuntimeException`:

```
package com.wrox.tourism.db;

public class NoSuchEntityException extends RuntimeException {

  public NoSuchEntityException(String message) {
    super(message);
  }

}
```

With the exception classes out of the way, let's move on to look at how our data access objects will operate, without (at this stage) looking at the actual code. Once we've thought through how each of the methods will work, we'll look at the actual data access object classes for `Attraction`, `Event`, and `UserRole`.

Create Methods

Each data access object defines one create method, which takes as an argument an instance of the corresponding entity class, and can throw `CreateException`. The steps involved in implementing the create method are:

1. The data access object was given a `Connection` when it was instantiated, however we had better check that it's still valid. If the connection is closed, we throw an `IllegalStateException`.

2. Create a `PreparedStatement` from the connection, passing it the specific SQL to create this type of entity.

3. Set the input parameters of the `PreparedStatement` from the entity object attributes. In our case, the entity object may be an `Attraction`, `Event` or `UserRole` object.

4. Execute the SQL. If the update count is not equal to 1, the insert operation wasn't done successfully so throw a `CreateException`.

5. If an `SQLException` was thrown in any of the above steps, check whether an entity already exists in the relevant table for the specified primary key. If it does exist, throw a `DuplicateKeyException`, or else throw a `RuntimeExecption`.

6. Finally, close the `PreparedStatement`. If an `SQLException` is thrown in the process we catch it and rethrow it as a `RuntimeException`.

> **Notice that we don't close the `Connection` here – the code that creates the data access object is responsible for obtaining a `Connection` from the pool, and for closing it (returning it to the pool) once it has finished with the data access object. We haven't forgotten about it – we'll see the code that obtains and closes the connection later.**

These steps are illustrated in the diagram below:

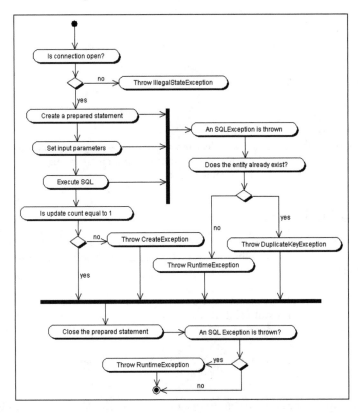

This is an **activity diagram**, the final type of UML diagram we will see in this chapter. It shows in diagramatic form the sequence of operations we just described. The dot at the top is where execution of the method starts, and it ends at the dot at the bottom of the diagram. Each rounded box represents an action performed, and each diamond represents a choice to be made.

Update Methods

Next, we'll look at the methods for updating the entities in the database. Each data access object defines one update method, which again takes as an argument an instance of the corresponding entity class. The activity diagram below illustrates the steps involved in updating the database:

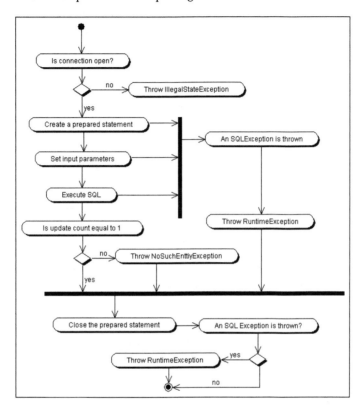

Working through this diagram, the steps involved in implementing the update method are:

1. If the connection is closed, throw an `IllegalStateException`.

2. Create a `PreparedStatement` from the connection, passing it the relevant SQL code to update the entity.

3. Set the input parameters of the `PreparedStatement` from the entity object attributes.

4. Execute the SQL. If the update count is not equal to 1, throw a `NoSuchEntityException`.

5. If an `SQLException` is thrown in any of the above steps, throw a `RuntimeException`.

6. Finally, close the `PreparedStatement`. If an `SQLException` is thrown in the process catch it and rethrow it as a `RuntimeException`.

Remove Methods

Next, let's look at the methods for removing the entities from the database. Each data access object defines one remove method, which takes the primary key of the corresponding entity as an argument. In our case:

❑   The primary key for the `Attraction` entity is a `String` representing the user id.

❑   The primary key for the `Event` entity is an `int` representing the event id.

❑   The primary key for the `UserRole` entity is two `Strings` representing the user id and role name.

The steps involved in implementing the remove method are:

1.   If the connection is closed, throw an `IllegalStateException`.

2.   Create a `PreparedStatement` from the connection, passing the delete SQL specific to the entity being deleted, as an argument.

3.   Set the input parameters of the `PreparedStatement` from the entity object passed to the method.

4.   Execute the SQL. If the update count is not equal to one throw a `NoSuchEntityException`.

5.   If an `SQLException` is thrown in any of the above steps, throw a `RuntimeException`.

6.   Finally, close the `PreparedStatement`. If an `SQLException` is thrown in the process catch it and rethrow it as a `RuntimeException`.

The activity diagram for the delete methods is very similar to that for update methods.

Finder Methods

The data access objects may define one or more finder methods to retrieve an entity or a collection of entities from the database; each will at least define a finder that takes a primary key value and returns an entity instance corresponding to that primary key. If the finder methods fail for some reason they throw `FinderException`.

Finder methods can be either single or multi object finders:

❑   Single object finder methods return a single instance of the entity; if no record meeting the specified criteria is found in the database method will throw `ObjectNotFoundException`.

❑   Multi object finders return a collection of entity instances; if no entities are found in the database for the specified criteria, an empty collection is returned.

Single Object Finders

Let's start by examining the logic for single object finders. The number and type of arguments taken by a finder method will depend on the `where` condition in the SQL code used to query the database; the methods for finding an entity by primary key will take the corresponding primary key values as arguments. The steps involved in implementing these finder methods are:

1. If the connection is closed, throw an `IllegalStateException`.

2. Create a `PreparedStatement` from the connection, with the relevant SQL select code for the entity being selected.

3. Set the input parameters of the `PreparedStatement` from the input arguments passed to the method.

4. Execute the SQL. If the result set is empty, throw an `ObjectNotFoundException`.

5. Create an entity instance, set its attribute values from the result set columns, and return the entity instance.

6. If an `SQLException` is thrown in any of the above steps, throw a `RuntimeExecption`.

7. Finally, close the `PreparedStatement`. If an `SQLException` is thrown in the process, catch it and rethrow it as a `RuntimeException`.

The activity diagram for single object finder methods is shown below:

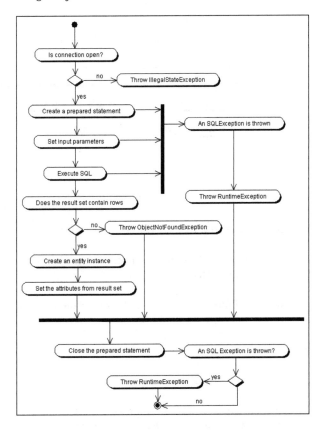

Multi Object Finders

Finally, we'll consider the logic for implementing multi object finders. Again, the number and type of arguments taken by a finder method depends on the `where` condition in the SQL code used to query the database. The activity diagram is as follows:

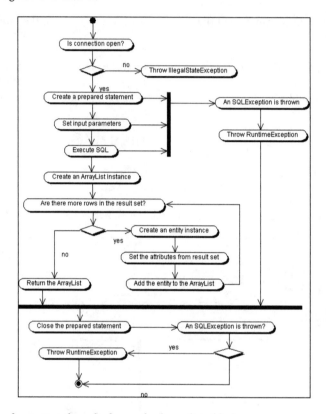

The steps involved in implementing these finder methods are listed below:

1. If the connection is closed, throw an `IllegalStateException`.

2. Create a `PreparedStatement` from the connection, with the relevant SQL select code for the collection of entities being selected.

3. Set the input parameters of the `PreparedStatement` from the input arguments passed to the method.

4. Execute the SQL.

5. Create an instance of `ArrayList`.

6. While there are more records in the result set, create entity instances, set the attributes from the result set columns and add to the `ArrayList` instance.

7. Return the `ArrayList` instance.

8. If an `SQLException` is thrown in any of the above steps, throw a `RuntimeException`.

9. Finally, close the `PreparedStatement`. If an `SQLException` is thrown in the process, catch it and rethrow it as a `RuntimeException`.

That completes our look at the generalities of how to implement these methods – let's turn now to implementing the specific data access objects for `Attraction`, `Event`, and `UserRole`.

AttractionDAO

`AttractionDAO` is the data access object class that encapsulates the data access calls for maintaining the state of `Attraction` entities. It defines the following methods:

❑ **create(Attraction attraction)**
This method creates a record in the `attraction` table from the attribute values of the `Attraction` object it is passed.

❑ **update(Attraction attraction)**
This method updates the `attraction` record in the database from the attribute values of the passed `Attraction` object.

❑ **remove(String userId)**
This method removes the `attraction` record with the specified `user_id` from the database.

❑ **findByPrimaryKey(String userId)**
This method finds the `attraction` record with the specified `user_id` and returns an `Attraction` object.

❑ **findAll()**
This method returns all the records from the `attraction` table as a collection of `Attraction` entity instances.

Let's have a look at the source code for the `AttractionDAO` class:

```
package com.wrox.tourism.db;

import com.wrox.tourism.entity.Attraction;

import java.sql.Connection;
import java.sql.PreparedStatement;
import java.sql.ResultSet;
import java.sql.SQLException;

import java.util.Collection;
import java.util.ArrayList;

public class AttractionDAO {

  private Connection con;
```

In the `constructor`, the JDBC connection for sending the SQL statements to the relation datastore is initialized:

```
public AttractionDAO(Connection con) {
  this.con = con;
}
```

The `create()` method takes an instance of the `Attraction` class. An instance of `PreparedStatement` is created, for executing the `insert` SQL statement; we then try to execute the statement:

```
public void create(Attraction attraction) throws CreateException {

  PreparedStatement ps = null;

  String sql = "INSERT INTO attraction VALUES (?,?,?,?,?,?)";

  try {

    if (con.isClosed()) {
      throw new IllegalStateException("error.unexpected");
    }

    ps = con.prepareStatement(sql);

    ps.setString(1,attraction.getUserId());
    ps.setString(2,attraction.getPassword());
    ps.setString(3,attraction.getName());
    ps.setString(4,attraction.getDescription());
    ps.setString(5,attraction.getWebSite());
    ps.setString(6,attraction.getAddress());
```

You'll notice the curious `String` value, `"error.unexpected"`, that is passed to the constructor for `IllegalStateException`. This value will be used later to look up the actual message we will display to the user explaining the error condition.

If we failed to create the record, a `CreateException` is thrown; if we suffered a `SQLException` due to an already existing record with the same primary key, a `DuplicateKeyException` is thrown. Whatever happens, we make sure to close the `PreparedStatement`:

```
    if (ps.executeUpdate() != 1) {
      throw new CreateException("error.create.attraction");
    }
  } catch (SQLException e) {
    try {
      findByPrimaryKey(attraction.getUserId());
    } catch (FinderException fe) {
      fe.printStackTrace();
      throw new RuntimeException("error.unexpected");
    }
    throw new DuplicateKeyException(
      "error.duplicate.attraction");
  } finally {
    try {
      if (ps != null)
```

```
        ps.close();
    } catch (SQLException e) {
      e.printStackTrace();
      throw new RuntimeException("error.unexpected");
    }
  }

}
```

The update() method takes an instance of Attraction class. An instance of PreparedStatement is created that is used for executing the update SQL statement. If the specified record is not found a NoSuchEntityException is thrown.

```
public void update(Attraction attraction) {

  PreparedStatement ps = null;

  String sql = "UPDATE attraction SET password = ?," +
      "name = ?,description = ?,web_site = ?,address = ? " +
      "WHERE user_id = ?";

  try {

    if (con.isClosed()) {
      throw new IllegalStateException("error.unexpected");
    }

    ps = con.prepareStatement(sql);
    ps.setString(1,attraction.getPassword());
    ps.setString(2,attraction.getName());
    ps.setString(3,attraction.getDescription());
    ps.setString(4,attraction.getWebSite());
    ps.setString(5,attraction.getAddress());
    ps.setString(6,attraction.getUserId());

    if (ps.executeUpdate() != 1) {
      throw new NoSuchEntityException(
        "error.removed.attraction");
    }

  } catch (SQLException e) {
    e.printStackTrace();
    throw new RuntimeException("error.unexpected");
  } finally {
    try {
      if (ps != null)
        ps.close();
    } catch (SQLException e) {
      e.printStackTrace();
      throw new RuntimeException("error.unexpected");
    }
  }

}
```

The remove() method takes the userId identifying the attraction record to be removed. An instance of PreparedStatement is created that is used for executing the delete SQL statement, and if the specified record is not found a NoSuchEntityException is thrown.

```
public void remove(String userId) {

  PreparedStatement ps = null;

  String sql = "DELETE FROM attraction WHERE user_id = ?";

  try {

    if (con.isClosed()) {
      throw new IllegalStateException("error.unexpected");
    }

    ps = con.prepareStatement(sql);
    ps.setString(1,userId);

    if (ps.executeUpdate() != 1) {
      throw new NoSuchEntityException(
        "error.removed.attraction");
    }

  } catch (SQLException e) {
    e.printStackTrace();
    throw new RuntimeException("error.unexpected");
  } finally {
    try {
      if (ps != null)
        ps.close();
    } catch (SQLException e) {
      e.printStackTrace();
      throw new RuntimeException("error.unexpected");
    }
  }

}
```

The findByPrimaryKey() method takes the userId for which the attraction record needs to be found. An instance of PreparedStatement is created that is used for executing the select SQL statement; if the record is not found an ObjectNotFoundException is thrown:

```
public Attraction findByPrimaryKey(String userId)
    throws FinderException {

  PreparedStatement ps = null;
  ResultSet rs = null;
  Attraction attraction = null;

  String sql = "SELECT * from attraction WHERE user_id = ?";

  try {
```

```
      if (con.isClosed()) {
        throw new IllegalStateException("error.unexpected");
      }

      ps = con.prepareStatement(sql);
      ps.setString(1,userId);
      rs = ps.executeQuery();

      if (rs.next()) {

        attraction = new Attraction();
        attraction.setUserId(rs.getString(1));
        attraction.setPassword(rs.getString(2));
        attraction.setName(rs.getString(3));
        attraction.setDescription(rs.getString(4));
        attraction.setWebSite(rs.getString(5));
        attraction.setAddress(rs.getString(6));

        return attraction;

      } else {
        throw new ObjectNotFoundException(
          "error.removed.attraction");
      }

    } catch (SQLException e) {
      e.printStackTrace();
      throw new RuntimeException("error.unexpected");
    } finally {
      try {
        if (ps != null)
          ps.close();
        if (rs != null)
          rs.close();
      } catch (SQLException e) {
        e.printStackTrace();
        throw new RuntimeException("error.unexpected");
      }
    }

  }
```

The findAll() method returns all the records from the attraction table and returns them as a collection of Attraction entity instances. An instance of PreparedStatement is created that is used for executing the select SQL statement; if an unexpected SQLException is thrown, it is caught and rethrown as a RuntimeException:

```
public Collection findAll() {

  PreparedStatement ps = null;
  ResultSet rs = null;
  ArrayList list = new ArrayList();

  String sql = "SELECT * from attraction ";
```

```
        try {

          if (con.isClosed()) {
            throw new IllegalStateException("error.unexpected");
          }

          ps = con.prepareStatement(sql);
          rs = ps.executeQuery();

          while(rs.next()) {

            Attraction attraction = new Attraction();
            attraction.setUserId(rs.getString(1));
            attraction.setPassword(rs.getString(2));
            attraction.setName(rs.getString(3));
            attraction.setDescription(rs.getString(4));
            attraction.setWebSite(rs.getString(5));
            attraction.setAddress(rs.getString(6));

            list.add(attraction);

          }

          return list;

        } catch (SQLException e) {
          e.printStackTrace();
          throw new RuntimeException("error.unexpected");
        } finally {
          try {
            if (ps != null)
              ps.close();
            if (rs != null)
              rs.close();
          } catch (SQLException e) {
            e.printStackTrace();
            throw new RuntimeException("error.unexpected");
          }
        }

      }

    }
```

EventDAO

The EventDAO class encapsulates the data access calls for maintaining the state of the Event entities, and defines the following methods:

❑ **create(Event event)**
This method creates a record in the event table from the attribute values of the Event instance it is passed.

❑ **update(Event event)**
This method updates the event record in the database from the attribute values of the passed Event entity instance.

❑ **`remove(int eventId)`**
This method removes the `event` record with the specified `event_id` from the database.

❑ **`findByPrimaryKey(int eventId)`**
This method finds the `event` record with the specified `event_id` and returns an `Event` instance.

❑ **`findAll(String userId)`**
This method returns all the records from the `event` table as a collection of `Event` entity instances, for the specified `user_id`.

Now let's look at the code for the `EventDAO` class; you'll see that it's very similar to the `AttractionDAO` class we just considered:

```
package com.wrox.tourism.db;

import com.wrox.tourism.entity.Event;

import java.sql.Connection;
import java.sql.PreparedStatement;
import java.sql.ResultSet;
import java.sql.SQLException;

import java.util.Collection;
import java.util.ArrayList;

public class EventDAO {

  private Connection con;
```

In the constructor, the JDBC connection for sending the SQL statements to the relation datastore is initialized:

```
public EventDAO(Connection con) {
  this.con = con;
}
```

The `create()` method takes an instance of the `Event` class, and creates an instance of `PreparedStatement` that is used to execute the `insert` SQL statement.

```
public void create(Event event) throws CreateException {

  PreparedStatement ps = null;

  String sql = "INSERT INTO event " +
      "(user_id,name,description,ticket_price) VALUES (?,?,?,?)";

  try {

    if (con.isClosed()) {
      throw new IllegalStateException("error.unexpected");
    }

    ps = con.prepareStatement(sql);
```

```
          ps.setString(1,event.getUserId());
          ps.setString(2,event.getName());
          ps.setString(3,event.getDescription());
          ps.setDouble(4,event.getTicketPrice());
```

If the method fails to create the record, a `CreateException` is thrown. Unlike the equivalent method in `AttractionDAO`, this method would never throw a `DuplicateKeyException` as the primary key for the `event` table is automatically generated by the database:

```
          if (ps.executeUpdate() != 1) {
            throw new CreateException("error.create.event");
          }
        } catch (SQLException e) {
          e.printStackTrace();
          throw new RuntimeException("error.unexpected");
        } finally {
          try {
            if (ps != null)
              ps.close();
          } catch (SQLException e) {
            e.printStackTrace();
            throw new RuntimeException("error.unexpected");
          }
        }

      }
```

The `update()` method takes an instance of the `Event` class. Again, an instance of `PreparedStatement` is created that is used for executing the `update` SQL statement, and if the specified record is not found a `NoSuchEntityException` is thrown:

```
    public void update(Event event) {

      PreparedStatement ps = null;

      String sql = "UPDATE event SET name = ?,description = ?," +
          "ticket_price = ? WHERE event_id = ?";

      try {

        if (con.isClosed()) {
          throw new IllegalStateException("error.unexpected");
        }

        System.out.println("event id:" + event.getEventId());

        ps = con.prepareStatement(sql);
        ps.setString(1,event.getName());
        ps.setString(2,event.getDescription());
        ps.setDouble(3,event.getTicketPrice());
        ps.setInt(4,event.getEventId());

        if (ps.executeUpdate() != 1) {
          throw new NoSuchEntityException(
```

```
      "error.removed.event");
    }

  } catch (SQLException e) {
    e.printStackTrace();
    throw new RuntimeException("error.unexpected");
  } finally {
    try {
      if (ps != null)
        ps.close();
    } catch (SQLException e) {
      e.printStackTrace();
      throw new RuntimeException("error.unexpected");
    }
  }

}
```

The `remove()` method takes the `eventId` identifying the `event` record to be removed. As usual, an instance of `PreparedStatement` is created that is used for executing the `delete` SQL statement. If the specified record is not found a `NoSuchEntityException` is thrown:

```
public void remove(int eventId) {

  PreparedStatement ps = null;

  String sql = "DELETE FROM event WHERE event_id = ?";

  try {

    if (con.isClosed()) {
      throw new IllegalStateException("error.unexpected");
    }

    ps = con.prepareStatement(sql);
    ps.setInt(1,eventId);

    if (ps.executeUpdate() != 1) {
      throw new NoSuchEntityException("error.removed.event");
    }

  } catch (SQLException e) {
    e.printStackTrace();
    throw new RuntimeException("error.unexpected");
  } finally {
    try {
      if (ps != null)
        ps.close();
    } catch (SQLException e) {
      e.printStackTrace();
      throw new RuntimeException("error.unexpected");
    }
  }

}
```

The `findByPrimaryKey()` method takes the `eventId` for which the `event` record needs to be found. In the normal way, an instance of `PreparedStatement` is created that is used for executing the `select` SQL statement. If the record is not found an `ObjectNotFoundException` is thrown:

```
public Event findByPrimaryKey(int eventId)
  throws FinderException {

  PreparedStatement ps = null;
  ResultSet rs = null;
  Event event = null;

  String sql = "SELECT * from event WHERE event_id = ? ";

  try {

    if (con.isClosed()) {
      throw new IllegalStateException("error.unexpected");
    }

    ps = con.prepareStatement(sql);
    ps.setInt(1,eventId);
    rs = ps.executeQuery();

    if (rs.next()) {

      event = new Event();
      event.setEventId(rs.getInt(1));
      event.setUserId(rs.getString(2));
      event.setName(rs.getString(3));
      event.setDescription(rs.getString(4));
      event.setTicketPrice(rs.getDouble(5));

      return event;

    } else {
      throw new ObjectNotFoundException("error.removed.event");
    }

  } catch (SQLException e) {
    e.printStackTrace();
    throw new RuntimeException("error.unexpected");
  } finally {
    try {
      if (ps != null)
        ps.close();
      if (rs != null)
        rs.close();
    } catch (SQLException e) {
      e.printStackTrace();
      throw new RuntimeException("error.unexpected");
    }
  }

}
```

The findAll() method returns all the records for the specified userId from the event table and returns them as a collection of Event entity instances. An instance of PreparedStatement is created that is used for executing the select SQL statement, and if an unexpected SQLException is thrown, it is caught and rethrown as a RuntimeException:

```
public Collection findAll(String userId) {

    PreparedStatement ps = null;
    ResultSet rs = null;
    ArrayList list = new ArrayList();

    String sql = "SELECT * from event WHERE user_id = ? ";

    try {

        if (con.isClosed()) {
            throw new IllegalStateException("error.unexpected");
        }

        ps = con.prepareStatement(sql);
        ps.setString(1,userId);
        rs = ps.executeQuery();

        while(rs.next()) {

            Event event = new Event();
            event.setEventId(rs.getInt(1));
            event.setUserId(rs.getString(2));
            event.setName(rs.getString(3));
            event.setDescription(rs.getString(4));
            event.setTicketPrice(rs.getDouble(5));

            list.add(event);

        }

        return list;

    } catch (SQLException e) {
        e.printStackTrace();
        throw new RuntimeException("error.unexpected");
    } finally {
        try {
            if (ps != null)
                ps.close();
            if (rs != null)
                rs.close();
        } catch (SQLException e) {
            e.printStackTrace();
            throw new RuntimeException("error.unexpected");
        }
    }

}
```

UserRoleDAO

The UserRoleDAO class encapsulates the data access calls for maintaining the state of the UserRole entities. You'll note that this class doesn't define an update() method, as the application doesn't need to update the records in this table. The methods defined by the UserRoleDAO class are:

- ❑ **create(UserRole userRole)**
  This method creates a record in the user_role table from the attribute values of the UserRole entity it is passed.

- ❑ **remove(String userId, String roleName)**
  This method removes the user_role record with the specified user_id and role_name from the database.

- ❑ **findByPrimaryKey(String userId, String roleName)**
  This method finds the user_role record with the specified user_id and role_name, and returns a UserRole entity instance.

We'll round off our consideration of the data access objects by looking at the code for UserRoleDAO:

```
package com.wrox.tourism.db;

import com.wrox.tourism.entity.UserRole;

import java.sql.Connection;
import java.sql.PreparedStatement;
import java.sql.ResultSet;
import java.sql.SQLException;

public class UserRoleDAO {

  private Connection con;
```

In the constructor, the JDBC connection for sending the SQL statements to the relation datastore is initialized:

```
public UserRoleDAO(Connection con) {
  this.con = con;
}
```

The create() method takes an instance of UserRole class. An instance of PreparedStatement is created that is used for executing the insert SQL statement. If the method fails to create the record, a CreateException is thrown.

```
public void create(UserRole userRole) throws CreateException {

  PreparedStatement ps = null;

  String sql = "INSERT INTO user_role VALUES (?,?)";

  try {

    if (con.isClosed()) {
      throw new IllegalStateException("error.unexpected");
    }

    ps = con.prepareStatement(sql);
    ps.setString(1,userRole.getUserId());
    ps.setString(2,userRole.getRoleName());

    if (ps.executeUpdate() != 1) {
```

```
        throw new CreateException("error.create.userRole");
      }

    } catch (SQLException e) {
      try {
        findByPrimaryKey(
          userRole.getUserId(),
            userRole.getRoleName());
      } catch (FinderException fe) {
        fe.printStackTrace();
        throw new RuntimeException("error.unexpected");
      }
      throw new DuplicateKeyException(
        "error.duplicate.userRole");
    } finally {
      try {
        if (ps != null)
          ps.close();
      } catch (SQLException e) {
        e.printStackTrace();
        throw new RuntimeException("error.unexpected");
      }
    }
  }

}
```

The remove() method takes the userId and roleName identifying the user_role record to be removed. As usual, an instance of PreparedStatement is created that is used for executing the delete SQL statement, and if the specified record is not found a NoSuchEntityException is thrown:

```
public void remove(String userId,String roleName) {

  PreparedStatement ps = null;

  String sql = "DELETE FROM user_role " +
      "WHERE user_id = ? AND role_name = ?";

  try {

    if (con.isClosed()) {
      throw new IllegalStateException("error.unexpected");
    }

    ps = con.prepareStatement(sql);
    ps.setString(1,userId);
    ps.setString(2,roleName);

    if (ps.executeUpdate() < 1) {
      throw new NoSuchEntityException(
        "error.removed.userRole");
    }

  } catch (SQLException e) {
    e.printStackTrace();
    throw new RuntimeException("error.unexpected");
  } finally {
```

```
        try {
          if (ps != null)
            ps.close();
        } catch (SQLException e) {
          e.printStackTrace();
          throw new RuntimeException("error.unexpected");
        }
      }

    }
```

The findByPrimaryKey() method takes the userId and roleName for which the user_role record needs to be found. An instance of PreparedStatement is created that is used for executing the select SQL statement; if the record is not found an ObjectNotFoundException is thrown:

```
public UserRole findByPrimaryKey(String userId, String roleName)
  throws FinderException {

  PreparedStatement ps = null;
  ResultSet rs = null;
  UserRole userRole = null;

  String sql = "SELECT * from user_role " +
      "WHERE user_id = ? AND role_name = ?";

  try {

    if (con.isClosed()) {
      throw new IllegalStateException("error.unexpected");
    }

    ps = con.prepareStatement(sql);
    ps.setString(1,userId);
    ps.setString(2,roleName);
    rs = ps.executeQuery();

    if (rs.next()) {

      userRole = new UserRole();
      userRole.setUserId(rs.getString(1));
      userRole.setRoleName(rs.getString(2));

      return userRole;

    } else {
      throw new ObjectNotFoundException(
        "error.removed.userRole");
    }

  } catch (SQLException e) {
    e.printStackTrace();
    throw new RuntimeException("error.unexpected");
  } finally {
    try {
```

```
        if (ps != null)
          ps.close();
        if (rs != null)
          rs.close();
      } catch (SQLException e) {
        e.printStackTrace();
        throw new RuntimeException("error.unexpected");
      }
    }
  }
}
```

And that's it – we've written all our data access objects, and we can now do all the manipulation of `Attraction`, `Event`, and `UserRole` objects we want without ever having to write another line of SQL code again!

Let's review where we've got to in implementing our application. Refering back to the high-level structure diagram we showed at the beginning of the chapter, you can see that we've sorted the database design, the entity model, and the data access objects; along the way we created a database connection pooling mechanism as well. We still have to write our business objects, action classes, and JSPs:

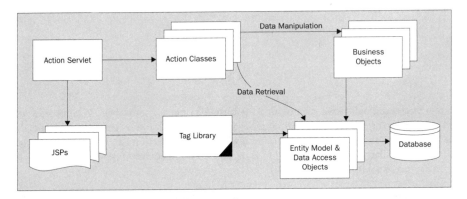

So we've come a long way, but there's still a lot to do. Time to get stuck into writing our business objects.

Business Objects

Business objects encapsulate the business rules associated with maintaining the entities in the system. In our application, we need to have business objects for maintaining `Attraction` and `Event` entities; when the business objects need to do data access, they call the data access objects. However, we don't need a business object for the `UserRole` entity, as instances of this entity are simply created and removed when attractions are registered and deregistered, to enable and disable access to the attractions through the JDBC realm.

Exception Handling

Just like the data access objects, our business objects need specialized exceptions for handling error conditions. There are two such exceptions, one each for attraction maintenance and event maintenance; we'll see these classes used when we come to write the business objects themselves.

AttractionException

This exception is thrown in the methods for maintaining `Attraction` entities:

```
package com.wrox.tourism.business;

public class AttractionException extends Exception {

  public AttractionException(String message) {
    super(message);
  }

}
```

EventException

This exception is thrown in the methods for maintaining `Event` entities:

```
package com.wrox.tourism.business;

public class EventException extends Exception {

  public EventException(String message) {
    super(message);
  }

}
```

Roles

We need one final thing before we start writing the business objects themselves. When a new attraction is registered, we need to create a record in the `user_role` table with the `user_id` as the specified user id and the `role_name` as "attraction", so that the newly created attraction can be successfully authenticated by our JDBC realm. Similarly, when an attraction is deregistered the corresponding record needs to be removed from the `user_role` table.

Rather than using the string "attraction" directly in the business methods, we will define this constant in an interface, so that if we ever need to change it we only need to change it in one place, rather than having to track down and change each place it occurs in our Java code.

```
package com.wrox.tourism.business;

public interface Role {

  public static final String ATTRACTION = "attraction";

}
```

AttractionBO

The `AttractionBO` class encapsulates the business logic for maintaining `Attraction` entities; it exposes three public methods:

❑ **registerAttraction(Attraction attraction)**
Registers a new attraction it is passed.

❑ **deregisterAttraction(String userId)**
Deregisters the attraction with the specified user ID.

❑ **updateAttraction(Attraction attraction)**
Updates the attraction it is passed.

Note that at this level we've moved away from any concerns over database access – our Struts action classes can call `AttractionBO` methods without caring about how the data is stored, and without taking any interest in the `user-role` table at all.

In addition this class defines a private method called from the `register()` and `update()` methods, which validates the `Attraction` entity that is passed:

❑ **validateAttraction(Attraction attraction)**
This method validates the `Attraction` by checking that valid data has been entered for all the attributes.

OK, let's have a look at the source code for the `AttractionBO` class:

```
package com.wrox.tourism.business;

import com.wrox.tourism.entity.Attraction;
import com.wrox.tourism.entity.Event;
import com.wrox.tourism.entity.UserRole;

import com.wrox.tourism.db.EventDAO;
import com.wrox.tourism.db.AttractionDAO;
import com.wrox.tourism.db.UserRoleDAO;
import com.wrox.tourism.db.CreateException;
import com.wrox.tourism.db.FinderException;

import com.wrox.tourism.db.util.ConnectionPool;

import java.sql.SQLException;
import java.sql.Connection;

import java.util.Iterator;

public class AttractionBO {
```

Whilst users of the class don't care about database connections, we will need database connections within the class when we come to use our data access objects. So that we can do that, the `AttractionBO` constructor gets an instance of the connection pool and stores it in an instance variable:

```
private ConnectionPool pool;

  public AttractionBO() {
    pool = ConnectionPool.getInstance();
  }
```

665

The `registerAttraction()` method performs a number of tasks:

1. First, we validate the `Attraction` entity we were passed by calling `validateAttraction()`

2. If the attraction was valid, we proceed to get a connection from the pool

3. Next we create an instance of `AttractionDAO`, passing it the connection we obtained from the pool

4. We then ask the data access object to create the attraction

5. Similarly, we create an instance of `UserRoleDAO`, passing it the connection

6. We then create an instance of the `UserRole` entity

7. Next we set the `userId` of the `UserRole` entity to the `userId` of the `Attraction` entity

8. Similarly, we set the `roleName` of the `UserRole` entity to `Role.ATTRACTION`

9. With that done, we ask the `UserRoleDAO` to create the `UserRole` entity in the database

10. If everything goes through fine, we commit the transaction, otherwise we roll the transaction back and throw an `AttractionException`

11. Finally, we close the connection to return it to the pool

The above steps are further illustrated in the sequence diagram below:

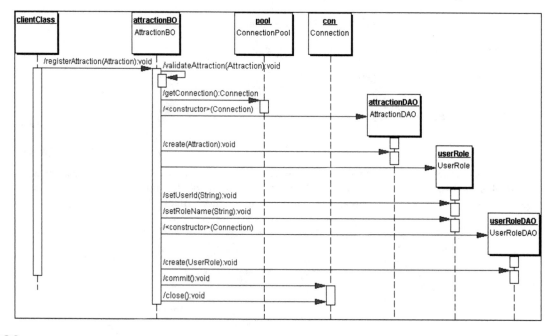

```
public void registerAttraction(Attraction attraction)
  throws AttractionException {

  validateAttraction(attraction);

  Connection con = null;

  try {

    con = pool.getConnection();

    AttractionDAO attractionDAO = new AttractionDAO(con);
    attractionDAO.create(attraction);

    UserRoleDAO userRoleDAO = new UserRoleDAO(con);
    UserRole userRole = new UserRole();
    userRole.setUserId(attraction.getUserId());
    userRole.setRoleName(Role.ATTRACTION);
    userRoleDAO.create(userRole);

    con.commit();

  } catch (Exception e) {
    try {
      if (con != null) {
        con.rollback();
        throw new AttractionException(e.getMessage());
      }
    } catch (SQLException sqle) {
      e.printStackTrace();
      throw new RuntimeException("error.unexpected");
    }
  } finally {
    try {
      if (con != null) {
        con.close();
      }
    } catch (SQLException sqle) {
      sqle.printStackTrace();
      throw new RuntimeException("error.unexpected");
    }
  }

}
```

The updateAttraction() method performs the following tasks:

1. First, it validates the Attraction entity passed in as the argument

2. It then gets a connection from the pool

3. Next, it creates an instance of AttractionDAO, passing it the connection that it just obtained from the pool

4. It then asks the data access object to update the attraction

5. If everything goes through fine it commits the transaction, or otherwise rolls it back and throws an `AttractionException`

6. Finally, it closes the connection

The above steps are further illustrated in the next sequence diagram:

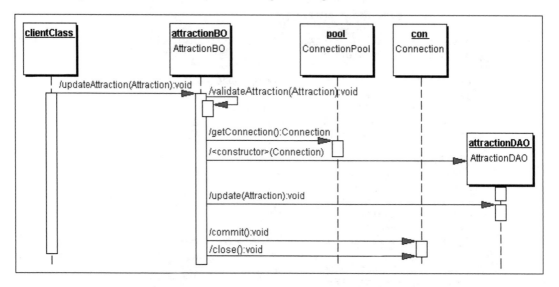

```
public void updateAttraction(Attraction attraction)
  throws AttractionException {

  validateAttraction(attraction);

  Connection con = null;

  try {

    con = pool.getConnection();

    AttractionDAO attractionDAO = new AttractionDAO(con);
    attractionDAO.update(attraction);

    con.commit();

  } catch (Exception e) {
    try {
      if (con != null) {
        con.rollback();
        throw new AttractionException(e.getMessage());
      }
    } catch (SQLException sqle) {
```

```
          e.printStackTrace();
          throw new RuntimeException("error.unexpected");
       }
    } finally {
       try {
          if (con != null) {
            con.close();
          }
       } catch (SQLException sqle) {
          sqle.printStackTrace();
          throw new RuntimeException("error.unexpected");
       }
    }
  }
}
```

The deregisterAttraction() method performs these tasks:

1. First, it again gets a connection from the pool

2. Then it creates an instance of AttractionDAO, passing it the database connection

3. Next, it asks the AttractionDAO object to remove the attraction

4. We also have to remove the user-role table entry, so it creates an instance of UserRoleDAO, again passing it the connection

5. The UserRoleDAO object is asked to remove from the database the UserRole entity corresponding to the attraction being removed

6. We still need to remove the attraction's events, so an instance of EventDAO is created, passing it the connection

7. The EventDAO object is asked to remove the Event entities associated with the attraction that is being removed

8. If everything goes through fine we commit the transaction, or else rollback the transaction and throw an AttractionException

9. Finally, we close the connection

The above steps are further illustrated in this sequence diagram:

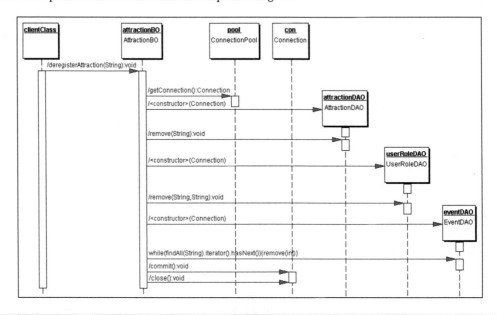

```
public void deregisterAttraction(String userId)
  throws AttractionException {

  Connection con = null;

  try {

    con = pool.getConnection();

    AttractionDAO attractionDAO = new AttractionDAO(con);
    attractionDAO.remove(userId);

    UserRoleDAO userRoleDAO = new UserRoleDAO(con);
    userRoleDAO.remove(userId,Role.ATTRACTION);

    EventDAO eventDAO = new EventDAO(con);
    Iterator it = eventDAO.findAll(userId).iterator();
    while(it.hasNext()) {
      Event event = (Event)it.next();
      eventDAO.remove(event.getEventId());
    }
    con.commit();

  } catch (Exception e) {
    try {
      if (con != null) {
        con.rollback();
        throw new AttractionException(e.getMessage());
      }
    } catch (SQLException sqle) {
      e.printStackTrace();
      throw new RuntimeException("error.unexpected");
```

```
      }
    } finally {
      try {
        if (con != null) {
          con.close();
        }
      } catch (SQLException sqle) {
        sqle.printStackTrace();
        throw new RuntimeException("error.unexpected");
      }
    }
  }
```

The last method is `validateAttraction()`, which ensures that the attributes of the `Attraction` entity are non-empty `String`s. We could of course enhance `validateAttraction()` to perform more complex validations, for example by checking that the `webSite` property is a valid URL:

```
  private void validateAttraction(Attraction attraction)
    throws AttractionException {

    if (attraction.getUserId().trim().equals("")) {
      throw new AttractionException("error.missing.userId");
    }

    if (attraction.getPassword().trim().equals("")) {
      throw new AttractionException("error.missing.password");
    }

    if (attraction.getName().trim().equals("")) {
      throw new AttractionException("error.missing.name");
    }

    if (attraction.getDescription().trim().equals("")) {
      throw new AttractionException("error.missing.description");
    }

    if (attraction.getWebSite().trim().equals("")) {
      throw new AttractionException("error.missing.webSite");
    }

    if (attraction.getAddress().trim().equals("")) {
      throw new AttractionException("error.missing.address");
    }

  }

}
```

EventBO

The `EventBO` class encapsulates the business logic for maintaining the `Event` entities, and exposes three public methods for maintaining `Event` entities:

❑ **`createEvent(Event event)`**
Creates a new event.

❑ **`updateEvent(Event event)`**
Updates the event.

❑ **`removeEvent(int eventId)`**
Removes the event with the specified ID.

In addition, like `AttractionBO`, this class defines a private method called from the register and update methods to validate the `Event` entity that is passed:

❑ **`validateEvent(Event event)`**
This method validates the `Event` by checking that valid data has been entered for all the attributes.

Let's have a look at the source code for the `EventBO` class:

```
package com.wrox.tourism.business;

import com.wrox.tourism.entity.Event;

import com.wrox.tourism.db.EventDAO;
import com.wrox.tourism.db.AttractionDAO;
import com.wrox.tourism.db.CreateException;
import com.wrox.tourism.db.FinderException;

import com.wrox.tourism.db.util.ConnectionPool;

import java.sql.SQLException;
import java.sql.Connection;

public class EventBO {
```

Just like `AttractionBO`, we store use the constructor to store an instance of the connection pool as an instance variable:

```
    private ConnectionPool pool;

    public EventBO() {
      pool = ConnectionPool.getInstance();
    }
```

The `createEvent()` method performs the following tasks:

1. First, it validates the `Event` entity that it was given

2. Gets a connection from the pool

3. Creates an instance of `AttractionDAO`, passing it the database connection

4. Checks whether the attraction user id specified in the `Event` is valid

5. Creates an instance of `EventDAO`, passing it the database connection

6. Creates the `Event` entity in the database

7. If everything goes through fine, commits the transaction, or else rolls it back and throws an `EventException`

8. Finally, closes the connection

The above steps are further illustrated in the sequence diagram below:

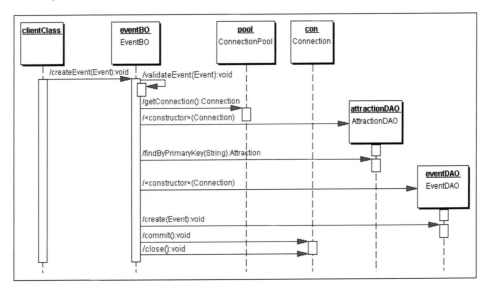

```
    public void createEvent(Event event) throws EventException {

      validateEvent(event);

      Connection con = null;

      try {

        con = pool.getConnection();
```

```
            AttractionDAO attractionDAO = new AttractionDAO(con);
            attractionDAO.findByPrimaryKey(event.getUserId());

            EventDAO eventDAO = new EventDAO(con);
            eventDAO.create(event);
    con.commit();
    } catch (Exception e) {
            try {
              if (con != null) {
                con.rollback();
                throw new EventException(e.getMessage());
              }
            } catch (SQLException sqle) {
              e.printStackTrace();
              throw new RuntimeException("error.unexpected");
            }
        } finally {
            try {
              if (con != null) {
                con.close();
              }
            } catch (SQLException sqle) {
              sqle.printStackTrace();
              throw new RuntimeException("error.unexpected");
            }
        }
    }

    }
```

The updateEvent() method performs these tasks:

1. Validates the Event entity

2. Gets a connection from the pool

3. Creates an instance of EventDAO, passing it the connection

4. Updates the Event entity in the database

5. If everything goes through fine, commits the transaction, or else rolls it back and throws an EventException

6. Finally, closes the connection

Again, the sequence diagram below illustrates these steps:

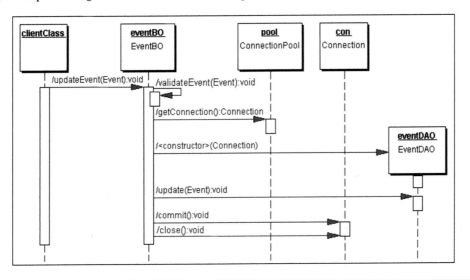

```
public void updateEvent(Event event) throws EventException {

  validateEvent(event);

  Connection con = null;

  try {

    con = pool.getConnection();

    EventDAO eventDAO = new EventDAO(con);
    eventDAO.update(event);

    con.commit();

  } catch (Exception e) {
    try {
      if (con != null) {
        con.rollback();
        throw new EventException(e.getMessage());
      }
    } catch (SQLException sqle) {
      e.printStackTrace();
      throw new RuntimeException("error.unexpected");
    }
  } finally {
    try {
      if (con != null) {
        con.close();
      }
    } catch (SQLException sqle) {
      sqle.printStackTrace();
      throw new RuntimeException("error.unexpected");
    }
  }

}
```

The removeEvent() method performs these tasks:

❑ Gets a connection from the pool

❑ Creates an instance of EventDAO, passing it the connection

❑ Removes the Event entity from the database

❑ If everything goes through fine, commits the transaction, or else rolls it back and throws an EventException

❑ Finally, closes the connection

The sequence diagram for this is as follows:

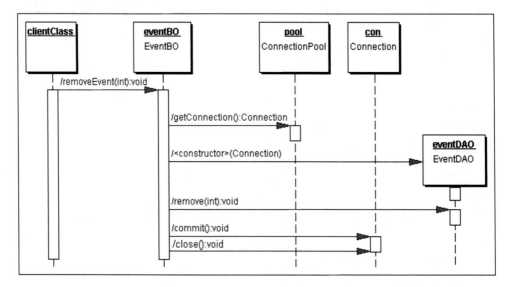

```
public void removeEvent(int eventId)
  throws EventException {

  Connection con = null;

  try {

    con = pool.getConnection();

    EventDAO eventDAO = new EventDAO(con);
    eventDAO.remove(eventId);

    con.commit();

  } catch (Exception e) {
    try {
      if (con != null) {
        con.rollback();
        throw new EventException(e.getMessage());
      }
```

```
      } catch (SQLException sqle) {
        e.printStackTrace();
throw new RuntimeException("error.unexpected");
      }
    } finally {
      try {
        if (con != null) {
          con.close();
        }
      } catch (SQLException sqle) {
        sqle.printStackTrace();
        throw new RuntimeException("error.unexpected");
      }
    }

  }
```

The `validateEvent()` method simply ensures that the attributes of the `Event` entity are populated:

```
private void validateEvent(Event event) throws EventException {

  if (event.getName().trim().equals("")) {
    throw new EventException("error.missing.name");
  }

  if (event.getDescription().trim().equals("")) {
    throw new EventException("error.missing.description");
  }

  if (event.getTicketPrice() < 0) {
    throw new EventException("error.missing.ticketPrice");
  }

}
```

Summary

And that's our business objects completed! We've come a long way since the start of the case study; let's have another look at that diagram of the system architecture and see what we've acomplished so far:

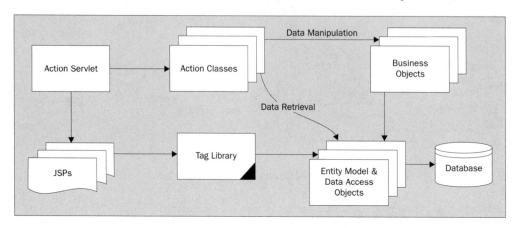

As you can see, we've now finished the right-hand part of this diagram: in the course of this chapter, we have:

❑ Examined the requirements for the application and identified the **use cases** that describe the ways users interact with it.

❑ Designed the overall **system architecture**, shown in the diagram above.

❑ Thought about **security** and how we prevent public users from doing things that only the managers of our registered tourist attractions should be able to do.

❑ Identified the **entities** that represent the data our application needs to store, created **database tables** to store the data in the long term, and written **entity classes** that represent the entities in our Java code.

❑ Created **data access objects** that allow the rest of the application to store, retrieve, update, and delete entities from the database without having to worry about JDBC or SQL code.

❑ Created **business objects** that contain certain rules about the entities and hide some of the complex interactions with the data access objects.

We still need to create the web tier: the action classes that respond to requests from users, and the JSPs that display the results of those actions. We'll cover these in the next chapter; with the great foundations we've laid already, it'll be easy!

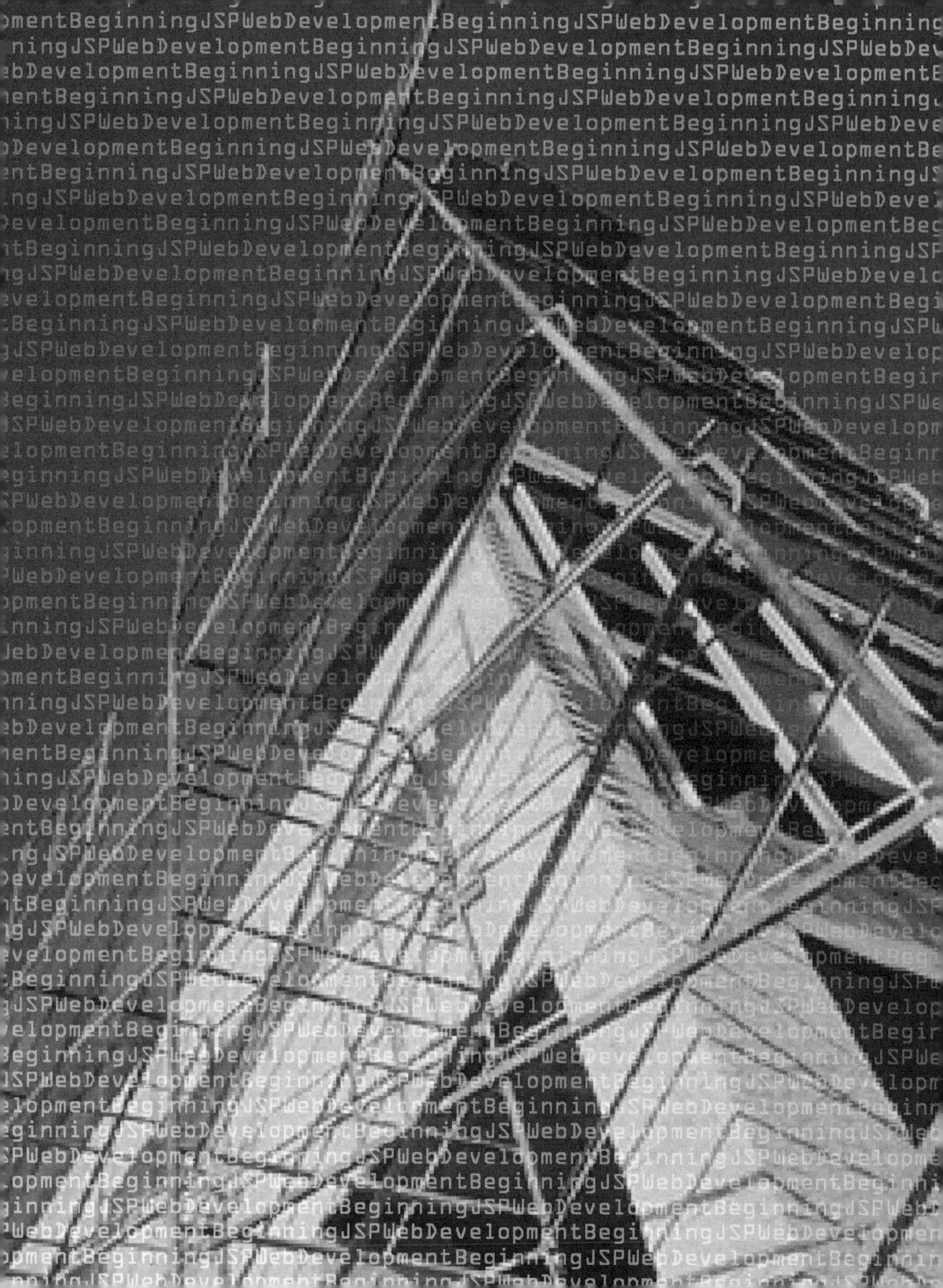
BeginningJSPWebDevelopment

Case Study:
The Web Interface

In the last chapter covered the design and development of the components for the application tier of our tourism database application; now we need to finish it off by creating the web "tier", the part of the application that actually interacts with the users by way of a dynamic web interface. Once that's done we'll tidy up all the loose ends and see how to deploy the application to get it up and running.

Implementing the Web Tier

So, without further ado, let's get stuck into implementing the web tier. There are quite a lot of things we need to do:

❑   Identify our Struts action forms

❑   Deal with error messages and internationalization

❑   Look at how we can use dynamic web page templates to make the page design easier

❑   Implement the role based menu

❑   Then, for each use case, we'll need to write the Struts action class and the JSPs that implement the view

Struts Action Forms

In the last chapter, when we created the entity objects, we mentioned that we would be reusing our entity objects as the Struts action forms as well, and identified `Attraction` and `Event` classes as the action form bean types associated with the forms for creating and editing attractions and events respectively. Accordingly, these classes both extend `org.apache.struts.action.ActionForm`. You won't always want to do this – it's not often true that the forms in your web page correspond exactly to the entities that you want to store in the database – but in this case we can take this short cut.

The excerpt shown below from the Struts configuration file illustrates how the action form beans are declared:

```
...
<form-beans>
  <form-bean name="attractionForm"
    type="com.wrox.tourism.entity.Attraction"/>
  <form-bean name="eventForm" type="com.wrox.tourism.entity.Event"/>
</form-beans>

...
```

This defines two action form beans, with the names `attractionForm` and `eventForm`, corresponding to our `Attraction` and `Entity` classes respectively. These names will be used later in the action mapping elements for associating the beans with action classes.

Error Handling and Internationalization

Proper handling of exceptions and informing the users about both expected and unexpected error conditions is a vital element of enterprise application development. In this section, we will have a look at how we can implement an efficient error handling mechanism for our application. One important aspect of sending error messages to the end users is that the messages should be sent to the users in their preferred language. Hence, error handling and internationalization are inter related.

As we saw near the start of Chapter 18, when we were considering application architecture, the HTTP requests coming in from the browser are routed to appropriate action classes. Depending on the type of request the action classes may use business objects and data access objects to fulfill the request, and the method calls on these objects may throw both expected and unexpected exceptions.

Method calls on instances of `AttractionBO` and `EventBO` may throw instances of `AttractionException` and `EventException` respectively. Similarly, method calls on data object instances may throw instances of `CreateException`, `RemoveException` or `FinderException` for expected error conditions and instances of subclasses of `RuntimeException` for unexpected error conditions.

If we start hard-coding the error messages in the exception constructors, when the exceptions are created, it will be difficult to internationalize the application. Therefore, as we saw Chapter 18, we instead specified a message *key* instead of a descriptive error message. When an exception is thrown in a business object or a data access object, the process is as follows:

❑ The business or data access object throws an exception

❑ The exception bubbles up to the action class

❑ The action class catches the exception and creates a Struts `ActionError` object, passing the exception message to its constructor

❑ This `ActionError` object is then added to a Struts `ActionErrors` object, and stored in request scope; this is done by the `saveErrors()` method defined in the `org.apache.struts.action.Action` class. The key used to store it in request scope is a default one provided by Struts.

❑ The response is then redirected back to the input page that caused the current action, which may use the Struts <html:errors> tag to display the error message

❑ The <html:errrors> tag queries a resources file specific to the end user's preferred language settings to produce an error message in the correct language

For more details on defining locale specific resources file and the use of Struts action error objects, refer back to Chapter 18.

The table below shows the message keys used for the data access exceptions:

Exception type	Thrown by	Message key used
CreateException	AttractionDAO	error.create.attraction
	EventDAO	error.create.event
	UserRoleDAO	error.create.userRole
DuplicateKeyException	AttractionDAO	error.duplicate.attraction
	UserRoleDAO	error.duplicate.userRole
ObjectNotFoundException	AttractionDAO	error.removed.attraction
	EventDAO	error.removed.event
	UserRoleDAO	error.removed.userRole
NoSuchEntityException	AttractionDAO	error.removed.attraction
	EventDAO	error.removed.event
	UserRoleDAO	error.removed.userRole
RuntimeException	AttractionDAO	error.unexpected
	EventDAO	error.unexpected
	UserRoleDAO	error.unexpected

The second table shows the message keys used for the business exceptions:

Exception type	Thrown by	Message key used
AttractionException	AttractionBO	error.missing.userId
		error.missing.password
		error.missing.name
		error.missing.description
		error.missing.address
		error.missing.webSite
EventException	EventBO	error.missing.name
		error.missing.description
		error.missing.ticketPrice

You should note that, if a business exception is caused by an exception thrown from a data access object call, the message key for the business exception will be the same as that defined for the data access exception. However, if the business exception is thrown by the validation methods defined in the business object, the message key will be one of the keys defined in the table on the previous page.

The message resources file for the default locale (which in this case is taken to be English) is called `TourismResources.properties`, and should be saved in the application's `WEB-INF/classes` directory. Its contents are as follows:

```
error.removed.attraction=
  <font color="red">Selected attraction has been removed</font>
error.create.attraction=
  <font color="red">Unable to create the attraction</font>
error.duplicate.attraction=
  <font color="red">Specified attraction already exists</font>

error.removed.event=
  <font color="red">Selected event has been removed</font>
error.create.event=
  <font color="red">Unable to create the event</font>
error.duplicate.event=
  <font color="red">Specified event already exists</font>

error.removed.userRole=
  <font color="red">Selected user role has been removed</font>
error.create.userRole=
  <font color="red">Unable to create the user role</font>
error.duplicate.userRole=
  <font color="red">Specified user role already exists</font>

error.missing.userId=
  <font color="red">Please enter the user id</font>
error.missing.password=
  <font color="red">Please enter the password</font>
error.missing.name=
  <font color="red">Please enter the name</font>
error.missing.description=
  <font color="red">Please enter the description</font>
error.missing.webSite=
  <font color="red">Please enter the web site</font>
error.missing.address=
  <font color="red">Please enter the address</font>
error.missing.ticketPrice=
  <font color="red">Please enter the ticket price</font>

error.unexpected=
  <font color="red">Unxpected error, Please contact webmaster</font>
```

If we wanted to add a French translation, we would name the file `TourismResources_fr.properties`; the German translations would be in `TourismResources_de.properties`, and so on. The name of the resources file (without the extension, in other words `"TourismResources"`) needs to be passed to the action servlet as an initialization parameter with the name `application`, as seen in this excerpt from the `web.xml` file:

```
...

<servlet>
  <servlet-name>action</servlet-name>
  <servlet-class>org.apache.struts.action.ActionServlet</servlet-class>
  <init-param>
    <param-name>application</param-name>
    <param-value>TourismResources</param-value>
  </init-param>
  <load-on-startup>2</load-on-startup>
</servlet>

...
```

Role Based Menu

All of the pages in the application include a menu, but the links we need to include vary depending on whether the current user is a member of the public or an authenticated attraction manager. In this section, we will have a look at how we can implement a generic menu JSP that can be included in all our web pages. The links we need to display on the menu can be categorized as:

❑   Links that need to be displayed for all users.

❑   Links that need to be displayed only for public users.

❑   Links that need to be displayed only for authenticated users.

For all users, we need to display:

❑   **Home**: This link points to the first page that is displayed when the web site is accessed: the page displaying a list of registered attractions with facilities for drilling down to view attraction details and associated events.

❑   **Register**: This link presents the users with the form for registering an attraction.

The one link that needs to be displayed only for public users is:

❑   **Logon**: This link can be used by registered attractions for logging on to the system. When users click on this link, the system presents a logon form and on successful authentication, the system presents a form populated with the details for the attraction associated with the logged-on user.

The links that need to be displayed only for authenticated users are:

❑   **Attraction Details**: This link displays the form for updating the attraction details for the logged-on user.

❑   **List Events**: Lists the events associated with the attraction.

❑   **Add Event**: This link presents the user with the form for adding a new event.

❑   **Deregister**: This link lets the user deregister the attraction.

❑   **Logoff**: This link logs off the currently logged-on user and presents the home page.

685

Putting all these together, we can see the two versions of the menu; on the left is the version shown to public users, and on the right is the version that authenticated attraction managers see:

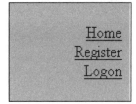

We will use the Struts logic tags `<logic:present>` and `<logic:notPresent>`, with the `role` attribute, for rendering the menu, to select which links to show by checking whether or not the `"attraction"` role is present. The links that need to be displayed only for public users are contained within the `notPresent` tag, and the links that need to be displayed only for authenticated users are inserted within the `present` tag, in each case with the value for role attribute as `"attraction"`. For more information on the Struts logic tags, refer back to Chapter 18.

The menu.jsp Page

Let's move on to look at the source code for the menu JSP, which we call `menu.jsp`. We start by importing the Struts HTML and logic tag libraries:

```
<%@ taglib uri="/html" prefix="html" %>
<%@ taglib uri="/logic" prefix="logic" %>

<br/>
<br/>
```

In all cases, we render the link for displaying the home page. `home.do` will be the Struts action corresponding to the application's home page:

```
<html:link href="home.do">Home</html:link>
 
<br/>
```

The second link displays the form for registering a new attraction; it points to `register.jsp`:

```
<html:link href="registerAttraction.jsp">Register</html:link>
 
<br/>
```

We use the Struts logic tag `<logic:notPresent>` to render the link for logging on only if the current user *isn't* logged in:

```
<logic:notPresent role="attraction">
  <html:link href="editAttraction.do">Logon</html:link>
   
  <br/>
</logic:notPresent>
```

Finally, we use the Struts `<logic:present>` tag to display the links specific to the authenticated users having the role `attraction`:

```
<logic:present role="attraction">
```

The first of these links displays the form for modifying attraction details:

```
<html:link href="editAttraction.do">Attraction Details</html:link>
 
<br/>
```

This link displays the list of events associated with the attraction:

```
<html:link href="listEvents.do">List Events</html:link>
 
<br/>
```

This link presents the users with a form for adding a new event:

```
<html:link href="editEvent.jsp">Add Event</html:link>
 
<br/>
```

This link deregisters the currently logged-on attraction:

```
<html:link href="deregisterAttraction.do">Deregister</html:link>
 
<br/>
```

And the final link logs off the currently logged-on attraction.

```
<html:link href="logoff.do">Logoff</html:link>
 
<br/>
</logic:present>
```

These links point to a variety of JSP pages and Struts actions; we'll look a little later at what these actually do in practice.

Web Page Dynamic Template

In Chapter 18 we saw how using dynamic templates can help us to modularize web page layouts, and in this section we'll come up with a template for our application's web pages. All of the pages will have:

❑ A header section for displaying a banner message

❑ A menu section on the left

❑ A main section on the right, for displaying the actual page content

❑ A footer section for displaying the user's logon status

To implement this using the Struts template tags we need to create a template JSP, and include this template JSP in all the other main JSPs. Our template will use an HTML table with the following layout:

❑ The first row contains a single cell for displaying the banner. Since the banner is going to be the same for all the JSPs we can hard-code the banner in the template JSP.

❑ The second row contains two cells. The first cell will contain the menu; since the logic for populating the menu is done using the Struts logic tags and the JSP file for the menu is always the same, we can include the menu.jsp file using the <jsp:include> action. The second cell will contain the main content, which is pushed in by the JSPs using the template. Hence, in this cell we can use the Struts <template:get> tag to get the content pushed in by the JSPs using the Struts template tag put.

❑ The third row will contain a single cell for displaying whether the user is currently logged on.

The template.jsp Page

So let's look at template.jsp, the page implementing our template. We start by importing the Struts template and logic tags:

```
<%@ taglib uri="/template" prefix="template" %>
<%@ taglib uri="/logic" prefix="logic" %>

<html>

 <head>
  <title>
   Welcome to Wroxton-on-Sea Tourism Authority
  </title>
 </head>

 <body>
  <center>
   <table height="100%" width="100%" cellpadding="0" cellspacing="0">
    <tr height="50" bgcolor="#CCCCCC">
```

In the first row of the table, we include the banner message:

```
    <td valign="center" align="center" colspan="3">
     <h1><i>Wroxton-on-Sea Tourism Authority</i></h1>
    </td>
   </tr>
   <tr>
```

In the second table row, the first cell simply includes the menu using the <jsp:include> action:

```
    <td width="15%" bgcolor="#CCCCCC" align="right" valign="top">
     <jsp:include page="menu.jsp"/>
    </td>
```

In the right-hand cell we include the main content using the Struts `<template:get>` tag:

```
        <td valign="top" align="center">
         <template:get name="content"/>
        </td>
        <td width="10%" bgcolor="#CCCCCC">
        </td>
       </tr>
       <tr height="10%" bgcolor="#CCCCCC">
```

Finally, in the bottom row of the table we use the Struts `<logic:present>` tag to display the currently logged-on user; we do this only if the currently logged-on user has the `attraction` role:

```
        <td valign="center" align="center" colspan="3">
         <logic:present role="attraction">
          You are currently logged on as
          <%= request.getRemoteUser() %>
         </logic:present>
        </td>
       </tr>
      </table>
     </center>
    </body>

   </html>
```

System Interactions

So what actually happens within the system for each of the use cases? In this section, we will be covering the sequence of events triggered by the application users' actions on the web pages. In most cases, we will map the request URL for these user actions to the Struts action servlet, and hence to the relevant action classes, depending on the action mappings defined in the Struts configuration file. The process is then as follows:

1. If the request involves data modification, the action classes delegate the data modification task to the appropriate business object.

2. The action classes use appropriate data access objects for retrieving the data required for the next view, and store the data as request scope beans.

3. The response is then forwarded to the relevant JSP defined in one of the local forwards for the action mapping that triggered the current action.

4. The JSP will use the relevant Struts custom tags to render the data stored as request scope beans.

Requests that don't involve either data modification or data retrieval will be mapped directly to JSP files, rather than going through Struts action classes, since there is nothing but presentation to be done.

To map the requests that need to be handled by Struts, we will declare the Struts action servlet in the web application deployment descriptor and add a servlet mapping element to map the request URL pattern `*.do` to the action servlet. As we saw earlier, the servlet requries an initialization parameter that defines the name of the resource file name:

```
  . . .

<servlet>
  <servlet-name>action</servlet-name>
  <servlet-class>org.apache.struts.action.ActionServlet</servlet-class>
  <init-param>
    <param-name>application</param-name>
    <param-value>TourismResources</param-value>
  </init-param>
  <load-on-startup>2</load-on-startup>
</servlet>

  . . .

<servlet-mapping>
  <servlet-name>action</servlet-name>
  <url-pattern>*.do</url-pattern>
</servlet-mapping>

  . . .
```

Welcome Page

OK, let's write some pages! The obvious place to start is with the initial page displayed when the users first access the web site; this displays a list of registered attractions and the menu, with the following links:

❑ A link for registering new attractions

❑ A link for logging on as registered attractions

❑ A link for coming back to the initial page from other pages

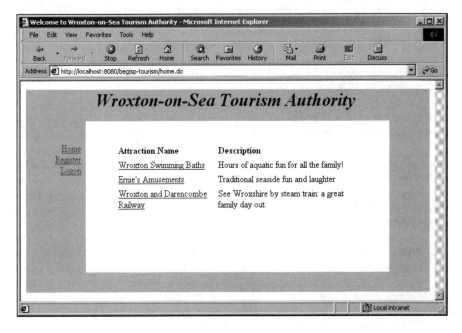

So, what are the internal system interactions associated with displaying this page? The sequence of events when users access the site is:

1. The request is first sent to `index.jsp`.

2. `index.jsp` redirects the user to the `home.do`.

3. Since all the requests ending with `*.do` are mapped to the Struts action servlet, the servlet forwards the request to the appropriate action class based on the action mapping specified in the configuration file.

4. In this case, the name of the action class is `com.wrox.tourism.action.HomeAction`.

5. The action class uses `AttractionDAO` to get a list of all registered attractions and stores the list as a request scope bean named `"attractionList"`. All the bean names are contained in the interface `com.wrox.tourism.action.BeanNames`.

6. The action class then finds a local action forward with the logical name `"success"` and forwards the response to that action forward.

7. This action forward maps to a physical resource called `home.jsp`.

8. This JSP uses the Struts template tags to insert into `home.jsp` the main content called `homeContent.jsp`.

9. `homeContent.jsp` uses the Struts bean and logic tags to render the attraction data that was stored as a request scope bean by the action class.

This is further illustrated in the sequence diagram below:

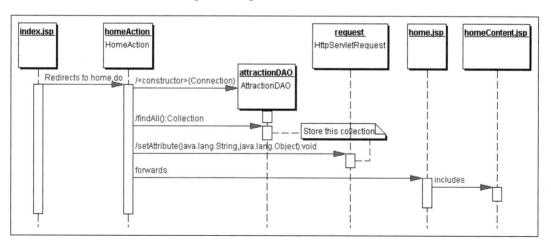

The index.jsp Page

Now we'll have a look at the code for `index.jsp`. The only thing this page does is that it redirects the browser to `home.do`, using the Struts `<logic:redirect>` tag:

```
<%@ taglib uri="/logic" prefix="logic" %>

<logic:redirect href="home.do"/>
```

The /home.do Action Mapping

The request URL /home.do is mapped to the corresponding action class in the Struts configuration file using the <action> element:

```
...
<action-mappings>
  ...
  <action path="/home"
    type="com.wrox.tourism.actions.HomeAction"
    unknown="true">
    <forward name="success" path="/home.jsp"/>
  </action>
  ...
</action-mappings>
...
```

The action class used is com.wrox.tourism.actions.HomeAction, and the action is defined as the default action for the application using the unknown attribute. It also defines a local forward named "success", mapping to the resource /home.jsp.

> **Note that when we talk of the URL /home.do this is relative to our particular web application. If, as we will show later, we set the server up so that the application is rooted at http://localhost:8080/begjsp-tourism/, then when we use the address /home.do within our Java code it actually refers to http://localhost:8080/begjsp-tourism/home.do.**

HomeAction

Now let's cover the implementation details for the action class HomeAction. The source code for this class is shown below:

```
package com.wrox.tourism.actions;

import org.apache.struts.action.ActionForm;
import org.apache.struts.action.ActionForward;
import org.apache.struts.action.Action;
import org.apache.struts.action.ActionMapping;
import org.apache.struts.action.ActionErrors;
import org.apache.struts.action.ActionError;
import org.apache.struts.action.ActionServlet;

import javax.servlet.http.HttpServletRequest;
import javax.servlet.http.HttpServletResponse;
import javax.servlet.ServletException;
```

```
import java.io.IOException;

import java.sql.Connection;
import java.sql.SQLException;

import java.util.Collection;

import com.wrox.tourism.db.util.ConnectionPool;
import com.wrox.tourism.db.AttractionDAO;

public class HomeAction extends Action {

  private ConnectionPool pool;
```

In the constructor we get the database connection pool instance and store it in a private instance variable:

```
public HomeAction() {
  pool = ConnectionPool.getInstance();
}
```

The `perform()` method is where the work gets done:

```
public ActionForward perform(ActionMapping mapping,ActionForm form,
  HttpServletRequest request,HttpServletResponse response)
    throws IOException,ServletException {

  Connection con = null;

  try {
```

First we get a connection from the pool:

```
con = pool.getConnection();
```

Then, with that connection, we create an instance of `AttractionDAO` and find a list of all registered attractions:

```
AttractionDAO attractionDAO = new AttractionDAO(con);
Collection col = attractionDAO.findAll();
```

We store the list as a request scope bean. All the bean names are enumerated in the interface called `BeanNames`, explained in the next section:

```
request.setAttribute(BeanNames.ATTRACTION_LIST,col);
```

The last step is to forward the request to `home.jsp`, which we configured as a local forward with the name "success":

```
return mapping.findForward("success");
```

Finally, if anything went wrong we perform some appropriate tidying up:

```
    } catch (SQLException e) {
      e.printStackTrace();
      throw new RuntimeException("Unable to get connection.");
    } finally {
      try {
        if (con != null)
          con.close();
      } catch (SQLException e) {
        throw new RuntimeException(e.getMessage());
      }
    }

  }

}
```

BeanNames

This interface simply contains constant `String` values that list the bean names we will be using in the application for storing request scope beans:

```
package com.wrox.tourism.actions;

public interface BeanNames {

  public static final String ATTRACTION_LIST = "attractionList";
  public static final String ATTRACTION_FORM = "attractionForm";
  public static final String EVENT_LIST = "eventList";
  public static final String EVENT_FORM = "eventForm";

}
```

The home.jsp Page

home.jsp is surprisingly short, since we're using the Struts templating mechanism. All it does to use the `<template:insert>` tag to insert the file `template.jsp`, and push the contents of `homeContent.jsp` into the template using the `<template:put>` tag:

```
<%@ taglib uri="/template" prefix="template" %>

<template:insert template="template.jsp">
  <template:put name="content" content="homeContent.jsp"/>
</template:insert>
```

The homeContent.jsp Page

And finally we reach `homeContent.jsp`. This file contains the main content that is displayed in the welcome page, and uses the `<logic:iterate>` tag to loop through the list of attractions; as you'll recall, the action class stored these as a request scope bean.

We use the `<bean:write>` tag to display the various attributes of each individual attraction entity. The attraction names are rendered as hyperlinks so that the users can drill down to view the attraction details and associated events.

So, first we import the Struts tag libraries:

```
<%@ taglib uri="/bean" prefix="bean" %>
<%@ taglib uri="/html" prefix="html" %>
<%@ taglib uri="/logic" prefix="logic" %>
<%@ taglib uri="/template" prefix="template" %>

<br/>
<br/>
```

Next up, the `<html:errors>` tag is used to render any error messages, if indeed any are present:

```
<html:errors/>

<table cellpadding="2" width="80%">
 <tr>
  <td>
   <b>Attraction Name</b>
  </td>
  <td>
   <b>Description</b>
  </td>
 </tr>
```

The `<logic:iterate>` tag loops through the list of attraction entities, which were stored under the name "attractionList". The current attraction is exposed as a bean named "attraction", and the type of the bean is defined as `com.wrox.tourism.entity.Attraction`:

```
<logic:iterate name="attractionList"
   id="attraction"
   scope="request"
   type="com.wrox.tourism.entity.Attraction">

 <tr>
  <td>
```

Within the loop, we use the `<bean:write>` tag to produce a hyperlink pointing to the resource `viewAttraction.do`, and passing the user id for the current attraction in the list as a request parameter. The text for the hyperlink is the name of the current attraction in the list:

```
   <a href="viewAttraction.do?userId=<bean:write name="attraction"
     property="userId"/>">
    <bean:write name="attraction" property="name"/>
   </a>
  </td>
```

You might find it a little hard to decipher what is going on here! An example should help: if an attraction had the userId `"pool"` and the name `"Wroxton-on-Sea Swimming Baths"`, the block of code above would produce the following HTML:

```
    <a href="viewAttraction.do?userId=pool">
    Wroxton-on-Sea Swimming Baths
    </a>
  </td>
```

Finally, we use `<bean:write>` once again to display the current attraction's description:

```
    <td>
     <bean:write name="attraction" property="description"/>
    </td>
   </tr>

  </logic:iterate>
 </table>
```

And that's it, our home page is finished! Time to make some coffee and congratulate ourselves, before moving on to the next screen.

View Attraction Details

This page displays a drilled-down view of an individual attraction and its associated events; it can be accessed from the welcome page by clicking on one of the attraction name links displayed in the list of attractions:

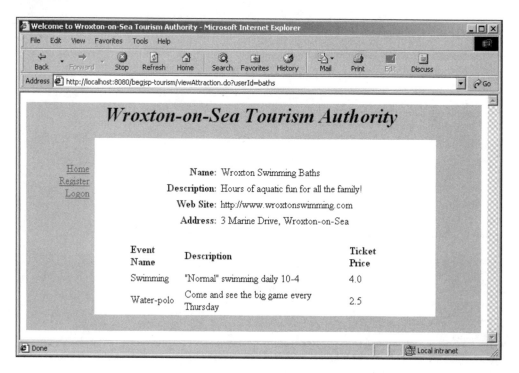

When the users click on an attraction name link the following sequence of events occurs:

1. The request is sent to the URL `viewAttraction.do`, which is mapped to the action class `com.wrox.tourism.actions.ViewAttractionAction`.

2. The action class gathers the user id for the selected attraction from the request parameter list.

3. It then creates an instance of `AttractionDAO` and finds the attraction entity object for the specified user id. This attraction entity object is then stored as a request scope bean.

4. Then the action class creates an instance of `EventDAO` and finds the list of events associated with the selected attraction by passing the user id. This list is also stored as a request scope bean.

5. The response is then forwarded to `viewAttraction.jsp`, which includes the JSP `viewAttractionContent.jsp` using the Struts template tags.

6. The file `viewAttractionContent.jsp` uses the appropriate Struts tags for rendering the attraction and event details.

7. If an exception occurs during the data access calls, action error objects are created by passing the exception's message, and the response is sent back to the input resource that is defined for the `/viewAttraction.do` action in the action mapping. In this case, the input resource is defined as `/home.do`, and so the JSP associated with `/home.do` will display the stored action errors using the `<html:errors>` tag.

Let's have a look at the sequence diagram that illustrates these events:

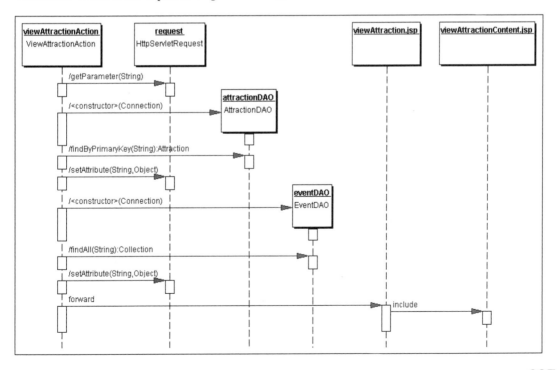

The /viewAttraction.do Action Mapping

The request URL /viewAttraction.do is mapped to corresponding action class by using the
<action> element in the Struts configuration file:

```
...
  <action path="/viewAttraction"
    type="com.wrox.tourism.actions.ViewAttractionAction"
    input="/home.do">
    <forward name="success" path="/viewAttraction.jsp"/>
  </action>
...
```

The action class used is com.wrox.tourism.actions.ViewAttractionAction. It also defines a
local forward named "success", mapping to the resource viewAttraction.jsp. The input
resource, to which the response has to be sent if an error occurs, is defined as home.do.

ViewAttractionAction

Onwards to the action implementation class, ViewAttractionAction. The source code for the
action class is shown below:

```
package com.wrox.tourism.actions;

import org.apache.struts.action.ActionForm;
import org.apache.struts.action.ActionForward;
import org.apache.struts.action.Action;
import org.apache.struts.action.ActionMapping;
import org.apache.struts.action.ActionErrors;
import org.apache.struts.action.ActionError;
import org.apache.struts.action.ActionServlet;

import javax.servlet.http.HttpServletRequest;
import javax.servlet.http.HttpServletResponse;
import javax.servlet.ServletException;

import java.io.IOException;

import java.sql.Connection;
import java.sql.SQLException;

import java.util.Collection;

import com.wrox.tourism.db.util.ConnectionPool;
import com.wrox.tourism.db.AttractionDAO;
import com.wrox.tourism.db.EventDAO;
import com.wrox.tourism.db.FinderException;
import com.wrox.tourism.entity.Attraction;

public class ViewAttractionAction extends Action {

  private ConnectionPool pool;
```

As with `HomeAction`, we store an instance of the connection pool in the constructor:

```
public ViewAttractionAction() {
  pool = ConnectionPool.getInstance();
}
```

`perform()` is again where the work gets done:

```
public ActionForward perform(ActionMapping mapping,ActionForm form,
  HttpServletRequest request,HttpServletResponse response)
    throws IOException,ServletException {

  Connection con = null;

  ActionErrors errors = new ActionErrors();

  try {
```

We get a connection from the pool:

```
    con = pool.getConnection();
```

Next, we need to get the user id for the selected attraction from the request parameter:

```
    String userId = request.getParameter("userId");
```

Create an instance of `AttractionDAO` and find the attraction entity object for the specified user id. Having found the attraction, we store it as a request scope bean:

```
    AttractionDAO attractionDAO = new AttractionDAO(con);
    Attraction attraction =
      attractionDAO.findByPrimaryKey(userId);
    request.setAttribute(BeanNames.ATTRACTION_FORM,attraction);
```

The next step is to look up the attraction's events, by creating an instance of `EventDAO` and finding the list of event entity objects for the specified user id:

```
    EventDAO eventDAO = new EventDAO(con);
    Collection col = eventDAO.findAll(userId);
```

We store the list of event entity objects as a request scope bean, and forward to `viewAttraction.jsp`:

```
    request.setAttribute(BeanNames.EVENT_LIST,col);
    return mapping.findForward("success");
```

Finally, we need to catch some possible errors:

```
  } catch (SQLException e) {
    e.printStackTrace();
    ActionError error = new ActionError("error.unexpected");
```

699

```
        errors.add(ActionErrors.GLOBAL_ERROR,error);
      } catch (Throwable e) {
        e.printStackTrace();
        ActionError error = new ActionError(e.getMessage());
        errors.add(ActionErrors.GLOBAL_ERROR,error);
      } finally {
        try {
          if (con != null)
            con.close();
        } catch (SQLException e) {
          throw new RuntimeException(e.getMessage());
        }
      }
    }
```

If an error occurred, we store the action errors in the request attribute list and forward the response to
/home.do.

```
        saveErrors(request,errors);
        return new ActionForward(mapping.getInput());

    }


  }
```

The viewAttraction.jsp Page

viewAttraction.jsp is another template-based page, so it simply uses `<template:insert>` to
insert the file template.jsp and pushes the contents of viewAttractionContent.jsp into the
template using `<template:put>`:

```
<%@ taglib uri="/template" prefix="template" %>

<template:insert template="template.jsp">
  <template:put name="content" content="viewAttractionContent.jsp"/>
</template:insert>
```

The viewAttractionContent.jsp Page

This file contains the main content that is displayed in the attractions details page. The attributes of the
attraction entity object are rendered on the screen using the `<bean:write>` tag, then use
`<logic:iterate>` to run through the list of events that the action stored in request scope

First, we import the Struts tag libraries:

```
<%@ taglib uri="/bean" prefix="bean" %>
<%@ taglib uri="/html" prefix="html" %>
<%@ taglib uri="/logic" prefix="logic" %>
<%@ taglib uri="/template" prefix="template" %>

<br/>
<br/>

<table cellpadding="2">
```

```
  <tr>
   <td align="right">
    <b>Name:</b>
   </td>
```

Next, we render the attraction name, description, web site, and address using the `<bean:write>` tag:

```
   <td>
    <bean:write name="attractionForm" property="name"/>
   </td>
  </tr>
  <tr>
   <td align="right">
    <b>Description:</b>
   </td>
   <td>
    <bean:write name="attractionForm" property="description"/>
   </td>
  </tr>
  <tr>
   <td align="right">
    <b>Web Site:</b>
   </td>
   <td>
    <bean:write name="attractionForm" property="webSite"/>
   </td>
  </tr>
  <tr>
   <td align="right">
    <b>Address:</b>
   </td>
   <td>
    <bean:write name="attractionForm" property="address"/>
   </td>
  </tr>

</table>

<br/>

<table cellpadding="2" width="80%">

  <tr>
   <td>
    <b>Event Name</b>
   </td>
   <td>
    <b>Description</b>
   </td>
   <td>
    <b>Ticket Price</b>
   </td>
  </tr>
```

Our final step is to use `<logic:iterate>` to loop through the list of event entities stored under the name "eventList". Each event in turn is made available as bean named "event", of type `com.wrox.tourism.entity.Event`:

```
<logic:iterate name="eventList"
  id="event"
  scope="request"
  type="com.wrox.tourism.entity.Event">


<tr>
```

For each event, we display its name, description, and the ticket price:

```
<td>
  <bean:write name="event" property="name"/>
</td>
<td>
  <bean:write name="event" property="description"/>
</td>
<td>
  <bean:write name="event" property="ticketPrice"/>
</td>
</tr>

</logic:iterate>
</table>
```

Another use case completed! In fact, we've nearly finished the pages that are publicly accessible, with only the register attraction use case left. Let's quickly move on to that.

Register Attraction

Registering a new attraction takes two separate actions from the end user:

❑ First, the user needs to click on the Register link on the menu; the system will then present the user with a form for entering the attraction details.

❑ The user then needs to fill in the details and submit the form. If he fails to fill in all the details, the system presents the form back to the user retaining all the data previously entered by the user and prompting the user to enter the missing information. Once the submitted form contains all required information, the system registers the attraction and sends a confirmation page back to the user.

Let's see what these screens look like. First, here's the screen that is displayed when the user clicks on the Register link on the menu:

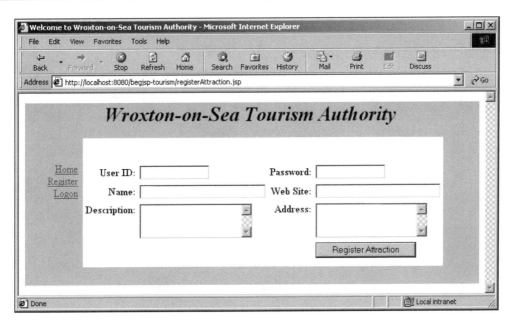

Next, we'll look at the screen that's displayed if the user clicks Register Attraction but some information is missing:

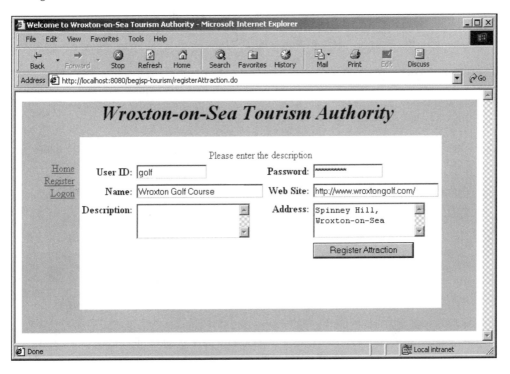

Finally, here's what the user will see when the attraction is successfully registered:

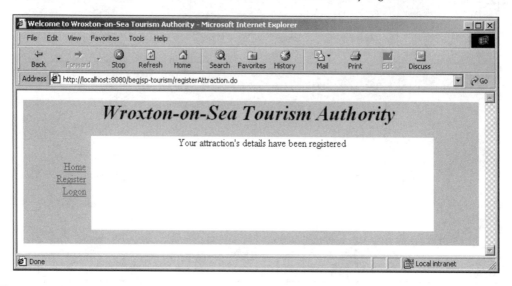

The internal system interactions associated with the various user actions in the process of registering a new attraction are listed below.

1. When the user clicks on the **Register** link on the menu, the system presents the user with `registerAttraction.jsp`, which includes `registerAttractionContent.jsp`. This page uses the Struts HTML tags to display the form and its elements.

2. When the user submits the displayed form for entering the attraction details, the action servlet will create an `Attraction` object, fill in its fields with the request parameters, and send the request to `/registerAttraction.do`, which is mapped to the action class `RegisterAttraction`.

3. The action class delegates the task of registering the attraction to the business object `AttractionBO`, passing it the `Attraction` object.

4. The business object validates the `Attraction` entity to check whether all the attributes are populated. If not it throws an `AttractionException`.

5. The action class catches this exception, retrieves the message key stored in the exception, creates an action error object passing the message key, saves the action errors objects in the request attribute list, and passes the control back to `registerAttraction.jsp`. The JSP will then use the Struts `<html:errors>` tag to render the error message, along with the form containing the data initially entered by the user.

6. If the entity object is valid then the business object delegates the task of creating an attraction record in the database to `AttractionDAO`. The data access object may throw a `CreateException` if the specified user id already exists; this exception is handled in the same way as explained in the last step.

7. If every thing goes fine, the action class forwards the response to
`confirmRegistration.jsp`, which displays a confirmation message to the user.

This sequence of events is depicted in the collaboration diagram below:

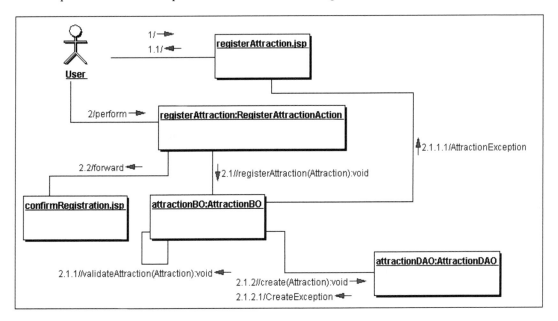

The **collaboration diagram** is the final type of UML diagram we'll be using; like the sequence diagram, this is used to show how different objects call each other. Having seen the other types of UML diagram you should be able to see fairly easily how it's put together.

The /registerAttraction.do Action Mapping

We want to map the request URL `/registerAttraction.do` to the corresponding action class, `com.wrox.tourism.actions.RegisterAttractionAction`. We need to tell the Struts action servlet that the form details should be saved in the `"attractionForm"` bean, which should be placed in request scope. We also define a local forward, `"success"`, pointing to `/confirmRegistration.jsp`; if there is an error, we'll send the user back to the input form, `/registerAttraction.jsp`.

Here's the extract from the Struts configuration file:

```
...
<action path="/registerAttraction"
  type="com.wrox.tourism.actions.RegisterAttractionAction"
  input="/registerAttraction.jsp"
  name="attractionForm"
  scope="request" >
  <forward name="success" path="/confirmRegistration.jsp"/>
</action>
...
```

The registerAttraction.jsp Page

We've seen this type of JSP before: it simply uses the template tags, and the content is in `registerAttractionContent.jsp`:

```
<%@ taglib uri="/template" prefix="template" %>

<template:insert template="template.jsp">
  <template:put name="content" content="registerAttractionContent.jsp"/>
</template:insert>
```

The registerAttractionContent.jsp Page

This is our first form page, and we'll be using the Struts HTML tags both to produce the final HTML `<form>` tags, and to produce the input elements within it. Using the Struts tags is handy because, if we are sent back to this page because of errors, the tags will automatically fill in the previously-entered values to save the user some work.

The form is associated with the `Attraction` form bean; when user clicks on the page's **Register Attraction** button this is what happens:

❑   The first time, the action servlet creates an instance of the `Attraction` bean and populates the bean attributes with the form values.

❑   The action servlet passes the `Attraction` bean to the relevant action class.

❑   Each time the form is sent back to the user because of any error, the JSP displays the error message using the `<html:errors>` tag and the form fields are pre-filled with the data entered by the user.

So, to start off we'll import the Struts tag libraries:

```
<%@ taglib uri="/bean" prefix="bean" %>
<%@ taglib uri="/html" prefix="html" %>
<%@ taglib uri="/logic" prefix="logic" %>
<%@ taglib uri="/template" prefix="template" %>
```

If there was an error message, we display it:

```
<br/>
<html:errors/>
<br/>

<table cellpadding="2">
```

We use the Struts `<html:form>` tag to render the form; as we specified in the Struts configuration file, this form is tied to the action form bean `attractionForm` which is of type `com.wrox.tourism.entity.Attraction`:

```
<html:form action="/registerAttraction.do" focus="userId">
  <tr>
   <td align="right">
    <b>User ID:</b>
   </td>
```

Now we'll display each input field in turn, using the `<html:text>` tag. The `property="userId"` syntax ties this form field to the `Attraction` bean's `userId` attribute:

```
<td>
 <html:text property="userId" size="15"/>
</td>
<td align="right">
 <b>Password:</b>
</td>
```

Similarly, we use the HTML tags to produce the password, name, website, description, and address fields. Note that, as appropriate, we use the `<html:password>` and `<html:textarea>` tags to produce the various types of HTML form elements:

```
<td>
 <html:password property="password" size="15"/>
</td>
</tr>
<tr>
<td align="right">
 <b>Name:</b>
</td>
<td>
 <html:text property="name" size="30"/>
</td>
<td align="right">
 <b>Web Site:</b>
</td>
<td>
 <html:text property="webSite" size="30"/>
</td>
</tr>
<tr>
<td align="right" valign="top">
 <b>Description:</b>
</td>
<td>
 <html:textarea property="description" rows="3" cols="20"/>
</td>
<td align="right" valign="top">
 <b>Address:</b>
</td>
<td>
 <html:textarea property="address" rows="3" cols="20"/>
</td>
</tr>
<tr>
<td>
</td>
<td>
</td>
<td>
</td>
```

Finally, the <html:submit> tags displays the submit button:

```
    <td>
      <html:submit value="Register Attraction"/>
    </td>
  </tr>
 </html:form>

</table>
```

RegisterAttractionAction

OK, so we've sorted the input form. What happens to the form data once it has been sent to the server? Let's look at the action class, RegisterAttractionAction:

```
package com.wrox.tourism.actions;

import org.apache.struts.action.ActionForm;
import org.apache.struts.action.ActionForward;
import org.apache.struts.action.Action;
import org.apache.struts.action.ActionMapping;
import org.apache.struts.action.ActionErrors;
import org.apache.struts.action.ActionError;
import org.apache.struts.action.ActionServlet;

import javax.servlet.http.HttpServletRequest;
import javax.servlet.http.HttpServletResponse;
import javax.servlet.ServletException;

import java.io.IOException;

import java.sql.Connection;
import java.sql.SQLException;

import java.util.Collection;

import com.wrox.tourism.business.AttractionBO;
import com.wrox.tourism.entity.Attraction;

public class RegisterAttractionAction extends Action {

  public ActionForward perform(ActionMapping mapping,ActionForm form,
    HttpServletRequest request,HttpServletResponse response)
      throws IOException,ServletException {

    ActionErrors errors = new ActionErrors();

    try {
```

The first thing we do is to create an instance of AttractionBO and tell it to register the new attraction. The perform() method is passed an ActionForm object containing the form data, which we need to cast to type Attraction:

```
        AttractionBO attractionBO = new AttractionBO();
        attractionBO.registerAttraction((Attraction)form);
```

If that was successful, we forward the request to `confirmRegistration.jsp`:

```
        return mapping.findForward("success");

    } catch (Throwable e) {
```

If something went wrong, on the other hand, we create an `ActionError`, passing the message key stored in the exception:

```
        e.printStackTrace();
        ActionError error = new ActionError(e.getMessage());
        errors.add(ActionErrors.GLOBAL_ERROR,error);
    }
```

We then store the action errors instance in the request and return to `registerAtrraction.jsp`:

```
        saveErrors(request,errors);
        return new ActionForward(mapping.getInput());

    }

}
```

The confirmRegistration.jsp Page

The last component for this use case displays a confirmation message on successful registration of the attraction. This JSP again uses the Struts template tags to insert the file `template.jsp`; however, in this case we don't need a separate JSP for the content as it's always the same. Instead, we set the `<template:put>` tag's `direct` attribute to `true`, which causes its `content` attribute to be directly inserted into the template:

```
<%@ taglib uri="/template" prefix="template" %>

<template:insert template="template.jsp">
  <template:put name="content"
    content="Your attraction's details have been registered"
    direct="true"/>
</template:insert>
```

Edit Attraction Details

Once an attraction is registered, its manager will want to be able to log in, edit its details, and start setting up details of events. Registered attractions may log on to the system by clicking on the Logon link on the menu; once the user is authenticated, the system displays a form for updating the details of the attraction associated with the logged on user. One of the links in the menu displayed after authentication is the Edit Attraction link, which also will display the form for updating attraction information; in fact, both the Logon and the Edit Attraction links point to the same web application resource:

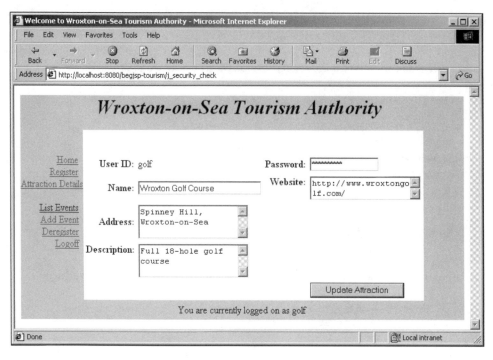

So, what's going on inside our system in this case?

1. Both the Logon and Edit Attraction links point to the web application resource `/editAttraction.do`.

2. If the user doesn't have the `attraction` role, the server will automatically redirect the user to the logon page, `login.jsp`, using HTTP form-based authentication.

3. The user enters their user id and password and submits the login form. The server checks their id and password, and if they match our database control is transferred to the action class `EditAttractionAction`.

4. The action class needs to find out who the user it; it does this by using the `getRemoteUser()` method on the `request` object.

5. An instance of `AttractionDAO` is used to retrieve the `Attraction` entity for the currently logged on user, by passing it the user id.

6. The entity object is then stored as a request scope bean, and the response is forwarded to `editAttraction.jsp`.

7. This JSP includes `editAttractionContent.jsp`, which uses the appropriate Struts tags to retrieve the bean and render its attribute values as an HTML form.

8. If an error occurs during the data access calls, an action errors object is saved in the request and control is sent to `/home.do`.

The diagram below illustrates these steps:

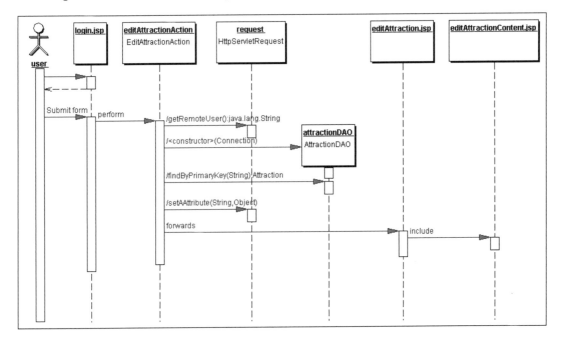

The /editAttraction.do Action Mapping

So, the user starts by requesting `editAttraction.do`, which we map to the corresponding action class as shown below:

```
...
<action path="/editAttraction"
  type="com.wrox.tourism.actions.EditAttractionAction"
  input="/home.do">
  <forward name="success" path="/editAttraction.jsp"/>
</action>
...
```

The action class is `com.wrox.tourism.actions.EditAttractionAction`, and we also define a local forward name "`success`" which maps to `editRegistration.jsp`. If an error condition arises, we want the response to be forwarded to `/home.do`.

The login.jsp Page

But before the request actually gets to `/editAttraction.do` we need to authenticate the user, and since we're using HTTP form-based authentication the server automatically directs them to our login page, `login.jsp`. This is just a simple page that inserts `loginContent.jsp` into the template:

```
<%@ taglib uri="/template" prefix="template" %>

<template:insert template="template.jsp">
  <template:put name="content" content="loginContent.jsp"/>
</template:insert>
```

711

The loginContent.jsp Page

loginContent.jsp displays the form for entering the user id and password. The Servlet specification tells us that the form's action must be defined as j_security_check, the name of the user id field must be j_username, and the name of the password field must be j_password:

```
<br/>
<br/>
<br/>
<table cellpadding="2">
<form action="j_security_check" focus="userId" method="post">
  <tr>
   <td align="right">
    <b>User ID:</b>
   </td>
   <td>
    <input type="text" name="j_username" size="15"/>
   </td>
  </tr>
  <tr>
   <td align="right">
    <b>Password:</b>
   </td>
   <td>
    <input type="password" name="j_password" size="15"/>
   </td>
  </tr>
  <tr>
   <td align="right">
   </td>
   <td>
    <input type="submit" value="logon"/>
   </td>
  </tr>
 </html:form>

</table>
```

EditAttractionAction

Since we're using the authentication features of the Servlet API, we don't need to worry any more about checking that the user is authenticated (beyond making sure our web.xml file lists the resources we need to protect). So we can move swiftly on to looking at the EditAttractionAction class, which needs to extract the attraction details and make them available to the form page:

```
package com.wrox.tourism.actions;

import org.apache.struts.action.ActionForm;
import org.apache.struts.action.ActionForward;
import org.apache.struts.action.Action;
import org.apache.struts.action.ActionMapping;
import org.apache.struts.action.ActionErrors;
import org.apache.struts.action.ActionError;
```

```
import org.apache.struts.action.ActionServlet;

import javax.servlet.http.HttpServletRequest;
import javax.servlet.http.HttpServletResponse;
import javax.servlet.ServletException;

import java.io.IOException;

import java.sql.Connection;
import java.sql.SQLException;

import java.util.Collection;

import com.wrox.tourism.db.util.ConnectionPool;
import com.wrox.tourism.db.AttractionDAO;
import com.wrox.tourism.entity.Attraction;

public class EditAttractionAction extends Action {

  private ConnectionPool pool;

  public EditAttractionAction() {
    pool = ConnectionPool.getInstance();
  }

  public ActionForward perform(ActionMapping mapping,ActionForm form,
    HttpServletRequest request,HttpServletResponse response)
      throws IOException,ServletException {

  Connection con = null;

  ActionErrors errors = new ActionErrors();

  try {
```

As usual, the first step is to get a connection from the database pool; then, we find out who the user is by looking in the `request` object:

```
con = pool.getConnection();
String userId = request.getRemoteUser();
```

Next, we create an instance of `AttractionDAO` and find the `Attraction` entity for this user id:

```
AttractionDAO attractionDAO = new AttractionDAO(con);
Attraction attraction =
  attractionDAO.findByPrimaryKey(userId);
request.setAttribute(BeanNames.ATTRACTION_FORM,attraction);
```

If everything went OK we forward the response to `editAttraction.jsp`:

```
return mapping.findForward("success");

} catch (SQLException e) {
  e.printStackTrace();
```

```
        ActionError error = new ActionError("error.unexpected");
        errors.add(ActionErrors.GLOBAL_ERROR,error);
    } catch (Throwable e) {
        e.printStackTrace();
        ActionError error = new ActionError(e.getMessage());
        errors.add(ActionErrors.GLOBAL_ERROR,error);
    } finally {
        try {
```

Finally, we make sure to release the database connection. If any errors occurred, we save the details in the request and send the user back to /home.do:

```
        if (con != null)
          con.close();
    } catch (SQLException e) {
        throw new RuntimeException(e.getMessage());
    }
    }
    saveErrors(request,errors);
    return new ActionForward(mapping.getInput());

  }

}
```

The editAttraction.jsp Page

As usual, we have a simple page that just uses the template tags to insert editAttractionContent.jsp:

```
<%@ taglib uri="/template" prefix="template" %>

<template:insert template="template.jsp">
  <template:put name="content" content="editAttractionContent.jsp"/>
</template:insert>
```

The editAttractionContent.jsp Page

editAttractionContent.jsp uses the Struts HTML tags to render the form and form elements for editing attraction details. Since the EditAttractionAction will have saved the Attraction details in request scope, the tags can access it to extract the current attraction details. First off, we import the Struts tag libraries:

```
<%@ taglib uri="/bean" prefix="bean" %>
<%@ taglib uri="/html" prefix="html" %>
<%@ taglib uri="/logic" prefix="logic" %>
<%@ taglib uri="/template" prefix="template" %>
```

If there were any error messages, we display them next:

```
<br/>
<html:errors/>
<br/>

<table cellpadding="2">
```

We use the `<html:form>` tag to render the form, specifying that when the user submits the form the data should be sent to `/updateAttraction.do`. In the next section we'll configure this URL; it will use the form bean `attractionForm` which is of type `com.wrox.tourism.entity.Attraction`:

```
<html:form action="/updateAttraction.do" focus="password">
 <tr>
  <td align="right">
   <b>User ID:</b>
  </td>
```

The next step is to display the user id as a static text, using the `<bean:write>` tag. (This screen can be used to change any attraction details *except* the user id.) But we will need to send the user id back to the server when updating the details, so we create a hidden input field using the `<html:hidden>` tag:

```
 <td>
  <bean:write name="attractionForm" property="userId"/>
  <html:hidden property="userId"/>
 </td>
```

The rest of the input fields are easy, and we use the `<html:password>`, `<html:text>`, and `<html:textArea>` tags to extract the attraction details and create the HTML form elements:

```
 <td align="right">
  <b>Password:</b>
 </td>
 <td>
  <html:password property="password" size="15"/>
 </td>
</tr>
<tr>
 <td align="right">
  <b>Name:</b>
 </td>
 <td>
  <html:text property="name" size="30"/>
 </td>
 <td align="right" valign="top">
  <b>Website:</b>
 </td>
 <td>
  <html:textarea property="webSite"/>
 </td>
</tr>
<tr>
 <td align="right">
  <b>Address:</b>
 </td>
 <td>
  <html:textarea property="address" rows="3" cols="20"/>
 </td>
</tr>
<tr>
```

```
    <td align="right" valign="top">
     <b>Description:</b>
    </td>
    <td>
     <html:textarea property="description" rows="3" cols="20"/>
    </td>
   </tr>
   <tr>
    <td>
    </td>
    <td>
    </td>
    <td>
    </td>
```

Lastly, we create the submit button itself:

```
    <td>
     <html:submit value="Update Attraction"/>
    </td>
   </tr>
  </html:form>

 </table>
```

Update Attraction

So we've created the form for users to modify attraction details; next we need to consider what happens when they click on the **Update Attraction** button in the form to update the details. The application needs to update the attraction details in the database, and if successful to display a page confirming that this has been done:

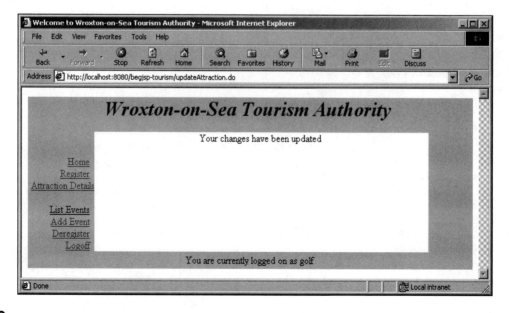

The sequence of internal system interactions triggered by the users submitting the attractions details form is as follows:

1. The action is sent to the request URL /updateAttraction.do.

2. This action is mapped to the action class UpdateAttractionAction.

3. The action class uses the business object AttractionBO to update the attraction details.

4. The business object delegates this task to the data access object AttractionDAO, after validating the data entered by the users.

5. If the details are successfully updated, the action class forwards the response to confirmUpdate.jsp.

6. If the business object or the data access object throws an exception, the action class creates an action error object, and sends the response back to editAttraction.jsp, which will use the Struts <html:errors> tag to display the error message.

The collaboration diagram below illustrates these steps:

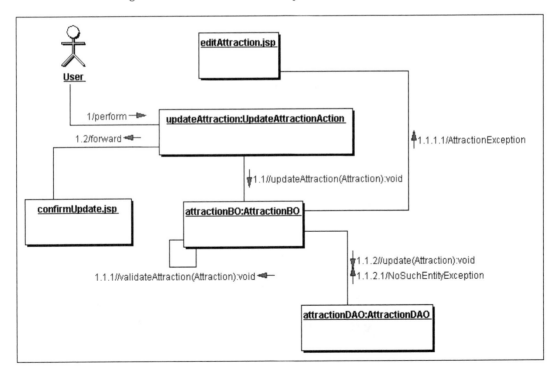

The /updateAttraction.do Action Mapping

The first step is to map the request URL /updateAttraction.do to the corresponding action class, com.wrox.tourism.actions.UpdateAttractionAction:

```
    ...
    <action path="/updateAttraction"
      type="com.wrox.tourism.actions.UpdateAttractionAction"
      input="/editAttraction.jsp"
      name="attractionForm"
      scope="request">
      <forward name="success" path="/confirmUpdate.jsp"/>
    </action>
    ...
```

This also defines a local forward named "success", mapping to confirmUpdate.jsp. If an error condition occurs, the page to return to is defined as editAttraction.jsp. Since this action will be receiving form data from the user, we associate it with the action form bean attractionForm.

UpdateAttractionAction

Let's move on to look at the action class itself, which has to take the form data and store it in the database:

```
package com.wrox.tourism.actions;

import org.apache.struts.action.ActionForm;
import org.apache.struts.action.ActionForward;
import org.apache.struts.action.Action;
import org.apache.struts.action.ActionMapping;
import org.apache.struts.action.ActionErrors;
import org.apache.struts.action.ActionError;
import org.apache.struts.action.ActionServlet;

import javax.servlet.http.HttpServletRequest;
import javax.servlet.http.HttpServletResponse;
import javax.servlet.ServletException;

import java.io.IOException;

import java.sql.Connection;
import java.sql.SQLException;

import java.util.Collection;

import com.wrox.tourism.business.AttractionBO;
import com.wrox.tourism.entity.Attraction;

public class UpdateAttractionAction extends Action {

  public ActionForward perform(ActionMapping mapping,ActionForm form,
    HttpServletRequest request,HttpServletResponse response)
      throws IOException,ServletException {

    ActionErrors errors = new ActionErrors();

    try {
```

We start by creating an instance of `AttractionBO` and calling the business method to update the attraction; we pass the action form as an argument. You'll see that, just like when we were considering `RegisterAttractionAction`, we need to cast the form to the `Attraction` class:

```
AttractionBO attractionBO = new AttractionBO();
attractionBO.updateAttraction((Attraction)form);
```

If everything works, we forward to `confirmUpdate.jsp`:

```
return mapping.findForward("success");

} catch (Throwable e) {
    e.printStackTrace();
    ActionError error = new ActionError(e.getMessage());
    errors.add(ActionErrors.GLOBAL_ERROR,error);
}
```

If, on the other hand, there were any errors we store them in the request and return to `editRegistration.jsp`:

```
saveErrors(request,errors);
return new ActionForward(mapping.getInput());

}

}
```

The confirmUpdate.jsp Page

Finally, we need to create a JSP that displays a confirmation message if the attraction details were successfully updated. As usual, we use the Struts template tags to acomplish this, but (like we did with `confirmRegistration.jsp`) we don't bother to create a separate JSP for the content. Instead, we set `direct="true"` on the `<template:put>` tag and use its `content` attribute to specify the message:

```
<%@ taglib uri="/template" prefix="template" %>

<template:insert template="template.jsp">
  <template:put name="content"
    content="Your changes have been updated"
    direct="true"/>
</template:insert>
```

Another use case out of the way. In fact, we're nearly there now; the remaining use cases are:

❑ List events
❑ Delete event
❑ Edit event
❑ Update event
❑ Deregister attraction
❑ Log off

719

Many of these event use cases will be very similar to the way we implemented the equivalent attraction use cases.

List Events

As we have already seen, each attraction may have zero or more events attached to it. Once an attraction logs on to the system, a link will be presented for browsing the list of events associated with the attraction; from the list, we will provide facilities to edit and delete individual events:

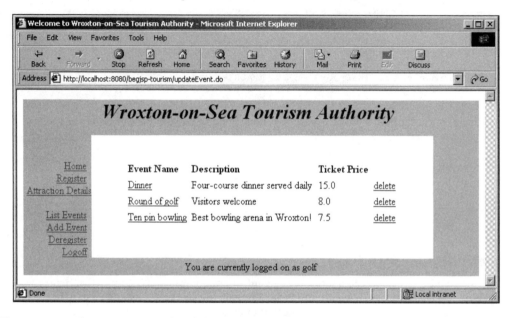

The sequence of events associated with listing the events is:

1. The request URL associated with listing the events is /listEvents.do.

2. This action is mapped to the action class ListEventsAction.

3. The action class first gets the remote user from the request object.

4. Then an instance of EventDAO is created and a list of events associated with the user is retrieved from the database.

5. This list is then stored as a request scope bean, and action forwards to listEvents.jsp.

6. This JSP includes listEventsContent.jsp, which uses the appropriate Struts tags to retrieve and render the information from the request scope bean.

7. If an error occurs during the data access calls, we store an action errors object, save it in the request, and return control to /editAttraction.do.

These events are illustrated in the next interaction diagram:

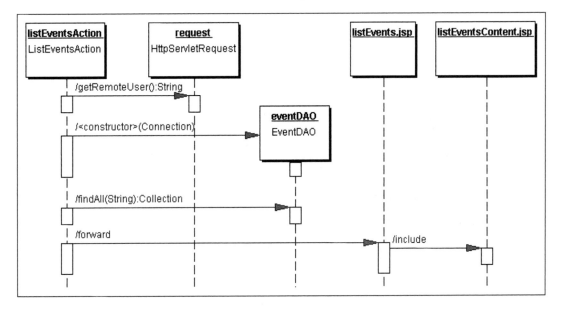

The /listEvents.do Action Mapping

As usual, we'll first see how we map the request URL to the action. In this case, we want to map
/listEvents.do to the action class com.wrox.tourism.actions.ListEventsAction. We
define a local forward named "success", pointing to listEvents.jsp; and if there are any errors,
the page we want to return to is /editAttraction.do:

```
...
<action path="/listEvents"
  type="com.wrox.tourism.actions.ListEventsAction"
  input="/editAttraction.do">
  <forward name="success" path="/listEvents.jsp"/>
</action>
...
```

ListEventsAction

Onwards to the action class itself:

```
package com.wrox.tourism.actions;

import org.apache.struts.action.ActionForm;
import org.apache.struts.action.ActionForward;
import org.apache.struts.action.Action;
import org.apache.struts.action.ActionMapping;
import org.apache.struts.action.ActionErrors;
import org.apache.struts.action.ActionError;
import org.apache.struts.action.ActionServlet;
```

```
import javax.servlet.http.HttpServletRequest;
import javax.servlet.http.HttpServletResponse;
import javax.servlet.ServletException;

import java.io.IOException;

import java.sql.Connection;
import java.sql.SQLException;

import java.util.Collection;

import com.wrox.tourism.db.util.ConnectionPool;
import com.wrox.tourism.db.EventDAO;
import com.wrox.tourism.entity.Attraction;

public class ListEventsAction extends Action {

  private ConnectionPool pool;

  public ListEventsAction() {
    pool = ConnectionPool.getInstance();
  }

  public ActionForward perform(ActionMapping mapping,ActionForm form,
    HttpServletRequest request,HttpServletResponse response)
      throws IOException,ServletException {

    Connection con = null;

    ActionErrors errors = new ActionErrors();

    try {
```

We're going to use the data access object directly, so we start by getting a connection from the pool, and looking up the user from the `request` object:

```
      con = pool.getConnection();
      String userId = request.getRemoteUser();
```

Next, we create an instance of `EventDAO` and get the list of events for the attraction that is currently logged on:

```
      EventDAO eventDAO = new EventDAO(con);
      Collection col = eventDAO.findAll(userId);
```

We store the list as a request scope bean and forward the response to `listEvents.jsp`:

```
      request.setAttribute(BeanNames.EVENT_LIST,col);

      return mapping.findForward("success");

    } catch (SQLException e) {
```

```
      e.printStackTrace();
      ActionError error = new ActionError("error.unexpected");
      errors.add(ActionErrors.GLOBAL_ERROR,error);
    } catch (Throwable e) {
      e.printStackTrace();
      ActionError error = new ActionError(e.getMessage());
      errors.add(ActionErrors.GLOBAL_ERROR,error);
    } finally {
      try {
        if (con != null)
          con.close();
      } catch (SQLException e) {
        throw new RuntimeException(e.getMessage());
      }
    }
  }
```

Finally, if an exception occurred we create an appropriate action errors object, store it in the request attribute list, and forward to /editAttractions.do:

```
    saveErrors(request,errors);
    return new ActionForward(mapping.getInput());

  }

}
```

The listEvents.jsp Page

listEvents.jsp is another simple JSP using the template tags to insert listEventsContent.jsp:

```
<%@ taglib uri="/template" prefix="template" %>

<template:insert template="template.jsp">
  <template:put name="content" content="listEventsContent.jsp"/>
</template:insert>
```

The listEventsContent.jsp Page

listEventsContent.jsp uses the Struts HTML tags to render the list of events. For each event we need to create two links: one pointing to /editEvent.do for editing the event, and one pointing to /deleteEvent.do for deleting it. In each case, we need to include the event id as a request parameter so our actions will know which event they are to work with.

The page starts off simply, by importing the Struts tag libraries:

```
<%@ taglib uri="/bean" prefix="bean" %>
<%@ taglib uri="/html" prefix="html" %>
<%@ taglib uri="/logic" prefix="logic" %>
<%@ taglib uri="/template" prefix="template" %>
```

```
<br/>
<html:errors/>
<br/>

<table cellpadding="2" width="80%">

 <tr>
  <td>
   <b>Event Name</b>
  </td>
  <td>
   <b>Description</b>
  </td>
  <td>
   <b>Ticket Price</b>
  </td>
  <td>
  </td>
 </tr>
```

Next we need to loop through the list of event entities that the action stored by the name "eventList". We use the `<logic:iterate>` tag to do this, exposing the current entity object in the list as a bean named "event", which will be of type `com.wrox.tourism.entity.Event`:

```
<logic:iterate name="eventList"
  id="event"
  scope="request"
  type="com.wrox.tourism.entity.Event">

 <tr>
```

First, we display an HTML link pointing to `editEvent.do`, passing the event id as a request parameter:

```
<td>
 <a href="editEvent.do?eventId=<bean:write name="event"
 property="eventId"/>">
  <bean:write name="event" property="name"/>
 </a>
</td>
```

In the next column we display the event description:

```
<td>
 <bean:write name="event" property="description"/>
</td>
```

After this comes the event ticket price:

```
  <td>
   <bean:write name="event" property="ticketPrice"/>
  </td>
```

Finally, we create the **delete** link pointing to `deleteEvent.do`, with the event id as a request parameter:

```
  <td>
   <a href="deleteEvent.do?eventId=<bean:write name="event"
   property="eventId"/>">
    delete
   </a>
  </td>
 </tr>

 </logic:iterate>
</table>
```

Delete Event

So we need to create actions for deleting and editing events. Let's start with the delete action.

Events may be deleted by clicking on the **delete** links displayed next to each event; on successful deletion, the system displays the refreshed list of events to the user. The sequence of internal system interactions is:

1. The request URL associated with listing the events is `/deleteEvent.do`.

2. This action is mapped to the action class `DeleteEventAction`.

3. The action class first gets the event id; this is passed as a request parameter.

4. Then an instance of `EventBO` is created, and the business method to delete the event is called. This in fact delegates the task to `EventDAO`.

5. The response is forwarded to `/listEvents.do`.

6. If an error occurs during the data access calls, an appropriate action errors object is populated in the request attribute list and the control is sent to `/listEvents.do`.

These events are illustrated in the interaction diagram below:

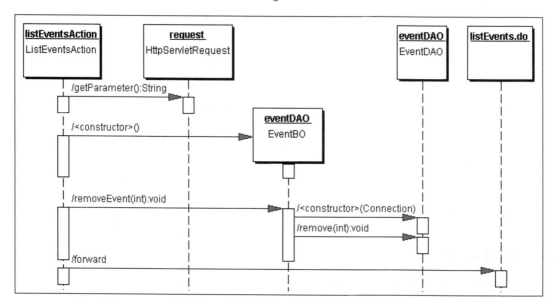

Action Mapping

We need to add an entry in the Struts configuration file to map the request URL /deleteEvent.do to the corresponding action class, com.wrox.tourism.actions.DeleteEventAction. We define a local forward named "success" mapping to /listEvents.do; this is also the resource to which we want to go in the event of an error condition:

```
  . . .
  <action path="/deleteEvent"
    type="com.wrox.tourism.actions.DeleteEventAction"
    input="/listEvents.do">
    <forward name="success" path="/listEvents.do"/>
  </action>
  . . .
```

DeleteEventAction

Let's take a look now at the source code for the action class:

```
  package com.wrox.tourism.actions;

  import org.apache.struts.action.ActionForm;
  import org.apache.struts.action.ActionForward;
  import org.apache.struts.action.Action;
  import org.apache.struts.action.ActionMapping;
  import org.apache.struts.action.ActionErrors;
  import org.apache.struts.action.ActionError;
  import org.apache.struts.action.ActionServlet;

  import javax.servlet.http.HttpServletRequest;
```

```
import javax.servlet.http.HttpServletResponse;
import javax.servlet.ServletException;

import java.io.IOException;

import java.sql.Connection;
import java.sql.SQLException;

import java.util.Collection;

import com.wrox.tourism.business.EventBO;
import com.wrox.tourism.entity.Attraction;

public class DeleteEventAction extends Action {

  public ActionForward perform(ActionMapping mapping,ActionForm form,
    HttpServletRequest request,HttpServletResponse response)
      throws IOException,ServletException {

    ActionErrors errors = new ActionErrors();

    try {
```

We start off by getting the event id from the request parameter:

```
    int eventId = Integer.parseInt(
      request.getParameter("eventId"));
```

Next, create an instance of `EventBO` and call the business method to remove the event:

```
    EventBO eventBO = new EventBO();
    eventBO.removeEvent(eventId);

    return mapping.findForward("success");
```

If an exception occurred, create an action errors object, store it in the request attribute list, and forward the response to /listEvents.do:

```
    } catch (Throwable e) {
      e.printStackTrace();
      ActionError error = new ActionError(e.getMessage());
      errors.add(ActionErrors.GLOBAL_ERROR,error);
    }
    saveErrors(request,errors);
    return new ActionForward(mapping.getInput());

  }

}
```

Edit Event

The other action users may perform from the event listing page is to edit an individual event, which they do by clicking on the event name links. This will display a form populated with the details of the selected events, which the users may modify and update:

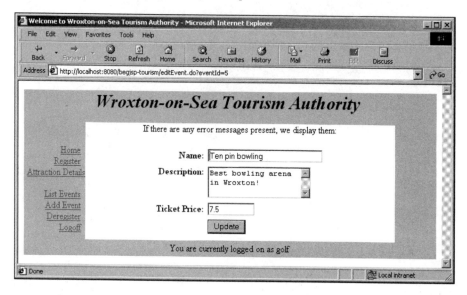

The sequence of events when the user clicks on an event name is:

1. The request URL associated with listing the events is `/editEvent.do`.

2. This action is mapped to the action class `EditEventAction`.

3. The action class first gets the event id that is passed as a request parameter.

4. Then an instance of `EventDAO` is created, and the `Event` entity object corresponding to the event id is retrieved.

5. The entity is then stored as a request scope bean, and the response is forwarded to `editEvent.jsp`.

6. This JSP includes `editEventContent.jsp`, which uses the appropriate Struts tags to render the bean attributes into a HTML form.

7. If an error occurs during the data access calls, an action errors object is stored in the request and control is sent to `/listEvents.do`.

These events are illustrated in the interaction diagram below:

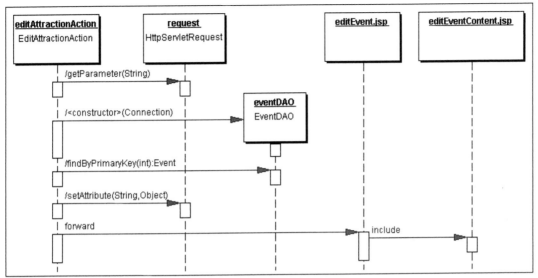

The /editEvent.do Action Mapping

Let's start, as usual, by mapping the request URL to the action class. /editEvent.do is the URL, and the action class is com.wrox.tourism.actions.EditEventAction. We also define a local forward named "success", mapping to /editEvent.jsp, and if an error condition occurs we want to return to /listEvents.do:

```
...
<action path="/editEvent"
  type="com.wrox.tourism.actions.EditEventAction"
  input="/listEvents.do">
  <forward name="success" path="/editEvent.jsp"/>
</action>
...
```

EditEventAction

The action class is rather reminiscent of EditAttractionAction:

```
package com.wrox.tourism.actions;

import org.apache.struts.action.ActionForm;
import org.apache.struts.action.ActionForward;
import org.apache.struts.action.Action;
import org.apache.struts.action.ActionMapping;
import org.apache.struts.action.ActionErrors;
import org.apache.struts.action.ActionError;
import org.apache.struts.action.ActionServlet;

import javax.servlet.http.HttpServletRequest;
```

```
import javax.servlet.http.HttpServletResponse;
import javax.servlet.ServletException;

import java.io.IOException;

import java.sql.Connection;
import java.sql.SQLException;

import java.util.Collection;

import com.wrox.tourism.db.util.ConnectionPool;
import com.wrox.tourism.db.EventDAO;
import com.wrox.tourism.entity.Event;

public class EditEventAction extends Action {

  private ConnectionPool pool;

  public EditEventAction() {
    pool = ConnectionPool.getInstance();
  }

  public ActionForward perform(ActionMapping mapping,ActionForm form,
    HttpServletRequest request,HttpServletResponse response)
      throws IOException,ServletException {

    Connection con = null;

    ActionErrors errors = new ActionErrors();

    try {
```

We start off by geting a connection from the pool, and extracting the event id that was passed as a request parameter:

```
con = pool.getConnection();
int eventId = Integer.parseInt(
  request.getParameter("eventId"));
```

Next, we create an instance of EventDAO and find the Event entity by passing it the event id:

```
EventDAO eventDAO = new EventDAO(con);
Event event = eventDAO.findByPrimaryKey(eventId);
```

Having located the Event entity we store it as a request scope bean (so that our JSP view can get to it) and forward it to editEvent.jsp:

```
request.setAttribute(BeanNames.EVENT_FORM,event);

return mapping.findForward("success");

} catch (SQLException e) {
```

```
      e.printStackTrace();
      ActionError error = new ActionError("error.unexpected");
      errors.add(ActionErrors.GLOBAL_ERROR,error);
   } catch (Throwable e) {
      e.printStackTrace();
      ActionError error = new ActionError(e.getMessage());
      errors.add(ActionErrors.GLOBAL_ERROR,error);
   } finally {
      try {
```

We mustn't forget to release the database connection:

```
      if (con != null)
         con.close();
   } catch (SQLException e) {
      throw new RuntimeException(e.getMessage());
   }
}
```

Lastly, if an exception occurred we create an appropriate action errors object, store it in the request attribute list, and forward to /listEvents.do:

```
      saveErrors(request,errors);
      return new ActionForward(mapping.getInput());

   }

}
```

The editEvent.jsp Page

This page simply uses the template tags to insert editEventContent.jsp into the template:

```
<%@ taglib uri="/template" prefix="template" %>

<template:insert template="template.jsp">
   <template:put name="content" content="editEventContent.jsp"/>
</template:insert>
```

The editEventContent.jsp Page

The content page for this use case, editEventContent.jsp, uses the Struts HTML tags to display the form and its contents; just like when we were coding the edit attraction details use case, the form fields will be automatically filled in with the existing event details. We will be using the page again a bit later, too, when we come to implement the Add Event menu link.

First off, we import the Struts tag libraries:

```
<%@ taglib uri="/bean" prefix="bean" %>
<%@ taglib uri="/html" prefix="html" %>
<%@ taglib uri="/logic" prefix="logic" %>
<%@ taglib uri="/template" prefix="template" %>
```

731

Chapter 20

If there are any error messages present, we display them:

```
<br/>
<html:errors/>
<br/>

<table cellpadding="2">
```

Next, we use the `<html:form>` tag to produce the form element in the page. Because the form is linked to `/updateEvent.do`, it is automatically tied to the action form bean `eventForm`, which is a `com.wrox.tourism.entity.Event` object:

```
<html:form action="/updateEvent.do" focus="name">
```

We need to produce a hidden input field containing the event id, which we do using the `<html:hidden>` tag. This field is automatically tied to the action form bean attribute `eventId`:

```
<html:hidden property="eventId"/>
<tr>
 <td align="right">
  <b>Name:</b>
 </td>
```

Next, we use the various Struts HTML tags to produce the necessary input fields in the page. They too are automatically tied to their corresponding bean attributes:

```
<td>
 <html:text property="name" size="30"/>
</td>
</tr>
<tr>
 <td align="right" valign="top">
  <b>Description:</b>
 </td>
 <td>
  <html:textarea property="description" rows="3" cols="20"/>
 </td>
</tr>
<tr>
 <td align="right">
  <b>Ticket Price:</b>
 </td>
 <td>
  <html:text property="ticketPrice" size="10"/>
 </td>
</tr>
<tr>
 <td align="right">
 </td>
```

Finally, we need a submit button:

```
<td>
 <html:submit value="Update"/>
</td>
```

```
    </tr>
  </html:form>

</table>
```

Update Event

So we've managed to display the event details for updating; next we need to make the system respond when the attraction manager submits this form. We don't need to create any new JSPs as, if the update was successful, we simply redisplay all the current attraction's events.

The sequence of internal system interactions triggered by the users submitting the event details form is as follows:

1. The form data is sent to the request URL /updateEvent.do.

2. This action is mapped to the action class UpdateEventAction.

3. The action class uses the business object EventBO to update the event details.

4. The business object delegates this task to the data access object EventDAO, after validating the data entered by the user.

5. If the details are successfully updated, the action class forwards to /listEvents.do.

6. If either the business object or the data access object throws an exception, the action class creates an action error object and sends the response back to editEvent.jsp. editEvent.jsp already includes the necessary <html:errors> tag to display the error message.

The collaboration diagram below illustrates these steps:

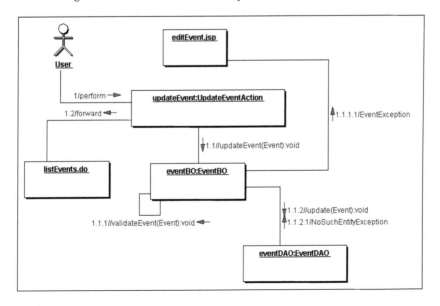

The /updateEvent.do Action Mapping

Let's start by mapping the action; we want to make the URL /updateEvent.do map to the action class com.wrox.tourism.actions.EditEventAction. listEvents.jsp is the "success" local forward which we will use if the update was successful; the input form (to which we want to return if there was an error) is defined as /listEvents.do.

```
...
  <action path="/updateEvent"
    type="com.wrox.tourism.actions.UpdateEventAction"
    input="/editEvent.jsp">
    <forward name="success" path="/listEvents.do"/>
  </action>
...
```

UpdateEventAction

Now let's have a look at the action class itself:

```java
package com.wrox.tourism.actions;

import org.apache.struts.action.ActionForm;
import org.apache.struts.action.ActionForward;
import org.apache.struts.action.Action;
import org.apache.struts.action.ActionMapping;
import org.apache.struts.action.ActionErrors;
import org.apache.struts.action.ActionError;
import org.apache.struts.action.ActionServlet;

import javax.servlet.http.HttpServletRequest;
import javax.servlet.http.HttpServletResponse;
import javax.servlet.ServletException;

import java.io.IOException;

import java.sql.Connection;
import java.sql.SQLException;

import java.util.Collection;

import com.wrox.tourism.business.EventBO;
import com.wrox.tourism.entity.Event;

public class UpdateEventAction extends Action {

  public ActionForward perform(ActionMapping mapping, ActionForm form,
    HttpServletRequest request, HttpServletResponse response)
      throws IOException, ServletException {

    ActionErrors errors = new ActionErrors();

    try {
```

First we cast the action form to the `Event` class, and set the user id to the remote user retrieved from the `request` object:

```
Event event = (Event)form;
event.setUserId(request.getRemoteUser());
```

This is where it gets slightly tricky. In a moment we're going to cheat slightly and reuse this action; it turns out that there's very little difference between updating an event and adding a new event, so we'll use the same action in both cases.

So we try to get the event id from the `Event` entity. However, if this is a new event rather than an update to an existing one, the event id will be zero, and so we will call the business method to *create* an event. If we have a non-zero event id the user must be trying to update an existing event, and so we call the business method to *update* that event:

```
int eventId = event.getEventId();

EventBO eventBO = new EventBO();

if (eventId == 0) {
  eventBO.createEvent(event);
} else {
  eventBO.updateEvent(event);
}
```

Whether we were creating a new event or updating an existing one, we forward the response to `/listEvents.do`:

```
return mapping.findForward("success");

} catch (Throwable e) {
  e.printStackTrace();
  ActionError error = new ActionError(e.getMessage());
  errors.add(ActionErrors.GLOBAL_ERROR,error);
}
```

If an exception occurred we create an appropriate action errors object, store it in the request, and forward to `editEvent.jsp`:

```
saveErrors(request,errors);
return new ActionForward(mapping.getInput());

  }

}
```

Add Event

The system also lets the users add new events to the attraction. This task involves the following steps:

1. First, the user clicks on the **Add Event** link on the menu, and the system displays `editEvent.jsp` with an empty form for entering the event details.

2. The user enters the event details and submits the form. The action for the form is `/updateEvent.do`, which maps to `UpdateEventAction`.

3. This class gets the event id from the passed action form.

4. If it is zero the action class calls the business method to create an event on the business object, otherwise it calls the business method to update the event details (as we explained in the last section).

5. If the update is successful, we forward to `/listEvents.do`.

6. If the business object or the data access object throws an exception the action class creates an action error object, and returns to `editEvent.jsp` to display the error message.

The action mapping, classes, and JSPs used for this use case have already been explained; the collaboration diagram is the same as that in the previous section on updating existing events.

Deregistering

Only two use cases left: deregistering, and logging off. We'll start with deregistering.

A logged-on attraction manager may deregister his attraction by clicking on the **Deregister** link in the menu. To do this, we need to remove the record from the `attraction` table, and all dependent records from the `event` and `user_role` tables. The sequence of events associated in deregistering an event is:

1. When the users click on the **Deregister** link the request is sent to the URL `/deregister.do`, which is mapped to the action class `DeregisterAttractionAction`.

2. The action class first retrieves the remote user from the `request` object.

3. Then an instance of `AttractionBO` is instantiated, and the business method to deregister the attraction is called passing the user id.

4. The business object uses `AttractionDAO` to remove the attraction record, `EventDAO` to remove all the associated event records, and `UserRoleDAO` to remove the user role record. Note that in the web tier we're not really interested in the details of how the attraction gets deleted: we just ask the business object to delete it.

5. Then we invalidate the user's session to log them out, **redirect** the user to `/home.do`.

6. If the business object throws an exception, the action class creates an action error object and returns to `/editAttraction.do`, which uses the `<html:errors>` tag to display the error message.

This series of events is illustrated in the sequence diagram below:

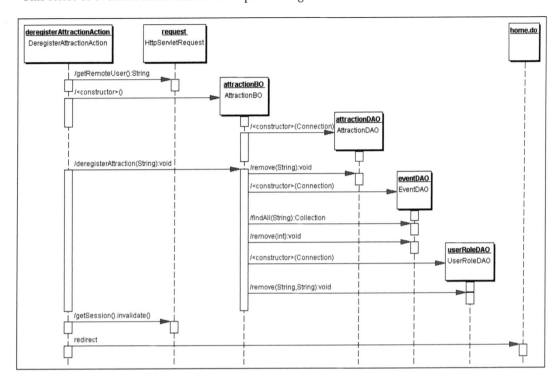

The /deregister.do Action Mapping

The request URL /deregister.do is mapped to the corresponding action class
com.wrox.tourism.actions.DeregisterAttractionAction

```
...
<action path="/deregisterAttraction"
   type="com.wrox.tourism.actions.DeregisterAttractionAction"
   input="/editAttraction.do">
   <forward name="success" path="/home.do" redirect="true"/>
</action>
...
```

This excerpt also defines a local forward named "success", mapping to the resource /home.do.
Please note that the redirect attribute is set to "true" for the local forward, which means that the
action servlet will send a message back to the browser redirecting it to /home.do. This is different from
the normal way of forwarding to a resource using the request dispatcher.

The reason for doing this is that the original request would have the security credentials for the
authenticated user; however, since we are deregistering the attraction we only want them to see the
menu links that public users see. The way to ensure that this happens is to invalidate the user session
(therefore logging them out of the site) and forcing them to make a fresh (non-authenticated) request for
the home page.

If an error occurs, we specify that the response should be forwarded to /editAttraction.do.

DeregisterAttractionAction

On to the action class:

```
package com.wrox.tourism.actions;

import org.apache.struts.action.ActionForm;
import org.apache.struts.action.ActionForward;
import org.apache.struts.action.Action;
import org.apache.struts.action.ActionMapping;
import org.apache.struts.action.ActionErrors;
import org.apache.struts.action.ActionError;
import org.apache.struts.action.ActionServlet;

import javax.servlet.http.HttpServletRequest;
import javax.servlet.http.HttpServletResponse;
import javax.servlet.ServletException;

import java.io.IOException;

import java.sql.Connection;
import java.sql.SQLException;

import java.util.Collection;

import com.wrox.tourism.business.AttractionBO;
import com.wrox.tourism.entity.Attraction;

public class DeregisterAttractionAction extends Action {

  public ActionForward perform(ActionMapping mapping,ActionForm form,
    HttpServletRequest request,HttpServletResponse response)
      throws IOException,ServletException {

    ActionErrors errors = new ActionErrors();

    try {
```

We need to find out which attraction we're trying to delete, so we get the remote user from the `request` object:

```
        String userId = request.getRemoteUser();
```

Next, we create an instance of `AttractionBO` and call the business method that deregisters the attraction:

```
        AttractionBO attractionBO = new AttractionBO();
        attractionBO.deregisterAttraction(userId);
```

An important step is to invalidate the user's session. This logs them off from the application, since they are now a normal, public user rather than an attraction manager:

```
request.getSession().invalidate();
```

If all that worked, we redirect the response to /home.do:

```
        return mapping.findForward("success");

    } catch (Throwable e) {
        e.printStackTrace();
        ActionError error = new ActionError(e.getMessage());
        errors.add(ActionErrors.GLOBAL_ERROR,error);
    }
```

If an exception occurred, we create an action errors object, store it as a request attribute, and forward it to /editAttraction.do:

```
        saveErrors(request,errors);
        return new ActionForward(mapping.getInput());

    }

}
```

Logging Off

The very last use case is logging off; congratulations on making it this far! Authenticated attraction managers users may log off from the system by clicking on the Logoff link on the menu. This will invalidate the current session (which makes the server forget that they were authenticated) and display the welcome page; since they are now logged off, only the links applicable to public users will be shown on the menu.

The sequence of actions is rather similar to that for deregistering, but for the (important) distinction that in this case we don't call the business method for deregistering the attraction! The sequence of events is:

1. When the users click on the Logoff link, the request is sent to /logoff.do, which is mapped to the action class LogoffAction.

2. The session is then invalidated and the response is **redirected** to /home.do.

3. If an exception is thrown, we create an action error object and go to /editAttraction.do.

The sequence diagram below illustrates this:

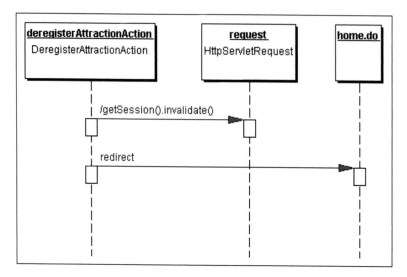

The /logoff.do Action Mapping

The request URL /logoff.do is mapped to corresponding action class, com.wrox.tourism.actions.LogoffAction. We define a local forward named "success" mapping to the resource /home.do. Note that, as with the /deregister.do action, the redirect attribute is set to "true" for this local forward. If an error occurs, we want to be forwarded to /editAttraction.do.

```
    . . .
    <action path="/logoff"
      type="com.wrox.tourism.actions.LogoffAction"
      input="/editAttraction.do">
      <forward name="success" path="/home.do" redirect="true"/>
    </action>
    . . .
```

LogoffAction

And so to our final action class:

```
    package com.wrox.tourism.actions;

    import org.apache.struts.action.ActionForm;
    import org.apache.struts.action.ActionForward;
    import org.apache.struts.action.Action;
    import org.apache.struts.action.ActionMapping;
    import org.apache.struts.action.ActionErrors;
    import org.apache.struts.action.ActionError;
    import org.apache.struts.action.ActionServlet;

    import javax.servlet.http.HttpServletRequest;
    import javax.servlet.http.HttpServletResponse;
```

```
import javax.servlet.ServletException;

import java.io.IOException;

import java.sql.Connection;
import java.sql.SQLException;

import java.util.Collection;

public class LogoffAction extends Action {

  public ActionForward perform(ActionMapping mapping,ActionForm form,
    HttpServletRequest request,HttpServletResponse response)
      throws IOException,ServletException {

  ActionErrors errors = new ActionErrors();

  try {
```

This action is nice and simple. First we invalidate the session:

```
    request.getSession().invalidate();
```

and then we redirect the response to /home.do:

```
    return mapping.findForward("success");

} catch (Throwable e) {
  e.printStackTrace();
  ActionError error = new ActionError(e.getMessage());
  errors.add(ActionErrors.GLOBAL_ERROR,error);
}
```

If an exception occurs, we create an action errors object, store it as a request attribute, and forward it to /editAttraction.do:

```
  saveErrors(request,errors);
  return new ActionForward(mapping.getInput());

  }

}
```

Configuring and Running the Application

We did it – that's all the Java code and JSPs for our application written! There were a lot of components to our site, but they're all pretty straightforward and self-contained. Hopefully you should be able to see that writing the site this way was a lot easier than creating a "bowl of spaghetti" type application, with everything tossed together so that it's hard to figure just which bits of code do what.

We do still have a little more work to do: we need to pull together all the entries we need to place in our deployment descriptor, web.xml, and we need to do the same for the Struts configuration file.

Deployment Descriptor

In this section, we will have a look at the complete listing of the deployment descriptor. As we have already seen, the deployment descriptor will contain the following pieces of information:

❑ Action servlet declaration

❑ Initialization parameter for the action servlet, to identify the application message resource

❑ Mapping the request URL *.do to the action servlet

❑ Database initialization servlet declaration

❑ Initialization parameters for the database initialization servlet

❑ "Welcome file" mapping pointing to /home.do

❑ Tag library declarations

❑ Security constraints

❑ Login configuration

The resources that should be accessible only by users with the attraction role are:

❑ /editAttraction.do: Edits the attraction details

❑ /updateAttraction.do: Updates the attraction details

❑ /deregisterAttraction.do: Deregisters the attraction

❑ /listEvents.do: Lists the events

❑ /editEvent.jsp: Presents a new form for adding events

❑ /editEvent.do: Edits an event

❑ /updateEvent.do: Updates an event

❑ /deleteEvent.do: Deletes an event

The source listing for the deployment descriptor is as follows:

```
<?xml version="1.0" encoding="ISO-8859-1"?>

<!DOCTYPE web-app
  PUBLIC "-//Sun Microsystems, Inc.//DTD Web Application 2.2//EN"
  "http://java.sun.com/j2ee/dtds/web-app_2_2.dtd">

<web-app>

  <!-- Standard Action Servlet Configuration -->
  <servlet>
    <servlet-name>action</servlet-name>
    <servlet-class>org.apache.struts.action.ActionServlet</servlet-class>
```

```xml
    <init-param>
      <param-name>application</param-name>
      <param-value>TourismResources</param-value>
    </init-param>
    <load-on-startup>2</load-on-startup>
</servlet>


<!-- Servlet for initialising datasources -->
<servlet>
  <servlet-name>dbInit</servlet-name>
  <servlet-class>com.wrox.tourism.db.util.DBInitServlet</servlet-class>
  <init-param>
    <param-name>driverClass</param-name>
    <param-value>org.gjt.mm.mysql.Driver</param-value>
  </init-param>
  <init-param>
    <param-name>jdbcURL</param-name>
    <param-value>jdbc:mysql://localhost:3306/tourism_db</param-value>
  </init-param>
  <init-param>
    <param-name>minCount</param-name>
    <param-value>1</param-value>
  </init-param>
  <init-param>
    <param-name>maxCount</param-name>
    <param-value>10</param-value>
  </init-param>
  <load-on-startup>1</load-on-startup>
</servlet>


<!-- Standard Action Servlet Mapping -->
<servlet-mapping>
  <servlet-name>action</servlet-name>
  <url-pattern>*.do</url-pattern>
</servlet-mapping>


<welcome-file-list>
  <welcome-file>index.jsp</welcome-file>
</welcome-file-list>


<!-- Struts Tag Library Descriptors -->
<taglib>
  <taglib-uri>/bean</taglib-uri>
  <taglib-location>/WEB-INF/struts-bean.tld</taglib-location>
</taglib>

<taglib>
  <taglib-uri>/html</taglib-uri>
  <taglib-location>/WEB-INF/struts-html.tld</taglib-location>
</taglib>

<taglib>
  <taglib-uri>/logic</taglib-uri>
  <taglib-location>/WEB-INF/struts-logic.tld</taglib-location>
</taglib>
```

```
<taglib>
  <taglib-uri>/template</taglib-uri>
  <taglib-location>/WEB-INF/struts-template.tld</taglib-location>
</taglib>


<!-- These actions require the user to be logged in as an attraction -->
<security-constraint>
  <web-resource-collection>
    <web-resource-name>Edit attraction</web-resource-name>
    <url-pattern>/editAttraction.do</url-pattern>
  </web-resource-collection>
  <web-resource-collection>
    <web-resource-name>Update attraction</web-resource-name>
    <url-pattern>/updateAttraction.do</url-pattern>
  </web-resource-collection>
  <web-resource-collection>
    <web-resource-name>Deregister attraction</web-resource-name>
    <url-pattern>/deregisterAttraction.do</url-pattern>
  </web-resource-collection>
  <web-resource-collection>
    <web-resource-name>List events</web-resource-name>
    <url-pattern>/listEvents.do</url-pattern>
  </web-resource-collection>
  <web-resource-collection>
    <web-resource-name>Add event</web-resource-name>
    <url-pattern>/editEvent.jsp</url-pattern>
  </web-resource-collection>
  <web-resource-collection>
    <web-resource-name>Edit event</web-resource-name>
    <url-pattern>/editEvent.do</url-pattern>
  </web-resource-collection>
  <web-resource-collection>
    <web-resource-name>Update event</web-resource-name>
    <url-pattern>/updateEvent.do</url-pattern>
  </web-resource-collection>
  <web-resource-collection>
    <web-resource-name>Delete event</web-resource-name>
    <url-pattern>/deleteEvent.do</url-pattern>
  </web-resource-collection>

  <auth-constraint>
    <role-name>attraction</role-name>
  </auth-constraint>
</security-constraint>


<!-- Require form-based login -->
<login-config>
  <auth-method>FORM</auth-method>
  <form-login-config>
    <form-login-page>/login.jsp</form-login-page>
    <form-error-page>/login.jsp</form-error-page>
  </form-login-config>
</login-config>

</web-app>
```

Struts Configuration

We have already covered all the elements of the Struts configuration file, `struts-config.xml`. The complete listing for this file is shown below:

```xml
<?xml version="1.0" encoding="ISO-8859-1" ?>

<!DOCTYPE struts-config PUBLIC
          "-//Apache Software Foundation//DTD Struts Configuration 1.0//EN"
          "http://jakarta.apache.org/struts/dtds/struts-config_1_0.dtd">

<struts-config>

  <form-beans>
    <form-bean name="attractionForm"
      type="com.wrox.tourism.entity.Attraction"/>
    <form-bean name="eventForm" type="com.wrox.tourism.entity.Event"/>
  </form-beans>

  <action-mappings>

    <action path="/home"
      type="com.wrox.tourism.actions.HomeAction"
      unknown="true">
      <forward name="success" path="/home.jsp"/>
    </action>

    <action path="/viewAttraction"
      type="com.wrox.tourism.actions.ViewAttractionAction"
      input="/home.do">
      <forward name="success" path="/viewAttraction.jsp"/>
    </action>

    <action path="/registerAttraction"
      type="com.wrox.tourism.actions.RegisterAttractionAction"
      input="/registerAttraction.jsp"
      name="attractionForm"
      scope="request">
      <forward name="success" path="/confirmRegistration.jsp"/>
    </action>

    <action path="/editAttraction"
      type="com.wrox.tourism.actions.EditAttractionAction"
      input="/home.do">
      <forward name="success" path="/editAttraction.jsp"/>
    </action>

    <action path="/updateAttraction"
      type="com.wrox.tourism.actions.UpdateAttractionAction"
      input="/editAttraction.jsp"
      name="attractionForm"
      scope="request">
      <forward name="success" path="/confirmUpdate.jsp"/>
    </action>

    <action path="/listEvents"
      type="com.wrox.tourism.actions.ListEventsAction"
      input="/editAttraction.do">
      <forward name="success" path="/listEvents.jsp"/>
```

```
      </action>

      <action path="/editEvent"
        type="com.wrox.tourism.actions.EditEventAction"
        input="/listEvents.do">
          <forward name="success" path="/editEvent.jsp"/>
      </action>

      <action path="/updateEvent"
        type="com.wrox.tourism.actions.UpdateEventAction"
        input="/editEvent.jsp"
        name="eventForm"
        scope="request">
          <forward name="success" path="/listEvents.do"/>
      </action>

      <action path="/deleteEvent"
        type="com.wrox.tourism.actions.DeleteEventAction"
        input="/listEvents.do">
          <forward name="success" path="/listEvents.do"/>
      </action>

      <action path="/deregisterAttraction"
        type="com.wrox.tourism.actions.DeregisterAttractionAction"
        input="/editAttraction.do">
          <forward name="success" path="/home.do" redirect="true"/>
      </action>

      <action path="/logoff"
        type="com.wrox.tourism.actions.LogoffAction"
        input="/editAttraction.do">
          <forward name="success" path="/home.do" redirect="true"/>
      </action>

  </action-mappings>

</struts-config>
```

Building the Application

Finally, we need to put all the pieces together.

1. We need to put all the pieces of the web application itself together. Create a folder called `begjsp-tourism`, inside Tomcat's webapps folder, to hold all the pieces of our application; its name will be something like `C:\jakarta-tomcat-4.0\webapps\begjsp-tourism`.

2. Inside it, you'll need to use this structure:

```
confirmRegistration.jsp
confirmUpdate.jsp
editAttraction.jsp
editAttractionContent.jsp
editEvent.jsp
editEventContent.jsp
home.jsp
homeContent.jsp
index.jsp
```

```
listEvents.jsp
listEventsContent.jsp
login.jsp
loginContent.jsp
menu.jsp
registerAttraction.jsp
registerAttractionContent.jsp
template.jsp
viewAttraction.jsp
viewAttractionContent.jsp

WEB-INF\
        createtables.sql
        struts-bean.tld
        struts-config.xml
        struts-html.tld
        struts-logic.tld
        struts-template.tld
        web.xml

WEB-INF\classes\
                TourismResources.properties
                compile.bat

WEB-INF\classes\com\wrox\tourism\actions\
                                BeanNames.java
                                DeleteEventAction.java
                                DeregisterAttractionAction.java
                                EditAttractionAction.java
                                EditEventAction.java
                                HomeAction.java
                                ListEventsAction.java
                                LogoffAction.java
                                RegisterAttractionAction.java
                                UpdateAttractionAction.java
                                UpdateEventAction.java
                                ViewAttractionAction.java

WEB-INF\classes\com\wrox\tourism\business\
                                AttractionBO.java
                                AttractionException.java
                                EventBO.java
                                EventException.java
                                Role.java

WEB-INF\classes\com\wrox\tourism\db\
                                AttractionDAO.java
                                CreateException.java
                                DuplicateKeyException.java
                                EventDAO.java
                                FinderException.java
                                NoSuchEntityException.java
                                ObjectNotFoundException.java
                                UserRoleDAO.java

WEB-INF\classes\com\wrox\tourism\db\util\
                                ConnectionPool.java
                                DBInitServlet.java
```

747

```
WEB-INF\classes\com\wrox\tourism\entity\
                                        Attraction.java
                                        Event.java
                                        UserRole.java

WEB-INF\lib\
            crimson.jar
            jaxp.jar
            struts.jar
```

The files `struts.jar`, `struts-bean.tld`, `struts-html.tld`, `struts-logic.tld`, and `struts-template.tld` come as part of Struts. `jaxp.jar` and `crimson.jar` are part of the Java API for XML Processing; copy these (don't move them!) from Tomcat's `server\lib` folder into our application's `WEB-INF\lib` folder.

3. Compile all the Java classes; you'll need to have the `struts.jar` file in the classpath for this to work. You'll find that in the code download for the book we've provided a Windows batch file `compile.bat` in the `WEB-INF\classes` directory; running this will compile all the code for you.

4. Use the MySQL command-line interface to create all the database tables from the scripts we described in Chapter 19.

5. Copy the MySQL JDBC driver file (`mm.mysql-2.0.4-bin.jar` or similar) into Tomcat's `common\lib` folder. Note that the application *won't* work if we just put it in the application's `WEB-INF\lib` directory – since we're using Tomcat's built-in authentication features Tomcat itself needs to know how to talk to the database.

6. Finally, you need to add an entry to Tomcat's `server.xml` file. You may find this file a bit intimidating, but what you need to do is find the bit about three fourths of the way through where it says:

```
        </Host>

      </Engine>

    </Service>
```

you want to add the following immediately before the `</Host>` entry:

```
    ...
        </Context>

        <Context path="/begjsp-tourism" docBase="begjsp-tourism" debug="0"
                reloadable="true">
          <Realm className="org.apache.catalina.realm.JDBCRealm" debug="99"
                driverName="org.gjt.mm.mysql.Driver"
                connectionURL="jdbc:mysql://localhost:3306/tourism_db"
                userTable="attraction" userNameCol="user_id"
                userCredCol="password" userRoleTable="user_role"
                roleNameCol="role_name" />
        </Context>
```

```
        </Host>

     </Engine>

  </Service>
...
```

7. All done. To run the application, you need to start your database server, start Tomcat, and point your web browser to http://localhost:8080/begjsp-tourism/. And explore!

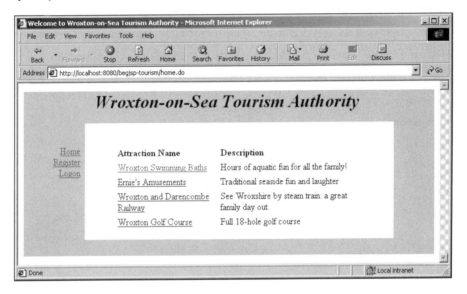

Enhancing the Application

You might find it interesting to experiment with adding extra features to our tourism database application, to get you started; here are some ideas:

❑ At the moment the internationalization only applies to the error messages, and we haven't actually added any translations of those messages. Try adding a new language; you could also try converting our JSPs so that rather than containing any English-specific text they use the `<bean:message>` tag to retrieve internationalized messages from the `TourismResources.properties` file.

❑ If there were a lot of attractions or events, our pages would get very large. You could try to modify the JSPs so that it lists these maybe ten at a time. There is a "pager" tag library which you might find useful for this; you can find it at http://jsptags.com/tags/navigation/pager/.

❑ Similarly, if the number of attractions is getting excessive users might appreciate the ability to search for an attraction rather than having to browse through the list.

❑ People who visit Wroxton-on-Sea often might be keen to register so that our site e-mails them when new attractions or events are added; this could be hidden inside our attraction and event business objects.

Summary

In the last two chapters we have designed and developed a real world web application built on Struts; we also covered:

- ❏ All aspects of the analysis, design, development and deployment phases of the project.

- ❏ Extensive usage of UML (Unified Modeling Language) for modeling both the dynamic and static aspects of the system.

- ❏ Almost all aspects of the Struts framework.

- ❏ Various aspects of security: authentication, authorization, custom security realms, etc.

- ❏ Using the Model 2 architecture for properly partitioning the web application.

- ❏ Use of business objects and data access objects.

- ❏ Database connection pooling.

- ❏ Internationalization.

- ❏ Dynamic template management.

We've come a long way since the start of the book; we hope you're just waiting to get started with developing your own web applications using JSP, Servlets, and Java. Have fun!

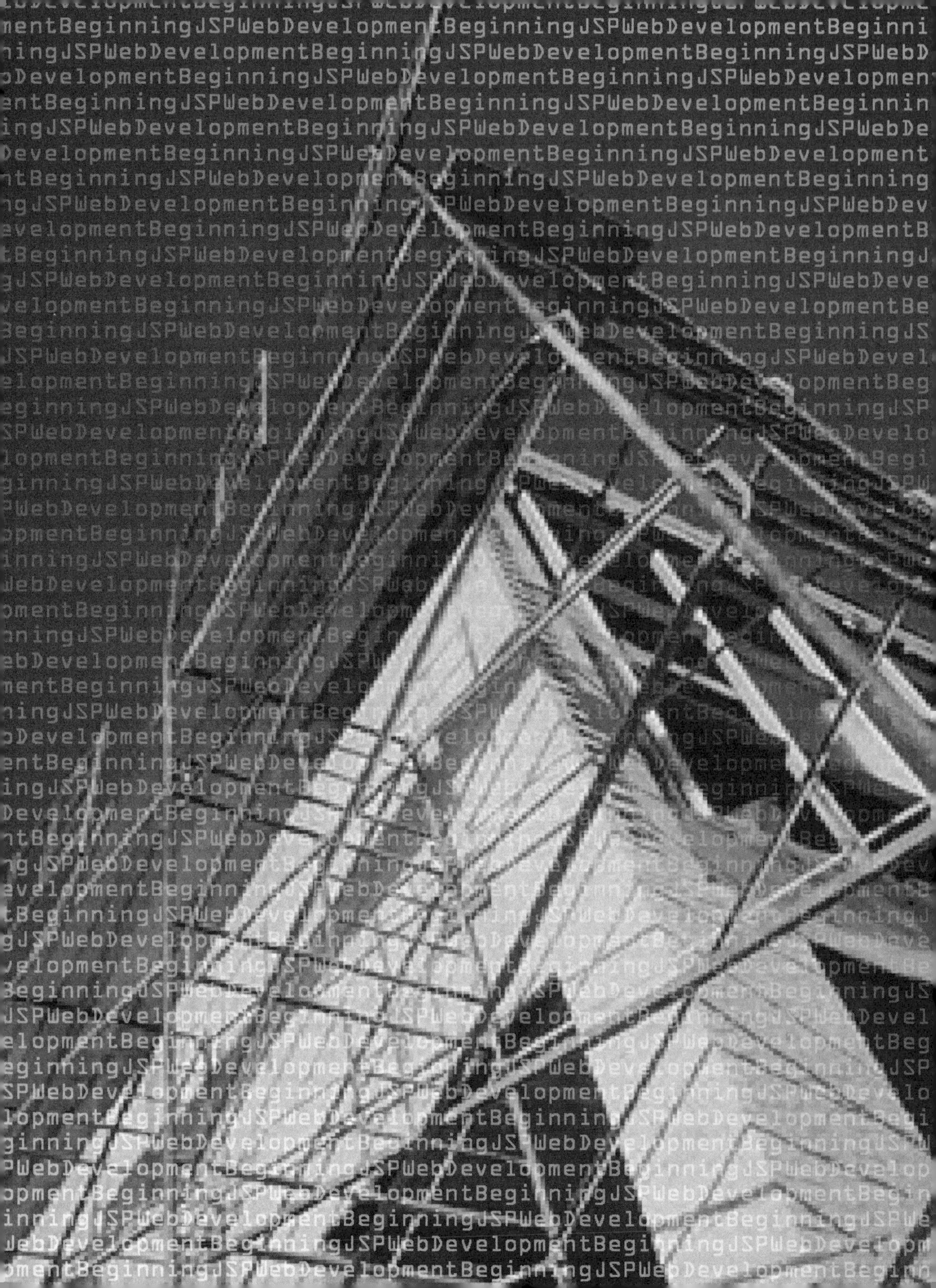
BeginningJSPWebDevelopment

JSP Syntax Reference

This appendix describes the syntax for JavaServer Pages 1.2. Our intention is to provide you with a reference that is complete and useful, but more compact than the specification. (The JSP 1.2 Proposed Final Draft specification weighs in at 243 pages!)

> **JSP specifications from version 1.0 upwards are available from http://java.sun.com/products/jsp/.**

This appendix looks in turn at:

❑   Various preliminary details: the notation we're using, how URLs are specified in JSP code, and the various types of commenting you can use.

❑   The JSP **directives** – the page, taglib, and include directives.

❑   JSP **scripting elements** – declarations, scriptlets, and expressions.

❑   JSP's **standard actions** including the `<jsp:useBean>`, `<jsp:setProperty>`, `<jsp:getProperty>`, `<jsp:include>`, and `<jsp:forward>` actions.

❑   A brief review of the syntax for using **tag libraries**.

❑   The **implicit objects** that are available within a JSP such as `request`, `response`, `session`, and `application`.

❑   Various predefined request and application **attributes** that you may find useful.

Preliminaries

Before we get stuck into the details, a few miscellaneous observations.

Notation

A word on the notation we've used in this appendix:

- ❑ *Italics* show what you'll have to specify.

- ❑ **Bold** shows the default value of an attribute. Attributes with default values are optional, if you're using the default. Sometimes, where the default value is a little complicated, we use **default** to indicate that the default is described in the following text.

- ❑ When an attribute has a set of possible values, those are shown delimited by |.

URL Specifications

URLs specified within JSP tags can be of two sorts:

- ❑ **Context-relative** paths start with a "/"; the base URL is provided by the web application to which the JSP belongs. For example, in a web application hosted at http://localhost:8080/begjsp-appendixA/, the URL "/urlspec.jsp" refers to http://localhost:8080/begjsp-appendixA/urlspec.jsp.

- ❑ **Page-relative** paths are interpreted relative to the JSP page in which they occur.

Comments

Two sorts of comments are allowed in JSP code – JSP and HTML:

```
<!-- HTML comments remain in the final client page.
    They can include JSP expressions.
-->

<%-- JSP comments are hidden from the final client page --%>
```

Remember too that within Java code (inside <% %>, <%! %>, or <%= %> tags) you can use standard Java comments:

```
<%
    /* This Java comments starts with a slash asterisk, and continues
        until we come to a closing asterisk slash
    */

    // This Java comment continues to the end of the current line
%>
```

Directives

Directives are instructions to the JSP container regarding page properties, importing tag libraries, and including content within a JSP.

The page Directive

The page directive specifies attributes for the page – all the attributes are optional, as the essential ones have default values, shown in bold.

```
<%@ page language="java"
        extends="package.class"
        import="package.class, package.*, ..."
        session="true|false"
        buffer="none|default|sizekb"
        autoFlush="true|false"
        isThreadSafe="true|false"
        info="Sample JSP to show tags"
        isErrorPage="true|false"
        errorPage="ErrorPage.jsp"
        contentType="TYPE|
                    TYPE; charset=CHARSET|
                    text/html; charset=ISO-8859-1"
        pageEncoding="default"
%>
```

❑   The default buffer size is defined to be *at least* 8kb.

❑   The errorPage attribute contains the relative URL for the error page to which this page should go if there's an un-handled error on this page.

❑   The specified error page file must declare isErrorPage="true" to have access to the Exception object.

❑   The contentType attribute sets the MIME type and the character set for the response.

❑   The pageEncoding attribute defines the character encoding for the JSP page. The default is that specified in the contentType attribute, or "ISO-8859-1" if none was specified there.

```
<%@ page language="java"
        isErrorPage="true" %>

<html>
<body>
<!-- The fully-qualified class that is the exception -->
<%= exception.toString() %>
<br>
<!-- The exception's message to the world -->
<%= exception.getMessage() %>
</body>
</html>
```

The taglib Directive

The taglib directive defines a tag library namespace for the page, mapping the URI of the tag library descriptor to a prefix that can be used to reference tags from the library on this page.

```
<%@ taglib uri="/META-INF/taglib.tld" prefix="tagPrefix" %>

...
```

```
<tagPrefix:tagName attributeName="attributeValue" >
  JSP content
</tagPrefix:tagName>

<tagPrefix:tagName attributeName="attributeValue" />
```

The include Directive

There are two include tags – the `include` directive and the `jsp:include` action.

The `include` directive includes a static file at translation time, adding any JSP in that file to this page for run-time processing:

```
<%@ include file="header.html" %>
```

See also the `jsp:include` action.

Scripting Elements

Scripting elements are used to include snippets of Java code within a JSP to declare variables and methods, execute arbitrary Java code, and display the result of Java expressions.

Declarations

The following syntax allows you to declare variables and methods for the page. These are placed in the generated Servlet *outside* the `_jspService()` method, in other words variables declared here will be instance variables of the Servlet:

```
<%!
  int i = 0;
  char ch = 'a';
  boolean isTrue(boolean b) {
    // Is this true?
  }
%>
```

Declaration tags are rarely used.

Scriptlets

Scriptlets enclose Java code (on however many lines) that is evaluated *within* the generated Servlet's `_jspService()` method to generate dynamic content:

```
<%
  // Java code
%>
```

756

Take care when using adjacent scriptlet blocks – this code:

```
<% if(user.isLoggedIn) { %>
    <p>Hi!</p>
<% } %>
<% else { %>
    <p>Please log in first...</p>
<% } %>
```

is not legal since the line break between the `<% } %>` and `<% else { %>` scriptlet blocks is treated as template text to be returned to the client.

Expressions

Expressions return a value from the scripting code as a `String` to the page:

```
<p>Hello there,
<%= userName %>
Good to see you.</p>
```

Standard Actions

The standard actions provide various facilities for manipulating JavaBeans components, including and forwarding control to other resources at request-time, and generating HTML to use the Java Plug-in.

<jsp:useBean>

The `<jsp:useBean>` tag checks for an instance of a bean of the given `class` and `scope`. If a bean of the specified class exists it references it with the `id`, otherwise it instantiates it. The bean is available within its `scope` with its `id` attribute.

You can include code between the `<jsp:useBean>` tags, as shown in the second example – this code will only be run if the `<jsp:useBean>` tag successfully instantiated the bean:

```
<jsp:useBean id="aBeanName"
             scope="page|request|session|application"
             typeSpecification
/>
```

or:

```
<jsp:useBean id="anotherBeanName"
             scope="page|request|session|application"
             typeSpecification
  <jsp.setProperty name="anotherBeanName"
                   property="*|propertyName" />
</jsp:useBean>
```

There is a lot of flexibility in specifying the type of the bean (indicated by *typeSpecification* above). You can use:

- ❏ class="*package.class*"
- ❏ type="*typeName*"
- ❏ class="*package.class*" type="*typeName*" (and with terms reversed)
- ❏ beanName="*beanName*" type="*typeName*" (and with terms reversed)

where:

- ❏ typeName is the class of the scripting variable defined by the id attribute; that is, the class that the bean instance is cast to (whether the class, a parent class or an interface the class implements).
- ❏ beanName is the name of the bean, as used in the instantiate() method of the java.beans.Beans class.

<jsp:setProperty>

The <jsp:setProperty> tag we used above sets the property of the bean referenced by name using the value:

```
<jsp.setProperty name="anotherBeanName"
                 propertyExpression
/>
```

The *propertyExpression* can be any of the following:

- ❏ property="*"
- ❏ property="*propertyName*"
- ❏ property="*propertyName*" param="*parameterName*"
- ❏ property="*propertyName*" value="*propertyValue*"

where:

- ❏ The * setting tells the tag to iterate through the request parameters for the page, setting any values for properties in the bean whose names match parameter names.
- ❏ The param attribute specifies the parameter name to use in setting this property.
- ❏ The value attribute can be any run-time expression as long as it evaluates to a String.
- ❏ Omitting value and param attributes for a property assumes that the bean property and request parameter name match.
- ❏ The value attribute String can be automatically cast to boolean, byte, char, double, int, float, long, and their class equivalents. Other casts will have to be handled explicitly in the bean's set*PropertyName*() method.

<jsp:getProperty>

The final bean-handling action is `<jsp:getProperty>`, which gets the named property and outputs its value for inclusion in the page as a `String`:

```
<jsp:getProperty name="anotherBeanName" property="propertyName" />
```

<jsp:param>

The `<jsp:param>` action is used within the body of `<jsp:forward>`, `<jsp:include>`, and `<jsp:plugin>` to supply extra name value parameter pairs. It has the following syntax:

```
<jsp:param name="parameterName" value="parameterValue" />
```

<jsp:forward>

To forward the client request to another URL, whether it be an HTML file, JSP or Servlet, use the following syntax:

```
<jsp:forward page="relativeURL" />
```

or:

```
<jsp:forward page="relativeURL" >
  <jsp:param name="parameterName" value="parameterValue" />
</jsp:forward>
```

where:

❑   The `page` attribute for `<jsp:forward>` can be a run-time expression

❑   The `value` attribute for `<jsp:param>` can be a run-time expression

<jsp:include>

The `<jsp:include>` action includes a static or dynamically-referenced file at run-time:

```
<jsp:include page="relativeURL" flush="true|false" />
```

or:

```
<jsp:include page="relativeURL"
             flush="true" >
  <jsp:param name="parameterName" value="parameterValue"/>
</jsp:include>
```

where:

- ❏ The `page` attribute can be the result of some run-time expression.

- ❏ The optional `flush` attribute determines whether the output buffer will be flushed before including the specified resource. The default value is `"false"`. (Note that in JSP 1.1 this attribute was mandatory and the only permissible value was `"true"`.)

- ❏ The `jsp:param` tag allows parameters to be appended to the original request, and if the parameter `name` already exists, the new parameter `value` takes precedence, in a comma-delimited list.

<jsp:plugin>

The `<jsp:plugin>` action enables the JSP to include a bean or an applet in the client page. It has the following syntax:

```
<jsp:plugin type="bean|applet"
            code="class"
            codebase="classDirectory"
            name="instanceName"
            archive="archiveURI"
            align="bottom|top|middle|left|right"
            height="inPixels"
            width="inPixels"
            hspace="leftRightPixels"
            vspace="topBottomPixels"
            jreversion="1.2|number"
            nspluginurl="pluginURL"
            iepluginurl="pluginURL" >
  <jsp:params>
    <jsp:param name="parameterName" value="parameterValue">
  </jsp:params>
  <jsp:fallback>Problem with plugin</jsp:fallback>
</jsp:plugin>
```

Most of these attributes are direct from the HTML spec – the exceptions are `type`, `jreversion`, `nspluginurl` and `iepluginurl`.

- ❏ The `name`, `archive`, `align`, `height`, `width`, `hspace`, `vspace`, `jreversion`, `nspluginurl`, and `iepluginurl` attributes are optional.

- ❏ The `<jsp:param>` tag's `value` attribute can take a run-time expression

- ❏ The `jreversion` is the Java Runtime Environment specification version that the component requires

- ❏ `nspluginurl` and `iepluginurl` are the URL where the Java plugin can be downloaded for Netscape Navigator and Internet Explorer

Tag Libraries

The syntax for using tag libraries is very similar to that for the standard actions, except of course that the tag names and attributes are defined in the tag library itself rather than by the JSP standard. Each tag library is associated with a **prefix**, by using the `taglib` directive to map the prefix to a URI identifying the tag library. For example, using the Jakarta Taglibs project's `request` tag library (http://jakarta.apache.org/taglibs/doc/request-doc/intro.html):

```
<%@ taglib uri="http://jakarta.apache.org/taglibs/request-1.0" prefix="req"
%>
```

Within the JSP, tags from the library can then be used by using the prefix defined in the `taglib` directive and the tag's name, for example:

```
<req:attributes id="loop">
 Name: <jsp:getProperty name="loop" property="name"/>
 Value: <jsp:getProperty name="loop" property="value"/>
</req:attributes>
```

The mapping between a particular URI (as used in the taglib directive) and the tag library descriptor can be set up in one of two ways. In JSP 1.2, it is possible to package tag libraries so that the mapping is automatic, based on settings contained in the tag library descriptor file. Alternatively, an entry can be made in the `web.xml` file to map a URI to a tag library descriptor file:

```
...
<taglib>
  <taglib-uri>http://jakarta.apache.org/taglibs/request-1.0</taglib-uri>
  <taglib-location>/WEB-INF/request.tld</taglib-location>
</taglib>
...
```

Implicit Objects

JSP defines a number of implicit objects that JSP scripting elements can make use of:

❑   request, of type `javax.servlet.http.HttpServletRequest`

❑   response, of type `javax.servlet.http.HttpServletResponse`

❑   out, of type `javax.servlet.jsp.JspWriter`

❑   session, of type `javax.servlet.http.HttpSession`

❑   application, of type `javax.servlet.ServletContext`

❑   exception, of type `java.lang.Throwable`

❑   config, of type `javax.servlet.ServletConfig`

❑   page, a reference to the implementing servlet class for the JSP

❑   pageContext, of type `javax.servlet.jsp.PageContext`

Appendix B gives details of these objects, and the methods that each makes available. There are many more classes and interfaces defined by the JSP and Servlet specifications; to find out more about them, you should consult the online documentation as described in Appendix D.

Predefined Attributes

The Servlet and JSP specifications define a number of special request and context (application) attributes.

Security-Related Attributes

These attributes are only available when a request has been made over SSL.

javax.servlet.request.cipher_suite

`javax.servlet.request.cipher_suite` is a request attribute of type `String` containing the cipher suite used for an SSL request.

javax.servlet.request.key_size

`javax.servlet.request.key_size` is a request attribute of type `Integer` containing the bit size that was used for an SSL request.

javax.servlet.request.X509Certificate

`javax.servlet.request.X509Certificate` is a request attribute of type `java.security.cert.X509Certificate` containing any certificate associated with an SSL request.

Inclusion-Related Attributes

These attributes are available when a Servlet or JSP is accessed via a `RequestDispatcher.include()` or a `<jsp:include>`.

javax.servlet.include.request_uri

`javax.servlet.include.request_uri` is a request attribute of type `String` containing the URI under which this included Servlet or JSP is being accessed.

javax.servlet.include.context_path

`javax.servlet.include.context_path` is a request attribute of type `String` containing the context path of the URI under which this included Servlet or JSP is being accessed.

javax.servlet.include.servlet_path

`javax.servlet.include.servlet_path` is a request attribute of type `String` containing the servlet path of the URI under which this included Servlet or JSP is being accessed.

javax.servlet.include.path_info

`javax.servlet.include.path_info` is a request attribute of type `String` containing the path info of the URI under which this included Servlet or JSP is being accessed.

javax.servlet.include.query_string

`javax.servlet.include.query_string` is a request attribute of type `String` containing the query string of the URI under which this included Servlet or JSP is being accessed.

Servlet Error Page Attributes

These attributes are only available within an error page declared in `web.xml`.

javax.servlet.error.status_code

`javax.servlet.error.status_code` is a request attribute of type `Integer` containing the status code of the Servlet or JSP that caused the error.

javax.servlet.error.exception_type

`javax.servlet.error.exception_type` is a request attribute of type `Class` that contains the type of the exception thrown by the Servlet or JSP. It is now redundant with the introduction of the `javax.servlet.error.exception` attribute.

javax.servlet.error.message

`javax.servlet.error.message` is a request attribute of type `String` containing the message contained within the exception thrown by the Servlet or JSP. It is now redundant with the introduction of the `javax.servlet.error.exception` attribute.

javax.servlet.error.exception

`javax.servlet.error.exception` is a request attribute of type `Throwable` containing the exception thrown by the Servlet or JSP.

javax.servlet.error.request_uri

`javax.servlet.error.request_uri` is a request attribute of type `String` containing the URI of the request that caused the Servlet or JSP to throw an exception.

JSP Error Page Attributes

This attribute is available within error pages declared in a JSP's `<%@ page %>` directive.

javax.servlet.jsp.jspException

`javax.servlet.jsp.jspException` is a request attribute of type `Throwable` containing the exception thrown by the JSP.

Temporary File Directory Attribute

This attribute allows a web application to make use of a temporary working directory.

javax.servlet.context.tempdir

`javax.servlet.context.tempdir` is a context attribute of type `java.io.File` referencing a temporary working directory that can be used by the web application.

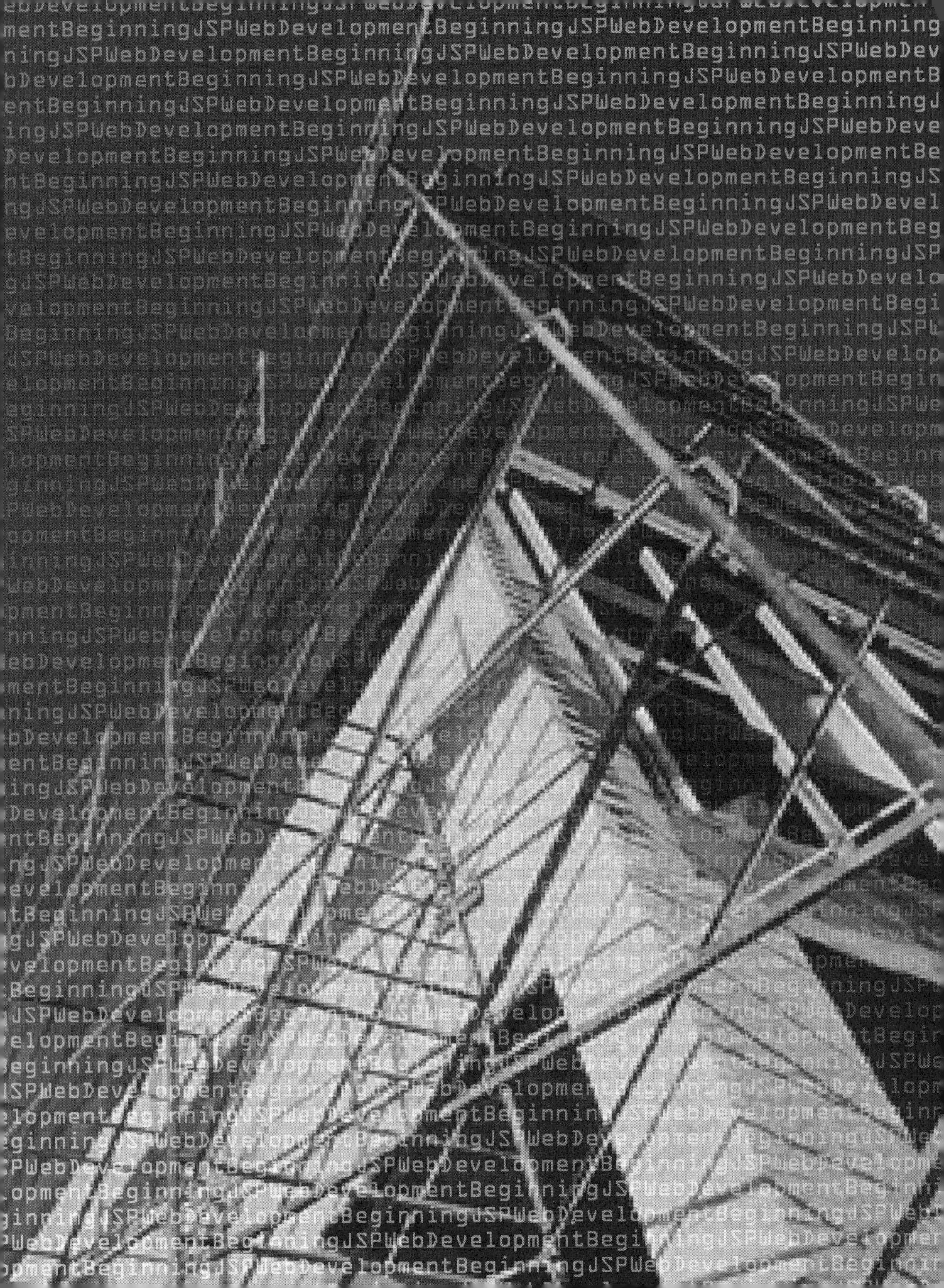
BeginningJSPWebDevelopment

JSP Implicit Objects

JSP defines a number of implicit objects that scripting elements can make use of. This appendix gives details of these objects, and the methods that each makes available. There are many more classes and interfaces defined by the JSP and Servlet specifications; to find out more about them, you should consult the online documentation as described in Appendix D.

*This appendix lists **all** the methods available for each object (except those defined in* `java.lang.Object`*), irrespective of which class or interface defines the methods.*

The implicit objects are:

- [ ] request
- [ ] response
- [ ] out
- [ ] session
- [ ] application
- [ ] exception
- [ ] config
- [ ] page
- [ ] pageContext

The request Object

The `request` object is an instance of a class that implements the `javax.servlet.http.HttpServletRequest` interface. It represents the request made by the client, and makes the following methods available:

```
public Object getAttribute(String name)
```

getAttribute() returns the value of the specified request attribute name. The return value is an Object or sub-class if the attribute is available to the invoking ServletRequest object, or null if the attribute is not available.

```
public java.util.Enumeration getAttributeNames()
```

getAttributeNames() returns an Enumeration containing the attribute names available to the invoking ServletRequest object.

```
public String getAuthType()
```

getAuthType() returns the name of the authentication scheme used in the request, or null if no authentication scheme was used.

```
public String getCharacterEncoding()
```

getCharacterEncoding() returns a String object containing the character encoding used in the body of the request, or null if there is no encoding.

```
public int getContentLength()
```

getContentLength() returns the length of the body of the request in bytes, or −1 if the length is not known.

```
public String getContentType()
```

getContentType() returns a String object containing the MIME type ("text/plain", "text/html", "image/gif", etc.) of the body of the request, or null if the type is not known.

```
public String getContextPath()
```

getContextPath() returns the part of the request URI that indicates the context path of the request. The context path is the first part of the URI and always begins with the "/" character. For servlets running in the root context, this method returns an empty String.

```
public Cookie[] getCookies()
```

getCookies() returns an array containing any Cookie objects sent with the request, or null if no cookies were sent.

```
public long getDateHeader(String name)
```

getDateHeader() returns a long value that converts the date specified in the named header to the number of milliseconds since January 1, 1970 GMT. This method is used with a header that contains a date, and returns −1 if the request does not contain the specified header.

```
public String getHeader(String name)
```

getHeader() returns the value of the specified header expressed as a `String` object, or `null` if the request does not contain the specified header.

    public java.util.Enumeration **getHeaders**(String *name*)

getHeaders() returns an `Enumeration` containing all of the values associated with the specified header name. The method returns an empty enumeration if the request does not contain the specified header.

    public java.util.Enumeration **getHeaderNames**()

getHeaderNames() returns an `Enumeration` containing all of the header names used by the request.

    public ServletInputStream **getInputStream**()
            throws java.io.IOException

getInputStream() returns a `ServletInputStream` object that can be used to read the body of the request as binary data.

    public int **getIntHeader**(String *name*)

getIntHeader() returns the value of the specified header as an `int`. It returns −1 if the request does not contain the specified header, and throws a `NumberFormatException` if the header value cannot be converted to an `int`.

    public java.util.Locale **getLocale**()

getLocale() returns the preferred locale of the client that made the request.

    public java.util.Enumeration **getLocales**()

getLocales() returns an `Enumeration` containing, in descending order of preference, the locales that are acceptable to the client machine.

    public String **getMethod**()

getMethod() returns the name of the HTTP method used to make the request. Typical return values are "GET", "POST", or "PUT".

    public String **getParameter**(String *name*)

getParameter() returns a `String` object containing the value of the specified parameter, or `null` if the parameter does not exist.

    public java.util.Map **getParameterMap**()

getParameterMap() returns a Map containing the request parameters.

```
public java.util.Enumeration getParameterNames()
```

getParameterNames() returns a Enumeration containing the parameters contained within the invoking ServletRequest object.

```
public String[] getParameterValues(String name)
```

getParamterValues() is used when a parameter may have more than one value associated with it. The method returns a String array containing the values of the specified parameter, or null if the parameter does not exist.

```
public String getPathInfo()
```

getPathInfo() returns any additional path information contained in the request URL. This extra information will be after the Servlet path and before the query string. It returns null if there is no additional path information.

```
public String getPathTranslated()
```

getPathTranslated() returns the same information as the getPathInfo() method, but translated into a real path.

```
public String getProtocol()
```

getProtocol() returns the name and version of the protocol used by the request. A typical return String would be "HTTP/1.1".

```
public String getQueryString()
```

getQueryString() returns the query string that was contained in the request URL, or null if there was no query string.

```
public java.io.BufferedReader getReader()
        throws java.io.IOException
```

getReader() returns a BufferedReader object that can be used to read the body of the request as character data.

```
public String getRemoteAddr()
```

getRemoteAddr() returns a String object containing the IP address of the client machine that made the request.

```
public String getRemoteHost()
```

getRemoteHost() returns a `String` object containing the name of the client machine or the IP address if the name cannot be determined.

```
public String getRemoteUser()
```

getRemoteUser() returns the login of the user making the request, or `null` if the user has not been authenticated.

```
public RequestDispatcher getRequestDispatcher(String path)
```

getRequestDispatcher() returns a `RequestDispatcher` object that acts as a wrapper around the resource located at the specified path. The path must begin with "/" and can be a relative path.

```
public String getRequestedSessionId()
```

getRequestedSessionId() returns the session ID that was specified by the client, or `null` if the request did not specify an ID.

```
public String getRequestURI()
```

getRequestURI() returns a subsection of the request URL, from the protocol name to the query string.

```
public StringBuffer getRequestURL()
```

getRequestURL() reconstructs the URL used to make the request including the protocol, server name, port number, and path, but excluding the query string.

```
public String getScheme()
```

getScheme() returns the scheme ("http", "https", "ftp", etc.) used to make the request.

```
public String getServerName()
```

getServerName() returns a `String` object containing the name of the server that received the request.

```
public int getServerPort()
```

getServerPort() returns the port number that received the request.

```
public String getServletPath()
```

getServletPath() returns the part of the request URL that was used to call the servlet, without any additional information or the query string.

```
public HttpSession getSession(boolean create)
public HttpSession getSession()
```

getSession() returns the HttpSession object associated with the request. By default, if the request does not currently have a session, calling this method will create one. Setting the boolean parameter create to false overrides this.

```
public boolean isRequestedSessionIdValid()
```

isRequestedSessionIdValid() returns true if the session ID requested by the client is still valid.

```
public boolean isRequestedSessionIdFromCookie()
```

isRequestedSessionIdFromCookie() returns true if the session ID came in from a cookie.

```
public boolean isRequestedSessionIdFromURL()
```

isRequestedSessionIdFromURL() returns true if the session ID came in as part of the request URL.

```
public boolean isSecure()
```

isSecure() returns true if the request was made using a secure channel, for example HTTPS.

```
public boolean isUserInRole(String role)
```

isUserInRole() returns a true if the authenticated user has the specified logical role, or false if the user is not authenticated.

```
public void removeAttribute(String name)
```

removeAttribute() makes the specified attribute unavailable to the invoking ServletRequest object. Subsequent calls to the getAttribute() method for this attribute will return null.

```
public void setAttribute(String name,
                         Object o)
```

setAttribute() binds a value to a specified attribute name. Note that attributes will be reset after the request is handled.

```
public void setCharacterEncoding(String env)
       throws java.io.UnsupportedEncodingException
```

setCharacterEncoding() overrides the character encoding used in the body of this request.

```
public static final String BASIC_AUTH
public static final String FORM_AUTH
public static final String CLIENT_CERT_AUTH
public static final String DIGEST_AUTH
```

These `String` constants are used to identify the different types of authentication that may have been used to protect the servlet. They have the values `"BASIC"`, `"FORM"`, `"CLIENT_CERT"`, and `"DIGEST"` respectively.

```
public String getRealPath(String path)
public boolean isRequestedSessionIdFromUrl()
```

These methods are deprecated and should not be used in new code – they exist for compatibility with existing code.

The response Object

The `response` object is an instance of a class that implements the `javax.servlet.http.HttpServletResponse` interface. It represents the response to be made to the client, and makes the following methods available:

```
public void addCookie(Cookie cookie)
```

`addCookie()` adds the specified cookie to the response (more than one cookie can be added).

```
public void addDateHeader(String name,
                          long date)
```

`addDateHeader()` adds a response header containing the specified header name and the number of milliseconds since January 1, 1970 GMT. This method can be used to assign multiple values to a given header name.

```
public void addHeader(String name,
                      String value)
```

`addHeader()` adds a response header with the specified `name` and `value`. This method can be used to assign multiple values to a given header name.

```
public void addIntHeader(String name,
                         int value)
```

`addIntHeader()` adds a response header with the specified name and `int` value. This method can be used to assign multiple values to a given header name.

```
public boolean containsHeader(String name)
```

`containsHeader()` returns `true` if the response header includes the specified header name. This method can be used before calling one of the `set()` methods to determine if the value has already been set.

```
public String encodeURL(String url)
```

773

encodeURL() encodes the specified URL by including the session ID or returns it unchanged if encoding is not needed. All URLs generated by a servlet should be processed through this method to ensure compatibility with browsers that do not support cookies.

```
public String encodeRedirectURL(String url)
```

encodeRedirectURL() encodes the specified URL or returns it unchanged if encoding is not required. This method is used to process a URL before sending it to the sendRedirect() method.

```
public void flushBuffer()
        throws java.io.IOException
```

flushBuffer() causes any content stored in the buffer to be written to the client. Calling this method will also commit the response, meaning that the status code and headers will be written.

```
public int getBufferSize()
```

getBufferSize() returns the buffer size used for the response, or 0 if no buffering is used.

```
public String getCharacterEncoding()
```

getCharacterEncoding() returns a String object containing the character encoding used in the body of the response. The default is "ISO-8859-1", which corresponds to Latin-1.

```
public java.util.Locale getLocale()
```

getLocale() returns the locale that has been assigned to the response. By default, this will be the default locale for the server.

```
public ServletOutputStream getOutputStream()
        throws java.io.IOException
```

getOutputStream() returns a ServletOutputStream object that can be used to write the response as binary data.

```
public java.io.PrintWriter getWriter()
        throws java.io.IOException
```

getWriter() returns a PrintWriter object that can be used to write the response as character data.

```
public boolean isCommitted()
```

isCommitted() returns true if the response has been committed, meaning that the status code and headers have been written.

```
public void reset()
```

`reset()` clears the status code and headers, and any data that exists in the buffer. If the response has already been committed, calling this method will cause an exception to be thrown.

```
public void resetBuffer()
```

`resetBuffer()` clears the content of the response buffer without clearing the headers or status code. It will throw an `IllegalStateException` if the response has been committed.

```
public void sendError(int sc,
                      String msg)
       throws java.io.IOException
public void sendError(int sc)
       throws java.io.IOException
```

`sendError()` sends an error response back to the client machine using the specified error status code. A descriptive message can also be provided. This method must be called before the response is committed (in other words, before the status code and headers have been written).

```
public void sendRedirect(String location)
       throws java.io.IOException
```

`sendRedirect()` redirects the client machine to the specified URL. This method must be called before the response is committed (in other words, before the status code and headers have been written).

```
public void setBufferSize(int size)
```

`setBufferSize()` requests a buffer size to be used for the response. The actual buffer size will be at least this large.

```
public void setContentLength(int len)
```

`setContentLength()` sets the length of response body.

```
public void setDateHeader(String name,
                          long date)
```

`setDateHeader()` sets the time value of a response header for the specified header name. The time is the number of milliseconds since January 1, 1970 GMT. If the time value for the specified header has been previously set, the value passed to this method will override it.

```
public void setContentType(String type)
```

`setContentType()` sets the content type of the response sent to the server. The `String` argument specifies a MIME type and may also include the type of character encoding, for example `"text/plain; charset=ISO-8859-1"`.

```
public void setHeader(String name,
                      String value)
```

775

`setHeader()` sets a response header with the specified `name` and `value`. If the value for the specified header has been previously set, the value passed to this method will override it.

```
public void setIntHeader(String name,
                         int value)
```

`setIntHeader()` sets a response header with the specified name and `int` value. If the `int` value for the specified header has been previously set, the value passed to this method will override it.

```
public void setLocale(java.util.Locale loc)
```

`setLocale()` specifies the locale that will be used for the response.

```
public void setStatus(int sc)
```

`setStatus()` sets the return status code for the response. The status code should be one of SC_ACCEPTED, SC_OK, SC_CONTINUE, SC_PARTIAL_CONTENT, SC_CREATED, SC_SWITCHING_PROTOCOLS, or SC_NO_CONTENT.

```
public static final int SC_CONTINUE
public static final int SC_SWITCHING_PROTOCOLS
public static final int SC_OK
public static final int SC_CREATED
public static final int SC_ACCEPTED
public static final int SC_NON_AUTHORITATIVE_INFORMATION
public static final int SC_NO_CONTENT
public static final int SC_RESET_CONTENT
public static final int SC_PARTIAL_CONTENT
public static final int SC_MULTIPLE_CHOICES
public static final int SC_MOVED_PERMANENTLY
public static final int SC_MOVED_TEMPORARILY
public static final int SC_SEE_OTHER
public static final int SC_NOT_MODIFIED
public static final int SC_USE_PROXY
public static final int SC_BAD_REQUEST
public static final int SC_UNAUTHORIZED
public static final int SC_PAYMENT_REQUIRED
public static final int SC_FORBIDDEN
public static final int SC_NOT_FOUND
public static final int SC_METHOD_NOT_ALLOWED
public static final int SC_NOT_ACCEPTABLE
public static final int SC_PROXY_AUTHENTICATION_REQUIRED
public static final int SC_REQUEST_TIMEOUT
public static final int SC_CONFLICT
public static final int SC_GONE
public static final int SC_LENGTH_REQUIRED
public static final int SC_PRECONDITION_FAILED
public static final int SC_REQUEST_ENTITY_TOO_LARGE
public static final int SC_REQUEST_URI_TOO_LONG
public static final int SC_UNSUPPORTED_MEDIA_TYPE
public static final int SC_REQUESTED_RANGE_NOT_SATISFIABLE
public static final int SC_EXPECTATION_FAILED
```

```
public static final int SC_INTERNAL_SERVER_ERROR
public static final int SC_NOT_IMPLEMENTED
public static final int SC_BAD_GATEWAY
public static final int SC_SERVICE_UNAVAILABLE
public static final int SC_GATEWAY_TIMEOUT
public static final int SC_HTTP_VERSION_NOT_SUPPORTED
```

These constants represent the status codes defined in the HTTP specification.

```
public String encodeUrl(String url)
public String encodeRedirectUrl(String url)
public void setStatus(int sc,
                      String sm)
```

These methods are deprecated and should not be used in new code – they exist for compatibility with existing code.

The out Object

The out object is an instance of the javax.servlet.jsp.JspWriter class. It is used to create the content returned to the client, and has the following useful methods available:

```
public abstract void clear()
        throws java.io.IOException
```

clear() clears the contents of the buffer; it throws an exception if some data has already been written to the output stream.

```
public abstract void clearBuffer()
        throws java.io.IOException
```

clearBuffer() clears the contents of the buffer, but does not throw an exception if some data has already been written to the output stream.

```
public abstract void close()
        throws java.io.IOException
```

close() flushes and then closes the output stream.

```
public abstract void flush()
        throws java.io.IOException
```

flush() flushes the output buffer and sends any bytes contained in the buffer to their intended destination. flush() will flush all the buffers in a chain of Writers and OutputStreams.

```
public int getBufferSize()
```

`getBufferSize()` returns the size in bytes of the output buffer.

```
    public abstract int getRemaining()
```

`getRemaining()` returns the number of bytes still contained in the buffer.

```
    public boolean isAutoFlush()
```

`isAutoFlush()` returns `true` if the buffer flushes automatically when an overflow condition occurs.

```
    public abstract void newLine()
            throws java.io.IOException
```

`newLine()` writes a new line character to the output stream.

```
    public abstract void print(boolean b)
            throws java.io.IOException
    public abstract void print(char c)
            throws java.io.IOException
    public abstract void print(int i)
            throws java.io.IOException
    public abstract void print(long l)
            throws java.io.IOException
    public abstract void print(float f)
            throws java.io.IOException
    public abstract void print(double d)
            throws java.io.IOException
    public abstract void print(char[] s)
            throws java.io.IOException
    public abstract void print(String s)
            throws java.io.IOException
    public abstract void print(Object obj)
            throws java.io.IOException
```

`print()` prints the specified primitive data type, `Object` or `String` to the client.

```
    public abstract void println()
            throws java.io.IOException
    public abstract void println(boolean x)
            throws java.io.IOException
    public abstract void println(char x)
            throws java.io.IOException
    public abstract void println(int x)
            throws java.io.IOException
    public abstract void println(long x)
            throws java.io.IOException
    public abstract void println(float x)
            throws java.io.IOException
    public abstract void println(double x)
            throws java.io.IOException
    public abstract void println(char[] x)
            throws java.io.IOException
```

```
public abstract void println(String x)
        throws java.io.IOException
public abstract void println(Object x)
        throws java.io.IOException
```

`println()` prints the specified primitive data type, `Object` or `String` to the client, followed by a newline character at the end. The no-argument version simply writes a newline character.

```
public void write(int c)
        throws IOException
public void write(char[] c)
        throws IOException
public void write(char[] c,
                int offset,
                int length)
        throws IOException
public void write(String str)
        throws IOException
public void write(String str,
                int offset,
                int length)
        throws IOException
```

`write()` writes to the client a single character, an array of characters, a portion of an array of characters, a `String`, or a portion of a `String`.

The session Object

The `session` object is an instance of a class that implements the `javax.servlet.http.HttpSession` interface. It can be used to store session state for a user, and makes the following methods available:

```
public Object getAttribute(String name)
```

`getAttribute()` returns the `Object` bound to the specified name in this session, or `null` if it doesn't exist.

```
public java.util.Enumeration getAttributeNames()
```

`getAttributeNames()` returns an `Enumeration` of `String` objects containing the names of all the objects bound to this session.

```
public long getCreationTime()
```

`getCreationTime()` returns the time when the session was created in milliseconds since midnight Jan 1, 1970 GMT.

```
public String getId()
```

getId() returns a `String` object containing a unique identifier for this session

```
public long getLastAccessedTime()
```

getLastAccessedTime() returns the last time a client request associated with the session was sent. The return value is the number of milliseconds since midnight Jan 1, 1970 GMT.

```
public int getMaxInactiveInterval()
```

getMaxInactiveInterval() returns the number of seconds the server will wait between client requests before the session is invalidated. A negative return value indicates the session will never time out.

```
public void invalidate()
```

invalidate() invalidates the session and unbinds any objects bound to it.

```
public boolean isNew()
```

isNew() returns true if the server has created a session that has not yet been accessed by a client.

```
public void removeAttribute(String name)
```

removeAttribute() removes the Object bound to the specified name from this session.

```
public void setAttribute(String name,
                          Object value)
```

setAttribute() binds an Object to the specified attribute name, in this session. If the attribute name already exists, the Object passed to this method will replace the previous Object.

```
public void setMaxInactiveInterval(int interval)
```

setMaxInactiveInterval() specifies the number of seconds the server will wait between client requests before the session is invalidated. If a negative value is passed to this method, the session will never time out.

```
public HttpSessionContext getSessionContext()
public Object getValue(String name)
public String[] getValueNames()
public void putValue(String name,
                      Object value)
public void removeValue(String name)
```

These methods are deprecated and should not be used in new code – they exist for compatibility with existing code.

The application Object

The `application` object is an instance of a class that implements the `javax.servlet.ServletContext` interface, and allows the page to obtain information about the web application in which it is running. It makes the following methods available:

```
public Object getAttribute(String name)
```

`getAttribute()` returns the value of the specified attribute name. The return value is an `Object` or sub-class if the attribute is available to the invoking `ServletContext` object, or `null` if the attribute is not available.

```
public java.util.Enumeration getAttributeNames()
```

`getAttributeNames()` returns an `Enumeration` containing the attribute names available to the invoking `ServletContext` object.

```
public ServletContext getContext(String uripath)
```

`getContext()` returns the `ServletContext` object for the resource at the specified path on the server. The path argument is an absolute URL beginning with "/".

```
public String getInitParameter(String name)
```

`getInitParameter()` returns a `String` object containing the value of the specified initialization parameter, or `null` if the parameter does not exist.

```
public java.util.Enumeration getInitParameterNames()
```

`getInitParameterNames()` returns a `Enumeration` containing the initialization parameters associated with the invoking `ServletContext` object.

```
public int getMajorVersion()
```

`getMajorVersion()` returns the major version of the Java Servlet API that the server supports. For servers supporting version 2.3 of the Servlet specification, this method will return 2.

```
public String getMimeType(String file)
```

`getMimeType()` returns the MIME type of the specified file or `null` if the MIME type cannot be ascertained. Typical return values will be "text/plain", "text/html", or "image/jpg".

```
public int getMinorVersion()
```

`getMinorVersion()` returns the minor version of the Java Servlet API that the server supports. For servers supporting version 2.3 of the Servlet specification, this method will return 3.

```
public RequestDispatcher getNamedDispatcher(String name)
```

getNamedDispatcher() returns a RequestDispatcher object that will be wrapped around the named servlet.

```
public String getRealPath(String path)
```

getRealPath() returns a String object containing the real path, in a form appropriate to the platform on which the servlet is running, corresponding to the given virtual path. An example of a virtual path might be "/blah.html".

```
public RequestDispatcher getRequestDispatcher(String path)
```

getRequestDispatcher() returns a RequestDispatcher object that acts as a wrapper around the resource located at the specified path. The path must begin with "/", and is interpreted relative to the current context root.

```
public java.util.Set getResourcePaths()
```

getResourcePaths() returns all the paths to resources held in the web application as Strings beginning with a "/".

```
public java.net.URL getResource(String path)
        throws java.net.MalformedURLException
```

getResource() returns a URL object that is mapped to the specified path, or null if there is no resource mapped to the path. The path must begin with "/" and is interpreted relative to the current context root.

```
public java.io.InputStream getResourceAsStream(String path)
```

getResourceAsStream() returns the resource at the specified path as an InputStream object.

```
public String getServerInfo()
```

getServerInfo() returns a String object containing information on the server on which the servlet is running. At a minimum, the String will contain the servlet container name and version number.

```
public String getServletContextName()
```

getServletContextName() returns the name of the web application, as specified in the <display-name> element in web.xml.

```
public void log(String msg)
public void log(String message,
                Throwable throwable)
```

`log()` is used to write a message to the servlet engine's log file. The second version writes both an explanatory message and a stack trace for the specified `Throwable` exception to the log file.

```
public void removeAttribute(String name)
```

`removeAttribute()` makes the specified attribute unavailable to the invoking `ServletContext` object. Subsequent calls to the `getAttribute()` method for this attribute will return `null`.

```
public void setAttribute(String name,
                         Object object)
```

`setAttribute()` binds a value to a specified attribute name.

```
public Servlet getServlet(String name)
        throws ServletException
public java.util.Enumeration getServlets()
public java.util.Enumeration getServletNames()
public void log(Exception exception,
                String msg)
```

These methods are deprecated and should not be used in new code – they exist for compatibility with existing code.

The exception Object

The `exception` object is an instance of the `java.lang.Throwable` class. It is available in error pages only, and represents the exception that occurred that caused control to pass to the error page. Its most useful methods are:

```
public String getMessage()
```

`getMessage()` returns the error message string of this `Throwable` object.

```
public String getLocalizedMessage()
```

`getLocalizedMessage()` returns a localized description of this `Throwable` object. (In many cases, this will return the same result as `getMessage()`.)

```
public String toString()
```

`toString()` returns a short description of this `Throwable` object. If an error message was supplied when the object was created, the result is the `Throwable` class's name, followed by a colon and a space, followed by that message.

```
public void printStackTrace()
public void printStackTrace(PrintStream ps)
public void printStackTrace(PrintWriter pw)
```

`printStackTrace()` prints information about this `Throwable` object, along with a listing of the method calls that led to the error condition arising. The output can be directed to the standard error stream, or to a specified `PrintStream` or `PrintWriter` object.

The config Object

The `config` object is an instance of the `javax.servlet.ServletConfig` interface. It is used to make initialization parameters available, and has the following methods:

    public String getInitParameter(String name)

`getInitParameter()` returns the value of the specified initialization parameter, or `null` if the parameter does not exist.

    public java.util.Enumeration getInitParameterNames()

`getInitParameterNames()` returns an `Enumeration` of `String` objects containing the names of all of the servlet's initialization parameters.

    public ServletContext getServletContext()

`getServletContext()` returns the `ServletContext` object associated with the invoking servlet. A `ServletContext` object contains information about the environment in which the servlet is running.

    public String getServletName()

`getServletName()` returns the name of the servlet. If the servlet is unnamed, the method will return the servlet's class name.

The page Object

The `page` object is a reference to the servlet object that implements this JSP page. JSP page authors do not often use this object.

The pageContext Object

The `pageContext` object is an instance of the `javax.servlet.jsp.PageContext` class, and is used by the container-generated servlet code for your JSP to access the various scopes available within the JSP. JSP page authors do not often use this object, though it is important when writing tag libraries.

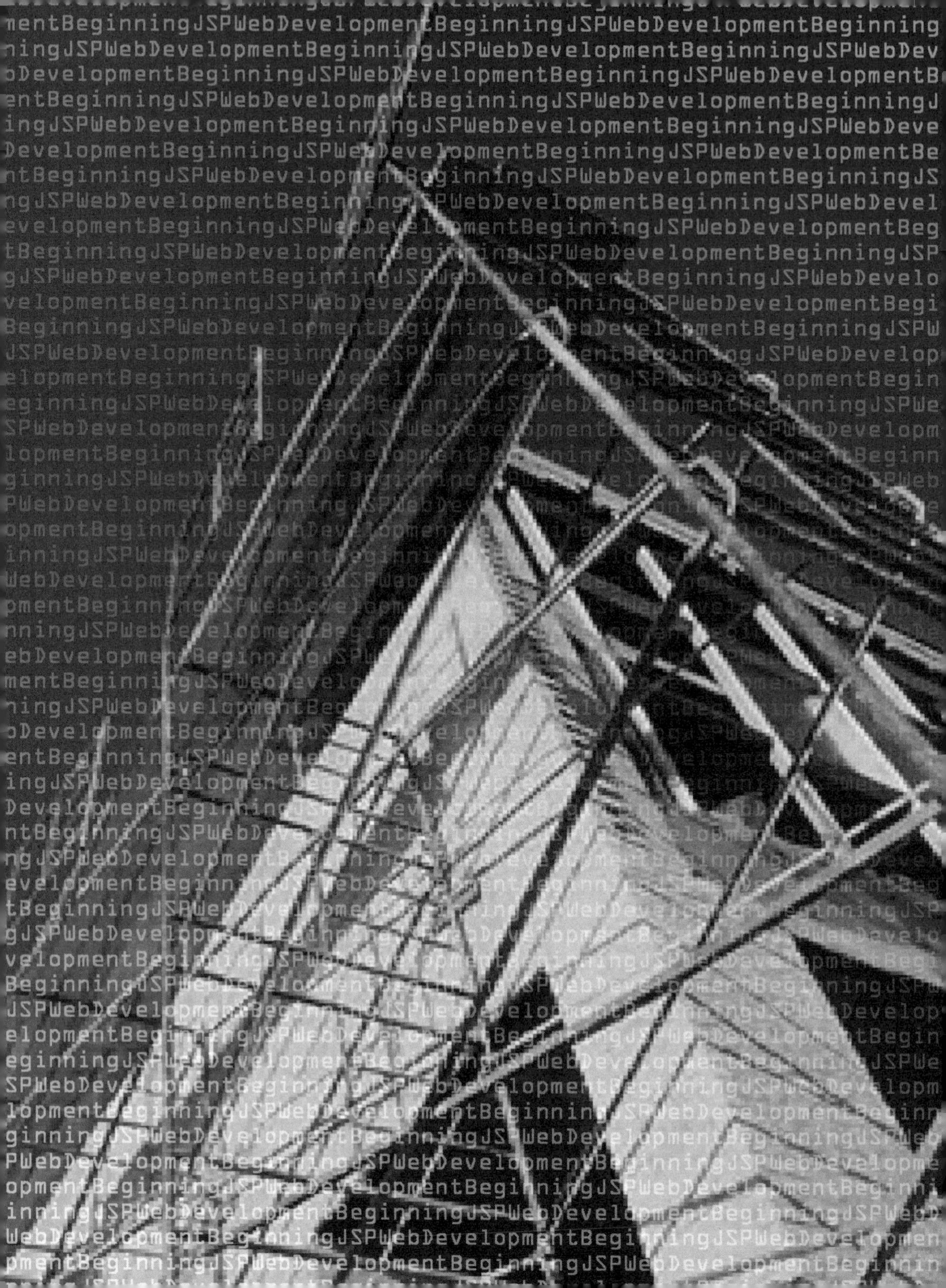

XML Data Formats

This appendix documents the three types of XML-based data we've encountered in the course of this book:

- ❑ The web application deployment descriptor file (web.xml)
- ❑ Tag library descriptor (.tld) files
- ❑ The Struts configuration file (struts-config.xml)

> *For full details, and for the XML format for JSP files, consult the Servlet and JSP specifications at http://java.sun.com/products/servlet/ and http://java.sun.com/products/jsp/ and the Struts documentation that's included in the download.*

We start, however, with a quick review of XML itself. This chapter is not a complete tutorial on XML, but should cover enough to get you up and running with reading and writing these XML-format files.

The Structure of XML Data

XML, the **eXtensible Markup Language**, is superficially similar to HTML but there are some notable differences:

- ❑ You can **define your own tags** (**elements**), to express the structure of your data.
- ❑ XML is **case-sensitive**: <Servlet> is not the same thing as <servlet>.
- ❑ Attribute values must be enclosed within **quotation marks**, attribute="value" or attribute='value'.
- ❑ Elements must be **correctly nested**, so that Hello! is illegal: it must be Hello!.
- ❑ Elements must be **closed**; if an element has no content you must either use <element></element> or the shortcut <element/>.
- ❑ An XML document must have one element at the top level, the **root element**. A minimal XML document would be:

```
<?xml version="1.0"?>
<root>
</root>
```

❑ This example also shows us that XML documents should begin with the XML prolog. This can also define the character encoding for the file, for example `<?xml version="1.0"? encoding="iso-8859-1">`.

Document Type Definitions

A **Document Type Definition** (**DTD**) is the way to specify the particular data format being used in an XML file. Since you can define your own tags, it's necessary to specify how they work: their names, the attributes they can have, and how they fit together.

Locating the DTD

The first thing we need to do is to tell the program reading our XML file which DTD is being used; we do this with the `DOCTYPE` declaration. This takes several forms, for example:

```
<!DOCTYPE photographs SYSTEM "photos.dtd">
```

This specifies that the DTD is contained in `photos.dtd` in the same folder as the XML file.

```
<!DOCTYPE photographs SYSTEM
 "http://www.quarry-siding.com/gallery/photos.dtd">
```

This specifies the location of the DTD as a URL. However, the method we will use here is to specify a **public identifier**, which may be recognized by the program reading the XML file allowing it to use its own local copy of the DTD rather than having to access the web. For example, the `DOCTYPE` declaration for the `web.xml` file reads:

```
<!DOCTYPE web-app
 PUBLIC "-//Sun Microsystems, Inc.//DTD Web Application 2.3//EN"
 "http://java.sun.com/j2ee/dtds/web-app_2_3.dtd">
```

The public identifier `"-//Sun Microsystems, Inc.//DTD Web Application 2.3//EN"` will be recognized by Tomcat.

It is also possible to include the DTD within the document itself; however, it is better just to reference it from your own file.

The Root Element

The `DOCTYPE` declaration also indicates what the root element of the document will be: it's specified by the entry after the word `DOCTYPE`. So, if the lines at the top of our `struts-config.xml` file are:

```
<!DOCTYPE struts-config PUBLIC
 "-//Apache Software Foundation//DTD Struts Configuration 1.0//EN"
 "http://jakarta.apache.org/struts/dtds/struts-config_1_0.dtd">
```

788

we are saying that the root element of this document is `<struts-config>`.

Elements

Elements are declared using the ELEMENT declaration. This specifies both the name of the element and the type of content it can accept, in this form:

```
<!ELEMENT name content-model>
```

For example:

```
<!ELEMENT photographs (photo+)>
```

A `<photographs>` element contains one or more `<photo>` elements.

```
<!ELEMENT photo (name,description?,gallery*,(color|bw))>
```

A `<photo>` element contains a `<name>` element, an optional `<description>` element, and 0 or more `<gallery>` elements, and either a `<color>` or a `<bw>` element.

```
<!ELEMENT name (#PCDATA)>
```

A `<name>` element contains character data, in other words text.

```
<!ELEMENT bw EMPTY>
```

The `<bw>` element may not have any content.

The full set of operators that can be used to describe element content is:

Symbol	Meaning
,	Strict ordering: elements must be in the specified order
|	One of the specified types of content must be used
+	1 or more
*	0 or more
?	Optional (0 or 1)
( )	Grouping

Attributes

We also need to declare the attributes that our elements can have. Attribute declarations have this form:

```
<!ATTLIST element-name attribute-defs>
```

And each attribute definitions has this form:

```
attribute-name attribute-type default-declarations
```

The possible attribute types are:

Attribute type	Meaning
CDATA	Textual data
ID	A textual value unique in the document
IDREF	A reference to an ID attribute in the document
NMTOKEN	Textual data without whitespace
NMTOKENS	Comma-separated list of NMTOKEN values
(true|false)	A restricted set of possible values, between (and) characters and separated by | characters

The possible default declarations are:

Default value declaration	Meaning
#REQUIRED	The attribute must be provided
#IMPLIED	The attribute is optional
#FIXED "default text"	The attribute must always have the supplied default value
"default text"	A default value may be supplied

Some examples:

```
<!ATTLIST forward name CDATA #REQUIRED>
```

The <forward> element has an attribute, name, which must be supplied and takes textual data.

```
<!ATTLIST action parameter CDATA #IMPLIED>
```

The <action> element has an attribute, parameter, which is optional and takes textual data.

```
<!ATTLIST action scope (request|session) #IMPLIED>
```

The <action> element has an attribute, scope, which is optional; however, if it is supplied, its value must be "request" or "session".

Entities

Finally, we come to entities. There are various types of entity, however the only one we encounter in any of the DTDs we're interested in are parameter entities, which are a simple form of textual substitution used in `struts-config.xml` to make the DTD more readable. For example, we can define an entity called `Boolean`:

```
<!ENTITY % Boolean "(true|false|yes|no)">
```

If we later use the sequence `%Boolean;` in our DTD, it is replaced with the text `(true|false|yes|no)` defined above. For example, this line:

```
<!ATTLIST forward redirect %Boolean; #IMPLIED>
```

would be interpreted as:

```
<!ATTLIST forward redirect (true|false|yes|no) #IMPLIED>
```

> **This has not been a comprehensive introduction to XML by any means. For more information, see *Beginning XML* from Wrox Press, ISBN 1-861003-41-2.**

Web Application Deployment Descriptor

The `DOCTYPE` declaration at the head of a Servlet 2.3 web application deployment descriptor (`web.xml`) file should be:

```
<!DOCTYPE web-app
  PUBLIC "-//Sun Microsystems, Inc.//DTD Web Application 2.3//EN"
  "http://java.sun.com/j2ee/dtds/web-app_2_3.dtd">
```

Note that within the `web.xml` file the ordering of elements is significant; failure to have the elements in the correct order is a common problem, especially when moving an application from an old web container that used a non-validating XML parser to a more recent one that does validate the XML. (In Servlet 2.3, validation of the `web.xml` file is recommended.)

Servlet 2.3-compatible web containers are also required to accept a `web.xml` file using the Servlet 2.2 format; this is included as an appendix to the Servlet 2.3 specification.

Common Elements

The `<description>`, `<display-name>`, and `<icon>` elements can occur in several places within `web.xml` and we will describe them only once, here.

<description>

The `<description>` element is used in a number of places within the `web.xml` file to provide a description of its parent element.

<display-name>

The <display-name> element contains a short name for its parent element, for GUI tools to display.

<icon>

The <icon> element references icons (GIF and JPEG formats must be accepted by tools) that will be used by a GUI tool to represent its parent element. It contains:

❑ An optional <small-icon> element containing the location within the application of a 16x16 pixel icon

❑ An optional <large-icon> element containing the location within the application of a 32x32 pixel icon

<web-app> – Root Element

The <web-app> element is the root element of the web.xml file. It contains:

❑ An optional (in other words 0 or 1) <icon> element

❑ An optional <display-name> element

❑ An optional <description> element

❑ An optional <distributable> element

❑ 0 or more <context-param> elements

❑ 0 or more <filter> elements

❑ 0 or more <filter-mapping> elements

❑ 0 or more <listener> elements

❑ 0 or more <servlet> elements

❑ 0 or more <servlet-mapping> elements

❑ An optional <session-config> element

❑ 0 or more <mime-mapping> elements

❑ An optional <welcome-file-list> element

❑ 0 or more <error-page> elements

❑ 0 or more <taglib> elements

❑ 0 or more <resource-env-ref> elements

❑ 0 or more <resource-ref> elements

❑ 0 or more <security-constraint> elements

❑ An optional <login-config> element

❑ 0 or more <security-role> elements

❑ 0 or more <env-entry> elements

❑ 0 or more <ejb-ref> elements

Subelements of <web-app>

The permissible subelements of <web-app> (other than those already described) are as follows.

<distributable>

The <distributable> element, if present, declares that this web application can be deployed in a distributed servlet container.

<context-param>

The <context-param> element declares a context initialization parameter. It contains:

- ❑ A <param-name> element containing the parameter's name
- ❑ A <param-value> element containing the parameter's value
- ❑ An optional <description> element (see earlier description)

<filter>

The <filter> element declares a filter. It contains:

- ❑ An optional <icon> element
- ❑ A <filter-name> element containing the filter's name
- ❑ An optional <display-name> element
- ❑ An optional <description> element
- ❑ A <filter-class> element containing the filter's class name
- ❑ 0 or more <init-param> elements containing initialization parameters for the filter

Each <init-param> element contains:

- ❑ A <param-name> element containing the parameter name
- ❑ A <param-value> element containing the parameter value
- ❑ An optional <description> element

<filter-mapping>

The <filter-mapping> element is used to map a filter to a servlet or a set of URLs. It contains:

- ❑ A <filter-name> element containing the name of a filter declared by a <filter> element
- ❑ Either a <url-pattern> element containing a URL pattern to match, or a <servlet-name> element containing the name of a servlet declared by a <servlet> element

<listener>

The <listener> element is used to declare an application listener. It contains:

- ❑ A <listener-class> element containing the listener's class name.

<servlet>

The <servlet> element declares a servlet. It contains:

- ❑ An optional <icon> element
- ❑ A <servlet-name> element containing the servlet's name
- ❑ An optional <display-name> element
- ❑ An optional <description> element
- ❑ Either a <servlet-class> element containing the listener's class name, or a <jsp-file> element containing the location within the web application of a JSP file
- ❑ 0 or more <init-param> elements
- ❑ An optional <load-on-startup> element indicating that the servlet should be loaded when the web application starts up, and containing an optional positive integer value indicating the order in which servlets should be started. If a <jsp-file> was specified, then the JSP should be precompiled and loaded
- ❑ 0 or more <security-role-ref> elements

Each <init-param> element contains:

- ❑ A <param-name> element containing the parameter name
- ❑ A <param-value> element containing the parameter value
- ❑ An optional <description> element

A <security-role-ref> element maps a role name called from within the servlet, and the name of a security role defined for the web application. It contains:

- ❑ An optional <description> element
- ❑ A <role-name> element containing the role name used within the servlet
- ❑ A <role-link> element containing the name of a role defined in a <security-role> element

<servlet-mapping>

The <servlet-mapping> element maps a servlet to a URL pattern. It contains:

- ❑ A <servlet-name> element containing the name of a servlet declared by a <servlet> element
- ❑ A <url-pattern> element containing a URL pattern to match

<session-config>

The <session-config> element configures the session tracking for the web application. It contains:

- ❑ An optional <session-timeout> element containing the default session timeout for this web application, which must be a whole number of minutes

794

<mime-mapping>

The `<mime-mapping>` element maps a filename extension to a MIME type. It contains:

- ❏ An `<extension>` element containing a filename extension
- ❏ A `<mime-type>` element containing a defined MIME type

<welcome-file-list>

The `<welcome-file-list>` element defines an ordered list of welcome files. It contains:

- ❏ 1 or more `<welcome-file>` elements containing a filename to use as a welcome file

<error-page>

The `<error-page>` element maps an error code or exception type to a resource ("error page") to use if that error condition arises. It contains:

- ❏ Either an `<error-code>` element containing an HTTP error code, or an `<exception-type>` element containing the class name of a Java exception type
- ❏ A `<location>` element containing the location of the error page resource within the web application

<taglib>

The `<taglib>` element declares a JSP tag library. It contains:

- ❏ A `<taglib-uri>` element containing a URI to identify the tag library
- ❏ A `<taglib-location>` element containing the location within the web application of the tag library descriptor file (`.tld` file)

<resource-env-ref>

The `<resource-env-ref>` element declares that the web application references an administered object. It contains:

- ❏ An optional `<description>` element
- ❏ A `<resource-env-name>` element containing the name of the resource environment
- ❏ A `<resource-env-ref-type>` element containing the type of the resource environment reference – J2EE web containers are required to support `javax.jms.Topic` and `javax.jms.Queue`

<resource-ref>

The `<resource-ref>` element declares that the web application references an external resource. It contains:

- ❏ An optional `<description>` element
- ❏ A `<res-ref-name>` element containing the name of the resource factory reference

❑ A `<res-type>` element specifying the type of the data source

❑ A `<res-auth>` element indicating whether the application code signs on to the resource programmatically, or whether the container should sign on based on information supplied by the application deployer. Contents must be either `Application` or `Containers`.

❑ An optional `<res-sharing-scope>` element specifying whether connections can be shared. Contents must be either `Shareable` (the default) or `Unshareable`.

`<security-constraint>`

The `<security-constraint>` element applies security constraints to one or more collections of web resources. It contains:

❑ An optional `<display-name>` element

❑ One or more `<web-resource-collection>` elements

❑ An optional `<auth-constraint>` element

❑ An optional `<user-data-constraint>` element

A `<web-resource-collection>` element identifies a set of resources within the application; it can be qualified by specifying particular HTTP method(s). (By default, the security constraint applies to all HTTP methods.) It contains:

❑ A `<web-resource-name>` element containing the name of the web resource collection

❑ An optional `<description>` element

❑ 0 or more `<url-pattern>` elements, each containing a URL pattern to match

❑ 0 or more `<http-method>` elements, each containing the name of an HTTP method

An `<auth-constraint>` element indicates that certain user roles should be permitted to access these web resources. It contains:

❑ An optional `<description>` element

❑ 0 or more `<role-name>` elements each containing a role referenced in a `<security-role-ref>` element, or the special name * that indicates all roles in this application

A `<user-data-constraint>` element indicates how data transmitted between the client and the application should be protected. It contains:

❑ An optional `<description>` element

❑ A `<transport-guarantee>` element containing the text NONE, INTEGRAL, or CONFIDENTIAL. NONE means that no transport guarantee is required, INTEGRAL means that the data must not be able to be changed in transit, and CONFIDENTIAL means that others should not be able to view the data.

`<login-config>`

The `<login-config>` element configures the authentication mechanism for this application. It contains:

- ❑ An optional `<auth-method>` element specifying the authentication mechanism. Must contain the text BASIC, DIGEST, FORM, or CLIENT-CERT.

- ❑ An optional `<realm-name>` element specifying the realm name for HTTP basic authorization

- ❑ An optional `<form-login-config>` element to configure form-based authentication. Contains a `<form-login-page>` element specifying the login page, and a `<form-error-page>` element specifying the error page used if login is unsuccessful.

<security-role>

The `<security-role>` element declares a security role used in the web application's security-constraints. It contains:

- ❑ An optional `<description>` element

- ❑ A `<role-name>` element containing the name of the role

<env-entry>

The `<env-entry>` element declares an application's environment entry. It contains:

- ❑ An optional `<description>` element

- ❑ An `<env-entry-name>` element containing the environment entry's name

- ❑ An optional `<env-entry-value>` element containing the environment entry's value

- ❑ An `<env-entry-type>` element containing the environment entry value's Java type. Legal values are java.lang.Boolean, java.lang.String, java.lang.Integer, java.lang.Double, and java.lang.Float.

<ejb-ref>

The `<ejb-ref>` element declares a reference to an Enterprise JavaBean. It contains:

- ❑ An optional `<description>` element

- ❑ An `<ejb-ref-name>` element containing the JNDI name of the EJB

- ❑ An `<ejb-ref-type>` element containing the expected type of the EJB, either Entity or Session

- ❑ A `<home>` element containing the type of the EJB's home interface

- ❑ A `<remote>` element containing the type of the EJB's remote interface

- ❑ An optional `<ejb-link>` element specifying that this EJB reference is linked to the named EJB in the encompassing J2EE application

- ❑ An optional `<run-as>` element specifying the security role (defined for this application) that should be propagated to the EJB

Document Type Definition
Here's the DTD for the Web Application Deployment
Descriptor:

```
<!DOCTYPE web-app PUBLIC "-//Sun Microsystems, Inc.//DTD Web Application
2.3//EN" "http://java.sun.com/dtd/web-app_2_3.dtd">

<!ELEMENT web-app (icon?, display-name?, description?, distributable?,
                   context-param*, filter*, filter-mapping*, listener*,
                   servlet*, servlet-mapping*, session-config?,
                   mime-mapping*, welcome-file-list?, error-page*, taglib*,
                   resource-env-ref*, resource-ref*, security-constraint*,
                   login-config?, security-role*, env-entry*, ejb-ref*)>
<!ELEMENT filter (icon?, filter-name, display-name?, description?,
                  filter-class, init-param*)>
<!ELEMENT filter-name (#PCDATA)>
<!ELEMENT filter-class (#PCDATA)>
<!ELEMENT filter-mapping (filter-name, (url-pattern | servlet-name))>
<!ELEMENT icon (small-icon?, large-icon?)>
<!ELEMENT small-icon (#PCDATA)>
<!ELEMENT large-icon (#PCDATA)>
<!ELEMENT display-name (#PCDATA)>
<!ELEMENT description (#PCDATA)>
<!ELEMENT distributable EMPTY>
<!ELEMENT context-param (param-name, param-value, description?)>
<!ELEMENT param-name (#PCDATA)>
<!ELEMENT param-value (#PCDATA)>
<!ELEMENT listener (listener-class)>
<!ELEMENT listener-class (#PCDATA)>
<!ELEMENT servlet (icon?, servlet-name, display-name?, description?,
                   (servlet-class|jsp-file), init-param*, load-on-startup?,
                   security-role-ref*)>
<!ELEMENT servlet-name (#PCDATA)>
<!ELEMENT servlet-class (#PCDATA)>
<!ELEMENT jsp-file (#PCDATA)>
<!ELEMENT init-param (param-name, param-value, description?)>
<!ELEMENT load-on-startup (#PCDATA)>
<!ELEMENT servlet-mapping (servlet-name, url-pattern)>
<!ELEMENT url-pattern (#PCDATA)>
<!ELEMENT session-config (session-timeout?)>
<!ELEMENT session-timeout (#PCDATA)>
<!ELEMENT mime-mapping (extension, mime-type)>
<!ELEMENT extension (#PCDATA)>
<!ELEMENT mime-type (#PCDATA)>
<!ELEMENT welcome-file-list (welcome-file+)>
<!ELEMENT welcome-file (#PCDATA)>
<!ELEMENT taglib (taglib-uri, taglib-location)>
<!ELEMENT taglib-uri (#PCDATA)>
<!ELEMENT taglib-location (#PCDATA)>
<!ELEMENT error-page ((error-code | exception-type), location)>
<!ELEMENT error-code (#PCDATA)>
<!ELEMENT exception-type (#PCDATA)>
<!ELEMENT location (#PCDATA)>
<!ELEMENT resource-env-ref (description?, resource-env-ref-name,
```

```
                              resource-env-ref-type)>
<!ELEMENT resource-env-ref-name (#PCDATA)>
<!ELEMENT resource-env-ref-type (#PCDATA)>
<!ELEMENT resource-ref (description?, res-ref-name, res-type, res-auth,
                        res-sharing-scope?)>
<!ELEMENT res-ref-name (#PCDATA)>
<!ELEMENT res-type (#PCDATA)>
<!ELEMENT res-auth (#PCDATA)>
<!ELEMENT res-sharing-scope (#PCDATA)>
<!ELEMENT security-constraint (display-name?, web-resource-collection+,
                               auth-constraint?, user-data-constraint?)>
<!ELEMENT web-resource-collection (web-resource-name, description?,
                                   url-pattern*, http-method*)>
<!ELEMENT web-resource-name (#PCDATA)>
<!ELEMENT http-method (#PCDATA)>
<!ELEMENT user-data-constraint (description?, transport-guarantee)>
<!ELEMENT transport-guarantee (#PCDATA)>
<!ELEMENT auth-constraint (description?, role-name*)>
<!ELEMENT role-name (#PCDATA)>
<!ELEMENT login-config (auth-method?, realm-name?, form-login-config?)>
<!ELEMENT realm-name (#PCDATA)>
<!ELEMENT form-login-config (form-login-page, form-error-page)>
<!ELEMENT form-login-page (#PCDATA)>
<!ELEMENT form-error-page (#PCDATA)>
<!ELEMENT auth-method (#PCDATA)>
<!ELEMENT security-role (description?, role-name)>
<!ELEMENT security-role-ref (description?, role-name, role-link)>
<!ELEMENT role-link (#PCDATA)>
<!ELEMENT env-entry (description?, env-entry-name, env-entry-value?,
                     env-entry-type)>
<!ELEMENT env-entry-name (#PCDATA)>
<!ELEMENT env-entry-value (#PCDATA)>
<!ELEMENT env-entry-type (#PCDATA)>
<!ELEMENT ejb-ref (description?, ejb-ref-name, ejb-ref-type, home, remote,
                   ejb-link?, run-as?)>
<!ELEMENT ejb-ref-name (#PCDATA)>
<!ELEMENT ejb-ref-type (#PCDATA)>
<!ELEMENT home (#PCDATA)>
<!ELEMENT remote (#PCDATA)>
<!ELEMENT ejb-link (#PCDATA)>
<!ELEMENT run-as (#PCDATA)>
```

In addition, all elements have an implied id attribute, for example:

```
<!ATTLIST web-app id ID #IMPLIED>
```

Tag Library Descriptor

The DOCTYPE declaration at the head of a JSP 1.2 tag library descriptor (.tld) file should be:

```
<!DOCTYPE taglib
 PUBLIC "-//Sun Microsystems, Inc.//DTD JSP Tag Library 1.2//EN"
 "http://java.sun.com/dtd/web-jsptaglibrary_1_2.dtd">
```

Note that the ordering of elements within a tag library descriptor file is significant, and failure to have the elements in the correct order is a common problem.

JSP 1.2-compatible web containers are also required to accept a .tld file using the JSP 1.1 format; this is included as an appendix to the JSP 1.2 specification.

Common Elements

The <description>, <display-name>, <large-icon>, and <small-icon> elements can occur in several places within web.xml and so we will describe them only once – here.

<description>

The <description> element contains a description of the enclosing element.

<display-name>

The <display-name> element contains a short name for its parent element, for GUI tools to display.

<large-icon>

The <large-icon> element contains the location within the tag library of a 16x16 pixel JPEG or GIF image denoting the enclosing element

<small-icon>

The <small-icon> element contains the location within the tag library of a 32x32 pixel JPEG or GIF image denoting the enclosing element.

<taglib> – Root Element

The <taglib> element is the root element of a .tld file. It contains:

❑ A <tlib-version> element

❑ An optional <jsp-version> element

❑ A <short-name> element

❑ An optional <uri> element

❑ An optional <display-name> element

❑ An optional <small-icon> element

❑ An optional <large-icon> element

❑ An optional <description> element

❑ An optional <validator> element

❑ 0 or more <listener> elements

❑ 1 or more <tag> elements

Subelements of <taglib>

The permissible subelements of <taglib> (other than those already described) are as follows.

<tlib-version>

The <tlib-version> element contains the version number of the tag library.

<jsp-version>

The <jsp-version> element contains the JSP version that the tag library requires (1.2 by default).

<short-name>

The <short-name> element contains a short name for the tag library.

<uri>

The <uri> element contains a URI uniquely identifying the tag library.

<validator>

The <validator> element defines a validator to check that a JSP page uses the tag library correctly. It contains:

❑   A <validator-class> element containing the name of the TagLibraryValidator class

❑   0 or more <init-param> elements

An <init-param> element defines initialization parameters for the validator, and contains:

❑   A <param-name> element containing the parameter name

❑   A <param-value> element containing the parameter value

❑   An optional <description> element

<listener>

The <listener> element defines an event listener for the web application using the tag library. It contains:

❑   A <listener-class> element containing the name of the listener class

<tag>

The <tag> element defines a tag. It contains:

❑   A <name> element containing the tag's name

❑   A <tag-class> element containing the name of the tag handler class

❑   An optional <tei-class> element containing the name of the TagExtraInfo class for the tag

- ❑ An optional `<body-content>` element describing the body content of the tag: either `tagdependent`, `JSP`, or `empty`.

- ❑ An optional `<display-name>` element

- ❑ An optional `<small-icon>` element

- ❑ An optional `<large-icon>` element

- ❑ An optional `<description>` element

- ❑ 0 or more `<variable>` elements

- ❑ 0 or more `<attribute>` elements

A `<variable>` tag declares that this tag defines a scripting variable. It contains:

- ❑ Either a `<name-given>` element containing the name of the scripting variable, or a `<name-from-attribute>` element containing the name of the tag attribute that will give the scripting variable's name at run-time.

- ❑ An optional `<variable-class>` element containing the class of the scripting variable. The default is `java.lang.String`.

- ❑ An optional `<declare>` element whose contents indicate whether the scripting variable is to be defined; the default is `true`.

- ❑ An optional `<scope>` element whose contents indicate the scope of the scripting variable. Possible values are `NESTED` (the default), `AT_BEGIN`, or `AT_END`.

An `<attribute>` element defines an attribute of the tag. It contains:

- ❑ A `<name>` element containing the name of the attribute

- ❑ An optional `<required>` element whose contents indicate whether the attribute is required or optional. Legal values are `true`, `false` (the default), `yes`, and `no`.

- ❑ An optional `<rtexprvalue>` element whose contents indicate whether the attribute value can be a run-time expression scriptlet rather than a static value. Legal values are `true`, `false` (the default), `yes`, and `no`.

- ❑ An optional `<type>` element containing the type of the attribute's value. (For static values, this is always `java.lang.String`.)

Document Type Definition

Here's the DTD for a Tag Library Descriptor file:

```
<!NOTATION WEB-JSPTAGLIB.1_2 PUBLIC
        "-//Sun Microsystems, Inc.//DTD JSP Tag Library 1.2//EN">
<!ELEMENT taglib (tlib-version, jsp-version?, short-name, uri?,
                display-name?, small-icon?, large-icon?, description?,
                validator?, listener*, tag+) >
<!ATTLIST taglib
    id ID #IMPLIED
```

```
        xmlns CDATA #FIXED "http://java.sun.com/dtd/web-jsptaglibrary_1_2.dtd"
>

<!ELEMENT tlib-version (#PCDATA) >
<!ELEMENT jsp-version (#PCDATA) >
<!ELEMENT short-name (#PCDATA) >
<!ELEMENT uri (#PCDATA) >
<!ELEMENT description (#PCDATA) >
<!ELEMENT validator (validator-class, init-param*) >
<!ELEMENT validator-class (#PCDATA) >
<!ELEMENT init-param (param-name, param-value, description?)>
<!ELEMENT param-name (#PCDATA)>
<!ELEMENT param-value (#PCDATA)>
<!ELEMENT listener (listener-class) >
<!ELEMENT listener-class (#PCDATA) >
<!ELEMENT tag (name, tag-class, tei-class?, body-content?, display-name?,
               small-icon?, large-icon?, description?, variable*,
               attribute*) >
<!ELEMENT tag-class (#PCDATA) >
<!ELEMENT tei-class (#PCDATA) >
<!ELEMENT body-content (#PCDATA) >
<!ELEMENT display-name (#PCDATA) >
<!ELEMENT large-icon (#PCDATA) >
<!ELEMENT small-icon (#PCDATA) >
<!ELEMENT variable ( (name-given | name-from-attribute), variable-class?,
                    declare?, scope?) >
<!ELEMENT name-given (#PCDATA) >
<!ELEMENT name-from-attribute (#PCDATA) >
<!ELEMENT variable-class (#PCDATA) >
<!ELEMENT declare (#PCDATA) >
<!ELEMENT scope (#PCDATA) >
<!ELEMENT attribute (name, required? , rtexprvalue?, type?) >
<!ELEMENT name (#PCDATA) >
<!ELEMENT required (#PCDATA) >
<!ELEMENT rtexprvalue (#PCDATA) >
<!ELEMENT type (#PCDATA) >
```

In addition, all elements have an implied id attribute, for example:

```
<!ATTLIST tlib-version id ID #IMPLIED>
```

Struts Configuration File

The DOCTYPE declaration at the head of a Struts configuration (struts-config.xml) file should be:

```
<!DOCTYPE struts-config PUBLIC
 "-//Apache Software Foundation//DTD Struts Configuration 1.0//EN"
 "http://jakarta.apache.org/struts/dtds/struts-config_1_0.dtd">
```

Note that within the Struts configuration file the ordering of elements is significant. You should additionally note that:

❑ All URL paths are context-relative, in other words they must start with a / and are relative to the root of the web application.

❑ In addition to the attributes listed below, all elements in the Struts configuration file have an implied id attribute.

Common Elements

The <set-property>, <description>, <display-name>, <icon>, <large-icon>, and <small-icon> elements can occur in several places within the Struts configuration file, and so we will describe them only once – here.

<set-property>

The <set-property> element is used to configure JavaBeans components by specifying a property name and value. It has no content, but the following attributes:

❑ property specifies the name of the bean property to be set

❑ value specifies the new property value, in a string representation

<description>

The <description> element contains a description of the enclosing element.

<display-name>

The <display-name> element contains a short name for its parent element, for GUI tools to display.

<icon>

The <icon> element references icons that will be used by a GUI tool to represent its parent element. It contains:

❑ An optional <small-icon> element containing the location, relative to the file, of a 16x16 pixel icon

❑ An optional <large-icon> element containing the location, relative to the file, of a 32x32 pixel icon

<struts-config> – Root Element

The <struts-config> element is the root element of the Struts configuration file. It contains:

❑ An optional <data-sources> element

❑ An optional <form-beans> element

❑ An optional <global-forwards> element

❑ An optional <action-mappings> element

<data-sources> and <data-source>

The <data-sources> element contains 0 or more <data-source> elements.

Each <data-source> element defines a DataSource object that will be configured and then instantiated as a ServletContext attribute. It has the following attributes:

- ❏   key, defining the name of the ServletContext attribute under which the DataSource will be stored. The default is Action.DATA_SOURCE_KEY.

- ❏   type, defining the name of the DataSource class (which must implement javax.sql.DataSource). The default is org.apache.struts.util.GenericDataSource.

There are several additional attributes whose use is now deprecated as they only applied to the default DataSource class; you should instead use nested <set-property> elements to set these values:

- ❏   autoCommit, defining whether the data source should auto-commit transactions.

- ❏   description, giving a description for the data source.

- ❏   driverClass, defining the name of the JDBC driver to be used. (Required.)

- ❏   loginTimeout, specifying the maximum number of seconds to wait for a connection to be created or returned.

- ❏   maxCount, specifying the maximum number of connections.

- ❏   minCount, specifying the minimum number of connections.

- ❏   password, specifying the database password. (Required.)

- ❏   readOnly, specifying whether new connections should be read-only.

- ❏   url, specifying the JDBC URL to use. (Required.)

- ❏   user, specifying the database username. (Required.)

A <data-source> element contains:

- ❏   0 or more <set-property> elements

<form-beans> and <form-bean>

The <form-beans> element contains 0 or more <form-bean> elements. It also has a type attribute, but this is no longer used by Struts and you need not set its value.

Each <form-bean> element defines a form bean that will be configured to handle form submissions. It has the following attributes:

- ❏   className allows you to override the default class Struts uses to represent a form bean internally. You will not commonly use this attribute.

- ❏   name specifies a unique identifier for this form bean, which will be used to reference it <action> elements. (Required.)

❑ type specifies the name of the form bean class to be used, which must extend `org.apache.struts.action.ActionForm`. (Required.)

A `<form-bean>` element contains:

❑ An optional `<icon>` element

❑ An optional `<display-name>` element

❑ An optional `<description>` element

❑ 0 or more `<set-property>` elements

`<global-forwards>` and `<forward>`

The `<global-forwards>` element contains 0 or more `<forward>` elements, specifying named forwards that will be available to all Struts actions (unless overridden within an `<action>` element). It also has a `type` attribute, but this is no longer used by Struts and you need not set its value.

The `<forward>` element maps a logical name to a web resource, and has the following attributes:

❑ `className` allows you to override the default class Struts uses to represent a forward internally. You will not commonly use this attribute.

❑ `name` specifies a unique identifier for this forward, which will be used to reference it within your application. (Required.)

❑ `path` specifies the location of the web resource. (Required.)

❑ `redirect` allows you to specify whether control should be redirected to this resource (value `"true"`), rather than forwarding to it (`"false"`). The default is `"false"`.

A `<forward>` element contains:

❑ An optional `<icon>` element

❑ An optional `<display-name>` element

❑ An optional `<description>` element

❑ 0 or more `<set-property>` elements

`<action-mappings>` and `<action>`

The `<action-mappings>` element contains 0 or more `<action>` elements, which map request URLs to `Action` classes. It also has a `type` attribute, but this is no longer used by Struts and you need not set its value.

The `<action>` element maps a request path to an `Action` class. Its attributes are listed below; exactly one of `forward`, `include`, or `type` must be specified:

❑ `type` specifies the class name of the action class (which must extend `org.apache.struts.action.Action`) to be used to process requests for this mapping if the `forward` or `include` attribute is not included.

- ❏ `forward` specifies the path of the servlet or JSP that will process this request, instead of instantiating and calling the `Action` class specified by `type`.

- ❏ `include` specifies the path of the servlet or JSP that will process this request, instead of instantiating and calling the `Action` class specified by `type`.

The remaining `<action>` attributes are:

- ❏ `path` defines the path of the submitted request that will be processed by this action, starting with a "/" character. If Struts was used with an extension-based `<servlet-mapping>` element then the filename extension should be omitted here. (Required.)

- ❏ `name` specifies the name of the form bean (if any) associated with the action.

- ❏ `attribute` specifies the name of the request-scope or session-scope attribute under which the form bean is accessed, if it is something other than the bean's specified name. It is optional if `name` is specified, but otherwise is not allowed.

- ❏ `scope` specifies the scope (`"request"` or `"session"`) in which the form bean is located, if any. It is optional if `name` is specified, but otherwise is not allowed.

- ❏ `input` specifies the path of the input form to which control should be returned if a validation error is encountered. It is required if `name` is specified and the input bean returns validation errors, is optional if `name` is specified and the input bean does not return validation errors, and is not allowed if `name` is not specified.

- ❏ `parameter` specifies general configuration information for the action.

- ❏ `prefix` specifies a prefix used to match request parameter names to form bean properties, if any. It is optional if `name` is specified, but otherwise is not allowed.

- ❏ `suffix` specifies a suffix used to match request parameter names to form bean properties names, if any. It is optional if `name` is specified, but otherwise is not allowed.

- ❏ `unknown` specifies whether this action should be configured to handle all requests not handled by another action.

- ❏ `validate` specifies whether the form bean's `validate()` method should be called prior to calling the action.

- ❏ `className` allows you to override the default class Struts uses to represent an action mapping internally. You will not commonly use this attribute.

An `<action>` element contains:

- ❏ An optional `<icon>` element

- ❏ An optional `<display-name>` element

- ❏ An optional `<description>` element

- ❏ 0 or more `<set-property>` elements

- ❏ 0 or more `<forward>` elements

Document Type Definition

Here's the DTD for the Struts configuration file:

```
<?xml version="1.0" encoding="ISO-8859-1"?>

<!ENTITY % BeanName "CDATA">
<!ENTITY % Boolean "(true|false|yes|no)">
<!ENTITY % ClassName "CDATA">
<!ENTITY % Integer "CDATA">
<!ENTITY % Location "#PCDATA">
<!ENTITY % PropName "CDATA">
<!ENTITY % RequestPath "CDATA">
<!ENTITY % RequestScope "(request|session)">

<!ELEMENT struts-config (data-sources?, form-beans?, global-forwards?, action-
mappings?)>
<!ATTLIST struts-config  id               ID            #IMPLIED>

<!ELEMENT data-sources (data-source*)>
<!ATTLIST data-sources   id               ID            #IMPLIED>

<!ELEMENT data-source (set-property*)>
<!ATTLIST data-source    id               ID            #IMPLIED>
<!ATTLIST data-source    key              %BeanName;    #IMPLIED>
<!ATTLIST data-source    type             %ClassName;   #IMPLIED>
<!-- The following attributes are deprecated: use a nested set-property
     element to configure data source properties. -->
<!ATTLIST data-source    autoCommit       %Boolean;     #IMPLIED>
<!ATTLIST data-source    description      CDATA         #IMPLIED>
<!ATTLIST data-source    driverClass      %ClassName;   #IMPLIED>
<!ATTLIST data-source    loginTimeout     %Integer;     #IMPLIED>
<!ATTLIST data-source    maxCount         %Integer;     #IMPLIED>
<!ATTLIST data-source    minCount         %Integer;     #IMPLIED>
<!ATTLIST data-source    password         CDATA         #IMPLIED>
<!ATTLIST data-source    readOnly         %Boolean;     #IMPLIED>
<!ATTLIST data-source    url              CDATA         #IMPLIED>
<!ATTLIST data-source    user             CDATA         #IMPLIED>

<!ELEMENT form-beans (form-bean*)>
<!ATTLIST form-beans     id               ID            #IMPLIED>
<!-- The following attribute value is ignored -->
<!ATTLIST form-beans     type             %ClassName;
                                "org.apache.struts.action.ActionFormBean">

<!ELEMENT form-bean (icon?, display-name?, description?, set-property*)>
<!ATTLIST form-bean      id               ID            #IMPLIED>
<!ATTLIST form-bean      className        %ClassName;   #IMPLIED>
<!ATTLIST form-bean      name             %BeanName;    #REQUIRED>
<!ATTLIST form-bean      type             %ClassName;   #REQUIRED>

<!ELEMENT global-forwards (forward*)>
<!ATTLIST global-forwards id              ID            #IMPLIED>
<!-- The following attribute value is ignored -->
```

```
<!ATTLIST global-forwards type          %ClassName;
                               "org.apache.struts.action.ActionForward">

<!ELEMENT forward (icon?, display-name?, description?, set-property*)>
<!ATTLIST forward          id           ID              #IMPLIED>
<!ATTLIST forward          className    %ClassName;     #IMPLIED>
<!ATTLIST forward          name         CDATA           #REQUIRED>
<!ATTLIST forward          path         %RequestPath;   #REQUIRED>
<!ATTLIST forward          redirect     %Boolean;       #IMPLIED>

<!ELEMENT action-mappings (action*)>
<!ATTLIST action-mappings id            ID              #IMPLIED>
<!-- The following attribute value is ignored -->
<!ATTLIST action-mappings type          %ClassName;
                               "org.apache.struts.action.ActionMapping">

<!ELEMENT action (icon?, display-name?, description?, set-property*, forward*)>
<!ATTLIST action           id           ID              #IMPLIED>
<!ATTLIST action           attribute    %BeanName;      #IMPLIED>
<!ATTLIST action           className    %ClassName;     #IMPLIED>
<!ATTLIST action           forward      %RequestPath;   #IMPLIED>
<!ATTLIST action           include      %RequestPath;   #IMPLIED>
<!ATTLIST action           input        %RequestPath;   #IMPLIED>
<!ATTLIST action           name         %BeanName;      #IMPLIED>
<!ATTLIST action           parameter    CDATA           #IMPLIED>
<!ATTLIST action           path         %RequestPath;   #REQUIRED>
<!ATTLIST action           prefix       CDATA           #IMPLIED>
<!ATTLIST action           scope        %RequestScope;  #IMPLIED>
<!ATTLIST action           suffix       CDATA           #IMPLIED>
<!ATTLIST action           type         %ClassName;     #IMPLIED>
<!ATTLIST action           unknown      %Boolean;       #IMPLIED>
<!ATTLIST action           validate     %Boolean;       #IMPLIED>

<!ELEMENT set-property EMPTY>
<!ATTLIST set-property     id           ID              #IMPLIED>
<!ATTLIST set-property     property     %PropName;      #REQUIRED>
<!ATTLIST set-property     value        CDATA           #REQUIRED>

<!ELEMENT description (#PCDATA)>
<!ATTLIST description       id           ID              #IMPLIED>

<!ELEMENT display-name (#PCDATA)>
<!ATTLIST display-name      id           ID              #IMPLIED>

<!ELEMENT icon (small-icon?, large-icon?)>
<!ATTLIST icon             id           ID              #IMPLIED>

<!ELEMENT large-icon (%Location;)>
<!ATTLIST large-icon       id           ID              #IMPLIED>

<!ELEMENT small-icon (%Location;)>
<!ATTLIST small-icon       id           ID              #IMPLIED>
```

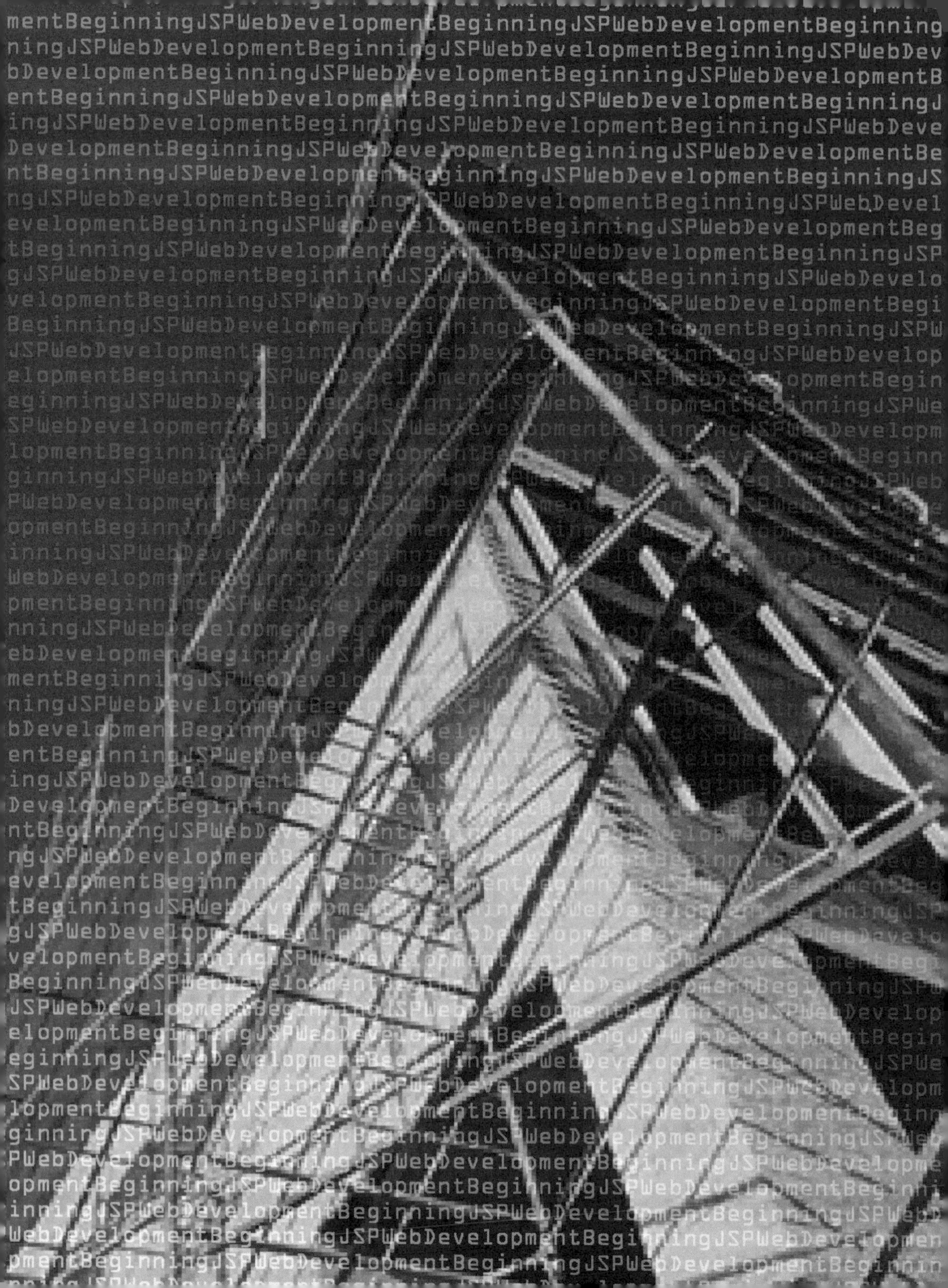
BeginningJSPWebDevelopment

Getting More Information

Java Development Kit Documentation

You should definitely download and install the Java Development Kit documentation; this provides a huge amount of information about the Java platform itself, such as:

- ❏ Instructions on using the Java command line tools (`javac`, `java`, and the like)
- ❏ Guides to Java features like I/O, networking, `.jar` files, and so on
- ❏ Most importantly, documentation on the various classes that make up the Java platform; these are commonly known as **Javadocs** because they are generated by a tool known as `javadoc`

You can download the documentation from http://java.sun.com/j2se/1.3/docs.html. It comes in the form of a `.zip` file, which you should unzip into your JDK directory (for example, into `C:\jdk1.3`). Once this is done, you can browse to the `index.html` to start reading – typically this means pointing your web browser to `C:\jdk1.3\docs\index.html`:

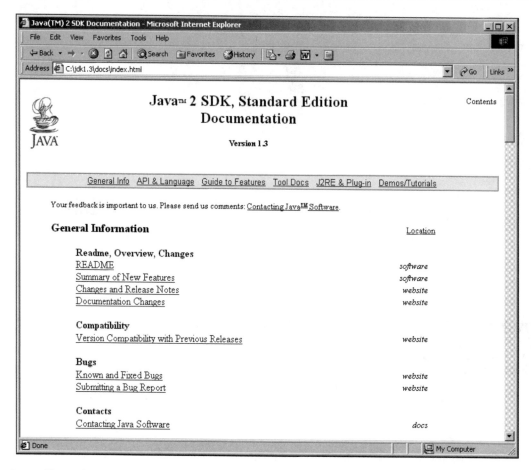

As you'll see if you scroll down this page, there is a lot of information; it's well worth spending some time exploring what's available. However, we'll focus here on one particular part of the documentation, the API guide. If you scroll down to the **API & Language Documentation** section, you'll find a link called **Java 2 Platform API Specification**. Clicking on this link takes you to the page seen opposite:

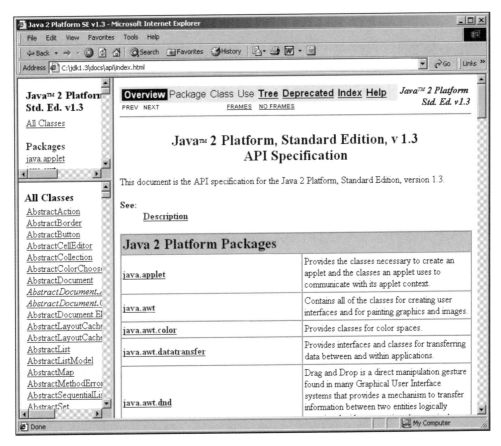

There is rather a lot of information here, too – there are a lot of classes and interfaces in the Java platform, in fact there are more than 1800 classes and interfaces listed! Fortunately they are all nicely categorized into packages, which makes it easier to find what you're looking for.

You'll see that the screen above is divided into three areas. The main area, on the right, initially contains a descriptive list of packages, while top left there is a quick summary of packages and bottom left is a complete list of classes and interfaces.

If you click on one of the package names in the list at the top left, the bottom left frame is replaced with a list of just the classes and interfaces in that package. Clicking on one of the package names in the main part of the screen replaces that frame with a descriptive overview of just that package.

So, let's say we're interested in the `java.io.File` class. In the top left frame we scroll down to `java.io`, and click on that link. The bottom left frame now contains just a list of the contents of that package; to get to the overview of that package, we click on the text `java.io` at the top of the bottom left frame:

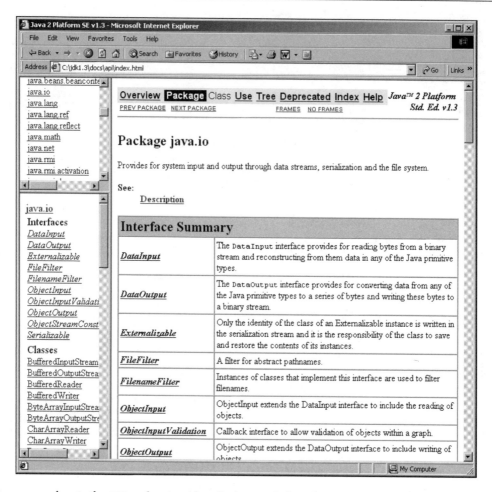

We can now locate the `File` class in either the bottom left or the main frames, and clicking on its link takes us to the documentation for that class:

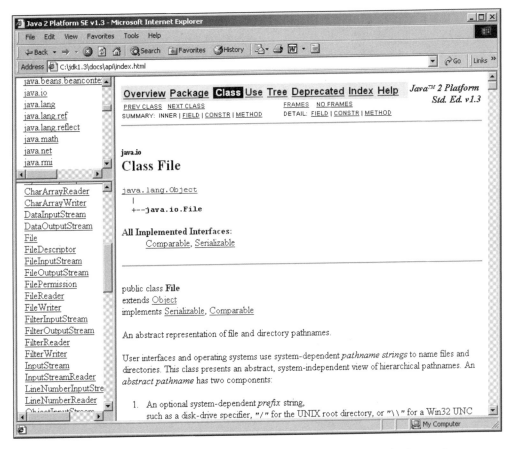

The documentation for each class is divided up into a number of sections. At the top is a summary showing the tree of classes that have been extended, and the interfaces that have been implemented, to get us to `java.io.File`, and below this is a textual description of the class.

Scrolling down, we start to get to the "meat":

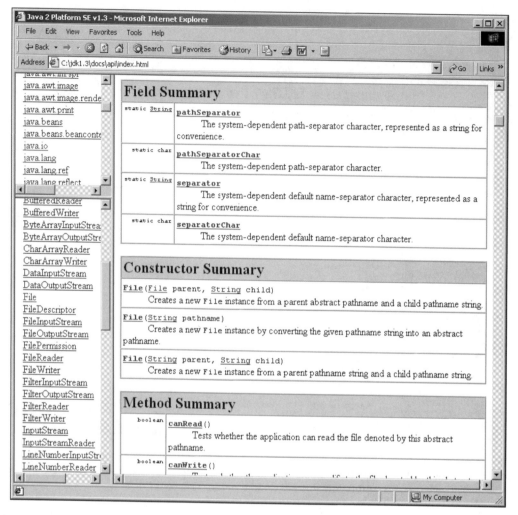

As you can see, we're given summaries of the fields, constructors, and methods declared for this class, with links to fuller descriptions further down the page. There is also a section listing methods inherited from the parent class.

Finally, towards the bottom, come detailed descriptions of each field, constructor, and method:

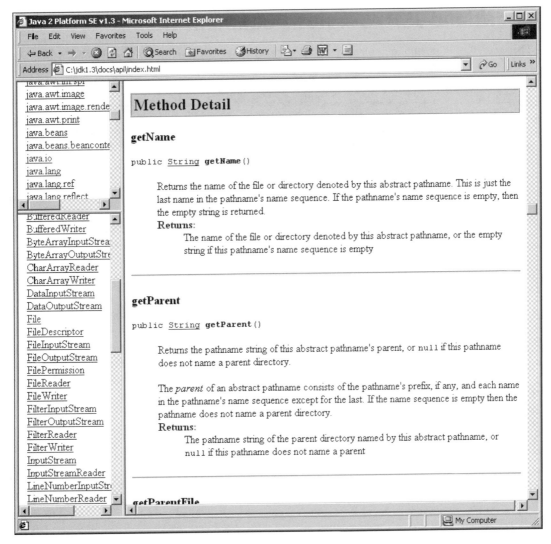

The whole set of API documents is liberally hyperlinked, and is actually very easy to find your way around.

Tomcat and JSP/Servlet Documentation

The second set of documentation you should know about is that which comes with Tomcat. When you installed Tomcat 4.0, you may have seen this page:

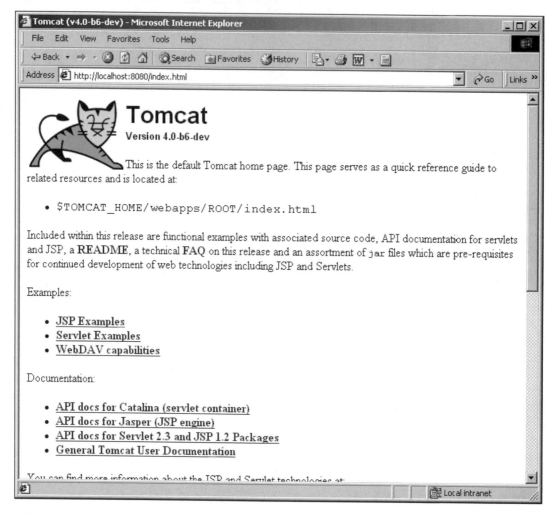

The two sections of this which are particularly interesting are the General Tomcat User Documentation section, and the API docs for Servlet 2.3 and JSP 1.2 Packages. The general documentation section is still a "work in progress", but provides useful documentation on the format of Tomcat's `server.xml` configuration file:

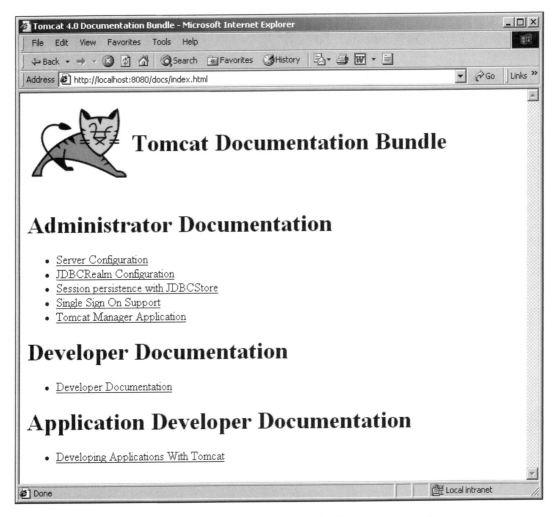

The Servlet and JSP API documentation is the Javadocs for the `javax.servlet`, `javax.servlet.http`, `javax.servlet.jsp`, and `javax.servlet.jsp.tagext` packages. You will find these documents handy to supplement the information in appendix B on the JSP implicit objects:

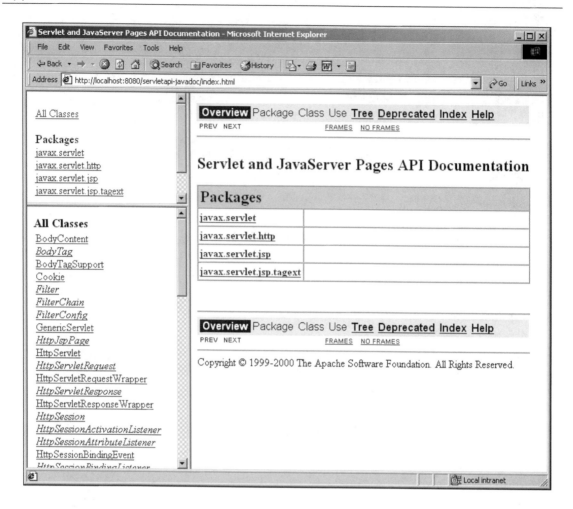

Other Resources

We've put together a list of some other resources you may find helpful as you continue to learn about JavaServer Pages and Java.

Several Wrox Press books will help you to take forward what you have learned in this book. You may be particularly interested in:

❑ *Beginning Java Objects*, by Jacquie Barker, ISBN 1-861004-17-6 teaches object-oriented programming in Java from the ground up, introducing the concepts of object orientation and how to model your system as a set of objects, then showing how to translate this into Java sources.

❑ *Beginning Java 2 – JDK 1.3 Edition*, by Ivor Horton, ISBN 1-861003-66-8 teaches the fundamentals of the Java programming language and APIs, together with how to use the Swing API to create graphical, client-side applications in Java.

❏ *Professional JSP, 2nd Edition*, ISBN 1-86100-4-95-8 takes you beyond what has been covered in this book with extensive coverage of advanced topics such as using XML with Java, more discussion of servlets, generating non-textual types of web content such as images and PDFs, and further use of the Struts framework.

❏ JavaServer Pages and servlets are only part of the **Java 2 Enterprise Edition (J2EE)**. *Professional Java Server Programming, J2EE Edition*, ISBN 1-861004-65-6 covers the whole J2EE platform – including XML, Enterprise JavaBeans, and the Java Message Service, giving you an excellent overview of the possibilities of Java technology.

Next, here are a few web sites that may be of use:

❏ Sun Microsystems' official web sites for JSP and servlets are at http://java.sun.com/products/jsp/ and http://java.sun.com/products/servlets/ respectively. These site are particularly useful for official information such as the JSP and servlet specifications (hard reading, though) and occasional articles.

❏ The Jakarta project, http://jakarta.apache.org/, has many useful subprojects offering useful (and free) server-side Java software. Particularly notable are Tomcat, the JSP/Servlet container we've been using throughout this book (http://jakarta.apache.org/tomcat/), the Struts framework (http://jakarta.apache.org/struts/), and the Taglibs project (http://jakarta.apache.org/taglibs/) which offers a host of ready-made JSP tag libraries ready for you to download and use.

❏ JSPInsider, http://www.jspinsider.com/ offers a host of JSP-related information including the helpful articles and useful (free) JavaBeans and tag libraries.

Lastly, there are a number of mailing lists that you may find helpful if you run up against problems in your code:

❏ The Wrox Programmer's Resource Centre, http://p2p.wrox.com/, has a number of Java mailing lists, including lists on JSP, tag libraries, and servlets.

❏ The Jakarta project also has mailing lists for their projects; each has a "user" list for questions about using the product, along with a "developer" list where the people who created the projects live. You'll probably mainly be interested in the "user" lists; see http://jakarta.apache.org/site/mail.html for more information.

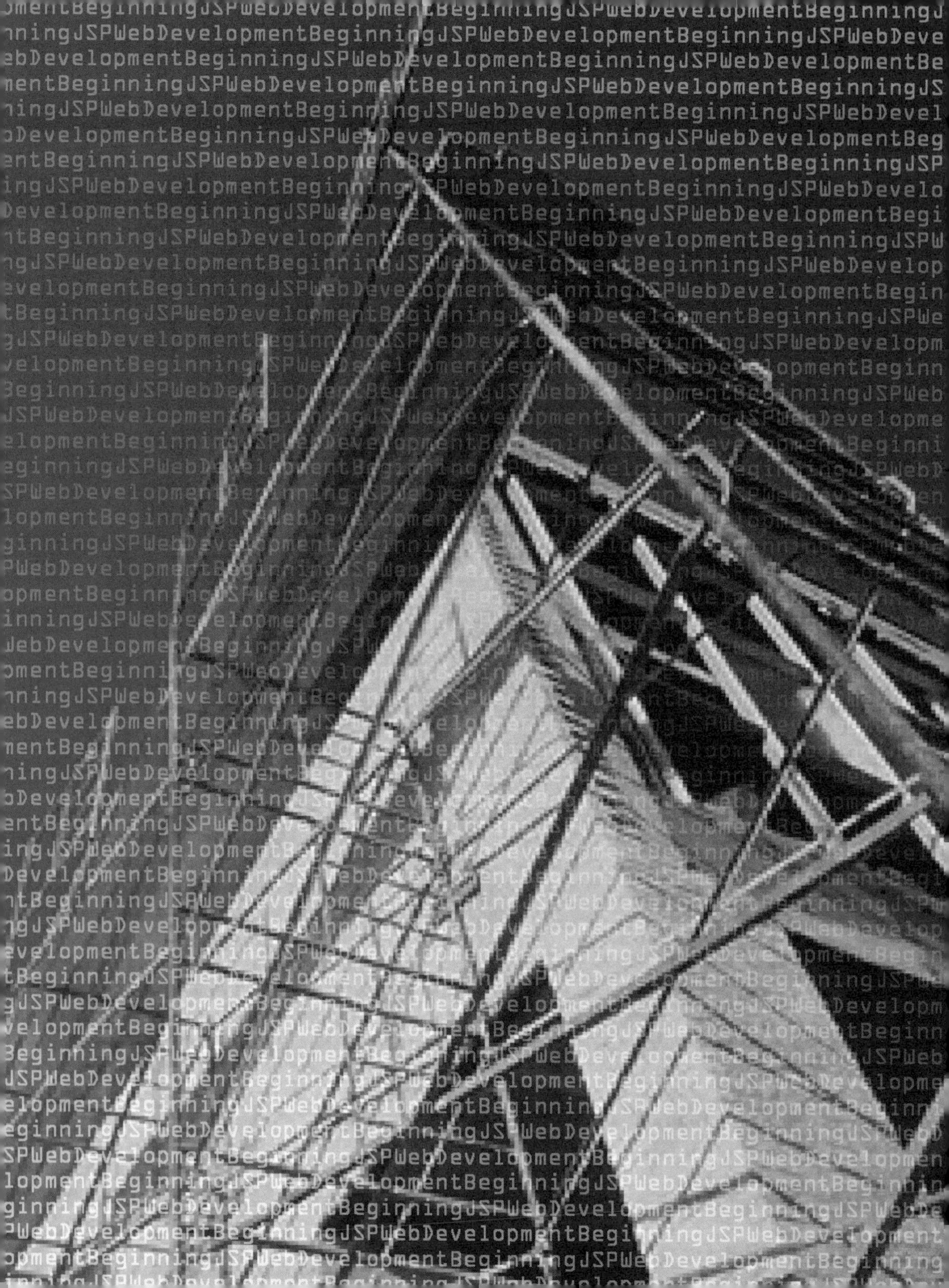

Support, Errata and p2p.wrox.com

One of the most irritating things about any programming book is when you find that bit of code you've just spent an hour typing simply doesn't work. You check it a hundred times to see if you've set it up correctly and then you notice the spelling mistake in the variable name on the book page. Of course, you can blame the authors for not taking enough care and testing the code, the editors for not doing their job properly, or the proofreaders for not being eagle-eyed enough, but this doesn't get around the fact that mistakes do happen.

We try hard to ensure no mistakes sneak out into the real world, but we can't promise that this book is 100% error free. What we can do is offer the next best thing by providing you with immediate support and feedback from experts who have worked on the book, and try to ensure that future editions eliminate these gremlins.

We also now commit to supporting you not just while you read the book, but once you start developing applications as well, through our online forums, where you can put your questions to the authors, reviewers, and fellow industry professionals.

In this appendix we'll look at how to:

- ❑ Enroll in the peer to peer forums at http://p2p.wrox.com
- ❑ Post and check for errata on our main site, http://www.wrox.com
- ❑ E-mail technical support with a query or feedback on our books in general

Between all three of these support procedures, you should get an answer to your problem very quickly.

The Online Forums at p2p.Online Forums

You can join the SQL mailing list (or any others which are of interest to you) for author and peer support. Our system provides **programmer to programmer™ support** on mailing lists, forums and newsgroups, all in addition to our one-to-one e-mail system, which we'll look at in just a while. Be confident that your query is not just being examined by a support professional, but by the many Wrox authors and other industry experts present on our mailing lists.

How To Enroll for Online Support

Just follow this four-step system:

1. Go to p2p.wrox.com in your favorite browser. Here you'll find any current announcements concerning P2P – new lists created, any removed and so on.

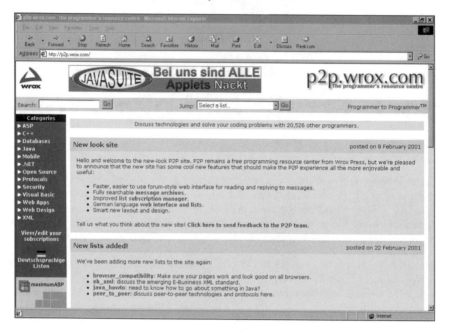

2. Click on the Java link in the left hand column.

3. Choose to access the beginning_jsp list.

4. If you are not a member of the list, you can choose to either view the list without joining it or create an account in the list, by hitting the respective buttons.

5. If you wish to join, you'll be presented with a form in which you'll need to fill in your e-mail address, name and a password (of at least 4 digits). Choose how you would like to receive the messages from the list and then hit Save.

6. Congratulations. You're now a member of the beginning_jsp mailing list.

Why This System Offers the Best Support

You can choose to join the mailing lists and you can receive a weekly digest of the list. If you don't have the time or facility to receive the mailing list, then you can search our online archives. You'll find the ability to search on specific subject areas or keywords. As these lists are moderated, you can be confident of finding good, accurate information quickly. Mails can be edited or moved by the moderator into the correct place, making this a most efficient resource. Junk and spam mail are deleted, and your own e-mail address is protected by the unique Lyris system from web-bots that can automatically hoover up newsgroup mailing list addresses. Any queries about joining, leaving the lists or any query about the list should be sent to: listsupport@p2p.wrox.com.

Support and Errata

The following section will take you step by step through the process of finding errata on our web site to get book-specific help. The sections that follow, therefore, are:

❏   Finding a list of existing errata on the web site

❏   Adding your own errata to the existing list

There is also a section covering how to e-mail a question for technical support. This comprises:

❏   What your e-mail should include

❏   What happens to your e-mail once it has been received by us

Finding an Erratum on the Web Site

Before you send in a query, you might be able to save time by finding the answer to your problem on our web site – http:\\www.wrox.com.

Each book we publish has its own page and its own errata sheet. You can get to any book's page by clicking on the Books link on the left hand side of the page.

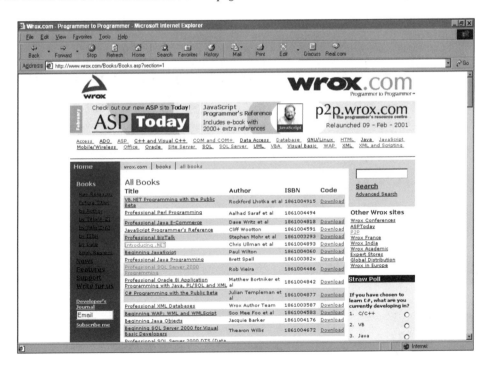

From here, find the book you are interested in and click the link. Towards the bottom of the page, underneath the book information at the right hand side of the central column is a link called Book Errata.

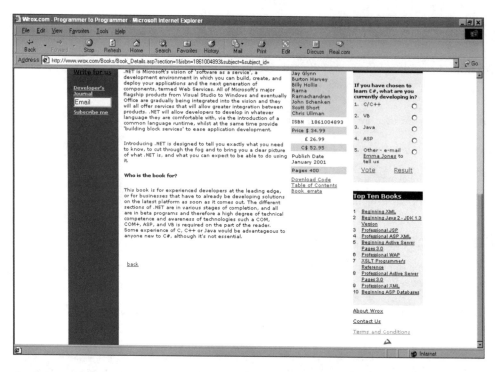

Simply click on this and you will be able to view a list of errata for that book:

Add an Erratum: E-mail Support

If you wish to point out an erratum to put up on the web site, or directly query a problem in the book with an expert who knows the book in detail, then e-mail support@wrox.com. A typical e-mail should include the following things:

- ❑ The **book name**, **last four digits of the ISBN** and **page number** of the problem in the Subject field
- ❑ Your **name**, **contact info** and details of the **problem** in the body of the message

We won't send you junk mail. We need the details to save your time and ours. When you send us an e-mail it will go through the following chain of support.

Customer Support

Your message is delivered to one of our customer support staff, who are the first people to read it. They have files on most frequently asked questions and will answer anything general immediately. They answer general questions about the book and the web site.

Editorial

Deeper queries are forwarded to the technical editor responsible for that book. They have experience with the programming language or particular product and are able to answer detailed technical questions on the subject, directly related to the book's contents. Once an issue has been resolved, the editor can post errata to the web site or reply directly to your e-mail as appropriate.

The Authors

Finally, in the unlikely event that the editor can't answer your problem, s/he will forward the request to the author. We try to protect the author from any distractions from writing. However, we are quite happy to forward specific requests to them. All Wrox authors help with the support on their books. They'll mail the customer and the editor with their response, and again all readers should benefit.

What We Can't Answer

Obviously with an ever-growing range of books and an ever-changing technology base, there is an increasing volume of data requiring support. While we endeavor to answer all questions about the book, we can't solve bugs in your own programs that you've adapted from our code. However, do tell us if you're especially pleased with the routine you developed with our help.

How To Tell Us Exactly What You Think

We understand that errors can destroy the enjoyment of a book and can cause many wasted and frustrated hours, so we seek to minimize the distress that they can cause.

You might just wish to tell us how much you liked or loathed the book in question. Or you might have ideas about how this whole process could be improved. In which case you should e-mail feedback@wrox.com. You'll always find a sympathetic ear, no matter what the problem is. Above all you should remember that we do care about what you have to say and we will do our utmost to act upon it.

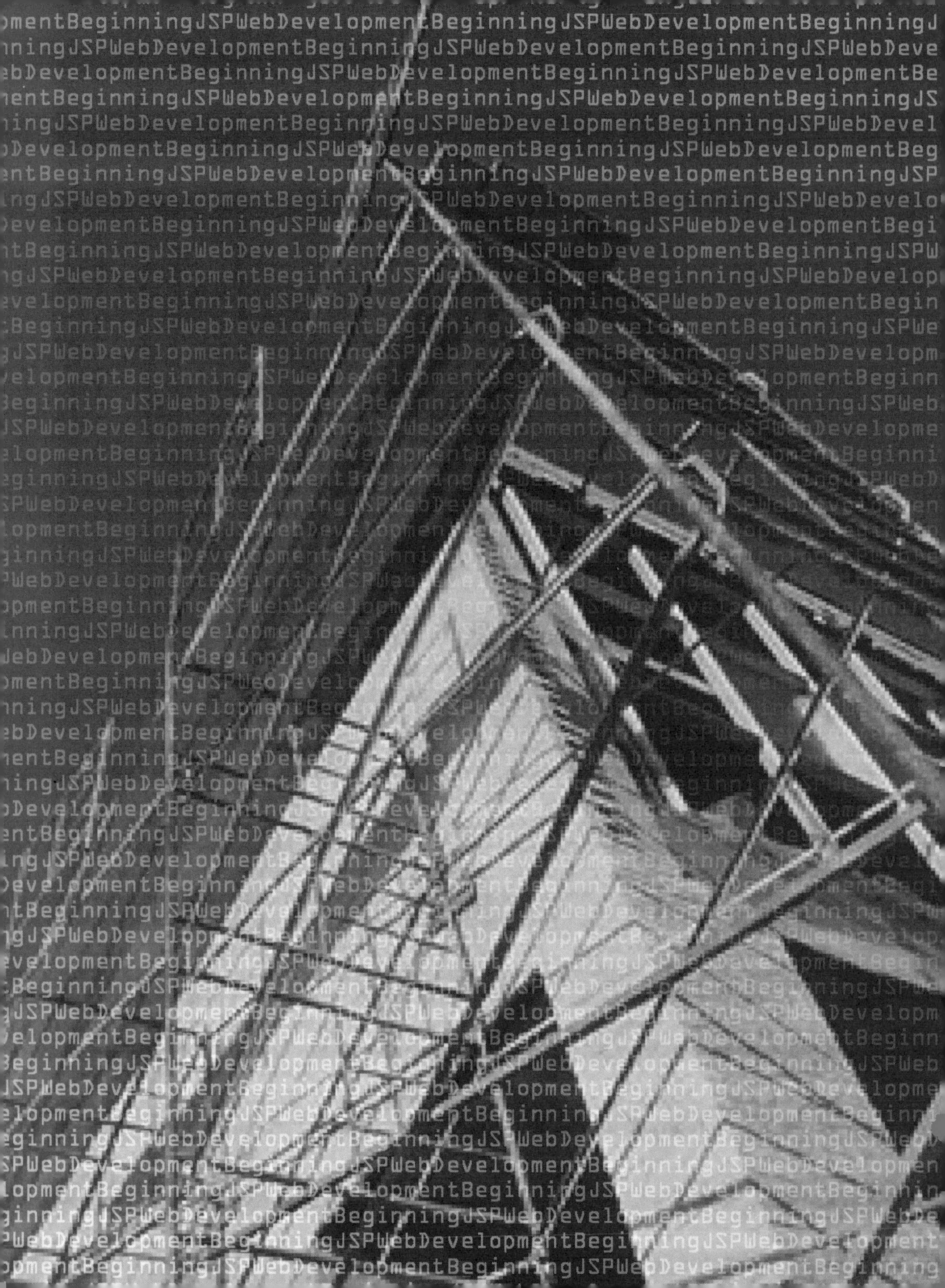
BeginningJSPWebDevelopment

Index

A Guide to the Index

The index is arranged hierarchically, in alphabetical order, with symbols preceding the letter A. Most second-level entries and many third-level entries also occur as first-level entries. This is to ensure that users will find the information they require however they choose to search for it.

I

U

V

W

X

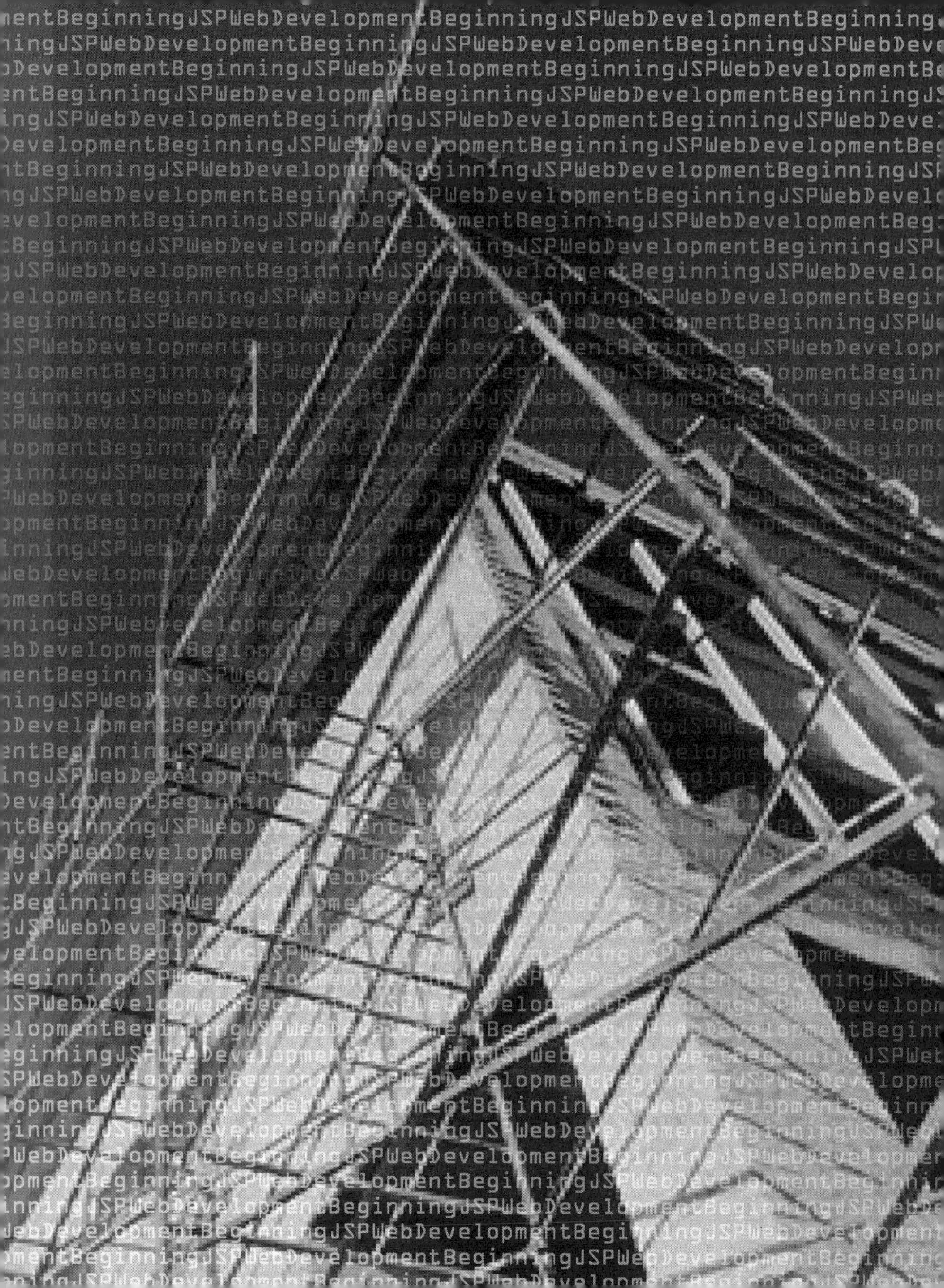
BeginningJSPWebDevelopment